COLLECTIVE INVESTMENT SCHEMES
IN LUXEMBOURG

Law and Practice

COLLECTIVE INVESTMENT SCHEMES IN LUXEMBOURG

Law and Practice

CLAUDE KREMER
Partner, Arendt & Medernach, Luxembourg
Lecturer, University of Luxembourg

ISABELLE LEBBE
Partner, Arendt & Medernach, Luxembourg

OXFORD
UNIVERSITY PRESS

OXFORD
UNIVERSITY PRESS

Great Clarendon Street, Oxford OX2 6DP

Oxford University Press is a department of the University of Oxford.
It furthers the University's objective of excellence in research, scholarship,
and education by publishing worldwide in

Oxford New York

Auckland Cape Town Dar es Salaam Hong Kong Karachi
Kuala Lumpur Madrid Melbourne Mexico City Nairobi
New Delhi Shanghai Taipei Toronto

With offices in

Argentina Austria Brazil Chile Czech Republic France Greece
Guatemala Hungary Italy Japan Poland Portugal Singapore
South Korea Switzerland Thailand Turkey Ukraine Vietnam

Oxford is a registered trade mark of Oxford University Press
in the UK and in certain other countries

Published in the United States
by Oxford University Press Inc., New York

British Library Cataloguing in Publication Data
Data available

Library of Congress Cataloging in Publication Data
Data available

Typeset by Cepha Imaging Private Ltd, Bangalore, India
Printed in Great Britain
on acid-free paper by
CPI Antony Rowe, Chippenham

ISBN 978-0-19-955976-3

1 3 5 7 9 10 8 6 4 2

INTRODUCTION TO THE FIRST EDITION
IN ENGLISH

Eight years have passed since the publication of the first edition of our compendium on undertakings for collective investment (UCIs) in French

Many new laws and regulations have been adopted during this period, mainly at the initiative of the EU authorities. This prompted the publication of a second edition in French in 2006.

It is not by accident that this book has come about. Although undertakings for collective investment have a long history in the Grand Duchy of Luxembourg, they had never previously been the subject of a systematic review and legal analysis. We could not allow this opportunity and challenge to pass.

Drafted by and for practitioners, this work is a handbook rather than a treatise. Its purpose is to enable the interested reader to understand the legal operation of UCIs and to provide immediate and practical answers. The law on UCIs is discussed by theme, from the creation of a UCI to its liquidation. The obligations connected with banking secrecy and the prevention of money laundering are discussed in detail, as are the tax rules governing UCIs and their participants. The impact of Community law on these aspects is explained in a separate chapter.

This edition also reflects recent legislative changes in the European Union and in the Grand Duchy of Luxembourg which impact on UCIs. Recent EU directives which affect UCIs include the 'Prospectus', 'MiFID', and 'Savings Taxation' Directives. Legislation passed in the Grand Duchy of Luxembourg in 2007 created the framework for the so-called 'specialized' investment funds, thereby increasing the types of UCIs available to qualified investors.

This edition in English is the result of a strong demand from all those market participants who are not familiar with the French language. It has been updated from the second edition in French published in November 2006 in all major aspects which are relevant, although some of them could not be analysed in as much detail as we would have liked. Furthermore, the proposed new regulation on coordinated UCITS, generally referred to as 'UCITS IV', has not been addressed, as, at the time of writing this introduction, no formal proposals from the European Commission have been adopted.

The English used in this edition has been monitored and improved by Denise Kinsella, an Irish lawyer based in Dublin. Denise is a former partner of the law firm Dillon Eustace and currently works as an independent director of, and consultant to, several Irish investment funds. We are most grateful for the significant improvements made by Denise, not only from a language point of view, but also in terms of clarity.

We also wish to thank our partners and associates at Arendt & Medernach for their specialist contributions to the contents of the book. We are extremely grateful for their support without which this work could not have been accomplished.

Last but not least, we would like to thank the readers of the previous editions—clients and friends—whose constructive comments have, we hope, allowed us to provide a more thorough analysis of the laws on collective investment schemes.

Claude Kremer and Isabelle Lebbe
Luxembourg
June 2008

PREFACE TO THE FIRST EDITION IN FRENCH

This work written jointly by Maîtres Claude Kremer and Isabelle Lebbe immediately impressed me on account of its thoroughness and, in particular, its scope. Whilst undertakings for collective investment have been the subject of many dissertations, I am not aware of any work that covers all of their aspects so completely.

The growing importance of UCIs for the financial market renders the contribution made by this book even more significant: designed as a reference tool, it can be used to track the development of a sector which has undergone persistent and permanent change in recent years. For that reason, I am convinced that it will become the virtually indispensable companion of practitioners, both in Luxembourg and elsewhere.

These pages show that Luxembourg has not only managed to create a general environment and a legal framework in which undertakings for collective investment can prosper, but that it has also built up a relevant body of legal opinion, which is explained clearly and fully in this book.

In conclusion, I sincerely hope that other authors will follow this example and write handbooks of similar quality for other market activities.

Jean-Nicolas Schaus
Director General
Commission de Surveillance du Secteur Financier
June 2000

CONTENTS—SUMMARY

CONTENTS

Contents

Contents

Contents

6. Parties Involved in the Operation of Undertakings for Collective Investment

Contents

9. Dissolution and Restructuring of Undertakings for Collective Investment

10. Undertakings for Collective Investment and Criminal Law

Contents

Contents

Contents

TABLE OF CASES

TABLES OF LEGISLATION, TREATIES, AND CONVENTIONS

EUROPEAN AND INTERNATIONAL LEGISLATION

Regulations

Directives

LIST OF ABBREVIATIONS

General

ABBL	*Association Luxembourgeoise des Banques et Banquiers* (Luxembourg Bankers' Association)
Act dr	*Actualités du droit* (Belgium)
ALFI	Association of the Luxembourg Fund Industry
Bull François Laurent	*Bulletin du Cercle François Laurent* (Luxembourg)
Cah dr eur	*Cahiers de droit européen* (Belgium)
CA	Court of Appeal (Luxembourg)
Cass b	*Cour de cassation belge* (Belgian Supreme Court of Appeal)
Cass fr	*Cour de cassation française* (French Supreme Court of Appeal)
Cass lux	*Cour de cassation luxembourgeoise* (Luxembourg Supreme Court of Appeal)
CESR	Committee of European Securities Regulators
CJEC	Court of Justice of the European Communities
CSSF	*Commission de Surveillance du Secteur Financier* (Commission for the Supervision of the Financial Sector)
D	*Recueil Dalloz* (France)
DAOR	*Droit des affaires—Ondernemingsrecht* (Belgium)
EC	European Communities
ECR	European Court Reports
EEA	European Economic Area, ie the EU Member States plus Iceland, Liechtenstein and Norway
Eligible Assets Directive	Commission Directive (EC) 2007/16 (see 'Legislation and Circulars' below)
ESC	European Securities Committee
EU	European Union, ie Austria, Belgium, Bulgaria, Czech Republic, Cyprus, Denmark, Estonia, Finland, France, Germany, Greece, Hungary, Ireland, Italy, Latvia, Lithuania, Luxembourg, Malta, Netherlands, Poland, Portugal, Romania, Slovakia, Slovenia, Spain, Sweden, United Kingdom
FATF	Financial Action Task Force on money laundering
FCP	*Fonds commun de placement* (common fund)
IML	*Institut Monétaire Luxembourgeois* (Luxembourg Monetary Institute), subsequently renamed the *Commission de Surveillance du Secteur Financier*
JCP	*Jurisclasseur périodique (La semaine juridique)* (France)
JDF	*Journal de droit fiscal* (Belgium)

JT	*Journal des tribunaux* (Belgium)
Larcier cass	*Larcier cassation* (Belgium)
LIR	Act of 4 December 1967 concerning the taxation of the income of natural persons and companies (*Tax Code*, volume 2, Editions de l'Imprimerie St-Paul)
Mémorial	*Mémorial, Journal officiel du Grand-Duché de Luxembourg* (official journal of the Grand Duchy of Luxembourg). The *Mémorial* encompasses the following three compendiums: the legislative compendium (*Mémorial* A), the administrative and economic compendium (*Mémorial* B), and the compendium of companies and associations (*Mémorial* C)
MiFID Directive	Directive (EC) 2004/39 (see 'Legislation and Circulars' below)
MTF	Multilateral trading facility
NAV	Net asset value
OECD	Organisation for Economic Cooperation and Development
OJ	Official Journal of the European Communities, subsequently renamed Official Journal of the European Union
Pas	*Pasicrisie* (Belgium)
Pas lux	*Pasicrisie luxembourgeoise* (Luxembourg)
RCJB	*Revue critique de jurisprudence belge* (Belgium)
RDC	*Revue de droit commercial belge* (Belgium)
Rec Lég Pl Fin	*Recueil de la législation sur la place financière de Luxembourg*, Central Legislation Department, 2006
Rec Lég Soc	*Recueil de la législation des sociétés et associations*, Central Legislation Department, 2003
Rép not	*Répertoire notarial* (Belgium)
Rev Banque	*Revue de la Banque* (Belgium)
Rev prat soc	*Revue pratique des sociétés* (Belgium)
Rev soc	*Revue des sociétés* (France)
Rev trim dr civ	*Revue trimestrielle de droit civil* (France)
SA	*Société anonyme* (limited company)
SARL	*Société à responsabilité limitée* (private limited company)
SCA	*Société en commandite par actions* (partnership limited by shares)
SCS	*Société en commandite simple* (limited partnership)
SE	*Société européenne* (European company)
SICAF	*Société d'investissement à capital fixe* (investment company with fixed capital)
SICAR	*Société d'investissement en capital à risque* (investment company in risk capital)
SICAV	*Société d'investissement à capital variable* (investment company with variable capital)
SIF	Specialized investment fund
Trib arr	*Tribunal d'arrondissement* (District Court)

UCI	Undertaking for collective investment
UCITS	Undertaking for collective investment in transferable securities
VAT	Value added tax
VaR	*Value at Risk*

Legislation and Circulars

1915 Act	Act of 10 August 1915 on commercial companies (*Rec Lég Soc* 41)
1929 Act	Act of 31 July 1929 on the taxation of financial holding companies (*Rec Lég Soc*, 249)
1983 Act	Act of 25 August 1983 on undertakings for collective investment (*Mémorial* A 1983, 1462)
1988 Act	Act of 30 March 1988 on undertakings for collective investment (*Rec Lég Soc*, 375)
1991 Act	Act of 19 July 1991 on undertakings for collective investment the securities of which are not intended to be placed with the public (*Rec Lég Soc*, 463)
1993 Act	Act of 5 April 1993 on the financial sector (*Rec Lég Pl Fin* 97)
Act of 23 December 1998	Act of 23 December 1998 establishing a supervisory commission for the financial sector (*Commission de Surveillance du Secteur Financier*) (*Mémorial* A 1998, 2985)
2002 Act	Act of 20 December 2002 on undertakings for collective investment and amending the Act of 12 February 1979, as amended, on value added tax (*Rec Lég Soc* 413)
Act of 22 March 2004	Act of 22 March 2004 on securitisation and amending: • the Act of 5 April 1993, as amended, on the financial sector; • the Act of 23 December 1998, as amended, creating a commission for the supervision of the financial sector (*Commission de Surveillance du Secteur Financier*); • the Act of 27 July 2003 on trusts and fiduciary contracts; • the Act of 4 December 1967, as amended, on income tax; • the Act of 16 October 1934, as amended, on wealth tax; • the Act of 12 February 1979, as amended, on value added tax; (*Mémorial* A 2004, 720)
Act of 15 June 2004	Act of 15 June 2004 on the investment company in risk capital (SICAR) (*Mémorial* A 2004, 1568)
Act of 12 November 2004	Act of 12 November 2004 on the prevention of money laundering and terrorist financing, transposing Directive (EC) 2001/97 of the European Parliament and of the Council of 4 December 2001 amending Council Directive

(EEC) 91/308 on prevention of the use of the financial system for the purpose of money laundering and amending:
- the Criminal Code;
- the Criminal Investigation Code;
- the Act of 7 March 1980, as amended, on the judicial organization;
- the Act of 23 December 1998, as amended, creating a commission for the supervision of the financial sector (*Commission de Surveillance du Secteur Financier*);
- the Act of 5 April 1993, as amended, on the financial sector;
- the Act of 6 December 1991, as amended, on the insurance sector;
- the Act of 9 December 1976, as amended, on the organization of the notarial profession;
- the Act of 10 August 1991, as amended, on the legal profession;
- the Act of 28 January 1984, as amended, on the organization of the profession of independent auditors;
- the Act of 10 June 1999 on the organization of the profession of qualified accountants;
- the Act of 20 April 1977, as amended, on the exploitation of gambling and betting on sports;
- the General Tax Code (*Abgabenordnung*);

(*Mémorial* A 2004, 2766)

Act of 10 July 2005 Act of 10 July 2005 on prospectuses for transferable securities:
- transposing Directive (EC) 2003/71 of the European Parliament and of the Council of 4 November 2003 on the prospectus to be published when securities are offered to the public or admitted to trading and amending Directive (EC) 2001/34;
- amending the Act of 23 December 1998 creating a commission for the supervision of the financial sector (*Commission de Surveillance du Secteur Financier*);
- amending the Act of 23 December 1998 on supervision of the markets in financial assets;
- amending the Act of 30 March 1988 on undertakings for collective investment;
- amending the Act of 20 December 2002 on undertakings for collective investment;
- amending the Act of 15 June 2004 on investment companies in risk capital;
- amending the Act of 10 August 1915 on commercial companies;

(*Mémorial* A 2005, 1726)

Act of 25 August 2006	Act of 25 August 2006:

- on the European company (SE), the *société anonyme à directoire et conseil de surveillance* and the *société anonyme unipersonnelle*;
- amending the amended Act of 10 August 1915 on commercial companies and certain other legal provisions;
- amending the Act of 19 December 2002 on the Trade and Companies Register and the accounting and annual financial statements of companies;
- amending the amended Act of 30 March 1988 on undertakings for collective investment;
- amending the Act of 20 December 2002 on undertakings for collective investment;
- amending the Act of 25 July 1990 on the status of directors representing the State or a legal person under public law in an SA;
- amending the Act of 4 December 1992 on the information to be disclosed when acquiring and divesting a material holding in a company listed on the stock exchange;
- amending the Act of 13 July 2005 on professional retirement institutions in the form of SEPCAVs and ASSEPs;

(*Mémorial* A 2006, 2684)

Act of 13 February 2007	Act of 13 February 2007 relating to specialized investment funds (SIFs) and amending:

- the amended Act of 20 December 2002 on undertakings for collective investment;
- the amended Act of 12 February 1979 concerning value added tax;

(*Mémorial* A 2007, 368)

Act of 13 July 2007	Act of 13 July 2007 on markets in financial instruments transposing:

- Directive (EC) 2004/39 of the European Parliament and of the Council of 21 April 2004 on markets in financial instruments amending Council Directives (EEC) 85/611 and (EEC) 93/6 and Directive (EC) 2000/12 of the European Parliament and of the Council and repealing Council Directive (EEC) 93/22;
- Article 52 of Commission Directive (EC) 2006/73 of 10 August 2006 implementing Directive (EC) 2004/39 of the European Parliament and of the Council as regards organizational requirements and operating conditions for investment firms and defined terms for the purposes of that Directive;

and amending:
- the Act of 5 April 1993, as amended, on the financial sector,
- the Act of 20 December 2002, as amended, on undertakings for collective investment,
- the Act of 12 November 2004 on combating money laundering and terrorist financing,
- the Act of 31 May 1999, as amended, on company domiciliation,
- the Act of 23 December 1998, as amended, creating a commission for the supervision of the financial sector (*Commission de Surveillance du Secteur Financier*),
- the Act of 6 December 1991, as amended, on the insurance sector,
- the Act of 3 September 1996 concerning the involuntary dispossession of bearer securities,
- the Act of 23 December 1998 concerning the monetary status and the central bank of Luxembourg (*Banque centrale du Luxembourg*),

and repealing:
- the Act of 23 December 1998, as amended, on supervision of the markets in financial assets,
- the Act of 21 June 1984, as amended, on futures markets (*Mémorial* A 2007, 2076)

Circular 91/75	IML Circular 91/75 of 21 January 1991
Circular 00/14	CSSF Circular 00/14 of 27 July 2000 on the adoption of the Act of 17 July 2000 amending certain provisions in the Act of 30 March 1988 with regard to undertakings for collective investment
Circular 02/77	CSSF Circular 02/77 of 27 November 2002 on the protection of investors in the event of NAV calculation error and correction of the consequences resulting from non-compliance with the investment rules applicable to undertakings for collective investment
Circular 02/80	CSSF Circular 02/80 of 5 December 2002 on the specific rules applicable to Luxembourg undertakings for collective investment ('UCI') pursuing alternative investment strategies
Circular 02/81	CSSF Circular 02/81 of 6 December 2002 on guidelines concerning the duties of auditors of undertakings for collective investment
Circular 03/87	CSSF Circular 03/87 of 21 January 2003 on the coming into force of the Act of 20 December 2002 on undertakings for collective investment
Circular 03/88	CSSF Circular 03/88 of 22 January 2003 on the classification of undertakings for collective investment governed by the

	provisions of the Act of 20 December 2002 on undertakings for collective investment
Circular 03/97	CSSF Circular 03/97 of 28 February 2003 on the publication in the electronic database for the financial centre ('*référentiel de la place*') of simplified and full prospectuses and the annual and half-yearly reports by undertakings for collective investment
Circular 03/108	CSSF Circular 03/108 of 30 July 2003 on Luxembourg management companies subject to Chapter 13 of the Act of 20 December 2002 on undertakings for collective investment, and Luxembourg self-managed investment companies subject to Article 27 or Article 40 of the Act of 20 December 2002
Circular 03/122	CSSF Circular 03/122 of 19 December 2003 on clarifications concerning the simplified prospectus
Circular 04/146	CSSF Circular 04/146 of 17 June 2004 on the protection of undertakings for collective investment and their investors against late trading and market timing practices
Circular 04/151	CSSF Circular 04/151 of 13 July 2004 on the information to be published in the listing particulars of the securities specified below: • shares and units of foreign UCIs whose securities are not publicly available, offered or sold in or from Luxembourg, and • securities redeemable or exchangeable for shares or units of UCIs or whose income and/or redemption is/are linked to underlying shares or units of UCIs
Circular 04/155	CSSF Circular 04/155 of 27 September 2004 on the compliance function
Circular 05/176	CSSF Circular 05/176 of 5 April 2005 on the rules of conduct to be adopted by undertakings for collective investment in transferable securities in relation to the use of financial derivative instruments
Circular 05/177	CSSF Circular 05/177 of 6 April 2005 on the abolition of any prior approval by the CSSF of advertising material issued by persons and companies supervised by the CSSF; revocation of point II of Chapter L of IML Circular 91/75; revocation of the two last sentences of point IV 5.11 of CSSF Circular 2000/15
Circular 05/178	CSSF Circular 05/178 of 11 April 2005 on administrative and accounting organization; outsourcing of IT services; revocation of point 4.5.2 of IML Circular 96/126 and replacement by point 4.5.2 of this Circular
Circular 05/185	CSSF Circular 05/185 of 24 May 2005 on Luxembourg management companies subject to the provisions of

	Chapter 13 of the Act of 20 December 2002 relating to undertakings for collective investment, as well as Luxembourg self-managed investment companies subject to the provisions of Article 27 or Article 40 of the Act of 20 December 2002 relating to undertakings for collective investment
Circular 05/186	CSSF Circular 05/186 of 25 May 2005 on the guidelines of the Committee of European Securities Regulators (CESR) regarding the application of transitional measures resulting from Directives (EC) 2001/107 and (EC) 2001/108 (UCITS III) amending Directive (EEC) 85/611 (UCITS I)
Circular 05/188	CSSF Circular 05/188 of 27 May 2005 on the coming into force of the Act of 12 November 2004 on combating money laundering and terrorist financing
Circular 05/210	CSSF Circular 05/210 of 10 October 2005 on the drawing-up of a simplified prospectus within the scope of Chapter 1 of Part III of the Act on prospectuses for securities
Circular 05/211	CSSF Circular 05/211 of 13 October 2005 on combating money laundering and terrorist financing and prevention of the use of the financial sector for the purpose of money laundering and terrorist financing
Circular 05/225	CSSF Circular 05/225 of 16 December 2005 on the concept of 'offer to the public of securities' as defined in the Act on prospectuses for securities and the consequential 'obligation to publish a prospectus'
Circular 05/226	CSSF Circular 05/226 of 16 December 2005 on a general overview of the Act on prospectuses for securities and technical specifications regarding communication to the CSSF of documents with a view to authorization or for filing and of notices for offers to the public and admissions to trading on a regulated market
Circular 06/241	CSSF Circular 06/241 of 5 April 2006 on the concept of risk capital under the Act of 15 June 2004 relating to the investment company in risk capital (SICAR)
Circular 06/267	CSSF Circular 06/267 of 22 November 2006 on technical specifications regarding the filing with the CSSF, in accordance with the Act on prospectuses for securities, of documents for approval or notification purposes and of notices for offers to the public of units/shares of Luxembourg closed-end UCIs and admissions of units/shares of Luxembourg closed-end UCIs to trading on a regulated market
Circular 06/272	CSSF Circular 06/272 of 21 December 2006 on technical specifications regarding the filing with the CSSF, in accordance with the Act on prospectuses for securities,

	of documents for approval or notification purposes and of notices for offers to the public of securities issued by SICARs and admissions of securities issued by SICARs to trading on a regulated market
Circular 07/277	CSSF Circular 07/277 of 9 January 2007 on the new notification procedure following guidelines issued by the Committee of European Securities Regulators (CESR) regarding the simplification of the UCITS notification procedure
Circular 07/283	CSSF Circular 07/283 of 28 February 2007 on the entry into force of the Act of 13 February 2007 relating to specialized investment funds
Circular 07/290	CSSF Circular 07/290 of 3 May 2007 on the definition of capital ratios pursuant to Article 56 of the amended Law of 5 April 1993 on the financial sector (application to investment firms and management companies subject to Chapter 13 of the Law of 20 December 2002 as amended)
Circular 07/307	CSSF Circular 07/307 of 31 July 2007 on the MiFID: Conduct of business rules in the financial sector
Circular 07/308	CSSF Circular 07/308 of 2 August 2007 on the rules of conduct to be adopted by undertakings for collective investment in transferable securities with respect to the use of a methodology for the management of financial risk, and the use of derivative financial instruments
Circular 07/309	CSSF Circular of 3 August 2007 on risk spreading in the context of specialized investment funds (SIFs)
Circular 07/310	CSSF Circular of 3 August 2007 on financial information to be provided by specialized investment funds (SIFs), as amended by CSSF Circular 08/348
Circular 08/339	CSSF Circular 08/339 of 19 February 2008 on the guidelines of the Committee of European Securities Regulators (CESR) concerning eligible assets for investment by UCITS
Circular 08/348	CSSF Circular 08/348 of 17 April 2008 on the changes to circulars IML 97/136 and CSSF 07/310
Circular 08/350	CSSF Circular 08/350 of 22 April 2008 on clarifications relating to the amendments introduced by the Act of 13 July 2007 on markets in financial instruments to the status of professionals of the financial sector (PFS) referred to in Articles 29-1, 29-2, 29-3, or 29-4 and designated as 'support PFS', as well as on the amendment to the prudential supervisory procedures for support PFS
Circular 08/356	CSSF Circular 08/356 of 4 June 2008 regarding rules applicable to UCIs which employ certain techniques and instruments relating to transferable securities and money market instruments

Directive 85/611	Council Directive (EEC) 85/611 of 20 December 1985 on the coordination of laws, regulations and administrative provisions relating to undertakings for collective investment in transferable securities (UCITS), as amended [1985] OJ L375/3
Directive 93/22	Council Directive (EEC) 93/22 of 10 May 1993 on investment services in the securities field [1993] OJ L141/27. Directive (EEC) 93/22 was repealed by Directive (EC) 2004/39 (MiFID). Its repeal took effect on 1 November 2007 (Article 69 of Directive (EC) 2004/39 as amended by Directive (EC) 2006/31 of 5 April 2006 [2006] OJ L114/60
Directive 2001/97	Directive (EC) 2001/97 of the European Parliament and of the Council of 4 December 2001 amending Directive (EEC) 91/308 of the Council on prevention of the use of the financial system for the purpose of money laundering [2001] OJ L344/76
Directive 2001/107	Directive (EC) 2001/107 of the European Parliament and of the Council of 21 January 2002 amending Council Directive (EEC) 85/611 on the coordination of laws, regulations and administrative provisions relating to undertakings for collective investment in transferable securities (UCITS) with a view to regulating management companies and simplified prospectuses [2002] OJ L41/20
Directive 2001/108	Directive (EC) 2001/108 of the European Parliament and of the Council of 21 January 2002 amending Council Directive (EEC) 85/611 on the coordination of laws, regulations and administrative provisions relating to undertakings for collective investment in transferable securities (UCITS), with regard to investments of UCITS [2002] OJ L41/35
Directive 2003/6	Directive (EC) 2003/6 of the European Parliament and of the Council of 28 January 2003 on insider dealing and market manipulation (market abuse) [2003] OJ L96/16
Directive 2003/48	Directive (EC) 2003/48 of the European Parliament and of the Council of 3 June 2003 on the taxation of savings income in the form of interest payments [2003] OJ L157/38
Directive 2003/71	Directive (EC) 2003/71 of the European Parliament and of the Council of 4 November 2003 on the prospectus to be published when securities are offered to the public or admitted to trading, and amending Directive (EC) 2001/34 [2003] OJ L345/65
Directive 2004/39 or MiFID	Directive (EC) 2004/39, 'MiFID' (Market in Financial Instruments Directive) of the European Parliament and of the Council of 21 April 2004 on markets in financial instruments amending Council Directives (EEC) 85/611 and (EEC) 93/6 and Directive (EC) 2000/12 of the European

	Parliament and of the Council and repealing Council Directive (EEC) 93/22 [2004] OJ L145/1 with effect from 1 November 2007 (Article 69 of Directive (EC) 2004/39 as amended by Directive (EC) 2006/31 of 5 April 2006 [2006] OJ L114/60)
Directive 2006/48	Directive (EC) 2006/48 of the European Parliament and of the Council of 14 June 2006 relating to the taking up and pursuit of the business of credit institutions (recast) [2006] L177/1
Directive 2006/73	Commission Directive (EC) 2006/73 of 10 August 2006 implementing Directive (EC) 2004/39 of the European Parliament and of the Council as regards organizational requirements and operating conditions for investment firms and defined terms for the purposes of that Directive [2006] OJ L241/26
Directive 2007/16 or Eligible Assets Directive	Commission Directive (EC) 2007/16 of 19 March 2007 implementing Council Directive (EEC) 85/611 on the coordination of laws, regulations and administrative provisions relating to undertakings for collective investment in transferable securities (UCITS) as regards the clarification of certain definitions [2007] OJ L79/11
EC Treaty	Treaty constituting the European Community, consolidated version published in 2002 OJ C325/33
Grand-Ducal Regulation of 13 July 2007	Grand-Ducal Regulation of 13 July 2007 relating to the organizational requirements and the rules of conduct in the financial sector and transposing Commission Directive (EC) 2006/73 of 10 August 2006 implementing Directive (EC) 2004/39 of the European Parliament and of the Council as regards organizational requirements and operating conditions for investment firms and defined terms for the purposes of that Directive (*Mémorial* A 2007, 2134)
Grand-Ducal Regulation of 8 February 2008	Grand-Ducal Regulation of 8 February 2008 relating to certain definitions of the law of 20 December 2002 as amended concerning undertakings for collective investment and implementing Commission Directive (EC) 2007/16 of 19 March 2007 implementing Council Directive (EEC) 85/611 on the coordination of laws, regulations and administrative provisions relating to undertakings for collective investment in transferable securities (UCITS) as regards the clarification of certain definitions (*Mémorial* A, 2008, 303)

1

INTRODUCTION

Definition of Undertaking for Collective Investment

Rather than introducing a general definition of undertaking for collective invest- **1.01**
ment (UCI), the authors of the 2002 Act, in line with the 1988 Act, sought to
define its constituent elements. Three basic criteria are required to constitute a
UCI. A UCI is an investment structure:

(1) the exclusive object of which is the collective investment of savings;

(2) which invests in assets (transferable securities or other assets) and operates in accordance with the principle of risk spreading;

(3) the funds of which, used for collective investment, have been raised from the public.

1.02 The first two criteria must always be met. The last—the raising of funds from the public—may be dispensed with in certain cases specified by law. All of these criteria were considered and clarified by the CSSF, the prudential authority for UCIs, in Circular 91/75.[1]

Collective investment of savings

1.03 The collective investment of savings is defined as the common investment of a number of individual investment contributions raised from the public. They may be invested in transferable securities or other assets.

1.04 Investment suggests that the purchase or sale of portfolio assets is carried out solely with the objective of generating a yield or capital gains. In contrast with other types of financial vehicles, a UCI does not acquire interests in order to obtain influence or control, albeit certain UCIs, such as those investing in venture capital assets, can in fact hold significant interests in certain companies. However, even in those circumstances, the UCI's main purpose is not to exercise control over the target company but rather to generate a return. The objective of a UCI is to show a capital gain once the company is sufficiently mature.

Investment according to the principle of risk spreading

1.05 Spreading investment risks avoids the excessive concentration of a UCI's investments and reduces investment risk. A minimum level of diversification of investments between assets of different types and issuers is required, although this requirement is interpreted differently, depending on the type of UCI.

Raising capital from the public

1.06 Capital is raised from 'the public' when it is raised from a group of investors which extends beyond a 'small circle of persons'.[2] There is no fixed minimum threshold beyond which the target investors cease to be a 'small circle of persons'.

---

[1] Ch B, I, Circular 91/75. A fourth criterion, not included as such in Circular 91/75, stipulates that Luxembourg-based UCIs must issue units or securities in accordance with Arts 2(2), 65(1), 69, and 73 of the 2002 Act. This requirement excludes certain structures from the scope of the legislation governing UCIs. See 2.161 below.

[2] Ch B, I, Circular 91/75.

The threshold in question is considered on a case-by-case basis by the CSSF, which does not, for example, regard family holding companies and investment clubs as collecting savings from the public albeit they are 'pursuing the objective of the collective investment of savings'.[3]

In the course of Parliamentary debates prior to the enactment of the 2002 Act it had been proposed not to regulate groups of investors comprising fewer than twenty persons.[4] An undertaking that does not wish to place its units with a larger number of investors therefore would not have come within the sphere of the 2002 Act. However, the legislation did not expressly provide for this clarification.   **1.07**

In addition the launch by a promoter of a UCI intended to be sold only to entities within its own group, is not a 'public' offering of units. Investors should be sought from 'outside' the group of companies rather than 'within' the relevant corporate group. A public offer is effected only when marketing efforts are targeted at a promoter's clientele or the clientele of one or more group entities.   **1.08**

A UCI must intend to place its units or shares with the public, regardless of whether or not it achieves this result. Failure to sell to the public does not automatically result in failure to satisfy the requirement, provided the UCI can demonstrate its bona fide intention to market its units or shares to the public.   **1.09**

There is no other definition of the term 'public'. The investor can be either institutional or private and an investor in the case of a 'public' offer is not required to meet any requirement as to status or capacity.   **1.10**

However, the term 'public' can have several meanings in the context of UCIs, depending on the situation. For example, in the context of raising funds for a UCI, it means a relatively large group of persons. In contrast, in other circumstances, it can be used to distinguish the type of investor concerned, for example to draw a distinction between well-informed investors and the 'general public'. This distinction is highly relevant in differentiating the scope of the 2002 Act and the Act of 13 February 2007 respectively. The 2002 Act refers to the public as an 'unrestricted circle of persons' whereas the Act of 13 February 2007, in limiting the eligibility of investors in funds authorized under the Act of 13 February 2007, to well-informed investors, refers to 'the public' as any investor who is not well informed.   **1.11**

Thus, it is not always necessary for a UCI to raise capital from the 'public'. The Act of 13 February 2007 permits the creation of UCIs 'whose units or shares are sold to one or more well-informed investors', and UCIs authorized under the Act of   **1.12**

---

[3] Ch B, II, Circular 91/75.
[4] This figure is mentioned in the Parliamentary documents for the Act of 2 August 2003, which amended the 1993 Act (*Parliamentary doc* No 5085, Explanatory Statement, 14).

13 February 2007 will therefore not necessarily raise funds from 'an unrestricted circle of persons', ie the 'public' as defined in the 2002 Act,[5] and can, indeed must, target a select investor group.[6]

Historical Background

1.13 UCIs have existed since the late nineteenth century, even though they only came into their own in the twentieth century. For instance, the years between 1880 and 1900 saw the rise in Scotland of the investment trust company whose objective was to invest in farm mortgages.[7] This Scottish innovation subsequently crossed the Atlantic to the United States, where it became a popular investment vehicle, especially after the First World War. Emboldened by their success, the managers of such investment companies borrowed increasingly large amounts for investment purposes. The assets managed by some of those companies were out of all proportion to their share capital, resulting in their demise during the Wall Street crash of 1929.

1.14 The Wall Street crash led to an increased interest by US investors in another type of UCI, the unit trust rather than a corporate structure. First constituted in England in 1868, this type of UCI initially ran into legal difficulties. One judge considered it a breach of English company law. While that judgment was overturned on appeal, it prompted the conversion into limited liability companies or liquidation of many such trusts.

1.15 In unit trusts, securities are bought and vested in a trustee, generally a regulated institution such as a bank or an insurance company. In return for payment/subscriptions for units, investors become the trust's beneficiaries and are issued with 'units' representing their rights. The management of a trust's portfolio is entrusted to a management company separate and distinct from the trustee.

1.16 The unit trust structure offered two major advantages compared with investment companies. First, securities acquired by a trust were held in the custody of a trustee

---

[5] An investment structure that does not canvass the public is not necessarily governed by the Act of 13 February 2007. An undertaking engaged in the collective investment of assets according to the principle of risk spreading, which reserves its units or shares for well-informed investors and does not canvass the public for funds, may either opt for application of the Act of 13 February 2007 and the regulations laid down by the CSSF or adopt, for example, the status of a non-regulated financial company whose activity is not supervised by the CSSF. For further explanations about these aspects, see 2.85 and 2.86 below.

[6] Art 1(1), Act of 13 February 2007, under which SIFs may reserve their securities for 'one or several well-informed investors'.

[7] The following discussion is mainly drawn from CO Merriman, *Unit Trusts and How They Work* (Pitman & Sons, 2nd edn, 1959) 1–10.

who was independent from the management company. Secondly, trust participants could at any time sell their units back to the trust, whereas an investment company was not entitled to buy back its own shares.

It was another fifty years before these structures re-emerged in Europe. The first **1.17** Swiss trust was created in 1930. Similarly, the successful sale in Great Britain of units in US trusts prompted British financiers to revive this type of product in 1931.

Nevertheless, the British investment community quickly distinguished itself from **1.18** its American counterpart. Chastened by the lessons learnt from the crash of 1929, the Americans had laid down extremely rigid management rules, whereas the British introduced ever greater flexibility. In a US trust, the composition of the portfolio had to be settled once and for all, and securities could be sold only under extremely strict conditions. The conditions imposed on trusts set up under English law were, from the outset, more flexible. The managers of English trusts were gradually authorized to sell portfolio securities when they considered this to be in the best interests of the unitholders, thereby boosting the popularity of this type of trust, of which there were 98 in England by 1939, covered by special regulations under the Prevention of Fraud (Investments) 1939 Act, which came into force on 8 August 1944.

The fund industry has continued to grow steadily ever since. In 1940, there **1.19** were 111 investment funds in the United States, comprising 43 companies and 68 trusts. By 1957, there were 167 funds, comprising 24 companies and 143 trusts.[8]

1959 saw the creation of the first investment fund in the Grand Duchy of **1.20** Luxembourg, under the prescient name 'FCP Eurunion'.[9] Broadly inspired by the trust structure described above, this was built around three components:

(1) a depositary bank responsible for keeping the securities in safe custody and overseeing their management;
(2) a management company responsible for managing and building up the portfolio;
(3) unitholders, the joint owners of the securities portfolio.

The relationships between the three parties were governed by management regulations.

---

[8] ibid 13.
[9] M-J Chèvremont, 'Évolution de l'industrie des fonds d'investissement en Europe et au Luxembourg en particulier', in Les fonds d'investissement, réglementation-fiscalité-évolution, Seminar held on 24 and 25 November 1988, *Association Luxembourgeoise des Juristes de Banque* (ALJB), *Institut Universitaire International Luxembourg* (IUIL) 5.

1.21   During the same period, ie in 1959 and 1960, the first incorporated investment funds emerged in the Grand Duchy of Luxembourg. In contrast with the English model, such companies were able to repurchase their own shares indirectly from their shareholders, under a structure involving the creation of a separate company known as a 'repurchase company'. Having waited a long time before creating a UCI based on the British model, the Grand Duchy of Luxembourg thus took an additional step, offering investors an opportunity that English investment companies were unable to provide.

1.22   Investment funds soon became an integral part of Luxembourg's investment scene, helped by a flexible and robust legal and regulatory environment, attractive tax treatment and the steadily growing expertise of local service providers. In 1970, there were 102 UCIs in the Grand Duchy of Luxembourg. In 2008, there are 3,105,[10] with aggregate net assets of €1,996,959 billion,[11] placing the Grand Duchy of Luxembourg second in the world behind the United States in terms of fund volumes.

Legal Sources

Specific laws and regulations applicable to UCIs

Chronological record of laws and regulations

Grand-Ducal Decree of 22 December 1972 concerning the supervision of investment funds

1.23   The Grand-Ducal Decree of 22 December 1972[12] was the first Luxembourg regulation to be adopted with regard to UCIs.[13] Prior to the adoption of that Decree, corporate UCIs had been created under the 1915 Act and for tax purposes were governed by the 1929 Act. This infrastructure was complemented by administrative decisions and recommendations, *inter alia*, from the Treasury Minister, the registration authority,[14] and the Banking Commissioner. This legal framework contained numerous loopholes and, especially for FCPs, turned out to be inadequate, as revealed by the IOS scandal towards the end of the 1960s.[15]

---

[10]   This figure comprises 1,259 traditional UCIs and 10,457 sub-funds of umbrella UCIs.

[11]   Figures for 31 May 2008; source: monthly press release published by the CSSF on the general situation of UCIs (July 2008 edition).

[12]   Grand-Ducal Decree of 22 December 1972 concerning the supervision of investment funds (*Mémorial* A 1972, 2112).

[13]   In the Grand Duchy of Luxembourg, the term *fonds d'investissement*, which is a literal translation of the English *investment fund*, was used until the 1983 Act introduced the concept of 'undertaking for collective investment', also found in Directive (EEC) 85/611.

[14]   *Administration de l'Enregistrement.*

[15]   Following a large-scale advertising campaign, Investors Overseas Services (IOS) persuaded more than 700,000 persons to subscribe for units in two FCPs it had created in the Grand Duchy of Luxembourg: the International Investment Trust and the Fund of Funds. Management of these

The Grand-Ducal Decree of 22 December 1972 was adopted in response to the **1.24** IOS scandal. The 1972 Decree defined the meaning of 'investment funds' for the first time[16] and conferred on the Banking Commissioner supervisory authority over all Luxembourg-based UCIs (whether of a contractual, corporate, or other type) and all foreign investment funds whose units or shares were offered to the public in or from the Grand Duchy of Luxembourg.[17] The Grand-Ducal Decree further required UCIs to have their accounts audited by an independent expert who, 'whilst providing assurances as to his probity and professional qualifications',[18] was also obliged to provide the Banking Commissioner with 'all information or certificates required by the Commissioner in the areas of expertise of the expert in the performance of the audit'.[19]

In regulations issued on 8 November 1974,[20] the Banking Commissioner set out **1.25** the rules governing the monthly financial reports to be prepared and submitted by UCIs under his supervision.

1983 Act concerning undertakings for collective investment

The rapid development of UCIs in the 1970s evidenced the need for more systematic **1.26** regulation of the organization, operation, and supervision of collective investment undertakings. Initially presented in Parliament on 31 December 1979,[21] comprehensive legislation was finally adopted four years later in the form of the 1983 Act.

In the preamble to the Bill, the government noted the absence of specific regula- **1.27** tions governing UCIs and stated that 'in order to protect savings, there is clearly an urgent need to specify the legal basis for such undertakings and to enact operating rules to eliminate any legal uncertainty in this area'.[22]

At the time, the government was aware of the need to align the regime for **1.28** Luxembourg-based UCIs with European Community law. In Parliamentary documents, it stressed the need to 'provide the parties concerned with an instrument capable of surviving, without amendment, the transposition into national law of EEC directives'.[23]

UCIs was a disaster. Moreover, their assets had no genuine substance. The investors lost nearly their entire investment.

[16] Art 1(1) of the Grand-Ducal Decree of 22 December 1972 concerning the supervision of investment funds (*Mémorial* A 1972, 2112).

[17] ibid Art 1(2).

[18] ibid Art 3(1).

[19] ibid Art 3(2).

[20] Approved by Ministerial Decree of 19 November 1974 concerning the approval of Banking Commissioner Reg No VM/1 of 8 November 1974 concerning the monthly financial reports to be prepared and submitted by the investment funds under his supervision (*Mémorial* A 1974, 1718).

[21] *Parliamentary doc* No 2366, Contents, 1.

[22] ibid Preamble, 18.

[23] ibid Preamble, 17.

1.29 The 1983 Act specifically governed the operation of FCPs. It introduced the SICAV, inspired by French legislation, into Luxembourg law. It also provided the legal framework for the other structures available to Luxembourg-based UCIs, and confirmed earlier regulations on the public offerings of units or shares in foreign UCIs in or from the Grand Duchy of Luxembourg.

1.30 The Grand-Ducal Regulation of 25 August 1983[24] determined the amount of fixed capital duty applicable to UCIs governed by the 1983 Act.

1.31 This was followed by the Grand-Ducal Regulation of 29 December 1983,[25] which laid down the rules governing the publication and filing of financial statements and reports by UCIs subject to supervision by the *Institut Monétaire Luxembourgeois*, which had succeeded[26] the Banking Commissioner under the Act of 20 May 1983.[27]

1988 Act concerning undertakings for collective investment

1.32 **Content** Already in the pipeline when the 1983 Act was approved, Directive 85/611 (the UCITS Directive) was adopted two years later and transposed into Luxembourg law by the 1988 Act.

1.33 The Directive coordinates the legislation of EEA Member States with regard to UCIs which invest in transferable securities and—since 2003—in other liquid financial assets (UCITS). It does not deal with other types of UCI, which Member States are free to regulate under local law and regulation.

1.34 Directive 85/611 could have been transposed into Luxembourg law simply by amending the 1983 Act. The government nevertheless felt that, 'in order to improve the previous regime in certain areas and . . . to permit broader application of the instrument of undertakings for collective investment', it was necessary to 'review the entire subject-matter and to develop a law governing all undertakings for collective investment'.[28]

---

[24] Grand-Ducal Regulation of 25 August 1983 determining the fixed duty applicable to the capital collected in undertakings for collective investment governed by the Act of 25 August 1983 (*Mémorial* A 1983, 1476).

[25] Grand-Ducal Regulation of 29 December 1983 concerning the publication and periodic submission of financial statements and reports by UCIs subject to supervision by the *Institut Monétaire Luxembourgeois* (*Mémorial* A 1983, 2676).

[26] Art 30, Act of 20 May 1983.

[27] Act of 20 May 1983 concerning the creation of the *Institut Monétaire Luxembourgeois* (*Mémorial* A 1983, 915), as amended by the Acts of 24 December 1984 (*Mémorial* A 1984, 2103), 22 December 1986 (*Mémorial* A 1986, 2403), 21 September 1990 (*Mémorial* A 1990, 734), 16 August 1991 (*Mémorial* A 1991, 1253), 5 April 1993 (*Mémorial* A 1993, 462), 23 December 1995 (*Mémorial* A 1995, 2303) and 22 April 1998 (*Mémorial* A 1998, 466).

[28] *Parliamentary doc* No 3172, Preamble, 32.

A Grand-Ducal Regulation of 30 March 1988[29] determined the amount of the **1.35** fixed capital duty applicable to UCIs governed by the 1988 Act, without changing the situation which had existed since 1983.

The 1988 Act was repealed by the 2002 Act with effect from 13 February 2007. **1.36** During the interim period, the two laws coexisted under a parallel system.

Because the 2002 Act contains most of the provisions of the 1988 Act, many **1.37** comments on the 1988 Act, particularly the Parliamentary documents preceding its enactment, remain relevant and the 1988 Act will be frequently referred to in this work.

Amendment of the 1988 Act

Act of 23 December 1994 The Act of 23 December 1994[30] introduced the first **1.38** change in the rate of the annual subscription tax paid by Luxembourg-based UCIs, as this tax had proved to be a disincentive for certain types of UCI wishing to establish in the Grand Duchy of Luxembourg, particularly money market funds.

This Act reduced the subscription tax to 0.03 per cent for UCIs investing in **1.39** money market instruments or cash and subscriptions by Luxembourg UCIs into other Luxembourg-based UCIs. The conditions for the application of the reduced tax rate and the qualifying criteria for money market instruments were set out in a Grand-Ducal Regulation of 14 April 1995.[31]

Act of 24 December 1996 The Act of 24 December 1996[32] further reduced the **1.40** subscription tax rate for certain types of Luxembourg-based UCIs to 0.01 per cent.[33] This reduction applied to UCIs investing in money market instruments and/or demand or time deposits, and institutional UCIs within the meaning of the 1991 Act which provided a framework for funds sold solely to institutional investors. In addition, subscriptions by Luxembourg UCIs into other Luxembourg-based UCIs were entirely exempted from subscription tax.

---

[29] Grand-Ducal Regulation of 30 March 1988 determining the fixed duty applicable to the capital collected in undertakings for collective investment governed by the Act of 30 March 1988 (*Mémorial* A 1988, 168).

[30] Art 12, Act of 23 December 1994 concerning State revenues and expenditure for the 1995 fiscal year (*Mémorial* A 1994, 2481), amending Art 108, 1988 Act.

[31] Grand-Ducal Regulation of 14 April 1995 adopted in application of Art 108 of the Act of 30 March 1988 concerning undertakings for collective investment, as amended by the Act of 23 December 1994 concerning State revenues and expenditure for the 1995 fiscal year (*Mémorial* A 1995, 906).

[32] Art 5, Act of 24 December 1996 amending certain direct and indirect tax provisions (*Mémorial* A 1996, 2911).

[33] For the sequence and stages of the reduction, see 11.63 *et seq* below.

1.41 Issued on the same day, another Grand-Ducal Regulation[34] defined the concept of a 'money-market instrument' and set out the terms and conditions governing the reduced tax rate.[35]

1.42 *Act of 29 April 1999* The Community legislature did not remain idle after adopting Directive 85/611. The scope of certain Community standards, including Directive 85/611, was extended to the EEA within the framework of the Agreement on the European Economic Area signed in Porto on 2 May 1992. Pursuant to Annexe IX to that Agreement and Protocol 1 on horizontal adaptations, all references in Directive 85/611 to the 'Community' or the 'common market' were deemed to refer to the EEA. The subsequent bankruptcy of Bank of Credit and Commerce International (BCCI) necessitated the increased supervision of financial intermediaries. This, in turn, necessitated the removal of obstacles such as business secrecy and bars on the disclosure of information between supervisory authorities. After Directive 85/611 had been modified to reflect these changes, the Luxembourg legislature had to make the corresponding adjustments to Luxembourg's national standards. This was the underlying purpose of the Act of 29 April 1999,[36] which amended the 1988 Act in the following areas:

(1) detailed provisions were added to step up cooperation between supervisory authorities;

(2) the audit obligations of UCI auditors were broadened;

(3) references in the 1988 Act to the EEC were partly replaced by references to the EEA.

1.43 *Act of 17 July 2000* Independently of the various Community initiatives, the Act of 17 July 2000[37] amended several further aspects of the 1988 Act, and included the following changes:

(1) the subscription tax was reduced to 0.01 per cent for sub-funds or unit classes sold to institutional investors in UCIs governed by the 1988 Act;[38]

---

[34] Grand-Ducal Regulation of 24 December 1996 adopted in application of amended Art 108, Act of 30 March 1988 concerning undertakings for collective investment, as amended by the Act of 24 December 1996 (*Mémorial* A 1996, 2914).

[35] The content of the Grand-Ducal Regulation of 24 December 1996 is identical to that of the Grand-Ducal Regulation of 14 April 1995, adopted in application of the Act of 23 December 1994.

[36] Act of 29 April 1999 concerning: (1) transposition of Directive (EC) 95/26 concerning the reinforcement of prudential supervision, in the amended Act of 5 April 1993 concerning the financial sector and in the amended Act of 30 March 1988 concerning undertakings for collective investment; (2) partial transposition of Art 7, Directive (EEC) 93/6 on the capital adequacy of investment firms and credit institutions, in the amended Act of 5 April 1993 concerning the financial sector; (3) various other modifications in the amended Act of 5 April 1993 concerning the financial sector; (4) modification of the Grand-Ducal Regulation of 19 July 1983 concerning the fiduciary contracts of credit institutions (*Mémorial* A 1999, 1301 *et seq*).

[37] Act of 17 July 2000 amending certain provisions of the Act of 30 March 1988 concerning undertakings for collective investment (*Mémorial* A 2000, 1226 *et seq*); commented upon in Circular 00/14.

[38] Art 108, para 3, 1988 Act.

(2) in umbrella UCIs, sub-funds were segregated vis-à-vis third parties so that the assets of an individual sub-fund could only be used to offset the liabilities of that particular sub-fund unless otherwise provided in the constitutive documents.[39]

Act of 21 December 2001   The Act of 21 December 2001[40] significantly changed   **1.44**
the tax regime of UCIs by reducing the subscription tax rate across the board from 0.06 to 0.05 per cent (other than in respect of money market funds and funds sold to institutional investors to which the reduced subscription tax rates referred to above continued to apply).[41]

Act of 19 July 1991 concerning undertakings for collective investment whose securities are not intended for the public

The 2002 Act and, before it, the 1988 Act apply only to UCIs whose units are   **1.45**
intended to be placed with the public. They do not cover investment structures sold to a small circle of informed investors. Because such structures could also benefit from the UCI regulatory infrastructure, the 1991 Act introduced the concept of institutional UCIs into Luxembourg law. It was replaced some fifteen years later by the Act of 13 February 2007 relating to specialized investment funds.

Act of 20 December 2002 with regard to undertakings for collective investment

Content   Despite a few upgrades, Directive 85/611 enjoyed limited success as   **1.46**
regards its stated objective of the free marketing of UCIs throughout Europe.

The UCI markets had grown considerably since 1985, with UCIs investing in   **1.47**
an increasingly diversified range of securities. Some of these, such as money market instruments, were still not considered transferable securities in all Member States. A UCI whose sole purpose was to invest in money market instruments was not freely able to distribute throughout Europe using the 'UCITS' passport in all markets. It could only claim the general principle of free movement of capital under the EC Treaty more or less respected by each host country. This was a frustrating situation for both the promoters of the relevant UCIs and the Community authorities, who wanted to give such products broader access to the internal market.

---

[39]   Art 111(2), 1988 Act.
[40]   Art 10, Act of 21 December 2001 reforming certain direct and indirect tax provisions (*Mémorial* A 2001, 3312 *et seq*), which amends Art 108(1), 1988 Act.
[41]   Since the coming into force of the 2002 Act, which abolishes the 1988 Act with effect from 13 February 2007, the latter has been amended again by the Act of 19 December 2003 (Art 12, Act of 19 December 2003 concerning the State revenue and expenditure budget for the fiscal year 2004 (*Mémorial* A 2003, 3687 *et seq*). The Act of 19 December 2003 grants total exemption from subscription tax to certain categories of institutional money market funds, amending both Art 129(3), Act of 2002 and Art 108(3), 1988 Act. The 1988 Act was then amended by the Act of 10 July 2005.

1.48 It was further felt that investor protection would be strengthened by regulating the status of management companies.

1.49 In addition, the fund industry expressed the need to simplify disclosure requirements, and called, *inter alia*, for the introduction of a simplified prospectus which could be provided to investors instead of the complete prospectus, thereby also facilitating the marketing of UCITS.

1.50 The overhaul of Directive 85/611 turned out to be a long and laborious process, finally culminating in two directives amending Directive 85/611, ie Directive 2001/107 and Directive 2001/108. The 2002 Act transposed these two directives into Luxembourg law following the structure of the 1988 Act other than in relation to new changes introduced to comply with new Community standards.

1.51 The 2002 Act is divided into five parts. Part I on UCITS transposed the new regime introduced by Directives 2001/107 and 2001/108 while retaining provisions from Part I of the 1988 Act which were not affected by the new Community legal framework. The changes mainly concerned the investment policies of UCITS to reflect the expanded range of authorized investments and related investment restrictions.

1.52 It is still possible to establish UCIs outside the Community framework pursuant to Part II of the 2002 Act, which, for the most part, is identical to Part II of the 1988 Act.

1.53 As in the 1988 Act, Part III contains a single provision with regard to the inward marketing into Luxembourg of foreign UCIs which are not UCITS.

1.54 A new Part IV on management companies reflects the new Community requirements for companies managing UCITS. It also covers the standards governing other types of management companies (ie those managing only UCIs other than UCITS), merging provisions from the 1988 Act with new provisions derived from Directive 2001/107.

1.55 Part V is very similar to Part IV of the 1988 Act and contains general rules applicable to UCITS and other UCIs. The new provisions inserted by the Luxembourg legislature deal with the simplified prospectus introduced under Directive 85/611, cooperation between the CSSF and foreign management company supervisory authorities, and new methods of publishing UCI sales documents.

1.56 Lastly, the law has two annexes. The first lists information to be supplied in sales documents (Schedule A to Directive 2001/107), periodic reports (Schedule B to Directive 2001/107), and the simplified prospectus (Schedule C to Directive 2001/107). The second annexe repeats the collective portfolio management functions listed in Directive 2001/107.

The 2002 Act came into force on 1 January 2003. Its implementation has been **1.57**
relatively complex in the light of the transition regime flowing from Directives
2001/107 and 2001/108 and included transitional arrangements to allow existing UCITS to conform to the new standards while also providing the benefit of
UCITS authorization and a European passport under Directives 2001/107 and
2001/108 for UCITS authorized under the 2003 Act.

To facilitate transitional arrangements, the Acts of 1988 and 2002 both had legal effect **1.58**
for a period of time until 13 February 2007 when the 1988 Act was finally repealed.

UCITS authorized between 13 February 2002 and 13 February 2004 were **1.59**
allowed to opt to operate under the 1988 Act until 13 February 2004 when
they were obliged to conform to the new UCITS rules. UCITS authorized
before 13 February 2002 (the effective date for Directives 2001/107 and
2001/108) were allowed to opt to operate under the 1988 Act until 13 February
2007 at which date they had to conform with the 2002 Act.

Management companies were also subject to a number of new rules under the 2002 **1.60**
Act. Companies managing UCIs other than UCITS have been governed by the
2002 Act since its effective date, ie 1 January 2003. Companies authorized before
13 February 2004 and mainly set up to manage one or more UCITS were permitted to postpone application of the new regime until 13 February 2007. As long as
they operated under the old rules, they were not entitled to apply for a European
passport. A UCITS governed by the 2002 Act could, until 13 February 2007, be
managed by a management company not yet in compliance with the new rules.[42]

Acts amending the 2002 Act
Act of 19 December 2003   The Act of 19 December 2003[43] exempted certain **1.61**
categories of institutional money market funds from subscription tax, provided
their residual portfolio maturity did not exceed ninety days and they had obtained
the highest possible rating from a recognized rating agency.

Act of 15 June 2004   The Act of 15 June 2004[44] extended the exemption from **1.62**
subscription tax to UCIs established as pension pooling vehicles.

Act of 10 July 2005   The Act of 10 July 2005 transposes Directive 2003/71,[45] **1.63**
generally referred to as the 'Prospectus Directive'. It sets out rules on the contents

---

[42]   This discussion needs to be considered in the light of the interpretations supplied by the
CESR. See Circular 05/186, which includes the CESR's recommendations.
[43]   Art 12, Act of 19 December 2003 concerning the State revenue and expenditure budget for
the fiscal year 2004 (*Mémorial* A 2003, 3687 *et seq*).
[44]   Art 45, Act of 15 June 2004 amending Art 129(3), 2002 Act.
[45]   Directive (EC) 2003/71 of the European Parliament and the Council of 4 November
2003 on the prospectus to be published when securities are offered to the public or admitted to
trading and amending Directive (EC) 2001/34 ([2003] OJ L345/64 *et seq*).

and dissemination of a prospectus in the case of a public offering or listing of transferable securities on a regulated market in Luxembourg. Insofar as they are governed by special legislation, UCIs generally fall outside its sphere of application with the exception of closed-end UCIs, ie UCIs whose unitholders are not allowed to redeem their units under any circumstances.[46] To avoid a combination of requirements for the issue of prospectuses by closed-end UCIs under both the 2002 Act and the Act of 10 July 2005, the 2002 Act was amended so that the issue of prospectuses by closed-end UCIs is exclusively governed by the Act of 10 July 2005.

1.64 The Act of 10 July 2005 also modified the treatment of foreign UCIs (other than coordinated UCITS) which are closed-ended within the meaning of the Act of 10 July 2005, to permit the marketing of their units in or from Luxembourg provided such closed-end UCIs comply with the Act of 10 July 2005.[47]

1.65 *Act of 13 February 2007*   The Act of 13 February 2007 slightly amended the 2002 Act, so as to exempt from subscription tax an investment in a SIF made by a UCI.[48]

Act of 13 February 2007 relating to specialized investment funds

1.66 The 1991 Act dealing with funds sold to institutional investors is a precise piece of legislation containing only seven articles and cross-referring for the most part to the 1988 Act. As a result of the repeal and replacement of the 1988 Act with new legislation on UCIs in 2002, it was necessary to amend the 1991 Act and the Luxembourg legislature took the opportunity of adopting a comprehensive and independent body of rules to replace the 1991 Act. This provided an opportunity to modernize the rules applying to institutional funds, bringing a larger pool of well-informed investors[49] within its scope, and to classify institutional funds as 'specialized investment funds'. The governing rules for specialized investment funds were simplified, although largely modelled on Part II of the 2002 Act. The main objective was to adapt the rules on institutional funds to meet an increased

---

[46] Closed-end UCIs are determined in juxtaposition to open-end UCIs, defined by Directive (EC) 2003/71 as follows: 'collective investment undertaking other than the closed-end type' means unit trusts and investment companies: (1) the object of which is the collective investment of capital provided by the public, and which operate on the principle of risk-spreading; (2) the units of which are, at the holder's request, repurchased or redeemed, directly or indirectly, out of the assets of these undertakings.

[47] Art 76, 2002 Act.

[48] Art 72, Act of 13 February 2007.

[49] For further details concerning the concept of well-informed investor, see 2.61 *et seq* below.

demand for alternative investment structures, such as hedge funds, real estate funds or private equity funds.[50]

Circulars issued by the supervisory authorities

Since the end of the 1970s, the supervisory authority has laid down, in the form of circulars, the rules governing the operation of UCIs and SICARs. However, the concept of a circular does not technically form part of Luxembourg's legal panoply.   **1.67**

The 2002 Act[51] permits the adoption of standards governing the operation or risk diversification of certain types of UCIs in the form of Grand-Ducal regulations subject to the recommendation of the supervisory authority. However, the CSSF has always preferred to issue circulars in order to ensure optimum flexibility and adaptability of its rules rather than recommending the adoption of Grand-Ducal regulations.   **1.68**

In the 1970s and 1980s, numerous circulars were issued by the CSSF (and its predecessors, the *Institut Monétaire Luxembourgeois* and the Banking Commissioner). Circular 91/75 of 21 January 1991 revised and reviewed the rules applicable to Luxembourg-based UCIs governed by the 1988 Act. The same circular repealed and replaced previous circulars. The application and interpretation of the 2002 Act is not yet covered by a general circular such as Circular 91/75, so that Circular 91/75 largely remains in force.   **1.69**

The main circulars on UCIs and SICARs currently in force are as follows: **1.70**

- IML Circular 91/75 of 21 January 1991;
- CSSF Circular 00/14 of 27 July 2000 on the adoption of the Act of 17 July 2000 amending certain provisions of the Act of 30 March 1988;
- CSSF Circular 02/77 of 27 November 2002 on the protection of investors in the event of net asset value calculation error and the correction of consequences resulting from non-compliance with the investment rules applicable to UCIs;
- CSSF Circular 02/80 of 5 December 2002 on the specific rules applicable to Luxembourg UCIs pursuing alternative investment strategies;
- CSSF Circular 02/81 of 6 December 2002 on guidelines concerning the duties of auditors of UCIs;

---

[50] For further details on the genesis of the Act of 13 February 2007, see M Moulla and M Chantalangsy, 'Presentation of the law of 2007 compared to other existing legislation governing collective investment structures—historical overview of the law of 2007' in *Specialised Investment Funds* (Arendt & Medernach, 2007) 14, 15.

[51] Arts 67, 72, and 75, 2002 Act.

- CSSF Circular 03/87 of 21 January 2003 on the coming into force of the 2002 Act;

- CSSF Circular 03/88 of 22 January 2003 on the classification of UCIs governed by the provisions of the 2002 Act;

- CSSF Circular 03/97 of 28 February 2003 on the publication in the electronic database for the financial centre ('*Référentiel de la place*') of simplified and full prospectuses and the annual and half-yearly reports by UCIs;

- CSSF Circular 03/108 of 30 July 2003 on Luxembourg management companies subject to the provisions of Chapter 13 of the 2002 Act, and Luxembourg self-managed investment companies subject to Article 27 or Article 40 of the 2002 Act;

- CSSF Circular 03/122 of 19 December 2003 on clarifications concerning the simplified prospectus;

- CSSF Circular 04/146 of 17 June 2004 on the protection of UCIs and their investors against late trading and market timing practices;

- CSSF Circular 04/151 of 13 July 2004 on the information to be published in the listing particulars of the securities listed below:

  - shares and units of foreign UCIs whose securities are not publicly available, offered or sold in or from Luxembourg, and

  - securities redeemable or exchangeable for shares or units of UCIs or whose income and/or redemption is/are linked to underlying shares or units of UCIs;

- CSSF Circular 04/155 of 27 September 2004 on the compliance function;

- CSSF Circular 05/176 of 5 April 2005 on the rules of conduct to be adopted by UCITS in relation to the use of financial derivative instruments;

- CSSF Circular 05/177 of 6 April 2005 on the abolition of any prior approval by the CSSF of advertising material used by persons and companies supervised by the CSSF; revocation of point II of Chapter L of IML Circular 91/75; revocation of the two last sentences of point IV 5.11 of CSSF Circular 2000/15;

- CSSF Circular 05/178 of 11 April 2005 on administrative and accounting organization; outsourcing of IT services; revocation of point 4.5.2 of IML Circular 96/126 and substitution with point 4.5.2 of Circular 05/178;

- CSSF Circular 05/185 of 24 May 2005 on Luxembourg management companies subject to the provisions of Chapter 13 of the 2002 Act, and Luxembourg self-managed investment companies subject to the provisions of Article 27 or Article 40 of the 2002 Act;

- CSSF Circular 05/186 of 25 May 2005 on the guidelines of the Committee of European Securities Regulators (CESR) regarding the application of transitional measures resulting from Directives (EC) 2001/107 and (EC) 2001/108 (UCITS III) amending Directive (EEC) 85/611 (UCITS I);

- CSSF Circular 05/188 of 27 May 2005 on the coming into force of the Act of 12 November 2004;

- CSSF Circular 05/210 of 10 October 2005 on the drawing-up of a simplified prospectus within the scope of Chapter 1 of Part III of the Act on prospectuses for securities;

- CSSF Circular 05/211 of 13 October 2005 on combating money laundering and terrorist financing and the prevention of the use of the financial sector for money laundering and terrorist financing purposes;

- CSSF Circular 05/225 of 16 December 2005 on the concept of 'offer to the public of securities' as defined in the Act on prospectuses for securities and the consequential 'obligation to publish a prospectus';

- CSSF Circular 05/226 of 16 December 2005 on the general overview of the Act on prospectuses for securities and technical specifications regarding communications to the CSSF of documents with a view to authorization or for filing and of notices for offers to the public and admissions to trading on a regulated market;

- CSSF Circular 06/241 of 5 April 2006 on the concept of risk capital under the Act of 15 June 2004;

- CSSF Circular 06/267 of 22 November 2006 on technical specifications regarding the filing with the CSSF, in accordance with the Act on prospectuses for securities, of documents for approval or notification purposes and of notices for offers to the public of units/shares of Luxembourg closed-end UCIs and admissions of units/shares of Luxembourg closed-end UCIs to trading on a regulated market;

- CSSF Circular 06/272 of 21 December 2006 on technical specifications regarding the filing with the CSSF, in accordance with the Act on prospectuses for securities, of documents for approval or notification purposes and of notices for offers to the public of securities issued by SICARs and admissions of securities issued by SICARs to trading on a regulated market;

- CSSF Circular 07/277 of 9 January 2007 on the new notification procedure following guidelines issued by the Committee of European Securities Regulators (CESR) regarding the simplification of the UCITS notification procedure;

- CSSF Circular 07/283 of 28 February 2007 on the entry into force of the Act of 13 February 2007;

- CSSF Circular 07/290 of 3 May 2007 on the definition of capital ratios pursuant to Article 56 of the 1993 Act (application to investment firms and management companies subject to Chapter 13 of the 2002 Act, as amended);

- CSSF Circular 07/307 of 31 July 2007 on the MiFID Directive: Conduct of business rules in the financial sector;
- CSSF Circular 07/308 of 2 August 2007 on the rules of conduct to be adopted by UCITS with respect to the management of financial risk and the use of derivative financial instruments;
- CSSF Circular 07/309 of 3 August 2007 on risk-spreading in the context of SIFs;
- CSSF Circular 07/310 of 3 August 2007 on financial information to be provided by SIFs, as amended by CSSF Circular 08/348;
- CSSF Circular 08/339 of 19 February 2008 on the guidelines of the Committee of European Securities Regulators (CESR) concerning eligible assets for investment by UCITS;
- CSSF Circular 08/348 of 17 April 2008 on the changes to Circulars IML 97/136 and CSSF 07/310;
- CSSF Circular 08/350 of 22 April 2008 on clarifications relating to the amendments introduced by the Act of 13 July 2007 to the status of professionals of the financial sector (PFS) referred to in Articles 29-1, 29-2, 29-3, or 29-4 and designated as 'support PFS', and on the amendment to the prudential supervisory procedures for support PFS;
- CSSF Circular 08/356 of 4 June 2008 regarding rules applicable to UCIs which employ certain techniques and instruments relating to transferable securities and money market instruments.

1.71 The circulars are a highly appropriate regulation tool for UCIs, which require a legal framework that can be easily and rapidly adapted to needs of the investment industry.

1.72 Since the constitutional reform of 19 November 2004,[52] the CSSF has been authorized to adopt regulations within the framework of its responsibilities, provided it has the necessary regulatory authority under the relevant law.

1.73 While the Constitution only refers to the adoption of regulations by the CSSF this does not of itself mean that the CSSF is restricted from prescribing circulars in areas where it has regulatory authority. Circulars are typically used to specify certain legal norms whereas the CSSF has adopted circulars as a means of informing

---

[52] Art 108*bis* of the Constitution, amended by the Act of 19 November 2004 with regard to (1) amendment of Arts 11(6), 32, and 76 of the Constitution; and (2) the creation of a new Art 108*bis* in the Constitution (*Mémorial* A 2004, 2784). This constitutional amendment followed the decision of 7 March 2003 of the Constitutional Court of the Grand Duchy of Luxembourg (*Mémorial* A 2003, 656) that the power to adopt regulations and decisions to implement legislation in accordance with Art 36 of the Constitution is in the hands of the Grand Duke. A law or regulation entrusting this power to an authority other than the Grand Duke is unconstitutional.

third parties of its general policy positions on various matters. As derogations from such positions are possible, it is difficult to argue that they decree or specify rigid legal norms. Circulars as issued by the CSSF are not so much a form of regulation as a tool to ensure transparency and adaptability.

Laws and regulations not limited to UCIs

Though not specifically limited to UCIs, two additional bodies of rules also apply in all standards governing such funds. **1.74**

The first is the 1915 Act, which has the status of a supplementary standard vis-à-vis UCIs.[53] It applies to situations not specifically legislated for by the 2002 Act and the Act of 13 February 2007. **1.75**

The second is the Luxembourg Civil Code, which governs the contractual structure underlying FCPs. It also governs civil companies in general and as such applies to investment companies, save to the extent otherwise provided for by the 1915 Act, the 2002 Act, or the Act of 13 February 2007. **1.76**

Role of the CSSF

General presentation

The CSSF is a public law body established with legal status by the Luxembourg State. Its object is to maintain prudential supervision of the financial sector.[54] Within this role, it oversees UCIs established or marketing their units in the Grand Duchy of Luxembourg.[55] It also supervises management companies of UCIs.[56] **1.77**

The CSSF actively engages in its supervisory duties in connection with UCIs. Its duties and involvement vary under the applicable regulations depending on whether the UCI is based in Luxembourg[57] or is a non-Luxembourg coordinated UCITS with a European passport, or a non-Luxembourg UCI which is not a UCITS. **1.78**

---

[53] Arts 26, 40, and 71, 2002 Act.
[54] Arts 2 and 3, Act of 23 December 1998 concerning the creation of a Commission for the supervision of the financial sector (*Mémorial* A 1998, 2985).
[55] For other comments on this issue, see 8.01 *et seq* below. See also A Elvinger. 'Le rôle des autorités de surveillance' *ALFI Yearbook 1994*, 33; C Kremer and J Baden, 'The role of the Luxembourg Monetary Institute in the supervision of undertakings for collective investment.' (February 1995) 3, 63, *World Fund Industry/Gestion collective internationale*.
[56] Arts 77 to 92, 2002 Act.
[57] Part I or Part II, 2002 Act or Act of 13 February 2007.

1.79 The CSSF also supervises management companies for UCIs based in Luxembourg. It supervises foreign entities only when operating under the European passport introduced by Directive 85/611. In such cases, its intervention is minimal as the primary regulatory authority is the supervisory authority in the company's home State.

1.80 Generally speaking, the CSSF has very extensive powers in its interpretation of the Act of 13 February 2007 and the 2002 Act. In the exercise of those powers, it has specified the meaning of certain concepts, such as overall risk connected with derivatives.[58] The 2002 Act also enables it to designate UCITS classes, which, whilst investing in transferable securities, cannot be regarded as coordinated UCITS entitled to the European passport under Directive 85/611. Last but not least, the 2002 Act refers to a proposed Grand-Ducal regulation to be issued in order to lay down specific rules with regard to certain provisions of the Act. As mentioned above, rather than recommending the adoption of a Grand-Ducal regulation, the CSSF has issued various circulars[59] detailing the principles adopted by it in its supervisory role in relation to matters not settled by the Act.

Supervision of UCIs

UCIs established in the Grand Duchy of Luxembourg

1.81 The CSSF is responsible for authorizing UCIs established in the Grand Duchy of Luxembourg. Accordingly, it receives the incorporation documents and various other documents and information about each UCI. If, after examining such papers, it believes that the investor information is adequate and reflects the applicable legal standards, it adds the UCI to the official list of UCIs. However, registration does not indicate approval of a UCI's investment objectives or investments, or of its ability to meet its objectives.

1.82 UCIs remain on the official list as long as they comply with the rules governing their operation and sales of units. The CSSF checks compliance against the monthly, semi-annual, and annual reports received from each UCI and against any other information requested by it. Similarly, it authorizes in advance proposed modifications to incorporation documents.

1.83 In addition, the CSSF is authorized to grant certain derogations from the 2002 Act.[60] It may waive the application of certain legal requirements for UCITS covered by Part I of the 2002 Act. It has more extensive powers in this regard with respect to UCIs governed by Part II of the 2002 Act and the Act of 13 February 2007.

---

[58] Circular 05/176.
[59] Primarily Circular 91/75 and, as regards SIFs, Circular 07/309.
[60] Arts 45(1) and 116, 2002 Act.

The CSSF exerts wider control over so-called 'self-managed' investment compa-   **1.84**
nies, which are subject to similar share capital and management obligations as
management companies themselves.[61]

The CSSF also has the power to impose penalties. In particular, it may remove   **1.85**
a UCI from the official list if it violates the laws and regulations governing its
operation or the sale of its units.

UCIs established in foreign countries

Coordinated UCITS

Coordinated UCITS benefit from the rules governing the free movement of   **1.86**
capital and freedom to provide services under Directive 85/611. This allows
coordinated UCITS approved by the supervisory authority of the Member State
in which they are established (the 'home State') to market their units freely in
another Member State of the EEA (the 'host State').

Only those aspects not covered by Directive 85/611 remain under the supervisory   **1.87**
authority of the host State, such as information to be provided to the public, as to
which the supervisory authority of the host State may lay down special
requirements.[62]

Pursuant to those principles, the CSSF has only limited authority over foreign   **1.88**
UCITS governed by Directive 85/611. Foreign UCITS must nevertheless inform
the CSSF of their intention to market their units in the Grand Duchy of
Luxembourg and provide it with certain documents. The CSSF may prohibit
marketing only on the grounds listed in Directive 85/611.[63]

Other UCIs under foreign law

Foreign open-end UCIs, within the meaning of the Act of 10 July 2005, other   **1.89**
than coordinated UCITS, must be authorized by the CSSF if they wish to market
their units in the Grand Duchy of Luxembourg. They are only authorized by the
CSSF when subject, in their home State, to permanent supervision by a supervisory authority created by law to protect investors. Such UCIs remain on the official list of the CSSF as long as they comply with the Luxembourg rules governing
their operation and sales of units.[64]

Foreign closed-end UCIs, within the meaning of the Act of 10 July 2005, may   **1.90**
market their units in the Grand Duchy of Luxembourg subject to compliance

---

[61] Art 27, 2002 Act. For details see 6.77 *et seq* below.
[62] Art 58, 2002 Act.
[63] Art 60, 2002 Act.
[64] Art 76, 2002 Act.

with the Act of 10 July 2005. They are not subject to the supervisory authority provided for by the 2002 Act.[65]

Supervision of management companies

Management companies established in the Grand Duchy of Luxembourg

1.91 The right to carry on the activity of a management company established in Luxembourg is subject to prior authorization. This is granted either by the CSSF or by the Minister with responsibility for the CSSF (in the case of a management company for foreign UCIs other than coordinated UCITS).[66] All applications are reviewed by the CSSF, whether or not the UCI in question is established in Luxembourg or another jurisdiction. This said, companies which only manage foreign UCIs other than coordinated UCITS require another type of authorization in Luxembourg than that for UCITS management companies. UCITS management companies may also manage UCIs other than coordinated UCITS, in which case they are subject to slightly different rules.

1.92 A management company seeking authorization must comply with a series of conditions set out in the 2002 Act[67] or, when it only engages in the management of foreign UCIs other than UCITS, the 1993 Act.[68] The same rules apply to a management company wishing to retain its authorization.[69] On an ongoing basis, the CSSF checks compliance by management companies with their obligations, particularly through the quarterly information they are obliged to supply.[70] The auditor of the relevant management company in fulfilling the auditor's role envisaged under the Acts of 2002[71] and 1993[72] also plays an important role in the continued retention of a management company's authorization.

1.93 Withdrawal of a management company's authorization is the ultimate penalty for non-compliance with the laws and regulations governing its authorization and activities. The CSSF determines whether an authorization should be withdrawn, although it does not have discretionary power to do so. An authorization may only be withdrawn when the CSSF observes that the management company in question comes within one of the situations listed in the 2002 Act[73] or in the 1993 Act,[74] as

---

[65] ibid.
[66] Arts 77(1) and 91(1), 2002 Act; Art 14(1), Act of 1993.
[67] Arts 77–80, 91, and 92, 2002 Act.
[68] Arts 15 to 22-1 and 28-8, 1993 Act.
[69] Arts 82–86, 91, and 92, 2002 Act; Art 23(4), 1993 Act.
[70] Section III, Circular 03/108.
[71] Arts 80 and 92, 2002 Act.
[72] Art 22, 1993 Act.
[73] Arts 78(5) and 91(5), 2002 Act.
[74] Art 23, 1993 Act.

the case may be. Under the 2002 Act the CSSF may grant management companies a limited period to comply with the applicable laws and regulations or to cease their activity.[75]

Management companies established in foreign countries

Management companies of UCITS approved as such in foreign countries may, by virtue of their European passport, establish themselves in Luxembourg or provide in Luxembourg the services set out in Directive 85/611 without having to seek additional authorization from the CSSF.[76] The notification procedure by which the authorities in the home State inform the CSSF, as set out in Directive 85/611, is the only applicable formality.[77] The CSSF has limited powers in this respect. It informs the management company of the general interest rules governing its activity in Luxembourg and any applicable rules of conduct if the company in question engages in Luxembourg in portfolio management for entities other than UCIs, the provision of investment advice or the acceptance of deposits.[78] The CSSF may decline permission to a management company wishing to market units of UCIs managed by it, if the CSSF notes that the activity violates the relevant provisions in Directive 85/611.[79]

1.94

The CSSF authorizes foreign management companies other than coordinated management companies when they want to manage a UCI in Luxembourg other than a coordinated UCITS[80] or a SIF. In principle, the CSSF requires such companies to be subject to prudential control in their country of origin, allowing it to trust in supervision it has every reason to consider effective.

1.95

---

[75] eg this power can be exercised by the CSSF when a management company no longer complies with the legal requirements with respect to share capital (Art 82, 2002 Act).

[76] See 6.195 below.

[77] Art 6a, Directive (EEC) 85/611.

[78] ibid Arts 6a, points 4 and 6, and 6b, points 3 and 4.

[79] ibid Art 6a, point 5.

[80] Art 93(3), 2002 Act.

2

CLASSIFICATION OF UNDERTAKINGS FOR
COLLECTIVE INVESTMENT

Classification of UCIs by Reference to their Investment and Sales Activities

2.01 The object of Luxembourg-based UCIs is the collective investment of capital raised from investors. Depending on the nature of the assets to be collectively invested (instruments governed by Directive 85/611 or other assets), the type of investor canvassed (traditional private investors or well-informed investors), the marketing method used (public offering or private placement), or the area in which the fund is marketed (inside or outside the EEA), Luxembourg-based UCIs fall into one of the following three categories:

(1) UCIs governed by Part I of the 2002 Act—such UCIs invest in transferable securities and other instruments authorized by Directive 85/611 and are therefore UCITS; they are eligible for the European passport created under Directive 85/611 and qualify as coordinated UCITS;

(2) UCIs governed by Part II of the 2002 Act—such UCIs may invest in assets other than those authorized by Directive 85/611 but are not eligible for a European passport since they fall outside the scope of application of Directive 85/611;

(3) so-called 'specialised' UCIs governed by the Act of 13 February 2007, which, while the nature of their investments is not restricted, must reserve their units for one or more well-informed investors.

These three categories of UCIs will be covered below.

UCITS governed by Part I of the 2002 Act

2.02 Part I of the 2002 Act applies to all 'undertakings for collective investment in transferable securities (UCITS) situated in the Grand Duchy of Luxembourg'[1] not specifically excluded from the status of coordinated UCITS. A coordinated UCITS is 'any undertaking . . . the exclusive object of which is the collective

---

[1] Art 2(1), 2002 Act.

investment in transferable securities and/or other liquid financial assets of capital obtained from the public . . . and whose units, at the holders' request, are directly or indirectly redeemed from its assets'.[2]

Thus it is the object of a UCI governed by the 2002 Act which determines whether **2.03** it is attributed the status of a coordinated UCITS or not. If a UCI's exclusive object is to invest in listed transferable securities and other instruments authorized by Directive 85/611 and it is not otherwise excluded from the ambit of the Directive, it will be governed by Part I of the 2002 Act as a coordinated UCITS unless it is exclusively marketed to well-informed investors and opts to be subject to the Act of 13 February 2007.

It is generally assumed, somewhat carelessly, that the term UCITS refers to *European-* **2.04** *type* or *coordinated* UCIs that may be marketed freely under the provisions of Directive 85/611 and which are subject to Part I of the 2002 Act. This, however, is not necessarily the case, as Directive 85/611 also refers to certain types of UCITS intentionally excluded from its scope of application including, for example, undertakings whose securities are marketed exclusively outside the EEA or are sold inside the EEA solely on a private placement basis. Such UCITS are not covered by Directive 85/611 because of the place or method of marketing of their units.

Other categories of UCITS are excluded because of their investment or borrowing **2.05** policies. Although such UCITS may be offered to the public in the EEA, they fall outside the scope of application of Directive 85/611 because Member States are not obliged to recognize them. In the Grand Duchy of Luxembourg, such categories are listed in Circular 03/88.[3] They include, for example, UCIs that use borrowing for investment in listed equities. While such UCIs buy transferable securities and are therefore 'UCITS', they do not benefit from the rights granted by Directive 85/611. In this work, such UCITS are sometimes referred to as *non-coordinated* UCITS.

Coordinated UCITS must meet four criteria: **2.06**

(1) their exclusive object must be the collective investment in listed transferable securities and other financial assets authorized by Directive 85/611;
(2) they must be open to the public of the EEA;
(3) they must redeem their units at the request of their investors;
(4) they must not be barred from coordinated status by reason of their investment and borrowing policy.

These criteria are described in greater detail in the following paragraphs.

---

[2] ibid Art 2(2).
[3] Section III, Circular 03/88.

Exclusive investment in transferable securities and other instruments governed by Directive 85/611

2.07 The fundamental scope of activity of coordinated UCITS is outlined in Directive 85/611,[4] according to which a UCITS must have as its *sole* object the collective investment in listed transferable securities and/or other liquid financial assets governed by Directive 85/611.

2.08 The designation 'UCITS' can be misleading here. Since its amendment in 2002, Directive 85/611 also governs UCIs whose exclusive object is to invest in money market instruments, units of UCIs, time deposits, and/or derivatives. Such UCIs are also considered to be 'UCITS'.

2.09 Like the 2002 Act,[5] Directive 85/611[6] provides that the status of coordinated UCITS is not accorded to 'investment companies whose assets are invested through subsidiary companies principally in assets other than transferable securities and other liquid financial assets' authorized by the Directive. This exclusion is difficult to interpret.

2.10 The object of a coordinated UCITS is, by definition, to invest in securities in accordance with the principle of risk spreading and the absence of controlling interests. In other words, interests in securities issued by different issuers over which the UCITS does not have any direct influence are acquired by UCITS. The issuers of securities held are not and cannot be its subsidiaries. The UCITS does not control the composition of the assets held by entities in which it invests nor their business operations.

2.11 Nevertheless, issuers of securities which may be held by coordinated UCITS can hold assets that the coordinated UCITS itself would not be authorized to acquire directly. For example, a coordinated UCITS can buy the shares of real estate property companies listed on a stock exchange or traded on a regulated market. The investment rules imposed by the 2002 Act prohibit the UCITS from acquiring a majority interest in such real estate companies. In economic terms, however, the portfolio of a UCITS investing in listed real estate companies represents real estate assets.[7] Precious metals afford a similar example.

2.12 However, if a UCI's object was to invest directly in assets other than transferable securities and other liquid financial assets authorized by the Directive, it would not be accorded the status of a coordinated UCITS.

---

[4] Arts 1 and 19.1 of Directive (EEC) 85/611, transposed into Arts 2 and 41, 2002 Act.
[5] Art 2(4), 2002 Act.
[6] Art 1.4, Directive (EEC) 85/611.
[7] Example given in the Parliamentary documents relating to the 1988 Act, *Parliamentary doc No 3172*, Comments on the Articles, 33.

These explanations call for an observation. Certain UCIs, particularly those **2.13** concentrating on investments in the real estate sector, may opt for either Part I or Part II of the 2002 Act, or even for the Act of 13 February 2007,[8] depending in particular on their investment objectives and strategies vis-à-vis their target assets.

Marketing to the public in the EEA

The status of coordinated UCITS was created in order to subject UCIs established **2.14** in the EEA to 'common basic rules . . . for their authorisation, supervision, structure and activities . . . and the information they must publish'.[9]

The preamble to Directive 85/611 refers to the need to coordinate national laws **2.15** governing UCIs 'with a view to bringing into line the conditions of competition between those undertakings at Community level, while at the same time ensuring more effective and more uniform protection for unitholders'.[10]

The status of a coordinated UCITS is not available to a UCI whose units are not **2.16** intended for investment by the public within the EEA. This does not mean that coordinated UCITS must market in all countries of the EEA to raise capital. It is sufficient for an undertaking to approach the public of a single Member State in order to obtain and maintain the status of a coordinated UCITS. In contrast, if only the public in a non-EEA country is canvassed or if the units of a coordinated UCITS are offered without promotion to the public, Directive 85/611 and therefore Part I of the 2002 Act do not apply.

UCITS whose units are reserved for sale to the public in non-EEA countries

Where a UCITS decides not to market its units within the EEA and formally **2.17** includes a prohibition to that effect in its constitutive documents, it falls outside the scope of Part I of the 2002 Act[11] and does not benefit from the European passport granted by Directive 85/611.

This reflects the rationale behind coordinated UCITS of promoting European **2.18** harmonization, mainly in the interests of EEA investors. When a UCITS is not marketed in EEA Member States, coordination becomes meaningless.

This does not mean that a non-coordinated UCITS which targets only the public **2.19** in a non-EEA country must prevent EEA residents from holding its units.

---

   [8]   As regards real estate SIFs, see M Kemp and C Martougin, 'Real estate SIFs—New opportunities for investments in real estate properties', in *Specialised Investment Funds* (Arendt & Medernach, 2007) 182.
   [9]   Fourth Recital in the preamble to Directive (EEC) 85/611.
   [10]   ibid Second Recital in the preamble.
   [11]   Art 3, third indent, 2002 Act.

2.20 A UCITS whose units are marketed only in non-EEA countries is regarded as non-coordinated, even when its units are listed on the Luxembourg Stock Exchange.[12]

2.21 This may seem surprising. In principle, a stock exchange listing is synonymous with a public offering in the area in which the stock exchange is established. However, if a UCI's units are listed only on the Luxembourg Stock Exchange but in fact are not marketed to the Luxembourg public directly and actively and are not marketed elsewhere in the EEA, the UCITS is not a coordinated UCITS.[13]

UCITS whose units are sold without promotion within the EEA

2.22 Undertakings that 'collect capital without promoting the sale of their units to the public in [the EEA] or any part [thereof]'[14] are excluded from Part I of the 2002 Act. Such UCITS may be available to the public but forego 'promotional activity' in their marketing efforts. The term 'promotional activity' is defined in Circular 03/88. It covers, in particular, the use of advertising resources—such as the press, radio, television, and advertising brochures[15]—or financial intermediaries or vendors.

2.23 An absence of advertising limits the circle of potential investors to certain categories of institutional investors or other individual investors who are particularly knowledgeable, whereas the objective of Directive 85/611 is to protect the general public. Thus UCITS without any promotional activities in the EEA cannot be accorded the status of coordinated UCITS.

2.24 In practice, the sale of units without promotional activity is often used by UCIs that plan to invest in listed transferable securities or other instruments authorized by Directive 85/611 but prefer not to be fettered by the investment restrictions applicable to coordinated UCITS, and wish to market within the EEA. By forgoing

---

[12] This case is mentioned in Section III, 3, Circular 03/88. The same example is given in the Parliamentary documents relating to the 1988 Act, *Parliamentary doc* No 3172, Comments on the Articles, 34.

[13] This position is confirmed by the Parliamentary documents relating to the 1988 Act, which come to the same conclusion, on the grounds that the concept of public offering is not defined in Luxembourg law. See *Parliamentary doc* No 3172, Comments on the Articles, 52. This remains true despite the new definition of public offering introduced by the Act of 10 July 2005. Circular 05/225 specifies that 'the effect of this definition is nevertheless limited to Part I of the Prospectus Act on public offerings of transferable securities subject to the Community harmonisation and to Chapter 1 of Part III of the Prospectus Act determining the rules applicable in Luxembourg to public offerings of transferable securities and equivalent securities outside the scope of application of the Prospectus Directive. The definition is not applicable to other areas, such as the marketing of units in open-end undertakings for collective investment (UCIs)'.

[14] Art 3, second indent, 2002 Act.

[15] Section III, 2, Circular 03/88. See also *Parliamentary doc* No 3172, Comments on the Articles, 34.

promotional activity, such UCITS avoid the investment and borrowing constraints imposed by Directive 85/611.

Mandatory redemption of units at the investors' initiative

One of the characteristics of a coordinated UCITS is its obligation to honour at all times redemption requests from investors. In other words, such a UCITS is 'open-ended'.[16]   **2.25**

Open-ended means that investors may redeem their units. A coordinated UCITS is not open-ended when it reserves to its management the right to determine when units may be redeemed, and does not permit investors the right to redeem at their own discretion. The open-ended concept is best expressed by saying that an investor may redeem his units when he wants to, not when decided by the UCI.   **2.26**

In practice, UCIs are sometimes closed-ended during the start-up period, for example for two years. Such UCIs announce in their constitutive documents and their sales documents that redemption will not be possible before expiration of the start-up period. This is frequently the case with UCIs investing in transferable securities with reduced liquidity, for example companies that have to reach a certain maturity before their securities can be listed. UCIs that buy such securities may have difficulty in selling them due to the absence of a liquid market, which in turn could impede the UCITS in satisfying redemption requests. UCITS can therefore reserve the right, in their constitutive documents, not to meet investor redemption requests for a given period, during which they fall outside the scope of Part I of the 2002 Act. In contrast, they automatically fall within the scope of Part I on the day investors acquire the right to request redemption, provided that they are not excluded for other reasons from Part I of the 2002 Act.[17]   **2.27**

Insofar as the opening up of a UCITS for redemptions at a future date is decided from inception, the prospectus must from the first date of issue alert investors to the 'lock up' period and describe its consequences, mainly with respect to the investment policy and inability of investors to redeem during the relevant period.[18]   **2.28**

'Open-ended' does not mean that a coordinated UCITS must accept all redemption requests received on the same day. Redemption of too many units could create liquidity problems and, in extreme cases, force the UCITS to sell part of its portfolio at a time when the investment manager would not otherwise have decided to   **2.29**

---

[16] The English term *open-ended* can lead to confusion in that *open-ended* can also mean 'open' for subscription. In this context, open-ended for redemption purposes determines whether the status of coordinated UCITS applies.

[17] Section III, 1, Circular 03/88.

[18] ibid.

sell assets. When redemption requests received for processing on the same day exceed a given specified threshold, the fund may reduce the requests proportionally and defer redemption of units in excess of the relevant threshold to subsequent dealing days. If this power is used, deferred redemption requests are processed on subsequent redemption days in priority to redemption requests received subsequently. In certain cases, UCITS may have to sell assets in order to fund redemption requests, prior to processing redemption requests received. The postponement conditions must be set out in the UCITS' constitutive documents and sales documents.[19]

2.30 Except in the above cases, a coordinated UCITS may not subject the exercise of redemption rights to terms and conditions that would render redemption practically impossible or arbitrarily complicated,[20] for example by charging excessively high redemption fees.

2.31 Nonetheless a coordinated UCITS may charge redemption fees, *inter alia*, to cover dealing costs on the sale of assets to meet redemption requests or to pay sales agents a deferred sales charge or transaction dealing charges levied by, for example, the UCITS transfer agent. Redemption fees are capped by the CSSF, especially when they are not paid to the UCITS. Fees can sometimes be based on a reducing scale by reference to the duration of ownership and are also appropriate if justified by certain features of the UCITS in question, for example in capital protected or guaranteed structures.[21] A UCITS' sales documents must specify the amount or rate of redemption fees, if any.

2.32 The 2002 Act specifies that it must be possible to redeem the units of a coordinated UCITS 'directly or indirectly out of the undertaking's assets'.[22]

2.33 The term 'indirectly' merits an explanation. Prior to the transposition of the European Directive on information for third parties and the protection of share capital,[23] Luxembourg company law did not allow SAs to redeem their own shares. To overcome this issue, the practice developed for UCI promoters to set up two

---

[19] Ch F, II, Circular 91/75.

[20] ibid.

[21] This practice is used for UCITS created for a limited time, whose yield or repayment of all or part of the subscription price is guaranteed by a third party. In such cases, the UCITS must give the investors an incentive not to request redemption before dissolution. In the case of excessive redemptions—requiring the fund to sell part of its portfolio—the projected yield may be jeopardized, subjecting the guarantor to an additional risk.

[22] Art 2(2), 2002 Act.

[23] Second Council Directive (EEC) 77/91 of 13 December 1976 on coordination of safeguards that are required in companies' Member States, within the meaning of the second paragraph of Art 58 of the Treaty, for the protection of the interests of members and others in respect of the formation of public limited liability companies and the maintenance and alteration of their capital, with a view to making such safeguards equivalent [1977] OJ L26/1.

companies: the investment company itself and another company for the purpose of redeeming the investment company's shares when requested by investors.[24] While this practice is no longer necessary, it is not prohibited by the 2002 Act, which allows the indirect redemption option provided for by Directive 85/611. This indirect redemption facility is regarded as a means of ensuring that the relevant UCITS is open-ended.[25]

'Action taken by a UCITS to ensure that the stock exchange value of its units does not significantly vary from their net asset value' is also regarded as equivalent to redemption.[26] The term 'significantly' is interpreted as a maximum deviation of 5 per cent.[27] In certain countries, listed UCITS do not redeem their units directly from investors but redeem them via the stock exchange. Such a repurchase is regarded as a redemption within the meaning of Directive 85/611 if, more generally, the UCI ensures that the stock exchange value of its units does not significantly vary from their net asset value. UCIs operating in this way are coordinated UCITS within the meaning of Directive 85/611, even if, technically, redemption takes place through the stock exchange.[28] **2.34**

Exclusion from coordinated status because of investment and borrowing policy

Directive 85/611 authorizes EEA Member States to determine categories of UCITS for which the status of coordinated UCITS may be inappropriate in the light of their investment and borrowing policies.[29] The 2002 Act adopts this exclusion option[30] and Circular 03/88 sets out four categories of excluded UCITS.[31] Such UCITS are governed by Part II of the 2002 Act or by the Act of 13 February 2007 and are further described below. **2.35**

---

[24] See R Kremer, 'Les organismes de placement collectif sur la place financière luxembourgeoise', Livre Jubilaire for the 75th anniversary of the Luxembourg Stock Exchange, Bourse de Luxembourg, 2004, 38.

[25] *Parliamentary doc* No 3172, Comments on the Articles, 33.

[26] Art 2(2), 2002 Act.

[27] This is based on Art 14.5 of Directive (EEC) 85/611, reflected in Art 33(5), 1988 Act (*Parliamentary doc* No 3172, Comments on the Articles, 33), but not taken up by the 2002 Act. Art 14.4 of Directive 85/611 sets out the conditions on which a SICAV may dispense with a depositary's services. This, *inter alia*, is the case when 80% or more of its shares are traded on a stock exchange. A SICAV without a depositary must trade on the market to prevent its stock price from deviating by more than 5% from the net asset value per share (Art 14.5, Directive 85/611).

[28] Towards a European market for undertakings for collective investment in transferable securities, Comments on the provisions of Directive 85/611, Office for Official Publications of the European Communities, No 11 (1988), 5 (hereinafter 'Towards a European market for UCITS').

[29] Art 2.1, fourth indent, Directive (EEC) 85/611.

[30] Art 3, fourth indent, 2002 Act.

[31] Section III, 4, Circular 03/88.

UCIs governed by Part II of the 2002 Act

2.36 The 2002 Act and Circular 03/88 provide an *a contrario* definition for UCIs governed by Part II of the 2002 Act, namely Luxembourg-based UCIs not subject to Part I, ie:

- UCIs that do not invest in listed transferable securities and/or other liquid financial assets authorized by Directive 85/611;
- UCIs that, while investing in listed transferable securities and/or other liquid financial assets authorized by Directive 85/611, are excluded from Part I of the 2002 Act.

UCIs excluded from Part I of the 2002 Act fall under four headings, discussed in the following paragraphs.

Closed-end UCITS

2.37 Closed-end UCITS are those that do not undertake to redeem units at the request of their investors. Such UCITS are automatically covered by Part II of the 2002 Act or the Act of 13 February 2007, even though they may invest primarily in listed transferable securities and/or other liquid financial assets authorized by Directive 85/611.

UCITS that raise capital without promoting the sale of their units to the public in the whole of the EEA or any part thereof

2.38 Certain UCITS may be open to the public but do not promote themselves within the EEA. This feature renders them subject to Part II of the 2002 Act or to the Act of 13 February 2007.

2.39 Promotional activity involves the use of advertising methods designed to reach a large public, such as advertising in the press, on the radio or television, or in widely distributed brochures. A UCI seeking to reach only carefully targeted, well-informed investors within the EEA, such as pension funds or insurance companies, without using broader promotional methods, is governed by Part II of the 2002 Act[32] or by the Act of 13 February 2007.

UCITS whose units, under their constitutive documents, may be sold only to the public in countries that are not members of the EEA

2.40 UCITS whose management rules or articles of incorporation reserve the marketing of units to investors in countries outside the EEA are governed by Part II of the 2002 Act or by the Act of 13 February 2007.

---

[32] Section III, 2, Circular 03/88.

The main objective of Directive 85/611 is to remove national barriers to the mar- **2.41**
keting of UCIs within the EEA. For that reason, UCIs marketed outside that
territory do not benefit from the provisions of the Directive and are therefore not
eligible for its European passport.

Specific categories of UCITS determined by the CSSF

In the course of drafting Directive 85/611, it became clear that certain UCITS, **2.42**
because of their investment and borrowing policies, would require certain derogations from the general legal provisions. At the time, this was of particular importance to UCIs investing a significant portion of their assets in start-ups whose
securities were not yet traded on a regulated market.

The authors of Directive 85/611 were aware of the issue.[33] They also understood **2.43**
that it would be necessary to be able to modify or implement derogations from the
general rules rapidly, as investment products would continue to evolve. Thus it
made sense to allow derogations from the general rules to be granted outside the
scope of the Directive itself.

It was therefore decided to exclude from the scope of the Directive those **2.44**
'categories of UCITS prescribed by the regulations of the Member States in
which such UCITS are situated, for which the rules laid down in Section V and
Article 36 are inappropriate in view of their investment and borrowing
policies'.[34]

The Grand Duchy of Luxembourg availed itself of the right of derogation pro- **2.45**
vided for in Directive 85/611. Pursuant to the authorization granted by the 2002
Act,[35] Circular 03/88[36] left the following UCIs outside the scope of Part I of the
2002 Act:

(1) so-called 'mixed' UCITS;
(2) UCITS investing in venture capital;
(3) UCITS which use borrowing for investment purposes (so-called 'leveraged
    funds');
(4) umbrella UCITS, of which at least one sub-fund is not subject to Part I of the
    2002 Act.

---

[33] 'Towards a European market for UCITS' (n 28 above) No 17, 7.
[34] Art 2.1 *in fine*, Directive (EEC) 85/611. The authors of the Directive were nevertheless concerned that the Member States would misuse the freedom granted to them in this respect. It was
planned to monitor application of this derogation by means of a report to be submitted by the
Commission of the European Communities 5 years after implementation of the Directive (Art 2.2
of Directive 85/611).
[35] Art 3, fourth indent, 2002 Act.
[36] Section III, 4, Circular 03/88.

2.46 Mixed UCITS are those whose investment policy allows them to invest at least 20 per cent of their net assets in securities which are neither listed transferable securities[37] nor other liquid financial assets authorized by Directive 85/611.

2.47 UCITS investing in venture capital are those whose focus is on investment in the securities of companies that have been recently constituted or which are still in the early development stage. They are subject to specific rules derogating from the general standards laid down in Part II of the 2002 Act.

2.48 Leveraged funds are UCITS whose investment policy provides for the permanent borrowing for investment purposes of amounts representing at least 25 per cent of their net assets.

2.49 Lastly, umbrella UCITS are subject to Part II of the 2002 Act when the investment or borrowing policy of one or more sub-funds does not meet the application criteria of Part I of the 2002 Act. In this situation the entire UCITS, and all of its sub-funds will be excluded from Part I. This may be either an advantage or a drawback. If a UCITS wishes to market all its sub-funds within the EEA, it should not create non-coordinated sub-funds which 'contaminate' the coordinated sub-funds. In contrast, this is a viable profile where a UCITS wishes to offer its investors sub-funds with a wide range of investment policies, such as investment in listed transferable securities and in venture capital instruments, without subjecting itself to the more restrictive rules and limitations applicable to coordinated UCITS.

Specialized investment funds within the meaning of the Act of 13 February 2007

History

2.50 The authors of the 1988 Act focused primarily on UCIs whose units were intended for direct investment by the public. It was felt that only the unsophisticated private investor needed to be protected by both the creation of an appropriate form of collective investment and a relatively strict legislative and regulatory framework. Well-informed investors, such as professionals of the financial sector, insurance companies, and pension funds, were targeted by the 1988 Act only insofar as their activities catered to the general public.

2.51 Yet there was also a demand for a regime that was similar to that for public UCIs but geared to the specific requirements of sophisticated investors. Such a regime was not available in the Grand Duchy of Luxembourg, whereas an appropriate framework existed in neighbouring countries such as France and Germany.

---

[37] Within the meaning of Art 41(1), 2002 Act.

This situation hampered Luxembourg's financial market and a rapid legislative **2.52** response was required. The legislature responded with the 1991 Act concerning undertakings for collective investment whose securities are not intended to be placed with the public. The Luxembourg legislature's approach to the needs of institutional investors took a number of factors into account.[38]

First of all, UCIs had demonstrated their value as a useful investment method **2.53** permitting segregation of invested assets and facilitating tracking of investment performance. There was no reason to deprive institutional investors of this advantage.

The legal frameworks created for UCIs—ie the FCP and the SICAF or SICAV **2.54** (investment companies with, respectively, fixed or variable capital)—had also proved to be useful investment mechanisms. It was therefore logical to continue to use them.

The operation of UCIs was also governed by specific rules. Transactions carried **2.55** out by UCIs are complex and call for considerable expertise. Accordingly, they require the services of specialized professionals, such as investment managers, depositaries, and administration agents. The role, obligations, and responsibilities of each type of service were carefully reviewed during the preparations for the 1988 Act. It was felt that the same system could be used to provide institutional investors with a robust and clearly defined legal framework.

Lastly, the institutional investor sometimes acted on behalf of or as a conduit for **2.56** the general public, which indirectly would be the beneficiary of a UCI's asset management. This was the position, in particular, in the case of insurance or accumulation products linked to UCIs, and foreign pension funds wishing to set up UCIs for the purpose of managing part of their assets in the Grand Duchy of Luxembourg. In all these cases, the UCI's sole shareholder would be the insurance company or pension fund. Both, however, acted on behalf of ultimate beneficial owners who could be a larger group of persons or even the general public. The ultimate beneficiary had to be borne in mind and it was regarded as important that the uninformed private investors hidden behind the institutional investor should also be protected.

For all those reasons, the regime created for institutional UCIs did not differ **2.57** materially from the regime created for public UCIs. The 1991 Act referred extensively to the provisions of the 1988 Act. Special attention, however, was given to the ownership of UCIs governed by the 1991 Act, which could consist only of 'institutional' investors.

---

[38] *Parliamentary doc* No 3467, Explanatory Statement, 2.

2.58 Shortly after the 1991 Act came into force, the CSSF issued an explanatory notice designed to facilitate the application of the 1991 Act by providing further information on a number of matters.[39]

2.59 A few years later, the CSSF's annual report confirmed a more flexible approach to the authorization of UCIs governed by the 1991 Act. With a view to faster processing of such applications, the CSSF then focused on promotional aspects and investment policy (including investment restrictions and risk spreading). In principle, the CSSF did not review participation conditions, participation rights and obligations, and equal treatment between participants, although it reserved the right to do so when considered necessary.[40]

2.60 After fifteen years of existence the 1991 Act was replaced by a more comprehensive law even better tailored to the expectations of well-informed investors. The Act of 13 February 2007 relating to specialized investment funds included the provisions of the 2002 Act likely to be appropriate to this type of UCI, amended as necessary to allow greater legal flexibility.

Scope of the Act of 13 February 2007

Concept of the well-informed investor

2.61 Not only is the SIF a specialized investment fund, it can also be characterized as a specialized investor(s) fund. Since investors in a SIF are sophisticated and well-informed, SIFs are subject to a more liberal set of rules than those laid down for traditional UCIs. This makes it possible, in particular, for a SIF to implement more specialized and flexible investment policies relating to such asset classes as derivatives, private equity, and real estate.

2.62 Only well-informed investors within the meaning of the Act of 13 February 2007 are allowed to invest in SIFs. This category of investors includes institutional investors, professional investors, and private investors fulfilling certain criteria.[41]

---

[39] Notice of 17 June 1992 with regard to the application of the Act of 19 July 1991 on undertakings for collective investment whose securities are not intended for investment by the public. This notice was withdrawn and replaced by a notice issued on 27 December 1999, which extended the previous text so as to extend the circle of investors capable of qualifying as institutional investors. For confirmation and a detailed explanation of this last point, see also the Annual Report of the CSSF for the 1999 financial year, 64.

[40] The reason for this position can be found in the status and knowledge of institutional investors, who are fully capable of judging these aspects for themselves (CSSF Annual Report for the 2004 financial year, 77).

[41] See V Pierlot and Y Benizri, 'A specialised investors fund?' in *Specialised Investment Funds*, (Arendt & Medernach, 2007) 24.

Concept of institutional investor Whilst the 1991 Act and subsequently the **2.63**
Act of 13 February 2007 refer to the institutional investor, they do not define that
concept, leaving leeway for a flexible and open-ended interpretation.

The legislature nevertheless sought to limit this interpretation by providing some **2.64**
key pointers in the Parliamentary documents accompanying the 1991 Act.
According to those documents, institutional investors are 'enterprises and organisations whose object entails responsibility for managing large amounts of money
and other assets'.[42] This is followed by a few examples: 'professionals of the financial sector itself, . . . insurance and reinsurance companies, . . . social security
institutions and . . . pension funds, . . . large financial corporations and . . . the
structures they set up to achieve their objectives'.

Holding companies do not feature among the examples given by the legislature. **2.65**
Their qualification as institutional investors is delicate and subtle. Whilst such
companies 'constitute, in principle, investors with an institutional purpose',[43] they
are not automatically accorded the status of institutional investor; that requires
prior examination of their ownership structure. For example, a Luxembourg-
based or foreign holding company or similar entity whose shareholders are all
institutional investors may itself qualify as an institutional investor.

Conversely, a holding company whose shareholders are all private investors is not, **2.66**
in principle, an institutional investor, save insofar as it falls within one of two
exceptions. The first exception relates to a holding company or similar entity
which can 'show that it has material substance, a separate structure and activity
from those of its shareholders, and which holds large financial interests'.[44] The
second applies to a family-owned holding company or similar entity through
which 'a family or branch of a family holds significant financial interests'.[45]

A UCI established in the Grand Duchy of Luxembourg or another country is **2.67**
invariably regarded as an institutional investor, even when its own investors
are not.

The status of institutional investor is also applied to local authorities, such as the **2.68**
governing body of a region, province, canton, commune or municipality, insofar
as they invest their own funds.

It is a more sensitive issue to confer the status of institutional investor on financial **2.69**
institutions wishing to invest the money of their private clients in SIFs. After

---

[42] *Parliamentary doc* No 3467, Comments on the Articles, 3. The CSSF uses this definition in its
notice of 27 December 1999.
[43] CSSF notice, 27 December 1999.
[44] ibid.
[45] ibid.

denying those financial institutions, for many years, the status of institutional investor when acting on behalf of private clients, the CSSF finally adopted a more flexible position. A credit institution or another professional of the financial sector established in the Grand Duchy of Luxembourg or a foreign country may use a SIF for its private clients, provided it acts on behalf of such clients under a discretionary management mandate. Moreover, such clients must not have the right to claim direct ownership of the units issued by the SIF, that right being restricted to the credit institution or any other professional of the financial sector.[46]

2.70 Likewise, from time to time one or more institutional investors might choose to create a UCI on behalf of private clients without granting the clients direct access to the units of the UCI and without a discretionary management mandate. Such a UCI may be constituted under either the 2002 Act or the Act of 13 February 2007, depending on whether the units ultimately will be held by the public at large—a distinction illustrated in the following example.[47]

2.71 A UCI that is ancillary to a life insurance or capitalization product may be structured as a SIF if the insurance company in question is its sole legal owner. In that case, the policyholders who have financed the fund have no right to its units. The only party taken into consideration for the purposes of classifying the UCI as a SIF is the insurance company, which is an institutional investor. The policyholders, who are the ultimate indirect beneficiaries of the units are not taken into consideration in classification of the UCI. In contrast, the status of SIF is not accorded to UCIs backing insurance products where the units acquired by the insurance company are transferred to the savers on maturity of the insurance policy. In those cases, the units are regarded as belonging to the public and are therefore covered by the 2002 Act.

2.72 **Concept of professional investor** A description of 'professional investor' is given in Directive 2004/39 (the Market in Financial Instruments Directive—MiFID). The Directive provides that such an investor 'possesses the experience, knowledge and expertise to make its own investment decisions and properly assess the risks that it incurs'.

2.73 More specifically, the concept of professional investor includes the following entities:

(1) entities which are required to be authorized or regulated to operate in the financial markets;[48]

---

[46] ibid.

[47] *Parliamentary doc* No 3467, Comments on the Articles, 2.

[48] In this respect, the following entities are mentioned in Annex II, I, of MiFID: credit institutions, investment firms, other authorized or regulated financial institutions, insurance companies, collective investment schemes and management companies of such schemes, pension funds

(2) large undertakings;[49]
(3) governments, public bodies that manage public debt, central banks, international and supranational institutions such as the World Bank, the IMF (International Monetary Fund), the ECB (European Central Bank), and the EIB (European Investment Bank);
(4) other institutional investors whose main activity is to invest in financial instruments.[50]

Under MiFID, a number of clients who do not meet the criteria set out above **2.74** may request or 'elect' to be treated as professional clients. They may be treated as such only if they meet several criteria pertaining to their knowledge, their expertise and, as the case may be, their assets.[51] Could the same treatment be requested under the Act of 13 February 2007 and thus allow a client other than those referred to above to invest in a SIF? The answer to this question is affirmative and the investor concerned will fall into the category of 'other well-informed investors' as described below.

The concepts of institutional and professional investors overlap to a large extent. **2.75** MiFID, in determining what constitutes a 'professional investor', does not distinguish between them and includes 'other institutional investors whose main activity is to invest in financial instruments'. However, professional investors arguably encompass a broader sphere than institutional investors. 'Professional investors' would include, in particular, large undertakings which meet certain criteria in terms of, for example, balance sheet total, net turnover, and own funds.

Concept of other well-informed investor Within the meaning of the Act of **2.76** 13 February 2007, the concept of well-informed investors not only includes institutional and professional investors but also any individual investor who satisfies the following conditions: he confirms in writing that he adheres to the status of 'well-informed investor', and (a) he invests a minimum of €125,000 in the SIF, or (b) he has been the subject of an assessment made by a credit institution, by an investment firm or by a management company within the meaning of Directive (EC) 2001/107 certifying his expertise, his experience, and his knowledge in adequately appraising an investment in the SIF.

Managing persons and other managers of SIFs The managing persons and **2.77** other persons involved in the management of a SIF are exempt from complying

---

and management companies of such funds, commodity and commodity derivatives dealers, locals and other institutional investors.

[49] According to MiFID, such undertakings must meet two of the following size requirements on a company basis: (1) balance sheet total: €20m; (2) net turnover: €40m; (3) own funds: €2m.

[50] According to MiFID, such investors also include entities dedicated to the securitization of assets or other financing transactions.

[51] Annex II, II of MiFID.

with the requirements set out above.[52] Their role in the management of the SIF signifies that they are sufficiently aware of the risks related to investments in this type of structure. They are allowed to acquire securities issued by a SIF managed by them without any other condition or assessment evidencing their knowledge, expertise, or minimum investment.

2.78 The CSSF considers that a SIF is responsible for checking the status of well-informed investor and setting up the relevant procedures in this respect.[53] The CSSF does not require the investors' names to be systematically communicated to it. Yet, it requires that SIFs should be able to communicate those names to it on request.

Scope of the Act of 13 February 2007 compared with the 2002 Act

2.79 The scope of the Act of 13 February 2007 was not determined as an alternative to that of the 2002 Act, so that the two are not necessarily mutually exclusive. The Act of 13 February 2007 applies only to UCIs in which all unitholders are 'well-informed investors'. The 2002 Act encompasses UCIs whose units are offered to an unrestricted circle of persons. A UCI which satisfies both authorization criteria, may opt to be governed by either of the two laws. Consequently, an ownership structure made up exclusively of well-informed investors does not necessarily entail application of the Act of 13 February 2007. It may be open to the public and so can opt for authorization under the 2002 Act.

2.80 In contrast, a SIF may not create sub-funds the units of which are intended for investors other than well-informed investors. For investors other than well-informed investors the relevant fund or sub-funds must be authorized under the 2002 Act and must market to the public to raise capital. In an umbrella UCI, the concept of the public is assessed at a consolidated level, with all sub-funds combined. Consequently, an umbrella UCI need not place the units of each sub-fund with the public, but can create both public sub-funds and sub-funds dedicated to well-informed or other investors and yet still meet the general condition of placement with the public stipulated by the 2002 Act.

2.81 When the only investors in a UCI organized under Part II of the 2002 Act are well-informed investors, the UCI can convert into a SIF governed by the Act of 13 February 2007. In such cases, it must cease any marketing to the public (considered as any non-institutional investor) and amend its constitutive documents and sales documents accordingly. Conversion does not interrupt the continuity of its legal status.

---

[52] Art 2(2), Act of 13 February 2007.
[53] CSSF Annual Report for 2007, 56.

This approach reflects the wishes expressed by the legislature in the 1991 Act. The **2.82**
legislature has also correctly noted that the 2002 Act need not necessarily apply to a
UCI whose units are held solely by institutional investors.[54] The protections afforded
by the 2002 Act are only essential for ordinary, non-sophisticated private investors.[55]

This reasoning applies only to UCIs governed by Part II of the 2002 Act. According **2.83**
to the CSSF, the provision in the 2002 Act that prohibits a coordinated UCITS
from converting itself into another type of UCI, also bars conversion of a UCITS
governed by Part I of the 2002 Act into a SIF.[56]

However, a SIF can broaden its ownership structure by marketing to the public, **2.84**
provided that it agrees to subject itself to the 2002 Act and adapts its constitutive
documents and sales documents accordingly.

Supplementary character of the Act of 13 February 2007

When a financial company limits its collective investment business, based on the **2.85**
principle of risk spreading, to a small number of well-informed investors, is it
automatically subject to the Act of 13 February 2007? The answer is—no. Where
canvassing is restricted to a small circle of persons, the status of UCI is not mandatory. Such a company may either opt to be governed by the Act of 13 February
2007 or remain outside its scope by adopting the rules governing financial companies which are not supervised by the CSSF.

Similarly, holding companies and comparable companies whose shareholders are **2.86**
all well-informed investors may convert to SIFs, provided that they comply with
the laws and regulations governing SIFs.

Legal regime governing specialized investment funds

Qualifying criteria

To be governed by the Act of 13 February 2007, a SIF must be situated in the Grand **2.87**
Duchy of Luxembourg. If it is an FCP, the registered office of its management

---

[54] *Parliamentary doc* No 3467, Comments on the Articles, 3.
[55] This idea had already been expressed in IML Circular 84/12, based on the 1983 Act, which
specified that, 'by providing for supervision by the supervisory authority, the legislature seeks to protect the non-sophisticated normal private investor canvassed by professional promoters'. Although
that text was not repeated in Circular 91/75, the aim seems to have remained the same.
[56] The legislature had nevertheless stated the opposite: see *Parliamentary doc* No 3467,
Comments on the Articles, 3: 'Article 1(5) of the Act of 30 March 1988, based on the corresponding
provision in the UCITS Directive, which prohibits undertakings governed by Part I from converting themselves into undertakings governed by Part II, does not appear to rule out such a conversion,
even for an undertaking governed by Part I. In fact, Article 1(5) is obviously intended to protect
the public against loss of the benefits afforded by the Directive, ie the rules on risk spreading and
borrowing limits and (at the level of the Directive) supervision. However, the public, which is the
only beneficiary of this protection, is not assumed to be involved in such undertakings.'

company must be located in Luxembourg. If it is an investment company, its registered office must be in Luxembourg.

Legal forms

2.88 A SIF may take the legal form of a UCI. It may also be incorporated as an SA, an SCA, an SARL, or a cooperative incorporated in the form of an SA.

Authorization of conducting persons

2.89 The new authorization procedure for conducting persons differs from the existing system for traditional UCIs. It is based on the procedure adopted for SICARs by the Act of 15 June 2004.[57]

2.90 The existing regime for UCIs not only requires authorization of a UCI's official conducting persons (directors of the investment company or of the FCP's management company) but also of all those who 'effectively determine the conduct of the activities of the UCI'.[58] Based on this definition, the CSSF has extended the authorization procedure for conducting persons to promoters and managers.

2.91 The Act of 13 February 2007 requires authorization only for those who formally represent a SIF, ie the managers in the case of an SARL, general partner(s) in the case of an SCA, director(s) in the case of an SA and a cooperative organized in the form of an SA, and the director(s) or manager(s) of an FCP's management company.[59]

2.92 Thus the CSSF does not require a promoter for SIFs and does not verify the status and financial situation of the manager to whom the conducting persons may delegate management. This simplification reflects investor quality. Since they are institutional, professional or other 'well-informed' investors, they have the necessary experience to assess the nature of the fund and the manager's qualification for themselves.

Role of the depositary

2.93 In a SIF, the depositary has a less onerous role than a depositary in a UCI governed by the 2002 Act. The legislature did not consider it necessary to require the depositary to verify the compliance of the UCI's operations with its constitutive documents. Consequently, all specific control duties of a depositary as provided for by the 2002 Act have been omitted.[60]

---

[57] Art 12, Act of 15 June 2004.
[58] Art 93(3), 2002 Act.
[59] Art 42(3), Act of 13 February 2007.
[60] ibid Arts 16, 33, and 40(2); Arts 18(2) and 34(3), 2002 Act; see also Y Lacroix and L Tristan, 'Parties and service providers involved in specialised investment funds' in *Specialised Investment Funds* (Arendt & Medernanch, 2007) 71.

Other simplifications

SIFs do not require CSSF authorization before starting business. They must apply **2.94** for authorization within one month following their organization.[61] However, this neither bars such UCIs from raising funds nor securing subscription commitments, nor does it prevent them from making their first investments.

In addition, for SIFs, rules governing communication with investors are reduced **2.95** to a minimum[62] and certain operating rules are simplified—particularly as regards the issue and redemption of units or shares[63] and payments made to investors[64]— and follow the rules in this regard adopted for SICARs.[65]

Classification of UCIs According to their Legal Form

Contractual UCIs

An FCP is a contractual UCI. The 2002 Act defines it as 'any undivided **2.96** co-ownership of [transferable] securities [and/or other liquid financial assets] managed in accordance with the principle of risk spreading on behalf of joint owners who are liable only up to the amount contributed by them and whose rights are represented by units intended for placement with the public by means of a public or private offering'.[66] The Act of 13 February 2007 provides a very similar description.[67]

In contrast with companies, FCPs do not have legal status and therefore do not **2.97** have the domicile necessary to determine their nationality. For that reason, it is important to start with an examination of the criteria by which they are subject to Luxembourg law, followed by an analysis of their operating rules under the 2002 Act and the Act of 13 February 2007.

Criteria determining the nationality of a common fund

Under the 2002 Act and the Act of 13 February 2007, an FCP is resident in **2.98** Luxembourg when the registered office of its management company is in the

---

[61] Arts 43 and 64, Act of 13 February 2007.
[62] ibid Arts 52–57.
[63] ibid Arts 8 and 28(2).
[64] ibid Arts 15, 29(2), and 31(1).
[65] See 13.71 below.
[66] Arts 5 and 65(1), 2002 Act. The definition of FCP in each of these articles is identical with one exception. Art 5 adds the adjective 'transferable' and refers to the 'other liquid financial assets mentioned in Article 41, paragraph (1)', to track the requirements for a coordinated UCITS.
[67] Art 4, Act of 13 February 2007; as regards FCP-SIF, see A-M Reuter and N Berck, 'Available Structures' in *Specialised Investment Funds* (Arendt & Medernach, 2007) 37.

Grand Duchy of Luxembourg.[68] That approach had already been laid down in the 1983 Act.[69] At that time, the legislature had reviewed several potential residence criteria.[70]

2.99 The most liberal approach would have been not to impose any objective residence criterion and to allow promoters to designate the applicable law. However, that approach seemed incompatible with the purpose of Luxembourg regulation, which is essentially designed to protect public savings and to impose operating rules intended to ensure reliable management.

2.100 Another solution would have been to limit the application of Luxembourg law to FCPs whose essential components are located in Luxembourg. In that case, Luxembourg law would have applied only if the management company and the depositary had their registered office in the Grand Duchy of Luxembourg and if all of a fund's units were offered to the public in the Grand Duchy of Luxembourg. That course seemed excessively liberal. It would have left too much leeway to promoters wishing to avoid the application of Luxembourg legislation.

2.101 A third possibility would have been to apply Luxembourg law to all FCPs of which at least one essential component (management company or depositary) is domiciled in the Grand Duchy of Luxembourg and which call on the public in Luxembourg. That solution was also dismissed, *inter alia*, in order to prevent funds from circumventing Luxembourg law by marketing exclusively in foreign markets. Eliminating the prerequisite of marketing to the public would not have worked either. It would have been incorrect to impose Luxembourg law on foreign funds merely because their depositary was a Luxembourg bank.

2.102 The legislature finally decided that the criterion for residence in Luxembourg should be the management company's domicile in Luxembourg, as the management company is an FCP's primary body. The management company manages and represents an FCP. Its location is therefore the appropriate gauge for determining an FCP's nationality.

Operating rules of a common fund

Requirement for an undivided collection of securities forming a common fund

2.103 An FCP is jointly owned since it is an undivided collection of securities. The term 'fund' simply means that the ownership right applies to a pool of assets.

2.104 A body of undivided assets represents the entitlements of one or more persons who jointly own undivided rights to the same asset or pool of assets. The entitlement of

---

[68] Arts 4 and 64, 2002 Act; Art 3, Act of 13 February 2007.
[69] Art 1(3), 1983 Act.
[70] *Parliamentary doc* No 2366, Comments on the Articles, 19 and 20.

each undivided owner is expressed in the form of a fraction and referred to as an undivided share.[71] The ownership of undivided assets is generally an undergone and provisional condition, mainly justified by the need for liquidation of common assets held, for example, in the context of an undivided estate.[72]

For UCIs, reference to undivided assets is not entirely adequate. In contrast to the definition of undivided ownership of assets contained in the Civil Code, an FCP is in principle created to last indefinitely. Its assets are actively managed on a going-concern basis. An FCP's status is better reflected in the idea of joint or common ownership. The individual rights of each unitholder in a pool of jointly owned assets are restricted by the rules/agreement as to the FCP's common ownership and purposes. The voluntary decision to acquire an interest in assets held for a common purpose justifies the relinquishment of certain individual ownership rights to such assets.[73] Having come to the same conclusion, several authors[74] have compared the co-ownership of a body of undivided assets through an FCP to the joint ownership of a building. Both may be regarded as constituting stable structures which have been arranged and are regulated for a specific purpose and are held on a joint ownership basis.

2.105

FCPs also have a number of special features additional to the features of undivided ownership as provided for in the Civil Code, such as the management of the unitholders' undivided assets by a management company, and the distinction drawn between an FCP as a collective investment undertaking and the individual rights of each participant to the units issued by the FCP.

2.106

Such major differences from the definition of undivided ownership in the Civil Code necessitated a distinct legal infrastructure for FCPs and, therefore, neither the 2002 Act nor the Act of 13 February 2007 applies the provision on undivided ownership laid down in the Civil Code.[75] This contrasts with the approach for investment companies, in respect of which the 2002 Act and the Act of 13 February 2007 specifically refer to the general law provisions of the 1915 Act.

2.107

---

[71] *Encycl Dalloz, Civil*, see 'Indivision', Nos 1 *et seq*, Nos 54 *et seq*.

[72] A Viandier, 'Les nouveaux fonds communs de placement' (1980) *Rev soc* 249.

[73] Y Chartier, 'Les nouveaux fonds communs de placement (Commentaire du titre Ier de la loi no 79-594 du 13 juillet 1979 et de ses textes d'application)'(1980) *JCP*, ed N, I, 3001, No 27; Viandier (n 72 above) 249.

[74] E Arendt, 'Statut juridique des fonds communs de placement et des sociétés d'investissement au Grand-Duché de Luxembourg', in Les organes collectifs de placement dans la perspective de la place financière de Luxembourg, Seminar held on 11 and 12 December 1970, International University of Comparative Sciences of Luxembourg, 12; Chartier (n 73 above) Nos 26–28; B Delvaux, 'Les sociétés d'investissement du type ouvert au Grand-Duché de Luxembourg' (1961) XVIII *Pas lux* 54 and 59.

[75] Nor, previously, was it applied by the 1983 Act and by the 1988 Act. This point was not amended in the 2002 Act and in the Act of 13 February 2007.

2.108 Thus the 2002 Act and the Act of 13 February 2007 created a new regime of undivided ownership for FCPs,[76] reflecting the interaction between traditional property law and the law governing UCIs. The operations of an FCP are analysed further below.

Internal operation of a common fund

2.109 An FCP does not have a legal personality. It exists by virtue of, and operates on the basis of, a network of contracts. The management regulations laid down by the management company are its constitutive document. That document provides essential information about an FCP's operation, such as its investment policy, its distribution policy,[77] and the issue and redemption procedures for units.[78] It also identifies the management company and the depositary.[79]

2.110 Once it has drawn up management regulations, the management company issues units representing an undivided share in the underlying assets which are acquired with the subscription proceeds from sale of units in the FCP. The acquisition of units, whether by subscription or otherwise, entails agreement by the unitholder with the management regulations. Participants in an FCP are deemed to have accepted the existing and future versions of the management regulations.[80] In principle, they have no entitlement to modify those regulations. Only the management company can amend the regulations. Hence the special status of the management regulations is, in essence, inviolate.[81]

2.111 The relationship between the management company and each participant is therefore rooted in two documents: the subscription agreement for the units and the management regulations. The subscription agreement obliges the participant to agree to be bound by the management regulations.

2.112 The other key aspect of the relationship between participants and the management company relates to the management of undivided assets. The basis of the management relationship is not contractual but legal. A management company's powers in this area flow directly from the law.[82] The 2002 Act imposes few limits

---

[76] Chartier (n 73 above) No 35; Viandier (n 72 above) 246.
[77] Arts 13(2) *b* and *c*, and 66, 2002 Act; Art 12(2) *b* and *c*, Act of 13 February 2007.
[78] Arts 13(2) *i* and *j*, and 66, 2002 Act.
[79] Arts 13(2) *a* and 66, 2002 Act; Art 12(2) *a*, Act of 13 February 2007.
[80] Arts 13(1) and 66, 2002 Act; Art 12(1), Act of 13 February 2007.
[81] Arendt (n 74 above) 13 and 14; Viandier (n 72 above) 261. Classification of the regulations as a multilateral participation contract (*contrat multilatéral d'adhésion*) does not seem applicable, despite the argument advanced by Delvaux (n 74 above) 43, since the management regulations do not create any link between the unitholders and the unitholders have no authority to amend them.
[82] In this respect, its classification as an industrial work contract (*contrat de louage d'industrie*), as proposed by certain authors (Arendt (n 74 above) 14 and Delvaux, (n 74 above) 58), seems inappropriate. The management company is the unitholders' legal rather than contractual

on these powers. It lays down only two requirements: a management company may act only in the interest of unitholders and it must comply with the management regulations.[83]

The reason for this legal authority is easily explained. As an FCP does not have a **2.113** separate legal personality, it is in principle unable to take decisions or to enter into commitments. Only participants acting collectively, through a common representative, can determine the rights and obligations attaching to the pool of undivided assets, and it was therefore necessary to vest management authority in an entity independent of the participants. The 2002 Act conferred that independence and necessary authority on the management company.

The legal basis for management authority explains the considerable freedom **2.114** granted to management companies to manage and administer FCPs to the exclusion of the FCP's participants.[84] A management company does not need to receive instructions from the participants and is not their agent.

The management company creates the fund, establishes the management regula- **2.115** tions and manages the FCP by virtue of powers conferred on it by the legislation. Its powers cannot be revoked by the participants unless the management regulations vest such a power in the general meeting of unitholders. Where no such powers are reserved under the management regulations, the irrevocable nature of powers conferred on the management company renders it virtually unassailable.[85]

Without the power to create or manage the FCP, unitholders do not, in principle, **2.116** have the power to terminate its existence. The 2002 Act deprives them entirely of the right to demand the winding up of the fund.[86]

Unitholders may express any dissatisfaction only through selling or redeeming **2.117** their units. In extreme cases, they may bring a liability suit against the management company. Whether or not the management company is at fault will depend on whether it has fulfilled its obligations with the 'diligence' of a 'salaried agent'.[87] Such a very limited sphere of powers explains the lack of legal relations as between participants in the same FCP.[88]

---

representative. As regards the management company's powers in respect of the portfolio securities, see also the Parliamentary documents connected with the 1983 Act (*Parliamentary doc* No 2366, Comments on the Articles, 24): 'The attribution of voting rights to the management company . . . should not be construed as a contractual mandate but as a legal power, since the management company is the legal representative of a group of undivided co-owners.'

[83] Arts 14(1) and 66, 2002 Act; Art 13(1), Act of 13 February 2007.
[84] Viandier (n 72 above) 245.
[85] Chartier (n 73 above) No 25.
[86] Arts 11(1) and 66, 2002 Act; Art 10, Act of 13 February 2007.
[87] Arts 15 and 66, 2002 Act; Art 14, Act of 13 February 2007.
[88] Viandier (n 72 above) 261.

2.118   The 2002 Act and the Act of 13 February 2007 do not provide unitholders with a prescribed framework for the adoption of decisions and the holding of meetings. That said, the management company remains free to create such a framework under the management regulations, if it so wishes.

2.119   Units issued in an FCP do not confer voting rights, save as may be provided for in the management regulations.[89] In practice, such a provision would be exceptional. However, the management regulations may grant unitholders decision-making powers, for example to approve certain changes in the management regulations or to extend the FCP's term as may be provided for in the management regulations.

External operation of a common fund

2.120   The most striking similarity between FCPs and the traditional concept of undivided assets lies in the absence of a formal legal status. Neither an FCP nor a body of undivided assets under civil law are legal persons with rights and obligations. Neither has the capacity to enter into contracts or to take legal action.

2.121   The 2002 Act and the Act of 13 February 2007 nevertheless limit the consequences of an FCP's lack of legal status, thereby distinguishing it from the concept of undivided assets as set out in the Civil Code.

2.122   The law provides, first of all, for the representation of an FCP. Legally authorized to manage an FCP, a management company must also be able to represent it and bind it to the performance of obligations. That fundamental aspect of its management powers is difficult to reconcile with the FCP's lack of legal status. How can one represent what does not exist? For that reason, the law specifies that a management company must act in its own name when acting on behalf of an FCP. In order to distinguish between actions and operations it carries out in its own interest, the management company must indicate in which cases it is acting on behalf of the FCP.[90]

2.123   The law adds that the management company 'shall exercise all rights attached to the securities comprising the portfolio of the common fund',[91] thus avoiding one of the drawbacks linked to the FCP's lack of legal status. In principle, only the owners of the undivided securities (ie the participants) should be entitled to exercise the rights attaching to such securities, notably voting rights. That exclusive voting right is protected by criminal sanctions in a number of countries, including the Grand Duchy of Luxembourg,[92] to which both the management company and the participants would have been subject in the absence of modifying legislation.

---

[89]   Arts 8(1) and 66, 2002 Act; Art 7(1), Act of 13 February 2007.
[90]   Arts 14(2) and 66, 2002 Act; Art 13(2), Act of 13 February 2007.
[91]   Arts 14(3) and 66, 2002 Act; also see Art 13(3), Act of 13 February 2007.
[92]   Art 162, 1915 Act.

It was therefore decided that the powers of a management company in this respect should be governed directly by statute.[93]

The law also limits the impact of the lack of legal status on the participants' liability. **2.124**

Under the Civil Code, joint owners are liable for the debts and charges attaching to the undivided assets jointly owned. If the assets are insufficient to pay all creditors, the joint owners may be held liable for debts in excess of their undivided fraction. **2.125**

The law disapplies this provision for unitholders in an FCP and provides that participants in an FCP are liable for the liabilities of the FCP only up to the amount contributed by them.[94] In other words, it provides for limited liability, in line with the rules governing SAs, for example. Thus an FCP's creditors cannot sue the participants directly. The FCP participants therefore enjoy a high level of protection. Should an FCP go bankrupt, they do not risk losing more than their investment. **2.126**

Similarly, the law provides that an FCP is not liable for the obligations of the management company or of unitholders. An FCP's liability extends only to the obligations and costs expressly imposed on it by its management regulations.[95] **2.127**

An FCP's status vis-à-vis third parties is similar to that of an investment company. It is represented by a specific entity, namely the management company. It has its own assets and liabilities. It also has a specific name.[96] It keeps separate accounts and publishes annual and, for UCIs and SIFs, semi-annual financial statements.[97] However, in contrast to a company, it does not have legal status. It has no independent will or interest.[98] In that respect, it remains an undivided body of assets. **2.128**

Incorporated UCIs

Incorporated UCIs are investment companies. In contrast to FCPs, the legal status of investment companies is invariably separate from that of its investors. This makes it unnecessary to interpose a management company between them and third parties. **2.129**

Investment companies are domiciled in Luxembourg when their registered office is situated in the Grand Duchy of Luxembourg. **2.130**

---

[93] See also Chartier (n 73 above) Nos 25 and 27 and Delvaux (n 74 above) 74; *Parliamentary doc* No 2366, Comments on the Articles, 24 and 25.

[94] Arts 5 and 65(1), 2002 Act; Art 4, Act of 13 February 2007.

[95] Arts 6 and 66, 2002 Act; Art 5, Act of 13 February 2007.

[96] Arts 13(2) *a*, and 66, 2002 Act; Art 12(2) *a*, Act of 13 February 2007.

[97] Art 109, 2002 Act; Art 52, Act of 13 February 2007.

[98] Viandier (n 72 above) 251 and Chartier (n 73 above) 32.

2.131 Theoretically, investment companies could take any corporate form allowed under Luxembourg law, ie they could be incorporated as a *société civile* (non-commercial company), or as *société commerciale* (SA, SCA, SE, or SARL), a *société coopérative* (cooperative society), *société en nom collectif* (general partnership), and SCS. In practice, however, the law and operational constraints limit the practical operation of the law to three or, at most, four types of company, as explained below. In this respect, a distinctions is made between SICAVs and SICAFs and further distinctions are made between investment companies governed by Part I of the 2002 Act, those governed by Part II of the Act, and those with a specialized investment status.[99]

Legal form of SICAVs (investment companies with variable capital)

2.132 As the French name indicates, a SICAV is a company whose capital may constantly vary. Its capital is at all times equal to the net asset value of the company, ie the value of its assets after deduction of liabilities. It fluctuates with changes in share subscriptions and redemptions, and with the valuation of assets.

2.133 The characteristic of equivalence of net asset value to capital has definite legal consequences.[100] In particular, a SICAV's shares do not have a nominal value but an accounting par value equal to the capital—or net asset value—divided by the number of shares in issue. The accounting par value varies in the same way as the capital. It is equal to the net asset value per share, ie the company's net asset value divided by the number of shares issued.

Investment companies with variable capital governed by Part I of the 2002 Act

2.134 SICAVs governed by Part I of the 2002 Act may only be incorporated as SAs:

—whose exclusive object is to invest their funds in transferable securities and/or other liquid financial assets . . . [authorized by the Directive] in order to spread the investment risks and to ensure for their shareholders the benefit of the result of the management of their assets, and

—whose shares are intended to be placed with the public by means of a public or private offer, and

—whose articles of incorporation provide that the amount of the capital shall at all times be equal to the net asset value of the company'.[101]

SICAVs constitute a very special type of SA. Their capital can change at any time without a decision by the shareholders.

---

[99] For further details, see Reuter and Berck (n 67 above) 42 *et seq*.
[100] See 4.67 *et seq* below.
[101] Art 25, 2002 Act.

Investment companies with variable capital governed by Part II of the 2002 Act

SICAVs governed by Part II of the 2002 Act likewise must adopt the legal form of an SA or an SE.[102] They are defined in the same way as SICAVs governed by Part I of the same law, save as regards their right to invest in all kinds of assets, not merely assets eligible under Directive 85/611. **2.135**

SICAVs, other than SIFs, may also opt for the status of European company. SICAVs that have completed this conversion may be called '*société européenne d'investissement à capital variable*' or 'SICAV-SE'.[103] No SICAV has opted for the status of SE so far. Therefore, such legal form will not be described at greater length in this work, save for the description set out below. **2.136**

The basic purpose of the new corporate form introduced by the SE is to facilitate cross-border mergers between companies and to create a company which can operate outside the constraints imposed by national systems of company law. **2.137**

The regime for SEs includes the regime applicable to SAs, together with certain complementary provisions shared by all Member States. Thus, the SE follows all rules for SAs but must also comply with additional obligations in order to obtain a Community passport. It is in fact admitted that 'the SE is broadly the same as a public limited company under the national law of the State in which its registered office is situated, subject to a few specific Community provisions . . .',[104] and that it is a 'variant of the species "public limited company"'.[105] **2.138**

The particular features of an SE concern its registered office and its incorporation method. An SE is incorporated according to particular formalities, listed below. In effect, an SE can be incorporated only in the following circumstances:[106] **2.139**

(1) the merger of SAs incorporated according to the laws of a Member State and established in at least two different Member States;
(2) the incorporation of a holding SE whose founders are SAs and/or SARLs incorporated according to the laws of a Member State and established in at least two different Member States or having a subsidiary in another Member State for at least two years;
(3) the incorporation of a subsidiary SE whose founders are companies under civil or commercial law set up to make a profit and established in at least two different Member States or having a subsidiary in another Member State for at least two years;

---

[102] Arts 69 and 71, 2002 Act.
[103] ibid Art 33.
[104] *Parliamentary doc* No 5352, Explanatory Statement, 30.
[105] ibid Comments on the Articles, 32.
[106] Arts 26*bis* and 26*ter*, 1915 Act.

(4) the conversion of an SA with a subsidiary in another Member State for at least two years.

The minimum capital for incorporating an SE is €120,000.[107]

2.140 Moreover, the parties must draw up an incorporation plan setting out the legal and economic aspects of the SE's incorporation and the consequences of adopting the form of an SE for the shareholders, other securities holders, and wage earners.[108] This plan is submitted for approval to the shareholders' general meeting and, as necessary, to the meetings of other securities holders at each of the companies participating in the SE's incorporation.[109]

2.141 An SE's registered office must be in the same Member State as its actual place of establishment.[110] This obligation provides a legislative solution to the problem identified by the European Court of Justice as to the nationality of companies whose registered office is established in a Member State other than that of their head office.[111]

2.142 The law stipulates, moreover, that the registered office may be transferred from one Member State to another without loss of legal personality.[112] In its preparatory work, the legislature indicated that the tax aspects connected with the transfer of a registered office would be covered in a separate law.[113]

SICAVs with the status of specialized investment fund

2.143 SICAVs that have opted for the status of SIF may be incorporated in the form of an SA and, unlike SICAVs established under the 2002 Act, may also be incorporated as an SCA, an SARL, or a cooperative incorporated in the form of an SA.[114]

2.144 An SCA is governed for the most part by the articles applicable to an SA.[115] It is distinguished from an SA by its ownership structure, made up of two types of partners. First, partners whose liability is limited to their investment. Their situation is similar to that of an SA's shareholders. They are known as limited partners.

---

[107] ibid Art 26*quater*.

[108] ibid Art 26*septies*.

[109] ibid Art 26.

[110] ibid Art 2.

[111] See the conclusions of Advocate General Dámaso Ruiz-Jarabo Colomer in C-208/00 *Überseering BV v Nordic Construction Company Baumanagement GmbH (NCC)*, points 33 and 69.

[112] Art 23(2), Act of 1915.

[113] *Parliamentary doc* No 5352, Explanatory Statement, 32.

[114] Art 25, Act of 13 February 2007; Reuter and Berck (n 67 above) 43 *et seq.*

[115] Art 103, 1915 Act. As regards SCAs, see F Bucher, 'Du bon usage de la commandite par actions' (1994) *Rev soc* 415; T Tilquin, 'Le renouveau de la société en commandite par actions, (1991) *Rev Banque* 89; T Tilquin, 'Quelques aspects de la transmission et de la continuité des sociétés familiales' in *Transmission et protection des entreprises familiales*, (Fédération des entreprises de Belgique, 1992) 69.

Secondly, and above all, there are one or more partners with joint and several unlimited liability for all commitments entered into by the company. Known as general partners, such partners are responsible for the management of the SCA. General partners may not be dismissed if they were appointed under the articles of incorporation.[116] They have wider powers than the members of boards of directors of SAs. Unless otherwise stipulated in the articles of incorporation, they can veto decisions adopted by the general meeting of limited partners. It is easy to understand why. General partners are personally liable and commit their personal assets as a result of their joint unlimited liability. Hence they must have the management powers necessary to protect their interests.

The general partners may, and frequently opt to, transfer their joint unlimited **2.145** liability to a company with limited liability (SA or SARL), to take on the role of general partner. The general partner would be incorporated, owned, and managed by those who intend to manage the SCA, and its shareholders' liability is limited to their investment. The interposition of a legal entity between an SCA and its conducting persons is a frequently used solution to the otherwise unlimited liability of the general partner.

The SARLs structure is only suitable for certain types of SIFs, as the number of **2.146** shareholders in an SARL is limited to forty[117] and an SARL may not offer shares to the public.[118] Moreover, an SARL's shares may be transferred only on certain terms specified in the 1915 Act which cannot be amended[119] in the articles of incorporation or contractually to allow more flexibility. These restrictions tend to discourage the promoters of SIFs whose shares are typically placed with numerous well-informed investors. In some other respects, however, the SARL may be an attractive solution as it is less regulated by the Act of 1915 than an SA and an SCA. The SARL share transfer restrictions may even turn out to be useful. They enable the promoter to exercise more control over the shareholding structure. In addition,

---

[116] The principle of irrevocability provides an excellent defence against changes in control over SCAs.

[117] Art 181, 1915 Act.

[118] ibid Art 188.

[119] ibid Arts 189 and 190. Pursuant to Art 189, *inter vivos* share transfers to non-shareholders require approval at a general meeting of shareholders representing at least three-quarters of the share capital. The same requirement is applied slightly less rigorously when shares are transferred to non-shareholders in the event of death. In that case, approval is not required for share transfers to reserved heirs, the surviving spouse or, to the extent permitted by the articles of incorporation, other legal heirs. Moreover, an heir who is not approved may require the company to buy the securities itself or arrange for their purchase by other shareholders or their transfer to an approved third party. If none of those measures is taken within three months from the date on which the heir serves notice, the heir may start proceedings for the premature dissolution of the company before expiry of its term. Article 190 subjects the acceptability of share transfers to compliance with the formalities laid down in Article 1690 of the Civil Code.

unlike an SCA, an SARL can be set up by a single shareholder. A SIF dedicated to a single investor can therefore be set up with the status of an SARL.

2.147 The legal form of a cooperative society organized as an SA is not used by any SIF, since its regulations are quite unsuited to this structure.

Legal forms of investment companies with fixed capital

2.148 SICAFs are more traditional companies. Their capital is equal to the amount of contributions received. In principle, the capital may be changed only pursuant to a decision of the general meeting of shareholders.

2.149 The shares of such companies can have both a nominal value and an accounting par value. The accounting par value fluctuates solely to reflect changes in the share capital, rather than changes in the value of the SICAF's portfolio. The company's investment results are reflected only in terms of the net asset value per share, which is equal to the company's net asset value divided by the number of shares in issue. In contrast to SICAVs, a SICAF's net asset value per share differs from the nominal value or accounting par value per share, which is equal to the share capital divided by the number of shares representing it.

Investment companies with fixed capital governed by Part I of the 2002 Act

2.150 The 2002 Act defines SICAFs governed by Part I as investment companies:

—other than investment companies with variable capital and

—whose exclusive object is to invest their funds in transferable securities and/or other liquid financial assets . . . [authorized by Directive 85/611] in order to spread the investment risks and to ensure for their shareholders or partners the benefit of the result of the management of their assets, and

—whose shares are intended to be placed with the public by means of a public or private offer, provided that the words '*société d'investissement*' (investment company) appear on all their deeds, announcements, publications, letters and other documents.[120]

2.151 No particular form is imposed on such companies. The promoters' choice is nevertheless limited by the fact that such companies are subject to the provisions applicable to the SA.[121] On an initial analysis, it would seem that a SICAF may only be established as an SA. However, that initial impression is not correct as a SICAF can also be incorporated as an SCA.

---

[120] Art 39, 2002 Act.
[121] Through Art 40, which refers to Art 26, 2002 Act.

Investment companies with fixed capital governed by Part II of the 2002 Act

SICAFs governed by Part II of the 2002 Act are companies other than companies **2.152** with variable capital and:

—whose exclusive object is to invest their funds in securities in order to spread the investment risks and to ensure for their investors the benefit of the result of the management of their assets, and

—whose shares are intended to be placed with the public by means of a public or private offer.[122]

The 2002 Act does not lay down, either directly or indirectly, any requirement as **2.153** to the form to be used for SICAFs established under that Act. A SICAF may therefore be set up using any of the company structures mentioned at the start of this section, though some of them are unlikely to be used in practice.

For instance, it is difficult to believe that investors would be willing to assume **2.154** unlimited personal liability for all commitments entered into by an investment company. That rules out the *société en nom collectif* (general partnership) and the *société civile* (non-commercial company). The *société en nom collectif* is characterized by the joint unlimited liability of its partners.[123] The partners in a *société civile* also assume personal unlimited liability, although they do not have joint liability.[124]

The fact that a SICAF has a fixed capital rules out the cooperative society, whose **2.155** capital is by definition variable.[125] That leaves the SA, the SCS or SCA, and the SARL as the structures of choice in practice. The SA and the SCA are the most common forms, mainly because their shares are easily transferable.

Another possible structure is the SCS. This type of company differentiates between **2.156** its partners in the same way as the SCA, that is to say, it comprises limited partners, whose liability is limited to their contribution, and general partners, who may not in principle be dismissed and who have joint unlimited liability for the company's commitments. It differs from SCAs in the ease with which its shares may be transferred. The shares held by an SCA's limited partners can be transferred as freely as an SA's shares. In contrast, transfers of shares issued by an SCS are subject to the formalities prescribed in the Civil Code.[126] That is, the company must first be notified of, or recognize, the transfer. That constraint makes the SCS unsuitable for SICAFs that intend to place their securities with the

---

[122] Art 73, 2002 Act.
[123] Art 14, 1915 Act.
[124] Art 1862, Civil Code.
[125] Art 113, 1915 Act.
[126] Art 21 of the 1915 Act refers indirectly to Art 1690 of the Civil Code with regard to transfers of receivables.

public. However, as the regime governing the SCS does not provide UCIs with any particular advantages, this form of company is hardly ever used.

2.157   A SICAF may also opt for the status of SARL.

SICAFs with the status of specialized investment fund

2.158   The situation of SICAFs organized as SIFs is quite similar to that of SICAFs governed by Part II of the 2002 Act. They can adopt the form of an SA, an SCA, an SARL, a cooperative incorporated in the form of an SA, a *société en nom collectif* (general partnership), a *société civile* (non-commercial company), or an SCS.[127]

Other legal forms of UCIs

2.159   Only a UCI falling within Part II of the 2002 Act or the Act of 13 February 2007 can adopt a form other than that of an FCP or investment company. Such UCIs may choose between all types of 'companies' and 'undertakings' without having to fulfil any other requirement, provided that they invest in 'assets' according to the principle of risk spreading.[128]

2.160   A UCI governed by Part II or a SIF can therefore be established as an association or a not-for-profit foundation.[129] In fact, the concept of a UCI is not incompatible with the pursuit of charitable or philanthropic purposes by a promoter or a group of investors. However, a UCI would need to have highly specific reasons, which may not be immediately identifiable, to justify such a legal form. In certain cases, donors can obtain tax relief on cash donations to bodies whose public interest is officially recognized.[130] That benefit may justify recourse to this more unusual type of UCI.

2.161   Is it possible that a bank or another entity holding both a discretionary (or other collective) management mandate and a portfolio with identical characteristics on behalf of a number of clients (for example via a joint account opened in the name of all participants) might be construed as managing a UCI? It seems difficult to reconcile such a collective management mechanism with the 2002 Act or with the Act of 13 February 2007, mainly for the following two reasons:

- first, such a collective mechanism cannot be considered an 'undertaking';
- secondly, and more fundamentally, such a system does not provide for the issue of securities, which is a *sine qua non* for UCIs.[131]

---

[127] Reuter and Berck (n 67 above) 48.
[128] Art 73, 2002 Act; Art 38, Act of 13 February 2007.
[129] Within the meaning of the amended Act of 21 April 1928 on associations and not-for-profit foundations ((2003) *Rec Lég Soc*, 541).
[130] Art 112, LIR
[131] Arts 2(2), 65(1), 69, and 73, 2002 Act.

This approach is confirmed by the grant of a special status for 'collective savings funds', **2.162** defined as 'collective undivided cash deposits managed on behalf of a minimum of twenty joint savers for the sole purpose of obtaining more attractive financial terms'.[132] The Explanatory Statement introducing the Parliamentary report on this legislative innovation distinguishes the concept of collective savings funds from collective investment schemes and other structures, *inter alia*, by virtue of the fact that collective savings funds do not satisfy either the legal definition for undertakings for collective investment or the definitions of other entities subject to CSSF oversight. The objective of protecting savers investing in those structures requires such structures to meet certain requirements, compliance with which is checked by the CSSF.[133]

Under certain circumstances, recourse to the legal mechanism of *fiducie* (trust)[134] **2.163** could result in the creation of a UCI.

In the capacity of a *fiduciaire* (trustee), a bank can legally hold a portfolio on **2.164** behalf of, and at the exclusive risk of, clients who, in the capacity of *fiduciants* (settlors), have signed a fiduciary agreement with the bank.

The bank would issue to the investors securities representing a portion of the **2.165** fiduciary assets. That would satisfy the condition that securities must be issued, although it may be asked how exactly such a structure would amount to an *undertaking* within the meaning of the 2002 Act.

Umbrella UCIs

Principles

The 2002 Act and the Act of 13 February 2007 allow UCIs to split their assets into **2.166** several portfolios, known as sub-funds, which are segregated by reason of their investment policy, accounting currency, or eligible investors. This enables each investor to choose between several currencies and types of assets within the same entity and to switch from one sub-fund to another without paying any back-end or front-end charges.[135]

By permitting the creation of umbrella UCIs, the legislator merely confirmed a **2.167** practice already in widespread use on the Luxembourg market.[136] As early as 1985,

---

[132] Art 28-7 of the 1993 Act, as introduced by the Act of 2 August 2003 (*Mémorial* A 2003, 2364).
[133] *Parliamentary doc* No 5085, Explanatory Statement, 14.
[134] Within the meaning of the Act of 27 July 2003 concerning trusts and fiduciary contracts (*Mémorial* A 2003, 2620), as amended by the Act of 22 March 2004.
[135] As regards the advantages of an umbrella structure, see Reuter and Berck, (n 67 above) 52 and 53.
[136] Until 1988, multiple-sub-fund UCIs did not have official existence but were tolerated by the administration. Remarkably enough, for practical needs the Luxembourg authorities even permitted derogations from the 1915 Act for multiple-sub-fund SICAVs.

the supervisory authority allowed the creation of such UCIs, subject to certain conditions.[137] With a few exceptions, such conditions are still applicable. They are set out in Circular 91/75.

2.168 By law, each UCI constitutes a single legal entity governed by one legal regime. For example, a UCI which has one or more sub-funds which do not comply with the restrictions specified by Part I of the 2002 Act cannot be regulated under both Part I and Part II of the 2002 Act. In such cases, only the rules of Part II of the 2002 Act are applicable.[138]

2.169 Segregation of the assets of an umbrella UCI involves a complex mechanism. As regards the relationships between unitholders, the law provides that each sub-fund must be treated as a separate entity unless otherwise stipulated in the constitutive documents.[139] When an investor joins a UCI, he must choose the sub-fund whose units he intends to buy. In so doing, he participates in the profits and the losses of that sub-fund. Investment results are shared at the sub-fund level rather than at the level of the overall UCI.

2.170 The status of third parties vis-à-vis sub-funds has also changed in recent years. For many years, liabilities incurred by individual sub-funds were not segregated as against third parties, so that the assets of the entire umbrella fund could be used to satisfy the liabilities of an individual sub-fund unless otherwise agreed with each third party.[140] Today, by virtue of the 2002 Act and the Act of 13 February 2007, a sub-fund's assets can only be used to satisfy the debts, commitments, and obligations incurred by that sub-fund, unless otherwise stipulated in the UCI's constitutive documents.[141]

2.171 The consequences of the choice of structure of an umbrella scheme differ according to whether the UCI is organized in the form of an FCP, a SICAV or a SICAF, and these are examined below.

Umbrella FCPs

2.172 A promoter who wishes to set up an umbrella FCP must comply with the rules of Circular 91/75.[142] The ability to assign different characteristics to the different sub-funds is limited in the following manner.

---

[137] Notice issued by the *Institut Monétaire Luxembourgeois*, 27 December 1985.
[138] Chs J, I, Circular 91/75. See also *Parliamentary doc* No 3172, Notice of the Chamber of Commerce, 3, and Notice of the *Conseil d'État*, 14.
[139] Art 133(5), 2002 Act; Art 71(5), Act of 13 February 2007.
[140] Art 111(2), old version, 1988 Act.
[141] Art 133(5), 2002 Act; Art 71(5), Act of 13 February 2007.
[142] Chs J, I, II and IV, Circular 91/75.

Uniformity is required as regards: **2.173**

(1) an FCP's operators (a single management company, a single depositary, a single auditor);

(2) the management regulations, which (subject to exceptions) must lay down standardized rules for the redemption of units, valuation of assets, suspension of the calculation of net asset value, and investment restrictions;[143]

(3) an FCP's overall currency of account, used for the combined financial statements of all sub-funds, as applicable after translation of the financial statements of sub-funds denominated in other currencies into the fund's overall currency;

(4) the generic name of the sub-funds, which may be complemented by a specific designation for each sub-fund;

(5) the form of the securities issued to express the rights of unitholders, distinguished only by the designation of the sub-fund for which they are issued.

Within the same FCP, investors must in principle be able to convert their units **2.174** from one sub-fund to another without paying fees or incurring unreasonable costs. Moreover, units must be issued and redeemed at the specific net asset value of the sub-fund for which they have been issued.

Lastly, investment and borrowing restrictions are calculated by reference to the **2.175** assets of the sub-fund concerned, save only as regards the percentage of securities held from a single issuer, which is determined at the level of the overall FCP, and the minimum net asset value of €1,250,000, which is applied to the overall FCP instead of each sub-fund. The rules applicable when the net asset value drops below two-thirds or even one-quarter of the minimum legal amount also apply to the umbrella scheme as a whole.

Umbrella SICAVs

In contrast to FCPs, SICAVs must be incorporated in the form of a company and **2.176** are required to adhere to the legal conditions laid down by the 1915 Act. This law does not provide for the incorporation of companies with sub-funds. The 2002 Act, in line with the 1988 Act, expressly provides such a framework for umbrella UCIs.

First, it introduced special rules on share values. Pursuant to the 1915 Act, securi- **2.177** ties representing the capital of an SA,[144] an SCA,[145] or an SARL[146] must be of

---

[143] This principle seems to have been called into question by the new contents of Arts 133(4) of the 2002 Act and 71(4) of the Act of 13 February 2007, which allow FCPs made up of several sub-funds to adopt separate management regulations for the characteristics and rules applicable to each sub-fund.

[144] Art 37, 1915 Act.

[145] Art 103, which refers indirectly to Art 37, 1915 Act.

[146] Art 182, 1915 Act.

equal value. However, because of the existence of sub-funds within an investment company, the accounting par value, which is equal to the net asset value per share, differs for each sub-fund, mainly in the light of its results. For that reason, the 2002 Act and the Act of 13 February 2007 deviate in this respect from the 1915 Act[147] and provide that shares or units in umbrella UCIs may be of different value, with or without an indication of accounting par value, depending upon the chosen legal form.[148] The accounting par value of each unit can vary from sub-fund to sub-fund.

2.178 As a SICAV's shares have different values, their respective voting rights could conceivably be different as well. However, the 2002 Act and the Act of 13 February 2007 do not deviate from the 1915 Act in this respect. Each share entitles its holder to one vote, regardless of its value.[149] Pursuant to Circular 91/75, the fact that shareholders have equal voting rights must be mentioned in the articles of incorporation of each umbrella investment company.[150]

2.179 The creation of sub-funds involves the issue of shares to which different privileges attach. The creation of specific share classes has several consequences under company law. In principle, any change in the rights attached to a given share class requires the unanimous approval of all unitholders or shareholders.[151] However, the 1915 Act lays down an important derogation from that rule for SAs and SCAs,[152] namely that modification of the specific rights of a share class does not require unanimous approval but approval by way of a resolution passed at a general meeting of the shareholders of each class at which the quorum and majority requirements for amendment of the articles of incorporation were satisfied.

2.180 It may be asked to what extent this principle and its derogation apply to umbrella SICAVs. The 2002 Act and the Act of 13 February 2007 each state that: 'with respect to relations between investors, each sub-fund shall be deemed to be a separate entity unless otherwise stipulated in the constitutive documents'.[153] That formulation may be construed as permitting independent treatment of each sub-fund in respect of certain rules of company law. That interpretation is reflected in Circular 91/75, which allows the articles of incorporation to include clauses

---

[147] See *Parliamentary doc* No 3172[1], Notice of the *Conseil d'État*, 14.

[148] Art 133(3), 2002 Act; Art 71(3), Act of 13 February 2007.

[149] Arts 67(4) and 195, 1915 Act.

[150] Ch J, III, 1, Circular 91/75.

[151] C Resteau, *Traité des sociétés anonymes*, Vol II, Swinnen, 3rd edn, by A Benoit-Moury and A Grégoire (1982), No 1297; G Ripert and R Roblot, *Traité de droit commercial*, Vol I, LGDJ, 15th edn, by M Germain (1993) Nos 1231 *et seq*; T Tilquin and V Simonart, *Traité des sociétés*, Vol I Kluwer Éditions juridiques Belgique, 1996 Nos 1030 and 1031.

[152] Arts 68 and 103, 1915 Act.

[153] Art 133(5), 2002 Act; Art 71(5), Act of 13 February 2007.

stipulating that decisions affecting the rights of the shareholders of only one sub-fund need only be submitted to a general meeting of the sub-fund concerned.[154]

As regards umbrella SICAVs, Circular 91/75 also stipulates certain requirements **2.181** linked more specifically to the status of UCIs.

Only one currency may be used to express the share capital of umbrella SICAVs.[155] **2.182** The share capital of the SICAV must be expressed in a given currency, which must be the same as that used for the accounting par value per share and for the company's annual financial statements. Different currencies may be used for different sub-funds and classes of shares within sub-funds. The net asset value of each sub-fund or class, and therefore of a sub-fund's or class's shares, is expressed in the sub-fund's or class's 'reference' or 'base' currency. This requirement must be clearly stipulated in the articles of incorporation of umbrella SICAVs.

The articles of incorporation of umbrella SICAVs must also list the circumstances **2.183** in which calculation of the net asset value per share may be suspended. In addition the articles of incorporation of umbrella funds must stipulate the circumstances in which calculation of the net asset value of a single sub-fund may be suspended.[156]

Finally, as for FCPs, Circular 91/75 specifies that investment and borrowing **2.184** restrictions must be applied to each individual sub-fund rather than to the overall UCI.[157] The only exception to this principle is the calculation of the percentage of securities held from a single issuer, which is calculated at the level of the UCI, with all sub-funds combined.[158]

Umbrella SICAFs

None of the 2002 Act or the Act of 13 February 2007 or Circular 91/75 distin- **2.185** guishes between SICAVs and SICAFs in laying down the principles applicable to the creation of sub-funds within the same UCI. Hence, the rules for SICAVs, as outlined previously, apply *mutatis mutandis* to SICAFs, save for one vital difference. The nominal value or accounting par value of a SICAF's shares remains the same, whether or not the fund has sub-funds. Only the net asset value per share varies from one sub-fund to another, according to the investment performance of each sub-fund. Thus, the provisions of the 1915 Act continue to apply as regards the nominal value or accounting par value per share of a SICAF.

---

[154] Ch J, III, 1, Circular 91/75.
[155] ibid Ch J, III, 2.
[156] ibid Ch J, III, 3.
[157] ibid Ch J, III, 4.
[158] ibid.

3

PERMITTED ACTIVITIES FOR UNDERTAKINGS FOR COLLECTIVE INVESTMENT

Permitted Activities for Coordinated UCITS

Permitted activities of a coordinated UCITS

Main activities

Introduction

3.01 The investment activity of a UCITS is strictly defined by Directive 85/611 and by the 2002 Act.[1] According to those texts, a UCITS' investments must consist 'solely' of the following securities:

(1) transferable securities listed or dealt in on a regulated market, situated either in the EEA or in a non-member country;

(2) money market instruments listed or dealt in on a regulated market in the EEA or in a non-member country and, provided the issuer meets certain conditions, over the counter;

---

[1] Art 19(1), Directive (EEC) 85/611 and Article 41(1), 2002 Act. The authors want to thank their partner M Eisenhuth and their colleague, Ms F Moreau, for their valuable contribution to these chapters.

(3) units/shares in UCIs;

(4) deposits at credit institutions;

(5) derivatives.

The term 'solely' does not prevent a coordinated UCITS from holding certain   **3.02**
securities other than the above assets, governed by Directive 85/611, subject to
compliance with certain criteria and limits as described below. It merely requires
that a UCITS' only investment objective must be to invest in such assets. A coordinated UCITS may never adopt another core policy, such as investing in privately
held companies or in buildings. On 19 March 2007, after more than two years of
cooperation and consultation with the CESR,[2] the European Commission adopted
the directive on eligible assets for UCITS[3] (the 'Eligible Assets Directive').

Directive 85/611, as amended by Directive 2001/108 and Directive 2001/107,   **3.03**
created the first European retail financial product. By harmonizing the features
of undertakings for collective investment, Directive 85/611 paved the way for
effective cross-border competition and a uniformly high level of protection of
investors in the European Union.

Since the adoption of Directive 85/611, the variety of financial instruments traded   **3.04**
on financial markets has considerably increased, leading to uncertainty in determining which categories of financial instruments are encompassed by the definitions
in Directive 85/611. This uncertainty gave rise to divergent interpretations of
Directive 85/611 across the European Union and a lack of uniformity in the
application of these legislative provisions.

In order to ensure uniform application of Directive 85/611, to help Member   **3.05**
States to develop a common understanding as to whether a given asset category is
eligible for a UCITS and to ensure that the definitions are understood in a manner
consistent with the principles underlying Directive 85/611, the European
Commission recognized the need to provide regulators and market participants
with more certainty as regards eligible assets.

The process

In October 2004, the European Commission issued a mandate to the CESR   **3.06**
requesting its technical advice, in its capacity as an independent advisory group,
in clarifying definitions of financial instruments in which a coordinated UCITS
can invest.

In accordance with Article 53(a) of Directive 85/611, which provides that technical   **3.07**
amendments may be made to Directive 85/611 to clarify definitions 'in order to

---

[2] Committee of European Securities Regulators.
[3] Commission Directive (EC) 2007/16 of 19 March 2007 implementing Directive (EEC)
85/611 as regards the clarification of certain definitions.

ensure uniform application of the directive throughout the Community', the CESR consulted widely with various industry participants before publishing its final advice in January 2006,[4] together with a feedback statement.

3.08 On 19 March 2007, following consideration of the CESR's advice, the European Commission then adopted the Eligible Assets Directive with regard to eligible assets for coordinated UCITS.

3.09 It is clear that the eligibility of an asset for a coordinated UCITS must now be assessed not only having regard to the requirements of Directive 85/611 but also as to whether it comes within the scope of the definitions as clarified by the text of the Eligible Assets Directive. The Eligible Assets Directive is accompanied by CESR guidelines 07-044 (the 'Eligible Assets Guidelines')[5] covering specific matters not included in the Eligible Assets Directive.

3.10 On 17 July 2007, the CESR published its additional guidelines (the 'Hedge Funds Indices Guidelines')[6] on the classification of hedge funds indices as financial indices. These guidelines form part of the Eligible Assets Guidelines.

3.11 Member States were obliged to transpose the Eligible Assets Directive and the two sets of guidelines into law as a single package of measures no later than 23 March 2008 and to apply those provisions no later than 23 July 2008. In Luxembourg, the Eligible Assets Directive and the two sets of guidelines have been transposed into national law by the Grand-Ducal Regulation of 8 February 2008 and the CSSF Circular 08/339 respectively.

Transferable securities

3.12 **Concept of transferable security**   Before 2002, Directive 85/611 did not define 'transferable security' and left its interpretation entirely at the discretion of national legislatures. The 1988 Act reflected the same flexibility: it did not describe this concept either. Consequently, it was left to the CSSF to define 'transferable security' in Circular 91/75.[7]

3.13 As the concept of transferable security was subsequently refined at European level, it was described more specifically in Directive 85/611 as revised and amended in 2002. Its definition, the same as the definition in Directive 93/22,[8] is very general, covering 'shares in companies and other securities equivalent to shares in companies

---

[4] CESR's advice on Clarification of Definitions concerning Eligible Assets for investment of UCITS dated January 2006 (ref CESR/06-005).

[5] CESR's guidelines concerning eligible assets for investment by UCITS dated March 2007 (ref CESR/07-044).

[6] CESR's guidelines concerning eligible assets for investment by UCITS—The classification of hedge fund indices as financial indices dated July 2007 (ref CESR/07-434).

[7] Ch F, III, 1, Circular 91/75.

[8] Art 1, point 4, Directive (EEC) 93/22.

("shares"), bonds or other forms of securitised debt ("bonds"), any other securities giving the right to buy such transferable securities by subscription or exchange', excluding the techniques and instruments covered by the Directive.

The Eligible Assets Directive and the Eligible Assets Guidelines further clarified **3.14** the requirements for a transferable security[9] as follows:

(1) the security must not expose the coordinated UCITS to losses beyond the amount paid for it or, in the case of a partly paid security, to be paid for it;

(2) the liquidity of the security must not compromise the UCITS' ability to repurchase or redeem its units at the request of any unitholder (transferable securities listed or dealt on a regulated market are deemed in principle to be liquid; if the liquidity is not certain, the UCITS must ensure that the liquidity for a given security is satisfied by considering certain additional criteria);

(3) there must be accurate, reliable, and regular prices for the security, either market prices or prices made available by valuation systems which are independent of issuers;

(4) there must be regular, accurate, and comprehensive information available to the market on the security or, where relevant, on the portfolio of the security; and

(5) the security must be negotiable.

In addition, the acquisition of any transferable security must be consistent with **3.15** the stated investment objectives of the coordinated UCITS and the risk of the security must be adequately captured in the risk management process of the coordinated UCITS.

Where the security embeds a derivative element (as fully detailed hereafter), the **3.16** derivative element must be taken into account in the calculation of the global risk exposure limit.

According to the CESR, investment in transferable securities benefits from a pre- **3.17** sumption of liquidity and negotiability if they are traded on a regulated market.

According to the CSSF's administrative practice, shares and units issued by a **3.18** closed-end UCI, ie a UCI not obliged to redeem its units or shares at the request of its investors,[10] are deemed transferable securities. Investment in shares and units of open-end UCIs is subject to rules other than those governing the purchase and ownership of transferable securities.

Pursuant to the Eligible Assets Directive and the Eligible Assets Guidelines,[11] **3.19** investments by a UCITS in closed-end funds are eligible, if the units issued by

---

[9] Art 2, Eligible Assets Directive and Item 17 of the Eligible Assets Guidelines.
[10] Ch F, III, 4, and Ch G, II, Circular 91/75.
[11] Art 2, Eligible Assets Directive and Item 17 of the Eligible Assets Guidelines.

such funds comply with the requirements stated for the transferable securities and with the following conditions:

(1) Closed-end funds established as an investment company or a unit trust are subject to corporate governance mechanisms applied to companies, and closed-end funds in contractual form are subject to corporate governance mechanisms equivalent to those applied to companies generally.

(2) The asset management activity carried on by or on behalf of the closed-end fund must be subject to appropriate investor protection safeguards. This means that where the asset management activity is carried out by another entity, as appropriate, that entity must be subject to national regulation for the purpose of investor protection.

Eligible transferable securities

3.20 *Transferable securities listed or dealt in on a regulated market*   Directive 85/611 provides that in order to be eligible for investment by a coordinated UCITS, a transferable security must be (a) admitted for listing or trading on a regulated market within the meaning of Directive 93/22, or (b) dealt in on another regulated market that is recognized, operates regularly, and is open to the public.[12]

3.21 The reference to regulated markets within the meaning of Directive 93/22 replaces the concept of 'stock exchanges' used previously in Directive 85/611. This substitution reflects the wish to harmonize the law as the concept of 'stock exchanges' was not defined in Directive 85/611, which led to many uncertainties and interpretation differences between Member States.

3.22 Directive 93/22 was repealed by the MiFID Directive, which came into force on 1 November 2007.[13] However, the MiFID Directive has had only a marginal impact on the concepts of 'regulated market' and 'other regulated market'.

3.23 Pursuant to Directive 93/22 and the MiFID Directive, regulated markets must meet the following criteria:[14]

(1) be included in the list issued by the Member State in which the market is organized;[15]

---

[12] According to the preparatory work for Directive (EC) 2001/108, the reference to listing or trading on a capital market rules out 'stocks and equivalent securities issued by Building Societies and Industrial and Provident Societies, whose ownership, in practice, can only be transferred by redemption by the issuing body' (Proposal for a Directive of the European Parliament and the Council modifying Directive 85/611 [1998] OJ C280/6).

[13] Art 69, MiFID Directive, as amended by Directive (EC) 2006/31 of 5 April 2006 [2006] OJ L114/60).

[14] For futher details on these criteria, see Art 4(14) and Title III on regualted markets in MiFID.

[15] Art 1, point 13, Directive (EEC) 93/22; Art 47, MiFID Directive. This list is published by the Commission of the European Communities in the OJ and on the website of the Commission of

(2) deal in the financial instruments mentioned in Section B of the Annexe to Directive 93/22, which became Section C in Annexe I of the MiFID Directive;[16]

(3) be in regular operation;

(4) be governed by minimum regulations;

(5) be regulated by the public authorities or by other legally appointed authorities; and

(6) guarantee minimum information and transparency conditions.

For other regulated markets, the CSSF also looked to Directive 93/22,[17] accord- **3.24**
ing to which a regulated market is one that meets the following conditions:

(1) liquidity;

(2) multilateral matching of orders (general matching of buy and sell orders in order to establish a single price); and

(3) transparency (dissemination of maximum information giving principals the possibility of monitoring trading in order to check that their orders were actually executed at the prevailing conditions).

Strict application of these criteria to certain markets sometimes generates difficul- **3.25**
ties that need to be settled individually. It is the responsibility of the UCITS directors, together with the depositary, to satisfy themselves whether a stock

---

the European Communities at <http://europa.eu.int/comm/internal_market/securities/docs/isd/reg.markets-provisions_en.pdf>.

[16] ie by virtue of Directive (EEC) 93/22, transferable securities, shares and units in UCIs, money market instruments, futures, forward rate agreements, interest rate swaps, currency swaps, or equity swaps, and options on any of the foregoing instruments, including currency and interest rate options. The MiFID Directive has extended this list to include: '(1) transferable securities; (2) money market instruments; (3) units in UCIs; (4) options, futures, swaps, forward rate agreements, and any other derivative contracts relating to securities, currencies, interest rates or yields, or other derivatives, financial indices, or financial measures which may be settled by physical or cash delivery; (5) options, futures, swaps, forward rate agreements, and any other derivative contracts relating to commodities that must be settled in cash or may be settled in cash at the option of one of the parties (otherwise than by reason of a default or other termination event); (6) options, futures, swaps, and any other derivative contract relating to commodities that can be physically settled provided that they are traded on a regulated market and/or an MTF; (7) options, futures, swaps, forwards, and any other derivative contracts relating to commodities, that can be physically settled not otherwise mentioned in Section C.6 and not being for commercial purposes, which have the characteristics of other derivative financial instruments, having regard to whether, *inter alia*, they are cleared and settled through recognized clearing houses or are subject to regular margin calls; (8) derivative instruments for the transfer of credit risk; (9) financial contracts for differences; (10) options, futures, swaps, forward rate agreements, and any other derivative contracts relating to climatic variables, freight rates, emission allowances, or inflation rates, or other official economic statistics that must be settled in cash or may be settled in cash at the option of one of the parties (otherwise than by reason of a default or other termination event), as well as any other derivative contracts relating to assets, rights, obligations, indices and measures not otherwise mentioned in this Section, which have the characteristics of other derivative financial instruments, having regard to whether, *inter alia*, they are traded on a regulated market or an MTF, are cleared and settled through recognized clearing houses, or are subject to regular margin calls.'

[17] CSSF Annual Report for 1999, 62.

exchange or a market meets the above criteria. Moreover, the UCITS directors should at all times be able to provide the CSSF with the necessary supporting information. Otherwise, application of the above criteria raises few interpretation difficulties in practice.

3.26   The CSSF has confirmed that the markets located in the countries of the European Union are to be considered as regulated. For markets situated outside the European Union, the CSSF, in compliance with the 2002 Act, confirms on a regular basis the markets it considers as regulated.[18] These confirmations can be given either following a specific request via a specific communication to the Luxembourg financial sector participants or in the CSSF annual reports.[19]

3.27   For example, the CSSF has, on a case-by-case basis, recognized as regulated the following markets: the over the counter (OTC) bond market organized by ISMA (International Securities Market Association); the OTC US markets regulated by the NASD and by the US SEC but not the US TRACE (Trade Reporting and Compliance Engine); the EASDAQ market; and the money market in the United Kingdom regulated by the Bank of England.

3.28   Regarding certain markets in Russia, the CSSF has recognized as regulated the Russian Trading System, and the Moscow Interbank Currency Exchange.[20] The CSSF has also confirmed that the new EuroMTF market operated by the Bourse de Luxembourg SA is to be considered as a regulated market which is operated regularly, is recognized, and is open to the public.[21]

3.29   In respect of stock exchanges, the CSSF confirmed a few years ago that exchanges recognized as such in their respective country by law or regulation should be recognized as eligible stock exchanges. These exchanges include in particular all FIBV ('*Fédération internationale des Bourses de Valeurs*' or 'World Federation of Exchanges') stock exchanges members.

3.30   Stock exchanges and other regulated markets on which transferable securities are bought must in principle be established in a member country of the EEA. If not, a UCITS may only have recourse to them provided 'the choice of the stock exchange or market has been provided for in the constitutive documents of the UCITS'.[22]

---

[18] Arts 1 and 41(1), 2002 Act.
[19] This was the case in the CSSF Annual Report for 2003, 85.
[20] CSSF Annual Report for 2005, 78. A coordinated UCITS, whose investment policy consists in investing part of or all of its assets in securities traded on the said Russian markets, must comply with the following requirements: the sales prospectus of the coordinated UCITS must make clear that the coordinated UCITS invests in securities traded on the Russian RTS Stock Exchange and MICEX; and the sales prospectus of the coordinated UCITS must include an appropriate risk description, allowing the investor to get a proper view of the coordinated UCITS' risk profile.
[21] ibid.
[22] Art 41(1) *c*, 2002 Act.

Previously, the CSSF interpreted the text literally and required that the constitutive documents of UCITS contain an exhaustive list of stock exchanges and markets targeted by the UCITS. This approach in fact hindered UCITS, which were unable to trade on newly emerging markets. Except when a UCITS voluntarily chooses to list specific markets, current practice is to refer in the constitutive documents to markets in all countries on all continents in order to maximize the scope of target markets. This practice does not appear to violate the spirit of Directive 85/611, as the European legislature did not want to restrict the geographical sphere of investments made by a UCITS.

3.31

Up to 10 per cent of the net assets of a coordinated UCITS can be invested in transferable securities not listed or dealt in on another regulated market. Pursuant to the Eligible Assets Directive, transferable securities not listed or dealt in on another regulated market must, however, in order to be eligible, fulfil the requirements listed above.

3.32

Newly issued transferable securities A coordinated UCITS may also invest in recently issued transferable securities not yet admitted to official listing on a regulated market.[23] Provided it meets the following conditions and complies with all other applicable investment restrictions, it is possible for a UCITS portfolio to hold only this type of transferable security.

3.33

In this respect, the following constraints apply:

3.34

(1) The terms of issue of the transferable securities in question must include an undertaking that application will be made for admission to official listing on a stock exchange or another regulated market. Moreover, the choice of stock exchange or market must have been provided for in the UCITS' constitutive documents.

(2) Admission to the stock exchange or other market must be obtained no later than one year after issue. This condition may raise practical difficulties when an issuer is unable to meet the initial timetable. In such a situation, the UCITS will be unintentionally in breach of the regulations. In principle, it will consequently be obliged to divest itself of such investments immediately. However, the 2002 Act treats the unintentional violation of the investment limits as a special situation. In the case of an unintentional breach, the UCITS is obliged to remedy the situation in the interests of the participants.[24] It is not obliged to sell the investments if this would be contrary to the investors' best interests. Thus a UCITS could determine not to divest itself of the recently

---

[23] Art 19.1(d) Directive (EEC) 85/611, transposed into Art 41(1)(d) 2002 Act. The provision on investments in newly issued transferable securities still refers to the concept of 'stock exchanges' but this is probably due to an oversight by the European legislature.
[24] Art 49(2), 2002 Act.

issued transferable securities immediately given the restricted market in the securities, and could await their final admission to the market in question.

3.35 The 2002 Act authorizes a UCITS to invest in newly issued money market instruments, subject to the conditions set out in the Act applicable to newly issued transferable securities.[25]

Money market instruments

3.36 **Concept of money market instrument** Directive 85/611, as amended in 2002, defines the concept of money market instruments and classifies these instruments as eligible investments for coordinated UCITS in the same way as transferable securities. A money market fund can therefore be classified as a coordinated UCITS. The conditions governing investment in money market instruments are very similar to those applicable to the purchase and ownership of transferable securities.

3.37 Like transferable securities, money market instruments are defined rather broadly in the Directive, which refers to 'instruments normally dealt in on the money market which are liquid, and have a value which can be accurately determined at any time'.[26]

3.38 The definition of money market instruments has been further clarified by the Eligible Assets Directive and the Eligible Assets Guidelines[27] which provide that:

- 'Liquid' means instruments which can be sold at limited cost in an adequately short timeframe taking into account the obligation of the UCITS to repurchase or redeem its units at the request of any unitholder.

- 'Value which can be accurately determined at any time' means instruments for which accurate and reliable valuation systems are available that enable the UCITS to calculate a net asset value in accordance with the value at which money market instruments held in the portfolio could be exchanged, between knowledgeable, willing parties in an arm's length transaction. These systems must be based on market data or on valuation models and include systems based on amortized costs.

- 'Normally dealt in on the money market' includes instruments which have a maturity at issuance of up to and including 397 days, a residual maturity of up to and including 397 days, or undergo regular yield adjustments in line with the above maturities. Furthermore, the risk profile, including credit and interest

---

[25] ibid Art 41(1)(d), 2002 Act. Here, Luxembourg law introduces an innovation compared with Directive (EEC) 85/611, which does not contain the same authorization (Article 19.1(d), Directive (EEC) 85/611).

[26] Art 1(9), Directive (EEC) 85/611 transposed into Art 1(18) of the 2002 Act.

[27] Art 3, Eligible Assets Directive and Items 18 and 19 of the Eligible Assets Guidelines.

rate risks, of such instruments must correspond to that of financial instruments which have the maturity or yield adjustments specified.

Instruments dealt on the money market include, for example, treasury and local authority bills, certificates of deposit, commercial paper, medium-term notes, and bankers' acceptances.[28]   **3.39**

Eligible money market instruments

Money market instruments listed or dealt in on a regulated market To constitute an authorized investment for a coordinated UCITS, a money market instrument must in principle be listed or dealt in on a regulated market.[29] The criteria for determining what constitutes a regulated market are the same as those for determining regulated markets in the context of transferable securities.   **3.40**

Money market instruments normally dealt in on the money market and which are admitted to or dealt in on a regulated market are presumed to be liquid and have a value which can be accurately determined at any time, unless there is information available to the UCITS that would lead to a different conclusion.   **3.41**

Money market instruments issued or guaranteed by certain entities A coordinated UCITS may buy a money market instrument not listed or dealt in on a regulated market, provided the following conditions are met:[30]   **3.42**

(1) The issue or the issuer of such instruments is itself regulated for the purpose of protecting investors and savings.

(2) The instrument has one of the following characteristics:

    (a) it has been issued or guaranteed by a central, regional, or local authority, or by a central bank of a Member State, the European Central Bank, the European Union, or the European Investment Bank, an international public institution of which one or more Member States are members, a non-Member State or, in the case of a Federal State, by one of the members making up the federation;

    (b) it has been issued by an undertaking whose securities are dealt in on a regulated market;

    (c) it has been issued or guaranteed by an establishment subject to prudential supervision, in accordance with criteria defined by Community law or by an equivalent supervision regime. Pursuant to the Eligible Assets Directive, this means an issuer which is subject to and complies with prudential rules and which is located in the EEA or which is located in a G11 country

---

[28] Preamble to Directive 2001/108, 4th Recital.
[29] Art 19.1(a),(b), and (c) Directive (EEC) 85/611 transposed into Article 41(1)(a),(b), and (c), 2002 Act.
[30] Article 19.1(h), Directive 85/611 transposed into Art 41(1)(h), 2002 Act.

(Belgium, Canada, France, Germany, Italy, Japan, the Netherlands, Sweden, Switzerland, the United Kingdom, and the United States), or which has at least an investment grade rating, or for which it can be demonstrated—based on an in-depth analysis of the issuer—that the prudential rules applicable to that issuer are at least as stringent as those laid down by Community law;

(d) it has been issued by other bodies belonging to the categories approved by the CSSF provided that investments in such instruments are subject to investor protection equivalent to that laid down in (a),(b), or (c) above, and provided that the issuer meets one of the following conditions:

(i) capital and reserves amount to at least €10 million and it presents and publishes its annual accounts in accordance with Directive 78/660,[31]

(ii) it is dedicated to the financing of a group of companies that includes one or more listed companies,

(iii) it is dedicated to the financing of securitization vehicles that benefit from a bank finance line.

3.43 Pursuant to the Eligible Assets Directive, in determining permissible money market instruments other than those dealt in on a regulated market and in respect of which the issue or the issuer is itself regulated for the purpose of protecting investors and savings:

- the same definition of money market instruments applies, except that money market instruments are regarded as 'normally dealt in on the money market' if either the maturity/yield adjustments or the risk profile criteria are fulfilled;

- appropriate information must be available for the instruments, including information which allows an appropriate assessment of the credit risks related to investment in such instruments; and

- the instruments must be freely transferable.

3.44 Up to 10 per cent of the net assets of the UCITS may be invested in money market instruments not fulfilling the requirements mentioned above.

Shares and units in UCIs

3.45 The amended Directive authorizes coordinated UCITS to invest in other coordinated UCITS.[32]

---

[31] Fourth Council Directive (EEC) 78/660, 25 July 1978, based on Article 54, paragraph 3, under g) of the Treaty and concerning the annual accounts of certain types of companies [1978] OJ L222/11.

[32] Art 19.1(e), Directive (EEC) 85/611 transposed into Art 41(1)(e), 2002 Act.

A coordinated UCITS may also invest part of its assets in a UCI other than coordi- **3.46** nated UCITS, provided it is a UCI 'within the meaning of Article 1, paragraph (2), first and second indents, of Directive 85/611'.[33] In other words, the relevant UCI, which need not necessarily be a coordinated UCITS, must also invest in transferable securities or other liquid financial assets within the meaning of Directive 85/611.

The phrase 'UCIs other than coordinated UCITS' covers UCIs established in **3.47** accordance with the national laws of an EEA Member State and not governed by the UCITS Directive as well as UCIs under the laws of a non-member country.[34]

Permissible UCIs must redeem their units or shares at the request of investors, **3.48** ie open-end UCIs. Shares and units in closed-end UCIs are considered transferable securities, which means that their purchase is subject to the general rules governing investment in transferable securities.[35]

An open-end UCI other than a coordinated UCITS is not necessarily an autho- **3.49** rized investment. It must also satisfy the following conditions:[36]

- it must be subject to supervision organized by the law and equivalent to that laid down for coordinated UCITS.

  Under the Eligible Assets Guidelines,[37] the following elements can be used to guide a decision on equivalence: Memoranda of Understanding (bilateral or multilateral), membership of an international organization of regulators, or other cooperative arrangements (such as an exchange of letters) to ensure satisfactory cooperation between the authorities; approval of the management company or the target open-end UCI, its rules and choice of depositary by the regulator; and authorization of the open-end UCI in an OECD country;

- the UCI must be supervised by authorities who cooperate sufficiently with the supervisory authorities of the investing UCITS;

- the UCI must offer investors a level of protection equivalent to that provided to investors in a coordinated UCITS (in particular as regards asset segregation, borrowing, lending and uncovered sales).[38]

  Under the Eligible Assets Guidelines,[39] the following criteria can be used as a guide of what constitutes equivalent investors protection: rules guaranteeing

---

[33] ibid.

[34] Explanatory Memorandum to the modified proposal for Directive (EC) 2001/108, 3 (document available on the website of the European Parliament under the heading 'Legislative Observatory').

[35] Ch F, III, 4, and Ch G, II, Circular 91/75.

[36] Article 19.1(e), Directive (EEC) 85/611 transposed into Art 41(1)(e), 2002 Act.

[37] Item 26, Eligible Assets Guidelines.

[38] This provision, *inter alia*, rules out investment in hedge funds that do not meet this requirement, particularly as regards the use of borrowings, loans and uncovered sales.

[39] Item 26, Eligible Assets Guidelines.

the autonomy of the management of the open-end UCI; management in the exclusive interest of the unitholders; the existence of an independent trustee/custodian with similar duties and responsibilities in relation to both safekeeping and supervision; the availability of pricing information and reporting requirements; redemption facilities and frequency; and restrictions in relation to dealings by related parties;

- the UCIs must issue half-yearly and annual reports.

3.50 The UCITS must be prohibited, under its constitutive documents, from investing more than 10 per cent of its assets in the units of other UCIs.[40] Directive 85/611 aims to prevent the 'cascade phenomenon'[41] of UCIs and does not regulate 'funds of funds of funds' structures falling outside its sphere of application.

3.51 Based on these rules, the CSSF does not include open-end real estate property funds in the category of other eligible UCIs as such funds do not invest in eligible securities within the meaning of the first and second indents of paragraph 2 of Article 1 of Directive 85/611. As regards the eligibility of real estate investment trusts as investments for UCITS, the CSSF treats such trusts as real estate property funds. Consequently, the holding thresholds of such vehicles depend, *inter alia*, upon whether or not their units can be redeemed at the investors' request.[42]

3.52 The CSSF has nevertheless confirmed that a UCITS may invest up to 10 per cent of its net assets in regulated open-end real estate funds subject to equivalent supervision.[43] In addition, the CSSF has confirmed in its 2005 annual report[44] that a UCITS may, pursuant to Article 41(2)(a) of the 2002 Act, invest up to 10 per cent[45] of its net assets in regulated open-end hedge funds (as well in regulated open-end funds of hedge funds) that are subject to equivalent supervision.[46] The requirement of compliance with the requirements relating to transferable securities does not apply any longer, as per the administrative practice of the CSSF, which did also recognize regulated open-end private equity funds as eligible under the above 10 per cent ratio.

---

[40] Art 19.1(e), fourth indent, Directive (EEC) 85/611 transposed into Art 41(1)(e), 2002 Act.

[41] Preamble to Directive (EC) 2001/108, 7th Recital.

[42] See CSSF Annual Report for 2004, 78.

[43] ibid.

[44] See CSSF Annual Report for 2005, 79.

[45] Art 41(2)(a), 2002 Act.

[46] Countries providing supervision equivalent to that of the CSSF are currently the following: all European Union Member States; all EFTA Member States (ie Iceland, Liechtenstein, Norway, and Switzerland); Isle of Man, Jersey, Guernesey, United States, Canada, Hong Kong, and Japan. Supervision in other jurisdictions is assessed, on a case-by-case basis, by the CSSF.

Deposits with credit institutions and incidental cash positions

The amended Directive permits deposits as authorized investments, subject to **3.53** compliance with the following cumulative criteria:[47]

(1) they must be repayable on demand;
(2) they must mature in no more than twelve months;
(3) they must be made with a credit institution whose registered office is in a Member State of the European Union or, if in a non-Member State, subject to prudential rules which are equivalent to those laid down in Community law.

The European legislature has abandoned the concept proposed in certain draft **3.54** amendments of Directive 85/611, of prohibiting deposits at the bank acting as the depositary of the coordinated UCITS in question.

Derivatives

Concept of derivatives   While the authors of Directive 85/611 defined the **3.55** concepts of transferable securities and money market instruments, they did not define derivatives. This probably reflects their objective of not excluding certain instruments by providing a rigid definition, as the products available on the derivatives markets are constantly changing or evolving.

Broadly, a derivative can be defined as 'a financial asset made up of a future right **3.56** or option derived from a contract or a promised contract whose value depends upon the price movements of one or more underlying assets or indices during the period between signature and settlement of the contract'.[48]

The CSSF confirmed in 2006[49] that warrants on transferable securities should be **3.57** considered as financial derivative instruments pursuant to Article 41(1)(g) of the 2002 Act.

Eligible financial instruments   Directive 85/611 specifies certain criteria to **3.58** enable a derivative to be categorized as an authorized investment for UCITS. These criteria concern (a) the asset underlying the instrument and (b) the market on which the instrument is traded.

A coordinated UCITS may only invest in derivatives if its constitutive **3.59** documents authorize direct investment in the assets underlying these derivatives.

---

[47] Article 19.1(f), Directive (EEC) 85/611 transposed into Article 41(1)(f), 2002 Act.
[48] G Nejman, *Les contrats de produits dérivés—Aspects juridiques* (Larcier, 1999) 15.
[49] See CSSF Annual Report for 2006, 89.

3.60   Moreover, the assets underlying financial instruments in which coordinated UCITS may invest must belong to one of the following categories:

- transferable securities,
- money market instruments,
- shares and units in UCIs,
- derivatives,
- financial indices,
- interest rates,
- foreign exchange rates,
- currencies, or
- financial instruments housing one or several characteristics of those assets.[50]

The financial instrument must also be traded on a regulated market or, if not, must be available for purchase over the counter subject to certain conditions.

3.61   The right to invest in over-the-counter instruments was debated during the preparation of Directive 2001/108, as such instruments have a higher counterparty risk than instruments traded on a regulated market.[51] This type of investment was finally authorized subject to certain conditions. The rules determining which markets are considered 'regulated' are described above.[52]

3.62   A derivative traded over the counter must meet the following conditions regarding the UCITS counterparty and the instrument itself.

3.63   The counterparty must be subject to prudential supervision and belong to one of the categories approved by the competent authorities of the Member State in which the coordinated UCITS is based. The derivative must be valued on a daily basis according to a reliable and verifiable method. Moreover, the UCITS must at all times be able to sell, settle, or close the derivative at fair value by means of an offsetting transaction.[53] Further developments in the criteria for determining the eligibility of derivatives are described in 3.303 *et seq* below.

Ancillary activities

3.64   Under the 2002 Act, the investments of a coordinated UCITS must consist exclusively of transferable securities and/or other liquid financial assets permitted by Directive 85/611. However, a coordinated UCITS may invest in other securities

---

[50] Art 8, Eligible Assets Directive.

[51] Opinion of the Economic and Social Committee [1999] OJ C116/47; Report of the Committee on Legal Affairs and Citizens' Rights, 19 (document available on the website of the European Parliament under the heading 'Legislative Observatory'; it questions whether 'effective supervision is not jeopardized' 'in view of the doubtful degree of transparency of over-the-counter derivatives'.

[52] See 3.23 above.

[53] The use of derivatives by UCITS is analysed in detail in 3.303 *et seq* below.

subject to the limits described below. A UCITS may also engage in ancillary activities necessary for its core investment business.

Unlisted transferable securities

A coordinated UCITS may invest no more than 10 per cent of its assets[54] in transferable securities other than those encompassed in its main investment policy.[55] **3.65**

Such 'other' transferable securities include, *inter alia*, unlisted transferable securities or recently issued securities not admitted to an official market within one year. The term also covers units in open-end UCIs that do not meet the eligibility conditions set forth in Directive 85/611. Pursuant to Article 41(2)(a) of the 2002 Act, the CSSF permits, for example, a UCITS to invest 10 per cent of its assets in regulated open-end real estate property funds, or regulated open-end hedge funds, or regulated open-end funds of hedge funds or regulated open-end private equity funds with equivalent supervision. **3.66**

Other money market instruments

A coordinated UCITS is authorized to invest up to 10 per cent of its assets in 'other money market instruments', ie in money market instruments that are not listed or dealt in on a regulated market, nor issued by an issuer who meets the conditions listed in the 2002 Act.[56] Such instruments must in any event satisfy the definition of money market instrument given in Directive 85/611 and in the Eligible Assets Directive.[57] According to this definition, such instruments must be liquid and have a value that can be accurately determined at all times. **3.67**

An additional threshold applies when a UCITS holds both unlisted transferable securities and other money market instruments. Together, such securities may not account for more than 10 per cent of a UCITS' assets.[58] **3.68**

---

[54] Directive 85/611 and the 2002 Act apply investment and borrowing limits and restrictions expressed as percentages of a UCITS' total assets, whereas Ch F, V of Circular 91/75 specifies that such percentages must be applied to a UCITS' net assets, which means that liabilities must be deducted from assets. When a UCITS may not borrow more than 10% of its assets, the nuance introduced by Circular 91/75 has no material impact in practice. It should, however, be abandoned by the CSSF as it is contrary to the text of Directive 85/611. The authors of this work have chosen to refer to Directive 85/611 and to express investment limits and restrictions in relation to the UCITS' assets. When a coordinated UCITS has several sub-funds, the investment and borrowing restrictions are calculated by reference to the assets of each sub-fund. However, the restriction prohibiting a UCITS from holding more than 10% of the securities of a single issuer applies to each separate sub-fund as well as to all sub-funds combined (Ch J, II and III, 4 of Circular 91/75).

[55] Art 41(2)(a), 2002 Act.

[56] ibid Art 41(2)(a).

[57] And transposed into Art 1(18) of the 2002 Act and Art 3, Eligible Assets Directive.

[58] Art 41(2)(a), 2002 Act.

Liquid assets

3.69 A UCITS may hold ancillary liquid assets.[59] However, neither Directive 85/611[60] nor the 2002 Act define the concept of 'liquid assets' or the term 'ancillary'.

3.70 In one of the recitals of Directive 2001/108,[61] the European legislature nevertheless provides a few explanations. The right to hold liquid assets on an ancillary basis applies to coordinated UCITS whose main investment policy is not to invest in bank deposits. The liquid assets held by a coordinated UCITS in accordance with this rule must therefore be ancillary to its core activities.

3.71 The European legislature also gives some examples of cases in which the holding of ancillary liquid assets by a coordinated UCITS would be considered justified, for example:

> . . . in order to cover current or exceptional payments; in the case of sales, for the time necessary to reinvest in transferable securities, money market instruments and/or in other financial assets provided for in this Directive; for a period of time strictly necessary when, because of unfavourable market conditions, investment in transferable securities, money market instruments and in other financial assets must be suspended.[62]

3.72 In the Grand Duchy of Luxembourg, the ancillary nature of liquid assets is interpreted flexibly. The term 'ancillary' means that liquid assets may not in themselves comprise the main investment objective.[63] A percentage is not stipulated. In special circumstances, such as a threatened stock market collapse, a UCITS whose objective is not to invest in bank deposits must nonetheless be able temporarily to hold its entire assets in liquid form in order to protect the interests of its investors, on the understanding that such liquid assets must be replaced by transferable securities or other financial liquid assets as soon as permitted by market conditions. In contrast, such a UCITS may not replace the transferable securities in its portfolio with a time deposit on the sole basis that the yield on liquid assets is currently higher than the return on transferable securities.[64]

---

[59] ibid Art 41(3).

[60] The authors of Directive 85/611 left this to the Member States. See 'Towards a European Market for undertakings for collective investment in transferable securities, Comments on the provisions of Directive 85/611', Office of Offical Publication of the European Communities (1988) (hereinafter 'Towards a European market for UCITS') No 90, 43.

[61] Preamble to Directive (EC) 2001/108, 9th Recital.

[62] ibid.

[63] Ch F, III, 3, Circular 91/75.

[64] Since bank deposits have become eligible financial assets like transferable securities, the debate on the 'ancillary' nature of liquid assets has become more of a theoretical discussion since, unlike in the past, a UCITS is no longer liable to violate the law due to unauthorized investment of cash.

Circular 91/75 clearly outlines the concept of liquid assets.[65] This term covers, **3.73** first of all, cash and short-term bank deposits. In contrast, it does not appear to cover medium- and long-term bank deposits. Unless the contemplated invest-ment policy is to invest in repayable deposits, a coordinated UCITS would find it difficult to justify a long-term investment in liquid assets, insofar as such invest-ments cannot be freed up rapidly for reinvestment in securities targeted by its main investment policy.

Circular 91/75 includes in the definition of liquid assets money market **3.74** instruments whose residual maturity does not exceed twelve months, provided that they are regularly traded. This is no longer appropriate since money market instruments have become assets eligible for UCITS. Money market instruments should therefore no longer be regarded as 'ancillary liquid assets', regardless of their initial or residual time to maturity.

Movable and immovable property

Investment companies may buy movable and immovable property which is **3.75** necessary for the pursuit of their business.[66] However, in practice, few investment companies avail themselves of this option. They generally appoint local service providers to provide administration and accounting services on their behalf, thus avoiding the need for an internal property infrastructure.[67]

The law does not extend the right to acquire property to the management companies **3.76** of FCPs. The movable and immovable property owned by such companies for business purposes is held in their own name and for their own account. Such property does not form part of an FCP's assets, making a specific investment rule unnecessary.

Borrowings

Coordinated UCITS may normally not borrow, as confirmed by Circular **3.77** 07/308,[68] which states clearly that borrowings may not be used for investment purposes. However, borrowing is permitted in two exceptional situations.[69]

First, a coordinated UCITS may need liquid assets, *inter alia*, to finance redemp- **3.78** tion requests from its investors. If the UCITS does not have the necessary liquid

---

[65] Ch F, III, 3, Circular 91/75.
[66] Article 41(2)(b), 2002 Act.
[67] This conclusion must be qualified when the investment company decides to manage itself in the meaning of Art 27 of the 2002 Act, in which case it must have its own 'substance'. See 6.77 below.
[68] CSSF Circular 07/308 of 2 August 2007 on the rules of conduct to be adopted by UCITS with respect to the management of financial risks and the use of financial derivative instruments, Section III.
[69] Art 50(2), 2002 Act.

assets, it may borrow up to 10 per cent of its assets, provided that the loan is short term.

3.79 Secondly, borrowing is exceptionally allowed when an investment company wishes to buy immovable property necessary for its business. In such cases, it may borrow up to 10 per cent of its assets.

3.80 The above two thresholds are not entirely cumulative. In all, a coordinated UCITS may not borrow more than 15 per cent of its assets.[70]

3.81 The 2002 Act also authorizes coordinated UCITS to buy currencies by means of back-to-back loans.[71] A back-to-back loan is a loan taken out when a UCITS wishing to make an investment borrows a currency while depositing with the lender or its agent a sum in another currency that is at least equivalent to the amount borrowed.[72]

Underwriting of securities

3.82 Can a UCITS act as an underwriter for securities issues? There is no clear answer to this question in either the 2002 Act or Circular 91/75. There seems, however, to be no bar to this activity. That said, one condition needs to be satisfied. The nature or volume of the securities that a UCITS agrees to buy may not violate the applicable investment restrictions set out in the 2002 Act.

Unauthorized activities

Precious metals

3.83 A coordinated UCITS may not acquire either precious metals or certificates representing them.[73] In contrast, it may invest in the securities of companies trading in precious metals.[74]

Uncovered sales of transferable securities

3.84 A UCITS may not carry out uncovered sales of transferable securities, money market instruments, units in UCIs, or derivatives.[75] The reason for this restriction is obvious since uncovered sales generate risks for the UCITS which are deemed incompatible with the need to protect investors.[76] However, UCITS are permitted to sell short synthetically by using financial derivative instruments, as is the case for

---

[70] ibid Art 50(2)(b).
[71] ibid Art 50(1).
[72] Ch F, IV, Circular 91/75.
[73] Art 41(2)(c), 2002 Act.
[74] The CSSF has confirmed the eligibility of Gold Bullion Securities when the latter are listed on the London or Paris Stock Exchanges. See CSSF Annual Report for 2006, 88.
[75] Art 42, Directive (EEC) 85/611 and Art 52, 2002 Act.
[76] For the concept of uncovered sales in connection with derivatives, see 3.253 and n 250 below.

130/30 UCITS. Such products generate short positions on individual stocks equivalent to 30 per cent of the value of a UCITS' assets via swaps or other derivatives which are balanced by long positions equal in value to 130 per cent of the UCITS' assets.

Similarly, a UCITS may not buy shares or units which expose it to unlimited liability, despite the fact that this is not specified in the 2002 Act. **3.85**

Loans and guarantees

A coordinated UCITS may not grant loans to or act as a guarantor on behalf of third parties.[77] **3.86**

The 2002 Act[78] qualifies this prohibition by specifying that UCITS may nonetheless acquire partly paid transferable securities, money market instruments, units in UCIs, and derivatives. That may seem a surprising distinction. On first analysis, a UCITS' agreement to honour future calls for funds on partly paid transferable securities seems to indicate a credit agreement, and therefore borrowing by the UCITS. Indeed, that was the position taken by the 1983 Act, which authorized the acquisition of partly paid transferable securities provided 'the unpaid fraction of such transferable securities does not exceed the overall limits . . . for borrowing and the unpaid amount'.[79] **3.87**

That is not the reasoning followed by Directive 85/611, which authorized the exception on the grounds that a UCITS' agreement to pay the unpaid fraction of such shares could not be regarded as 'contrary to the prohibition on acting as a guarantor'.[80] **3.88**

It might also be asked whether a coordinated UCITS is authorized to pledge all or part of its portfolio to third parties.[81] The 1983 Act prohibited management companies[82] from granting a pledge or any other lien[83] on an FCP's assets. Such transactions are no longer prohibited by the 2002 Act and are therefore possible in principle, provided the pledge is offered in the UCITS' interest. **3.89**

Investment limits for coordinated UCIs

Obligation to pursue a policy based on the principle of risk spreading

Directive 85/611 and subsequently the 2002 Act lay down relatively complex risk-spreading rules, some of which apply only to particular types of instruments issued by the same issuer, while others restrict aggregate investment in a single issuer. **3.90**

---

[77] Art 51(1), 2002 Act.
[78] ibid Art 51(2).
[79] Art 7(5) of the 1983 Act. This requirement was not maintained in the 2002 Act, whose wording in this respect is an accurate transcription of the text of Directive (EEC) 85/611.
[80] 'Towards a European market for UCITS' (n 60 above) No 158, 82.
[81] eg to its depositary, to guarantee commitments entered into vis-à-vis that party.
[82] But not SICAVs or other types of UCI.
[83] Art 7(4), 1983 Act.

The legislature's objective was to limit a UCITS' counterparty risk, ie 'the risk that the co-contracting party is unable to honour its obligations on settlement of a transaction'.[84] The degree of this risk depends on the UCITS' market, the quality of the counterparty or the guarantees provided with certain securities issues. This explains the derogations applicable to most rules laid down by Directive 85/611 and by the 2002 Act. That said, there are sometimes so many exceptions that it becomes difficult to maintain sight of the principle.

3.91 Counterparty risk is measured pragmatically. Several legal persons may be considered as a single 'counterparty' where the legislature holds that the 'counterparty' risk applies to a number of different entities, albeit the various entities may have individual legal personality. This is the case for companies which are members of a group within the meaning of recognized international accounting rules.

3.92 Conversely, a single legal entity may sometimes include several separate issuers in application of the rules described below. This is the case when an issuer is a legal entity with multiple sub-funds, in which case the sub-funds must be considered separate asset and liability pools. The Luxembourg legislature has taken the need for segregation of assets and liabilities of sub-funds of UCITS into account, treating each sub-fund as a separate issuer for the purpose of risk-spreading rules.[85]

Application of the concept of 'group'

3.93 In order to avoid an 'excessive concentration of investments with the same issuer, the same entity or the same group of issuers or linked entities',[86] Directive 85/611 considers companies belonging to the same group as part of the same entity for the purpose of risk-spreading rules.

3.94 Companies that, by virtue of Directive 83/349 on consolidated accounts[87] or in accordance with recognized international accounting rules must prepare consolidated accounts are considered companies within the same group. In order to determine the extent to which a company belongs to a group in terms of the accounting regulations, Directive 83/349 introduces several criteria, such as entitlement to majority voting rights;[88] the right to appoint or remove a majority of members of a company's board of directors, management, or supervisory board;[89]

---

[84] Nejman, (n 48 above) 24.

[85] Arts 46(1) and 49(3), 2002 Act.

[86] Explanatory Memorandum to the modified proposal for Directive (EC) 2001/107, 4 (document available on the website of the European Parliament, under the heading 'Legislative Observatory'). The European legislature holds that such a concentration 'could be contrary to the principle of risk spreading integrated in the Directive, possibly aggravating the risk of loss.'

[87] Seventh Council Directive (EEC) 83/349 of 13 June 1983, based on Article 54, paragraph 3, under g) of the Treaty with regard to consolidated accounts [1983] OJ L193/1.

[88] Art 1.1(a), Seventh Council Directive (EEC) 83/349 (n 87 above) [1983] OJ L193/2.

[89] Art 1.1(b) Seventh Council Directive (EEC) 83/349 (n 87 above) [1983] OJ L193/2.

the right to exercise a dominant influence over the company in question, whether contractually or by virtue of a provision in the articles of incorporation,[90] or ownership of an interest[91] in the company within the meaning of Directive 78/660; as well as the existence of a single management structure for the company in question and its parent undertaking.[92]

The reference to recognized international accounting rules is intended to apply limits equivalent to investment in issuers established in EEA Member States to issuers in non-member countries. The concept of group defined by Directive 83/349 applies only to companies governed by the national laws of EEA Member States. However, to extend its sphere of application to entities belonging to non-member countries would have required UCITS managers to undertake extensive inquiries to determine the degree of compliance by target companies with the criteria laid down by Directive 83/349. It was considered more sensible to refer to recognized international accounting rules, given that many non-Community regulations apply similar principles and definitions to consolidated accounts to those specified by Directive 83/349. **3.95**

However, this does not eliminate the practical difficulties caused by application of the group concept. It is still necessary to obtain information about an issuer's ownership and interests, which may delay certain investments. If such information subsequently turns out to be incomplete, the UCITS may be in violation of its investment restrictions, resulting in potential liability for its operators. **3.96**

This is why the Luxembourg legislature, in the Explanatory Statement to the 2002 Act,[93] took care to subject application of the group concept to two qualifications. **3.97**

The legislature first specifies that correct evaluation of an issuer's membership in a group and determination of the identity of an issuer's affiliates are a best endeavours obligation, not an absolute obligation. The Explanatory Statement adds that the scope of the duties resulting from this obligation must be evaluated reasonably. It states, for example, that a merger should not be taken into account as long as it is not effective and publicly known. **3.98**

---

[90] Art 1.1(c), Seventh Council Directive (EEC) 83/349 (n 87 above) [1983] OJ L193/2.

[91] According to Art 17 of the Fourth Council Directive (EEC) 78/660 of 25 July 1978, based on Article 54 paragraph 3 under g) of the Treaty with regard to the annual accounts of certain types of companies [1978] OJ L222/11, a participating interest is characterized by 'rights in the capital of other undertakings, whether or not represented by certificates, which, by creating a durable link with those undertakings, are intended to contribute to the company's activities. The holding of part of the capital of another company shall be presumed to constitute a participating interest when it exceeds a percentage fixed by the Member States' (this percentage is fixed at 20% for Luxembourg (Art 221, 1915 Act)).

[92] Article 1.2(b), Seventh Council Directive (EEC) 83/349 (n 87 above) [1983] OJ L193/3.

[93] *Parliamentary doc* No 5033, Explanatory Statement, Comments on the Articles, 56–57; *Parliamentary doc* No 5033[1], Opinion of the *Conseil d'État*, 22.

3.99 The Explanatory Statement also limits the consequences of violation of an investment restriction as a result of the incorrect determination of a group's structure. It repeats the principle that accidental violation of an investment limit must be corrected in the interests of the investors. In practice, this principle permits two possible approaches. It can apply only to situations where, as a result of changes in a corporate group in which a UCITS holds securities, the UCITS exceeds its authorized investment in the group in question. It can apply to situations where a UCITS' assessment of a group's structure transpires to be wrong, thereby resulting in a breach of its investment restrictions. Such assessment errors can often turn out to be excusable and do not amount to violation of the manager's best endeavours obligation. In such cases, breach of an investment limit due to an error of this kind should be considered accidental and therefore covered by the principle mentioned specifically by the legislature.[94]

3.100 Accidental violation of an investment restriction has two consequences—the necessity of rectifying of the UCITS' situation and the liability of the UCITS managers. The added requirement that correction must be in the investors' interest allows the UCITS not to sell the excess securities immediately if it is considered that this would be contrary to the best interests of the investors. In addition, UCITS managers will not be liable for inadventent breach, as described and applied in CSSF Circular 02/77.[95]

Separate asset and liability pools within the same issuer

3.101 A legal entity may consist of several separate asset and liability pools which do not assume liability for the liabilities of other asset and liability pools.

3.102 A typical example of such a structure is the Luxembourg UCI, which under the 2002 Act may create several sub-funds whose assets and liabilities are independent from each other. Other examples of this kind of structure can be found in foreign UCIs and in financing or securitization vehicles under Luxembourg or foreign law.[96] When an issuer has established a series of separate asset and liability pools, its counterparty's risk in respect of the UCITS is limited to the particular pool committed on behalf of the UCITS. In the absence of guidelines in Directive 85/611 on this point, the Luxembourg legislature has adopted a flexible and pragmatic approach.[97] In the 2002 Act, the legislature specifies that every sub-fund of a given issuer must be considered a separate issuer insofar as the assets

---

[94] Art 49(2), 2002 Act.
[95] Section II, Circular 02/77.
[96] *Parliamentary doc* No 5033³, Amendments adopted by the Finance and Budget Committee, 6; *Parliamentary doc* No 5033⁴, Complementary Opinion of the *Conseil d'État*, 1; *Parliamentary doc* No 5033⁵, Report of the Finance and Budget Committee, 10.
[97] Arts 46(1) and 49(3) of the 2002 Act.

of each sub-fund are exclusively available to satisfy the entitlements of investors in and creditors of the specific sub-fund.[98]

Investment restrictions applicable by type of instrument

Transferable securities and money market instruments

Rules of 10 per cent and 40 per cent   A coordinated UCITS may not invest more **3.103** than 10 per cent of its assets in transferable securities or money market instruments issued by the same issuer.[99] This rule reflects the basic principle of spreading investment risks. However, there are many exceptions, dictated by the particular features of certain issues or types of products.

The obligation to spread risks and to limit investment in any one issuer to 10 per **3.104** cent is strengthened by the requirement to limit the aggregate value of transferable securities and money market instruments exposed to issuers in which a UCITS invests more than 5 per cent of its net assets, to 40 per cent of total net assets[100] (the '5/10/40' rule). However, transferable securities and money market instruments acquired by virtue of the two exceptions of 25 per cent and 35 per cent described below[101] are not taken into account in calculating the threshold of 40 per cent.

A UCITS which only invests in transferable securities and which does not intend to **3.105** take advantage of the two exceptions described below, therefore must hold at least sixteen lines of investment: four representing a maximum of 10 per cent each, accounting for up to 40 per cent of its assets, and twelve others representing a maximum of 5 per cent each, accounting for the remaining 60 per cent of its assets.

However, this additional risk-spreading obligation does not apply to all autho- **3.106** rized investments. The threshold of 40 per cent does not restrict investment in liquid assets when these take the form of deposits at financial institutions subject to prudential supervision,[102] nor does it apply to derivatives transactions entered into over the counter with such institutions.[103]

Exception of 20 per cent   The principle that a group must be considered a single **3.107** issuer for the purpose of applying risk-spreading rules is subject to an important qualification. The basic threshold of 10 per cent investment per issuer is raised to 20 per cent when applied to the same group.[104]

---

[98] *Parliamentary doc* No 5033, Comments on the Articles, 57; *Parliamentary doc* No 5033[1], Supplementary Opinion of the *Conseil d'État*, 23.
[99] Art 43(1), 2002 Act.
[100] ibid Art 43(2).
[101] ibid Art 43(5).
[102] ibid Art 43(2).
[103] ibid.
[104] ibid Art 43(5), 2002 Act.

3.108 As the application of this rule was open to interpretation by market participants in Luxembourg, the CSSF has clarified the application of the notion of group in respect of the risk-spreading rules contained in Article 43 of the 2002 Act.[105]

3.109 *Exception of 25 per cent* The above-mentioned limit of 10 per cent per issuer may be raised to 25 per cent for certain debt securities issued by credit institutions based in the EEA and subject by law to particular supervisory rules designed to protect the holders of such debt securities, including the issuer's legal obligation to invest the revenues from such bonds in assets that are adequate to cover the liabilities arising from the issue. Such assets must moreover be allocated on a priority basis to the repayment of the capital and accrued interest in the event of default by the issuer.[106]

3.110 An additional limit applies to purchases of these types of debt securities. A UCITS wishing to invest in such securities and thus wishing to invest more than 5 per cent of its assets per issuer must limit the total value of such investments to 80 per cent of its assets.[107]

3.111 *Exception of 35 per cent* The ceiling of 10 per cent issuer may be raised to 35 per cent where the transferable securities or money market instruments to be acquired by a UCITS are issued or guaranteed by a sovereign State, a local authority in an EEA Member State, or a public international organization of which one or more EEA Member States are members.[108]

3.112 *Exception of 100 per cent* The CSSF may authorize a coordinated UCITS to invest up to 100 per cent of its assets in transferable securities and money market instruments issued or guaranteed by a sovereign State, local authorities in EEA Member States, or public international organizations of which one or more EEA Member States are members.[109] In practice, such authorization is

---

[105] In its annual report of 2005, the CSSF considered that the notion of group, as defined in Art 43(5) of the 2002 Act, does not apply with respect to the application of the limits referred to in Art 43(1) and (2) of the 2002 Act. Consequently, the CSSF considers that the notion of 'body' referred to in Art 43(1), which sets out that a UCITS may invest not more than 10% of its assets in transferable securities or money market instruments issued by the same body, should be interpreted as 'issuer'. The restrictions set out in Art 43(2) also apply to the individual issuer. Furthermore, the CSSF considers that the consolidation of accounts allows the presentation of the accounts of a group of companies with common interests and considers that the companies comprised within the scope of consolidation are part of the same group. Consequently, Art 43(5) applies to all the consolidated companies, irrespective of the consolidation method applied. Moreover, the CSSF has decided, by analogy with the provisions of Art 43(2), that the investment restriction relating to the notion of group provided for by Art 43(5), last indent, applies to all instruments (including deposits and transactions on derivatives).

[106] Art 43(4), 2002 Act. Note that debt securities issued by Luxembourg banks in the form of *lettres de gage* constitute transferable securities within the meaning of Art 43(4), 2002 Act.

[107] ibid.

[108] ibid Art 43(3).

[109] ibid Art 45(1).

implicit by virtue of the approval of a UCITS' constitutive documents and sales literature.

Interestingly, the concept of risk spreading may thus vary significantly depending on the issuer's creditworthiness—ie solvency—without violating Directive 85/611. Under the regulations, where the risk of insolvency of an issuer is remote or theoretical as, for example, in the case of government issuer, a UCITS may invest 100 per cent of its assets in transferable securities and money market instruments issued or guaranteed by a single issuer. **3.113**

That said, the principle of risk-spreading must still be respected. A coordinated UCITS must hold securities comprised in no fewer than six different issues, and securities comprised in the same issue may not exceed 30 per cent of the total. In other words, the legislature has assumed that risk spreading may be achieved by factors other than an issuer's identity. A UCITS is regarded as having diversified its risk when it holds transferable securities and/or money market instruments in at least six different issues, whose maturities, terms of issue, interest rates, and payment conditions may vary. **3.114**

Although the 2002 Act applies to all sovereign States, the CSSF grants authorization only if it considers that unitholders in the relevant UCITS will have the same protection as that available under the risk-spreading rules in Luxembourg.[110] **3.115**

To highlight the exceptional character of this derogation, the 2002 Act requires the States, local authorities, and international organizations in which a UCITS plans to invest more than 35 per cent to be specified in its constitutive documents.[111] **3.116**

In addition, to ensure transparency, a UCITS' sales literature must draw the investor's attention to the authorization granted by the CSSF. This is generally achieved by the use of bold characters to attract investors' attention.[112] **3.117**

Index tracker funds Owing to the risk-spreading obligations described above, index tracker funds—ie funds whose object is to replicate a precise stock or bond index in terms of composition or performance—would not be eligible for the status of coordinated UCITS without the application of derogations.[113] **3.118**

---

[110] ibid.

[111] ibid Art 45(2).

[112] ibid Art 45(3).

[113] ibid Art 44(1). The concept of 'replication of the composition of a stock index' as used by Directive (EC) 2001/108, seems to refer to precise replication of the weighting of each stock in the index. This kind of replication is frequently impossible owing to the investment limits—even when somewhat relaxed—imposed on coordinated UCITS. Moreover, operating costs would make it impossible for a UCITS to reproduce the performance of an index when replicating exactly its composition. It therefore seems that 'replication of the composition of a stock index' must not be taken literally. Index tracker funds are coordinated UCITS which, without exactly replicating the

Yet such funds cater to industry and investor demand. Replication of an index which covers a broad range of securities implies a degree of risk spreading. Moreover, the publication nature of an index allows investors to compare and measure the performance of the replicating UCITS.

3.119   These considerations convinced the European legislature that they should authorize the creation of index tracker funds within the framework of Directive 85/611.[114] The legislature removed the principal barrier by laying down a specific risk-spreading rule for such funds. That said, their use was subjected to limits in order to prevent abuse.

3.120   Index tracker funds that meet certain legal conditions are not subject to the risk-spreading thresholds of 10 and 40 per cent[115] or the exceptions described above. These have been replaced by a limit of 20 per cent for investments in shares and/or bonds issued by the same body.[116] The ceiling of 20 per cent may be raised to a maximum of 35 per cent when justified by exceptional market conditions,[117] for example (as referenced in the Directive) the 2002 Act refers particularly to 'regulated markets where certain transferable securities or money market instruments are highly dominant.' The authorization to invest up to 35 per cent is granted only in respect of a single issuer.[118] The Eligible Assets Guidelines specify[119] that the simplified prospectus of the UCITS should provide appropriate information to investors in respect of the extended rules.

3.121   To benefit from these exceptional risk-spreading rules, an index tracker fund must offer certain assurances as to the index it aims to replicate.[120] In order to

---

composition of an index, endeavour to replicate its performance. This has been confirmed by the Eligible Assets Directive, which considers that the replication of a stock or debt securities index shall be understood as a reference to replication of the composition of the underlying assets of the index, including through the use of derivatives or other techniques and instruments as referred to in Art 21(2) of Directive (EEC) 85/611 and in Art 11 of the Eligible Assets Directive.

[114] 'The proposed risk-spreading rules would also recognise the widespread use of new investment management techniques such as techniques enabling investment in alternative shares but which replicate the weightings applied to the securities basket on which the index in question is based.' Opinion of the Economic and Social Committee [1999] OJ C116/44.

[115] Surprisingly, for index tracker funds Directive (EEC) 85/611 does not expressly disapply the rule that the total value of transferable securities and money market instruments from issues in which a UCITS invests more than 5% of its assets may not exceed 40% of total assets. This seems to be an oversight by the European legislature. In fact, application of such a limit to index-based funds would make it impossible to replicate a considerable number of recognized indices such as the DAX 30, the CAC 40 and the BEL 20. This is why this omission by the European legislature was 'rectified' when the Directive was transposed into the 2002 Act. Art 44 of the 2002 Act raises the limits imposed by Art 43 to 20%, which includes the restriction of 5/40%.

[116] Art 44(1), 2002 Act.

[117] ibid Art 44(2).

[118] ibid.

[119] Item 25, Eligible Assets Guidelines.

[120] Art 44(1), 2002 Act.

'avoid misuse of replication of indices',[121] Directive 85/611 and the Eligible Assets Directive[122] require prior recognition by the CSSF[123] on the basis of the criteria listed below. In addition, financial indices can serve as the underlyings of derivatives (used to track or gain exposure to an index), based on the same criteria. The composition of the index must be sufficiently diversified, which implies that the following criteria are fulfilled:

(1) the index is composed in such a way that price movements or trading activities regarding one component do not unduly influence the performance of the whole index;
(2) where the index is composed of assets eligible for UCITS, its diversification is established if the exposure of the UCITS versus the components of such underlying index does not exceed 20 per cent of its net assets for each component (such limit being increased to 35 per cent for one single component);
(3) where the index is composed of assets other than those eligible for UCITS, it has to be diversified in a way which is equivalent to that provided for in (b) above.

If financial derivative instruments are used for risk-diversification purposes and not **3.122** for tracking an index, there is no need to look at the underlying components of the individual indices to ensure that they are sufficiently diversified provided that the UCITS' exposure to the individual indices complies with the 5/10/40 per cent ratios. The index represents an adequate benchmark for the market to which it refers which implies that the following criteria are fulfilled:

(1) the index measures the performance of a representative group of underlyings in a relevant and appropriate way;
(2) the index is revised or rebalanced periodically to ensure that it continues to reflect the markets to which it refers following criteria which are publicly available;
(3) the underlyings are sufficiently liquid, which allows users to replicate the index, if necessary.

In summary, these criteria can be taken to refer to an index whose provider uses a **3.123** recognized methodology which generally does not result in the exclusion of a major issuer in the market to which it refers. It is published in an appropriate manner, which implies that the following criteria are fulfilled:

(1) the publication process relies on sound procedures to collect prices and to calculate and publish the index value, including pricing-procedures for components where a market price is not available; and

---

[121] Explanatatory Memorandum to the modified proposal for Directive (EC) 2001/108, 10 (document available on the website of the European Parliament, under the heading 'Legislative Observatory').
[122] Art 12, Eligible Assets Directive.
[123] Art 44(1), 2002 Act.

(2) material information on matters such as index calculation and rebalancing methodologies, index changes, or information relating to any operational difficulties in providing timely or accurate information is provided on a public and timely basis.

3.124 In summary, these criteria will be met when the index is accessible to the public and when the index provider is independent of the index-replicating UCITS. The latter condition does not prevent index providers and the relevant UCITS being part of the same group, provided that conflicts of interest are adequately managed.

3.125 Lastly, the benefit of exceptional risk-spreading rules is only available to index tracker funds whose constitutive documents provide for replication of an index.[124]

3.126 It should be noted that the CESR[125] is considering that derivatives on commodity futures indices, commodity indices, and property indices may be classified as eligible investments for coordinated UCITS.

3.127 Finally, following an intense debate, the Hedge Funds Indices Guidelines issued in July 2007[126] elaborate on the circumstances in which hedge funds indices can be considered as financial indices under the Eligible Assets Directive. The matter is of importance for UCITS which seek to gain exposure to hedge funds through derivatives on hedge funds indices, as Article 19(1)(g) of Directive 85/611 states that derivatives are eligible investments for UCITS, provided that their underlyings, among other things, are financial indices.

3.128 The CESR had carved out the issue of hedge funds indices from its review of eligible assets, highlighting issues and publishing consultation papers on the subject in October 2006 and February 2007 respectively. Given the relative immaturity of hedge funds indices and widespread debate across the industry as to their suitability for retail investors, the CESR expressed concerns about including these within the UCITS regime. However, hedge funds indices are now confirmed as eligible for inclusion in coordinated UCITS' portfolios subject to certain criteria being met:

(1) The hedge funds indices must comply with the conditions laid down in Article 9 of the Eligible Assets Directive, relating to financial indices, meaning that they must be sufficiently diversified, represent an adequate benchmark for the market to which they refer, and be published in an appropriate manner. The determination of how to consider each of these conditions can be found

---

[124] ibid.
[125] Item 22, Eligible Assets Guidelines.
[126] CESR's guidelines concerning eligible assets for investment by UCITS—The classification of hedge funds indices as financial indices dated July 2007 (réf CESR/07-434).

in the Eligible Assets Guidelines as the Hedge Funds Indices Guidelines do not impose any new requirements.

(2) The methodology of construction of the indices should provide for the selection and rebalancing of their components on the basis of predetermined rules and objective criteria. Indeed, the objective selection of components using predetermined rules is a key distinction between hedge fund indices and funds of hedge funds.

(3) The indices providers must not accept payments from potential index components in order to be included in the indices, as the compilation of the indices would not then be objective and this would be contrary to the adequate benchmark and objective component principles.

(4) The hedge funds indices' methodology should not allow any retrospective changes to previously published indices' values, ie backfilling.

(5) When gaining exposure to hedge funds indices by means of an over-the-counter financial derivative instrument, the UCITS should comply with the UCITS requirements applicable to the counterparty to the derivative instrument, valuation of the instrument and the UCITS' ability to close out a position at any time. The UCITS should also respect applicable conditions regarding calculation of the risk exposure and issuance of a risk-management process.

(6) The UCITS needs to carry out appropriate due diligence before investing in a specific hedge funds index. It should make an appropriate overall assessment of the quality of a particular hedge funds index based on the following criteria:

(a) the comprehensiveness of the index methodology (whether the methodology contains an adequate explanation of subjects such as the weighting and classification of components (ie on the basis of the investment strategy of the selected hedge funds) and whether the index represents an adequate benchmark for the kind of hedge funds to which it refers;

(b) the availability of information about the index (whether there is a clear narrative description of what the index is trying to represent, whether the index is subject to independent audits (ie that the index methodology has been followed, that the index is calculated correctly), and how frequently the index is published (and whether this affects the ability of the UCITS to calculate its own net asset value); and

(c) the treatment of the index components—having regard to such matters as whether the number of its components achieves sufficient diversification or the procedures by which the index provider carries out any due diligence on the net asset value calculation procedures of the index's components.

The UCITS must keep a record of its assessment.

With regard to the publication of the hedge funds indices, it is important to note   **3.129** that this matter will relate directly to the net asset value calculation frequency of the underlying hedge funds. It is also worth noting in this respect that the necessity to obtain greater clarity in terms of hedge funds valuations is recognized in the report published by the International Organization of Securities Commissions (IOSCO) in November 2007 relating to the valuation of assets by hedge funds.[127] This report aims to deal also with the issues specific to hedge funds indices on an international level.

3.130 In conclusion, the Hedge Funds Indices Guidelines are aimed at increasing consumer protection in this market. This shows a growing international acceptance of advanced investment management techniques.

3.131 **Bank deposits** A UCITS may not invest more than 20 per cent of its assets in deposits with the same entity. The 2002 Act does not specify whether this limit applies to liquid assets which a UCITS (other than a UCITS investing in bank deposits) may hold on an 'ancillary basis'.[128]

Derivatives

3.132 *Limits applicable to derivatives* There is no risk-spreading rule for transactions in derivatives[129] traded on a regulated market within the meaning of the Directive, as the European legislature no doubt felt that investors are adequately protected by the operating rules of such markets.

3.133 In contrast, for derivatives traded over the counter, UCITS are subject to restrictions on counterparty risk. This counterparty risk may not exceed one of the following thresholds:

- 10 per cent of a UCITS' assets when the counterparty is a credit institution established in an EEA Member State or in a non-member country—however, if it is established in a non-member country, the counterparty must be subject to prudential rules equivalent to those provided for by Community legislation;

- 5 per cent of the UCITS' assets in all other cases.[130]

3.134 Such counterparty risk may be reduced by the use of collateral. In this case, the CSSF requires that the collateral granted to the UCITS must have a certain level

---

[127] See OICV-IOSCO, 'Principles for the valuation of hedge funds portfolios', Final report, Report of the Technical Committee of the International Organization of Securities Commissions, (November 2007).

[128] The parliamentary preparations for the 2002 Act are not very useful here. The *Conseil d'État*, the highest administrative court, suggested that the issue be settled expressly, which the Finance and Budget Committee did not consider desirable. *Parliamentary doc* No 5033[1], Opinion of the *Conseil d'État*, 22 and *Parliamentary doc* No 5033[5], Report of the Finance and Budget Committee, 9. In the absence of a clear regulation, the CSSF takes the view that the 20% rule also applies to liquid assets held on an ancillary basis.

[129] For further details in the area of derivatives, see 3.188 *et seq* and 3.306 *et seq* below.

[130] Art 43(1), 2002 Act.

of diversification. However, the limits set out in the 2002 Act[131] need not be met in this respect, except as regards the entity responsible for holding the collateral. The credit risk linked to such an entity must be reduced in accordance with the deposit limits provided for by the 2002 Act.[132]

When a transferable security or a money market instrument contains an embedded derivative, the embedded derivative must be taken into account in calculating counterparty exposure limits.[133]   **3.135**

Limits applicable to assets underlying derivatives   The risks to which the assets   **3.136** underlying derivatives included in the portfolio of a coordinated UCITS are exposed must be taken into account in determining compliance with the UCITS' investment limits.[134] In other words, when a coordinated UCITS directly holds a particular asset[135] in addition to a derivative whose underlying comprises the same asset, both the direct position and the indirect exposure obtained through the derivative must be aggregated to calculate the investment limit.

However, some of the investment limits and restrictions described here do not   **3.137** apply to over-the-counter transactions with financial institutions subject to prudential supervision.[136]

The risks connected with the underlying assets are calculated based on the current   **3.138** value of the underlying assets, the counterparty risk, the foreseeable market trends, and the time available to liquidate positions.[137] The methods used to value the risks connected with underlying assets are not specified.[138] Directive 85/611 leaves the implementation of specific regulations in this regard to each EEA Member State.

As with any general rule, there is an exception to the transparency of derivatives   **3.139** with regard to risk spreading. The risk-spreading requirement does not apply to

---

[131] Arts 43 to 45, 2002 Act.

[132] ibid Art 43(1).

[133] ibid Art 42(3).

[134] Art 21.3(3), Directive (EEC) 85/611.

[135] The asset must be a transferable security or a money market instrument the text does not refer to units of UCIs. Article 21.3(3), Directive (EEC) 85/611, does not refer expressly to Art 24, which defines the investment limits applicable to investments in the units of UCIs. The rationale for this seeming inconsistency appears to lie in the principle of risk spreading inherent in the assets of UCIs. However, in Circular 07/308, the CSSF extends this limitation to units of UCIs and UCITS referred to in Art 46 of the 2002 Act.

[136] See 3.338 *et seq* below.

[137] Art 42(3), 2002 Act.

[138] A coordinated UCITS (or its management company) is nevertheless obliged to employ a 'risk-management process which enables it to monitor and measure at any time the risk of positions held and their contribution to the overall risk profile of the portfolio; in particular, it must employ a process for accurate and independent assessment of the value of over-the-counter derivative instruments' (Art 42(1), 2002 Act).

derivatives whose underlying asset is an index, as exposure to a single issuer is intrinsically diluted in this type of instrument.[139] Investment in derivatives on indices should not be combined with the individual issuer limits described above.[140]

3.140 **Units in UCIs**   A coordinated UCITS may not invest more than 20 per cent of its assets in the units of a single UCI. The European legislature was more flexible in this area than with direct investment in transferable securities, on the grounds that the target UCI already complied with the risk-spreading obligation.[141]

3.141 In principle, the investments made by the underlying UCI are not transparent. The transferable securities, money market instruments, and other securities that comprise the portfolios of the underlying UCIs are not considered as direct holdings of the coordinated UCITS in question. Such assets are not added to those of the investing coordinated UCITS in calculating risk-spreading limits.[142] However, there is one exception, in order to limit 'funds of funds of funds' type structures. The constitutive documents of the underlying UCIs must prohibit investment of more than 10 per cent of their assets in the units of other UCIs.[143]

3.142 Every sub-fund of an underlying UCI is considered as a separate issuer, provided that it forms a distinct asset and liability pool, and thus complies with the principle that commitments to third parties are segregated.[144]

3.143 A coordinated UCITS may therefore invest all of its assets in a single target coordinated UCITS provided the assets and liabilities of each of the sub-funds of the target coordinated UCITS are segregated. In this case, a foreign coordinated UCITS could be a single investment target for a Luxembourg-based UCITS.

3.144 Investment in UCIs other than coordinated UCITS may not account for more than 30 per cent of a UCITS' assets.[145]

3.145 Pursuant to Article 41(2)(a), of the 2002 Act, the CSSF permits a UCITS to invest 10 per cent of its net assets in regulated open-end real estate property funds,

---

[139] See Report of the Economic and Monetary Committee, 15 (available on the website of the European Parliament, under the heading 'Legislative Observatory').

[140] Art 42(3), 2002 Act.

[141] Explanatory Memorandum to the proposal for Directive (EC) 2001/108, 5th Recital [1998] OJ C280/6.

[142] Art 46(2), 2002 Act.

[143] ibid Art 41(e), 2002 Act. In its modified proposal for a Directive, the Commission of the European Communities specifies that compliance with this limit by underlying funds must be verified during the initial investment, based on the articles of incorporation of each such fund (Explanatory Memorandum to the modified proposal for Directive 2001/108, 12 (available on the website of the European Parliament, under the heading 'Legislative Observatory')).

[144] Art 46(1), 2002 Act.

[145] Art 24.2, Directive (EEC) 85/611 transposed into Art 46(2), 2002 Act.

regulated hedge funds and funds of hedge funds as well as regulated open-end private equity funds subject to equivalent supervision.

Combined limits per issuer

In addition to limits on investment in particular securities issued by a single issuer, there are broader restrictions per issuer when the securities to be taken into consideration are in several legal categories.   **3.146**

Limit of 20 per cent   As a general rule, a UCITS may not expose more than one-fifth of its assets to the counterparty risk of a particular issuer. Consequently, a UCITS' cumulative investments in the securities issued by a single entity may not account for more than 20 per cent of its assets, whether or not such securities are classified as transferable securities or money market instruments. This limit of 20 per cent also includes deposits and transactions in over-the-counter derivatives with the same entity.[146] In contrast, units of UCIs are not included, owing to their inherent risk diversification.   **3.147**

As explained above, transactions in derivatives traded on a regulated market are not covered by the risk-spreading rules and are not taken into account in calculating the 20 per cent limit.   **3.148**

Exception of 35 per cent   When certain conditions are met, a UCITS may exceed the limit of 10 per cent per issuer and invest up to 25 per cent or even 35 per cent of its assets in transferable securities or money market instruments issued by a single entity.   **3.149**

The scope in this regard derives from a determination of the aggregate investment limits per issuer and the types of assets issued by the particular issuer as held by the UCITS. Transferable securities or money market instruments issued by a single entity may represent up to 25 per cent or 35 per cent of a UCITS' assets. However, such an investment may not expose the UCITS to an overall counterparty risk exceeding 35 per cent of its assets. When a UCITS exercises its right to invest more than 10 per cent of its assets in the transferable securities and money market instruments of a single issuer, it may in no circumstances invest more than 35 per cent of its assets in a combination of transferable securities and money market instruments issued and deposits or over-the-counter derivatives whose counterparty is the same issuer.[147]   **3.150**

In other words, a coordinated UCITS may at most hold the securities of three different issuers, respectively representing two investments of 35 per cent and one investment of 30 per cent.   **3.151**

---

[146] Art 43(2), 2002 Act and Circular 07/308, Section III, 2, 4.
[147] Art 43(5), 2002 Act.

3.152 This limit does not apply to investment by a UCITS in transferable securities and/or money market instruments issued or guaranteed by a sovereign State, certain international organizations and local authorities in which a UCITS is authorized to invest up to 100 per cent of its assets.[148]

Prohibition on pursuing a takeover policy

3.153 The following rules reflect a different objective to the aims outlined above, the object of which is to diversify risk. Those described below are designed to prevent a coordinated UCITS from being used for purposes other than collective investment.

3.154 A coordinated UCITS could endeavour to buy a large volume of securities of the same issuer in order to exercise control, without violating the principle of risk spreading. However, such control exceeds a UCITS' function, which is limited to investment in the interests of its participants.[149] For that reason, such actions are prohibited for coordinated UCITS.

Acquisition of shares with voting rights

3.155 A coordinated UCITS is not authorized to acquire a proportion of shares enabling it to exercise 'significant influence' over the management of an issuer.[150] This applies both to investment companies and to management companies for all the FCPs managed by it and which fall within the scope of Part I of the 2002 Act. An FCP does not have an independent will. Only the management company, acting through the FCP—and, where applicable, one or more other FCPs—could control another entity. The prohibition on acquiring a controlling stake must therefore be applied to the management company. Consequently, the investment restriction in respect of a single issuer may have to be considered in the context of the investment activities of several UCIs.

3.156 The meaning of 'significant influence' is determined in the light of the national law applicable to the issuer whose securities are acquired. Prior to Directive 85/611, the laws of certain EEA Member States (including those of Italy, Germany, and Greece) required an intention to acquire control of an issuer. That intention was reflected in a threshold fixed at 5 per cent. This approach was not followed by other countries, including the Grand Duchy of Luxembourg. During the preparations for Directive 85/611, Member States linking the concept of 'significant influence' to a percentage argued that their UCITS could be disadvantaged compared with UCITS based in more flexible countries. Their viewpoint was partly accepted.

---

[148] ibid Art 45.
[149] 'Towards a European market for UCITS' (n 60 above) No 108, 55–56.
[150] Art 48(1), 2002 Act.

Directive 85/611 adopted a halfway position by referring to the national law applicable to the issuer whose shares were acquired.[151] The Council of the European Communities advised the competent national authorities to ensure that percentage limits reflecting the concept of significant influence in other Member States be respected by investment and management companies from their relevant country investing in such Member States. Accordingly, Member States applying such limits were to notify the Commission of the European Communities, which was charged with informing all other Member States.[152] Hence, when an issuer is situated in a country with an influence threshold based on a given percentage, a Luxembourg UCITS must comply with that threshold. Where there is no such threshold, the UCITS must refer to other applicable criteria under the legislation concerned.[153]

3.157

Acquisition of other transferable securities

As a general rule, the 2002 Act prohibits coordinated UCITS from controlling other entities. For that reason, in addition to the limitations on acquisition of shares with voting rights, a coordinated UCITS may not acquire more than 10 per cent of the following securities:[154]

3.158

- non-voting shares of the same issuer,
- debt securities of the same issuer,
- money market instruments from the same issuer.

This limit is raised to 25 per cent for units issued by a single UCITS and/or other UCI.[155] In principle, according to the authors of Directive 85/611, such a holding does not allow the UCITS to control the underlying fund.[156]

This restriction also applies to all debt securities issued by the same issuer. The rule is stricter than that laid down by Part II of the 2002 Act, which only applies to 'securities of the same kind' issued by the same entity,[157] making it possible to distinguish between types of debt securities.

3.159

---

[151] Art 25.1, Directive 85/611.

[152] 'Towards a European market for UCITS' (n 60 above) No 111, 58–59.

[153] *Parliamentary doc* No 3172, Comments on the Articles, 45.

[154] Art 48(2), 2002 Act.

[155] Division of a target UCI into sub-funds does not affect application of this 25% rule. The percentage is calculated by reference to all sub-funds. The *Parliamentary documents* on the 2002 Act are clear on this point: 'The 25% rule is a control rule, not a risk-spreading rule, and therefore applies to the UCI overall, irrespective of its status as a fund with multiple sub-funds' (*Parliamentary doc* No 5033, Comments on the Articles, 58). The *Conseil d'État* proposal to introduce this clause in the law has not survived. The legislature wanted the law only to include the text of the Directive (*Parliamentary doc* No 5033[1], Opinion of the *Conseil d'État*, 24; *Parliamentary doc* No 5033[5], Report of the Finance and Budget Committee, 9).

[156] Common Position (EC) No 24/2001 adopted by the Council on 5 June 2001, [2001] OJ C297/48.

[157] Chapter G, II, b, Circular 91/75.

3.160 For both debt securities and UCI units and money market instruments, the 2002 Act allows a UCITS temporarily to exceed the thresholds above if, at the time of acquisition, the gross amount of debt securities or the net amount of the securities issued cannot be calculated.[158]

Exceptions and derogations

3.161 **State and supranational issuers**   Generally, the rules prohibiting the acquisition of controlling interests do not apply where the transferable securities and money market instruments to be acquired by a coordinated UCITS have been issued or guaranteed by an EEA Member State or its local authorities, a non-EEA member country, or public international organizations of which one or more EEA Member States are members.[159]

3.162 These are the same exceptions as those applied in the context of risk diversification, justified by the status—government or government-related—of certain issuers.

3.163 **Investment in intermediaries in a given country**   In certain circumstances the applicable control/risk diversification rules may apply to an entity other than the UCITS itself, for example when a UCITS is unable to invest directly in a given country[160] due to legislative restrictions in that country. Certain emerging markets permit investment in their territory only through specially approved companies. This was the case regarding Taiwan when Directive 85/611 was being prepared. To circumvent this difficulty, Directive 85/611 and, subsequently, the 2002 Act allow coordinated UCITS not to apply the percentage thresholds applicable to individual issuers if the investment is made via a company established in a country which is not an EEA Member State and which invests its assets mainly in the securities of entities from that country (ie an intermediary investment company). Such participation must constitute the only legal means by which the UCITS can invest in the securities of issuers from the country in question. In such cases, the risk-diversification rules apply to the intermediary rather than to the UCITS.[161]

3.164 **'Sandwich' subsidiaries**   The rules prohibiting the acquisition of a controlling interest do not apply to an investment company's ownership of shares in the capital of subsidiaries whose management, advice, or marketing activities are carried out exclusively on its behalf in the countries in which such subsidiaries are located, in regard to the repurchase of units at unitholders' request.[162] Like all the other rules and exceptions above, this derogation is derived directly from Directive 2001/108.

---

[158] Art 48(2), 2002 Act.
[159] Art 48(3)(a),(b), and (c), 2002 Act.
[160] Art 48(3)(d), 2002 Act.
[161] ie the contents, described above, of Arts 43, 46, and 48(1) and (2), 2002 Act.
[162] Art 48(3)(e), 2002 Act and Art 25(3)(e), Directive (EEC) 85/611.

The scope of the rule that a subsidiary must be situated in the country in which it **3.165** carries on its activities, in regard to the repurchase of units at unitholders' request, is not easily determined. The text can be interpreted two ways. According to the first interpretation, this rule would mean that the activities carried on by the subsidiary would always have to include redemption of units at the request of unitholders, which would have to occur in the country in which the subsidiary is established.[163] The second, which is a more liberal interpretation, would mean that reference to the redemption of units would not necessarily require the subsidiaries to conduct redemption activity but merely that, when redemptions are carried on, they must be carried on in the country in which the subsidiary is established.

This choice has practical consequences since Luxembourg-based UCITS often **3.166** use subsidiaries to optimize the tax treatment of their investments. The text of Directive 85/611 and the 1988 Act are not specific about the scope of this rule.

In such cases, the investment company creates a subsidiary financed with a capital **3.167** endowment, supplemented where necessary by a loan, to hold the portfolio of transferable securities or other financial liquid assets the investment company plans to acquire. This structure may give investment companies the benefit of a network of double taxation treaties, which it would have been unable to claim in the absence of such a subsidiary.

The CSSF has allowed this practice on the grounds that the search for the most **3.168** attractive tax regime in the investors' exclusive interest may be regarded as a management activity within the general meaning of the term. This approach is unlikely to be challenged since Directive 2001/108 has not changed the reference to management activities.

For example, Luxembourg-based investment companies have been authorized to **3.169** establish subsidiaries in Mauritius in order to invest in India, in Cyprus in order to invest in Russia, and in Labuan in order to invest in South Korea. More recently, investment companies have started to use Luxembourg subsidiaries.

Is the use of subsidiaries for tax optimization purposes affected by the added rule **3.170** in Directive 2001/108, namely that a subsidiary must carry on its activities in the country in which it is situated in regard to the repurchase of units at unitholders' request? This would be the case if such subsidiaries were obliged to include the repurchase of units at unitholders' request in their activities. However, this does not appear to have been the wish of the authors of Directive 2001/108, as disclosed by a perusal of the preparatory work for the Directive.

---

[163] See L De La Mettrie and M Lambion, 'UCITS III: Quel avenir pour les sociétés "sandwich"?' (April 2002) AGEFI Luxembourg 11.

3.171 When amending Directive 85/611, the Commission of the European Communities wanted to restrict the establishment of subsidiaries in non-Member States on the grounds that this could weaken the effective supervision of UCITS.[164] It therefore proposed limiting the prohibition on sandwich subsidiaries to subsidiaries established in non-EEA member countries.[165]

3.172 The Economic Committee criticized this approach in its opinion on the proposal of the Commission of the European Communities. It recommended a more liberal stance on the grounds that the prohibition of sandwich subsidiaries in non-member countries could have negative consequences, especially because it would prevent the use of subsidiaries for tax optimization purposes.[166]

3.173 The Commission of the European Communities modified its proposal for a Directive accordingly, adopting the wording currently found in Directive 85/611 and the 2002 Act for the derogation, explaining that the derogation was mainly to facilitate the redemption of units by UCITS and acknowledging that this activity could also take place in non-member countries. It specified that 'these subsidiaries may not have any other objective than to provide management, advisory or marketing services'.[167] It did not express any wish to change the meaning of 'management, advisory or marketing services' compared with the previous version of the Directive, nor did it specify the activities to be carried on in the country in which the subsidiary would be established.

3.174 As this point in the version proposed by the Commission of the European Communities was not the subject of further discussion, the preparations for the Directive do not contain other useful information.

3.175 The Explanatory Memorandum to the Directive does not provide information to determine whether investment companies may no longer use sandwich subsidiaries for tax purposes; instead, it refers to the obligation for UCITS to act at all times in the interest of the unitholders, adding that this obligation 'and, in particular, the objective of increasing cost efficiencies, never justify a UCITS undertaking measures which may hinder the competent authorities from exercising

---

[164] Explanatory Memorandum to the proposal for Directive 2001/108, 14th Recital [1998] OJ C280/7.

[165] Art 1.12 of the proposal for Directive 2001/108 [1998] OJ C280/11.

[166] 'If the competent authorities believe that they are actually capable of supervising the activities of a non-European subsidiary and that this does not jeopardise the interests of unitholders, there is no need for a general prohibition. Such a prohibition could have a negative effect if, for example, it were to make it impossible for a UCITS to benefit from the advantages provided for in double taxation treaties between non-Member States' (Opinion of the Economic and Social Committee [1999] C116/49).

[167] Explanatory Statement to the modified proposal for Directive 2001/108, 11 (available on the website of the European Parliament, under the heading 'Legislative Observatory').

effectively their supervisory functions'.[168] The CSSF has always subjected the use of investment subsidiaries to several conditions in order to ensure that investor protection is not reduced compared with direct investment, which are normally as follows:

(1) the investment company must hold the subsidiary's entire capital;
(2) the subsidiary may not carry on activities other than holding investments on behalf of the parent company;
(3) the subsidiary's shares must be issued in registered form;
(4) a majority of the subsidiary's directors must be directors of the investment company;
(5) in the investment company's semi-annual and annual financial statements, the subsidiary must be regarded as transparent—the investment company's accounts must include a list of final investments made through the subsidiary;
(6) the subsidiary must comply with the investment restrictions applicable to the parent company, calculated by reference to the parent company's net assets;
(7) the accounts of the investment company and of the subsidiary must be audited by the same auditor;
(8) the investment company's Luxembourg-based depositary must be fully able to perform its legal tasks in respect of the assets held by the subsidiary;
(9) the use of a subsidiary must be mentioned in the investment company's prospectus;
(10) the subsidiary may either be incorporated as a special purpose vehicle or as an open-end fund as the 2002 Act is silent on the corporate form to be taken by the subsidiary.

As the use of subsidiaries by Luxembourg-based investment companies therefore does not prevent the CSSF from effectively exercising its supervisory functions, such use should be authorized even for purposes other than the repurchase of units at the unitholders' request. **3.176**

The derogation concerning the use of subsidiaries provided for by Directive 85/611[169] does not apply to coordinated FCPs. FCPs may nevertheless use a subsidiary by virtue of another provision in Directive 85/611,[170] which allows coordinated UCITS to employ techniques and instruments relating to transferable securities provided that such techniques and instruments are used for the purpose of efficient portfolio management. Recourse to a subsidiary is regarded as such a technique. **3.177**

---

[168] Explanatory Memorandum to Directive (EC) 2001/108, 15th Recital.
[169] Art 25(3)(e), Directive (EEC) 85/611, and Art 48(3)(e), 2002 Act.
[170] Art 21, Directive (EEC) 85/611, and Art 42(2), 2002 Act.

3.178   In the cases described above, subsidiaries are not used to circumvent the investment rules and restrictions laid down by Directive 85/611. In fact, they are merely a means to optimize portfolio management, since the investment restrictions apply to a UCI as though its subsidiary did not exist.[171]

Tolerated non-compliance with investment restrictions for coordinated UCITS

3.179   Directive 85/611 and the implementing provisions in the 2002 Act provide for certain cases in which non-compliance by a coordinated UCITS with the investment restrictions described above is not penalized.

3.180   First of all, during a start-up period set at six months from the authorization date, a recently formed UCITS may derogate from some of the risk-diversification rules described above.[172] The date of the launching of the coordinated UCITS (ie when the UCITS is opened for subscriptions, rather than its authorization date) can be considered as the commencement date for the derogation. The derogation does not relieve a UCITS from the obligation to comply with the principle of risk spreading but allows it not to comply with certain investment restrictions laid down in the 2002 Act. The 'grace' period of six months, which is not renewable, applies to each new sub-fund of a UCITS.

3.181   Moreover, a UCITS exercising subscription rights attached to transferable securities which form part of its assets, is not restricted by the applicable investment limits.[173]

3.182   Lastly, if investment limits are exceeded due to circumstances beyond a UCITS' control or pursuant to the exercise of subscription rights, the sales effected by such a UCITS must primarily be designed to regularize its situation in the interests of the unitholders and shareholders. In these circumstances, when a limit is

---

[171] The Luxembourg interpretation of Directive (EEC) 85/611 concerning investment subsidiaries was disputed by the *Commission Bancaire et Financière*, the supervisory authority for UCITS in Belgium. According to the *Commission Bancaire et Financière*, such subsidiaries carry on an investment activity rather than a management, advisory, or marketing activity as permitted by Art 25(3)(e), of Directive (EEC) 85/611; such a structure would violate the letter and the spirit of Directive (EEC) 85/611 and could harm the interest of UCITS from other Member States which impose a stricter interpretation of that text. Consequently, the *Commission Bancaire et Financière* refused to register Luxembourg-based UCITS whose constitutive documents and sales literature provided for the right to use such subsidiaries. The case was referred to the Belgian *Conseil d'État*, which rejected the arguments of the *Commission Bancaire et Financière* (CE, 4 June 1997, No 66556, *Fleming Flagship v. État Belge, Rev Banque*, 8/1997, 588 *et seq*, note by M Tison; see also Commission Bancaire et Financière, *Annual report* (1995–96) 132–3, (1996–97) 140–2).

[172] Art 49(1), 2002 Act. Those rules are laid down by Arts 43, 44, 45, and 46, 2002 Act. See 3.109 *et seq* above.

[173] Art 49(1), 2002 Act.

exceeded, the relevant UCITS is not obliged to immediately sell that portion of the portfolio held in breach of the applicable restrictions. On the contrary, in the interests of unitholders and shareholders, such a sale should if at all possible be made without realizing a loss. The correction of the breach situation should always be made having regard to the market conditions at the time of the breach.

Conditions surrounding investment in UCI units

Special criteria apply when the target UCITS or other target UCI is linked to the UCITS wishing to make the investment. Two types of links are possible. The two UCIs may be managed directly or by delegation by the same management company, or the target UCI may be managed by a company with which the management company of the investing UCITS is connected by common management or control or by a substantial direct or indirect holding.   **3.183**

In such cases, the investing UCITS may not be charged subscription or redemption fees for assets invested in units of the linked UCI.[174]   **3.184**

More generally, a UCITS that invests a substantial proportion of its assets in other eligible UCITS/UCIs has certain disclosure obligations.[175] The terms 'substantial proportion of assets' have been clarified recently by the CSSF. Indeed, as no reference is made in the 2002 Act to the percentage investment in UCITS/UCIs which would constitute the UCITS as a 'fund of funds', the CSSF has confirmed that a UCITS (or a sub-fund of such UCITS if the UCITS is set up as an umbrella UCITS) will be regarded as a 'fund of funds' if more than 50 per cent of its net assets are invested in other eligible UCITS or UCIs.   **3.185**

Such a UCITS must disclose in its prospectus the maximum level of the management fees that may be charged both to the UCITS itself and to the other UCITS/UCIs in which it intends to invest. However, how this maximum amount should be interpreted remains unclear. The CSSF has confirmed recently that in calculating the maximum fee payable, rebated commissions may be deducted from the management fees.   **3.186**

A UCITS must also draw the investors' attention to its policy of investment in the units of UCITS/UCIs.[176] In its annual report, it must indicate the maximum percentage of management fees charged directly and at the level of the UCIs in which it invests.[177]   **3.187**

---

[174] ibid Art 46(3).
[175] ibid.
[176] ibid Art 47(2). This also applies to all promotional documents used by UCITS.
[177] ibid Art 46(3).

Conditions surrounding investment in derivatives

3.188 In addition to the above risk-spreading rules,[178] derivatives are subject to the principle of risk limitation and various obligations as regards investor information, risk management, and reports for the CSSF.

Risk limitation

3.189 Global exposure to derivative instruments may not exceed the total net asset value of a coordinated UCITS.[179]

3.190 When a transferable security or a money market instrument embeds a derivative, the embedded element must be taken into account for the purpose of measuring this limit.[180] This has been reiterated by the Eligible Assets Directive, which clearly states that the derivative element of the transferable security or money market instrument must be taken into account for the calculation of the global risk exposure limit.[181]

Investor information

3.191 The prospectus of a coordinated UCITS authorized to invest in derivatives must state that it is so authorized. It must also specify whether such operations may be carried out for the purpose of hedging or with the aim of meeting investment goals. In addition, it must mention the possible consequences of the use of financial derivative instruments on the risk profile of the coordinated UCITS in question. This information must be prominently stated.[182]

3.192 Moreover, when a coordinated UCITS invests principally in derivatives, the prospectus and any other promotional literature must include a prominent statement drawing the investor's attention to its investment policy.[183]

---

[178] See 3.132 *et seq* above. See also for further details 3.333 *et seq* below.

[179] Art 42(3), 2002 Act. The preparations for Directive (EC) 2001/108 specify that 'complete correlation between the underlying portfolio and the derivatives risk is unnecessary but the fund must be able to meet its commitments' (Opinion of the Economic and Social Committee [1999] OJ C116/47). The idea behind this rule is that the fund must be able to satisfy its commitments (Report of the Economic and Monetary Committee, 34 (available on the website of the European Parliament, under the heading 'Legislative Observatory').

[180] Art 42(3), 2002 Act.

[181] Art 10, Eligible Assets Directive.

[182] Art 47(1), 2002 Act.

[183] ibid Art 47(2). It was originally planned to include this notice in the prospectus of any UCITS investing in futures and options. Rightly, the Economic and Social Committee pointed out that such a broad sphere of application could turn out to be counter-productive as derivatives 'can be used to create funds which are perfectly suited to inexperienced investors where such a notice could spark confusion.'

Risk management process

A coordinated UCITS (or its management company) must provide for and employ a risk-management process enabling it to monitor and measure at any time the risks associated with its investments and their contribution to the overall risk profile of its portfolio. Indeed, in the introduction of Circular 07/308,[184] the CSSF states that UCITS must devote greater efforts and resources to risk quantification and oversight because the 2002 Act has expanded the list of financial instruments in which UCITS may invest. **3.193**

A UCITS must in particular employ a process for accurate and independent assessment of the value of over-the-counter derivative instruments.[185] **3.194**

Reporting to the competent authorities

A coordinated UCITS (or its management company) must regularly inform the CSSF of the types of derivatives, the underlying risks, the quantitative limits, and the risk management methods adopted by it.[186] In this respect, Circular 07/308 provides that a UCITS must provide the CSSF with appropriate documentation in respect of the risk-management process put in place. A coordinated UCITS (or its management company) must conduct an internal self-evaluation in order to determine the possible variances of its risk-management process from the provisions of Circular 07/308. The minimum content of any risk-management procedure is also provided by the Circular. **3.195**

Permitted Activities for UCIs other than Coordinated UCITS

Investment objectives of UCIs governed by Part II of the 2002 Act and by the Act of 13 February 2007

Investment in *valeurs* (securities)

According to the 2002 Act,[187] the investments of a UCI within the framework of Part II must consist of '*valeurs*'. Circular 91/75 uses the same term without explaining it further. The Act of 13 February 2007 provides no further explanation either, whilst using the same concept.[188] As a general rule, '*valeur*' can be **3.196**

---

[184] I. General Provisions, Circular 07/308.
[185] Art 42(1), 2002 Act.
[186] ibid.
[187] ibid Art 65, 69, and 73.
[188] Art 1(1), Act of 13 February 2007.

defined as the 'price at which an object may be exchanged or sold, particularly its price in money.'[189]

3.197   In the context of the 2002 Act and of the Act of 13 February 2007, the word *'valeur'* must be understood broadly, ie including 'by extension certain services or certain goods'.[190] It refers more precisely to goods in which it is possible to invest. An investment is an 'operation whereby money is used to buy a good whose value is expected to increase'.[191] The word *valeur* is here used in the strict meaning of the word, ie 'something which is worth money, a thing'.[192]

3.198   A *'valeur'* is therefore an asset one buys in the hope that its purchase price will generate profit over time. This is the purpose for which the asset is kept and not consumed. Thus, the concept of *'valeur'* covers goods which meet the following two conditions, both of which are necessary and which are sufficient in themselves: (a) it must be possible to retain such goods (b) in order to see their value increase. The first of these conditions rules out consumables, ie goods which are used up when used for the first time,[193] unless the use for which such goods are intended does not rule out their consumption.[194] The second, ie an increase in value, may refer to the expectation of income or the prospect of a capital gain.

3.199   The question of whether a good is a *'valeur'* does not depend upon its purchase price. For instance, caviar is expensive but not a *valeur*. In contrast, gold is expensive and a *valeur*. A share is a *valeur* but need not be expensive at all.

---

[189]   Definition given in *Le Petit Larousse*, Grand format, 1999.

[190]   Definition given in *Vocabulaire Juridique*, Association Henri Capitant, chief editor G Cornu, (Presses Universitaires de France, 6th edn, 2004) 935.

[191]   ibid.

[192]   ibid.

[193]   H De Page and R Dekkers, *Traité élémentaire de droit civil beige*, Vol V (Bruylant, 2nd edn, 1975) 540.

[194]   As intention can influence the consumable nature of goods (H De Page and R Dekkers, (n 193 above) 544), this concept is intrinsically linked to the use for which an item is intended. For example, 'by their nature, consumables are sometimes used for other purposes than the consumption for which they were designed' (ibid). A classic example is afforded by fruit or game prepared for display. A retailer lends fruit or game to another retailer, not to be eaten but to decorate his shop. This is use *ad pompam et ostentationem*. Assigned for use *ad pompam et ostentationem*, such articles cannot be consumed (J Hansenne, *Les Biens*, Vol I (Ed. Collection Scientifique de la Faculté de Droit de Liège, 1996) 17; H De Page and R Dekkers, ibid; H De Page and R Dekkers, *Traité élémentaire de droit civil belge*, Vol IV, ibid 478). In this case, such articles cannot be considered consumables. Their use modifies their status and the legal rules by which they are governed. For instance, a consumable such as wine can meet the above two conditions and thus be qualified as a *'valeur'* in the meaning of the 2002 Act. That said, it is necessary to distinguish between 'ordinary' wines and 'fine' wines. A fine wine differs primarily from an ordinary wine in that it improves with age and gradually becomes more valuable. This is why its buyer may prefer not to consume it but to keep it in the hope of realizing a capital gain. Indeed, this happens so often that a special market for fine wines with a certain age and a certain value has evolved. In this case, the wine is no longer classified as a consumable. Such fine wines can be qualified as a *'valeur'* in the meaning of the 2002 Act since (a) they are intended to be kept, (b) in order to increase their value.

Whether or not a good is a *'valeur'* does not depend on its physical composition. **3.200**
Mass-produced pottery is not a *valeur* since, in principle, it does not increase in
value over time, whereas pottery painted by a famous artist is a *valeur*.

The concept of *'valeur'* seems adequate given its flexibility, since it covers every **3.201**
type of asset acceptable in consideration of another.[195] It is supported by the practices of the CSSF, which authorizes UCIs to invest in such diverse assets as properties, futures and commodities, art works, or even certain fine wines. Lastly, it
allows Part II of the 2002 Act to cover all UCIs not governed by Part I.

Consequences

The flexibility of investment objectives for UCIs governed by Part II of the 2002 **3.202**
Act and by the Act of 13 February 2007 has a drawback in that those UCIs are not
eligible for a European passport. When they wish to market their units outside their
home country, their structure, operation, and unit sales become subject to the
requirements of the supervisory authorities in the host country. This situation may
rule out marketing in countries whose terms are impossible to meet or too stringent.

The reason for this constraint is clear. In the eyes of the supervisory authorities of **3.203**
EEA Member States, only UCIs governed by uniform rules pursuant to Directive
85/611 may offer adequate investor protection guarantees. More 'exotic' UCIs are
required to comply with constraints known only in their home State. Foreign
supervisory authorities may therefore have legitimate concerns about them,
within the reasonable limits fixed by the Community concepts of the free movement of capital and the freedom to provide services.

Investment and borrowing limitations applicable to UCIs governed by Part II of the 2002 Act or by the Act of 13 February 2007

General presentation of investment restrictions applicable to UCIs governed by Part II of the 2002 Act or by the Act of 13 February 2007

Neither the 2002 Act nor the Act of 13 February 2007 lists the investment **3.204**
restrictions applicable to UCIs. The 2002 Act refers to the specification of investment limits under a Grand-Ducal regulation.[196] However, as that regulation was

---

[195] The Parliamentary documents accompanying the 1983 Act tend to reflect this idea.
The question that arose at the time was whether to authorize UCIs other than FCPs and SICAVs
to invest in a wide range of securities, such as undivided entitlements to securities representing
property ownership. The object was to authorize as wide a range of investment activities as possible.
The legal framework was to cover every potential development in the area of investment on the
Luxembourg market (*Parliamentary doc* No 2366[5], Supplementary Opinion of the Chamber of
Commerce, 4; *Parliamentary doc* No 2366[8], Report of the Special Committee, 13).
[196] Arts 67(1) for FCPs, 72(1) for SICAVs, and 75(1) for other types of UCI.

never adopted, the CSSF set out the investment limits that must be observed in a Circular.[197]

3.205 As a general rule, the objective of the CSSF is to lay down appropriate rules for each type of investment. The idea is to satisfy a UCI's needs whilst protecting investors. This approach of necessity requires a certain capacity to adapt. The strategies and techniques used by UCIs to invest and to make their portfolios profitable continue to evolve rapidly. If provided with adequate reasons, the CSSF may therefore grant derogations from the following rules.

3.206 The investment restrictions applicable to UCITS governed by Part II of the 2002 Act or by the Act of 13 February 2007 are considerably less than those for coordinated UCITS.

3.207 As regards UCITS governed by Part II of the 2002 Act, investment restrictions consist of three 10 per cent limits. Unless it has been granted a derogation by the CSSF, a UCITS governed by Part II may not:[198]

(1) invest more than 10 per cent of its net assets in securities not listed on a stock exchange or dealt in on another regulated market that operates regularly and is recognized and open to the public;

(2) invest more than 10 per cent of its net assets in securities issued by a single issuer; or

(3) acquire more than 10 per cent of the securities of the same kind issued by a single issuer.

3.208 This principle is qualified by one exception, which concerns securities issued or guaranteed by OECD member States, their local authorities, or supranational institutions and organizations at Community, regional, or world level. A UCITS governed by Part II may invest its entire assets in a single issue of that type.

3.209 The fact that the limit for holding securities issued by a single local entity is to be calculated exclusively by reference to securities 'of the same kind' issued by that issuer allows for a qualified application of the restriction. For example, a distinction may be made between several categories of debt securities.

3.210 For other types of UCI governed by Part II of the 2002 Act, uniformly prescribed investment restrictions were not desirable. It is impossible to prescribe in advance appropriate limits for investment in every type of asset. For that reason, the CSSF has adopted a pragmatic attitude and imposes, in each individual case, the requirements it regards as most appropriate to ensure an adequate spread of risk.

---

[197] Ch G, II, Circular 91/75; Circular 07/309 for SIFs.
[198] ibid.

For certain categories of UCI, the CSSF has established specific standards, as we shall see below,[199] whereas the rules are laid down case by case for other categories.[200] **3.211**

With respect to SIFs only one risk-spreading principle applies. As interpreted by the CSSF, it consists of three limits.[201] **3.212**

The first limit relates to securities of the same kind issued by a given entity. It may be determined on the basis of either the SIF assets or those of one of its sub-funds, or on the basis of the subscription commitments secured by the SIF, respectively one of its sub-funds. The limit precludes a SIF or a SIF's sub-fund from investing more than 30 per cent of its assets or subscription commitments in securities of the same kind issued by the same issuer. **3.213**

There are two exceptions to this limit: **3.214**

(1) It does not apply to investments in UCIs when the underlying UCI must comply with risk-spreading requirements which are at least as stringent as those laid down for SIFs. Therefore, *master/feeder* structures may be established. A SIF may invest all its assets in a foreign UCI. It is irrelevant whether the target UCI is regulated or not. Only the investment limits with which it must comply are relevant.

(2) It is not applicable to securities issued or guaranteed by an OECD member State or its local authorities, or by supranational bodies or institutions.

The second limit also relates to securities issued by the same issuer, yet it applies to uncovered sales which could be carried out by a SIF. After such sales have been effected, a SIF may not hold a short position in securities of the same type issued by a given entity which accounts for more than 30 per cent of its assets. **3.215**

Finally, the third limit applies to the use of derivatives by a SIF. In contrast with the two first limits, it does not refer to a defined percentage. It requires 'a similar level of risk-spreading' '*via* appropriate diversification of the underlying assets'.[202] Similarly, it requires a limitation of the counterparty risk in an OTC transaction 'having regard to the quality and qualification of the counterparty'.[203] **3.216**

---

[199] See 3.224 *et seq* below.
[200] eg UCIs investing in receivables are subject to specific standards, developed on a case-by-case basis by the CSSF, and therefore not included in Circular 91/75. The CSSF requires compliance with certain rules, one of which does not allow a debtor to transfer his debt. At present, very few UCIs invest mainly in receivables and the above rules will no doubt be reviewed and refined as this type of UCI gains ground in the future. The Act of 22 March 2004 provides for the creation of securitization companies and funds. Although not actual UCIs in the meaning of the laws governing UCIs, such vehicles may subject themselves to supervision by the CSSF and invest in receivables of any kind. Thus they can become an alternative to UCITS for this type of investment.
[201] Circular 07/309.
[202] ibid.
[203] ibid.

3.217 None of those three limits is absolutely mandatory. Derogations may be granted by the CSSF, provided they have been duly substantiated. Conversely, the CSSF may require the SIF to comply with additional investment restrictions, where that investment policy of that SIF so requires.[204]

3.218 The rules applicable to investments by SIFs are therefore not numerous and rather liberal. The only requirement is the risk-spreading obligation which the legislator has not quantified or laid down in law. The applicable limits have been set forth in a circular by the CSSF.[205] Hence, SIFs are particularly well-suited to investment policies in private equity,[206] real estate,[207] or derivatives.[208]

Borrowing by UCIs governed by Part II of the 2002 Act

Principle

3.219 A UCI governed by Part II of the 2002 Act may in principle borrow no more than an amount corresponding to 25 per cent of its net assets.[209] Loans may be taken out for all purposes, particularly for investment.[210]

Exceptions

3.220 **UCIs using debt for leverage purposes** No maximum borrowing limits are set for leveraged funds, for which there is a minimum borrowing requirement of 25 per cent of net assets. Each case is judged separately by the CSSF, having regard to the characteristics of each proposal.

3.221 **UCIs investing mainly in real property** Real estate property funds may borrow up to 50 per cent of the aggregate market value of their property portfolio. Exemptions from this rule may be granted on submission to the CSSF giving adequate reasons as to why a derogation should be granted.[211]

3.222 **UCIs pursuing alternative investment strategies** These UCIs may borrow at all times for investment purposes, but only from reputable professionals specializing in this type of transaction.

---

[204] ibid.

[205] Circular 07/309.

[206] See C De Boeck and E d'Anterroches, 'SIF: a new investment vehicle suitable for private equity' in *Specialised Investment Funds* (Arendt & Medernach, 2007) 214.

[207] See M Kemp and C Martougin 'Real estate SIFs—New opportunities for investments in real estate poperties' in *Specialised Investment Funds* (Arendt & Medernach, 2007) 182.

[208] See H Schwabe and F Brülin, 'SIF hedge funds—opportunities to establish "unrestricted" hedge funds in a regulated environment' in *Specialised Investment Funds* (Arendt & Medernach, 2007) 198.

[209] Ch G, III, Circular 91/75.

[210] ibid.

[211] Ch I, III, 4.3, Circular 91/75. The Circular mentions only buildings but also seems to take into account other types of real property, such as holdings in property companies.

Borrowings are limited to 200 per cent of a UCI's net assets. Consequently, the **3.223** value of a UCI's net assets may not exceed 300 per cent of its net asset value. In certain cases, the debt ratio may be raised to a maximum of 400 per cent.[212]

Specific standards for certain UCIs governed by Part II of the 2002 Act

Non-coordinated funds of funds

Investment restrictions

When the objective of a UCI is to invest 20 per cent or more of its net assets in the **3.224** units of open-end UCIs other than coordinated UCITS or equivalent UCIs, it will be subject to regulation under Part II of the 2002 Act. If the UCI whose units it buys itself complies with the obligation to spread risks and to refrain from acquiring controlling interests, the investment rules are less strict.

Three major principles govern investment by a fund of funds other than a coordi- **3.225** nated UCITS.

The first concerns the triple limit of 10 per cent. When the risk-spreading **3.226** obligations to which the target UCIs are subject are comparable to those provided for UCIs governed by Part II of the 2002 Act, this triple limit of 10 per cent is in principle not applicable to the fund of funds.

The second principle is that a foreign open-end UCI within the meaning of **3.227** the Act of 10 July 2005, other than a coordinated UCITS, may not be publicly marketed in the Grand-Duchy of Luxembourg if it is not subject in its country of origin to permanent supervision by a supervisory authority provided for by law in order to protect investors.[213] A Luxembourg-based fund of funds may not be set up to avoid this rule but an intention of avoiding this rule cannot be automati- cally assumed from the stated objective of investing exclusively in unregulated foreign UCIs.

According to the third principle, a fund of funds may not invest all of its assets in **3.228** a single UCITS. In doing so it would change its basic purpose and be reclassified as a participant in a master/feeder structure.[214] This type of structure is authorized in the Grand-Duchy of Luxembourg but subject to stricter requirements.

The CSSF only authorizes master/feeder structures subject to certain conditions. **3.229** In the past, the CSSF only allowed a feeder fund under Luxembourg law to invest all of its assets in a master fund if the master fund was also governed by the laws of

---

[212] See 3.286 below.
[213] Art 76, 2002 Act.
[214] For further details on the *master/feeder* structure, see 2.157 above.

the Grand-Duchy of Luxembourg. The system has now become more flexible. A Luxembourg-based feeder fund may be authorized, on a case-by-case basis, to invest in a foreign master fund, even if from an unregulated jurisdiction, provided the master fund is subject to equivalent investment restrictions to those applicable to UCIs governed by Part II of the 2002 Act and provided the depositary of the feeder fund has a 'transparent' right of inspection of the master fund's assets.

3.230   Lastly, a Luxembourg-based fund of funds may not freely invest in an open-end UCI which itself invests in another open-end UCI (*fund of fund of funds*). The CSSF may grant this right on the making of a submission giving justifiable reasons.

Other rules

3.231   Circular 91/75 lays down the following principles for UCIs whose main objective is investment in other open-end UCIs:[215]

- the intention to invest in other UCIs must be disclosed in the prospectus, as must the asset allocation strategy used to spread investments between different types of target UCIs and the other elements of the fund of fund's investment policy;

- where a fund of funds plans to invest in other UCIs established by the same promoter, the prospectus must disclose the type of costs that may arise as a result of such investment. Investors must, for instance, be informed when agents involved in both the investing UCI and the target UCI are paid a fee by each UCI, even though they in fact provide services to only one of them.

UCIs investing mainly in risk capital

Investment restrictions

3.232   UCIs investing mainly in risk capital are defined as those 'whose investment policy provides for the investment of 20 per cent or more of their net assets in risk capital, [ie] investment in the securities of companies which have been recently created or are still in a growth phase'.[216] Such companies are not listed because they have not yet attained the size necessary to enter the stock market.[217] Such UCIs are known as risk capital funds or venture capital funds.

3.233   For such UCIs, Circular 91/75 created a special regime based on their specific needs and constraints.[218] This regime has been superseded by the rules laid down

---

[215]   Ch G, II, Circular 91/75.
[216]   Ch C, II, 4.1, Circular 91/75.
[217]   Ch I, Introduction, Circular 91/75.
[218]   See also C Kremer and J Baden, 'L'investissement par les organismes de placement collectif luxembourgeois dans les marchés émergents', Notes financières de la Banque générale du Luxembourg, No 56 (March/April 1996) 20.

in the Act of 15 June 2004, which created the SICAR and specified the rules for this type of investment.[219]

Risk capital funds include private equity funds.[220] As a general rule, investment by **3.234** risk capital funds is subject to a single constraint, ie appropriate investment risk spreading. Accordingly, Circular 91/75 does not permit such UCIs to invest more than 20 per cent of their net assets in a single company.[221]

Other rules

The rules governing risk capital funds lay down particular requirements to protect **3.235** investors. Those requirements are threefold in nature. They concern the conducting persons and investment advisers of the funds concerned, the nature of the securities they may issue and the information they must disclose.

First of all, the conducting persons of such UCIs must be able to demonstrate that **3.236** they have specific experience in their area of activity, ie the risk capital market. The same applies to investment advisers working for such UCIs.[222]

Secondly, the value of the bearer shares issued by such UCIs and their denominations **3.237** must be equivalent to at least €12,394.68. The same applies to registered shares.[223]

Thirdly, the prospectuses of such UCIs must contain the following information: **3.238**

(1) a description of the investment risks inherent in their investment policy;[224]
(2) more specifically, a notice stating that only persons able to risk the amounts invested by them should invest in such UCIs, and that they should allocate only part of their long-term investment portfolio to such an investment, as this type of investment entails a higher-than-average risk;[225]
(3) a description of the nature of the potential conflicts of interest between such UCIs and their investment advisers, as well as the persons comprising the latter's management bodies;[226] and
(4) an indication of the assets on which the fees of investment advisers and the management bodies are charged, if such fees are higher than those normally paid to such parties in more traditional UCIs. More specifically, investors

---

[219] See 13.01 *et seq* below.
[220] Since the introduction of the Act of 15 June 2004 on risk capital investment companies, there has been a parallel regime for investment in private equity. This regime is described in detail in Ch 12 below. The Act of 13 February 2007 also has a decisive impact on the structuring of such investment funds.
[221] Ch I, I, 2, Circular 91/75.
[222] ibid Ch I, I, 1.
[223] ibid Ch I, I, 4.1.
[224] ibid Ch I, I, 4.4.
[225] ibid.
[226] ibid.

must be informed whether the excess remuneration compared with traditional UCIs is also payable on the assets of the UCI that are not invested in risk capital.[227]

3.239 Futhermore, the annual and semi-annual financial statements of such UCIs must indicate:[228]

(1) the performance of the companies whose securities are acquired;

(2) the amount of the capital gains or losses realized on the sale of each portfolio item; and

(3) specific information about potential conflicts of interest between the UCI, its investment advisers, and the persons comprising the latter's management bodies.

UCIs investing mainly in real property

Investment restrictions

3.240 Real estate property funds are those that invest mainly in real property. The concept of *valeur immobilière* (property asset) is relatively broad. It not only includes the buildings owned by the UCI but also holdings in property companies[229] and the claims on such companies.[230] The UCI must be able to sell units in such property companies at least as easily as property rights held directly. *Valeur immobilière* further includes long-term property utilization rights (the right to surface areas, long-term leases, etc) as well as options on *valeurs immobilières*.[231]

3.241 Like UCIs investing in risk capital and UCIs investing in futures and/or options contracts, UCIs that mainly invest in property funds are not subject to the general investment restrictions laid down by Part II of the 2002 Act.[232]

3.242 Such funds are subject to only one limit, adopted in order to ensure compliance with the fundamental principle of risk spreading. In order to comply with this obligation, a real estate property fund may in principle not invest more than 20 per cent of its net assets in a single *valeur immobilière*.[233] This limitation applies at the time when the *valeur* in question is acquired. Such funds may nevertheless

---

[227] ibid Ch I, I, 4.2.

[228] ibid Ch I, I, 4.3.

[229] Insofar as such transferable securities are listed, UCIs investing mainly in such securities may adopt the status of coordinated UCITS.

[230] ie according to Circular 91/75 (Ch I, III), their exclusive object and purpose are to acquire, assign, sell, rent, and lease buildings.

[231] Ch I, III, Circular 91/75.

[232] ibid Ch I, III, 2. As regards the rules applicable to real estate funds, as foreseen by Part II of the 2002 Act, see Kemp and Martougin (n 207 above) 185–8.

[233] On the understanding that property with related economic viability is also considered part of a 'single *valeur immobilière*'.

derogate from this rule for a period of up to four years from the closure of the UCI's initial offer period for subscription.[234] The CSSF may further grant additional individual derogations based on valid reasons.[235]

This investment restriction calls for one comment. It is unfortunately not based on a UCI's total assets but only on its net assets. Real estate property funds are permitted to borrow up to 50 per cent of the value of all their buildings. A UCI using this extended borrowing right proportionally reduces the amount of its net assets and is thus penalised by the investment restriction. The investment ceiling of 20 per cent per property asset is not based on the value of all property assets held by the fund but on the net value of its property portfolio.   **3.243**

There is no good reason for this. The reason for the 20 per cent cap is to spread investment risk. The rationale is to offset investment in possibly unprofitable buildings with more profitable investments. The fact that part of the portfolio is leveraged does not affect this objective and should not be taken into consideration in calculating the 20 per cent ceiling, which should be calculated by reference to the total assets held by the UCI.   **3.244**

Other rules

Real estate property funds are subject to derogations from the general regime applicable to UCIs governed by Part II of the 2002 Act as regards their investment restrictions[236] and the extent to which they may borrow.[237] However, there are other standards that are applied.   **3.245**

First, Circular 91/75 authorizes real estate property funds to restrict their obligation to redeem their own shares.[238] Such restrictions may be judicious, sometimes to the point of being mandatory in view of 'the features of a UCI's investment policy',[239] ie the lack of liquidity of property assets.   **3.246**

Secondly, real estate property funds are governed by the specific requirements listed in Circular 91/75, which are in line with those applicable to risk capital funds. The requirements in question apply to the management bodies and the advisers of real estate property funds, to asset valuations and to the contents of prospectuses and promotional literature and the annual and semi-annual reports of such UCIs. For   **3.247**

---

[234] Ch I, III, 2(2), Circular 91/75.

[235] eg the CSSF allows real estate property funds in special cases to invest more than 20% of their net assets in a single property company. In this case, it sets an acceptable threshold, which may vary from case to case.

[236] See 3.206 *et seq* above.

[237] See 3.219 above.

[238] Ch I, III, 3, Circular 91/75. By way of example, the Circular cites the right for real estate property funds to set a redemption payment time enabling them to collect sufficient liquid assets.

[239] ibid.

instance, their managers and, as the case may be, their investment advisers may only be persons with specific experience in property investments.[240]

3.248 They are further required to appoint at least one independent property expert with specific property valuation experience in order to maintain their professional standards.[241] Such an expert has two types of task to perform. At the time of closure of the financial year, he verifies the valuation of buildings and land owned by the UCI or the property companies in which the UCI invests. Secondly, he values buildings or land bought or sold by the UCI, except for buildings or land sold within six months of their latest valuation. His valuation is the benchmark value. The purchase or sale price may not be significantly higher or lower than the benchmark value, save in exceptional circumstances, in which case valid reasons must be given. In the event of a major discrepancy, the next financial report must include a management explanation.

3.249 Valuation of a real estate property fund's minority interests in property companies is also subject to several constraints.[242] Where such holdings are not listed on a stock exchange or dealt in on another regulated market which operates regularly and is recognized and open to the public, they are consolidated at the end of the year with the real estate property fund's results or at least valued at their probable realization value, estimated in good faith according to the principle of prudence. In contrast, where such holdings are listed or dealt in on a regulated market, they are valued at their stock exchange or market value.

3.250 Moreover, the accounts of real estate property funds and affiliated property companies, ie those whose capital or loans are owned as to 50 per cent or more by real estate property funds, must be audited by the same person.[243] The accounts of all such entities are, in principle, closed or cut off at the same date. Moreover, they must be consolidated every six months, which does not rule out the application of other laws and regulations relating to consolidation.

3.251 As regards investor information, Circular 91/75 requires a real estate property fund's prospectus to provide particulars of the following:

(1) the risks attached to investment in the fund;[244]

(2) the nature of the fees and other charges to be paid by the fund;[245]

(3) the method used to calculate and charge such fees and other charges;[246]

---

[240] ibid Ch I, III, 1.
[241] ibid Ch I, III, 4.2.
[242] ibid Ch I, III, 4.4.
[243] ibid.
[244] ibid Ch I, III, 4.5.
[245] ibid.
[246] ibid.

(4) if the fees of the investment advisers and managers are higher than those normally paid to such parties in more traditional UCIs, the extent to which such excess remuneration is payable on assets not invested in real property;[247] and

(5) any redemption restrictions applying to the units of such UCIs.[248]

Lastly, a real estate property fund's annual and semi-annual reports must contain the following information:[249]   **3.252**

- a valuation of its property portfolio;

- a list of the properties held by the fund and its affiliated property companies, including the purchase price, the insurance value, and the valuation of each property;

- the basic principles used to consolidate the UCI's accounts with those of affiliated property companies.

UCIs pursuing alternative investment strategies

Concept

The concept of 'alternative' UCIs has no uniformly recognized legal meaning. Such UCIs are defined instead in contrast to 'traditional' UCIs, and both types of UCI together constitute the two major categories of investment fund which are distinguished from each other by learned opinion.[250]   **3.253**

'Traditional' UCIs[251] are those which buy positions ('long' positions) in asset categories which themselves are considered 'traditional', such as liquid shares issued in developed markets, bonds and other liquid fixed and variable rate financial instruments with a high rating, or units in other traditional UCIs.   **3.254**

Traditional UCIs use derivatives only for the purpose of hedging and efficient portfolio management. They do not make uncovered sales on portfolio assets and do not seek to leverage through borrowing.   **3.255**

'Non-traditional'[252] UCIs make uncovered sales[253] of traditional assets while taking long or short positions in high-risk assets, such as stocks and bonds issued   **3.256**

---

[247] ibid Ch I, III, 4.1.

[248] ibid Ch I, III, 3.

[249] ibid Ch I, III, 4.4.

[250] For a detailed analysis of this classification and the operating method of certain types of alternative funds, see P Cottier, *Hedge Funds and Managed Futures* (Haupt, 3rd edn, 2000). There may be slight differences in the classifications adopted by various authors. This work does not appear to be the right place to discuss them. However, the informed reader will be able to find them while looking through the many publications referred to by Cottier.

[251] ibid 7.

[252] ibid 8.

[253] The concept of 'uncovered sale' is defined in Circular 03/88. According to Commission Recommendation (EC) 2004/383 of 27 April 2004 on the use of derivative financial instruments

in emerging markets, high yield and junk bonds, private equity, risk or venture capital, distressed securities, asset and mortgage-backed securities, convertible bonds, commodities, derivatives traded on regulated markets or over the counter, and structured products.

3.257 Non-traditional UCIs are classified as alternative funds and non-classical funds. This category also includes hedge funds and futures funds. Hedge funds[254] are UCIs which:

- invest in derivatives, and/or
- are authorized to make uncovered sales, and/or
- seek significant leverage by borrowing.

3.258 Futures funds[255] take long or short positions in derivatives traded on regulated markets where the assets underlying such derivatives are commodities or derivatives.

Futures funds are a sub-category of hedge funds. In contrast with hedge funds, futures funds invest exclusively in derivatives traded on regulated markets. The term UCIs 'pursuing alternative investment strategies' referred to below covers the entire category of hedge funds.

Regulatory framework

3.259 The regulatory framework applicable to UCIs 'pursuing alternative investment strategies' is supplied by Circular 02/80.[256] Previously, this category of UCI was not covered by specific rules in the Grand-Duchy of Luxembourg. Granted, Circular 91/75 contains operating rules for UCIs whose primary objective is to invest in futures and options;[257] however, actual investment in derivatives is merely a limited aspect of alternative investment strategies. Uncovered sales, securities borrowing, recourse to a prime broker, and the search for high leverage are other aspects of such strategies that are not mentioned in Circular 91/75.

---

for UCITS ([2004] OJ L144), Recital No 9: 'Uncovered sales are all transactions in which the UCITS is exposed to the risk of having to buy securities at a higher price than the price at which the securities are delivered and thus making a loss and the risk of not being able to deliver the underlying financial instrument for settlement at the time of the maturity of the transaction.' Although provided in a different context, this definition remains entirely valid in connection with alternative UCIs.

[254] Cottier (n 250 above) 17; Schwabe and Brülin (n 208 above) 198 and, for the strategies of those funds, 203 *et seq.*

[255] Cottier (n 250 above) 11.

[256] For further discussion of alternative funds based in Luxembourg, see C Niedner and F Kass, 'Les fonds alternatifs en droit luxembourgeois' in *Droit bancaire et financier au Luxembourg*, Vol 4 (Larcier, 2004), 1581.

[257] Ch I, II, Circular 91/75.

Before the adoption of Circular 02/80, the practice of the CSSF was to approve **3.260**
alternative funds on a case-by-case basis. This approach had two drawbacks. First,
the potential promoters of alternative funds were frequently unaware of the
restrictions which the CSSF might apply to such products. The absence of specific
regulations was a deterrent to domiciling such UCIs in Luxembourg. Secondly,
the particular rules laid down on a case-by-case basis by the CSSF were not
universally applicable due to the absence of global analysis and codification in a
general regulation. This made it impossible to use rulings given in particular
circumstances as precedents for future projects.

These were the shortcomings Circular 02/80 was intended to address by laying **3.261**
down 'specific rules applicable to Luxembourg undertakings for collective investment ("UCI") pursuing alternative investment strategies'. The Circular was
'issued in the context of the existing legal framework', specifying that such UCIs
are subject to Part II of the 1988 Act[258] as 'the rules set forth in chapter 5 of said
Act are not appropriate for such UCIs'.[259]

This is an interesting observation. As we have seen, the Acts of 2002 and 1988 **3.262**
allow UCITS to avoid coordinated status by belonging to certain categories laid
down by the CSSF for which the coordinated status is inappropriate 'because of
their investment or borrowing policy'.[260] The wording of Circular 02/80 makes it
clear that alternative funds form such a category of non-coordinated UCITS. This
is an important detail, since such vehicles frequently hold transferable securities
portfolios. This would make them, at first sight, candidates for the status of
coordinated UCITS, which would make it impossible for them to pursue certain
alternative strategies, such as uncovered sales.

The extended scope of application of the 2002 Act does not affect this reasoning. **3.263**
It merely prompts a broader array of UCITS to adopt coordinated status, since the
eligible assets now also include money market instruments, units in UCITS, bank
deposits, and derivatives. That said, the 2002 Act still allows the CSSF to refuse to
grant coordinated status to certain categories of UCIs because of their investment
and/or borrowing policy.[261] The CSSF has already ruled out certain categories of
UCIs,[262] to which it has now added alternative funds. Recourse to alternative
strategies allows this category of UCIs to remain subject to Part II of the 2002 Act
even if their portfolios include liquid financial assets in which coordinated UCITS
may also invest.

---

[258] At present it is necessary to include Part II of the 2002 Act, which Circular 02/80 does not do
since it was adopted before the 2002 Act came into force.
[259] Preamble, Circular 02/80.
[260] Ch C, II, 4, Circular 91/75.
[261] Art 3, 2002 Act.
[262] See Circular 03/88.

Investment restrictions

3.264 Long portfolios   The long portfolio of an alternative fund includes primarily transferable securities and money market instruments. It may also include the units of other alternative UCIs. Technically speaking, a UCI investing in other alternative UCIs has the characteristics of a fund of hedge funds.

3.265   Nothing prevents an alternative UCI from combining the two types of portfolio, turning it into a hybrid alternative UCI.

3.266   *Transferable securities and money market instruments*   According to Circular 02/80,[263] alternative UCIs are authorized to invest in transferable securities and money market instruments, subject to the following restrictions:

(1) as regards the types of securities they may buy—they may not invest more than 10 per cent of their assets in transferable securities which are not quoted on a stock exchange or dealt on another regulated market;

(2) as regards control over the issuer—they may not buy more than 10 per cent of securities of the same nature issued by the same issuer;

(3) as regards risk diversification—they may not invest more than 20 per cent of their assets in the securities of the same issuer.

3.267   These restrictions are not applicable to investments in securities issued or guaranteed by a member country of the OECD or by one of its regional authorities, nor do they apply to securities issued by supranational institutions or organizations at Community, regional or world level.

3.268   Lastly, they do not apply to investments in the units of open-end UCIs, which are governed by special rules.

3.269   *Investment in units of open-end UCIs*   An alternative fund will frequently be constituted as a fund of alternative funds. This is due to the way in which alternative products are structured and managed. Most alternative managers offer management services by selling units in funds they have created or whose assets they are managing. This allows them to limit the number of client accounts[264] under management, avoiding the administrative costs generated by the management of many individual accounts as well as potential conflicts of interests in allocating assets among these accounts.

3.270   Investment in a fund managed by such a manager may frequently be the only way an alternative UCI can access the investment management skills of a selected manager. The CSSF recognizes this situation. Accordingly, Circular 02/80 contains special rules for investment in open-end funds.

---

[263] Section D, Circular 02/80.
[264] Often referred to as 'managed account'.

In accordance with the principle of risk spreading, Circular 02/80 does not permit **3.271**
a UCI to invest more than 20 per cent of its net assets in the securities of a single
target UCI.[265] As is the case for UCITS governed by Part I of the 2002 Act, the
CSSF permits sub-funds of an umbrella scheme to be regarded as a separate UCI
in application of this rule on the basis that each sub-fund forms a separate asset
and liability pool within the target UCI.[266] Thus, an alternative UCI may invest
its entire assets in five sub-funds of a single UCI.

The Circular does not specify the geographical location of target UCIs. **3.272**

In practice, an investing UCI sometimes wishes to control a UCI in which it **3.273**
invests. Such control may also turn out to be inevitable if the target UCI has not
yet attracted other investors. Circular 02/80 allows an investing UCITS to hold
up to 100 per cent of the securities issued by another UCI. When the target UCI
has several sub-funds, an additional restriction applies. If the investing UCI wishes
to hold more than 50 per cent of the securities issued by the target UCI, the total
value of the investment made by the investing UCI in the target UCI may not
represent 50 per cent or more of the net assets of the investing UCI.[267]

The reason for this restriction is as follows. When a Luxembourg-based UCI **3.274**
invests its entire assets in several sub-funds of the same foreign UCI, the CSSF
may argue that the foreign UCI is marketed indirectly in Luxembourg. According
to the 2002 Act, a foreign open-end UCI within the meaning of the Act of 10 July
2005 may only be marketed publicly in Luxembourg when subject in its country
of origin to regulations equivalent to those in force in the Grand-Duchy of
Luxembourg.[268] In contrast, the CSSF holds that target funds are not indirectly
marketed in Luxembourg when a Luxembourg-based UCI divides its investments
between two or more foreign UCIs.

Thus Circular 02/80 stipulates that the proportion of control over a target **3.275**
UCI may exceed half the securities issued by it provided the investing UCI also
limits the proportion of units bought in the target UCI to half of its own
net assets.

The above risk-spreading obligations and restrictions on control do not apply if **3.276**
the target UCI is subject to risk-spreading principles similar to those provided for
the Luxembourg-based UCIs governed by Part II of the 2002 Act and, in its
country of origin, is submitted to permanent supervision by a supervisory authority
set up by the law in order to protect investors.[269]

---

[265] Section C, Circular 02/80.
[266] ibid.
[267] ibid.
[268] Art 76, 2002 Act.
[269] ibid.

3.277 Nevertheless, the absence of such restrictions must never result in an excessive concentration of investments in a single target UCI. Circular 02/80 does not define 'excessive' concentration, although it states that, for the purpose of applying this limit, each sub-fund in a target UCI must be considered a separate UCI provided it adheres to the principle of segregating the liabilities of such sub-funds. Thus investment in a single target UCI remains possible if the UCI's sub-funds are legally segregated.

3.278 Investment in other UCIs may raise problems with liquidity, depending upon their redemption conditions. The investing UCI must take this characteristic into account at the time of investment. Circular 02/80 specifies that an investing UCI must verify that the portfolios of target UCIs are sufficiently liquid to be able to meet its redemption obligations when required to process redemption.

3.279 Although such situations can occur in practice, Circular 02/80 does not discuss investment by alternative UCIs in other funds of alternative funds. The CSSF allows such investments on precise conditions designed to avoid layering of costs and a lack of transparency regarding investments made by the target UCIs.[270]

3.280 **Short portfolios** Circular 02/80 authorizes alternative UCIs to carry out uncovered sales. Such sales are only authorized when they involve highly liquid transferable securities. They are, moreover, subject to precise risk-spreading rules.[271]

3.281 *Liquidity requirement* In principle, alternative UCIs may only make uncovered sales of transferable securities listed on a stock exchange or dealt in on another regulated market. Exceptionally, a UCI may hold short positions in transferable securities that do not meet this condition if such securities are highly liquid and do not represent more than 10 per cent of the UCI's assets.[272]

---

[270] Legitimate reasons for investing in a fund of alternative funds include the following two. First, the selection of effective managers and thus of the funds created by them is an extremely demanding skill which calls for sophisticated knowledge of alternative product management. The lack of information about such managers and the extensive analysis required makes it particularly difficult to select effective managers. The investing UCI must closely monitor the selected managers and continually assess the availability of other managers capable of replacing them. This is why the composition of a sufficiently diversified portfolio of managers is a long and costly effort requiring the services of specialists. Only a few sufficiently large funds of funds can afford to do so without burdening their assets unduly. Secondly, direct investment by an alternative UCI in funds created by managers of alternative products may hamper risk diversification. Such managers agree only to manage significant amounts, which reduces the leeway for investors to use several. This may prompt a fund to invest in larger funds of funds whose size allows them to spread their investments over several managers and thus limit the impact of less effective management by one of them.

[271] Section A, Circular 02/80.

[272] ibid Section A, A.1(a).

Moreover, an alternative UCI may not hold a short position representing more than 10 per cent of the securities of the same type issued by the same issuer.[273] **3.282**

Risk spreading   An alternative UCI is subject to three risk-spreading rules. The first applies when a UCI makes an uncovered sale. The other two must be applied continually until the short position has been settled. These restrictions are as follows: **3.283**

(1) the sum of the settlement price for uncovered sales involving transferable securities issued by the same issuer may not represent more than 10 per cent of the UCI's assets;[274]
(2) the unrealized loss resulting from uncovered sales involving transferable securities issued by the same issuer may not represent more than 5 per cent of the UCI's assets;[275]
(3) the sum of unrealized losses resulting from uncovered sales must remain less than 50 per cent of the UCI's assets.[276]

An unrealized loss within the meaning of the above two restrictions is the amount obtained after subtracting the price at which a security is sold short from the market value at which the short position may be covered. A UCI whose unrealized loss on one or more uncovered sales exceeds the above thresholds must immediately close its short position. This is why Circular 02/80 requires a UCI at all times to hold the assets necessary to close its position. **3.284**

A forward sale of transferable securities for which a UCI has adequate coverage is no longer an 'uncovered sale' and is not used to calculate the unrealized losses referred to above. According to Circular 02/80, a UCI's delivery of security on its assets to third parties in order to guarantee liabilities towards such third parties is not considered adequate coverage.[277] **3.285**

Borrowing and leverage   An alternative UCI is at all times authorized to borrow money in order to finance its investments provided it borrows from reputable professionals specializing in this type of transaction. Such borrowings may represent up to 200 per cent of a UCI's net assets. Consequently, the gross asset value of an alternative UCI can, in principle, represent up to 300 per cent of its net assets. When an alternative UCI pursues a strategy with a high correlation between long and short positions,[278] it may borrow up to 400 per cent of its net assets. **3.286**

---

[273] ibid Section A, A.1(b).
[274] ibid Section A, A.1(c).
[275] ibid.
[276] ibid Section A, A.3.
[277] ibid Section A, A.4.
[278] eg market neutral and relative value strategies.

Circular 02/80 specifies, moreover, that the CSSF may set higher limits based on submissions giving appropriate justification for this.[279]

3.287 The leverage generated by borrowing can be increased by the use of derivatives. Circular 02/80 obliges UCIs to set an overall limit by disclosing in their prospectuses the maximum leverage generated by a combination of borrowings and investment in derivatives.

3.288 **Derivatives** Alternative UCIs are authorized to use all types of derivatives, particularly futures, forwards, options, and swaps. Commodity futures are also permitted. These instruments may be traded on regulated markets or over the counter. In the second case, the over-the-counter counterparty must be a reputable professional specializing in this type of transaction.

3.289 The margins called on derivative instruments, when traded on an organized market, may not exceed:

- 5 per cent of the UCI's assets per individual derivatives contract;[280]
- 50 per cent of the UCI's total assets.[281]

These same limits are calculated in respect of a UCI's commitments when the UCI trades on the over-the-counter market.

3.290 For derivatives with one single underlying commodity relating to one single type of futures contracts, the margin or (for over-the-counter derivatives) the commitment must remain at less than 20 per cent of a UCI's assets.

3.291 An alternative UCI may not borrow to finance margin deposits and must have a cash reserve at least equal to its margin deposits.[282]

3.292 **Cumulative application of restrictions** The aggregate commitment created by uncovered sales of transferable securities and the use of derivatives may not exceed 100 per cent of a UCI's assets.[283]

Other portfolio management techniques

3.293 *Securities lending* When an alternative UCI makes uncovered sales, Circular 02/80 authorizes it to borrow securities from reputable professionals specializing in this type of transaction.

3.294 Although not specified in Circular 02/80, the UCI is also authorized to lend securities. In this case, the rules stipulated in Circular 08/336 should apply.

---

[279] Preamble, last paragraph, Circular 02/80.
[280] ibid Section E, E.1.
[281] ibid.
[282] ibid Section E, E.1, points 1 and 2.
[283] ibid Section E, third paragraph, Circular 02/80.

Repurchase agreements and related transactions   Alternative UCIs are allowed to   **3.295**
carry out such transactions[284] subject to compliance with certain conditions, set
out in Circular 08/336.

Recourse to a prime broker

Concept   Hedge funds and futures funds generally use one or more prime bro-   **3.296**
kers to help them to implement their investment strategies. Prime brokers carry
out and clear transactions between parties. They open the accounts to which the
UCI's margin deposits, as required on the various option and futures markets, are
paid. The prime broker can also grant a UCI the credit lines necessary to finance
overdrafts. It further acts on behalf of the UCI in securities lending, borrowing,
and repurchase transactions. Lastly, it offers risk management services and other
administrative or IT services. In exchange for these services, the UCI places most
of its buy and sell orders through the prime broker.[285]

Circular 02/80 does not discuss the relationship between an alternative UCI and   **3.297**
its prime broker(s). The term 'prime broker' is not mentioned in the Circular
itself, although the Circular does require money lenders to UCIs to be reputable
professionals specializing in this type of transaction and the name of such professionals to be mentioned in the prospectus.

Rules on collateral   When a prime broker lends a UCI securities and money, it   **3.298**
obtains collateral which is subject to certain restrictions. The Circular does not
limit the type or form of collateral, which may take the form of the traditional
pledge. Guarantee mechanisms based on transfer of ownership are also
permitted.[286]

When the collateral granted by a UCI has the effect of transferring ownership,   **3.299**
Circular 02/80 limits the counterparty risk that the UCI may assume vis-à-vis the
prime broker. The difference between the value of the assets the UCI assigns by
way of collateral in (a) security or cash borrowing transactions, and (b) security
loans connected with uncovered sales, and the value of the amounts owed to
the lending prime broker may not exceed 20 per cent of the UCI's asset value.[287]
The purpose of this rule is to limit the counterparty risk incurred by UCIs towards
prime brokers.

---

[284] See 3.424 below for a description of this type of transaction.
[285] For the role of the prime broker, see Cottier, (n 250 above) 34.
[286] This refers to the technique of transferring ownership by way of guarantee in accordance with
the Act of 5 August 2005 on financial guarantee agreements (*Mémorial* A 2005, 2212), repealing
the previous Act of 1 August 2001 on the transfer of ownership by way of guarantee. This allows the
UCI to grant an equivalent guarantee under foreign law (eg the technique of outright transfer of
ownership or rehypothecation provided for in Anglo-Saxon law).
[287] Section B, Circular 02/80.

3.300 *Interaction with depositary* A prime broker may also be appointed directly by the depositary as custodian of the UCI's assets. In practice, the UCI is often a party to the prime broker agreement, which thus becomes a tripartite arrangement. The accounts at the prime broker are opened in the name of the UCI with the right for the depositary to have at all times direct access to information on these accounts. Insofar as the prime broker is free to dispose of the assets received by way of security from the UCI, the depositary loses control over them, which deviates from the general law provisions on the supervision obligations incumbent upon depositaries of Luxembourg-based UCIs. In the light of market practices, the CSSF allows the prime broker to act as global sub-depositary for the depositary provided it is a reputable professional recognized as such in this business.[288]

3.301 **Promoter and conducting persons** Circular 02/80 specifies that, owing to the high investment risks attendant upon alternative strategies, the CSSF pays close attention to the 'reputation, experience and financial resources of the promoters'.[289] The same applies to the professional qualifications and experience of the 'conducting persons, management bodies and as applicable the investment managers and the investment advisors'.[290] The latter must be able to show 'confirmed experience in the area of the proposed investment policy'.[291]

Transparency rules

3.302 Circular 02/80 stipulates certain requirements as regards the contents of the prospectus of an alternative UCI:[292]

(1) It must describe the investment risks inherent in the investment policy and the potential losses which may result from uncovered sales of transferable securities, and must warn investors that such losses can be unlimited. It must further inform investors about the risks generated by the use of derivatives and other techniques and the risk that the UCI may not be able to fulfil redemption requests due to the low liquidity of its assets.

(2) It must mention the proposed leverage of the UCI.

(3) It must contain a description of the UCI's futures and options trading strategy.

---

[288] In the case of SIFs, the role of the depositary of an alternative UCI is scaled back insofar as the depositary is released from the obligation to check the regularity of transactions, incumbent upon depositaries of UCIs governed by the 2002 Act.

[289] Preamble, Circular 02/80.

[290] ibid.

[291] ibid Section G.

[292] ibid Section H.

Use by UCITS of Derivatives and Portfolio Management Techniques

Introduction

In its initial version, Directive 85/611 allowed coordinated UCITS to use derivatives and portfolio management techniques. However, it did not regulate their use, merely authorizing UCITS to 'employ techniques and instruments relating to transferable securities, provided that they are used for the purpose of efficient portfolio management'.[293] It allowed UCITS, moreover, to use techniques and instruments 'intended to provide protection against exchange risks in the context of the management of their assets and liabilities'.[294] These techniques and instruments were therefore only allowed to optimize management techniques and hedge portfolios, which had to consist solely of transferable securities. Literally copying the provisions in Directive 85/611, the 1988 Act left it to Circular 91/75 to provide the relevant regulatory framework. Coordinated UCITS governed by the 1988 Act were authorized, within certain limits, to use derivatives and various portfolio management techniques, such as securities lending.[295]

3.303

Directive 2001/108, as transposed into the 2002 Act, radically changed this situation. The approach adopted by Directive 2001/108 in relation to financial derivative instruments, rather than aiming at regulating every single detail, was to lay down the principles in relation to the use of financial derivative instruments in order to maintain sufficient flexibility for future market developments.[296] Derivatives may now be strategic investment tools, whereas they used to be merely incidental management or portfolio hedging tools. They have become a new category of eligible assets, just like money market instruments, units in UCITS, and bank deposits.

3.304

In addition to this innovation, the 2002 Act retains the authorization for coordinated UCITS to use techniques and instruments involving transferable securities and money market instruments 'for the purpose of efficient portfolio management'.[297] The scope of this provision has changed, however. Under the 1988 Act, this text was the only source authorizing coordinated UCITS to use derivatives and certain portfolio management techniques. The 2002 Act changed

3.305

---

[293] Art 21.1, Directive (EEC) 85/611 in its wording of 1985.

[294] ibid Art 21.2.

[295] Ch H, Circular 91/75. For a detailed analysis of the regime under the 1988 Act, see C Kremer and I Lebbe, *Les organismes de placement collectif en droit luxembourgeois* (Larcier, 1st edn, 2001) paras 246–283.

[296] Art 41(1)(g), 2002 Act.

[297] ibid Art 42(2).

this rationale. First, it created a potential second status for derivatives. Derivatives can now not only be used as direct investment targets by UCITS, they may also be used to manage and hedge portfolios made up of other securities, on the understanding that such a use is subject to the same restrictions as investment in the derivatives themselves.[298] Secondly, the 2002 Act continues to authorize the use of portfolio management techniques such as securities lending and repurchase and reverse repurchase agreements.

Recourse to derivatives

3.306 Coordinated UCITS governed by the 2002 Act may use derivatives as a direct investment target. This is expressly stated in the 2002 Act, which lists these instruments among eligible asset categories.[299]

3.307 Directive 2001/108 and the 2002 Act do not provide a definition of 'financial derivative instruments', in practice generally referred to as 'derivatives'. The European legislature probably did not want to provide a definition, which was bound to lack the flexibility needed to keep up with the ongoing changes in, and growing sophistication of, instruments of this type. According to learned opinion, the expression designates 'any asset whose value or price is "derived" from an underlying asset to create leverage and which is not recognised in the balance sheet'.[300] Derivatives are generally classified into three categories: futures, swaps, and options.[301]

3.308 Neither Directive 2001/108 nor the 2002 Act imposes a weighting on such investments compared with other assets in the portfolio of a coordinated UCITS. UCITS have considerable freedom in this respect. They may invest exclusively in derivatives or combine more traditional portfolios with derivative investment strategies. Mixed UCITS are therefore conceivable, with bank deposits or transferable securities accompanied by a range of derivatives in which a UCITS invests according to an investment strategy approved by the manager.

3.309 Moreover, as in the past, coordinated UCITS under the 2002 Act may continue to use derivatives for the purpose of 'efficient portfolio management'.[302] This includes situations in which such instruments are used exclusively for hedging purposes. The expression 'sound portfolio management' used in the 1988 Act[303]

---

[298] ibid.
[299] ibid Art 41(1)(g).
[300] See H de Vauplane and J–P Bornet, *Droit des marchés financiers* (Litec, 1998) para 698, 586 and the references quoted in this text.
[301] ibid.
[302] Art 42(2), 2002 Act.
[303] Art 41(1), 1988 Act.

was not clarified by the legislature or the CSSF. Circular 91/75 stated that this concept included the use of such instruments for hedging and other purposes.[304] Under the 2002 Act, a coordinated UCITS may continue to use such instruments if it is believed they will help the UCITS to improve portfolio management. However, the 2002 Act specifies that their use must be subject to the same conditions and limits as those applied to derivatives used for investment purposes.[305] Consequently, the rules and restrictions set out below apply regardless of the reasons why a UCITS may use derivatives.

Eligibility criteria

According to the 2002 Act, coordinated UCITS may only use derivatives that comply with certain utilization criteria. **3.310**

Tradability

The 2002 Act first of all authorizes instruments traded on regulated markets, ie the same type of markets as those used to deal in the transferable securities and money market instruments in which UCITS may invest.[306] Next, it authorizes derivatives traded over the counter. According to the 2002 Act, derivatives include equivalent instruments settled in cash.[307] **3.311**

Composition of underlying assets

A coordinated UCITS can only invest in derivatives if the assets underlying these instruments are themselves eligible investments for UCITS. This makes it impossible, for example, to use derivatives whose direct underlying assets are precious metals or other commodities. **3.312**

The following underlying assets are authorized:[308] **3.313**

- transferable securities and money market instruments dealt in on a regulated market,
- units of coordinated UCITS or other eligible UCIs,
- derivatives themselves,
- currencies,
- financial indices,
- interest rates, and
- foreign exchange rates.

---

[304] Ch H, I, 2, Circular 91/75.
[305] Art 42(2), 2002 Act.
[306] See 3.23 above.
[307] Art 41(1)(g), 2002 Act.
[308] ibid.

The obligation that the underlying asset itself must be UCITS eligible applies to all derivatives, whether traded on a regulated market or over the counter.

3.314 The 2002 Act further specifies that there must be a link between the assets underlying derivatives and the investment objectives of the UCITS in question, as outlined in its constitutive documents.[309] A UCITS may not invest in derivatives to avoid compliance with, or change the investment objectives set out in, its constitutive documents or its prospectus.[310] For example, a UCITS that rules out direct or indirect investment in assets other than money market instruments may not invest in derivatives whose underlying assets reflect the performance of shares.

3.315 Difficulties may occur with derivatives based on a financial index made up of assests or of derivatives on assets that the UCITS is not authorized to hold directly, such as commodities. The same problem arises when the financial index on which a derivative is based consists of a representative basket of UCIs with alternative strategies; such UCIs cannot be considered eligible assets.

3.316 Is a UCITS authorized to invest in such derivatives when the immediately underlying asset of the index is either an ineligible asset (for example commodities) or is eligible (for example a futures contract) but the asset in turn underlying the first underlying is an ineligible asset (for example a futures contract on commodities)? In other words, must the principle of transparency be applied at several levels in order to find out whether one is in compliance with Directive 85/611? It is assumed that the UCITS aims at synthetic replication of the financial index by banning the purchase and delivery of the assets underlying the index.

3.317 The 2002 Act does not appear to prohibit UCITS from stopping at the first level of underlying assets without taking further levels of underlying assets into account, since the index on which the derivative is based can be qualified as a financial index.

3.318 No provision in the 2002 Act requires the assets making up the financial index to be themselves eligible assets within the meaning of the 2002 Act. If Directive 2001/108 had wanted to impose such a condition, it would have been worded to refer explicitly not only to direct underlying assets but also to indirect underlying assets.

3.319 However, is true that Recital No 13 in the preamble to Directive 2001/108 specifies that 'transactions in derivatives may never be used to circumvent the rules and principles set out in this Directive'. It would nevertheless be wrong to use this point to support a restrictive interpretation. A recital in the preamble to a European directive does not in itself set a legal standard. Its purpose is to explain the reason for the obligations in the directive in order to facilitate their interpretation.

---

[309] ibid.
[310] ibid Art 42(2).

Recital No 13 in the preamble to Directive 2001/108 is intended to remind the **3.320** reader that application of provisions on derivatives must never allow UCITS to violate other rules in the Directive. For example, a UCITS may not use derivatives resulting in the delivery of ineligible assets such as commodities when a futures contract is settled.

If UCITS could not expose themselves indirectly to ineligible assets such as com- **3.321** modities, this reasoning would also prohibit investment in the listed shares of companies in such sectors as energy, agriculture, etc. This type of reasoning would, further, make it impossible for UCITS to invest in listed companies whose object is to buy and manage buildings, based on the idea that the 2002 Act does not permit even indirect investment in real property.

Directive 2001/108 does not make transparency at successive levels an absolute **3.322** principle. The only thing that matters is that the index is in itself eligible as a finan- cial index, independently of the content of the assets underlying the components of the index.

This reasoning is strengthened by the principle, set out in the Directive, that a **3.323** UCITS which invests in derivatives based on an index is exempt from the obliga- tion to apply the principle of transparency, within the framework of risk-spreading rules.[311] Transparency is also ignored where the underlying assets are units in UCITS or other eligible UCIs.[312] Why should one subject the eligibility of assets underlying the index to the principle of transparency when not required to do so by the Directive?

The matter has been further clarified by the Eligible Assets Directive, which has **3.324** imposed the additional criteria for determining the eligibility of financial deriva- tive instruments:[313]

(1) the transfer of the credit risk of an asset independently from the other risks associated with that asset is permitted;
(2) the financial derivative instruments must not result in the delivery or transfer of assets other than those eligible for UCITS, including in the form of cash;
(3) the risks of the financial derivative instruments must be adequately captured by the risk management process of the UCITS, and by its internal control mechanisms in the event of a disparity in information available to the UCITS and the counterparty to the credit derivative as a result of the potential access by the counterparty to non-public information on firms in respect of which credit derivatives are issued.

---

[311] ibid Art 42(3), paragraph 3.
[312] See 3.340 below.
[313] Art 8, Eligible Assets Directive.

Counterparties

3.325 A transaction involving over-the-counter derivatives exposes a UCITS to a counterparty risk insofar as the contracting party may not be able to honour its obligations vis-à-vis the fund.[314] This is why Directive 2001/108 requires counterparties to this type of transaction to comply with certain quality criteria. Only transactions entered into with financial institutions subject to prudential supervision are authorized in order to limit counterparty risk. In addition the counterparty must belong to one of the categories authorized by the CSSF in this respect.[315] Such categories have not been further defined by the CSSF but one may argue that all investment firms as defined by Directive (EC) 2004/39, whether established in Luxembourg or in any Member State of the EEA, are entitled to be considered as approved counterparties by the CSSF. With respect to counterparties established outside the EEA, the CSSF must therefore determine whether the prudential control over foreign institutions can be considered sufficient. This may be the case, for example, where the counterparty is subject to consolidated supervision by the mother company or parent company situated within the EEA. The CSSF has also confirmed the necessity for the counterparty to be a financial institution specializing in these types of activities.

3.326 This condition with respect to the status of the counterparty applies only to derivatives traded on over-the-counter markets. On regulated markets, the counterparty risk is addressed by specific protection measures, reducing the importance of a counterparty's quality.[316]

Valuation and liquidity

3.327 Over-the-counter derivatives must be valued on a daily basis according to a reliable and verifiable method. Moreover, a UCITS must at all times be able to sell, settle or close derivatives at fair value by means of an offsetting transaction.[317]

3.328 This condition applies only to derivatives traded over the counter. In principle, the operating rules of regulated markets adequately guarantee the reliability of valuations and liquidity in derivatives at all times.

3.329 The legislature's concern with valuation and liquidity is easy to understand. Derivatives allow UCITS to contract considerable commitments which must be capable of accurate measurement. It is vital to ensure that positions can at all times be valued correctly. Moreover, UCITS must be able to settle their positions on a daily basis, for example when expecting a downturn of the financial markets on

---

[314] For a definition of counterparty risk, see 3.363 below.
[315] Art 41(1)(g), 2002 Act.
[316] See 3.364 below.
[317] Art 41(1)(g), 2002 Act.

which their derivatives are positioned. They must be able to do so by selling their holdings or by liquidating or closing their positions by means of offsetting transactions.[318] The Eligible Assets Directive and the Eligible Assets Guidelines have clarified these issues.

The term 'Fair Value' is defined (as per the International Accounting Standards **3.330** definition) as 'the amount for which an asset could be exchanged or a liability settled between knowledgeable, willing parties in an arm's length transaction'.[319] A 'reliable and verifiable valuation' shall mean a valuation by the UCITS corresponding to the fair value which does not only rely on market quotations by the counterparty and which fulfils the following criteria:

(1) The basis for the valuation is either a reliable up-to-date market value of the instrument, or, if such a value is not available, a pricing model using an adequate recognized methodology.
(2) The verification of the valuation is carried out by one of the following:

  (a) an appropriate third party independent of the counterparty to the OTC financial derivative instrument, at an adequate frequency and in such a way that the UCITS is able to check the verification;
  (b) a department within the UCITS which is independent from the department in charge of managing the assets and which is adequately equipped for such purpose.[320]

According to Circular 07/308,[321] the reference to reliable and verifiable valuation **3.331** is interpreted as a valuation by the UCITS, which corresponds to the fair value, which is not based solely on market prices supplied by the counterparty, and which complies with the following criteria:

(1) The valuation is based on a current market value, which was established in a reliable manner for the instrument, or, if no such value is available, on a valuation model using an appropriate and recognized methodology.
(2) The verification of the valuation shall be effected by one of the following entities:

  (a) an appropriate third party, independent of the counterparty to the OTC derivative instrument, which will verify the value at an appropriate frequency and pursuant to methods allowing the UCITS to check the verification; or
  (b) a department of the UCITS which is independent of the department overseeing asset management and which is appropriately equipped for this purpose.

---

[318] ibid.
[319] Art 8(3), Eligible Assets Directive.
[320] ibid Art 8(4).
[321] Section IV.2, Circular 07/308.

3.332   Circular 07/308 further mentions that the UCITS may, if applicable, use valuation tools, such as data, provided by a third party subject to satisfying itself that they are appropriate prior to using them in the valuation process. Valuation models provided by a party linked to the UCITS (for example a dealing room through which the UCITS settles its derivative transactions) and which have not been reviewed by the UCITS, are not acceptable. Circular 07/308 finally provides that if it is not possible to value a particular product in this manner, a UCITS may not acquire the product, even if the investment policy expressly allows it. In principle, the CSSF may request that the valuation method for OTC derivative instruments be disclosed in the description of the risk management process to be submitted to the CSSF.

Limits and utilization conditions

Transparency of underlying assets

3.333   **Principle**   A UCITS may invest in derivatives provided the risks to which the underlying assets are exposed do not exceed the limits imposed by the 2002 Act on UCITS with respect to direct investment by UCITS in such assets.[322] In other words, when a coordinated UCITS invests directly in a financial asset and exposes itself indirectly to the same asset through a derivative, both the direct position and the indirect exposure on the asset must be taken into account when determining whether the UCITS complies with the investment limits applicable to such asset. This rule is demonstrated by the following example.

3.334   A UCITS directly holds ABC shares, accounting for 4 per cent of its assets. It also buys a futures contract under which it agrees to buy ABC shares at a price representing 7 per cent of its assets. Under the 2002 Act, a UCITS may not invest more than 10 per cent of its assets in transferable securities issued by the same entity.[323] In our example, the UCITS will have breached the investment restriction of 10 per cent per issuer when entering into the futures contract.

Exceptions

3.335   *Exception for index-based derivatives*   When a UCITS invests in derivatives based on an index, the underlyings thereof are not taken into account in calculating the investment restrictions applicable to the underlying assets.[324] This rule is illustrated by the following example.

3.336   A UCITS directly holds ABC shares, which represent 10 per cent of its assets. The UCITS buys a futures contract on the CAC 40 index (the ABC stock is

---

[322]   Art 42(3), 2002 Act.
[323]   ibid Art 43(1).
[324]   ibid Art 42(3), paragraph 3.

part of this index). The indirect risk incurred by the UCITS on the ABC stock through the futures contract is not taken into consideration in calculating the ratio of 10 per cent per issuer referred to above.

This exception also applies when the purpose of the UCITS is to replicate the composition of a stock or bond index.[325]   **3.337**

Exception for over-the-counter derivatives   Pursuant to the 2002 Act, the total   **3.338** exposure to transferable securities held by a UCITS in issuers in each of which it invests more than 5 per cent of its assets may not exceed 40 per cent of the value of its assets.[326] In applying the principle of transparency to underlying assets, this limit is not exceeded when additional exposure is obtained to the same issuer through over-the-counter derivative transactions. This can also be demonstrated by the following example.[327]

A UCITS directly owns five holdings, each of which accounts for 8 per cent of its   **3.339** assets. One of these holdings is the ABC stock. The UCITS buys a swap under which it agrees to buy an amount of ABC shares representing 2 per cent of its assets. The risk generated for the UCITS by the ABC stock under this contract will not be taken into account in calculating the 5/40 per cent ratio.

Exception for derivatives based on an underlying asset other than a transferable   **3.340** *security or a money market instrument*   The principle of transparency in connection with the assets underlying derivatives applies only when such assets are transferable securities or money market instruments. For example, when the underlying assets are represented by units in UCITS or other eligible UCIs, the fund is not required to add together its direct positions and its indirect positions through derivatives.[328]

Embedded derivatives   Embedded derivatives are derivatives contained in   **3.341** composite transferable securities or money market instruments. Pursuant to Directive 2001/108, the 2002 Act includes a new provision by virtue of which, when a transferable security or a money market instrument contains a derivative, the derivative must be taken into account for the purpose of applying each of the restrictions described above. This makes it easier to assess the market and counterparty risks connected with the derivative. The asset underlying the derivative is factored into the risk-spreading ratios.[329]

---

[325] In the meaning of ibid Art 44(1).
[326] ibid Art 43(2).
[327] ibid.
[328] According to the transparency rule set out in Art 42(3) of the 2002 Act, the risks to which underlying assets are exposed may not exceed the investment limits stipulated in Art 43 of the 2002 Act. Art 43 does not set investment restrictions on investments in units in UCITS, which can be found in Art 46 of the 2002 Act.
[329] ibid Art 42(3), paragraph 4.

3.342   In view of this, the 2002 Act does not provide a precise definition or an exhaustive list of embedded derivatives. However, the Eligible Assets Directive and the Eligible Assets Guidelines[330] have provided some clarifications in this respect.

3.343   *A new category*   The category of embedded derivatives within the meaning of the 2002 Act is unlikely to be very generic. While most structured products combine transferable securities or money market instruments with derivatives, these products cannot all be considered to be embedded derivatives in the meaning of the 2002 Act.

3.344   Pursuant to the Eligible Assets Directive, securities which are backed by or linked to the performance of other assets (often referred to as 'structured financial instruments') constitute transferable securities if they comply with the criteria set out under chapter I above. Whether the assets backing the security are themselves eligible for a coordinated UCITS is not relevant for this purpose. This approach is based on the consideration that Directive 85/611 does not require a 'look-through approach'.

3.345   However, if the linked asset is an embedded financial derivative instrument, the linked asset must be included in the calculation of the global risk exposure. But, not all forms of linkage to other assets necessarily embed a derivative element.

3.346   Pursuant to the Eligible Assets Directive, there is only an embedded derivative element if the linkage would constitute an embedded derivative element under the criteria developed for the identification of embedded financial derivative instruments as detailed below. This means that there should be an identifiable host contract whose cash flows are modified by the linkage.

3.347   In consequence, transferable securities and money market instruments embedding a financial derivative instrument means transferable securities and money market instruments that contain a component which fulfils the following criteria:

- by virtue of that component, some or all of the cash flow that otherwise would be received by the transferable security/money market instrument which functions as the host contract can be modified according to a specified interest rate, financial instrument price, foreign exchange rate, index of prices or rates, credit rating or credit index, or other variable, and therefore vary in a way similar to a stand-alone derivative;

- its economic characteristics and risks are not closely related to the economic characteristics and risks of the host contract;

- the embedded element has a significant impact on the risk profile and pricing of the transferable security/money market instrument.[331]

---

[330]   Art 10, Eligible Assets Directive and item 23, Eligible Assets Guidelines.

[331]   Based on these criteria: (A) A collateralized debt obligation (CDO) should not be considered to embed a derivative within the meaning of the 2002 Act, particularly when it meets the following criteria: (a) active management of underlying assets provided their management (i) is implemented

A transferable security or a money market instrument shall not, pursuant to the **3.348** Eligible Assets Directive, be regarded as embedding a financial derivative instrument where it contains a component which is contractually transferable independently of the transferable security or money market instrument. Such a component will be deemed to be a separate financial instrument.

The Eligible Assets Guidelines provides a list of structured financial instruments **3.349** which could be assumed by UCITS to embed a financial derivative instrument:

- credit linked notes;[332]
- structured financial instruments whose performance is linked to the performance of a bond index;
- structured financial instruments whose performance is linked to the performance of a basket of shares, with or without active management;
- structured financial instruments with a nominal value fully guaranteed whose performance is linked to the performance of a basket of shares, with or without active management;
- convertible bonds; and
- exchangeable bonds.

In practice, the CSSF relies on the CESR's approach in determining whether **3.350** particular instruments could be assumed by a UCITS to embed a financial derivative instrument, unless the contrary is established through persuasive arguments.

Concept of global exposure

A coordinated UCITS must ensure that the global exposure linked to the deriva- **3.351** tives used by it does not exceed the total net value of its portfolio.[333] It is the wish of the European legislature, anxious to protect public savings, that UCITS should limit the risks to which they expose investors. This is the rationale behind the prohibition on UCITS borrowing for investment purposes or making uncovered sales of transferable securities and derivative instruments. The same concern explains the rationale behind investment in derivatives being subject to precise restrictions. These restrictions include the rule that the maximum loss a UCITS may suffer through investment in such instruments is the total net value of its portfolio.

---

by a professional, (ii) is intended to modify the portfolio according to market opportunities, and (iii) concerns diversified underlying assets, and/or (b) debt subordination; (B) euro medium-term notes whose underlying risk is spread and asset backed securities should not include derivatives in the meaning of the 2002 Act.

[332] Thus, a credit default swap (CDS) in the form of a credit linked note (CLN) embeds a derivative instrument. On the contrary, an asset backed security (ABS) structured with derivative contracts in order to hedge a currency risk does not embed a derivative instrument. The investor's main risk derives much more from the way the ABS is structured than from the derivative contracts.

[333] Art 42(3), 2002 Act.

Although not specified in Directive 2001/108, for the purpose of this limit, the concept of 'portfolio' includes liquid and all other assets held by the UCITS, in such a way that it can be considered equivalent to the net assets of the UCITS.[334]

3.352 By limiting the global exposure connected with derivatives to its net asset value, a UCITS cannot be exposed to a maximum loss that exceeds its entire assets and liabilities.

3.353 Surprisingly, the European legislature has said very little about the concept of global exposure, ie the limit on the use of derivatives. Its interpretation is a delicate task given the need for UCITS to preserve some room for manoeuvre in order to balance the two objectives of maximizing the gains from derivatives while ensuring adequate investor protection.

3.354 The CSSF, in Circular 07/308, has clearly confirmed that global exposure is restricted to market risk only, contrary to what was stated in the former CSSF Circular 05/176.[335] Global exposure therefore need not take account of counterparty risk as counterparty risk is already subject to specific limits imposed by the 2002 Act.

3.355 **Market risk** The market risk is 'the risk represented by the change in price or value of an instrument resulting in a loss for the operator'.[336] Pursuant to the 2002 Act, the market risk attached to a derivative is measured according to three criteria:[337]

(1) the current value of the underlying assets;
(2) the foreseeable market trend; and
(3) the time available to liquidate positions.

3.356 The meaning of 'current value of underlying assets' differs according to the derivatives concerned and also to whether the UCITS is regarded as 'sophisticated' or 'non-sophisticated'. Indeed, Circular 07/308, in Appendix 1, clearly distinguishes the calculation principles for the commitment to be taken into account in determining global exposure for non-sophisticated UCITS and the criteria that should be met when calculating global exposure through the value at risk method for sophisticated UCITS.

3.357 When using the commitment method for non-sophisticated UCITS the market risk reflects the market value of the underlying assets, adjusted by the option's delta for options on stocks and bonds and warrants.

---

[334] This interpretation was confirmed by Section 2.1 of Circular 05/176.
[335] CSSF Circular 05/176.
[336] de Vauplane and Bornet (n 300 above) No 357.
[337] Art 42(3), 2002 Act.

For index and bonds futures, the commitment is based on the market value of the contract or the underlying assets. **3.358**

For forward exchange contracts, interest rate swaps, and currency swaps, the commitment equals the principal of the contract. For credit default swaps, the commitment calculation differs depending on whether the UCITS is a protection buyer (in this case, the commitment equals the sum of the premiums to be paid during the entire life of the contract) or whether the UCITS is a protection seller (in this case, the commitment is the contract's notional value). The determination of the commmitmnent in the case of a total return swap is the contract notional value, irrespective of whether the UCITS is a protection buyer or seller. **3.359**

The amount of the resulting commitment may be increased or reduced by weighting the market risk according to two criteria. **3.360**

First, the foreseeable market trend needs to be taken into consideration. Application of this rule can help to lower the initial risk determined according to the previous criteria. Analysis of the volatility of a futures contract may lead to the conclusion that, even in a worst-case scenario, the contract value is unlikely to drop below a certain threshold. Conversely, application of the same rule may aggravate the risk, for example in the case of a call option without a hedge whose underlying asset increases in value over time. **3.361**

Next, the time available to liquidate the position needs to be measured. This may result in modification of the initial risk (which is in principle lowered) to the extent that the UCITS is able to settle its position before maturity. The capacity to liquidate a position in a liquid market on a daily basis normally reduces the maximum loss. **3.362**

Counterparty risk The counterparty risk, also known as the credit risk, is 'the risk that an operator does not honour an obligation to its counterparty'.[338] **3.363**

On regulated markets, the counterparty risk is in principle transferred to the clearing house.[339] On such markets, the final buyer and the final seller do not know each other. Both use the services of a commission agent.[340] The obligations of operators on such markets depend upon the type of derivative in which they trade. In the case of option contracts, a premium is paid as soon as the order is executed. In the case of futures, positions not settled during the same day are valued on a daily basis at the clearing price. The spread between two valuations results in a margin call (when the difference is negative) or a margin payment (when it is positive). Margins must be paid before the start of the next trading session. **3.364**

---

[338] de Vauplane and Bornet (n 300 above) Nos 357 and 712.
[339] ibid No 712, and Nejman (n 48 above) No 52.
[340] For the detailed legal rules governing such transactions, see de Vauplane and Bornet (n 300 above) Nos 590 *et seq.*

In other words, on regulated markets a UCITS counterparty exposure is to the clearing house and is limited to margin calls.[341]

3.365 In contrast, counterparty risk can be much higher on over-the-counter markets. The counterparty risk for an over-the-counter derivative is calculated by reference to the daily valuation of the instrument. This principle is illustrated by the following example.

3.366 Under a swap agreement, a UCITS agrees to swap the income generated by its bond portfolio for the notional income generated by a composite stock index. After offsetting the two sides of the contract, the balance may be positive or negative during the contract, depending on the market trend. If positive, the UCITS runs a credit risk vis-à-vis the counterparty, equal to the amount owed to it by its counterparty. In calculating the overall exposure, this risk must be added to the market risk.

3.367 The credit risk may be reduced by collateral in favour of the UCITS should the counterparty default. Collateral could take the form of a pledge or ownership transfer by way of guarantee. A margin deposit may also reduce the counterparty risk in the case of contracts settled by offsetting positions.

3.368 In transactions involving over-the-counter derivatives, the counterparty risk must not exceed a maximum of 10 per cent of a UCITS' assets when the counterparty is a credit institution. This threshold is lowered to 5 per cent of assets in all other cases.[342] Moreover, a credit institution counterparty must have its registered office in an EEA Member State. If its registered office is situated in a non-member country, the institution must be subject to prudential rules considered by the CSSF to be equivalent to those provided for by Community legislation.[343] Circular 07/308 clarifies that the calculation can be limited to over-the-counter derivatives (and need not to take into account derivatives executed on a market involving a clearing house meeting certain conditions).[344] This circular then describes the detailed rules for calculating the counterparty risk, followed by acceptable methods for mitigating the counterparty risk, including netting techniques and the effect of the UCITS receiving collateral.

3.369 Circular 07/308 specifies that counterparty risk incurred vis-à-vis an issuer or its group may not exceed a maximum of 20 per cent as stipulated by the 2002 Act.[345] Logically, this ceiling must be the cap applicable to the UCITS' aggregate investment in transferable securities or money market instruments, deposits, and risks

---

[341] ibid No 677.
[342] Art 43(1), 2002 Act.
[343] ibid Art 43(1) in combination with Article 41(1)(f).
[344] Section III.2, Circular 07/308.
[345] Art 43(2) and (5), 2002 Act.

connected with over-the-counter derivatives transactions. It cannot be limited to investment in over-the-counter derivatives only, since the laws and regulations do not expressly provide for this.[346]

Calculation of global exposure   The global exposure connected with derivatives   **3.370** is equal to market risk, and is separate from calculation of counterparty risk. While calculation of counterparty risk generally raises no particular difficulties, calculation of market risk can be a highly sophisticated exercise.

Reference to the current value of the underlying assets is the simplest method, ie   **3.371** a commitment approach whereby positions in financial instruments are converted into equivalent positions in underlying assets. The resulting commitment is at all times equal to the overall exposure incurred and the maximum authorized 'leverage'.

The advantage of this method is its easy application. Its drawback is that it ignores   **3.372** two risk weighting criteria, ie the foreseeable market trend and the time available to liquidate positions.

This was the rationale behind the development of sophisticated risk calculation   **3.373** models based on value at risk (VaR), which may be described as follows.

VaR models can be used to measure the risk of loss attached to a portfolio of finan-   **3.374** cial assets, ie the risk that the sales value of the portfolio decreases due to changing market factors (interest rates, exchange rates, stock prices, commodities prices) or due to instability of these factors according to portfolio sensitivity, volatility, and the correlations between these factors. VaR measures the potential loss when directly linked to the probability of changes in the simulated risk factors.[347]

In VaR models, the risk is defined as the maximum potential loss on a particular   **3.375** date for a particular level of confidence. For example, the probability that a portfolio with a VaR of €1 million per day whose estimated confidence level is 99 per cent will lose more than €1 million the following day is only 1 per cent.[348]

VaR therefore measures the maximum potential loss during a given period of   **3.376** ownership, with a predetermined probability that the real loss may be higher. As VaR does not take account of losses caused by abnormal market situations, its estimation must be conducted through stress testing of worst-case scenarios

---

[346] The increase in the investment threshold to 20% for investment in securities issued by a single group only applies to transferable securities, money market instruments, and deposits, not to derivatives. See Circular 107/308, 13.

[347] Working paper of the European Parliament, Economic Affairs Series ECON 118 FR, 'The Functioning and Supervision of International Financial Institutions', collective work, Vol 1, (February 2001) 58.

[348] S Das, *Swaps/Financial Derivatives—Products, Pricing, Applications and Risk Management*, Vol 2 (Wiley Finance, 3rd edn, 2003) 59.

reflecting risk factors influencing the portfolio in question. These tests measure the effect on the portfolio composition of extreme market movements not reflected in the reference scenario.[349]

3.377 For example, stress tests could use 19 October 1987 (the date on which the S&P 500 index fell by 22.3 standard deviations) or another, less extreme reference date, to measure the impact of an extreme movement on the price of US stocks.[350]

3.378 Regardless of the method used to calculate VaR, it must be subjected to back testing. Back testing shows the reliability and accuracy of past VaR estimates. It is used to determine the number of days during the reference period on which portfolio losses exceeded the corresponding VaR measurement.

3.379 These methods generally lower the leverage obtained by using the commitment method, since they take account of a whole series of market risk weighting factors that are simply ignored by the commitment method.

3.380 The overall exposure run by a UCITS does not just depend upon positions taken by investment in derivatives. It is also likely to be influenced by other portfolio elements and related management techniques (such as securities lending and repurchase and reverse repurchase agreements). The UCITS must use a risk management method whose sophistication depends upon the nature of the assets and the extent to which it uses derivatives. This method is described below.[351]

Prudential lines of conduct

3.381 Although Directive 2001/108 lays down principles allowing a coordinated UCITS to use derivatives, it does not set precise limits on their use. For instance, it does not specify in detail how the global exposure limit for derivatives must be determined. It does not stipulate the maximum leverage allowed for derivatives. Similarly, the text does not clearly define the method required to calculate the counterparty risk on derivatives. While a UCITS may not take short positions in derivatives, the Directive does not clarify the concept of uncovered sales. The 2002 Act, which accurately replicates Directive 2001/108, does not shed additional light on this issue due to the absence of concrete guidance by the EU authorities.

---

[349] P Embrechts and H Furrer, 'VaR, stress testing and related risk management techniques for hedging funds' in *The new generation of risk management for hedge funds and private equity investments* (Institutional Investor Books, 2003) and the references mentioned therein, 408.

[350] JC Hull, *Options, Futures and Other Derivatives* (Prentice Hall, 5th edn, 2002) 360.

[351] See 3.443 below.

This situation prompted the Commission of the European Communities to **3.382** issue a recommendation regarding the use of financial derivative instruments by coordinated UCITS.[352]

Based on this text, the CSSF issued in 2005 a circular outlining the practice to be **3.383** adopted by coordinated UCITS when using derivatives.[353] The content of Circular 05/176 is almost the same as the text of the recommendation issued by the European Commission, differing only in certain details. As its title suggests, it outlined a code of conduct from which the CSSF may permit deviation in individual cases according to the specific characteristics of the UCITS in question.

Circular 05/176 was replaced on 2 August 2007 by Circular 07/308, which **3.384** provides UCITS with rules of conduct to be followed for the implementation of their risk-management process. Circular 07/308 is limited to financial risks directly covered by the 2002 Act, namely the global exposure, the counterparty risk, and the concentration risk.

The content of Circular 07/308 will be examined below. It specifies seven basic **3.385** aspects, discussed in the following seven paragraphs.

Risk measurement system   Here, Circular 07/308 merely repeats the principle **3.386** already laid down in the 2002 Act,[354] ie that UCITS must use risk-measurement systems geared to their risk profile in order to ensure accurate measurement of all significant risks. This is essential to protect investors. A UCITS must apply adequate risk measurement procedures allowing it at all times to monitor, measure, and manage the risks connected with each position and their contribution to the portfolio's global risk profile.

Risk limitation rules   First of all, Circular 07/308 notes that, under the **3.387** 2002 Act,[355] UCITS must make sure the global exposure connected with derivatives does not exceed the total net value of their portfolio. More precisely, the global exposure may not exceed 100 per cent of the UCITS' net asset value. In other words, the total exposure assumed by a UCITS may not exceed 200 per cent of the net asset value.[356]

---

[352] Commission Recommendation of 27 April 2004 on the use of derivative financial instruments for undertakings for collective investment in transferable securities (UCITS), (EC) 2004/383 [2004] OJ L144/34.

[353] Circular 05/176.

[354] Art 42(1), 2002 Act.

[355] ibid Art 42(3).

[356] Section III.1.2.2, Circular 07/308. When a derivative provides adequate coverage for another commitment of the UCITS, the derivative is not taken into account in calculating global exposure limits. The principle of *netting* is authorized for both the commitment method and the VaR approach.

3.388 Next, the global exposure may not be increased by more than 10 per cent by means of temporary borrowings, ie the total exposure may never exceed 210 per cent of the net asset value.[357]

3.389 **Measurement of market risk** Market risk measurement methods must be geared to the risk profile of the UCITS in question. Circular 07/308 distinguishes between 'non-sophisticated' UCITS and 'sophisticated' UCITS. According to Circular 07/308, a UCITS is considered 'non-sophisticated when it uses derivative instruments to a limited extent or acquires less complex positions in derivative instruments or financial derivative instruments solely for hedging purposes'.[358]

3.390 On the other hand, Circular 07/308 defines[359] a sophisticated UCITS as a UCITS making extensive use of financial derivative instruments and/or making use of more complex strategies or instruments.

3.391 For non-sophisticated UCITS, market risk must be measured according to the commitment approach, whereby the derivative positions of a UCITS are converted into equivalent positions in the underlying assets, on the understanding that buy and sell positions on the same underlying asset may be offset.[360]

3.392 Certain other factors must also be taken into consideration, particularly the global exposure assumed by the UCITS due to the use of derivatives, the nature, aim, number, and frequency of the contracts entered into by the UCITS and the management techniques adopted by it.[361]

3.393 In the case of options, a UCITS should use the market value of the underlying asset, adjusted by the delta approach, based on sensitivity of a change in the option price to marginal changes in the price of the underlying financial instruments.

3.394 The conversion of forwards, futures, and swap positions should in principle depend upon the precise nature of the underlying contracts. In most cases, the market value of the underlying contract or the notional, depending upon the nature of the contract, will provide an appropriate basis for calculation.

3.395 In the case of sophisticated UCITS, a value at risk (VaR) approach must be applied on a regular basis.[362] In this type of approach, the maximum potential loss a UCITS portfolio could suffer is estimated within a given time horizon and confidence level. The UCITS must use stress tests to facilitate management of the risks connected with possible abnormal market movements. In addition, the

---

[357] Section III, Circular 07/308.
[358] ibid Section III.1.1.
[359] ibid.
[360] ibid Section III.1.2.2. The netting principle is accepted regardless of the maturities of the underlying assets.
[361] ibid.
[362] See 3.373 above.

following parameters should be used: a 99 per cent unilateral confidence interval; a holding period equivalent to one month (20 days); an effective observation period (history) of risk factors of at least one year (250 days), unless a shorter observation period is justified by a significant increase in price volatility; a quarterly data update; and a daily calculation in principle.[363]

Circular 07/308 further distinguishes between the use of of a 'relative VaR limitation' which may not exceed two times the VaR of a reference portfolio of the same market value as the UCITS. This circular describes how the relevant reference portfolio must be determined by the UCITS. With respect to sophisticated UCITS which are unable or for which it is not appropriate to determine a reference portfolio (such as an 'absolute return' type UCITS), an absolute VaR on all of the portfolios' positions must be determined and the maximum VaR may not exceed a threshold of 20 per cent.[364] **3.396**

Circular 07/308 also allows a UCITS to use an internal risk measurement model. Such models must be subject to appropriate safeguards and prior approval by the CSSF and be in compliance with the criteria set out in Appendix 2 of Circular 07/308.[365] **3.397**

Measurement of leverage The concept of leverage is not defined in Directive 2001/108 or the 2002 Act, nor does Circular 07/308 provide a definition.[366] **3.398**

Circular 07/308 recommends the commitment method to measure the leverage effect of non-sophisticated UCITS. **3.399**

In the case of sophisticated UCITS, the leverage effect is calculated according to the VaR approach and the resulting stress tests.[367] **3.400**

Limitation and reduction of counterparty risk Circular 07/308 specifies that derivative transactions on a market with a clearing house are considered to be free from counterparty risk. However, the clearing house must meet the following three conditions: **3.401**

(1) it must be backed by an appropriate completion guarantee;
(2) it must mark derivative positions every day to the market; and
(3) it must make margin calls at least once a day.[368]

---

[363] Appendix 2, Circular 07/308.
[364] ibid Section III.1.3.2.
[365] ibid Section III.1.3.3.
[366] The leverage effect can be defined as the 'ratio between the potential gain (or loss) of a given product and the initial investment' (P Chabardes and F Delclaux, *Les produits dérivés* (Gualino Editeur, 1999) 150).
[367] As regards leverage for sophisticated UCITS, the text of Circular 07/308 refers to the beforementioned European recommendation. This recommendation requires the use of a comparison basis such as the *VaR/stress test* value of a benchmark portfolio reflecting the UCITS investment policy or the *VaR/stress test* value of another appropriate benchmark for a method based on VaR and stress tests, which is not required by the Circular.
[368] Section III.2, Circular 07/308.

3.402 In contrast, over-the-counter derivative transactions will generate a counterparty risk for UCITS. This counterparty risk may be reduced by using collateral subject to certain conditions.[369] This risk must be measured according to the maximum potential loss which would be incurred by the UCITS if the counterparty defaulted, not on the basis of the notional value of the over-the-counter contract.[370]

3.403 The counterparty risk connected with over-the-counter instruments must be determined according to the method laid down in Circular 07/308.[371] Subject to appropriate justification, the CSSF allows UCITS to use an alternative method.

3.404 Circular 07/308 also allows UCITS to receive collateral to reduce their counterparty risk. Such collateral must meet the following criteria:

(1) it must be valued at market price at a calculation frequency that is at least equal to the frequency at which the net asset value of the UCITS in question is calculated;

(2) it must present limited risks, be adequately diversified, liquid and not present a significant, positive correlation with the counterparty's credit status;

(3) it must consist of cash deposits and financial instruments equivalent to cash, debt instruments with an external credit rating at least equivalent to 'investment grade' and shares and convertible bonds which are comprised in a main index;

(4) it must be held by a third party custodian not related to the provider or be legally secured from the consequences of default by a related party; and

(5) the UCITS must at all times be able to enforce the collateral in full.

3.405 A UCITS may reduce its counterparty risk to the extent of its collateral, provided the value of such collateral, valued at market price and subjected to adequate discounts, exceeds the value of the amount exposed to the risk.[372]

---

[369] ibid Section III. 2.3.2(b).

[370] ibid Section III.2.3.

[371] Circular 07/308 merely transposes in this connection the method laid down in Directive (EC) 2000/12 of the European Parliament and of the Council of 20 March 2000 relating to the taking up and pursuit of the business of credit institutions [2000] OJ L126/1, without making any express reference to such Directive. This Directive, now replaced by Directive (EC) 2006/48, sets the following rules for estimating the risks connected with interest rate swaps, currency swaps, or other benchmark or index swaps. The mark-to-the-market approach applies in three stages: (1) it is first necessary to determine current market values for contracts (valuation at market price) in order to find the current replacement cost of all contracts with positive values; (2) then to obtain a figure for potential future credit exposure, the notional principal amounts or underlying values are multiplied by one of the percentages stipulated in Annexe III to Directive (EC) 2000/12, which differ according to the nature and residual maturity of the contract; and (3) the sum of the current replacement cost and the potential future credit exposure is multiplied by a weighting coefficient stipulated in Art 43 of the Directive, which varies according to the nature of the relevant counterparty.

[372] Section III.2.3.2(b), Circular 07/308.

Lastly, Circular 07/308 specifies that a UCITS may net its over-the-counter derivative positions vis-à-vis the same counterparty as long as the netting procedures comply with the conditions set out in Part 7 of Annex III of Directive (EC) 2006/48, and are based on legally binding agreements (like an ISDA Master Agreement).[373] This is one of the ways to mitigate counterparty risk, the other being providing financial collateral by way of a guarantee. **3.406**

Issuer risk concentration limits   Pursuant to Directive 85/611 and the 2002 Act, the risks to which the assets underlying the derivatives are exposed may not exceed the risk spreading limits laid down in the Directive and the 2002 Act.[374] The CSSF extends this limitation to units of UCIs and UCITS referred to in Article 46. This provision only affects, in principle, those financial derivative instruments whose underlying assets entail an issuer risk, namely those based on an ownership deed or debt security.[375] **3.407**

Circular 07/308 specifies that, in accordance with commitment method applicable to non-sophisticated UCITS, derivatives must be converted into equivalent positions on underlying assets for the purpose of determining issuer risk. The method used for this must be appropriate to the type of instrument concerned. In the case of options, it recommends the market value of the underlying asset, adjusted by the option's delta. In certain cases, when demanded by the complexity of the financial instrument, an alternative method may be used based on the maximum potential loss linked to the instrument in question. This loss is considered to be the maximum threshold assessment of the solvency risk.[376] **3.408**

The exception to this transparency rule is when the derivative is based on an index.[377] Circular 07/308 specifies the criteria that must be met by the index in question. It stipulates, *inter alia*, that the UCITS may not use derivatives based on a self-composed index with the intention of circumventing the concentration limits provided for in the 2002 Act.[378] Lastly, Circular 07/308 specifies that, for the application of the 20 per cent net asset value-limit at group level, the counterparty risk must be added to the issuer risk of the same entity or group.[379] **3.409**

Cover for derivatives transactions   According to the 2002 Act, coordinated UCITS are not authorized to take short positions in transferable securities, money market instruments, or derivatives.[380] **3.410**

---

[373] ibid Section III.2.3.2.
[374] Art 42(3), 2002 Act.
[375] Section III.2.3.2, Circular 07/308.
[376] ibid Appendix 1.
[377] Art 42(3), 2002 Act; see also 3.335 above.
[378] Section III.3.2, Circular 07/308.
[379] ibid Section III.2.4.
[380] Art 52, 2002 Act.

3.411 Circular 07/308 adds several important points about the concept of coverage in connection with derivatives. First, Circular 07/308 allows a UCITS to enter into derivatives contracts which, automatically or at the choice of the UCITS counterparty, provide for physical delivery of the underlying financial instrument at the maturity or strike date. However, physical delivery must be the ordinary practice in the case of the instrument in question. In such cases, the UCITS portfolio must contain the underlying financial instrument for cover purposes,[381] or if the UCITS deems that the underlying financial instrument is sufficiently liquid, it may hold other liquid assets (including liquidities) as coverage on the condition that these assets (after applying appropriate safeguards, ie discounts), held in sufficient quantities, may be liquidated at the time for delivery of the underlying financial instrument.

3.412 Lastly, a UCITS is not obliged to hold the particular underlying instrument for cover purposes when the derivative is settled in cash, whether automatically or at the discretion of the UCITS. In this case, the following assets provide acceptable coverage:

(1) cash;
(2) liquid debt securities (for example government bonds) subject to appropriate safeguard measures (particularly 'haircuts'); and
(3) other highly liquid assets the CSSF may accept in view of their correlation with the asset underlying the derivative, subject to the above-mentioned safeguard measures (investment grade debt instruments, shares comprised in a main index, etc).[382]

3.413 The definition of 'liquid' applies to instruments that can be converted into cash at very short notice at a price corresponding closely to the present value of the financial instrument on its market. It is up to the entity in charge of risk management to check regularly whether the coverage available to UCITS, either in the form of the underlying derivative instrument or in the form of liquid assets, is sufficient to meet future obligations.[383]

3.414 The CSSF leaves it up to the UCITS itself to determine the method by which it will determine the coverage level for contracts which are payable in cash.[384]

3.415 All financial instruments underlying derivatives must comply with Directive 2001/108 and conform to the investment policy of the UCITS concerned.[385]

---

[381] Section IV.1, Circular 07/308.
[382] ibid.
[383] ibid.
[384] ibid.
[385] ibid.

Portfolio management techniques

The 2002 Act allows coordinated UCITS to use techniques and instruments **3.416** related to transferable securities and money market instruments for 'efficient portfolio management'.[386] This includes the use of such portfolio management techniques as securities lending and repurchase and reverse repurchase agreements, and certain other techniques analysed in the following paragraphs. The Eligible Assets Directive provides that techniques and instruments relating to transferable securities and money market instruments should be economically appropriate (this implies that they are used in a cost-effective way), and entered into for one or more of the following specific aims:

- the reduction of risk,
- the reduction of cost, or
- the generation of additional capital or income for the UCITS with an appropriate level of risk which is consistent with the risk profile of the UCITS and the UCITS risk-diversification rules.

In addition, the risks must be adequately captured by the risk-management process of the UCITS.

On 4 June 2008, the CSSF released Circular 08/356,[387] which is of immediate **3.417** application. The techniques and instruments covered by Circular 08/356 are securities lending transactions, sales with right of repurchase transactions, and reverse repurchase transactions/repurchase transactions.

For all of these types of transactions, the counterparty must be subject to pruden- **3.418** tial supervision rules considered by the CSSF as equivalent to those provided by Community law.

Securities lending transactions

The UCITS may enter into securities lending transactions, provided that the **3.419** following conditions are complied with:

(1) The UCITS may lend the securities included in its portfolio to a borrower either directly or through a standardized lending system organized by a recognized clearing institution or through a lending system organized by a financial institution subject to prudential supervision rules considered by the CSSF as equivalent to those prescribed by Community law and specializing in these types of transactions.

---

[386] Art 42(2), 2002 Act.
[387] CSSF Circular 08/356 regarding rules applicable to UCIs which employ certain techniques and instruments relating to transferable securities and money market instruments.

(2) The UCITS must ensure that the volume of the securities lending transactions is kept at an appropriate level or that it is entitled to request the return of the securities lent in a manner that enables it, at all times, to meet its redemption obligations and that these transactions do not jeopardize the management of its assets in accordance with its investment policy.

(3) In its financial reports, the global valuation of the securities lent on the reference date for these reports must be disclosed.

Purchase with option to repurchase transactions (*achat à rémére*)

3.420 Acting as buyer, the UCITS may agree to purchase securities with a repurchase option. These transactions consist of the purchase of securities with a clause reserving for the seller (counterparty) the right to repurchase the securities sold from the UCITS at a price and time agreed between the two parties at the time when the contract is entered into.

3.421 Entering into purchase with option to repurchase transactions is subject to the following conditions:

(1) During the duration of the agreement, the UCITS may not sell the securities which are the subject of the agreement before the counterparty has exercised its option or until the deadline for the repurchase has expired, unless the UCITS has other means of coverage.

(2) The UCITS must maintain the value of the purchase with repurchase option transactions at a level such that it is able, at all times, to meet its redemption obligations towards its unitholders.

(3) The securities that may be the subject of purchase with a repurchase option transaction are limited to:
   (a) short-term bank certificates or money market instruments such as those defined within Directive (EC) 2007/16 of 19 March 2007 implementing Council Directive EEC 85/611 on the coordination of laws, regulations and administrative provisions relating to certain UCITS as regards the clarification of certain definitions;
   (b) bonds issued or guaranteed by a Member State of the OECD or by their local public authorities or by supranational institutions and undertakings with EU, regional or worldwide scope;
   (c) shares or units issued by money market UCIs calculating a daily net asset value and being assigned a rating of AAA or its equivalent;
   (d) bonds issued by non-governmental issuers offering an adequate liquidity;
   (e) shares quoted or negotiated on a regulated market of an EU Member State or on a stock exchange of a Member State of the OECD, on the condition that these shares are included in a main index.

(4) The securities purchased with a repurchase option must comply with the UCITS' investment policy and must, together with the other securities that the UCITS holds in its portfolio, globally comply with the UCITS' investment restrictions.

(5) In its financial report, the UCITS must provide separate information on the securities purchased with a repurchase option, disclosing the total amount of the open transactions on the date of reference of these reports.

Sale of securities with a repurchase option (*vente à réméré*)

Acting as the seller, the UCITS may agree to sell securities with a repurchase **3.422** option. These transactions consist of the sale of securities with a clause reserving for the UCITS the right to repurchase the securities from the purchaser (counterparty) at a price and at a time agreed between the two parties at the time when the contract is entered into.

Entering into sale with option to repurchase transactions is subject to the **3.423** following conditions:

(1) The UCITS must ensure that, at maturity of the repurchase option, it holds sufficient assets to be able to settle, if applicable, the amount agreed for the repurchase of the securities by the UCITS.

(2) In its financial report, the UCITS must provide separate information on securities sold with a repurchase option, disclosing the total amount of the open transactions on the date of reference of these reports.

Reverse repurchase agreement transactions (*opérations de prise en pension*)

The UCITS may enter into reverse repurchase agreement transactions, which **3.424** consist of a forward transaction at the maturity of which the seller (counterparty) has the obligation to repurchase the asset sold and the UCITS the obligation to return the asset received under the repurchase agreement.

Entering into reverse repurchase transactions is subject to the conditions set out **3.425** in point 2(b)(e) of Circular 08/356 for purchase with option to repurchase transactions.

Furthermore, the UCITS may, during the duration of the reverse repurchase **3.426** agreement, not sell or pledge/give as security the securities purchased under the contract, unless it has other means of coverage.

Repurchase agreement transactions (*opérations de mise en pension*)

The UCITS may enter into repurchase agreement transactions, which consist of **3.427** a forward transaction at the maturity of which the UCITS has the obligation to repurchase the asset sold and the buyer (the counterparty) the obligation to return the asset received under the transaction.

3.428 The entering into repurchase agreement transactions is subject to the conditions set out in point 3 (a) and (b) of Circular 08/356 for the sale of securities with a repurchase option. Furthermore, the UCITS must ensure that the volume of the repurchase agreement transactions is kept at a level such that it is able, at all times, to meet its redemption obligations towards unitholders/ shareholders.

Receipt of an appropriate guarantee/collateral

Common conditions to securities lending transactions, sale or purchase with option to repurchase transactions, and/or reverse repurchase/repurchase transactions

3.429 The risk exposure of the UCITS to a single counterparty arising from one or more securities lending transactions, sale or purchase with option to repurchase transactions, and/or reverse repurchase/repurchase transactions may not exceed 10 per cent of its assets when the counterparty is a credit institution referred to in Article 41(1)(f) of the 2002 Act or 5 per cent of its assets in other cases. The UCITS must value the collateral received on a daily basis.

3.430 The agreement concluded between the UCITS and the counterparty must include provisions to the effect that the counterparty must provide additional collateral at very short notice if the value of the collateral provided following valuation is insufficient to secure the amount to be covered. Furthermore, the agreement must, if appropriate, provide for safety margins that take into consideration exchange risks or market risks inherent to the assets accepted as collateral.

3.431 Collateral must normally take the form of:

(1) liquid assets (liquid assets include not only cash and short-term bank certificates, but also money market instruments as defined within the Eligible Assets Directive—a letter of credit or a guarantee on first-demand given by a first class credit institution not affiliated to the counterparty is considered as equivalent to liquid assets);

(2) bonds issued or guaranteed by a Member State of the OECD or by their local public authorities or by supranational institutions and undertakings with EU, regional, or worldwide scope;

(3) shares or units issued by money market UCIs calculating a daily net asset value and being assigned a rating of AAA or its equivalent;

(4) shares or units issued by UCITS investing mainly in bonds/shares mentioned in (5) and (6) below;

(5) bonds issued or guaranteed by first class issuers offering an adequate liquidity; or

(6) shares admitted to or dealt in on a regulated market of a Member State of the European Union or on a stock exchange of a Member State of the OECD, on the condition that these shares are included in a main index.

Collateral given in any form other than cash or shares/units of a UCI/UCITS must be issued by an entity not affiliated to the counterparty. **3.432**

In the case of cash collateral, which may expose the UCITS to a credit risk vis-à-vis a financial or credit institution, the UCITS must take the applicable limits on deposits to which it is subject into consideration. **3.433**

Cash collateral must not be held by the counterparty, unless it is legally protected in the event of default or insolvency of the counterparty. Collateral in a form other than cash must not be held by the counterparty, unless it is adequately segregated from the counterparty's own assets. **3.434**

The collateral must be readily available at all times, either directly or through the medium of a first class financial institution or a wholly-owned subsidiary of such an institution, in such a manner that the UCITS can appropriate or realize the assets provided as collateral, without delay, if the counterparty does not comply with its obligation to return the securities. **3.435**

The UCITS must ensure that its contractual rights relating to the relevant transactions will permit it, in the event of liquidation, reorganization, or in any other similar situation affecting the UCITS to discharge its obligations to return the assets received as collateral, if and to the extent that the restitution cannot be effected on the terms initially agreed. **3.436**

During the duration of the agreement, the collateral cannot be sold or given as a security, or pledged, except when the UCITS has other means of security. **3.437**

Specific conditions applicable to securities lending transactions

For each securities lending transaction, the UCITS must receive collateral not less in value during the lifetime of the lending agreement, than 90 per cent of the global valuation (interests, dividends, and other eventual rights included) of the securities lent. **3.438**

Reinvestment of cash provided as a guarantee

The UCITS may reinvest cash collateral subject to the following conditions: **3.439**

(1) The reinvestments may only be made in:
   (a) shares or units in money market UCIs calculating a daily net asset value and having a rating of AAA or its equivalent;
   (b) short-term bank deposits;

    (c) money market instruments as defined in the Eligible Asset Directive;

    (d) short-term bonds issued or guaranteed by a Member State of the European Union, Switzerland, Canada, Japan, or the United States, or by their local authorities, or by supranational institutions and undertakings with EU, regional, or worldwide scope;

    (e) bonds issued or guaranteed by first class issuers offering an adequate liquidity; and

    (f) reverse repurchase agreement transactions.

(2) Financial assets other than bank deposits and units or shares of UCIs acquired by means of reinvestment of cash received as collateral, must be issued by an entity not affiliated to the counterparty. Furthermore, financial assets other than bank deposits must not be retained for safekeeping by the counterparty, unless they are segregated in an appropriate manner from the counterparty's own assets.

(3) Bank deposits must in principle not be retained for safekeeping by the counterparty, unless they are legally protected in the event of default of the counterparty.

(4) The financial assets may not be pledged/given as a guarantee, except when the UCITS has sufficient liquid assets enabling it to return the guarantee by a cash payment.

(5) Short-term bank deposits, money market instruments, and bonds referred to in (b) to (d) above must be eligible investments within the meaning of Article 41(1) of the 2002 Act.

(6) The reinvestment of cash received as collateral is not subject to the diversification rules generally applicable to the UCITS, provided, however, that the UCITS must avoid an excessive concentration of its reinvestments, both at issuer level and at instrument level. Reinvestments in assets referred to in (a) and (e) above are exempt from this requirement.

(7) If the short-term bank deposits referred to in (b) above are likely to expose the UCITS to a credit risk vis-à-vis the institution with which the deposit is placed, the UCITS must take this into consideration for the purpose of the limits on deposits.

(8) The reinvestment must, in particular if it creates a leverage effect, be taken into account in the calculation of the UCITS' global exposure. Any reinvestment of cash collateral in financial assets providing a return in excess of the risk free rate, is subject to this requirement.

(9) Reinvestments must be specifically mentioned with their respective value in an appendix to the financial reports of the UCITS.

Other portfolio management techniques

Use of a subsidiary

3.440 A coordinated UCITS may use a subsidiary for investment purposes as a portfolio management technique. Such a subsidiary may indirectly give the parent UCITS the benefit of a network of treaties against double taxation which it would not have been able to claim without such a subsidiary. Viewed in this light, the search for the most attractive tax regime in the exclusive interest of the investors is a portfolio management technique within the meaning of the 2002 Act.

The rules and conditions governing the use of subsidiaries by coordinated UCITS **3.441** are discussed in a separate paragraph in this work, to which the reader is referred.[388]

Asset pooling and other income balancing techniques

In the same way as for use of subsidiaries, pooling assets between the sub-funds of **3.442** a particular UCITS with multiple sub-funds and other techniques to balance income between sub-funds are also portfolio management techniques authorized under the 2002 Act.

Use of risk-management methods

The 2002 Act requires every coordinated UCITS to use a risk-management **3.443** method allowing it at all times to check and measure the exposure generated by its positions and their contribution to the general risk profile of the portfolio.[389] This risk-management method is not restricted to derivatives but applies to all portfolio securities.

Similarly, a UCITS must use a method permitting accurate and independent **3.444** valuation of over-the-counter derivatives.[390]

A UCITS must regularly inform the CSSF of the types of derivatives, underlying **3.445** risks, quantitative limits, and methods chosen to estimate the risks connected with derivative transactions.[391] Section V of Circular 07/308, headed 'Information to be provided to the Commission',[392] describes the information which must be submitted to the CSSF, including the following principal obligations:

• the drawing up and providing of clear and precise documentation with respect to the risk-management process at the time of set-up of the UCITS in line with the requirements of the circular; and

• the drawing up and providing of updated documentation and information each time a change to the UCITS or the launch of a new sub-fund would entail changes to the risk-management process previously used.

---

[388] See 3.164 *et seq* above.
[389] Art 42(1), of the 2002 Act.
[390] ibid.
[391] ibid.
[392] This section then describes, in six sub-sections, the information which the description of the risk-management process must comprise.

Aspects of lege ferenda

3.446 The use of derivatives and portfolio management techniques by coordinated UCITS is a constantly evolving subject. Neither Directive 2001/108 nor the 2002 Act clearly describe all the rules in this area. The Commission recommendation of 27 April 2004, culminating in Circular 07/308, provided 'guidelines' (*sic*) which were not binding in any way. However, the Eligible Assets Directive and the Eligible Assets Guidelines now detail the conditions under which derivatives and portfolio management techniques may be used.

3.447 The clarifications brought by these documents on eligible assets are welcome and Member States will now benefit from a consolidated regulatory and legal framework applying harmonized rules in respect of investments of UCITS.

3.448 UCITS offer investment opportunities in such asset types as listed closed-end real estate, hedge, and commodities funds which are already allowed in Luxembourg, provided that they comply with the criteria prescribed for transferable securities and notwithstanding the fact that the underlying assets are not necessarily eligible assets. Investment in open-end regulated hedge funds, real estate funds, and private equity funds is also permissible under the 10 per cent trash ratio. The UCITS Directive has also brought flexibility in terms of, for example, the newly permitted extended use of financial derivative instruments allowing the implementation of new investment strategies for UCITS, thereby continually responding to the growing needs of funds' promoters

4

ESTABLISHMENT OF UNDERTAKINGS FOR COLLECTIVE INVESTMENT

The Role of the Promoter

Definition

Luxembourg-based UCIs must always have a promoter. This principle is never-theless subject to a major exception under the framework for SIFs,[1] whereby such funds can be established in the Grand Duchy of Luxembourg without the need for a promoter as described in this chapter. This exception also applies to SICARs. **4.01**

---

[1] *Parliamentary doc* No 5616.

That said, the promoter's role is not described in any law or regulation. The 2002 Act does not give a definition, nor do the Parliamentary documents provide an explanation.

4.02 The concept of promoter is used in Circular 91/75. The provision dealing with the filing requirements in connection with a UCI's authorization application specifies that information should be provided with respect to 'promoter(s)', including recent financial statements of the promoter.[2]

4.03 The concept of promoter is therefore exclusively based on the administrative practices of the CSSF, which has gradually defined and developed it. According to the CSSF, the promoter is defined as 'anyone who establishes a UCI, who is the driving force behind or triggers the establishment of a UCI, who determines its business profile and who benefits from its results'.[3]

4.04 Because of the promoter's decisive involvement in the launch and management of UCIs, the CSSF holds it liable for any damage to third parties resulting from deficiencies in the management or administration of a UCI. In view of its role, the CSSF regards the promoter as a 'conducting person' within the meaning of the 2002 Act.[4]

4.05 The CSSF's interpretation is less justifiable for UCITS governed by Part I of the 2002 Act, which are now subject to strict capitalization, substance, and management quality requirements. There seems to be less need than in the past to appoint a responsible promoter to assist the conducting persons. It is possible that the CSSF may therefore review its position with respect to promoters of UCITS governed by Part I of the 2002 Act.

4.06 Pursuant to the 2002 Act,[5] the 'financial group (e.g. bank) promoting the UCITS' must be referred to in the simplified prospectus to be issued by UCITS governed by Part I. This requirement of the 2002 Act flows directly from Directive 2001/107 and should be interpreted in the context that EU Member States tend to consider the promoter as the distributing entity. For example, in France the term 'promoter' has been replaced by 'marketer', defined as the 'institution which takes the initiative to market the UCITS'.[6]

---

[2] Ch K(e), Circular 91/75.

[3] CSSF memorandum on the selective approach to UCI promoters. This is the memorandum in which the CSSF explains its interpretation of the concept of promoter as described in the present chapter.

[4] According to Art 93(3), 2002 Act, the conducting persons (*dirigeants*) of a UCI are the persons who represent the UCI or the depositary or who effectively determine the policy of the UCI.

[5] Annex I, Sch C, 2002 Act.

[6] Art 10 of the *Instruction de l'Autorité des Marchés Financiers*, No 2005-02 of 25 January 2005 with regard to the complete prospectus of UCITS authorized by the AMF. This document is available on the website of the Autorité des Marchés Financiers <http://www.amf-france.org>.

Authorization conditions

According to the CSSF, the legislature intended to subject a UCI's authorization **4.07** to a series of prerequisites, including the qualifications and reputation of its conducting persons. Those requirements reflect the desire to avoid loss to investors who entrust investment managers with their assets and to protect the reputation and credibility of the financial market of the Grand Duchy of Luxembourg.[7]

Accordingly, the CSSF will refuse to authorize a new UCI governed by the 2002 **4.08** Act if it is not convinced that its promoters and other service providers involved in its administration, management, and auditing have the professional reputation and experience required for the performance of their duties.[8] This CSSF requirement does not apply to the promoter of a SIF or a SICAR.

The promoter of a UCI regulated under the 2002 Act must, moreover, have suf- **4.09** ficient financial resources to cover claims for damages resulting from managerial and administrative faults, negligence, irregularities, or shortcomings. The purpose of this rule is to ensure that the liability of a UCI's conducting persons is not just theoretical or illusory.[9]

Legal basis for the liability of the promoter of a UCI governed by the 2002 Act

According to the CSSF, the promoter's role is, *inter alia*, to make good all dam- **4.10** age caused by managerial and administrative faults, negligence, irregularities, or shortcomings in the management and administration of the UCITS.[10] However, this liability is not rooted in any specific law or regulation. Hence, the promoter's liability appears to be more of a professional rule of conduct than a legal obligation. Only general legal provisions apply. Thus, a promoter may be held liable for its own acts and omissions in managing, administering, or distributing a UCI. However, it may also have to assume liability for those for whom it has agreed to be responsible. Moreover, in its capacity as an employer, it may be held liable for the acts and omissions of any of the UCI's conducting persons employed by it.

The promoter's liability does not mean that the promoter alone bears the cost of **4.11** compensating the investors or other third parties. It may in turn take action against those who caused the damage or helped to bring it about.

---

[7] CSSF memorandum on the selective approach to UCI promoters. See also Circular 02/77.
[8] ibid.
[9] ibid.
[10] ibid.

Practical applications

4.12 The CSSF generally wishes to see the name of the promoter(s) of a UCI other than a SIF included in the UCI's prospectus. Alternatively, it may require a commitment letter in which the promoter acknowledges its responsibilities and undertakes to compensate investors in the above-mentioned circumstances.

4.13 Because of the key role of the promoter, as a matter of practice the CSSF requires it, in principle, to be willing to provide most of the board members of the management company or the investment company. However, this requirement sometimes raises practical problems. For example Anglo-Saxon UCI promoters frequently wish to appoint a majority of independent directors in order to give investors additional reassurance that the UCI or its management company will always act in their exclusive interest. The CSSF recognizes this particular need and consequently allows the majority of board directors to be selected from outside the promoter's group. In that case, it nevertheless informs the promoter that this does not in any way reduce its potential liability.[11]

4.14 The nomination of directors by the promoter is liable to generate conflicts of interest as the promoter also typically provides the UCI with other services, such as investment management or head office functions. In this case, it is advisable to implement measures designed to prevent such conflicts.

4.15 Lastly, a UCI falling under the 2002 Act must at all times be supported by a promoter authorized by the CSSF, which will not allow a promoter to resign or to be replaced by an unauthorized promoter.

Co-promotion of UCIs

4.16 In some cases, the promoter does not have the financial resources required by the CSSF. In that event, the authorization requirements will differ according to whether or not the promoter plays an active management role in the UCI.[12]

4.17 If it plays an active management role, the promoter must be backed by a third party who has adequate financial resources. This third party must have the funds necessary to cover potential damages.

4.18 If the promoter is not involved in management, the UCI's management and administration must be delegated to managers and other qualified service providers. In that event, the criterion of adequate financial resources will apply to the service providers. The fact that this criterion applies to the service providers

---

[11] CSSF memorandum on the composition of management bodies of a Luxembourg UCI.
[12] CSSF memorandum on the selective approach to UCI promoters.

must, moreover, be set out clearly in the agreements signed with each service provider.[13]

Constitutive Documents and Sales Literature

Arrangement of constitutive documents and sales literature

Constitutive documents

Contractual UCIs

Management regulations

In the Grand Duchy of Luxembourg, a contractual UCI takes the form of an FCP. **4.19** An FCP's constitutive document, known as the 'management regulations', sets out the fund's operating rules and the relationship between the management company and the unitholders. By law,[14] the unitholders are deemed to accept the provisions of the management regulations through the acquisition of units in the FCP. The management company alone has the power to draw up the management regulations of an FCP.[15] It acts as the legal representative of the body of unitholders.[16]

In practice, management regulations are frequently counter-signed by an FCP's **4.20** depositary. They may further stipulate that they may not be amended without the depositary's prior consent. This provision is not imposed by the 2002 Act. However, the reason for its inclusion is obvious. In performing its duties of monitoring and verifying the fund's assets, the depositary must certify that the FCP's transactions comply with the management regulations. It must therefore have taken official cognisance of that document before it came into force and must have checked whether its contents comply with the law. While it may attest to this in a separate instrument, the depositary's agreement is frequently reflected in counter-signature of the regulations.

Contents of management regulations

The minimum contents of the management regulations are laid down in law, **4.21** which requires them to contain at least the information described below.[17] When an FCP has several sub-funds, the kind of information to be supplied for each sub-fund varies according to its objectives.

---

[13] ibid.
[14] Arts 13(1) and 66, 2002 Act; Art 12(1), Act of 13 February 2007.
[15] ibid.
[16] For a more detailed analysis of the legal nature and functions of management companies, see 6.31 *et seq* below.
[17] Arts 13(2) and 66, 2002 Act; Art 12(1), Act of 13 February 2007.

General contents of management regulations

4.22 *Name and duration of the FCP* The management regulations must indicate the fund's name and duration, as well as the names of the management company and of the depositary.[18] This is vital information, since it permits identification of the FCP and its main service providers.

4.23 *Investment policy and restrictions* The management regulations must describe the investment policy 'according to its proposed specific objectives and the criteria for achieving them'.[19] Specific objectives may include, for example, obtaining a high yield or regular revenues for the unitholders. The investment policy is defined by reference to various criteria, such as the nature and quality of the FCP's assets or the geographical or sector mix of the contemplated investments. It does not have to be described in detail as that is the purpose of the prospectus.

4.24 The management regulations must also describe the investment restrictions governing asset management. The 2002 Act and the Act of 13 February 2007 do not lay down any detailed specifications. For example, the management regulations of an FCP with the status of a coordinated UCITS may merely refer to the investment restrictions imposed by the 2002 Act. However, if such an FCP wishes to restrict its investments beyond the limits set by law, this will have to be mentioned explicitly in the management regulations. The prospectus must in any event give a detailed description of the investment restrictions adopted by the FCP.

4.25 *Distribution policy* The management regulations must provide information on the revenue distribution policy planned by the management company for the FCP.[20] They must specify whether the fund's revenues are capitalized or whether, and to what extent, they are distributed to the unitholders. In order to give the management company adequate flexibility, the regulations may, *inter alia*, make capitalization (or distribution) of revenues the general rule and reserve the right to deviate from that basic policy in the interests of the unitholders.

4.26 *Remuneration of the management company* The management regulations must list the remuneration and expenditure that the management company is authorized to charge against the fund's assets.[21] This discloses to unitholders the type of costs which will be borne by their common portfolio. The management regulations must also specify the methods of calculation of remuneration of service providers. They must, for example, state whether the management company's remuneration is calculated by reference to the FCP's net assets or total assets or whether other pricing mechanisms are used. They must, where appropriate,

---

[18] Arts 13(2)(a) and 66, 2002 Act; Art 12(2)(a), Act of 13 February 2007.
[19] Arts 13(2)(b) and 66, 2002 Act; Art 12(2)(b), Act of 13 February 2007.
[20] Arts 13(2)(c) and 66, 2002 Act; Art 12(2)(c), Act of 13 February 2007.
[21] Arts 13(2)(d) and 66, 2002 Act; Art 12(2)(d), Act of 13 February 2007.

indicate whether the management company is authorized to charge a performance fee and specify the indices or other benchmark criteria used to calculate such fee.

Other commitments and costs of the FCP   In order to protect unitholders against **4.27** any unwarranted commitments which an unscrupulous management company might charge to an FCP managed by it, the law stipulates that an FCP is answerable only for the obligations and expenses expressly imposed upon it by its management regulations.[22] The management regulations must therefore include an exhaustive list of all costs and charges that may be paid from the fund's assets, such as the remuneration payable to the service providers who participate in the FCP's operation. The management company cannot require the FCP to bear expenses not provided for in the management regulations.

In contrast with the position as regards the management company's remunera- **4.28** tion, the management regulations are not required to specify the exact amount and methods of calculating such expenses, details of which need be given only in the complete and simplified prospectuses of the FCP.

Publication of management regulations   The management regulations must specify **4.29** the way in which their contents, and any amendments thereto, are to be published.[23]

Closing date of the FCP's accounts   The management regulations must specify the **4.30** opening and closing dates of an FCP's financial year.[24] That period does not necessarily have to coincide with the calendar year. In principle, an FCP's financial year may not last longer than twelve months. Exceptionally, an FCP's first financial year may be extended to eighteen months. As a general rule, the closing date must coincide with the end of a given month, though derogations may be granted for valid reasons.

Dissolution of the FCP   The management regulations must indicate in what cir- **4.31** cumstances and on what grounds an FCP may be dissolved.[25] In that respect, they may specify whether such a decision is to be left to the discretion of the management company or whether approval from a general meeting of unitholders is required. In addition to such contractual cases, there are legal grounds for dissolution. These need not be mentioned in the management regulations, since they flow directly from the law.

Procedures for amendment of management regulations   The management regula- **4.32** tions must specify under what conditions and subject to what formalities they may be modified.[26]

---

[22]   Arts 6 and 66, 2002 Act; Art 5, Act of 13 February 2007.
[23]   Arts 13(2)(e) and 66, 2002 Act; Art 12(2)(e), Act of 13 February 2007.
[24]   Arts 13(2)(f) and 66, 2002 Act; Art 12(2)(f), Act of 13 February 2007.
[25]   Arts 13(2)(g) and 66, 2002 Act; Art 12(2)(g), Act of 13 February 2007.
[26]   Arts 13(2)(h) and 66, 2002 Act; Art 12(2)(h), Act of 13 February 2007; also see 2.109 *et seq* above.

4.33 *Procedure for the issue of units* The management regulations must provide information about the method used to issue units and their issuing frequency.[27] The management company is not obliged to always issue new units, even if the FCP is a coordinated UCITS. An FCP may be closed for subscription after the initial subscription period. It may also accept subscriptions solely according to a timetable set by the management company to reflect investment opportunities or the FCP's target size. Such restrictions must be set out in the management regulations, if only in general terms.

4.34 According to the 2002 Act, an FCP's units must be issued at a price based on the FCP's net asset value.[28] There is no exception to this rule, whether the FCP is a coordinated UCITS or another type of UCI. In contrast, FCPs established as SIFs are free to set their own issue price for their units.[29]

4.35 The issue price of units may be increased by costs and fees.[30] Those costs usually remunerate services provided by distributors in the placement of units. They may also be related to the so-called swing pricing,[31] ie a pricing method which includes security dealing and transaction costs in the net asset value in the case of new or departing investors. As a rule, the net amount of subscriptions and redemptions is taken into account. If the fund's capital activity leads to a net inflow, the net asset value is increased; if dealing activity results in a net outflow, the net asset value is reduced.

4.36 Two types of swing pricing are possible:

- full swing: the net asset value is swung on every dealing date on a net deal basis, regardless of the size of the net capital flow;

- partial swing: the net asset value is swung only when the capital activity exceeds a certain amount expressed as a monetary amount or as a percentage of the net assets.

4.37 When swing pricing is used, a number of elements must be considered, such as the basis on which the net asset value swing is calculated (real costs, flat-rate method, or a combination of both elements), the frequency with which the swing method is to be revised or, in case of partial swing, the calculation method for the swing threshold. It is also important to determine whether the swung net asset value is to be taken into account for the calculation of costs and fees, including the performance fee.

---

[27] Arts 13(2)(i) and 66, 2002 Act; Art 12(2)(i), Act of 13 February 2007.
[28] Arts 9(1) and 66, 2002 Act.
[29] Art 8, Act of 13 February 2007.
[30] ibid.
[31] See ALFI's communication on swing pricing which is available at <http://www.alfi.lu> under the heading 'Brochures'.

In some cases, swing pricing can increase volatility and result in an increased risk **4.38** of 'tracking error' between a fund and the index against which it is benchmarked. In this respect, specific warnings should be included in the prospectus.

Must swing pricing take into account contributions and redemptions in kind? **4.39** The answer should in principle be no, except when such contributions require security transactions.

The law does not require the management regulations to specify when subscribers **4.40** must pay the issue price to the FCP.[32] Because the management regulations are required to provide information about the issuing procedure, and because time limits for payment are an essential element of the issuing procedure, the management regulations should provide some indications regarding those limits. There seems, however, to be no bar to the management company setting such time limits, provided details are given in the complete and simplified prospectuses.

Redemption procedure The management regulations must describe the redemp- **4.41** tion procedure.[33] In coordinated UCITS, redemption must take place at the unitholders' request. For other types of UCI, the management regulations may expressly restrict investors' rights to redeem their units on request, or subject redemption to special terms, which must be disclosed.

The regulations must also indicate the cases in which redemption may be **4.42** suspended.

Lastly, as with the issue of units, the management regulations must specify a time **4.43** limit for paying the redemption price.

Valuation of the FCP's assets The management regulations must specify the **4.44** criteria used to value the fund's assets.[34]

The 2002 Act leaves considerable leeway in this area. In principle, officially listed **4.45** securities are valued at 'the last known stock exchange price', whereas unlisted securities are valued at 'their probable realisation value, estimated with care and in good faith'.[35] The management regulations may nevertheless provide otherwise, in which case the chosen criteria must be described in detail.

The Act of 13 February 2007 refers to the fair value as being determined accord- **4.46** ing to the principles set forth in the management regulations.[36] The management

---

[32] For SICAVs, Arts 28(4) and 71, 2002 Act require the articles of incorporation to stipulate time limits for payment in respect of share issues.

[33] Art 13(2)(j) 2002 Act; Art 12(2)(i), Act of 13 February 2007.

[34] Arts 9(3) and 66, 2002 Act; Art 9, Act of 13 February 2007.

[35] Arts 9(3) and 66, 2002 Act.

[36] Art 9, Act of 13 February 2007; see also I Dubourdieu, F Moreau and A Baratelli, 'Functioning of the SIF structure' in *Specialised Investment Funds* (Arendt & Medernach, 2007) 109.

regulations may permit derogation from the fair value concept and selection of another means of valuation. This option to derogate can be explained by the variety of investment policies which may be carried out by a SIF, which may mean that the use of the fair value approach may be inadequate for certain types of assets. As required, alternative accounting principles may be substituted for the fair value, provided that shareholders or unitholders are treated equally and that the financial information obtained on such basis is reliable.[37]

4.47 The fair value concept is often based on the principles set down and issued by specialized professional associations, such as the European Venture Capital Association (EVCA) in the private equity area, or the Royal Institution of Chartered Surveyors (RICS) as regards real estate assets.[38]

4.48 *Reference currency of the FCP* Although not required by law, the management regulations must state the currency in which the net assets are expressed, this is known as the FCP's reference (or 'base') currency. There is no restriction in this regard, save that the currency must be freely convertible. If an FCP's assets are denominated in a currency other than the reference currency, they must be translated into the reference currency according to the procedure laid down in the management regulations.

4.49 **Specific information about sub-funds** The 2002 Act and the Act of 13 February 2007 do not clearly indicate how the above rules are to apply to umbrella type FCPs. They merely specify that such an FCP may lay down in separate management regulations the characteristics and rules applicable to each sub-fund.[39] An FCP can therefore conceivably use several sets of management regulations, provided the fund preserves a common base of essential rules for the fund's consistent operation. This solution is similar to the principles applicable to pension funds, which may apply more than one set of pension regulations.[40] The Parliamentary debates relating to the 2002 Act specify that the legal regime for FCPs has not been changed in this respect.[41]

---

[37] *Parliamentary doc* No 5616, Comments on the Articles, 21.

[38] ibid.

[39] Art 133(4), 2002 Act; Art 71(4), Act of 13 February 2007.

[40] Art 68(1), Act of 13 July 2005 on professional retirement institutions in the form of *société d'épargne-pension à capital variable* (sepcav—pension-savings companies with variable capital) and *association d'épargne-pension* (assep—pension-savings associations), amending Art 167(1), Act of 4 December 1967, as amended, on income tax (*Mémorial* A 2005, 1860). See C Kremer and A Contreras, 'Les fonds de pension soumis au contrôle prudentiel de la Commission de Surveillance du Secteur Financier' in *Droit Bancaire et Financier au Luxembourg*, Vol 4 (Larcier, 2004) 1749.

[41] The text mainly clarifies certain points and does not amend the rules provided for by Art 111, 1988 Act (*Parliamentary doc* No 5033, Comments on the Articles, 66; also see *Parliamentary doc* No 50331, Opinion of the *Conseil d'État*, 35, which nevertheless points out that the right to issue separate management regulations for every sub-fund is a new provision of the law).

When the promoter of an FCP wants the fund to be governed by one set of management regulations without ruling out the launch of new sub-funds in the future, certain legal requirements should be considered. For example, how should one describe the investment policy of sub-funds not yet in existence at the time when the fund is established? In practice, there are two possible solutions. **4.50**

The first is to structure the management regulations in such a way that the characteristics of each sub-fund are disclosed in a schedule forming an integral part of the regulations. As and when new sub-funds are established, more schedules are added. The drawback of this method is its inconvenience. Like the management regulations themselves, successive schedules must be lodged with the registry of the District Court and be published in the *Mémorial* in order to become valid vis-à-vis third parties.[42] These may turn out to be cumbersome formalities, especially when a new sub-fund is to be launched on the market with all due haste.[43] **4.51**

A simpler method is to keep the wording of the management regulations general, stating, for example, that the management company is authorized at any time to establish new sub-funds, the characteristics of which have not yet been settled. This practice accords with the provisions of the 2002 Act, which requires the management regulations to indicate an FCP's investment policy 'according to its proposed specific objectives and the criteria for achieving them'.[44] **4.52**

The management regulations must therefore specify the types of sub-funds that may be established (sub-funds investing in, for example, equities, bonds, mixed portfolios, other assets, such as liquid assets, or other financial instruments). However, the regulations may authorize the management company to determine the precise components of sub-funds' portfolios and their geographical, sectoral, and currency mix at the time of their establishment. The details of the investment policy and the investment restrictions applicable to the various sub-funds must be set out in the complete and simplified prospectuses, which must be updated from time to time. **4.53**

There is no such flexibility in respect of the revenue distribution policy, which must be described in the management regulations pursuant to the 2002 Act and the Act of 13 February 2007.[45] **4.54**

---

[42] Arts 13(1) and 66, 2002 Act; Art 12(1), Act of 13 February 2007.

[43] In practice, a similar method has emerged for families of FCPs managed by the same management company, other than for structures with umbrella funds. In order to avoid the need, when creating new FCPs, to publish management regulations the contents of which will be very broadly the same as those of existing FCPs, a separate set of general management regulations is published at the outset and special regulations are additionally adopted for each FCP. The special regulations provide that the general regulations are applicable to the FCP in question and set out the additional provisions or derogations which are to apply. The advantage of this method is that it prevents successive publication of similar regulations and minimizes publication formalities and costs.

[44] Arts 13(2)(b) and 66, 2002 Act; Art 12(2)(b), Act of 13 February 2007.

[45] Arts 13(2)(c) and 66, 2002 Act; Art 12(2)(c), Act of 13 February 2007.

4.55   This is a more stringent provision. The management company may not wait until a sub-fund is launched before defining its distribution policy in the prospectus. It must comply with the regulations, which must specify whether the sub-funds capitalize or distribute the capital gains and income generated by the various portfolios. That said, the management regulations may authorize the management company to deviate, in exceptional circumstances, from the distribution policy described if this is in the interests of the unitholders. In practice, this difficulty is frequently avoided by creating two unit classes—distribution and accumulation units—within each sub-fund, so that unitholders may opt for the distribution policy of their choice by subscribing for units in the preferred class.

4.56   According to Circular 91/75, the management regulations must set out the redemption conditions applicable to each sub-fund (assuming the FCP is open for redemption), and the rules governing asset valuation, suspension of net asset value calculation, and investment restrictions, all of which must be consistent as between sub-funds[46] although derogations from this principle may be permitted for justified reasons.

4.57   The management company's remuneration must also be specified in the management regulations, normally per sub-fund.[47] In practice, the precise fee applicable need not be disclosed as the management regulations must merely specify the maximum rate, whilst the actual rate of each sub-fund can be specified in the complete and simplified prospectuses.

4.58   The reference currency in which the net assets of each sub-fund are expressed need not necessarily be the same for all sub-funds. It is not necessary to specify the reference currency for each sub-fund in the management regulations, rather only to state the fund's consolidated reference or base currency, ie the currency used to express the overall position, obtained by consolidating the financial statements for all sub-funds.[48]

4.59   Umbrella type FCPs constitute a single legal entity.[49] However, liability is segregated as between sub-funds so that liability for a sub-fund's debts attaches only to the assets of that sub-fund, unless otherwise stipulated in the management regulations.[50]

---

[46] Ch J, II, Circular 91/75.
[47] Arts 13(2)(d) and 66, 2002 Act; Art 12(2)(d), Act of 13 February 2007.
[48] Ch J, II, Circular 91/75.
[49] In the context of FCPs, this wording, used by the 2002 Act, is incorrect, since such funds do not have legal personality.
[50] Art 133(5), 2002 Act; Art 71(5), Act of 13 February 2007.

Corporate UCIs

Articles of incorporation

In the Grand Duchy of Luxembourg, incorporated UCIs are, in principle, consti- **4.60**
tuted in the form of investment companies. Unlike FCPs, investment companies
have a legal personality separate from their members.

As in the case of an FCP's management regulations, an investment company's **4.61**
articles of incorporation are the basic instrument in which a UCI's essential characteristics and operating rules are laid out. They are adopted in the form of a
notarized deed. After adopting the articles of incorporation, an investment company's founders, who generally act on behalf of the promoter(s) or initiator(s), call
a general meeting to appoint the first board of directors.

Contents of the articles of incorporation

The contents of an investment company's articles of incorporation differ in sev- **4.62**
eral ways from those of management regulations. This is due to a number of factors. First of all, a company's operating rules are based on the 1915 Act, which
means that the articles of incorporation may be less explicit. Secondly, an investment company's shareholders have more influence over a UCI's business than an
FCP's unitholders. The shareholders of a corporate UCI appoint and dismiss the
board of directors and may thereby control the way in which the company's business is managed. Unitholders in an FCP do not have that power. For that reason,
an FCP's management regulations must provide certain assurances regarding its
operations and set out certain rules with which the management company must
comply. Whilst it is true that the management company has the unilateral power
to amend the rules applicable to an FCP, the unitholders are entitled to divest
themselves of their units, for example by means of redemption before such amendments come into force. No such assurances are required in respect of investment
companies.

For example, the law does not require the articles of incorporation to specify the **4.63**
investment policy, which is determined by the UCI's management body and described
in the complete and simplified prospectuses. Similarly, an investment company's
articles of incorporation do not necessarily prescribe the distribution policy.

In other respects, however, the contents of the constitutive documents of incorpo- **4.64**
rated and contractual UCIs are similar, since both types of UCI carry on the same
business.

SICAVs   SICAVs are subject to the provisions applicable to SAs or SEs insofar as **4.65**
no derogation is provided for by the 2002 Act.[51] When they are governed by the

---

[51] Arts 26 and 71, 2002 Act.

Act of 13 February 2007, SICAVs may also be incorporated in a form other than an SA (SCA, SARL, or cooperative society organized in the form of an SA).[52] Such SICAVs are governed by the rules applicable to the particular type of company subject to derogations allowed under the Act of 13 February 2007.

4.66 A SICAV's articles of incorporation are therefore very similar to those of a traditional SA, SCA, or SARL, apart from two differences. As its name indicates, a SICAV has a variable capital and its object is to be an investment company.

4.67 *Contents of articles of incorporation with respect to the variable nature of the capital* A SICAV's articles of incorporation stipulate that the amount of capital must at all times be equal to the value of the company's net assets.[53] Variations in the capital are effected automatically as and when the net asset value of the SICAV increases or decreases, without the necessity of completion of an official filing of capital increase or decrease.[54] The net asset value may increase because of capital gains or revenues generated by portfolio items or because of the receipt of additional subscription proceeds. Conversely, the net asset value decreases when a SICAV suffers capital losses, or incurs costs, or when investors redeem shares.

4.68 In principle, a SICAV's articles of incorporation vest in the board of directors or the board of managers the power to issue new shares at any time without calling a general meeting of shareholders or unitholders.[55] As a result, a SICAV benefits at all times from unlimited authorized capital, save to the extent restricted by the articles of incorporation.[56]

4.69 The 2002 Act and the Act of 13 February 2007 further provide that a SICAV's shareholders may not claim preferential subscription (pre-emption) rights to newly issued shares, unless the articles of incorporation expressly grant this right.[57]

4.70 The variable nature of the capital also means that shares in a SICAV do not have a nominal value.[58] This characteristic is described in the articles of incorporation.

4.71 As regards SICAVs governed by the 2002 Act, shares must be fully paid up,[59] whereas shares issued by SICAV-SIFs must be paid up as to 5 per cent of the subscribed amount.[60]

---

[52] Art 25, Act of 13 February 2007.
[53] Arts 25 and 69, 2002 Act; Art 25, Act of 13 February 2007.
[54] Arts 29(1) and 71, 2002 Act; Art 29(1), Act of 13 February 2007.
[55] Arts 28(1)(a) and 71, 2002 Act; Art 28(1), Act of 13 February 2007.
[56] ibid. This distinguishes a SICAV from a traditional SA, where capital increases are reserved for the general meeting, which may delegate this exclusive power for a maximum period of five years to the board of directors when building up authorized capital.
[57] Arts 29(3) and 71, 2002 Act; Art 29(3), Act of 13 February 2007.
[58] Arts 28(8) and 71, 2002 Act; Art 28(7), Act of 13 February 2007.
[59] Arts 28(8) and 71, 2002 Act.
[60] Art 28(3), Act of 13 February 2007.

Moreover, SICAVs are not subject to the constraints imposed by the 1915 Act on traditional SAs for the payment of interim dividends.[61] The board of directors of a SICAV is not required to be authorized under the articles of incorporation to pay interim dividends. **4.72**

SICAVs are not obliged to establish a legal reserve,[62] although such a provision may be made in the articles of incorporation if so desired by the founders. **4.73**

Contents of the articles of incorporation with respect to the investment company's **4.74** *activity* Whether subject to Part I or Part II of the 2002 Act or even to the Act of 13 February 2007, SICAVs may, in principle, have identical articles of incorporation. However, when a SICAV is not a coordinated UCITS, it may restrict or even withdraw the investors' right to request redemption.

The shares of a SICAV other than a SIF[63] are issued and redeemed at a price based **4.75** on the net asset value.[64] This is reflected in the articles of incorporation. For that reason, the articles of incorporation lay down the principles and methods used to value the SICAV's assets.

According to the 2002 Act, officially listed securities must be valued at the 'last **4.76** known stock exchange price', whereas unlisted securities must be valued at their 'probable realisation value' unless the articles of incorporation stipulate specific rules.[65] SICAVs have considerable leeway in this respect.

For its part, the Law of 13 February 2007 refers to the concept of fair value, whilst **4.77** conceding derogations to that principle.[66]

A SICAV-SIF may also establish other issue or redemption prices, such as a fixed **4.78** amount determined in advance and increased or reduced, as the case may be, by an interest rate.

The articles of incorporation also prescribe time limits for paying the price of **4.79** newly issued or redeemed shares[67] and the conditions under which share issues and redemptions may be suspended.[68]

The articles of incorporation determine the frequency with which issue and **4.80** redemption prices are calculated.[69] Where a SICAV is a coordinated UCITS, the

---

[61] Arts 32(3) and 71, 2002 Act; Art 31(3), Act of 13 February 2007.
[62] Arts 32(2) and 71, 2002 Act; Art 31(2), Act of 13 February 2007.
[63] Art 28(2), Act of 13 February 2007.
[64] Art 28(2), 2002 Act. However, the obligation to redeem shares at net asset value only applies to SICAVs governed by Part I, since Art 71, 2002 Act does not refer to Art 28(2)(b), 2002 Act.
[65] Arts 28(4) and 71, 2002 Act.
[66] Art 28(4), Act of 13 February 2007; also see 4.33 above.
[67] Arts 28(4) and 71, 2002 Act; Art 28(2), Act of 13 February 2007.
[68] Arts 28(5) and 71, 2002 Act; Art 28(5), Act of 13 February 2007.
[69] Arts 28(6) and 71, 2002 Act.

minimum frequency is, in principle, twice a month.[70] In other cases it is, in principle, once a month, subject to derogations for justifiable reasons.[71] A SIF[72] does not have to calculate its net asset value more than once a year.

4.81 SICAVs governed by the 2002 Act may not issue founder shares which are not representative of the share capital. A SICAV-SIF, however, is allowed to do so.[73]

4.82 Lastly, the articles of incorporation prescribe 'the nature of the costs to be borne by the SICAV'.[74] For SICAVs, the legislature has used more general wording than for FCPs. A SICAV's constitutive documents do not have to set out the costs to be borne by the UCI in the same detail as an FCP's management regulations. Such details only have to be provided in the complete and simplified prospectuses of the SICAV.

4.83 **SICAFs** SICAFs are generally incorporated as SAs or SCAs. The contents of a SICAF's articles of incorporation are similar to those of a SICAV's articles of incorporation. Likewise, the contents of the articles of incorporation of SICAFs subject to Part I or Part II of the 2002 Act or to the Act of 13 February 2007 are not necessarily the same.

4.84 *Differences between the articles of incorporation of SICAFs and SICAVs* There are several differences between the articles of incorporation of SICAFs and SICAVs. To begin with, SICAFs have a fixed capital. That capital does not automatically change when the net asset value changes, as is the case with SICAVs. It is the responsibility of a general meeting of shareholders to lay down a SICAF's share capital in the articles of incorporation, to increase or reduce it, or to authorize the board of directors to increase it within the authorized capital limits specified in the articles of incorporation. The authority to increase capital may not exceed five years but can be renewed.[75]

4.85 Secondly, the nominal or accounting par value of a SICAF's shares must be stated in the articles of incorporation.

4.86 Thirdly, a SICAF's articles of incorporation must provide for allocation of part of the profits to a legal reserve, in contrast to SICAVs.

4.87 A SICAF's articles of incorporation may provide for the issue of partly paid shares,[76] in contrast with SICAVs governed by the 2002 Act.[77]

---

[70] Art 116(1), 2002 Act.
[71] Art 116(1), 2002 Act and Ch G, I, Circular 91/75.
[72] Arts 31 and 71, 2002 Act.
[73] ibid.
[74] Arts 28(7) and 71, 2002 Act; Art 28(6), Act of 13 February 2007.
[75] Art 32, 1915 Act.
[76] Art 40, 2002 Act does not make Art 28(8), 2002 Act applicable to SICAFs governed by Part I. Moreover, Ch 11, 2002 Act does not prohibit SICAFs falling within the sphere of Part II from issuing partly paid-up shares.
[77] However, the issue of partially paid-up securities is allowed for SICAVs and SICAFs which opt for the status of SIF.

Lastly, in contrast with the shareholders in a SICAV, a SICAF's shareholders nor- **4.88** mally have preferential subscription (pre-emption) rights. The general law provisions laid down by the 1915 Act have broader application to SICAFs. Existing shareholders have a preferential subscription right, subject to the right of the general meeting to introduce a derogation, or to authorize the board of directors to introduce a derogation within the limits of the authorized capital, on terms set out in the articles of incorporation.[78]

Differences between the articles of incorporation of (a) SICAFs governed by Part I **4.89** *and (b) SICAFs governed by Part II of the 2002 Act or by the Act of 13 February 2007* SICAFs governed by Part I differ in two essential respects from those governed by Part II of the 2002 Act or by the Act of 13 February 2007.

First, SICAFs subject to Part II of the 2002 Act or to the Act of 13 February 2007 **4.90** are not prohibited from issuing founder shares. The issue of founder shares and the legal regime applying to them should, however, be provided for in the articles of incorporation.[79]

Secondly, insofar as provided for by their articles of incorporation, SICAFs gov- **4.91** erned by Part II of the 2002 Act or by the Act of 13 February 2007 may issue and redeem shares at a price based on criteria other than the net asset value, such as the stock market price, if justified by the circumstances. Examples of this are to be found, in particular, in the real estate property fund sector.

Umbrella type investment companies The regime applicable to umbrella type **4.92** FCPs[80] is also broadly applicable to umbrella type investment companies, notably the rules on investment and borrowing restrictions and the rules on suspension of net asset value calculations.

Additionally, the articles of incorporation of an umbrella type investment com- **4.93** pany must specify that each share confers an equal voting right at general meetings, even though the value of the shares may differ from sub-fund to sub-fund.[81] Moreover, the articles of incorporation distinguish between decisions affecting all shareholders, adopted by the common general meeting, and decisions connected with the special rights of the shareholders in individual sub-funds, as adopted at separate general meetings of the relevant sub-funds.

Similarly, the articles of incorporation prescribe the currency in which the share **4.94** capital must be denominated, on the understanding that the aggregate capital of

---

[78] Art 32-3, 1915 Act.
[79] The prohibition contained in Art 31 and (by reference) Art 40, 2002 Act, precluding SICAVs in general and SICAFs governed by Part I from issuing founder shares, is mentioned neither in Ch 11, 2002 Act with regard to SICAFs governed by Part II, nor in the Act of 13 February 2007.
[80] See 2.172 *et seq* above.
[81] Ch J, III, Circular 91/75.

the sub-funds must be denominated in a single currency. The net asset value of each sub-fund may, however, be expressed in the sub-fund's own reference currency.

4.95   Lastly, even though the investment company as a whole constitutes a single legal entity with only one set of articles of incorporation,[82] the assets of a given sub-fund can be used only to pay the debts of the sub-fund itself, unless otherwise provided for in the articles of incorporation.[83]

Sales literature

Complete prospectus

Principles

4.96   Each Luxembourg-based UCI publishes a complete prospectus, the contents of which must enable investors to make an informed judgment concerning the proposed investment.[84]

4.97   In principle, the constitutive documents of a UCI governed by the 2002 Act form an integral part of, and are annexed to, the prospectus.[85] However, they do not have to be appended if the prospectus informs the unitholders where such documents can be obtained or consulted.[86]

4.98   Schedule A to the 2002 Act specifies certain information which must be included in the complete prospectus of a UCI governed by that Act. As such information may also be found in the constitutive documents annexed to the complete prospectus,[87] certain UCI promoters prefer to publish prospectuses containing information which is primarily related to the UCI's investment policy and its cost structure, while the more legal aspects are disclosed in the annexed constitutive documents. This is a useful approach for FCPs, whose management company may amend the management regulations without seeking approval from the unitholders. In contrast, this approach may not be so useful in the case of investment companies, whose articles of incorporation may only be amended by a resolution of the general meeting of shareholders. In any event, there should no longer be any necessity for FCPs or coordinated investment companies to publish a more

---

[82] An investment company cannot have separate articles of incorporation for a sub-fund, contrary to what is allowed for FCPs, which may have separate management regulations (Art 133(4), 2002 Act; Art 71(4), Act of 13 February 2007).

[83] Art 133(5), 2002 Act; Art 71(5), Act of 13 February 2007. The wording of these Articles suggests that the constitutive documents may provide for joint liability of the sub-funds vis-à-vis third parties. As a general rule, it is hard to see why an umbrella fund would be structured in such a way.

[84] Art 110(1), 2002 Act; Art 53, Act of 13 February 2007.

[85] Art 111(1), 2002 Act.

[86] ibid Art 111(2).

[87] ibid Art 110(2).

succinct prospectus in this manner, as they must now in any event publish a simplified prospectus summarizing the complete prospectus.

The drafting of a SIF prospectus uses a different rationale. By definition, such a **4.99**
UCI is exclusively dedicated to well-informed investors who are better qualified to inquire into the proposed investment by reading the documentation provided to them and ask salient questions of the promoter of the fund, if necessary. Therefore, the legislature did not set out any minimum content for a prospectus issued by a SIF. It merely indicated that the prospectus 'must include the information necessary for investors to be able to make an informed judgment of the investment proposed to them and, in particular, of the risks attached thereto'.[88] In practice, this requirement is construed as referring for the most part to information such as that set out in Schedule A to the 2002 Act. The prospectus of a SIF differs only slightly from the prospectus of a UCI governed by the 2002 Act.

The 2002 Act requires the essential elements of the prospectus to be kept up to **4.100**
date.[89] A UCI must review the contents of its prospectus from time to time in order to ensure that the prospectus continues to reflect the actual situation. However, the essential elements may, and sometimes are, updated in the periodic financial reports.[90] Essential changes, such as adjustment of the investment policy or restrictions, are published in the semi-annual or annual report issued at the time when such changes come into force. In such cases, the prospectus is simply updated at a later date.

The Act of 13 February is less stringent. The essential elements of the prospectus **4.101**
must be updated only when additional securities are issued to new investors.[91] As regards SIFs which do not issue securities on a continual basis, where there is a change in an essential element, the prospectus is required to be amended only for subsequent closings, provided that new investors are allowed to make subscriptions on such closings.

Minimum information for UCIs governed by the 2002 Act

The complete prospectus of a UCI must contain at least the information indi- **4.102**
cated in Schedule A to the 2002 Act. That information differs slightly between FCPs and investment companies because of their structural differences. For example, an FCP's prospectus contains information about the management company, which is not found in the prospectus of an investment company. The general information to be supplied in the prospectus is reviewed below. The distinctions between FCPs and investment companies are only explained where necessary.

---

[88] Art 53, Act of 13 February 2007; see also Circular 07/309, which states that the prospectus 'must include quantifiable restrictions evidencing the fulfilment of the principle of risk spreading'.
[89] Art 112, 2002 Act.
[90] Ch L, I, 1, Circular 91/75.
[91] Art 54, Act of 13 February 2007.

4.103 The 2002 Act allows the CSSF to adapt the contents of Schedule A as regards UCIs governed by Part II of the 2002 Act.[92]

4.104 Circular 91/75[93] also lays down rules of conduct regarding the provision of information, such as the obligation to state that no information may be relied on other than that included in the prospectus and the documents referred to in the prospectus. The CSSF may, moreover, require the publication of any additional information which it considers necessary in order to provide the public with complete, objective information. Finally, a UCI may, in principle, only carry out the transactions mentioned in its prospectus. This applies especially to the use of derivative techniques and instruments.[94]

4.105 **Structure of UCIs and, as the case may be, their management company** The prospectus must specify the form adopted by the investment company or, as the case may be, the FCP's management company. It must also provide the names of such companies, their term (when limited), their registered office and their principal place of business (if not the same as the registered office), their incorporation date, and the amount of their capital.[95]

4.106 **Investment policy and restrictions** The prospectus must describe the investment policy the UCI plans to pursue, including the type of assets to be acquired, the geographical mix, and, as the case may be, the issuer's economic sector. The financial objectives must also be explained (long-term capitalization, short-term realization of capital gains, etc). The UCI may also pursue other objectives, such as humanitarian goals (for example assistance to developing countries) or political-economic aims (for example faster accession of applicant countries to the European Union).

4.107 The prospectus must also list the investment restrictions a UCI is obliged or has decided to apply, and the derivative techniques and instruments it may use. Lastly, it must state the UCI's borrowing limits.[96]

4.108 **Historical performance of UCIs** The complete prospectus must describe the UCI's past results. In view of the naturally open-ended nature of this kind of information, the 2002 Act allows performance information to be attached to the prospectus, which consequently does not have to be modified whenever performance information is updated.[97]

---

[92] Art 110(7), 2002 Act.
[93] Ch L, Circular 91/75.
[94] ibid.
[95] Annex I, Sch A, points 1.1 and 1.2, 2002 Act.
[96] ibid point 1.15.
[97] ibid point 5.1.

Standard investor profile for which a UCI has been developed   To allow inves-   **4.109**
tors to judge for themselves whether or not investment in a particular UCI is
appropriate for them, the complete prospectus must describe the profile of a
typical investor for whom the UCI has been developed.[98]

Conducting persons of UCIs   Because the knowledge and reputation of the   **4.110**
conducting persons may be critical in the context of the performance of the UCI,
the prospectus gives relatively detailed information about them, notably the name
and function of each of the members of managing bodies, the board of directors,
and the supervisory board. In the case of FCPs, this information is provided in
respect of the management company's conducting persons.

Where conducting persons carry on significant activities on behalf of other enti-   **4.111**
ties, this must be mentioned in the prospectus,[99] which must also indicate any
other UCIs managed by the management company.[100]

Units and shares in UCIs   The prospectus must describe the nature and princi-   **4.112**
pal characteristics of the units or shares issued by the UCI. This type of information
includes, *inter alia*, an indication of the nature of the rights represented by the units
or shares, as well as a description of some of the specific rights conferred by the units
or shares (for example voting rights, rights to dividends,[101] and rights to the return
of assets in the case of liquidation). The form of security held (registered or bearer)
must also be stated, as must the right, if any, to issue fractions of shares.[102]

The unit or share issue, redemption, and conversion procedures must also be   **4.113**
described. Similarly, the prospectus must give a full explanation of the issue,
redemption, and conversion price calculation methods, the calculation frequency,
publication procedures, and any additional costs—such as issue, redemption, and
conversion charges—as well as redemption and subscription fees (including costs
relating to swing pricing).[103] It must also indicate the circumstances under which
redemption may be suspended.[104]

The prospectus must mention the exact time limit for accepting orders.[105] As this   **4.114**
time limit necessarily precedes calculation of the net asset value, that net asset
value is unknown whenever a subscription, redemption, or conversion order is
issued (forward pricing).[106]

---

[98]   ibid point 5.2.
[99]   ibid point 1.8.
[100]   ibid point 1.3.
[101]   Including an indication of the frequency and payment methods of such distributions.
[102]   Annex I, Sch A, point 1.10, 2002 Act.
[103]   See 4.35 above.
[104]   Annex I, Sch A, points 1.12 and 1.13, 2002 Act.
[105]   Section I(a), Circular 04/146.
[106]   ibid.

4.115   Lastly, the prospectus must mention any stock exchanges or other markets on which the units or shares are traded.[107]

4.116   **Liquidation of UCIs**   The prospectus must state the grounds on which the UCI may be placed in liquidation and the procedures to be followed in that regard.[108]

4.117   **Financial information**   The prospectus must describe the rules adopted by the UCI for the valuation of its assets and the determination and allocation of its revenues.[109]

4.118   It must also provide information about the remuneration and charges paid by the UCI to its management company, its depositary, or third parties and about any other costs and fees which may be borne by the UCI or its investors, distinguishing between costs borne by the unitholders or shareholders and those borne by the UCI.[110]

4.119   It must indicate the closing date for accounting purposes and the auditor appointed to verify the financial statements.[111]

4.120   **Information about the depositary and the investment advisers**   The prospectus must give details in respect of the depositary (name, legal form, core business, registered office, and, as the case may be, principal place of business) and any external investment advisers who maintain contractual relations with the UCI and whose fees are discharged from the UCI's assets. The depositary and investment advisers must be named and their other significant activities disclosed and the principal terms of their contracts with the UCI disclosed.[112]

4.121   **Tax treatment of UCIs**   The prospectus must contain a summary of the tax rules applicable to the UCI which are of concern to the investors, such as the existence of withholding taxes (if any) on distributions made by the UCI.[113]

4.122   **Circulation of information**   The prospectus must describe the method used to circulate information about the UCI, including information about the locations where the UCI's constitutive documents and financial reports are publicly available.[114]

4.123   **Risk profile of UCIs**   The complete prospectus must include a clear and easily understandable description of the UCI's risk profile. This requirement applies regardless of the type of instrument targeted by the investment policy.[115]

---

[107]   Annex I, Sch A, point 1.11, 2002 Act.
[108]   ibid point 1.10.
[109]   ibid points 1.14 and 1.16.
[110]   ibid points 1.18 and 6.1.
[111]   ibid points 1.6 and 1.7.
[112]   ibid points 2 and 3.
[113]   ibid point 1.5.
[114]   ibid point 4.
[115]   Art 110(1), 2002 Act.

Umbrella funds

Umbrella funds must issue a single complete prospectus for all their sub-funds, **4.124** which must specify that obligations of a given sub-fund are binding only on the sub-fund concerned, unless otherwise specified in the constitutive documents of the UCI.[116] It must mention the historical performance and standard investor profile of each sub-fund.[117] In addition, the prospectus must set out the information required by Circular 91/75[118] to be included in an FCP's management regulations[119] and an investment company's articles of incorporation.[120]

Circular 91/75 allows the establishment of individual complete prospectuses for **4.125** each sub-fund in addition to the main prospectus.[121] Such documents must inform investors that:

(1) the sub-fund concerned is not a separate legal entity but coexists with other sub-funds that together form the umbrella fund;

(2) a sub-fund's commitments are binding only on the sub-fund itself unless otherwise provided for in the constitutive documents;[122]

(3) as regards relations between investors, each sub-fund is regarded as a separate entity with its own costs, revenues, capital gains, and capital losses;

(4) there is a consolidated prospectus in which all sub-funds are described; and

(5) the consolidated prospectus may be obtained at the location specified in the sub-fund prospectus.

Simplified prospectus

Principles

Following the practice adopted by certain Member States who required the **4.126** publication of a 'key features' type document summarizing the most important elements of regulated collective investment schemes,[123] the European legislature introduced a requirement to publish a document which was less exhaustive than a complete prospectus but easier to understand for the non-sophisticated investor. The simplified prospectus complements the complete

---

[116] Ch L, Circular 91/75 does not yet reflect the change made in this respect by the Act of 17 July 2000, which amended certain provisions of the 1988 Act (*Mémorial* A 2000, 1226). Prior to the enactment of that law, the commitments accepted by a sub-fund were binding on the entire UCI unless otherwise agreed with the creditors concerned.

[117] Annex I, Sch A, point 5.3, 2002 Act.

[118] Ch L, I, 2, Circular 91/75.

[119] See 4.21 *et seq* above.

[120] See 4.62 *et seq* above.

[121] ibid.

[122] Chapter L, I, 2, of the Circular is to be read in the light of the amendment of Art 111(2) of the 1988 Act introduced by the above-mentioned Act of 17 July 2000. Also see Art 133(5), 2002 Act.

[123] Particularly including France, Belgium, and the United Kingdom.

prospectus[124] and is a summary document which, in clear and understandable language,[125] provides the essential information contained in the complete prospectus. Simplified prospectuses facilitate understanding of the operation of the UCIs to which they refer and allow investors to judge and compare similar funds.[126]

4.127   The purpose of the simplified prospectus is not just to improve investor information but also to facilitate cross-border marketing of UCITS. The only prerequisite for distributing a simplified prospectus in the host Member State, once the UCI or its management company has completed the formalities for obtaining a European passport, is to get it translated into an official or approved language in the host State.[127] Only UCITS governed by Part I of the 2002 Act are obliged to prepare and publish a simplified prospectus.[128]

4.128   The requirements for the contents of a simplified prospectus as specified in Directive 85/611 are mandatory and a host Member State cannot require the filing of any addtional document or notice.[129]

4.129   A simplified prospectus must be updated at least once a year,[130] particularly with respect to investment performance, the total expense ratio, and the portfolio turnover rate.[131] This information may also be given in a leaflet attached to the prospectus, such that any changes are limited to the leaflet. Other changes may also be required from time to time and the 2002 Act requires key information in the simplified prospectus to be kept up to date.[132]

---

[124]   During the preparations for Directive (EC) 2001/107, complete prospectuses were noted as being documents 'drafted by and for lawyers' and 'quite simply incomprehensible for investors' (Report of the Committee on Legal Affairs and Citizens' Rights, point 3.6, 14 (available on the website of the European Parliament under the heading 'Legislative Observatory')).

[125]   The authors of Directive (EC) 2001/107 stress the need for simple language in this document, which must contain 'useful and factual information and a description of the risk profile characterizing the product offered' (Report of the Economic and Monetary Committee, 35 (available on the website of the European Parliament under the heading 'Legislative Observatory')).

[126]   Report of the Economic and Monetary Committee, 35.

[127]   Arts 56 and 110(3), 2002 Act. Also see Art 28.3, Directive (EEC) 85/611.

[128]   Art 109(3), 2002 Act.

[129]   Art 28.3, Directive (EEC) 85/611; Explanatory memorandum to the modified proposal for Directive (EC) 2001/107, 8 (available on the website of the European Parliament under the heading 'Legislative Observatory'). The Commission of the European Communities also stresses the 'unique and intangible character (apart from translation needs)' of the simplified prospectus. This document is a 'commercial reference tool, the outcome of the Commission's maximum harmonisation approach in this respect' (Communication of the Commission to the European Parliament, point 3.2.2.7, SEC/2001/1004 final (available on the website of the European Parliament under the heading 'Legislative Observatory')).

[130]   Section I, Circular 03/122.

[131]   ibid.

[132]   Art 112, 2002 Act.

Both the simplified prospectus and each update require prior approval by the **4.130**
CSSF.[133]

Contents

The content of the simplified prospectus is set out in detail in Schedule C to **4.131**
Directive 85/611, transposed in Schedule C to Annex I of the 2002 Act. The
simplified prospectus consists of five sections, respectively outlining a summary of
the UCITS, investment information, financial data, commercial information,
and certain general explanations.

When a UCITS has several sub-funds, its simplified prospectus must provide **4.132**
investment information and financial and commercial data for each sub-fund.

Summary of the UCITS   In this brief presentation of the UCITS, the simplified **4.133**
prospectus notes the date on which the fund was established and the Member
State in which it was constituted, as well as any relevant information about the
existence of more than one sub-fund, the name of the management company if
appointed by the UCITS, and the projected term of the fund if established for a
limited period. Lastly, the summary must mention the fund's depositary, the auditor, and the promoter.[134]

Investment information   The section dealing with the fund's investments **4.134**
describes its objectives, investment strategy, and risk profile, as applicable, including information about the use of financial derivative instruments. Information
about the historical performance of the UCITS is also provided when these figures
are available. This information is accompanied by a warning that past performance is no guarantee of future results. The section also describes the profile of the
typical investor for whom the UCITS is intended.

In Circular 03/122, the CSSF specifies the way in which all of this information **4.135**
must be presented in the simplified prospectus.[135]

As the wording clearly indicates, a 'brief definition of the UCITS' objectives' is a **4.136**
description of the fund's purpose. In the case of guaranteed funds, this is followed
by an outline of guarantees received and any restrictions applicable to these guarantees. In the case of index-based funds, the section must also include the name of
the replicated index and a description of the desired degree of replication.[136]

The paragraph dealing with the fund's investment strategy describes the main **4.137**
categories of eligible financial assets. It mentions whether the purpose of the

---

[133] Section III, Circular 03/122.
[134] Here, the concept of promoter has the meaning described at 4.02 above.
[135] Section II (a), Circular 03/122.
[136] ibid.

UCITS is to invest in certain markets (sectoral, geographical, or other) or in certain types of assets (equities, bonds, or other). It specifies whether the fund intends to use derivatives, if any, for its investment strategies or only for hedging purposes. In the case of index-based funds, it describes the strategy pursued to replicate the index.[137]

4.138 The description of the fund's risk profile must cover the general risks connected with investment in a fund, regardless of its type, and the specific risks attributable to the characteristics of the UCITS in question. It is a qualitative, not quantitative, description which is required. The CSSF expressly requires the insertion of two types of risk warnings for investors. The first warns investors against market risk, which may mean investors are likely not to recover their full investment. The second refers them to the complete prospectus for a more detailed description of risks.[138]

4.139 Historically, the past performance of a UCITS could have been described in different ways. The 2002 Act does not specify either the reference period for calculating performances or the form required for presentation to investors (graph, histogram, or simply a written description). The absence of specified requirements is likely to give rise to widely varying practices by promoters and funds, thereby impeding the ability of investors to compare different UCITS.

4.140 Thus Circular 03/122 complements and specifies the information required under the 2002 Act.[139] A fund's past performance should be represented in a histogram showing returns for the previous three financial years or, if the fund was organized less than three years before, the financial years completed so far. Past performance is based on net asset value after reinvestment of dividends.

4.141 When a UCITS is managed according to a benchmark index, its past performance is compared with that of the benchmark. The same kind of comparison is required when a UCITS or its investors pay a performance fee tied to a benchmark index.[140]

4.142 **Financial information** The simplified prospectus must inform investors about costs and fees, including the management fee and any performance fee. A distinction must be made between costs and fees borne by investors and by the UCITS' assets.

4.143 The CSSF does not require the simplified prospectus to mention either the total expense ratio (TER) or the portfolio turnover rate (PTR). These two types of information are in fact not required by Directive 2001/107.[141]

---

[137] ibid.
[138] ibid.
[139] ibid.
[140] Section II(b), Circular 03/122.
[141] Some members of the Contact Committee instituted by Art 53, Directive (EEC) 85/611 were nevertheless strongly in favour of making them mandatory. This plan was finally abandoned

The CSSF nevertheless allows promoters to include the total expense ratio and the **4.144** portfolio turnover rate in the simplified prospectus. Promoters who do so must comply with certain criteria intended to harmonize the presentation of this information.

The total expense ratio, defined as the ratio between the gross amount of a UCITS' **4.145** costs and its average net asset value, is calculated annually on an ex-post basis. Generally, it refers to the UCITS' financial year.[142] The CSSF specifies the costs and the average net asset value to be taken into account. The average net asset value is based on the UCITS' net assets as valued on every net asset value calculation date.

The costs to be taken into account are the charges borne directly by the UCITS, **4.146** including management costs and fees, performance fees, administrative costs, deposit, distribution and registration costs, and the fees of auditors and legal advisers. The inclusion of transaction costs is optional. A simplified prospectus must always indicate whether these costs are included in the total expense ratio. The ratio does not include costs borne by investors, such as subscription and redemption fees.

Promoters wishing to publish a total expense ratio may also have to calculate a **4.147** synthetic ratio. This occurs when a UCITS invests more than 20 per cent of its net assets in investment funds which publish a total expense ratio according to Circular 03/122. Any Luxembourg-based UCITS publishing a total expense ratio and investing at least 20 per cent of its net assets in other Luxembourg-based funds which also calculate and publish such a ratio in accordance with Circular 03/122 must add to this ratio a synthetic ratio reflecting this investment. When funds in which a UCITS holds securities do not publish a total expense ratio in accordance with Circular 03/122, the UCITS' simplified prospectus must state that it is unable to calculate a synthetic ratio for the relevant portion of assets.

The portfolio turnover rate, when mentioned in the simplified prospectus of a **4.148** UCITS, must be calculated according to the following formula, defined in Circular 03/122:[143]

Turnover = [(Total 1-Total 2)/M]*100
where:
Total 1 = Total transactions in securities during the period under review = X + Y
where X = securities purchases and Y = securities sales
Total 2 = total transactions in the units/shares of UCITS during the period under review = S + T

---

due to lack of agreement between the representatives of the national authorities and the European Commission.

[142] Section II(c), Circular 03/122.
[143] ibid.

where S = subscriptions of units/shares of UCITS and T = redemptions of units/shares of UCITS

M = monthly average assets of the UCITS.

4.149   The other financial information a simplified prospectus must include is a summary of the applicable tax treatment, a description of subscription and redemption fees, and any other costs and fees, distinguished according to whether they are borne by the investors or the fund.

4.150   **Commercial information**   The commercial information details the conditions under which units may be purchased and sold and, as applicable, converted, the frequency with which and the conditions under which dividends are distributed, and the publication frequency, place and method of subscription, redemption, and conversion prices.

4.151   **Additional information**   The additional information listed in Schedule C must include a notice informing investors that the complete prospectus and the annual and semi-annual reports are available upon request, free of charge, both before and after subscription. It must further indicate the competent authority and a contact capable of providing further explanations. Lastly, it must mention the prospectus publication date.

Umbrella funds

4.152   When a UCITS has more than one sub-fund, the required investment, financial, and commercial information must be provided for each sub-fund.[144] However, a fund can issue a general simplified prospectus with a specific appendix for each sub-fund. Insofar as the general information is identical for all funds, it can be included in the general part and does not have to be reproduced systematically in each appendix.

4.153   The total expense ratio must be calculated for each sub-fund. When a UCITS issues several categories of units, it must also calculate this ratio for each category.[145] The portfolio turnover rate must also be determined for each sub-fund.[146]

Other publications

4.154   The 2002 Act does not govern the use of sales literature other than the complete and simplified prospectus. That said, the use of advertising materials is authorized. Such materials need no longer be vetted in advance by the CSSF even if they have not been checked by the supervisory authorities of the country in which they

---

[144] Annex I, Sch C, *in fine*, 2002 Act.
[145] Section II(c), Circular 03/122.
[146] ibid.

are to be used. This does not mean that there are no restrictions as regards the contents of these documents. Issuers of advertisements must comply with the rules of conduct in force in the Luxembourg or foreign financial sector and may not include misleading investor information. This is achieved by stating the existence of a prospectus, naming the location where it may be obtained, and by informing the investors about the risks connected with the proposed investment.[147]

The Act of 13 February 2007 is even less precise. Given the limited pool of investors allowed to subscribe as well as their sophistication, the legislature did not deem it necessary to regulate the use of advertising material. **4.155**

Publication of constitutive documents and sales literature

Constitutive documents

Publication

The management regulations of an FCP are drawn up and signed by the management company, following which they are lodged with the registry of the District Court. The lodgement is published in the *Mémorial*.[148] Amendments of the regulations are similarly filed. The management company's representatives or their agents take care of these publication formalities insofar as the drafting and modification of the management regulations do not require the services of a notary. **4.156**

An investment company's articles of incorporation are adopted and amended by notarized deed, after which the notary lodges the instrument with the trade and companies register and arranges its publication in the *Mémorial*. **4.157**

Effect between the parties

The management regulations come into force in respect of the unitholders at a predetermined moment as specified in the management regulations, which may be when the regulations are signed, are lodged with the registry of the District Court, or are published in the *Mémorial*, or on the occurrence of any other event prescribed in the management regulations. **4.158**

The same applies to amendment of the management regulations. The regulations may provide that any amendment of their contents is to come into effect with respect to the unitholders on the date it is signed and prior to publication by means of a notice in the *Mémorial* (although such publication is required vis-à-vis legal effect with third parties). An FCP's unitholders are not 'third' parties but are themselves party to the regulations. **4.159**

---

[147] Art 117, 2002 Act and Circular 05/177.
[148] Arts 13(1) and 66, 2002 Act; Art 12(1), Act of 13 February 2007.

4.160 An investment company exists as soon as the founders have signed the deed of incorporation before a notary. Any amendment of the articles of incorporation becomes applicable to the shareholders when validly approved by them at a general meeting.

Validity vis-à-vis third parties

4.161 In the absence of an express provision in the 2002 Act or the Act of 13 February 2007, the validity vis-à-vis third parties of an FCP's establishment and amendments to the management regulations would appear to follow the above-mentioned rules, pursuant to ordinary contract law.[149]

4.162 This is not the position as regards the incorporation[150] of investment companies and the amendment of their constitutive documents. Any amendment of the articles of incorporation is ineffective vis-à-vis third parties prior to publication in the *Mémorial*, since third parties will not be aware of it before such publication.

Sales literature

4.163 Every complete and simplified prospectus authorized by the CSSF is stamped, showing the *nihil obstat* from that authority. This stamp does not reflect a positive assessment by the supervisory authority of the quality of the securities offered for sale.[151]

4.164 The 2002 Act requires the simplified prospectus to be offered free of charge to investors before subscription.[152] Subscription may take place without the subscriber's having read the prospectus or having received a copy, provided he has been offered this document free of charge.[153] The complete prospectus and the latest annual and semi-annual reports (with respect to UCIs other than SIFs) need only be provided to investors on request, provided they are offered free of charge.[154]

4.165 The 2002 Act allows the CSSF to publish or to have other parties publish the complete and simplified prospectuses and the annual and semi-annual reports of UCITS in any way it considers appropriate.[155] This provision reflects the joint wish of the CSSF and the Luxembourg Stock Exchange to facilitate electronic access to

---

[149] However, no UCI other than a SIF may place its units or shares with the public without being entered on the official list of UCIs. An application must be filed with the CSSF within, at most, one month from a UCI's formation or incorporation.

[150] ibid.

[151] Art 96, 2002 Act; Art 44, Act of 13 February 2007.

[152] Art 115(1), 2002 Act.

[153] Ch L, IV, Circular 91/75.

[154] Art 115(1), 2002 Act; Art 57(1), Act of 13 February 2007.

[155] Art 114(2), 2002 Act.

these documents.[156] The need for express legal authorization is probably due to the CSSF's wish to validate this publication method and to make it mandatory, notwithstanding, for instance, the existence of copyright in the documents involved.

Centrale de Communications Luxembourg SA (CCLux) has launched a specific **4.166** platform known as the 'market reference database' in order to receive and disseminate prospectuses and financial reports sent to it for this purpose by the CSSF. This gives investors access to a central database on Luxembourg-based UCIs other than SIFs.[157]

The obligation to be published in the market reference database only applies to **4.167** UCIs governed by the 2002 Act.

In Circular 03/97, the CSSF allows for the granting of derogations from the obli- **4.168** gation to publish the required information in the market reference database, provided adequate justification is given. A request for derogation could, for example, be made on account of confidentiality concerns when distribution of the relevant UCI will be limited to a very restricted circle of investors.

In principle, a prospectus is issued in the market reference database after approval **4.169** by the CSSF. At the UCI's request, publication may be postponed until it begins to market its units.[158]

Annual reports are released on the market reference database within four months **4.170** following the end of the financial year. Semi-annual reports are published within two months following the end of the period under review.[159]

The above-mentioned publication rules for prospectuses apply only in the terri- **4.171** tory of the Grand Duchy of Luxembourg. Subscription conditions may differ in other countries in which a UCI's units or shares are marketed and must be complied with.[160]

Entry on the List of UCIs

A UCI may carry on its activities in the Grand Duchy of Luxembourg only when **4.172** it has been authorized by the CSSF and included in the CSSF's list of UCIs.[161]

---

[156] Circular 03/97.
[157] ibid.
[158] ibid.
[159] ibid.
[160] ibid. SIFs are, however, not required to publish semi-annual reports. Their annual reports are to be released within 6 months following the end of the financial year (Art 52(1) and (2), Act of 13 February 2007).
[161] This is different for SIFs pursuant to Arts 42(1), 43, and 64, Act of 13 February 2007.

4.173 Authorization of a UCI governed by the 2002 Act requires the promoter and its agents to liaise with the CSSF once the constitutive documents and the sales literature are prepared. Drafts of these documents are submitted to the CSSF, which sends its comments and recommendations to the promoter or its agents. Its comments are taken into account and are discussed where necessary or appropriate with the inspector charged with reviewing the application file. On completion of this procedure, the definitive versions of these documents are finalized and the UCI can be established.

4.174 Once authorized, a UCI may begin business. Five copies of its complete prospectus and, as applicable, its simplified prospectus are sent to the CSSF to be stamped.[162] The CSSF sends written confirmation that the UCI has been added to its list and returns two duly stamped copies of the prospectus. The visa stamp means that the CSSF has no objection to the contents of the prospectus but may not be used for advertising purposes.[163] It does not reflect a positive assessment by the CSSF on the quality of the securities offered by the UCI.[164]

4.175 Given the sophistication of the investors to which it is dedicated, a SIF is permitted to gather subscriptions and commitments to subscribe before it is authorized by the CSSF.[165] It may also start its investment activity without being authorized. This does not mean that a SIF need not be authorized. The legislature simply allows for the possibility of postponement by a SIF of authorization but in the interim period a SIF can market and invest capital raised.

4.176 The ability for a SIF to launch its capital gathering and capital investment activities in advance of authorization has to be used carefully as the CSSF can impose changes to the operation or management of a SIF on application for authorization even though the SIF may already have been launched. In this event, it may be necessary to revert to investors and renegotiate with them. In order to avoid this kind of inconvenience, a prior consultation with the CSSF is highly recommended where there is any doubt about the CSSF's agreement on any aspect of the proposed operation of the SIF to be launched.

4.177 Pursuant to the 2002 Act and to the Act of 13 February 2007, applications for entry on the list of UCIs must be filed with the CSSF within one month following constitution or formation of a UCI.[166]

---

162 Ch L, I, 3, Circular 91/75; Section III, Circular 03/122.
163 ibid.
164 Art 96, 2002 Act.
165 Arts 42(1), 43, and 64, Act of 13 February 2007; for further details on this *ex post* agreement process, see A Contreras and J-N Fassin, 'Supervision' in *Specialised Investment Funds* (Arendt & Medernach, 2007) 77–79.
166 Art 94(1), 2002 Act; Art 43, Act of 13 February 2007.

As regards UCIs governed by the 2002 Act, the law distinguishes between the   **4.178**
constitutive documents of the UCI, which will not have been checked by the
CSSF prior to constitution or formation of the UCI (and are required to be filed
on application for authorization), and the offering document relating to securities
to be issued by the UCI to the public, which requires prior review by the CSSF. It
is immaterial whether the offering is public or private. As a UCI's establishment is
not necessarily tied to a simultaneous securities offer, the authors of the 2002 Act
did not wish to delay the UCI's establishment until the moment of authorization,
as the authorization application process need only commence within a month of
formation.[167] In practice, however, a UCI governed by the 2002 Act is established
following verbal approval by the CSSF of all documents accompanying the
registration application.

The list of UCIs authorized by the CSSF is published in the *Memorial*.[168] The   **4.179**
entry on the official list of UCIs is maintained subject to continuing observance
by the relevant UCI of all applicable laws, regulations, or agreements.[169]

---

[167] This solution was already provided for in the 1983 Act (Art 42(1)). While the law does not
provide for the imposition of penalties when the deadline of one month is exceeded, under Arts
22(1)(d), 23, and 66 of the 2002 Act, an FCP is automatically placed in liquidation when its net
assets are less than one-fourth of the legal minimum of €1,250,000 for more than 6 months.

[168] Art 94(1), 2002 Act; Art 43(1), Act of 13 February 2007.

[169] Art 94(2), 2002 Act; Art 43(2), Act of 13 February 2007.

5

SECURITIES ISSUED BY UNDERTAKINGS FOR COLLECTIVE INVESTMENT

5.01 In this chapter we will examine the different types of securities a UCI may issue, the rights they represent, and the conditions governing their transfer.

5.02 There is a fundamental distinction between units issued by FCPs and shares issued by investment companies. FCPs are essentially contractual schemes and may therefore issue all kinds of units, to which they may attach significantly varying rights. In contrast, investment companies are subject to the requirements applicable to the type of company that they have chosen. The promoters' creativity must fit into a stricter framework and investment companies must take a series of binding laws and regulations into account.

5.03 A further distinction can be drawn between the different types of securities UCIs may issue. First of all, they may consist of units or shares, ie securities representing an interest in the net assets, in the case of units of an FCP, or in the share capital of an investment company, in the case of shares in an investment company. Investment companies may also issue founder shares in exchange for contributions not reflected in their share capital. Lastly, UCIs may issue bonds or similar securities representing claims on the assets of an FCP or debts of an investment company.

5.04 These three types of securities will be discussed in the following three sections.

Units and Shares Issued by UCIs

Types and forms of units and shares of UCIs

Units issued by common funds

5.05 According to the 2002 Act and to the Act of 13 February 2007, an FCP's units represent the co-ownership rights of the investors, as joint owners of the

FCP's assets.[1] An FCP's units represent one or more portions of ownership of the fund.[2] As FCPs do not have a legal personality, they themselves may not issue units. Instead units are created and issued by the FCP's management company.[3]

The 2002 Act and the Act of 13 February 2007 are virtually silent on the rights **5.06** and obligations attaching to an FCP's units. The legislation incidentally[4] states that units may carry voting rights, implying that they generally do not. It adds that unitholders may not require the partition or dissolution of FCPs[5] and, lastly, specifies that ownership of units automatically entails acceptance of the provisions of the management regulations.[6] In all other respects, an FCP's founders are free to create the rights and obligations attaching to the holding of units issued by the fund.

An FCP's units may be issued in the form of registered or bearer securities. The **5.07** issue of registered units may, depending on the circumstances, be accompanied by the issue of registered certificates for their holders, representing ownership of one or more FCP units. Alternatively, the management company may decline to issue certificates and simply supply to the registered owner written confirmation of an entry in the register of the fund's registered units.[7]

If certificates are issued they must be signed by an FCP's management company **5.08** and depositary. Their signatures do not have to be handwritten but may be reproduced mechanically.[8]

An FCP's units may be issued in fractional amounts. These must always be **5.09** registered and may not carry any voting rights, which can attach only to whole units.[9]

Shares in SICAVs

SICAVs governed by the 2002 Act must be incorporated in the form of an SA[10] **5.10** and are, therefore, subject to the rules governing such companies, save insofar as the 2002 Act derogates from those rules.[11] Units in such companies are more precisely known as shares and, accordingly, are described as such below. There is no nominal value for registered shares and bearer shares.

---

[1] Arts 5 and 65(1), 2002 Act.
[2] ibid Arts 8(1) and 66.
[3] ibid.
[4] ibid.
[5] ibid Arts 11(1) and 66; Art 10, Act of 13 February 2007.
[6] Arts 13(1) and 66, 2002 Act; Art 12(1), Act of 13 February 2007.
[7] Arts 8(1) and 66, 2002 Act; Art 7(1), Act of 13 February 2007.
[8] ibid.
[9] ibid. Unit fractions can be grouped to form a whole unit.
[10] Or of an SE. See 2.134 *et seq* above.
[11] Arts 26 and 71, 2002 Act.

5.11   SIFs may opt for the status of SA, SCA, SARL, or cooperative society organized in the form of an SA.[12] They may issue every type of security permitted to be issued by the relevant form of company under the 1915 Act.

5.12   The rights attaching to a SICAV's shares are described neither in the 2002 Act nor in the Act of 13 February 2007, although this does not mean the founders have unlimited freedom to specify rights in this regard. The rights attaching to shares are subject to precise rules in the 1915 Act, as we shall see below.

Equal value of shares: principles and exceptions

5.13   According to the 1915 Act,[13] 'the capital of *sociétés anonymes* [SAs] is divided into shares of equal value, with or without mention of value'. Hence, each share represents an identical fraction of the share capital.

5.14   This requirement is in principle applicable to SICAVs, in accordance with the intention expressed in the 2002 Act and in the Act of 13 February 2007.[14] However, the rule that shares have equal value is difficult to comply with for SICAVs having several share classes. SICAVs frequently issue shares of different classes, for example when creating several sub-funds. In umbrella type SICAVs, the value of shares belonging to a given sub-fund is equal to the value of that sub-fund's assets less the liabilities attributable to the sub-fund. The value of a SICAV's shares will therefore differ from one sub-fund to the next.

5.15   Additional share classes can be created for a SICAV as a whole (when it does not have multiple sub-funds) or within an individual sub-fund. In the latter case, classes are superimposed on the class of shares arising from the compartmentalization of the SICAV into sub-funds (each sub-fund constituting a different 'class' of shares).

5.16   For example, a sub-fund may issue accumulation and distribution shares, whose value will be equal at the moment of creation. As dividends are declared on the distribution shares, the portion of the sub-fund's net assets attributable to the accumulation shares (and the net asset value attributable to the accumulation shares) increases. As the value of accumulation shares increases above the value of the distribution shares (which is reduced to reflect distributions made), the value of assets attributable to the two classes diverges and continues to diverge throughout the life of the sub-fund.

5.17   Other types of share class are also possible, for example different costs may be charged to different classes. By way of illustration, it is possible to create an

---

[12]   Art 25, Act of 13 February 2007.
[13]   Art 37, 1915 Act.
[14]   Arts 26 and 71, 2002 Act; Art 26, Act of 13 February 2007.

'institutional' share class, which pays a reduced proportion of a SICAV's management, administration, and marketing costs than the costs attributed to shares issued to 'private investors'. The favourable treatment of such institutional shares can be justified by the higher minimum investment threshold applicable to the institutional share class.

Another example is the creation of share classes in currencies other than the relevant fund's base or reference currency (in which the net assets are expressed), for example to facilitate distribution of shares in different markets. Through the use of derivative techniques and instruments, the portion of assets attributable to such a share class is typically hedged against fluctuations in the SICAV's or sub-fund's reference currency. The costs and benefits of such techniques and instruments are allocated to the net asset value of the shares of the relevant currency class, resulting in those classes having a different value from other classes. **5.18**

In all these examples, a single portfolio of assets is attributable to several share classes, whose unequal values result only from the different apportionment of certain rights and revenues (such as distributions) or commitments and charges (such as management costs or the expense of currency hedging). **5.19**

Yet more types of classes—not necessarily resulting in different values—are also conceivable, for example shares to which a sliding scale of redemption charges determined by the period of ownership of shares applies or the level of sophistication of the fund's management techniques.[15] **5.20**

In respect of umbrella type SICAVs, the 2002 Act[16] and the Act of 13 February 2007[17] derogate from the 1915 Act and provide that the shares issued by such companies may have different values. This exception, however, applies only to umbrella funds. **5.21**

Does this mean that the shares of an ordinary SICAV may not have different values? This question calls for a qualified answer. It is traditionally accepted that this rule is public policy and may not be deviated from by the articles of incorporation.[18] However, it is important to analyse the reason for its existence. **5.22**

The authors of the 1915 Act sought to establish equal treatment of shareholders in respect of voting rights. The intention was that shareholders making identical contributions should be accorded the same voting powers. **5.23**

---

[15] For a detailed discussion of such practices, see the Annual Report of the CSSF for 1999, 65 and 66.

[16] Art 133(3), 2002 Act.

[17] Art 71(3), Act of 13 February 2007.

[18] For a critical analysis of this issue, see J Delvaux, *Le Droit des sociétés au Grand-Duché de Luxembourg* (Université de Luxembourg, 1999) Ch 3, para 3.2.3.4.1.

5.24 That principle has already been weakened by SAs other than investment companies. There is no bar to issuing shares at a premium. As the amount of the premium may vary from issue to issue, the price of the vote attaching to a share is not always the same, albeit identical voting power results. This practice weakens the principle of equal treatment of all shareholders and raises the question of whether that principle can still be regarded as a matter of public policy and hence mandatory.

5.25 A SICAV's articles of incorporation frequently permit the conversion of shares from one class to another, enabling shareholders to exchange their shares for a different number of shares—and therefore voting rights—in another class, provided the overall value of the exchanged securities remains the same. Where such conversion is cost free, shareholders wishing to exercise their voting rights are not affected by the coexistence of shares with different values within the same SICAV.

5.26 Instead of creating several share classes within a single SICAV to, for example, differentiate between accumulating and distributing shares, it would of course be possible to create several investment companies or to divide an investment company's assets into sub-funds with the same asset composition but with each sub-fund having a different share class (for example accumulation or distribution), or a different reference currency or cost structure. It would nevertheless be desirable to adapt the 2002 Act and the Act of 13 February 2007.[19]

5.27 The merit of this solution is that it avoids the potential problem discussed in this section (ie that the derogation permitting shares issued by SICAVs to have different values applies only to umbrella funds). However, it involves the coexistence of several UCIs or sub-funds, which is likely to make their management or administration more cumbersome and costly.

Form of shares

5.28 A SICAV's shares can be issued in registered or bearer form. Regardless of their form, they must carry a sequence number.[20]

Registered shares

5.29 Registered shares are represented only by an entry in the share register.[21] Shareholders may be given a certificate proving registration, but that does not represent the shares in question. Information on the shares can be found in the

---

[19] The problem is different for FCPs, since the 1915 Act does not apply to them and neither the 2002 Act nor the Act of 13 February 2007 requires equal value as between classes of units in an FCP, reflecting the fact that an FCP's units do not, in principle, carry voting rights.

[20] Art 37, 1915 Act.

[21] ibid Art 40.

register, which, according to the 1915 Act, must contain 'the exact name of each shareholder and an indication of the number of shares or share fractions held by him, any payments made, any transfers together with the dates of transfers and details of any conversions of shares into bearer securities, if authorised by the articles of incorporation'.[22]

Reference to payments may be unnecessary in the sense that shares of a SICAV **5.30** governed by the 2002 Act must be fully paid up,[23] but is justified when the fund issues fractional shares or when shares are issued by a SIF.

Bearer shares

Bearer shares are represented by a security. They do not exist until they are **5.31** printed.[24] Once printed and put into circulation, they incorporate the shareholder's rights. Their form is governed by the 1915 Act, with one exception the 2002 Act and the Act of 13 February 2007 specify that they may not indicate their accounting par value or the portion of the share capital they represent, but must specify the minimum share capital of the SICAV.[25] This requirement is logical for a company whose capital can vary at all times, particularly as regards the performance of its investments. Pursuant to the ordinary law governing SAs, a SICAV's bearer shares must further indicate: 'the date of the company's deed of incorporation and its publication, . . . the number and nature of each share class, a brief statement of the contributions and the conditions on which they are made, any special benefits attributed to the founders, the company's term, and the day, time and municipality in which the annual general meeting is held'.[26]

Bearer shares also bear signatures, in principle those of two directors. Unless other- **5.32** wise stipulated in the articles of incorporation, they may be handwritten, printed, or stamped. However, the board of directors may authorize a given person other than a director to affix one of the two signatures. Such an authorization must be published in the *Mémorial*.[27] The signature of that person may be handwritten only.

---

[22] ibid Art 39

[23] Arts 28(8) and 71, 2002 Act. Partial payment is nevertheless permitted for SIFs (Arts 28(3) and 39(6), Act of 13 February 2007).

[24] In contrast with foreign law systems, Luxembourg legislation does not provide for paperless bearer shares. Despite this legislative void, 'statutory' rules on paperless shares have emerged, under which a company issues a 'global' bearer certificate which factors in the total amount of the share capital to be covered by the planned share issue. Such shares—or share fractions—are not themselves issued in the form of a printed certificate but merely recorded in a bearer securities account opened on the depositary's books in the investor's name. The virtue of this practice is that it makes it unnecessary for the issuing company to print costly bearer certificates. However, since this practice is not endorsed by an express legal provision, rapid adjustment of company law would be desirable.

[25] Art 28(8) and (9) and Art 71, 2002 Act; Art 28(8), Act of 13 February 2007.

[26] Art 41, 1915 Act.

[27] ibid.

Share fractions

5.33   A SICAV's shares may be issued in fractional amounts,[28] which also bear a sequence number.

5.34   Share fractions do not carry voting rights except when, in aggregate, they are sufficient to constitute a whole share. They are useful when an investor does not subscribe for a specific number of shares but subscribes for shares up to a given monetary amount. In such cases, a SICAV may issue a share fraction corresponding to the balance of the subscription in order to avoid having to repay that balance to the subscriber and so generating additional administrative formalities and costs.

5.35   In contrast to the rules applying to FCPs, the 2002 Act and the Act of 13 February 2007 do not require a SICAV's share fractions to be registered. They may take the form of bearer certificates.

Shares in SICAFs

5.36   The rules governing shares in SICAFs are more complex. A SICAF may take several legal forms, depending on whether the SICAF in question comes under Part I or Part II of the 2002 Act or under the Act of 13 February 2007.[29] The following paragraphs examine only those rules governing securities issued by the two most prevalent types of SICAF, ie the SA and the SCA. The rules governing SARLs will be outlined only for the sake of completeness, since that legal form is rarely used in practice.

SICAFs incorporated in the form of an SA

5.37   The regime for shares of SICAFs incorporated in the form of an SA is almost the same as that for shares of SICAVs.

5.38   However, there are a few differences, due to the fact that the capital of SICAFs is, by definition, fixed. A SICAF's capital can vary only if the formalities for increasing or reducing the capital of an SA are complied with. It is not modified by a SICAF's investment performance. Consequently, in contrast to SICAVs:

(1)   a SICAF's shares have a nominal value or accounting par value, which must be stated in the articles of incorporation[30] and on any bearer shares;[31]

(2)   the nominal value or accounting par value of all shares issued by a SICAF is the same, even when there are several share classes with different net asset values;

(3)   the amount of the share capital must be indicated on any bearer shares.[32]

---

[28]   Art 37, 1915 Act. This applies to share fractions.
[29]   See 2.150 above.
[30]   Art 27(7), 1915 Act.
[31]   ibid Art 41.
[32]   ibid.

SICAFs incorporated in the form of an SCA

When created in the form of an SCA, a SICAF issues two types of shares. **5.39**

Shares of the first type are governed by the same legal rules as for shares issued by **5.40**
SAs[33] and are referred to as 'shares' in the 1915 Act[34]. They represent the share
capital of the SCA and, in principle, are issued in favour of the company's limited
partners but may also be subscribed for by general partners. There is only
one minor difference between such shares and those issued by an SA, and this
concerns the form of bearer shares. Bearer shares must be signed by the managers,[35]
whose signature may not be delegated to anyone else.

The second type of shares issued by SICAFs incorporated in the form of an SCA is **5.41**
known as a '*part d'intérêt*'. This type of share specifically represents the corporate
rights attaching to a general partner. Its status is similar to that of shares issued
by *sociétés de personnes* (partnerships) such as the *société en nom collectif* (general
partnership) and the SCS. It may not take the form of a bearer share and, in principle, cannot be transferred.

SICAFs incorporated in the form of an SARL

In an SARL, securities representing the partners' rights in the share capital must **5.42**
always be registered. They cannot be traded. The 1915 Act defines them as 'certificates of interest held by specific persons'[36], without otherwise prescribing the form
in which they may be issued.

Rights attaching to the units and shares of UCIs

Rights of units in common funds

General presentation

The 2002 Act and the Act of 13 February 2007 are somewhat vague concerning **5.43**
the rights attaching to units in an FCP.

That leaves considerable freedom in this area, subject to three legal constraints. **5.44**
First, the ownership of units does not confer the power to require an FCP's
partition or dissolution.[37] Secondly, ownership of a unit automatically entails
acceptance of the provisions of the management regulations.[38] Lastly, the right to
information of investors in FCPs is covered by strict rules.

---

[33] ibid Art 103.
[34] ibid Art 106.
[35] ibid.
[36] Art 188, 1915 Act.
[37] Arts 11(1) and 66, 2002 Act; Art 10(1), Act of 13 February 2007.
[38] Arts 13(1) and 66, 2002 Act; Art 12(1), Act of 13 February 2007.

5.45 In other respects, an FCP's founders have very wide discretion in attaching rights to the units. Such rights can include, for example, the grant of voting rights to the units, which can be exercised in relation to a wide range of decisions (which must be specified in the regulations), or preferential subscription rights for newly issued units, rights to call general meetings or rights to dividends, which may be preferential or even cumulative, or any other types of rights imaginable.

Right to information

5.46 This section deals only with the information to be disclosed during the life of an FCP. The contents of the constitutive documents and sales literature required on creation have already been discussed.[39]

5.47 An FCP's participants must be provided with the information listed below, which is required by the 2002 Act or by the Act of 13 February 2007.

5.48 One of the major concerns of the European legislature is to ensure that investors receive correct and adequate information. For that reason, it provided in 1985 that every prospectus must always contain the information needed by investors to make an informed judgment about the proposed investment.[40] As regards UCIs governed by the 2002 Act, this requirement means that a dated and up-to-date prospectus must be released whenever one of an FCP's essential components is modified.[41] An FCP's prospectus may, however, be updated by the issue of its periodic financial reports, ie its semi-annual and annual reports.[42] As for SIFs, the prospectus must be updated only when new securities are issued to new investors.[43]

5.49 In 2002, the legislature added the requirement for funds to issue a simplified prospectus in addition to the complete prospectus. The simplified prospectus summarizes the essential information contained in the complete prospectus, in a language and presentation style which is easy to understand for the average investor. Quite logically, it required only coordinated UCITS to disseminate a simplified prospectus. The Luxembourg legislature followed suit, not wishing to impose excessive constraints on UCIs governed by Part II of the 2002 Act or the Act of 13 February 2007.[44]

5.50 The updated complete prospectus does not necessarily have to be delivered to all participants in the FCP. The law merely requires it to 'be delivered free of charge to subscribers on request'.[45]

---

[39] See 4.19 *et seq* and 4.96 *et seq* above.
[40] Art 28.1, Directive (EEC) 85/611, also see Art 110(1), 2002 Act and Ch L, I, 1, Circular 91/75; as regards SIFs, see Art 53, Act of 13 February 2007.
[41] Art 112, 2002 Act and Ch L, I, 1, Circular 91/75.
[42] ibid Ch L, I, 1.
[43] Art 54, Act of 13 February 2007.
[44] Art 109(3), 2002 Act.
[45] Art 115(1), 2002 Act; Art 57(1), Act of 13 February 2007.

In other words, the law does not require an FCP to supply a complete prospectus   **5.51**
to everyone wishing to subscribe for its units; nor does it have to prove that subscribers for its units have acquainted themselves with the document, which merely
has to be available free of charge on request.[46] This is not the case with the simplified
prospectus, which the law requires to be 'offered to subscribers free of charge
before conclusion of a contract'.[47] Subscribers can also be briefed by means of a
simplified marketing brochure. However, marketing brochures are not governed
by the provisions of the 2002 Act for simplified prospectuses. Typically the marketing brochure, if used, is attached to the subscription form, refers to the
availability of the prospectus on request,[48] and informs subscribers about the
essential components of the FCP whose securities they would be buying.

Every FCP must publish financial reports on the state of its assets and liabilities.   **5.52**
UCIs governed by the 2002 Act must publish annual and semi-annual reports,[49]
whereas only annual reports are required for SIFs.[50]

An FCP's annual report covers an entire financial year. It must be audited by an   **5.53**
authorized independent auditor[51] and published within four months following
the end of the financial year concerned.[52] That period is extended to six months
for SIFs.[53]

An FCP's semi-annual report covers the first six months of the financial year.[54] It   **5.54**
must be published within two months following the end of the period concerned.[55]
In contrast to the annual report, it need not be audited by an independent
auditor.

Semi-annual and complete annual reports are made available in accordance with   **5.55**
the same principles as those applying to the complete prospectus described above.
Such documents do not have to be supplied on each subscription but must be
offered free of charge to subscribers who request a copy.[56] When they relate to a
UCI governed by the 2002 Act they must be delivered free of charge, on request,

---

[46] Ch L, IV, Circular 91/75.
[47] Art 115(1), 2002 Act.
[48] Ch L, IV, Circular 91/75.
[49] Art 109(1), 2002 Act.
[50] Art 52(1), Act of 13 February 2007.
[51] Art 113(1), 2002 Act; Art 55(1), Act of 13 February 2007.
[52] Art 109(2), 2002 Act
[53] Art 52(2), Act of 13 February 2007.
[54] Art 109(1), 2002 Act.
[55] ibid Art 109(2); and Ch L, III, 1, Circular 91/75. For a newly created UCI, the first interim
report may cover a period of 8 months, in principle reckoned from the date of the UCI's registration
on the official list. The first annual report may cover an extended period of, at most, 18 months from
the registration date.
[56] Art 115(1), 2002 Act; Art 55(1), Act of 13 February 2007.

to unitholders.[57] Lastly, they must be kept available to the public at the places specified in the prospectus.[58]

5.56   When a semi-annual or annual report contains errors or omissions, the FCP does not necessarily have to publish an amended report,[59] but the CSSF reserves the right to require it to do so.

5.57   Every FCP governed by the 2002 Act must publish the issue and sales price and, as the case may be, the redemption price of its units.[60] Prices of UCITS governed by Part I of the 2002 Act must in principle be published at least twice a month and whenever units are issued, sold, or redeemed.[61] In accordance with the 2002 Act, the CSSF may, however, permit a UCITS to reduce the publication frequency to no less than once a month,[62] provided that such a derogation does not prejudice the interests of the unitholders. UCIs covered by Part II of the 2002 Act enjoy greater flexibility. They have to publish the issue and sales price and, as the case may be, the redemption price of their units only once a month.[63] The 2002 Act authorizes the CSSF to derogate from this frequency without fixing a limit.[64] UCIs are sometimes authorized to limit publication to the occasions when they produce their semi-annual and annual reports and whenever they issue or redeem units. A SIF is required to report its net asset value only once a year.

5.58   Advertising material circulated by FCPs governed by the 2002 Act does not have to be submitted for verification to the CSSF even when it is to be distributed in the Grand Duchy of Luxembourg.[65] The 2002 Act merely requires such advertising documents to indicate the existence of a prospectus and the places where it may be obtained.[66] The CSSF has added to these requirements for compliance with the applicable rules of conduct of the financial sector, whether in Luxembourg or elsewhere. These rules include a ban on misleading advertising and the obligation to inform investors correctly of the risks connected with the proposed investment.[67]

---

[57]   Art 115(2), 2002 Act; Art 57(2), Act of 13 February 2007.
[58]   Art 115(3), 2002 Act.
[59]   Ch L, III, 3, Circular 91/75.
[60]   The CSSF takes the view that publication of such prices does not necessarily mean publication in specialized newspapers or other gazettes. It is enough to make them available at the UCI's registered office or at any other place mentioned in the prospectus.
[61]   Art 116(1), 2002 Act.
[62]   ibid.
[63]   Provided they do not issue, sell, or redeem their units more frequently, as such transactions must systematically be published: Art 116(2), 2002 Act.
[64]   ibid.
[65]   Circular 05/177.
[66]   Art 117, 2002 Act.
[67]   Circular 05/177.

Rights of shares in investment companies

The corporate framework of investment companies entails the application of a   **5.59**
series of standards governing the rights attaching to their shares.

Such rights are traditionally divided into two categories. First, there are rights of   **5.60**
association, which determine the conditions governing participation in general
meetings and the instruments and methods available to monitor, or even challenge, the company's management. The second category consists of ownership
rights, ie the rights to a return of capital and to share in the profits. The nature and
scope of these rights is broadly the same, regardless of the type of company chosen.
There are, however, some differences, which are discussed below.

Rights of association

Right to attend general meetings

All shares carry the right to attend general meetings, regardless of the company by   **5.61**
which they are issued. That is a matter of public policy and hence not open to
derogation under the articles of incorporation or a contract.[68]

Voting rights

Principles   For many years, voting rights were regarded as an essential right of   **5.62**
association, which therefore could not be limited or withdrawn. The rule[69] that
every shareholder may participate, without limitation, in deliberations with the
same number of votes as his number of shares is imperative, and applies despite
any clause to the contrary in the articles of incorporation.

That principle was weakened when the 1915 Act permitted the issue of non-   **5.63**
voting shares by SAs and, indirectly,[70] by SCAs. This means that two share classes
can coexist in SAs and SCAs, distinguished by the scope of their voting rights.

Ordinary shares   All ordinary shares have the same voting rights. There is no   **5.64**
distinction according to whether they are fully paid up or not.[71]

The voting rights attaching to ordinary shares may be suspended in the situations   **5.65**
listed exhaustively in the 1915 Act. For example, voting rights are suspended in
the case of shares issued by an SA that have been redeemed[72] by or pledged[73] to the

---

[68] J Van Ryn, *Principes de droit commercial* (Bruylant, 1954) Vol I, 352.
[69] For SAs, this is Art 67(4) of the 1915 Act, which applies to SCAs by virtue of Art 103 of that
Act; the equivalent for SARLs is Art 195 of the 1915 Act.
[70] Art 103, 1915 Act.
[71] Arts 67(4), 103, and 195, 1915 Act. Note, however, that the voting right attached to shares
that have not been paid up is suspended under Art 67(7) of the 1915 Act for as long as these
payments, officially called and due, have not been made.
[72] Art 49-5, 1915 Act.
[73] ibid Art 49-7.

SA as security and which it does not cancel but rather holds in its assets. The same rules on suspension of voting rights apply to SCAs,[74] and to the indirect purchase and holding of treasury stock by SAs or SCAs through subsidiaries.[75]

5.66 Shareholders can restrict their freedom to exercise their voting rights in voting agreements. Debated for many years,[76] the lawfulness of this type of agreement was finally determined by the Belgian Supreme Court in a ruling of 1989.[77] In that decision, the Court held that shareholder agreements are lawful 'when they do not eliminate the shareholder's right to participate in corporate decisions, reflect the interests of the company itself, and are wholly free from fraudulent intent'.[78] Although not yet enshrined in Luxembourg law, this legal precedent tends to be followed by our courts.[79]

5.67 **Non-voting shares**   SAs or SCAs may also issue so-called 'non-voting shares'. Shares of this type should more appropriately be qualified as shares 'with reduced voting rights', since they carry voting rights in certain circumstances listed in the 1915 Act.

5.68 The legal framework for non-voting shares is relatively strict. Most of the applicable rules reflect public policy and govern the issue and conversion of such shares and the circumstances in which they carry voting rights.

5.69 *Issuing terms and procedures*   A decision to issue non-voting shares may be taken at the time of incorporation of the company, as part of a capital increase or by conversion of ordinary shares.[80] The maximum number of non-voting shares to be issued or converted is determined by the general meeting of shareholders.[81]

5.70 The issue of non-voting shares is subject to certain conditions designed to strengthen non-voting shareholders' ownership rights.[82] Thus:[83]

(1) non-voting shares may not represent more than half of the share capital;

---

[74] ibid Art 103.

[75] ibid Art 49*bis*, 1915 Act, introduced by the Act of 12 March 1998 transposing Council Directive (EEC) 92/101 of 23 November 1992 amending Directive (EEC) 77/91 on the formation of public limited-liability companies and the maintenance and alteration of their capital, and amending the modified Act of 10 August 1915 on commercial companies (*Mémorial* A 1998, 356) and Art 103 of the 1915 Act.

[76] See in this regard, P Van Ommeslaghe, 'Les conventions d'actionnaires en droit belge' (1989) *Rev prat soc* 309.

[77] Belgian *Cour de Cassation*, 13 April 1989. For a commentary on that decision, see D Michiels (1990) *JT* 751; J-M Nelissen Grade, 'De la validité et de l'exécution de la convention de vote dans les sociétés commerciales' (1991) *RCJB* 214; Van Ommeslaghe (n 76 above) 312.

[78] ibid.

[79] Delvaux (n 18 above) Ch 3, para 3.2.3.4.2.

[80] Art 45(1), 1915 Act.

[81] ibid Art 45(2).

[82] *Parliamentary doc* No. 2890[1], Message from the Minister of Justice to the Speaker of the Parliament, 2.

[83] Art 44(1), 1915 Act.

(2) non-voting shares must confer a right to a preferential[84] and cumulative[85] dividend corresponding to a percentage of their nominal or accounting par value as fixed in the articles of incorporation—they may also carry a right to an additional share in the profits;

(3) non-voting shares must confer a preferential right to repayment of capital—they may also carry a right to share in the distribution of any liquidation surplus.

Such conditions must be fulfilled at all times. Where they are not—or are no longer—fulfilled, non-voting shares automatically recover their voting rights.[86]   **5.71**

Since neither the 2002 Act nor the Act of 13 February 2007 address the question   **5.72** of the issue of non-voting shares, non-voting shares could theoretically be issued by both SICAVs and SICAFs. However, the legal status of SICAVs precludes them from issuing such securities, since compliance with all of the above-mentioned conditions is extremely complicated for such a company, in that its shares do not have a stable nominal value or accounting par value needed to calculate the right to preferential and cumulative dividends.

Exercise of reduced voting rights   The rights of non-voting shareholders to prefer-   **5.73** ential and cumulative dividends are carefully protected. Whenever profits are paid out, such shareholders are the first to receive their entitlement. If the preferential right is disregarded, such shareholders are automatically given voting rights to enable them to claim their entitlements.[87] The general shareholders' meeting may decide not to declare a dividend for a given financial year. When such a decision is made twice, in two successive financial years, non-voting shares are accorded voting rights until such time as the preferential and cumulative dividends due have been paid in full.[88] The same sanction applies when preferential and cumulative dividends are only partly paid for two successive financial years despite the availability of distributable profits.[89]

Non-voting shares are accorded voting rights only when distributable profits exist   **5.74** but are not paid to the holders of those shares. Such rights are not accorded when preferential dividends cannot be paid due to the lack of distributable profits.[90] In those circumstances, no shareholder may claim a dividend. The preferential

---

[84]   ie paid before any other.

[85]   ie a dividend 'that may be paid from the profits of years after the year concerned, if the profits of that year do not permit the payment of a preferential dividend or permit the payment of only a partial preferential dividend' (J-M Van Hille, *La société anonyme, Aspects juridiques et pratiques*, supplement (Bruylant, 1992) 54).

[86]   Art 44(2), 1915 Act.

[87]   ibid.

[88]   Art 46(2), 1915 Act.

[89]   ibid.

[90]   This concept has a special meaning in the context of UCIs. See 5.102 below.

dividends due for such a financial year are cumulative, however, and will therefore be added to the dividends due for subsequent financial years.[91]

5.75 In addition to those cases in which voting rights are accorded by way of sanction, holders of preference shares can vote at general meetings held to vote on various matters listed in the 1915 Act.[92]

5.76 Whether or not they may exercise voting rights, the holders of non-voting shares are entitled to attend general meetings. They must be sent the notices calling meetings and the reports and other documents which, under the 1915 Act, must be sent to the company's shareholders or made available to them,[93] within the same time limits as for ordinary shareholders.[94]

5.77 Compliance with the rules governing the quorum required for general meetings is determined differently depending on whether or not voting rights are attached to preference shares. If voting rights attach, the holders of non-voting shares are taken into account in calculating the quorum. If not, they are ignored.[95]

Preferential subscription right

5.78 The preferential subscription right allows the existing shareholders of an SA or SCA to subscribe in cash to capital increases prior to third parties. Each shareholder has a preferential subscription right proportionate to his share capital entitlement.[96] The preferential subscription right can, in principle, be assigned by shareholders who do not wish to exercise it.

5.79 The preferential subscription right offers shareholders three forms of protection. Exercise of this right enables shareholders to preserve their proportionate interest in the share capital and therefore their voting power within the company after each capital increase effected by cash contributions. It also avoids loss of value to shareholders when new shares are issued at a discount to the true value of the existing shares. Lastly, it may render it very difficult, if not impossible, for a third party to become a new shareholder.

5.80 The rules on preferential subscription rights differ as between SICAVs and SICAFs. In principle, a SICAV's shareholders may not claim preferential

---

[91] *Parliamentary doc* No 2890¹, Message from the Minister of Justice to the Speaker of the Parliament, 3; Report of the Legal Committee, 7.

[92] ie the issue of new shares with preferential rights, the determination of the preferential and cumulative dividend attaching to non-voting shares, conversion of non-voting preference shares into ordinary shares, reduction of share capital, modification of the corporate object clause, the issue of convertible bonds, early dissolution of the company, and conversion of the company into a company with another legal form (Art 46(1), 1915).

[93] ibid Art 47.

[94] ibid.

[95] ibid Art 46(3).

[96] For SAs, Art 32-3(1), 1915 Act, which applies to SCAs by virtue of Art 103 of that Act.

subscription rights when new shares are issued,[97] although the articles of incorporation may provide otherwise, in which case they will determine the scope and conditions of exercise of this right.

In contrast, in SICAFs incorporated in the form of SAs or SCAs, the preferential **5.81** subscription rights of existing shareholders must in principle be respected.[98] In that respect, the 2002 Act and the Act of 13 February 2007 do not derogate from the 1915 Act.

Capital increases effected by cash contributions must therefore always be **5.82** preceded by a notice to the shareholders,[99] which must state the period during which the preferential subscription right may be exercised. The notice must be published in the *Mémorial* and in two newspapers distributed in the Grand Duchy of Luxembourg. A registered letter to each shareholder will suffice as notice if all the shares are registered. The period during which the preferential subscription rights may be exercised is fixed by the board of directors and may not be less than thirty days from the opening of subscriptions.

A shareholder may assign his preferential subscription right if he does not wish to **5.83** exercise it. The assignment of subscription rights is subject only to the restrictions on assignment of the shares to which the subscription right is attached.[100] A shareholder who does not exercise or assign his preferential subscription right can also receive its value in cash. Subscription rights not exercised during the subscription period must be sold publicly by the company.[101] According to the Law of 1915, the shareholders entitled to the particular rights can claim the sale proceeds for five years.

The preferential subscription right is not mandatory. The law authorizes excep- **5.84** tions to and limitations on the pre-emption rights, subject to certain conditions.

First, the general meeting voting on a capital increase or the grant of authorization **5.85** of the board of directors to increase the capital, can restrict or abolish the preferential subscription right or authorize the board of directors to do so.[102] The notice to attend the general meeting must include notice of the proposed resolution. The board of directors must also present to the general meeting a report explaining the reasons for limiting or removing the preferential subscription right and explaining the proposed issue price.

---

[97] Arts 29(3) and 71, 2002 Act; Art 29(3), Act of 13 February 2007.
[98] Except when an investment company is incorporated in the form of an SARL, since the 1915 Act does not provide for any preferential subscription rights in such companies.
[99] Art 32-3(3), 1915 Act.
[100] ibid Art 32-3(4).
[101] ibid Art 32-3(7).
[102] ibid Art 32-3(5).

5.86   The general meeting may also organize alternative procedures for exercising the preferential subscription right.[103] For example, the general meeting could provide for exercise of the right within a shorter period than thirty days.

5.87   Secondly, the articles of incorporation may authorize the board of directors to eliminate or restrict preferential subscription rights within the framework of the authorized capital. An authorization to so limit or restrict preferential rights will endure for the same length of time as the authorized capital.

5.88   As a general rule, where several share classes have been established,[104] the articles of incorporation can provide for the exercise of preferential subscription rights firstly by the class in which new shares are issued and subsequently by other share classes.

Right to information

5.89   The rights of an investment company's shareholders to information are equivalent to those detailed above in relation to FCPs.[105] These constitute the minimum information requirements to be supplied to unitholders in UCIs. However, because investment companies have corporate status, they also must comply with the obligations with respect to provision of information to shareholders as set out in the 1915 Act. These obligations apply primarily to SAs and SCAs.

5.90   SAs and SCAs are, for example, required to provide their shareholders with the following information or documents:

(1)   the report presented by the board of directors when an extraordinary general meeting is convened to consider whether to restrict or remove preferential subscription rights of existing shareholders, explaining the reasons for the restriction or removal and the calculation of the issue price of new shares proposed to be issued;[106]

(2)   the share register, which all shareholders are entitled to consult at the registered office;[107]

(3)   details on the acquisition of the company's own shares at the direction of the board of directors in order to avoid serious and imminent damage to the company—in this instance, the general meeting following the acquisition of the company's shares must be informed of the objective of the acquisition(s), the number of shares acquired, their nominal value, or, in the absence of a

---

[103]   Delvaux (n 18 above) Ch 5, para 5.2.3.2.2.4.5.5.

[104]   eg when shares are issued in a given class, they may initially reserve the exercise of the preferential subscription right to shareholders from that class, so that the other shareholders are deferred to a second round before exercising their right (Art 32-3(2) of the 1915 Act).

[105]   See 5.46 above.

[106]   Arts 32-3(5), 47, and 103, 1915 Act.

[107]   ibid Arts 39, 47, and 103.

nominal value, their accounting par value, the consideration paid for the shares, and the fraction of the subscribed capital they represent;[108]

(4) conflicts of interest of directors and the consequences of such conflicts, which must be reported to the first general meeting held following the occurrence and disclosure by the relevant director of any conflicts of interest;[109]

(5) infringements of the law or of the articles of incorporation by directors in the performance of their management duties, which must be reported to the first general meeting held after the directors who were not at fault become aware of the relevant infringements;[110]

(6) acts of the directors which exceeded their powers under the articles of incorporation, which must be specifically mentioned in the notice calling the extraordinary general meeting and, if this is not done, may not be properly ratified by the shareholders;[111]

(7) the salaries, emoluments and benefits of any kind allocated to the director responsible for day-to-day management, which must be disclosed annually to the ordinary general meeting;[112] and

(8) certain information about mergers, demergers, or similar transactions contemplated by the company.[113]

As with FCPs, the semi-annual and annual financial reports of an investment company **5.91** incorporated in the form of an SA or SCA must be published. Investment companies with the status of SIF are not required to draft and publish semi-annual reports. Certain particulars must be mentioned, due to the fact that UCIs are companies. As the annual financial reports are approved by the directors prior to approval by the general meeting of shareholders,[114] they are made publicly available at the registered office two weeks before the ordinary general meeting.[115] They are also sent to the registered shareholders together with the notice calling the meeting. Lastly, they are supplied free of charge to any shareholder on request, at least two weeks prior to the general meeting.

The following documents are also made available at the registered office two weeks **5.92** before the ordinary general meeting of an SA or SCA:

• a list of the company's portfolio securities; and
• for SICAFs, a list of shareholders whose shares are not fully paid up, including the number of shares not fully paid up and the domicile of the relevant shareholders.[116]

---

[108] ibid Arts 49-2(2), 47, and 103.
[109] ibid Arts 47, 57, and 103.
[110] ibid Arts 47, 59, and 103.
[111] ibid Arts 47, 74, and 103.
[112] ibid Arts 47, 60, and 103.
[113] ibid Arts 47, 264, 267, 277, 278, 281, 292, 295, 306, 307, 308*bis*-2 to 308*bis*-7, and 308*bis*-9.
[114] ibid Arts 74, and 103.
[115] ibid Arts 73, and 103.
[116] ibid. This also applies to SIFs using their right to issue partly paid-up shares.

5.93 An SARL's partners must at all times be permitted access to the annual report at the registered office.[117] In SARLs with more than twenty-five partners, that right is available only in the two weeks prior to the general meeting.

5.94 The obligation for UCIs to publish their annual financial statements within four months—within six months for SIFs[118]—following closure of their financial year influences the date of their annual general meeting, which must be held to approve the financial statements within the four-month or six-month period, as the case may be.

Right to call a general meeting

5.95 An investment company's shareholders may, in certain circumstances, require the directors to call a general meeting. In SAs and SCAs, this right is available to shareholders who, alone or together, represent at least one tenth of the share capital.[119] In SARLs, the right may be exercised by partners representing more than half of the share capital.[120]

Right to sue for the company's dissolution

5.96 Every shareholder in an investment company may in principle petition the courts to dissolve the investment company for valid reasons.[121] This right is rarely exercised in practice, given the right of shareholders to request redemption.

Financial rights

Right to share in profits

5.97 **Principles** Every company is incorporated 'in order to enable shareholders participate in the resulting profits'.[122] Without the objective of making and sharing profits, there is no basis on which to form a company. Each partner or shareholder must be able to share in the profits. Agreements depriving one or more partners or shareholders of all or substantially all profits are void as a matter of public policy.[123]

---

[117] Art 198, 1915 Act.
[118] Art 52(2), Act of 13 February 2007.
[119] Arts 70 and 103, 1915 Act.
[120] ibid Art 196.
[121] Arts 99 for SAs, 103 for SCAs and 180-1 for SARLs. As to the concept of valid reasons, see in particular A Benoit-Moury, 'Des justes motifs de dissolution des sociétés commerciales. De l'article 1871 du Code civil à l'article 102 des LCSC' in *Liber Amicorum Jan Ronse* (E Story-Scientia, 1986) 147; P-A Foriers, 'Les situations de blocage dans les sociétés anonymes' (1992) *RDC*, 477.
[122] Art 1832, Civil Code.
[123] ibid Art 1855. Clauses intended to infringe the social pact by granting the whole benefits to a single partner/shareholder or by excluding from any contribution to losses one or several partners'/shareholders' equity in the company are prohibited. Clauses which may not be intended to achieve this result but in fact have the same effect are also prohibited. According to the Court of Appeal in Brussels, the judge must 'elicit the principal objective of the relevant provisions, so as to determine if in the parties' minds the agreement merely provides for the transfer of certain rights or, on the contrary, it enables a partner to avoid any contribution to losses' (CA Brussels, 10 November 2006, *TRV*, 2007, 183, note T Vlietinck; *L'Echo* (summary, E Houpin), 19 July 2007, 11). See also Cass B,

As long as this basic rule is respected, all methods of dividing profits between the shareholders/partners are allowed. For example, it is possible to organize the unequal distribution of profits and losses despite equal contributions or, conversely, to provide for equal distribution despite unequal contributions. A partner's or shareholder's right to participate in the profits may be subject to conditions, such as a minimum profit. The partners or shareholders may also agree to divide profits on a different basis than losses. In the absence of agreement to the contrary, the Civil Code lays down rules by virtue of which everyone participates in the profits in proportion to his contribution to the share capital.[124]

5.98

A partner's or shareholder's right to participate in profits applies to all profits generated by the company. Profits may be distributed during the company's life in the form of dividends. Distribution of profits by way of dividend is not mandatory and the payment of dividends is subject to certain specific rules, which will be examined separately.

5.99

Right to receive dividends In contrast to the right to participate in profits, which is an essential right for every partner or shareholder, partners or shareholders do not have an absolute right to receive dividends, even when a company makes profits. Undistributed profits must be retained within the company.

5.100

A company's results are recognized annually in the balance sheet and profit and loss account, giving rise to the custom of declaring a dividend if the financial statements show a distributable profit.[125]

5.101

In SICAFs, the general meeting has exclusive authority to determine the profit to be paid out.

5.102

Where such a company is incorporated in the form of an SA or SCA, its board of directors or manager is authorized to declare interim dividends subject to compliance with the following basic conditions and formalities:[126]

5.103

(1) the articles of incorporation must authorize the payment of interim dividends;
(2) an accounting report must be prepared to show that there are profits available for distribution;

---

5 November 1998 (Torraspapel/SRIW), at <http://www.cass.be> (18 October 2001); De Riemacker, *JT*, 1999 (summary), 131; (1999) *Rev not b* 181; M Coipel, 'Réflexions sur le portage d'actions au regard de l'article 1855 du Code civil. Le porteur et le lion' (1986) *RCJB* 542; 'Encore l'article 1855, alinéa 2, du Code civil: réflexions additionnelles en faveur d'une interprétation renouvelée d'un texte controversé' (1995) *RDC* 132; P-A Foriers, 'Portage et clause léonine (observations sur le champ d'application de l'article 1855 du Code civil' in *Hommage à Jacques Heenen* (Bruylant, 1994) 149; I Lebbe and P-E Partsch, 'L' article 1855, alinéa 2, du Code civil et les opérations sur titres' (1997) *Rev prat soc* 81.

[124] Art 1853, Civil Code.
[125] Th Tilquin and V Simonart, Traité des sociétés (Kluwer Editions juridiques Belgique, 1996) Vol I 407.
[126] Arts 72-2 and 103, 1915 Act.

(3) the amount to be distributed may not exceed the amount of profit made since the end of the previous financial year plus retained earnings and available reserves, less losses brought forward and sums to be transferred to reserves;

(4) the decision to declare interim dividends may not be taken more than two months after the reference date of the accounting report referred to above;

(5) the decision to distribute interim dividends may not be taken within six months of previous financial year end;

(6) a decision to distribute a second interim dividend may not be taken within three months of the date of declaration of the first interim dividend;

(7) the company's auditors must verify compliance with the above conditions and certify compliance in a report to the board of directors before the distribution is effected.

5.104 Dividends may not under any circumstances be distributed if the distribution would reduce the company's assets to an amount less than one-and-a-half times the total amount of the company's liabilities to its creditors as reported in the preceding year's annual financial statements.[127] In that respect, a SICAF differs from SAs or SCAs which are not regulated entities, and which may not make distributions which would reduce their net assets to less than the amount of the subscribed capital plus non-distributable reserves.[128]

5.105 Historically speaking, this difference probably stems from the limited borrowing powers of SICAFs, which would typically have lower borrowings than ordinary companies. SICAFs' creditors would not therefore require the same level of protection as within traditional companies. As a result, SICAFs can finance distributions to their partners or shareholders from capital and non-distributable reserves as long as the prescribed ratio between assets and liabilities is respected.

5.106 With respect to SICAVs, the power to authorize distributions is likewise vested in the general meeting, with the board of directors having power to pay only interim dividends. There are, however, two principal differences when compared with SICAFs.

5.107 First, a SICAV's net assets may be distributed as long as its net assets do not fall below the legal minimum capital requirement of €1,250,000.[129] Unless otherwise stipulated in the articles of incorporation, distributions may thus be made from a SICAV's current income (interest, dividends, and other investment revenues) and capital gains. Capital gains may be distributed even when not realized. There is no obligation first to deduct capital losses, whether realized or not.

---

[127] ibid Arts 72-3 and 103, which apply to SICAFs whose shares are intended to be placed with the public, thereby excluding certain SIFs from the scope of their provisions.

[128] ibid Arts 72-1(1) and 103.

[129] Arts 32(1) and 71, 2002 Act; Art 29(1), Act of 13 February 2007.

Secondly, interim dividends approved by the board of directors are not subject to **5.108** the conditions and requirements applicable to SICAFs.[130]

Right to repayment of capital

In any company (including any investment company), the rights of shareholders **5.109** to repayment of capital will be realized ultimately on liquidation of the relevant company. However, in the case of investment companies, shareholders are generally repaid following a request for redemption of their units or shares.[131] In SICAVs and SICAFs governed by Part I of the 2002 Act, shareholders may exercise the right to request redemption at any time, in accordance with the redemption procedures set down in the prospectus.[132] In contrast, SICAVs and SICAFs governed by Part II of the 2002 Act or by the Act of 13 February 2007 may reserve the right to refuse redemption.

The right to redemption of subscriptions made exists only insofar as the invest- **5.110** ment company has sufficient net assets to satisfy redemption requests. Where the net assets are insufficient to meet redemption requests, repayment can be restricted to a proportionate amount of the initial contribution, or may even be impossible.

In any company (including any investment company), the right to reimburse- **5.111** ment of an investor's contribution is limited to the nominal value or accounting par value of the relevant shares or units. Transactions that have the effect of lowering the nominal value or accounting par value of the shares diminish the shareholder's right to reimbursement of his contribution by the same proportion. Application of this principle to SICAVs has astonishing consequences. In a SICAV, the accounting par value of the shares is equal to the fraction of the net assets attributable to each share. Shares in a SICAV have a par value which corresponds to their net asset value. The value of the reimbursable contribution fluctuates therefore as the value of the net assets changes. It matches the profits made on the shareholder's initial investment. Reimbursement of a contribution and participation in the profits amount to the same thing.

Lastly, the right to reimbursement of a contribution applies not to the contribution **5.112** itself but to its economic value. An investor who contributes securities to an investment company may not claim those securities when recovering his investment. He is entitled only to assets equivalent in value to the net asset value of shares held at the time of redemption.

---

[130] Arts 32(3) and 71, 2002 Act; Art 31(3), Act of 13 February 2007.
[131] The terms 'redemption' or 'repurchase' are used incorrectly in the 2002 Act. Since the issue of units is not a sale, a UCI's recovery of its own units or shares should be termed a 'purchase'.
[132] Arts 28(1)(b) and 40, 2002 Act.

Issue of units or shares of UCIs

Issue of units by common funds

5.113 The issue of units by FCPs is governed by the 2002 Act or by the Act of 13 February 2007, depending on the particular type of collective investment scheme, and by the management regulations.[133] The authors of management regulations have considerable flexibility in defining the scope of the rules applicable to issues of units as the 2002 Act and the Act of 13 Febuary 2007 are not explicit on the point.

5.114 There is one significant exception to this flexibility in the case of UCIs governed by the 2002 Act, namely the price at which units may be issued. The issue price must be based on the net asset value of the fund's units,[134] ie the FCP's net asset value[135] divided by the number of units outstanding, to which costs and commissions may be added.[136] The CSSF requires that such costs and commissions are reasonable by reference to market standards.

5.115 A SIF, however, may issue its units at the price calculated in accordance with its management regulations.[137]

5.116 The 2002 Act prohibits FCPs from issuing units prior to payment of the net issue price.[138] It also requires the issue price to be paid to the fund 'within the usual time limits'.[139] These two rules do not apply to SIFs and deserve to be explained.

5.117 The first rule applies to the material rather than the legal aspects of issuing units. Legally, a unit is issued when the management company accepts a subscription request which triggers automatically an increase in the unit capital. In return, the FCP represented by its management company becomes the creditor of the subscriber for the amount of the subscription price to be paid. As soon as the capital management company receives payment, it will no longer have a claim in respect of the amount received and issues either a certificate representing the subscriber's units or confirmation of entry of ownership in the register. The 2002 Act obliges the management company to defer delivery of such certificates or confirmations to subscribers prior to receipt by the fund of the issue price. This precaution prevents the circulation of certificates for units for which payment has not been

---

[133] The management regulations must describe the procedures for issuing units (Arts 13(2)(i) and 66, 2002 Act; Art 12(2)(i) Act of 13 February 2007).

[134] Arts 9(1) and 66, 2002 Act.

[135] Which is equal to total assets minus liabilities.

[136] Arts 9(1) and 66, 2002 Act. The maximum expenses and commissions may be fixed in a Grand-Ducal Regulation to be adopted pursuant to a proposal or recommendation of the CSSF. This option has not yet been used.

[137] Art 8, Act of 13 February 2007.

[138] Arts 9(2) and 66, 2002 Act.

[139] ibid.

received. The management regulations may also make the legal issue of units subject to, or conditional on, receipt of the subscription price.

The second rule permits the management regulations to fix the time limit by **5.118** which the issue price must reach the FCP subject to receipt of payment 'within the usual time limits'. Subscribers are generally afforded several days to effect payment. If payment is not made, the FCP will redeem the units, generally at the net asset value ruling on the redemption date. If their value has dropped since the subscription date, the subscriber is, in principle, liable for the difference.

The 2002 Act does not define the expression 'within the usual time limits', which **5.119** can be interpreted several ways, depending on the type of investor and the type of UCI. For example, a venture capital fund could stipulate that the issue price would not be immediately payable in full but could be scheduled or deferred according to the fund's expected investment possibilities and needs. It goes without saying that payment for units is not a pre-condition for a bonus issue of units. That point is nevertheless expressly stated in the 2002 Act.[140]

The 2002 Act and the Act of 13 February 2007 prohibit the issue of units in three **5.120** instances. The first is where the business of the FCP cannot be carried on if there is no management company or depositary.[141] The second is where the FCP's continuity is jeopardized because its management company or depositary goes into liquidation, or is declared bankrupt, or seeks a composition with its creditors, suspension of payment, court-controlled administration, or similar measures.[142] The third and last case is the situation in which the FCP has gone into liquidation.[143]

The 2002 Act does not provide for the voluntary suspension by an FCP of the issue **5.121** of units. Directive 85/611 does not address this point either. Such a suspension is nonetheless possible when provided for in the management regulations.

The issue of units by an FCP governed by the 2002 Act is monitored by its depositary, **5.122** which ensures that units are issued in accordance with the law and the management regulations.[144] The depositary of a SIF is not required to carry out such monitoring.

Issue of shares by SICAVs

SICAVs are subject to the general rules applicable to companies, as provided in the **5.123** 1915 Act. Units of SICAVs are issued in accordance with those general standards, save for a few exceptions, as examined below.

---

[140] ibid.
[141] ibid Arts 12(3)(a) and 66, 2002 Act; Art 11(2)(a) Act of 13 February 2007.
[142] Arts 12(3)(b) and 66, 2002 Act; Art 11(2)(b), Act of 13 February 2007.
[143] Arts 22(3) and 66, 2002 Act; Art 20(3), Act of 13 February 2007.
[144] Arts 18(2)(a) and 66, 2002 Act.

5.124 The most significant distinction from the general provisions of company law is that the capital of SICAVs is variable. SICAVs may at any time issue shares without complying with the rules on capital increases laid down by company law. A SICAV does not need to convene a general meeting to amend the articles of incorporation or to use a notary's services for the purpose of increasing its issued capital. Capital increases fall within the remit of the board of directors' general powers. The capital may be increased at any time[145] without the need for compliance with any specific formalities.[146]

5.125 The 2002 Act and the Act of 13 February 2007 also deviate from the 1915 Act as regards shareholders' preferential subscription rights.[147] Preferential rights of shareholders would impede a SICAV's ability to issue shares and consequently a SICAV's shareholders do not have preferential subscription rights unless otherwise stipulated in the articles of incorporation.

5.126 The issue price of a SICAV's shares is regulated in the same way as that of an FCP's units. With respect to SICAVs governed by the 2002 Act, the price is based on the net asset value of the company's shares, ie it is derived by dividing the SICAV's net asset value by the number of shares outstanding.[148] That price may be supplemented by costs and commissions,[149] the amount of which is monitored by the CSSF. SICAVs authorized as SIFs enjoy more flexibility in this regard. The issue price of their shares may be based on their net asset value or on any other price, such as a fixed amount determined in advance or the stock exchange price of those shares.[150]

5.127 As with FCPs, the 2002 Act makes the issue of shares conditional on payment of the issue price within the usual time limits.[151] Although this concept has already been discussed,[152] its application to SICAVs other than SIFs calls for two additional remarks.

5.128 First, the articles of incorporation must determine the time limits within which the subscription price is to be paid,[153] although the articles may provide that the

---

[145] ibid Arts 28(1)(a) and 71; Art 28(1)(a), Act of 13 February 2007.

[146] This derogation is authorized at European level by Art 1(2) of Second Council Directive (EEC) 77/91 of 13 December 1976 on coordination of safeguards which, for the protection of the interests of members and others, are required by Member States of companies within the meaning of the second paragraph of Article 58 of the Treaty, in respect of public limited liability companies and the maintenance and alteration of their capital [1977] OJ L26/1.

[147] Arts 29(3) and 71, 2002 Act; Art 29(3), Act of 13 February 2007.

[148] Arts 28(2)(a) and 71, 2002 Act.

[149] The maximum expenses may be fixed by Grand-Ducal regulation, although no such measure has yet been adopted.

[150] Art 28(2), Act of 13 February 2007.

[151] Arts 28(3) and 71 of the 2002 Act.

[152] See 5.116 above.

[153] Arts 28(4) and 71 of the 2002 Act.

issue price must be paid within a time frame determined by the board of directors and specified in the prospectus.

Secondly, subscriptions are irrevocable pursuant to the general provisions of **5.129** company law and may not be tied to either a condition precedent or a condition subsequent.[154] The validity of a subscription cannot be affected as such by failure to pay the subscription price. Only allocation of the share to the shareholder, ie delivery of a certificate to the holder or entry in the share register, is suspended for so long as the issue price has not been paid to the SICAV.

A SICAV's articles of incorporation must set out the circumstances in which the **5.130** issue of shares may be suspended.[155] Any decision to suspend the issue of shares must be reported promptly to the CSSF and the supervisory authorities of the EEA Member States in which the SICAV markets its shares.[156]

As with FCPs, the depositary of a SICAV governed by the 2002 Act must ensure that **5.131** the shares are issued in accordance with the law and the articles of incorporation.[157] This obligation has not been tracked through into the Act of 13 February 2007 and therefore does not apply to the depositary of a SIF.

Issue of shares by SICAFs

SICAFs are a more traditional type of company than SICAVs. Their capital is not **5.132** variable but fixed, like that of other SAs, SCAs, or SARLs. For that reason, the issue of shares by a SICAF requires compliance with the formalities prescribed by the 1915 Act in respect of capital increases, ie principally, approval by the general meeting of shareholders[158] and modification of the articles of incorporation. In SAs and SCAs, the general meeting may authorize the board of directors or, as the case may be, the managers, to increase the capital up to a given amount, the 'authorized capital'. Such authorization is valid for at most five years but may be renewed by the general meeting.[159]

When issuing shares, a SICAF incorporated in the form of an SA or SCA must, in **5.133** principle, allow the existing shareholders to exercise their preferential subscription rights. The company's articles of incorporation may nonetheless authorize the board of directors to deviate from this rule within the limits of the authorized capital. The general meeting of partners or shareholders may also derogate from this rule or authorize the board to do so.[160]

---

154 Van Ryn, (n 68 above) 336.
155 Arts 28(5) and 71, 2002 Act; Art 28(5), Act of 13 February 2007.
156 ibid.
157 Arts 34(3)(a) and 71, 2002 Act.
158 Arts 32, 103, and 199, 1915 Act.
159 ibid Arts 32 and 103.
160 ibid Arts 32-3(5). As regards the preferential subscription right, see 5.78 *et seq* above.

5.134 The issue of shares by SICAFs is subject to various special rules due to their status as UCIs.

5.135 Thus, calculation of the price of shares issued by a SICAF governed by Part I of the 2002 Act, is regulated in the same way as for SICAVs,[161] as is the suspension of the issues of shares[162] and the time limit for payment of the subscription price for shares.[163]

5.136 In contrast, in the case of SICAFs governed by Part II of the 2002 Act or the Act of 13 February 2007, only the suspension of the issues of shares is regulated.[164] The articles of incorporation of such SICAFs can provide for suspension of the issue of shares. As the 2002 Act and the Act of 13 February 2007 lay down no other provisions with respect to share capital, the articles of incorporation of a SICAF governed by Part II of the 2002 Act or the Act of 13 February 2007 could specify that the issue price of shares is the official stock market price.[165]

5.137 Lastly, as is the case for an FCP, the depositary of a SICAF governed by the 2002 Act is responsible for making sure that shares are issued in accordance with the law and the articles of incorporation.[166] The depositary of a SIF does not have this responsibility.

Transfer of units or shares of UCIs

5.138 The 2002 Act and the Act of 13 February 2007 contain few provisions regarding the transfer of the units or shares of a UCI. The legislation mostly assumes and provides for the repurchase by a UCI of its own units or shares at the request of the investors. Other permissible types of assignment are governed by general law, ie the Civil Code and, as applicable, the 1915 Act.

5.139 For that reason, we analyse the transfer of UCI units and shares below in three steps. We will firstly examine the legal or contractual restrictions on transfer, which apply regardless of the type of transfer. Next we will review the rules governing the transfer of units and shares as between investors. Lastly, we will look at the regime for transferring units and shares to the UCI that has issued them.

---

[161] Arts 28(2)(a) and 40, 2002 Act.
[162] ibid Arts 28(5) and 40.
[163] ibid Arts 28(3) and 40.
[164] ibid Arts 28(5) and 75(6); Arts 28(5) and 40(2), Act of 13 February 2007.
[165] Art 28(2)(a), 2002 Act requires SICAVs governed by Part I to issue shares on the basis of the net asset value per share. Art 40, 2002 Act makes that article applicable to SICAFs governed by Part I. However, it is not included among the provisions which Arts 73 *et seq* of the 2002 Act apply to SICAFs governed by Part II.
[166] Arts 34(3), 40, and 75(6), 2002 Act.

Restrictions on the assignment of units and shares of UCIs

The units of FCPs and the shares of investment companies can, in principle, be **5.140** assigned in the manner set out below.[167] The transfer of units/shares is at times restricted by law or by agreement.

Legal restrictions on the assignment of units and shares

Legal restrictions on the assignment of units and shares apply exclusively to invest- **5.141** ment companies. They vary according to the securities to be assigned and the companies by which they are issued. SAs, SCAs, and SARLs are subject to restrictions.

In an SA, shares that have not yet been issued cannot be assigned. The 1915 Act[168] **5.142** renders void the assignment of shares in a company not yet incorporated or shares to be issued following a capital increase.[169]

The restriction on the right to trade in an SARL's shares is more important as, in **5.143** principle, assignment to a person who is not a partner always requires authorization from the partners.[170] The required approval must be given by a resolution passed at a general meeting of partners representing at least three-quarters of the issued capital. There are no requirements for approval for a transfer to an existing partner.

Contractual restrictions on the assignment of units and shares

Contractual restrictions in common funds

As a general rule, the transfer of an FCP's units can be subject to any type of **5.144** contractual restriction, as set out in the management regulations or in agreements between unitholders, provided the units remain negotiable. Any restriction on the right to assign units must therefore be for a limited time and reflect a legitimate interest.[171]

---

[167] These discussions are partly based on an article: I Lebbe, 'La vente d'un fonds de commerce ou la cession de titres de sociétés—Aspects du droit commercial' (1994) Vol 4 *Act dr* 833.

[168] Art 43, 1915 Act.

[169] However, see, J Kirkpatrick, 'Le régime de la cession d'actions futures d'une société anonyme en droit positif belge et *de lege ferenda*' in *Hommage à Jacques Heenen* (Bruylant, 1994) 221.

[170] If not yet a partner, the buyer must be approved by a general meeting of partners representing at least three-quarters of the issued capital. Assignment to a non-partner after death also requires the approval of the partners representing three-quarters of the rights owned by the surviving parties. An assignment is void if this condition is not met. However, the authorization of assignments after death is not required in respect of transfers to the spouse, the reserved heirs and insofar as provided for in the articles of incorporation, the other legal heirs of the transferor (Art 189, 1915 Act).

[171] *Encycl Dalloz, Droit civil,* v° 'Inaliénabilité', para 66, paras 68 *et seq*; A Delège, 'Inaliénabilité', *Rép not* Vol II, Book 7 (Larcier, 1979) para 45.

Restrictions under the articles of incorporation and contractual restrictions in investment companies

5.145   There is a distinction between SAs and SARLs as regards contractual restrictions and restrictions under the articles of incorporation in relation to the assignment of shares. In an SA, the right of assignment is a principle from which the company may only derogate within strict limits established by case law. Assignments between partners in SARLs may be subjected to contractual restrictions similar to those provided for in SAs (ie mainly authorization or pre-emption clauses). As regards assignments to non-partners, only clauses imposing requirements for approval by a larger majority than provided for by law (as outlined above) are permissible.[172]

5.146   SAs can impose clauses restricting assignment of their shares, provided they remain negotiable. For example, some observers believe that an SA may not require that new shareholders be subject to approval by a particular body or person on a discretionary basis, since that would effectively enable such body or person to prevent the assignment of securities.[173] Clauses prohibiting assignment, such as veto clauses, must be temporary and must be justified by a legitimate interest.[174]

5.147   Authorization clauses[175] and pre-emption clauses[176] are used most frequently by SAs. That said, the effects of penalties set out in the relevant company's articles or shareholders agreement for any failure of a transferor to comply with authorization or pre-emption clauses are not always clear.

5.148   It is widely agreed that assignments in breach of an authorisation clause in the articles of incorporation are void vis-à-vis the company whose securities are assigned,[177] albeit they will be valid between the parties involved in the transaction, subject to the assignee's right to allege fraud, error, or the doctrine of latent defects.

5.149   The situation is different when a pre-emption clause in the articles of incorporation is violated. Traditionally, this type of breach is sanctioned in one of the following two ways: the beneficiary of the clause (for example the other shareholders) is

---

[172]   L Metzler, *Le régime juridique et fiscal des sociétés à responsabilité limitée dans le grand-duché de Luxembourg* (Imprimerie de la Cour Victor Buck, 1933) 78.

[173]   The situation would be different if it were easy for the assignor to find another buyer (Van Ommeslaghe (n 76 above) 294–7).

[174]   Delvaux (n 18 above) Ch 3, para 3.2.8.2.1, which mentions clauses valid for 3 or 5 years as examples of permissible clauses; Van Ommeslaghe (n 76 above) 294.

[175]   ie clauses rendering the assignment of securities subject to authorization by the board of directors or a group of shareholders.

[176]   ie clauses entitling the board of directors or a group of shareholders to acquire a shareholder's securities by pre-emption when he wishes to sell them.

[177]   In the company's eyes, the seller remains the owner of the securities (P De Wolf and B Feron, 'Les conventions d'actionnaires, une évolution inachevée' (1991) DAOR 32).

awarded damages or the assignment is declared null and void where the assignee acted in bad faith at the time of the transaction.[178] Those two penalties can be combined when avoidance of the transaction is not sufficient to compensate the loss caused by violation of the clause. The second penalty where the assignee acted in bad faith is to nullify the assignment and to allocate the securities to a holder of the pre-emption right who is willing to pay the price agreed pursuant to the clause (the pre-emption clause must specify the means of calculating the price).[179] That penalty would be a form of redress in kind. Lastly, certain commentators[180] hold that such assignments are void vis-à-vis the company.

In the case of non-compliance with an authorization or pre-emption clause specified **5.150** in a shareholders' agreement but not provided for in the articles of incorporation, a transfer can only be declared void on the basis of collusion by the parties to the transfer. As a third party to the shareholders' agreement, the company may not plead invalidity of the assignment.[181] It is also possible to obtain damages for breach of the shareholders' agreement.

Transfer of units and shares between investors

Transfer of units in common funds

Because FCPs are purely contractual structures, transfers of rights to the jointly **5.151** owned assets represented by their units would have been subject to stringent requirements. For that reason, the 2002 Act and the Act of 13 February 2007 simply refer to the provisions governing the transfer of shares in SAs, which provide for a less onerous regime.[182]

There is a distinction drawn depending on whether the units to be transferred are **5.152** bearer or registered units.

Bearer units

When a bearer security is issued, the represented right merges with the written **5.153** document.[183] Consequently, a bearer share is a form of tangible movable property subject, *inter alia*, to the mandatory rules laid down in the Civil Code.[184] Consequently, as between successive purchasers, a purchaser with actual possession

---

[178] In that event, the assignee is penalised as a third party complicit in the violation of the clause.
[179] See De Wolf and Feron (n 177 above) 34; P Van Ommeslaghe and X Dieux, 'Examen de jurisprudence (1979 à 1990), Les sociétés commerciales (suite)' (1993) *RCJB* 716–18.
[180] See in particular Van Ryn (n 68 above) Vol I, No 545, 364.
[181] Van Ommeslaghe, (n 76 above) 304.
[182] Arts 8(2) and 66, 2002 Act; Art 7(2), Act of 13 February 2007; Arts 40 and 42, 1915 Act.
[183] J Van Ryn and J Heenen, *Principes de droit commercial* (Bruylant, 2nd edn, 1981) Vol III, 103.
[184] Arts 1141 and 2279, Civil Code.

will be preferred and remain the owner, even if his purchase agreement with the same vendor bears a later date, provided that he acted in good faith when he acquired the bearer share. Moreover, his possession has the force of title: someone who possesses something in good faith and who can show just title and claim valid possession is the owner by law.

5.154   The 1915 Act[185] provides that an assignment of title to bearer shares is effected simply by delivery. The 1915 Act does not alter the rules of ordinary law concerning the assignment of tangible movable property: bearer units are assigned simply by agreement and delivery of the relevant property from one party to another and the assignment is immediately valid as against third parties.[186]

Registered units

5.155   The rights attached to registered units are not represented by a physical document and the property interest in registered units remains intangible. Granted, it may be proven by the unitholder's entry in the share register or by the production of a certificate recording registration, but such mechanisms are merely forms of proof, rather than title documents embodying a unitholder's rights.[187]

5.156   Like bearer units, a binding agreement for the sale of registered units is created as soon as the transferor and transferee have exchanged an agreement.[188]

5.157   However, other conditions have to be satisfied before a sale is valid vis-à-vis the FCP and other third parties. The parties may choose either[189] to record the transfer in a declaration dated and signed by the assignor and the assignee or their respective representatives and entered in the share register or to follow the rules on the assignment of claims set out in the Civil Code.[190] The FCP's management company may also accept a transfer recorded in correspondence or other documents constituting the agreement between the assignor and the assignee and enter it in the register, which will render the transfer valid vis-à-vis third parties.

---

[185]   Art 42, 1915 Act.

[186]   Formalities such as those provided for by Art 1690 of the Civil Code are therefore not required in the case of transfer of tangible movable property. The requirement of delivery of title merely refers to the rule of proof contained in Art 2279 of the Civil Code: 'possession of movable property amounts to title', meaning that possession raises a presumption of proper acquisition of ownership by the possessor unless and until the contrary is proven; see C Resteau, Traité des sociétés anonymes (Editions Swinnen, 3rd edn, 1982) Vol I, para 599, 382.

[187]   K Geens, 'Quelques aspects de la clause d'agrément dans la société anonyme' (1989) *Rev prat soc* 325, and the references cited in that article.

[188]   Resteau (n 186 above) Vol I, para 683*bis*, 420; Van Ryn (n 68 above) Vol I, para 535, 359.

[189]   Art 40, 1915 Act, referred to by Arts 8 and 66, 2002 Act, and by Art 7, Act of 13 February 2007.

[190]   Art 1690, Civil Code.

Transfer of shares in investment companies

Share transfers in investment companies incorporated in the form of an SA follow **5.158** the same rules as for transfers of FCP units. The comments for FCPs apply *mutatis mutandis.*

Share transfers in SARLs must be recorded in a notarial or private deed.[191] Such **5.159** transfers become valid vis-à-vis third parties only once they have been notified to the company or have been accepted by it in accordance with the rules of the Civil Code.[192]

Redemption of units and shares issued by UCIs

The redemption of units or shares is one of the key features of the regime govern- **5.160** ing UCIs, especially when they are subject to Part I of the 2002 Act. UCIs are required to buy units or, to use the erroneous but widely accepted expression, to 'redeem'[193] their units or shares on request from their investors.[194] That does not prevent them from redeeming units or shares on their own initiative in certain circumstances.

The legal rules governing the redemption of units or shares vary depending on the **5.161** type of UCI and the UCI's status. The regime applicable to investment companies also depends on the type of redemption, as explained below.

Redemption of units issued by FCPs

FCPs governed by Part I of the 2002 Act are, in principle, obliged to redeem their **5.162** units at the unitholders' request,[195] in contrast to FCPs governed by Part II of the 2002 Act or by the Act of 13 February 2007, which can be established as closed-end schemes or otherwise restrict the terms on which units can be redeemed.

The redemption of units by FCPs subject to Part I of the 2002 Act is governed by **5.163** the provisions of the 1915 Act, which apply to the transfer of units in general,[196] in addition to the specific constraints prescribed by the 2002 Act, which flow from Directive 85/611.

The redemption price for units redeemed by FCPs governed by Part I of the 2002 **5.164** Act must be based on the net asset value of the units after deduction of any applicable

---

[191] Art 190, 1915 Act.
[192] Art 1690, Civil Code.
[193] As already explained, the terms 'redemption' or 'repurchase' are used incorrectly in both the 2002 Act and the Act of 13 February 2007. As the issue of units is not a sale, a UCI's recovery of its own units or shares should be termed a 'purchase'.
[194] Art 2(2), 2002 Act.
[195] ibid Art 11(2).
[196] ibid Arts 8(2) and 66; Arts 40 and 42, 1915 Act.

commissions and costs.[197] The amount of commissions and costs must be disclosed in the prospectus. These pricing constraints do not apply to FCPs subject to Part II of the 2002 Act[198] or to FCPs that have opted for the SIF status.[199]

5.165 FCPs can either cancel redeemed units or keep them for resale to other investors. There are no provisions with respect to how they are treated in the FCP's records[200] or the price at which they may subsequently be sold.

5.166 There is no fund value threshold below which redemption may no longer be processed.[201] While the 2002 Act[202] and the Act of 13 February 2007[203] each prohibit distributions that reduce an FCP's net assets to less than €1,250,000, the restriction does not apply to redemptions.

5.167 Although, in principle, units may be redeemed on an ongoing basis in FCPs governed by Part I of the 2002 Act, redemptions may be suspended in certain circumstances. The management company does not have the discretion to determine such circumstances, which must fulfil the following cumulative criteria laid down by the 2002 Act:[204]

(1) suspension must be in the interests of the unitholders;

(2) the circumstances justifying suspension must be exceptional;

(3) those circumstances must be described in the management regulations; and

(4) the suspension procedure must be set out in the management regulations.

The decision to suspend redemptions must be reported promptly to the CSSF and to the supervisory authorities in the EEA Member States in which the FCP's units are marketed.[205]

5.168 There are also circumstances in which redemptions must be suspended by FCPs. In such cases, the management company has no choice but to comply with the law and the directives of the CSSF. The common denominator of those circumstances,

---

[197] Art 11(3), 2002 Act.

[198] The provisions of Arts 65 *et seq* of the 2002 Act have not made Art 11(3) of the 2002 Act, which requires FCPs governed by Part I to redeem their units at their NAV, applicable to FCPs governed by Part II.

[199] Art 8, Act of 13 February 2007.

[200] Note that Arts 18(2)(a) and 66, 2002 Act require the depository of an FCP to ensure that when units are cancelled, they are cancelled in accordance with the law and the management regulations. However, those articles do not appear to prescribe automatic cancellation of units. They have not been incorporated in the Act of 13 February 2007.

[201] Provided that the provisions of Art 24, 2002 Act and of Art 22 Act of 13 February 2007 are complied with; by virtue of those provisions, the supervisory authority must be informed when an FCP's NAV falls below two-thirds of the legal minimum.

[202] Arts 16 and 66, 2002 Act.

[203] Art 15, Act of 13 February 2007.

[204] Art 12(1)(a), 2002 Act.

[205] ibid Art 12(2).

listed in the 2002 Act or in the Act of 13 February 2007, is that the FCP's management is at risk for some reason. Those cases are specifically listed as follows:

(1) the laws, regulations, or agreements concerning the activity and operation of an FCP are not observed;[206]
(2) the FCP no longer has a management company;[207]
(3) the FCP no longer has a depositary;[208]
(4) the management company or the depositary is placed in liquidation or declared bankrupt or seeks a composition with its creditors, suspension of payment, or court-controlled management, or some similar measure;[209] or
(5) more generally, where suspension is in the interests of the unitholders or the public.[210]

Both the redemption procedure and the suspension conditions must be described in an FCP's management regulations[211] and complete prospectus.[212]   **5.169**

Lastly, the depositary of an FCP governed by the 2002 Act must ensure that the redemption and, as the case may be, the cancellation of units takes place in accordance with the law and the management regulations.[213] The depositary of a SIF does not have an equivalent obligation.   **5.170**

Redemption of shares issued by SICAVs

Redemption can be effected in one of three ways in SICAVs: **5.171**

(1) redemption at the shareholder's request;[214]
(2) redemption by the company with the shareholder's agreement; or
(3) compulsory redemption of shares under the articles of incorporation.

A SICAV which redeems its own shares acquires an interest in its own capital and assets, made up of rights vis-à-vis the company itself but without value vis-à-vis creditors.   **5.172**

Consequently, the 1915 Act, the 2002 Act, and, to a very limited extent, the Act of 13 February 2007 require that redemptions of shares comply with specific conditions and formalities, which differ according to the type of redemption and what happens to the shares redeemed (ie whether they are cancelled or not).   **5.173**

---

[206] ibid Arts 12(1)(b) and 66; Art 11(1), Act of 13 February 2007.
[207] Arts 12(3)(a) and 66, 2002 Act; Art 11(2)(a), Act of 13 February 2007.
[208] ibid.
[209] Arts 12(3)(b) and 66, 2002 Act; Art 11(2)(b), Act of 13 February 2007.
[210] Arts 12(1)(b) and 66, 2002 Act; Art 11(1), Act of 13 February 2007.
[211] Art 13(2)(j), 2002 Act; Art 12(2)(i), Act of 13 February 2007.
[212] Annex I, Sch A, para 1.13, 2002 Act; Art 53, Act of 13 February 2007, this information is particularly relevant to investors.
[213] Arts 18(2)(a) and 66, 2002 Act.
[214] As referred to in Art 2(2), 2002 Act.

5.174 Redemption of its own shares by an SA or SCA is regulated by Articles 49-2 to 49-5 of the 1915 Act which specify notably the circumstances in which shareholder's agreement is needed for redemption. Redemption of redeemable shares is governed by Article 49-8 of the 1915 Act. Those provisions constitute the transposition into Luxembourg law of the Second Council Directive 77/91.[215] The Act of 1915 must therefore be interpreted according to that Directive.

5.175 Hence, redemptions of shares by a SICAV are, in principle, subject to the 1915 Act. There is one exception to this principle,[216] namely where the SICAV immediately cancels the redeemed shares and reduces its capital. In those circumstances, most of the constraints contained in the 1915 Act are not applicable. As the common practice of SICAVs is to cancel shares immediately following redemption, in practice the provisions of the Act of 1915 frequently do not apply in the case of SICAVs. Nonetheless, certain rules apply to all types of redemptions.

Redemption of shares at the shareholder's request

5.176 Redemption of shares at the shareholder's request will be effected in response to a request from a shareholder that the SICAV redeem all or part of his shares in the company. A SICAV governed by Part I of the 2002 Act must permit shareholders to redeem their shares when they so wish. On redemption, shares may be cancelled immediately, which is the usual practice, or treated as an asset of the SICAV.

5.177 **Immediate cancellation of shares** A SICAV is required at all times to maintain a minimum capital of €1,250,000.[217] Thus it would seem that a SICAV may not redeem and cancel all shares issued as a means of liquidation of the SICAV. In these circumstances, shares redeemed may not be cancelled but should be recorded by the SICAV as 'assets', which are not subject to the same minimum threshold restriction.

5.178 Unless otherwise stipulated in the articles of incorporation, the redemption decision (which is merely a formality, as shareholders have to request redemption) may be taken by the board of directors, or by a representative thereof, or by the general meeting of shareholders.[218]

5.179 **No immediate cancellation of shares** Where a SICAV decides not to cancel the redeemed shares but prefers to record them under assets, for example to avoid diminution of capital below the required minimum threshold, a distinction must

---

[215] Arts 19–22 and 39, Second Council Directive (EEC) 77/91 of 13 December 1976 on coordination of safeguards which, for the protection of the interests of members and others, are required by Member States of companies within the meaning of the second paragraph of Article 58 of the Treaty, in respect of the formation of public limited liability companies and the maintenance and alteration of their capital, with a view of making such safeguards equivalent [1977] OJ L26/1.

[216] Arts 29(2) and 71, 2002 Act; Art 29(2), Act of 13 February 2007.

[217] Arts 29(2) and 71, 2002 Act; Art 29(2), Act of 13 February 2007.

[218] Arts 49-2 to 49-5 and 49-8, 1915 Act, which restrict this freedom, do not apply.

be drawn between SICAVs governed by the 2002 Act and SICAVs which have opted for the status of SIF.

The Act of 13 February 2007 differs from the requirements of the 1915 Act as it **5.180** provides that shares of a SIF are redeemed 'in accordance with the conditions and procedures provided for in the articles of incorporation'.[219] A SIF's founders are free to set up the regime they deem the most appropriate. The 2002 Act does not contain any similar provision, so that the rules set out in the 1915 Act are fully applicable to UCIs other than SIFs.

In principle, the prohibition on reducing net assets below €1,250,000 does **5.181** not apply to a redemption with a view to a subsequent resale, as redemption of shares for subsequent resale does not necessarily reduce the net assets but is of a speculative nature comparable to a SICAV's day-to-day transactions, conducted in the hope of generating a capital gain for the benefit of the SICAV on the shares it has acquired for subsequent resale.

The 1915 Act lays down strict rules for the purchase and holding of own shares by **5.182** UCIs governed by the 2002 Act.

The acquisition of its own shares by a SICAV other than a SIF is subject to the **5.183** following rules:[220]

(1) a general meeting of shareholders must authorize the purchase and lay down the conditions, including the maximum number of shares which may be acquired, the minimum and maximum consideration that may be paid, and the term of the authorization granted, which may not be longer than eighteen months;
(2) the nominal value or, failing that,[221] the accounting par value of shares held by the company may not exceed 10 per cent of the subscribed capital;[222]
(3) the net asset value may not become less than the subscribed capital plus non-distributable reserves;[223] and
(4) the purchased shares must be fully paid up.[224]

Generally, the board of directors does not have authority to decide whether **5.184** to acquire a company's own shares, and requires authorization from a general meeting of shareholders, which may be granted by a majority of the shareholders

---

[219] Art 28(2), Act of 13 February 2007.
[220] Art 49-2(1), 1915 Act.
[221] This is always the case with SICAVs, whose shares cannot have a nominal value. SICAFs can opt for shares without a nominal value, in which case such shares only have a par value.
[222] The concept of subscribed capital, as applied to SICAVs, refers to their capital, which is at all times equal to their NAV (Arts 25 and 69, 2002 Act).
[223] This condition must always be fulfilled by SICAVs, whose capital is always equal to their NAV.
[224] This condition is already met by SICAVs by virtue of Arts 28(8) and 71, 2002 Act.

present or represented at such meeting. The majority required at the shareholders' meeting is a simple majority.

5.185 Authorization from the general meeting of shareholders is not necessary if the objective of the company in acquiring the shares is to prevent serious and imminent damage to the company.[225] In such an event, the board of directors may take the decision to purchase the company's own shares, subject to the obligation to inform the next general meeting of the reasons for and purpose of the acquisitions, the number and nominal value of shares acquired or, failing that, the accounting par value of the purchased shares, the fraction of the subscribed capital they represent, and the consideration paid.

5.186 Authorization from the general meeting is likewise unnecessary where the company acquires shares for distribution to its employees.[226] This is largely a theoretical possibility in the case of UCIs.

5.187 SICAVs holding their own shares are subject to the following rules:[227]

(1) When the shares are recognized as assets in the balance sheet, the company must set aside a non-distributable reserve equal to the amount of the book value of the shares.

(2) The voting rights attached to the shares held by the company are suspended.

(3) The company's management report must disclose:

    (a) the reasons for the acquisitions made during the financial year;

    (b) the number, the nominal value, or the accounting par value of such shares bought and sold during the year and the fraction of the subscribed capital they represent;

    (c) the number, the nominal value, or the accounting par value of all the shares bought and held in portfolio and the fraction of the subscribed capital they represent; and

    (d) the consideration, if any, paid for the shares.

5.188 On cancellation by the company of own shares held, it is no longer necessary to provide for a non-distributable reserve. Recorded as a liability, the reserve is used to offset own shares recorded as an asset, as those shares cannot be regarded as genuine assets vis-à-vis creditors. When 'own' shares are removed from the balance sheet, the non-distributable reserve becomes redundant.

---

[225] Art 49-2(2), 1915 Act. A few examples of serious and imminent damage are given in the *Parliamentary documents*, including the case of a 'sudden price collapse making it impossible to set aside the necessary provisions'. In certain cases, a SICAV's board of directors may therefore decide on its own whether to repurchase the SICAV's shares on the stock market in order to align the stock market price with their NAV (*Parliamentary doc* No 2474, Comments on the Articles, 24).

[226] Art 49-2(3), 1915 Act.

[227] ibid Art 49-5.

The strict framework described above does not apply where the regulations **5.189** stipulate that the shares are 'redeemable'.[228]

Redemption at the initiative of the company with the shareholder's consent

A SICAV may invite its shareholders to redeem their shares. Because the consent **5.190** of each selling shareholder is implicit in such cases, the applicable rules are those described under paras 5.176 *et seq* above for redemption at the shareholder's initiative.

Compulsory redemption of redeemable shares

A SICAV's articles of incorporation may provide that the company's shares are **5.191** redeemable on the SICAV's initiative. If so, in the circumstances specified by the articles of incorporation, the SICAV can compulsorily redeem shares held by shareholders.

In practice, the articles of incorporation of investment companies frequently **5.192** provide that their issued shares are redeemable by the relevant company in certain circumstances. Such circumstances would include the redemption of shares held by certain types or categories of investors, for example those to whom the relevant scheme is not marketed.

Immediate cancellation of shares As indicated above, the only mandatory **5.193** constraint on redemption of share capital is to maintain a minimum level of share capital of €1,250,000.

No immediate cancellation of shares If a SICAV other than a SIF[229] decides **5.194** not to reduce its capital but to retain redeemed shares as balance sheet assets, repurchase is subject to the following conditions:[230]

(1) The articles of incorporation must have authorized redemption of the redeemable shares prior to the relevant subscription and set out the repurchase conditions and procedures.
(2) A non-distributable reserve in an amount equal to the nominal value or, failing that, the accounting par value of the redeemed shares must be maintained in the balance sheet. In the context of SICAVs, the reserve must be equal to the net asset value of the shares at the time of repurchase. Such a reserve is not required when the shares are redeemed with the proceeds of a new issue created specifically to finance the repurchase.

---

[228] See 5.191 *et seq* below.
[229] Art 28(2), Act of 13 February 2007 derogates from the 1915 Act insofar as it leaves a SIF's founders free to determine in the SIF's articles of incorporation the redemption regime of securities issued by the SIF.
[230] Art 49-8, 1915 Act.

(3) The shares may only be redeemed with distributable amounts or the proceeds of a new issue the purpose of which is to finance the repurchase.

(4) The premium, if any, paid to the shareholders on redemption may only be taken from distributable amounts.

(5) Only fully paid up shares may be repurchased.

(6) The repurchase transaction must be published in the *Mémorial*.

5.195 The conditions to be satisfied by SICAVs subject to the Act of 2002 under points (3), (4), and (5) above, do not raise particular problems, since their shares are always fully paid up and the concept of distributable amounts has a specific meaning with respect to SICAVs.[231]

5.196 In contrast to the provisions of the 1915 Act governing redemptions effected with the shareholder's consent,[232] the non-distributable reserve set aside on redemption of redeemable shares, which must match the net asset value of the repurchased shares, must be kept on the balance sheet even if such shares are subsequently cancelled, thereby reducing the SICAV's capital.

5.197 The reserve is in place for a particular reason. It was provided for by a Community Directive[233] in order to protect creditors. The creation of a non-distributable reserve requires the company to retain a portion of the profits equal to the amount taken from the capital. Consequently, the reserve must be created and kept on the balance sheet regardless of whether or not the redeemed shares are cancelled. Indeed, the 1915 Act specifies that such a reserve may only be used to increase the capital or to be distributed to the shareholders as part of a repayment of capital and does not require that the maintenance of the reserve is subject to retention of the shares as assets on the balance sheet.

Rules applicable to all redemptions by SICAVs

5.198 As with FCPs, redemptions follow the general rules applicable to share transfers, as supplemented by special rules set out in the 2002 Act or the Act of 13 February 2007, and in the 1915 Act.

5.199 The redemption price to be paid by a SICAV governed by Part I of the 2002 Act is equal to the net asset value of the shares[234] as calculated at the time of redemption, less any applicable costs and commissions.[235] No such rule applies to SICAVs governed by Part II of the 2002 Act[236] or to SICAVs with SIF status, which may

---

[231] Art 29(2), 2002 Act. See 5.106 *et seq* above.

[232] Art 49-5, 1915 Act.

[233] Art 39, Second Council Directive (EEC) 77/91(see n 215 above).

[234] Art 28(2)(b), 2002 Act.

[235] ibid.

[236] ibid Art 28(2)(b) requires SICAVs governed by Part I to redeem their shares at net asset value per share. Art 71 of the Act does not make that article applicable to SICAVs governed by Part II.

therefore, *inter alia*, redeem their shares by reference to the stock exchange value, if so provided for by the articles of incorporation.

SICAVs must always pay the redemption price to shareholders within the time limit specified in the articles of incorporation.[237]   **5.200**

SICAVs may, and indeed must, suspend redemptions in certain situations.   **5.201**

First of all, the articles of incorporation can specify the circumstances in which redemptions are to be suspended.[238] In contrast to the provisions of the 2002 Act and the Act of 13 February 2007 with respect to FCPs,[239] the 2002 Act and the Act of 13 February 2007 do not restrict suspension to exceptional situations where the suspension is appropriate in the circumstances and can be justified in the interests of shareholders. However, SICAVs governed by Part I of the 2002 Act must logically comply with those criteria for suspension which flow from Directive 85/611,[240] even if not expressly prescribed by the 2002 Act.   **5.202**

SICAVs governed by the 2002 Act must immediately report the suspension of redemptions to the CSSF and the supervisory authorities of the EEA Member States in which the shares of such SICAVs are marketed.[241]   **5.203**

The CSSF may also impose the suspension of redemptions. In this respect also, the 2002 Act deviates to some extent from Directive 85/611 by authorizing the CSSF to suspend redemptions where a SICAV fails to comply with the laws, regulations, and articles of incorporation governing its activity and operation.[242] The CSSF has the same powers with respect to SIFs.[243] Suspension must be in the interests of the shareholders.[244] Directive 85/611 authorizes the Member States of the EEA to provide for redemptions to be suspended 'in the interest of the investors or of the public'.[245] The Grand Duchy of Luxembourg has made only limited use of these powers with regard to SICAVs.   **5.204**

The depositary must verify that the redemption and, as the case may be, the cancellation of shares by or on behalf of a SICAV, complies with the law and the articles of incorporation,[246] unless the SICAV is governed by the Act of 13 February 2007, which does not impose this obligation on depositaries of SIFs.   **5.205**

---

[237] Arts 28(4) and 71, 2002 Act; Art 28(2), Act of 13 February 2007.
[238] Arts 28(5) and 71, 2002 Act; Art 28(5), Act of 13 February 2007.
[239] Art 12(1)(a), 2002 Act; Art 11(1), Act of 13 February 2007.
[240] Art 37(2)(a), Directive (EEC) 85/611.
[241] Arts 28(5) and 71, 2002 Act.
[242] ibid.
[243] Art 28(5), Act of 13 February 2007
[244] Arts 28(5) and 71, 2002 Act; Art 28(5), Act of 13 February 2007.
[245] Art 37(2)(b), Directive 85/611.
[246] Arts 34(3) and 71, 2002 Act.

Redemption of shares by a SICAF

Principles

5.206 The criteria governing redemptions by SICAFs are relatively similar to those applicable to SICAVs and are also based on both the 2002 Act or the Act of 13 February 2007, as the case may be, and the 1915 Act.

5.207 There are many similarities between the provisions applicable to redemptions by SICAVs and SICAFs governed by Part I of the 2002 Act. The obligation to redeem shares at the shareholder's request,[247] legal determination of the redemption price,[248] the reasons and procedure for suspension of redemption,[249] and the depositary's duty of supervision[250] apply to both. The chapter in the 2002 Act applicable to SICAFs governed by Part I merely cross-refers to the corresponding criteria for SICAVs.[251] However, there are a number of differences with respect to the procedure and conditions applicable to the redemption and holding of shares, areas in which the 1915 Act distinguishes between SICAVs and SICAFs.

5.208 SICAFs governed by Part II of the 2002 Act or by the Act of 13 February 2007 enjoy a wider discretion with respect to redemption procedures than those governed by Part I. Their obligations with respect to redemption criteria are limited to the depositary's task of verifying compliance of the redemption (and, as the case may be, the cancellation of the shares) with the law and the articles of incorporation,[252] the circumstances in which redemptions can be suspended, and certain provisions in the 1915 Act. There is no mandatory basis for determining the redemption price, ie it does not have to be based on the net asset value.[253]

Redemption at the shareholder's request

5.209 Pursuant to the 1915 Act,[254] the only condition applicable to the redemption of shares by a SICAF which proposes to place its shares with the public[255] is that it may not reduce its net asset value to less than the subscribed capital plus non-distributable reserves.

---

[247] See 5.176 above.
[248] See 5.199 above.
[249] See 5.201 above.
[250] See 5.205 above.
[251] Art 40, 2002 Act.
[252] Art 75(6), 2002 Act.
[253] Arts 73 *et seq*, 2002 Act do not render Art 28(2)(b), of that Act (which requires SICAVs governed by Part I to redeem their shares at their NAV) applicable to SICAFs governed by Part II. Likewise, Art 28(2)(b), of the 2002 Act has not been incorporated into the Act of 13 February 2007.
[254] Art 49-3(g), 1915 Act.
[255] This requirement excludes de facto certain SICAFs incorporated as SIFs from the scope of the provision.

Where redeemed shares are not immediately cancelled, they may continue to be **5.210** held by the SICAF subject to compliance with the following conditions:[256]

(1) the establishment of a non-distributable reserve, in an amount equal to the amount at which the shares are recorded as assets;
(2) the suspension of the voting rights attaching to the redeemed shares; and
(3) the inclusion of specific notices in the annual management report.

These reduced requirements with respect to redemptions apply only to SICAFs **5.211** when a shareholder requests redemption from the SICAF. If redemptions are effected at the SICAF's initiative, whether with or without the shareholder's consent, the rules specified below apply.

Redemption at the company's initiative with the shareholder's consent

When a redemption proposed by a SICAF requires the shareholder's consent, the **5.212** limits and conditions set out in the 1915 Act apply fully to the redemption and holding of such shares,[257] whether they are immediately cancelled or not.

Redemption of redeemable shares

The redemption and holding by a SICAF of so-called 'redeemable' shares is sub- **5.213** ject to the rules specified in the 1915 Act, as described above.[258]

Founder Shares Issued by UCIs

Founder shares, sometimes known as 'founding shares', are securities issued in **5.214** consideration of a contribution which does not form part of a company's capital.[259] Founder shares may be issued to facilitate the establishment of the company, to remunerate certain contributions, or to grant specific rights to their owners. They may be issued at any time during the company's existence.

Such securities may not be issued by FCPs, which do not distinguish between dif- **5.215** ferent types of share capital and shareholders' equity.

Only SICAVs which have opted for the status of SIF and SICAFs governed by **5.216** Part II of the 2002 Act are permitted to issue founder shares. Other investment companies would need authorization pursuant to a Grand-Ducal regulation, which has not yet been passed.[260]

---

[256] Art 49-5, 1915 Act.
[257] See 5.181 *et seq* above.
[258] See 5.191 *et seq* above.
[259] Delvaux (n 18 above) Ch 3, para 3.3.1; Van Ryn (n 68 above) Vol I, para 349, 366.
[260] Arts 31, 40, and 71, 2002 Act.

5.217   The authors of the 1983 Act (as endorsed by the authors of the 1988 and 2002 Acts) held the view that a UCI's promoters should not be accorded extensive rights with respect to the distribution of profits or any liquidation surplus, or over a fund's management and administration. The issue of founder shares would have enabled the establishment of such rights, which is why they are not authorized. Nevertheless, the legislature has not entirely ruled out the possibility of creating such securities, since founder shares could provide a transparent way of remunerating the promoters. Hence the possibility of a derogation by Grand-Ducal regulation[261] was provided for in the legislation.

5.218   Because investors in a SIF require less protection, SIFs are not subject to the same restriction and are not prohibited by law from issuing founder shares.

5.219   The 2002 Act mentions founder shares and 'all types of similar securities'.[262] This expression encompasses other securities which represent a contribution which does not form part of the share capital, such as bonus shares (*actions de jouissance*).[263]

5.220   What makes founder shares different from other shares is that they do not form part of the share capital. They do not enjoy in full the rights of and protections in place for ordinary shareholders, for example with respect to creditors, and are therefore subject to more flexible rules. The consideration given by holders of founder shares for the issue of founder shares may be an 'in kind' form of consideration, for example in the form of effort (*apport en industrie*), such as advice about the company's incorporation or management, rather than a cash contribution. It would not be possible, under the 1915 Act, to issue shares in consideration of an 'intangible' contribution in the form, for example, of know-how.[264]

5.221   The concept of contribution also distinguishes between founder shares and bonds. A capital contribution in respect of ordinary shares is subject to risk arising from unforeseen corporate developments. The loan represented by bonds, as it constitutes a debt of the company, must in principle be repaid regardless of the results of the company's business.

---

[261]   *Parliamentary doc* No 2366, Comments on the Articles, 37; *Parliamentary doc* No 2366[8], Report of the Special Committee, 11.

[262]   Art 31, 2002 Act.

[263]   Art 69-1, 1915 Act. Bonus shares may be issued to replace shares issued by the company, reimbursed from its profits, and subsequently cancelled. Such shares carry the same rights as the cancelled shares except for the right to reimbursement of the contribution and the right to distribution of a first dividend declared on shares that have not been reimbursed.

[264]   Art 26-3, 1915 Act. However, see Art 37 of the 1915 Act, which imposes application of Art 26-1 of the same Act on verification of contributions in kind.

The rights attaching to founder shares may be determined at the company's **5.222**
discretion,[265] with a few exceptions. A holder of founder shares is not entitled to
repayment of share capital, as founder shares do not constitute capital, nor are
they entitled to a preferential right to subscribe for new shares, that right being
reserved in principle for existing ordinary shareholders.[266]

In all other respects, the privileges attached to founder shares are determined by **5.223**
the articles of incorporation,[267] including the right to a dividend, the right to the
liquidation surplus, and voting rights. Such rights are usually granted to founder
shareholders.

Companies have greater leeway to determine the rules governing founder shares **5.224**
than those governing other shares. This latitude makes founder shares an interesting instrument and, *inter alia*, an excellent substitute for non-voting shares, the
issue of which is more strictly regulated.

Bonds Issued by UCIs

Principles

Bonds are securities representing loans contracted by a company. Such securities **5.225**
may be traded and confer on their holders equal claims on the company when
issued to represent the same loan or debt.

Bonds may be issued by SAs,[268] SCAs[269] and, within very narrow limits, SARLs.[270] **5.226**
Bonds issued by SAs and SCAs are covered by legal provisions designed to protect
their holders, although the provisions are not always mandatory. Most can be
avoided by subjecting debt issues to foreign law,[271] while others remain applicable
regardless of the governing law chosen.

The issue of bonds by UCIs

The 1915 Act does not authorize FCPs to issue bonds. This does not, however, **5.227**
prevent the issue of other debt securities by a management company acting on
behalf of an FCP.

---

[265] Art 37, 1915 Act.
[266] ibid Art 32-3(1) and (5).
[267] ibid Art 27(11).
[268] ibid Arts 79–98.
[269] ibid Art 103.
[270] Such companies may not offer bonds to the public (ibid Art 188).
[271] ibid Art 95.

5.228   In contrast, investment companies organized in the form of an SA or SCA may borrow by issuing bonds, subject to the laws and regulations governing borrowings by investment companies.[272]

Types of bonds that may be issued

5.229   In addition to the general rules laid down in respect of bonds, the law provides for four special types of bonds:[273]

- bonds with share subscription rights;
- bonds convertible into shares;
- mortgage bonds; and
- bonds redeemable by the drawing of lots.

5.230   This list does not preclude the issue of other types of bonds, subject to compliance with the mandatory requirements of Luxembourg law and, more particularly, company law.

Form of bonds

5.231   As is the case with shares, bonds may be in registered or bearer form.

5.232   Registered bonds are entered in the bonds register and may be transferred subject to the same conditions as for registered shares.

5.233   Bearer bonds are represented by a written document containing a series of notices listed in the 1915 Act.[274] The transfer of bonds is subject to the same conditions as those applicable to the transfer of bearer shares.[275]

5.234   Bonds always have a nominal value,[276] which may be denominated in euros or in any other currency.

Issue of bonds

5.235   As in the case of other types of borrowings, the decision to issue bonds lies in principle with the investment company's board of directors.

5.236   However, in the case of a SICAF which issues bonds convertible into shares and bonds with share subscription rights, as such securities may result in a capital increase, the board of directors must have regard to the company's authorized

---

[272]   See 3.77 *et seq* and 3.219 *et seq* above.
[273]   Arts 32-4, 94-6, and 96, 1915 Act.
[274]   ibid Art 84.
[275]   ibid.
[276]   ibid.

capital limits approved by the shareholders in general meeting for a maximum of five years. Conversion or share subscriptions may take place subsequently, after expiry of the resolution specifying the authorized capital.[277]

There are no such constraints for SICAVs, whose capital is allowed to fluctuate. **5.237**

In SICAFs, the formalities applicable to the issue of convertible bonds and bonds **5.238** with subscription rights are the same as those prescribed for capital increases.[278] Existing shareholders must have a preferential right to subscribe for bonds in cash, save for any derogation adopted or authorized[279] by the general meeting of shareholders.[280]

Moreover, in the case of conversion, convertible bonds normally entail a contribu- **5.239** tion to increase the company's capital. For that reason, they are valued by an independent auditor,[281] who prepares and presents a report at the time of issue of the convertible bonds. The report covers the exchange ratio between the bonds and shares, as described in the general issue terms.[282] As the 2002 Act and the Act of 13 February 2007 do not derogate from the 1915 Act as regards the formalities applicable to contributions in kind, a valuation report is required for both SICAFs and SICAVs incorporated as SAs or SCAs.

The share capital is increased after bond conversion or share subscription. In the **5.240** case of SICAFs, this increase is recorded in a notarial deed executed by the board of directors and based on the subscription documents.[283] Any issue premium must be paid in full.[284]

Essential rights of bondholders

The following essential rights are attached to all bonds, either as part of the loan **5.241** components or because they reflect provisions of the 1915 Act from which derogation is not permitted.

Right to interest

Because bonds represent borrowings on the part of the company, they entitle the **5.242** holder to the payment of interest, which may be at a fixed or floating rate and may be payable on a series of due dates or even on redemption.

---

[277] ibid Art 32-4. See also, to the same effect, Delvaux (n 18 above) Ch 3, para 3.4.7.
[278] ibid Art 32-4.
[279] In the context of the authorized capital.
[280] Art 32-3, 1915 Act.
[281] Art 32-4 that, via Art 32-1, refers to Art 26-1, 1915 Act.
[282] Delvaux (n 18 above) Ch 3, para 3.4.7.
[283] Art 32-4, which refers to Art 32-1, 1915 Act.
[284] Art 32-4, which refers to Art 32-2, 1915 Act.

5.243 In principle, neither the amount nor payment of such interest may depend on the company's performance. The interest is due even in the event of losses being incurred by the company.

Right to the repayment of principal

5.244 The borrowing represented by the bonds must be repaid to the bondholders at the scheduled maturity date(s). In principle, this right subsists regardless of the company's performance.

Right to information

5.245 During the two weeks preceding the annual general meeting of shareholders, bondholders are entitled to review the following documents at the registered office of the company:[285]

(1) the balance sheet and the profit and loss account;
(2) a list of the company's portfolio securities;
(3) a list of shareholders who have not yet paid up their shares, including the number of their shares and their domicile; and
(4) the auditors' report.

Right to attend general meetings of shareholders

5.246 Bondholders may attend all of the company's general meetings of shareholders.[286]

5.247 In principle, bondholders may not vote at general meetings of shareholders, with four exceptions, namely circumstances in which a general meeting of shareholders is called to change the company's nationality; to increase the shareholders' commitments; to change the company's form; or to change the corporate object. Such decisions affect the company's very essence and could jeopardize the rights of the bondholders or shareholders by depriving them of their framework of legal protection or of the restrictions imposed on the powers of the company's conducting persons by the company's object clause.[287] Thus, such decisions must also be approved by the general meeting of bondholders,[288] whose vote must either be unanimous[289] or satisfy special conditions as to the quorum and majority

---

[285] ibid Art 85, 1915 Act.
[286] ibid.
[287] However, it is difficult to understand why the legislature has given bondholders the right to vote on increased commitments for the shareholders.
[288] Except in the case of a merger, demerger, or similar operation (Art 67-1(3), 1915 Act).
[289] ibid Art 67-1(1).

required.[290] If necessary, a second general meeting is convened for consideration of the relevant issues.[291]

Additional rights of bondholders

Certain additional rights apply to bondholders when the bond issue is not governed by foreign law, as follows.   **5.248**

Right to take certain measures at general meetings

The bondholders may hold a general meeting to consider any amendment to the conditions of the loan represented by their securities or, more generally, to protect their interests.   **5.249**

The decisions that the general meeting of bondholders is authorized to take are listed in the 1915 Act.[292] Most require a strict quorum and majority.[293]   **5.250**

Right to appoint a representative

Bondholders have an inalienable right but are not obliged to appoint a representative. The bondholders' representative has the status of agent. He may be appointed by the general meeting of bondholders, the company or, in an emergency, the president of the district court hearing commercial cases and ruling in summary proceedings.[294] As a general rule, his powers are determined by the general meeting of bondholders.[295]   **5.251**

When appointing such a representative, the bondholders are deemed to waive their individual right to take action.[296]   **5.252**

---

[290] ibid Art 67-1(3).
[291] ibid.
[292] ibid Art 94-2.
[293] ibid Arts 94-2 to 94-4.
[294] ibid Art 87(1) and (2).
[295] ibid Art 88.
[296] ibid Art 94-5.

6

PARTIES INVOLVED IN THE OPERATION OF UNDERTAKINGS FOR COLLECTIVE INVESTMENT

Conducting Persons of UCIs

6.01   The general business of all Luxembourg-based UCIs is conducted by persons invested with broad management and administration powers ('conducting persons' or '*dirigeants*'). Depending on a UCI's legal form, the type of conducting person varies. FCPs are managed by a management company while investment companies are run by a board of directors or a management board (in a two-tier structure) (SA), or a general partner (SCA), or a board of managers (SARLs). These management bodies may delegate all or part of their daily management duties to other natural or legal persons, who must also be regarded as conducting persons. The 2002 Act and the Act of 13 February 2007 render the appointment of conducting persons subject to authorization by the CSSF, on account of their importance in ensuring the proper conduct of the UCI's business.

The legal status of the administration and management bodies and their delegates, **6.02** their respective spheres of authority, their potential civil and criminal liability and the conditions and procedures for their authorization will be discussed in this chapter.

Principles

The nature and status of a UCI's conducting persons varies according to whether **6.03** the UCI is a corporate or contractual scheme.

Incorporated UCIs

Incorporated UCIs can take various different legal forms.[1]   **6.04**

SAs with a one-tier management structure

The most traditional form is the SA with fixed or variable capital, which is managed **6.05** by the board of directors, whose appointment and termination of appointment is controlled by the shareholders in general meeting.[2] The board of directors has the power to carry out all acts necessary or expedient for the achievement of the corporate object.[3] The CSSF requires that there be at least three directors on the board of an SA, even if the UCI has only one shareholder.

SAs with a two-tier management structure

In SAs which have opted for a two-tier management structure, the board of direc- **6.06** tors is replaced by a supervisory board and a management board.[4]

The management board is the management body of the company and has the power **6.07** to take any action necessary or useful to realize the company's corporate object.[5]

---

[1] See 2.129 *et seq* above.
[2] Art 51, 1915 Act.
[3] ibid Art 53.
[4] See also J-P Spang, 'Réflexions sur la Société Européene et le droit commun des sociétés' (2005) No 36 ALJB 13–14; T-P Winandy, *Manuel et droit des sociétés* (Legitech, 2008) 509 *et seq*.
[5] Art 60*bis*-7(1), 1915 Act.

6.08 The number of a management board's members or the rules for determining the number of members are laid down in the articles of incorporation of the SA, failing which they are determined by the supervisory board.[6] The Act of 25 August 2006 provides that in single-shareholder SAs or in SAs whose capital is less than €500,000, the management board may have only one member.[7]

6.09 The members of the management board are appointed by the supervisory board or by the shareholders in general meeting where provided for in the articles of incorporation.[8] They may also be removed by the supervisory board or, where provided for in the articles of incorporation, by the general meeting.[9]

6.10 The management board is continuously supervised by the supervisory board, which means, *inter alia*, that it must, at least every three months, make a written report to the supervisory board on the progress and foreseeable development of the company's business.[10] In addition, the management board must promptly pass to the supervisory board any information on events likely to have a significant impact on the company's situation.[11]

6.11 Save for its obligations towards the supervisory board, the management board assumes the same functions,[12] is subject to the same operating, meeting and decision rules,[13] and the same liability regime as the board of directors.[14] The measures designed to prevent conflicts of interest at the management board are directly derived from the relevant rules applicable to the board of directors.[15] Given those similarities, references made to the board of directors in this work are to be understood as applying to the management board as well, unless otherwise specified.[16]

6.12 The supervisory board supervises the management of the company by the management board and is not authorized to interfere with the management.[17] It has an unlimited right to inspect all the transactions of the company and may

---

[6] ibid Art 60*bis*-2(1).

[7] ibid Art 60*bis*-2(2).

[8] ibid Art 60*bis*-3.

[9] ibid Art 60*bis*-5.

[10] ibid Art 60*bis*-12(2).

[11] ibid Art 60*bis*-12(3).

[12] See ibid Art 60*bis*-7(1) for the management board and Art 53 for the board of directors.

[13] See ibid Art 60*bis*-8 for the management board and Art 60 for the board of directors.

[14] See ibid Art 60*bis*-10 for the management board and Art 59 for the board of directors.

[15] See ibid Art 60*bis*-18 for the management board and Art 57 for the board of directors.

[16] Also see Art VIII, Act of 25 August 2006, according to which: 'Any legal or regulatory provision on commercial companies referring to the "board of directors" of an SA is to be understood as referring to the management board of the company—provided that the SA has a management board and a supervisory board, unless reference is made to the supervisory board due to the nature of the task concerned.'

[17] Art 60*bis*-11, 1915 Act.

inspect, but not remove, the books, correspondence, minutes, and generally all the records of the company.[18]

The supervisory board is made up of at least three members, unless the company has been incorporated by a sole shareholder, in which case it may have only one member.[19] **6.13**

The liability regime applicable to the members of the supervisory board is also modelled on that of the directors.[20] Measures designed to prevent conflicts of interest follow the same approach as for directors.[21] **6.14**

For obvious reasons related to the prevention of conflicts of interest, the members of the supervisory board may not act as members of the board of managers.[22] **6.15**

In practice, this two-tier structure may prove useful to UCIs. In particular it allows promoters to maintain a certain control over the company's local management as the management board will have members residing in Luxembourg, whereas the promoter or the founders of the company active in the supervisory board will be in a position to supervise the management of the company. **6.16**

SCAs

A second legal form is the SCA, which is available only to SICAFs governed by the 2002 Act and to investment companies established as SIFs. SCAs are managed by one or more general partners appointed under the articles of incorporation.[23] **6.17**

Unless otherwise stipulated in the articles of incorporation, the general partner has the right to veto any decision taken or ratified by the general meeting of shareholders, insofar as such decision concerns relationships between the company and third parties or is intended to amend the articles of incorporation.[24] In return, the general partner has unlimited and joint liability for the company's commitments, whereas the liability of the investors, the limited partners, is limited to their investment commitment.[25] In principle, a general partner cannot be dismissed unless otherwise stipulated in the articles of incorporation.[26] This enables the UCI's promoter to maintain a degree of control over the SCA. In contrast, the directors of an SA may be dismissed at any time by the general meeting of shareholders. **6.18**

---

[18] ibid Art 60*bis*-12.
[19] ibid Art 60*bis*-14; Art 51.
[20] ibid Art 60*bis*-14; Art 51*bis*, second indent.
[21] ibid Art 60*bis*-18 for the supervisory board and Art 57 for the board of directors.
[22] ibid Art 60*bis*-17(1).
[23] ibid Art 107.
[24] ibid Art 111.
[25] ibid Art 102.
[26] L Fredericq, *Traité de droit commercial belge* (Éditions Fecheyr, 1950) Vol IV, para 202 and Vol V, para 552; G Ripert and R Roblot, *Traité de droit commercial* (LGDJ, 15th edn, 1993) Vol I, para 1619.

SARLs

6.19 A third legal form, which is also possible only for SICAFs governed by the 2002 Act and for investment companies established as SIFs, is the SARL, which is managed by one or more managers who can be dismissed only for legitimate reasons unless otherwise stipulated in the articles of incorporation.[27] This type of company is normally unsuitable for UCIs open to the public because of restrictions on assignment of its shares.

6.20 The conducting persons of any investment company, regardless of its legal form, can decide to delegate management to a management company. When this occurs within the framework of Directive 85/611, it releases the investment company from a number of obligations, which will then be performed by the management company appointed by it.

6.21 The SA remains the most widespread form of incorporated UCI. For that reason, only the regime applicable to its conducting persons will be examined below. However, most of this discussion applies equally to the other two above-mentioned legal forms and can, in principle, be transposed for such companies, save for a few special features described further below.[28]

Contractual UCIs

6.22 According to the 2002 Act and the Act of 13 February 2007, which refers to the 2002 Act in this respect, FCPs must be managed by a management company incorporated in the form of an SA, an SARL, a cooperative society or an SCA, whose capital is represented solely by registered shares.[29]

6.23 The 1983 Act had already stipulated that only a company could manage an FCP.[30] The Parliamentary debates at the time of its enactment show several reasons for this approach. First of all, a company inherently enjoys greater continuity and therefore offers private investors a stronger guarantee of consistency. Secondly, a management company is subject to prior authorization by the CSSF. Supervision by the CSSF ensures that the management company has the financial resources needed to fulfil its obligations. Lastly, management companies were not, in 1983, permitted to pursue activities other than the management of FCPs. They were

---

[27] Art 191, 1915 Act.

[28] ibid Art 103 applies the SAs provisions to SCAs. Consequently, the rules on liability and delegation of authority governing the functioning of an SA's board of directors are broadly applicable to an SCA's general partner. The same applies to an SARL's managers, for whom the provisions of Arts 191 *et seq* of the 1915 Act lay down virtually identical rules of conduct and liability rules.

[29] Arts 77(1) and 91(1), 2002 Act.

[30] Art 2(1), 1983 Act.

therefore highly specialized[31] and entitled to the special tax status afforded to holding companies governed by the 1929 Act.[32]

The 1983 Act also reserved the management of FCPs to SAs. No convincing reason was given for that exclusive right, which was not maintained in the 1988 Act and in the 2002 Act.   **6.24**

The management company is critical for an FCP as an FCP cannot exist without it. That does not, however, preclude the replacement of a management company by another.[33]   **6.25**

A management company is governed by one of two sets of rules, depending on the status of the UCIs managed by it.   **6.26**

When the ordinary business of a management company is the collective management of UCITS in the form of FCPs and/or investment companies, it is granted the status of a 'harmonised' management company. It agrees to a series of investor protection rules in exchange for a passport allowing it to offer its services throughout the EEA. This is why it is sometimes referred to as a 'coordinated' management company.   **6.27**

Other management companies, ie those that manage only UCIs governed by Part II of the 2002 Act or by the Act of 13 February 2007, are subject to less strict rules but do not have a passport to carry on their business in other countries. Like coordinated management companies, they require prior authorization from the CSSF,[34] which may be withdrawn in certain circumstances.[35]   **6.28**

The 2002 Act allows management companies, regardless of their status, to manage several separate FCPs.[36] When a management company manages several UCIs, the Luxembourg tax administration regards it as a commercial company subject to the ordinary tax regime for corporations.[37]   **6.29**

The authorized activities of a management company are relatively limited and differ according to whether the company is coordinated or not.   **6.30**

Non-coordinated management company

A non-coordinated management company may not carry out functions other than the management of UCIs that are also non-coordinated.[38] This restriction   **6.31**

---

[31] *Parliamentary doc* No 2366, Comments on the Articles, 20–21.
[32] ibid 21 and *Parliamentary doc* No 3172, Comments on the Articles, 35.
[33] Arts 21(a) and 66, 2002 Act.
[34] ibid Art 91(1).
[35] ibid Art 91(5).
[36] ibid Arts 77(2) and 91(1).
[37] For the tax treatment of management companies, see 11.86 *et seq* below.
[38] Art 91(1), 2002 Act.

has its roots in an earlier version of Directive 85/611,[39] which stipulated that a management company's activity must be limited to the management of UCIs. The 1988 Act extended an equivalent requirement to management companies of non-coordinated UCIs. The purpose of this rule was to ensure optimum specialization of management companies and to avoid the risk of conflicts of interest with other activities, in order to protect investors.[40] Although Directive 85/611 has been amended in this respect, the principle has been maintained for management companies other than those governed by the Directive.

6.32 'UCI management' is the only permitted activity for non-coordinated management companies but is described neither in the 2002 Act nor in the Act of 13 February 2007. This management activity can best be determined by describing and classifying the services typically provided by management companies.

6.33 First, the management company assumes a UCI's strategic management. Its main purpose is to create one or more FCPs and to manage their assets. In this capacity it exercises the same prerogatives as the board of directors or managers of an investment company.

6.34 A management company may also provide certain limited asset management services on behalf of a UCI. In doing so, it acts as an agent for the principal management body. It can provide management services to incorporated UCIs in addition to FCPs created by other management companies. The UCIs that benefit from this service may be based in Luxembourg or in another country.

6.35 The asset management activity conducted by a non-coordinated management company may be carried out only in respect of UCIs. A non-coordinated management company is not authorized to act as an asset manager, whether for private investors or institutional investors.[41]

6.36 Secondly, a management company may assume the administrative management of UCIs. This concept covers all head office functions. Services may be provided both to FCPs, whether established by the particular management company or not, and to incorporated UCIs. The UCIs that benefit from this service need not be based in Luxembourg. Obviously, the provision of all or part of the head office functions connected with foreign UCIs from Luxembourg should be permissible under the relevant foreign tax or regulatory rules applicable to the UCIs in question.

---

[39] Art 6, Directive (EEC) 85/611 in its wording of 1985.

[40] 'Towards a European Market for undertakings for collective investment in transferable securities, Comments on the provisions of Directive 85/611', Office of Official Publication of the European Communities (1988) (hereinafter 'Towards a European market for UCITS') No 38, 19–20; *Parliamentary doc* No 3172, Comments on the Articles, 35.

[41] eg asset management on behalf of pension funds does not fall within the scope of activities allowed for non-coordinated management companies.

An entity other than a management company which intends to provide similar services to UCIs is, with respect to the provision of such services, governed by the 1993 Act as an administrative agent of the financial sector.[42]

Thirdly, the management of UCIs may to some extent include the distribution or sale of units in UCIs. This is always true for FCP units issued by the management company on behalf of an FCP created by it. It is worthwhile noting that distribution of units in third-party UCIs is also considered as an investment service within the meaning of the 1993 Act.[43]   **6.37**

The distribution of units incidentally requires the opening and maintenance by the management company of the accounts in which units purchased by investors are recorded. While such accounts may in principle recognize only the units of FCPs created by the particular management company, the CSSF nonetheless allows such accounts to be established to record for the benefit of investors units issued by other UCIs if such funds are linked to the management company by the same promoter or the same financial group. Such an activity is not considered the management company's professional activity and is therefore permissible.   **6.38**

Coordinated management company

A coordinated management company is more tightly regulated and has access to a broader range of activities. Directive 85/611 takes a relatively flexible view of the 'collective portfolio management' of FCPs and investment companies. The functions envisaged in this concept are listed in the Directive, which specifies that the list is not exhaustive and that other activities may be added.[44] Collective portfolio management covers three types of functions, ie (1) portfolio management, (2) administration,[45] and (3) marketing.   **6.39**

Directive 85/611 no longer limits the activities of the management companies governed by it to management of UCIs. In additional to management of UCITS, other functions may also be added.[46] The additional services mentioned in Directive 85/611 are the management of investment portfolios on a discretionary client-by-client basis in accordance with the mandates given by investors where   **6.40**

---

[42] Art 29-2, 1993 Act.

[43] In the 1993 Act, distributors of units in UCIs are a special kind of financial market professional whose activity is to distribute units in UCIs that may be marketed in the Grand Duchy of Luxembourg (Art 24-7, 1993 Act).

[44] Art 5.2, Directive (EEC) 85/611 and Art 77(2), 2002 Act.

[45] The administration activity defined in Annexe II of Directive (EEC) 85/611 includes a fund's legal and accounting management services, processing requests for information from clients, valuing the portfolio and the units (including tax aspects), verifying compliance with applicable regulations, keeping the register of unitholders, distributing income, issuing and redeeming units, settling contracts (including sending certificates), and recording and safekeeping records of transactions.

[46] Art 5.3, Directive (EEC) 85/611 and Art 77(3), 2002 Act.

such portfolios include one or more of the instruments listed in MiFID.[47] The other incidental services authorized by the Directive are investment advice regarding those instruments[48] and the safekeeping and administration of units in UCIs.[49, 50]

Powers and functions of the management bodies and their delegates

6.41   This section will examine the legal nature of the functions and powers, first, of the management bodies of an investment company and, secondly, of the management company of an FCP. It also considers the powers that may be delegated within investment companies and FCPs.

Management bodies *stricto sensu*

Board of directors of an investment company incorporated as an SA with a one-tier management structure

6.42   **Legal nature of the functions of the board of directors**   The directors of an SA are 'agents appointed for a fixed term, whether shareholders or not, who may be dismissed and who are paid a salary or provide their services free of charge'.[51]

6.43   **Powers of the board of directors**   Pursuant to the 1915 Act,[52] the board of directors has authority to carry out 'all acts necessary or expedient for the achievement

---

[47]   ie transferable securities, money market instruments, shares and units in UCIs, options, futures, swaps, future rate agreements and all other derivatives related to transferable securities, currencies, interest rates or yields or other derivatives, financial indices or financial instruments that can be settled by physical delivery or in cash, options, futures, swaps, future rate agreements and all other derivatives related to commodities, which must be settled in cash or may be settled in cash at the request of one of the parties (otherwise than through default or another incident resulting in termination), options, futures, swaps and all other derivatives related to commodities which can be settled by physical delivery, provided they are traded on a regulated market and/or an MTF, options, futures, swaps, forwards and any other derivative contracts relating to commodities that can be physically settled not otherwise mentioned in Section C.6 of MiFID and not being for commercial purposes, which have the characteristics of other derivative financial instruments, having regard to whether, *inter alia*, they are cleared and settled through recognized clearing houses or are subject to regular margin calls, derivative instruments for the transfer of credit risk, financial contracts for differences, options, futures, swaps, forward rate agreements and any other derivative contracts relating to climatic variables, freight rates, emission allowances or inflation rates or other official economic statistics that must be settled in cash or may be settled in cash at the option of one of the parties (otherwise than by reason of a default or other termination event), and any other derivative contracts relating to assets, rights, obligations, indices and measures not otherwise mentioned in Section C of MiFID, which have the characteristics of other derivative financial instruments, having regard to whether, *inter alia*, they are traded on a regulated market or an MTF, are cleared and settled through recognized clearing houses or are subject to regular margin calls.

[48]   Art 5.3(b), Directive 85/611 and Art 77(3)(b), 2002 Act.

[49]   ibid.

[50]   For other particulars, see 6.90 *et seq* below.

[51]   Art 50, 1915 Act.

[52]   ibid Art 53.

of the corporate object'. As the French name of this body—the *conseil d'administration*—suggests, that includes actual administrative acts[53] and all acts involving the management of corporate assets.[54]

Acts 'reserved by the law or the articles of incorporation for the general meeting' **6.44**
fall outside the authority of the board of directors.[55] Whilst that restriction is obvious—and valid vis-à-vis third parties—for acts reserved by law to the general meeting of shareholders,[56] the situation is less clear as regards restrictions on the board's powers contained in the articles of incorporation. Whilst such restrictions may curb the board of directors' internal acts, they are never valid vis-à-vis third parties even when published in the *Mémorial*.[57] The object of this rule is to protect third parties. Parties entering into a contract with a company do not first have to verify that the board is authorized by the articles of incorporation to conclude each contemplated transaction. That protection also applies to acts falling outside the sphere of the corporate object, provided that the third party concerned acted in good faith, ie that it could not have known, in the relevant circumstances, that the act in question went beyond the scope of the corporate object.[58]

Management board of an investment company incorporated as an SA with a two-tier management structure

Legal nature of the management board's functions   The members of the man- **6.45**
agement board are considered as the company's representatives, in the same way as directors are.[59]

The management board's powers   The management board has the power to **6.46**
take 'any action necessary or useful to realise the corporate object, with the exception of those powers reserved by law or the articles of incorporation to the supervisory board and to the general meeting'.[60]

---

[53]   ie in the context of UCIs, mainly the so-called head office tasks.
[54]   Mainly the purchase and sale of transferable or other securities making up a UCI's portfolio.
[55]   Art 53, 1915 Act. See, *inter alia*, J Van Ryn, *Principes de droit commercial*, (Bruylant, 1st edn, 1954) Vol I, 442 *et seq*; P Wauwermans, *Manuel pratique des sociétés anonymes* (Bruylant, 1933) 307 *et seq*.
[56]   Such as the appointment or dismissal of the board members or modification of the articles of incorporation.
[57]   Conversely, third parties are likewise precluded from relying on them vis-à-vis the company in order to evade having to perform their obligations (P-E Partsch, 'Dans quelle mesure le conseil d'administration d'une société anonyme belge peut-il adopter des décisions sans réunion physique de ses membres?'(1995) *Rev prat soc*, 201).
[58]   Art 60*bis*, 1915 Act; Cass b, 12 November 1987, RCJB, 1989, 387, according to which third parties may not claim that an act is outside the scope of the corporate object in order to release themselves from their commitments vis-à-vis the company.
[59]   Art 60*bis*-10, 1915 Act.
[60]   ibid Art 60*bis*-7(1).

6.47 The rules governing the enforceability as against third parties of any limitations on the powers of the management board deriving either from the articles of incorporation or from a decision of the relevant corporate bodies are the same as those mentioned above in connection with the board of directors.[61]

The management company of a common fund

6.48 **Legal nature of the management company's functions** The legal nature of the relations existing between a management company and third parties, on the one hand, and between the management company and the FCP (ie all unitholders), on the other, is described in the 2002 Act and in the Act of 13 February 2007.

6.49 The management company 'shall act in its own name *vis-à-vis* third parties but shall indicate that it is acting on behalf of the common fund' when so acting.[62] That provision was already included in the 1983 Act.[63] Since an FCP does not have legal personality, the management company is obliged to act on its behalf. To avoid confusion, the management company must indicate that it acts on behalf of the FCP, given that it may also act on its own behalf.[64]

6.50 The management company is the legal representative of the undivided co-ownership of assets constituting the FCP, ie the composite group of unitholders. Its powers are rooted directly in the law.[65]

6.51 **The management company's powers** The 2002 Act and the Act of 13 February 2007 provide that 'the management company shall manage the common fund in accordance with the management regulations and in the exclusive interest of the unitholders . . . It shall exercise all rights attached to the securities comprised in the portfolio of a common fund'.[66]

6.52 The management company's function in an FCP is similar to that exercised by the board of directors of an SA. It is responsible for the UCI's administration and management.[67]

6.53 In contrast to the board of directors of an SA, its powers are somewhat limited by those of the depositary. The 2002 Act requires a certain division of functions between the

---

[61] ibid Arts 60*bis*-7(4) and 60*bis*-9, 1915 Act.

[62] Arts 14(2) and 66, 2002 Act; Art 13(2), Act of 13 February 2007.

[63] Art 7(2) of the 1983 Act, itself inspired by Art 7 para 2, of the European Council recommendation on collective investment funds, the subject of Resolution (72) 28 adopted by the Committee of Ministers on 19 September 1972 during the 213th meeting of the Ministers' Deputies.

[64] *Parliamentary doc* No 2366, Comments on the Articles, 24.

[65] For a more detailed analysis of the relationship between an FCP's management company and the unitholders, see 2.109 *et seq* above.

[66] Arts 14(1) and (3) and 66, 2002 Act; Art 13(1), Act of 13 February 2007.

[67] In this context, it is the management company itself, not its board of directors or manager, in which those powers are vested; the board of directors or the manager of the management company in turn are the management organ of the management company.

management company and the depositary, the tasks of which include in particular, monitoring the activities of the management company whose instructions it carries out, 'save insofar as they conflict with the law or the management regulations'.[68]

The meaning and scope of this provision of the 2002 Act, designed to protect the **6.54** unitholders and to specify the matters coming within the responsibility of the depositary, will be examined later.[69] It is nevertheless clear that the management company's powers are in this respect more limited than those of an investment company's board of directors as a result of the depositary's inspection powers.

The situation of an FCP with the status of SIF is different in this respect. The **6.55** depositary of such a UCI is not responsible for monitoring the activity of its management company.

Delegates of management bodies

The following paragraphs deal with the conditions and limits permitting a UCI's **6.56** management bodies to delegate the powers vested in them by law.

Delegates of the board of directors or of the management board of an investment company incorporated as an SA

Defined as the principal management body,[70] the board of directors may not **6.57** entirely cede its powers to a third party. The same requirement applies to the management board. Those boards may nonetheless be assisted by agents in the performance of their management duties. They may delegate general day-to-day management tasks, the daily management of investments, daily administration, or the marketing of the company's units.[71]

Within the context of an investment company, delegation of certain functions **6.58** releases the board of directors or the management board from performing certain tasks. The scope of delegation varies according to the type of delegation. Thus:

(1) global daily management, which the 1915 Act does not define,[72] covers the investment management and daily administration activities referred to below

---

[68] Arts 18(2)(c) and 66, 2002 Act.

[69] See 6.344 *et seq* below.

[70] District Court of Luxembourg, 30 May 1980, Bull François Laurent, 1987, II, 80–1, confirmed by the Court of Appeal, 1 March 1982, Bull Droit & Banque No 4, 1984, 41 *et seq*, and by the Luxembourg Cour de Cassation, 19 May 1983, Bull Droit & Banque, No 4, 1984, 45 *et seq*.

[71] For details, see L Fredericq, *Traité de droit commercial belge* (Editions Fecheyr, 1950) Vol V, paras 456 and 459.

[72] As a general rule, according to case law and legal commentators, this consists in 'the carrying out of acts in the daily execution of the policy outlined by the board, which must be accomplished on a day-to-day basis in order to carry on the company's business and which, because of their lack of importance and the need for prompt solutions, do not justify intervention by the board of directors itself' (Belgian *Cour de Cassation*, 17 September 1968, Pas, 1969, I, 61).

and, for example, the authority to negotiate certain service agreements on behalf of the UCI, provided that they have been approved in principle by the board of directors;

(2) daily investment management includes the power to buy and sell securities and other components of the portfolio in accordance with the investment policy and restrictions laid down by the board of directors;

(3) daily administration consists of the performance of all of a UCI's head office tasks as required by current regulations; and

(4) the marketing of the investment company's units or shares to investors includes all actions involved in the distribution of such securities for investment by the target public.

In general, the board of directors of an investment company delegates most of the daily management of the company.

6.59   When all such management activities are delegated to a coordinated management company, coordinated investment companies are released from the obligation to comply with certain requirements that would otherwise have applied. The scope and consequences of this type of delegation are examined separately.[73]

6.60   **Global daily management delegation**   Pursuant to the 1915 Act,[74] daily management may be delegated globally to one or more directors, members of the management board, managers, or other officers of the company, to the exclusion of the members of the supervisory board. Their appointment, dismissal, and powers of delegates are regulated by the articles of incorporation or the competent bodies of the company.

6.61   Any restrictions on the powers of a management body[75] set out in the articles of incorporation or a contract are not binding insofar as they affect third parties. Daily management delegates do not have to produce to third parties any power of attorney proving their authority. They are merely required to show the capacity in which they act, provided the necessary notices have been published.[76]

6.62   Daily management requires widely varying degrees of intervention, depending on the type of UCI concerned. For example, the meaning of daily management of investments in the context of UCIs investing in listed securities with a high portfolio turnover differs considerably from that of real estate property funds or venture capital funds whose assets are acquired in the fulfilment of a longer-term strategy.

---

[73] See 6.69 *et seq* below.
[74] Arts 60 and 60*bis*-8, 1915 Act.
[75] C Resteau, *Traité des sociétés anonymes* (Swinnen, 3rd edn, 1982) Vol II, paras 897–898.
[76] ibid Vol II, para 1108.

It is possible to delegate an SA's daily management globally to one or more natural **6.63** persons who may be authorized to act individually or collectively. As global daily management can only be delegated en bloc, each delegate is in principle authorized to carry out all delegated management actions. When management is delegated to a committee, decisions may only be taken collectively and not by individual members of that group.

In addition, when delegating global powers, the board of directors or the manage- **6.64** ment board may assign specific responsibilities to certain delegates or to a committee. It may also allow the committee itself to delegate responsibilities to certain members. However, such arrangements and restrictions on powers have no validity vis-à-vis third parties, even when published,[77] but may influence the internal relations between the board of directors or the management board and the delegates.

All tasks delegated globally as part of the daily management are carried out under **6.65** the control of the board of directors or the management board, as the case may be, within the framework and limits set by the board. For example, the delegate reports regularly to the board of directors or the management board on the investments made by him. That does not release the board from the obligation to adjust its strategies from time to time to reflect changes in the economic environment and the markets.

Partial delegation of authority   General daily management delegation is not **6.66** always necessary in investment companies. In many cases, the board of directors or the management board may merely limit a manager's powers to management of the company's portfolio. That amounts to a special delegation.

Moreover, the board of directors or the management board of an investment com- **6.67** pany frequently divides the daily management functions between several agents, in which case one or more managers appointed to implement the investment policy will be working alongside other agents, normally banks or other financial service providers, who have been appointed with responsibility for the investment company's daily administration or distribution of units. These likewise constitute special delegations.

Similarly, principles of corporate governance call for the formation of special **6.68** committees made up of directors and/or specialists independent of the board of directors or the management board with responsibility for preparing, taking, and/or controlling some of the most sensitive decisions, including those requiring increased shareholder protection. The investment company or its management

---

[77] Arts 60 and 60*bis*-8, 1915 Act.

company may set up an audit committee,[78] a compensation committee,[79] or a supervision committee.[80]

6.69 **Delegation by a coordinated investment company to a 'designated' management company** The 2002 Act introduces a new distinction between coordinated investment companies that have 'designated' a management company and those that manage themselves. The board of directors in the former case assigns global management responsibility to the designated management company and primarily retains responsibility for oversight of the delegated activities. The management company may in turn delegate a number of functions within the limits laid down by the 2002 Act.[81]

6.70 A self-managed investment company is mainly managed by its board of directors, which may nevertheless delegate particular functions to third parties, especially a management company.

6.71 The Community legislature decided to create special rules for investment companies that manage their own activities 'in order to avoid any distortion of competition between UCITS constituted as investment companies and UCITS managed by management companies'.[82] It would have been inappropriate for contractual UCITS subject to a series of new obligations to have to compete with incorporated UCITS not subject to the new rules and thereby benefiting from an unfair advantage.

6.72 In contrast, a coordinated investment company governed by the new rules in the Directive which uses the services of an authorized management company is not obliged to comply with the new provisions which, in this case, apply at the level of the management company.

6.73 According to the 2002 Act, investment companies which have not 'designated' a management company are considered to be self-managed. The Act does not provide information about the scope of the delegation by such entities.

---

[78] Mainly charged with checking the quality and accuracy of the financial information supplied to third parties; risk evaluation and management procedures; the quality of internal control; the appointment, remuneration, and, as applicable, replacement of outside auditors; and, more generally, their independence vis-à-vis the investment company and its groups.

[79] Invested with authority to propose and verify the remuneration of the directors and other conducting persons of the company.

[80] Responsible for inspecting and reporting to the board of directors on compliance by the investment company and/or the management company with the applicable laws, regulations, and contracts.

[81] See 6.173 *et seq* below.

[82] Common Position (EC) No 23/2001 adopted by the Council on 5 June 2001 with a view to adopting a Directive of the European Parliament and of the Council amending Council Directive (EEC) 85/611 on the coordination of laws, regulations and administrative provisions relating to undertakings for collective investment in transferable securities (UCITS) with a view to regulating management companies and simplified prospectuses [2001] OJ C297/32.

The 2002 Act can be interpreted in two ways to determine which activities to **6.74** entrust to a management company. According to the first, a management company can be entrusted with a 'significant part' of management, which does not have to include intellectual management of investments. The second, stricter, interpretation holds that an investment company remains self-managed unless it delegates its administration, the intellectual management of its investments, and its marketing to a coordinated management company.[83] This is the interpretation adopted by the CSSF in Circular 03/108.

---

[83] Nothing in Directive (EEC) 85/611 contradicts the first interpretation. No provision requires or implies that an investment company that does not wish to be categorized as a self-managed company must delegate management of investments to a management company. The same observation applies to the preparatory work for Directive (EC) 2001/107. On the contrary, we read that, according to the Council of the European Communities, an investment company 'of which a large part of the activities is managed by a management company' cannot be considered self-managed (Common Position (EC) No 23/2001 adopted by the Council on 5 June 2001 with a view to adopting a Directive of the European Parliament and of the Council amending Council Directive (EEC) 85/611 on the coordination of laws, regulations and administrative provisions relating to undertakings for collective investment in transferable securities (UCITS) with a view to regulating management companies and simplified prospectuses [2001] OJ C297/33. By distinguishing between delegation of a 'large part' of UCITS management to a management company and less comprehensive delegations, the Council confirms implicitly that a management company is not required to exercise all investment management, administration, and marketing functions. An investment company that delegates its head office tasks to a management company could thus be released from the additional obligations imposed on self-managed investment companies, even if it keeps or delegates to another entity the intellectual management of its investments (for the opposite view see J Elvinger and IM Schmit, 'Les sociétés de gestion d'organismes de placement collectif en droit luxembourgeois', in *Droit bancaire et financier au Luxembourg* (Larcier, 2004) Vol 4, 1504). Head office services represent a large part of an investment company's activity, especially in connection with the protection of investor interests. In this respect, head office functions are at least as important as—and in certain circumstances even more important than—management of the UCITS' assets itself. This is, for example, the case with index-linked funds and money market funds. The second interpretation mainly reflects the spirit of the Directive. According to this interpretation, although its spirit is intrinsically invisible, it inspired the wording of certain provisions of Directive (EEC) 85/611. (This would, for instance, explain the fact that Art 5g of the Directive allows management companies to delegate 'one or more of their functions'. According to this view, the use of the plural indicates that the activities of a management company include intellectual management of investments. Similarly, reference in the same provisions to the 'main function of investment management' should not be read as opposed to the 'additional function' of investment management on a discretionary client-by-client basis for an entity other than a UCITS. It simply means that a management company must manage the assets of the investment companies by which it has been designated). Again, according to this interpretation, the European legislature wanted management of a UCITS' assets always to be effected by an entity subject to the obligations imposed on management companies by Directive (EC) 2001/107. It would thus be contrary to the spirit of the Directive to categorize an entity responsible only for the management of an investment company's head office as the 'designated' management company when the fund's investments are managed by the investment company itself or by an entity other than a management company. More importantly, this interpretation avoids the potential for abuse. The delegation of certain minor functions only to a management company could lead to widespread avoidance of the rules applicable to self-managed companies. Prohibiting this regime only when all administration, management, and marketing activities are entrusted to a management company is a simple and radical way to avoid misuse. This probably explains the CSSF's preference for the latter approach.

6.75 As interpreted by the CSSF, the 'designation' of a management company necessarily covers every aspect of the company's daily management. This raises the question of whether the provisions of the 1915 Act on the powers of the entity to whom daily management is delegated and the enforceability of the appointment are applicable. The answer should be in the affirmative since the 2002 Act does not specifically stipulate otherwise. The investment company should nevertheless be able to disregard these provisions and make the management company merely an agent but must ensure the management company is given all investment management, administration, and marketing functions listed by the law.

6.76 In any case, a management company's designation as the delegated daily manager has the advantage that it does not have to prove its representation powers when carrying out legal actions on behalf of the investment company. This same advantage can nevertheless become a source of concern for an investment company wishing to delegate to a management company only those functions that are strictly necessary to avoid the status of self-managed company. The extensive representative power of the delegated daily manager may give rise to a risk of abuse on the part of the management company, which could commit the investment company to actions or transactions it did not wish to conclude. Such concerns on the part of an investment company are more likely when the designated management company is not part of the promoter's corporate group.

6.77 The status of a self-managed investment company requires compliance with certain requirements not applicable to other companies.

6.78 On the date of its authorization, a self-managed investment company must have a minimum capital of €300,000.[84] No such minimum capital is imposed on investment companies that have designated a management company. The difference in treatment is due to the fact that the rules on ratios of own funds (shareholders' equity) to assets under management apply to the management companies designated by an investment company. An investment company that has designated a management company is therefore considered to be 'covered'[85] by the 'own funds' of its management company.

6.79 Next, a self-managed investment company must comply with prudential rules that are similar to those provided for management companies, *inter alia*, requiring a good administrative and accounting organization.[86]

6.80 A self-managed investment company is also subject to the same rules of conduct and delegation limits as management companies.[87]

---

[84] Art 27(1), 2002 Act.
[85] Preamble to Directive 2001/107, 13th Recital.
[86] Art 27(3), 2002 Act.
[87] ibid Art 27(2).

For the purpose of prudential surveillance by the CSSF, a self-managed investment company supplies the CSSF every three months with information on its financial situation and its profit and loss account.[88] **6.81**

Delegates of the management company of a common fund

The 2002 Act does not provide for the delegation of powers by management companies. Since it is not prohibited, such delegation is in principle possible and may be organized in a similar way to the delegations permitted for investment companies.[89] **6.82**

Status of coordinated management companies

When Directive 85/611 was initially adopted, one particularly important class of player in the investment fund industry remained sidelined from Community coordination, ie management companies, whose role and responsibilities were becoming gradually more essential as the investment fund sector continued to develop. The need for these companies to have a clear and uniform legal framework enabling them to operate on a level playing field throughout the EEA could no longer be ignored. More generally, many financial operators were subject to Community standards allowing them to exercise their freedom of establishment and their freedom to provide services while protecting the market and investors. The time had come for management companies to benefit from a similar legal framework. This was one of the objectives of Directive 2001/107. Below, we will examine its rules on head office, the status of conducting persons, prudential rules, rules of conduct, and delegation conditions. **6.83**

Permissible activities for coordinated management companies

Until the 2002 Act came into force, management companies were not authorized to carry on functions other than UCI management. The purpose of this restriction was to protect investors by ensuring optimum specialization of management companies and avoiding the risk of conflicts of interest with other activities.[90] **6.84**

Even though still relevant, these objectives have been superseded by the need to allow management companies to 'achieve important economies of scale'.[91] Directive 85/611, as amended by Directive 2001/107, extended the range of **6.85**

---

[88] Section IV, Circular 03/108.

[89] The delegation available under Art 60, 1915 Act is not applicable in this context, since that Article applies only to SAs, whereas here it is the management company itself that delegates its powers.

[90] 'Towards a European market for UCITS' (n 40 above) No 38, pp 19–20; *Parliamentary doc* No 3172, Comments on the Articles, 35.

[91] Preamble to Directive (EC) 2001/107, 9th Recital.

activities such companies are authorized to carry on to certain exhaustively listed additional functions. That said, management of UCIs remains their primary function, without which they are not allowed to engage in any of the additional activities permitted by Directive 85/611.

Principal function: management of UCIs

6.86 As defined by Directive 85/611 and the 2002 Act, a coordinated management company is one 'whose usual activity is the management of UCITS taking the form of FCPs and/or investment companies (collective portfolio management of UCITS), including the functions mentioned in Annexe II'.[92] Annexe II to the 2002 Act specifies that three types of functions are 'included in the collective portfolio management activity' of UCITS, ie (a) portfolio management, (b) administration, and (c) marketing.

6.87 The services mentioned in this connection under the administration activity defined in Annexe II are: legal and accounting services for the funds in question; the processing of requests for information from clients; portfolio valuation and calculation of the value of units (including tax aspects); verification of compliance with regulations; keeping the register of unitholders; distribution of income; the issue and redemption of units; settlement of contracts (including the mailing of certificates); and the registration and administration of transactions. This is in fact the head office activity described in greater detail at 6.361–6.415 below.

6.88 Prior to implementation of Directive 2001/107, the exact scope of the concept of 'management of UCIs' remained uncertain and subject to divergent interpretations throughout the EEA. In Luxembourg, management of UCIs included intellectual and administrative management and, within limits, the marketing of UCI units. The current definition in Directive 85/611 and the 2002 Act does not alter this practice fundamentally.

6.89 In addition to coordinated UCITS, coordinated management companies are authorized to manage UCIs with a different status, such as UCIs governed by Part II of the 2002 Act, by the Act of 13 February 2007, or foreign UCIs. The 2002 Act nevertheless requires management companies engaged in such activities to be subject to prudential supervision.[93] This prudential supervision requirement entails few legislative or regulatory constraints except perhaps the obligation to report the services provided to such UCIs to the CSSF.[94] Most management obligations imposed on coordinated management companies by the 2002 Act and CSSF circulars only concern services supplied to UCITS.

---

[92] Art 1a, point 2, Directive (EEC) 85/611.
[93] Art 77(2), 2002 Act.
[94] Elvinger and Schmit (n 83 above) 1506.

Additional and incidental functions

In addition to its primary function as a manager of UCIs, a management com-   **6.90**
pany may carry on a few activities regulated by MiFID and exhaustively listed in
the 2002 Act. The first is discretionary management of the portfolios of private
and institutional investors, especially pension funds, insofar as such portfolios
include one or more of the instruments mentioned in Section B of Annexe II of
the 1993 Act.[95] This reference to the 1993 Act permits management companies
to manage a diverse range of:

(1) transferable securities;
(2) money market instruments;
(3) shares and units in UCIs;
(4) options, futures, swaps, future rate agreements, and all derivatives related to
     transferable securities, currencies, interest rates or yields, or other derivatives,
     financial indices or financial instruments that can be settled by physical delivery
     or in cash;
(5) options, futures, swaps, future rate agreements, and all other derivatives
     related to cash or physically settled commodities[96] not otherwise mentioned
     in Section C.6 of MiFID and not being for commercial purposes, which have
     the characteristics of other derivative financial instruments having regard to
     whether, *inter alia*, they are cleared and settled through recognized clearing
     houses or are subject to regular margin calls;
(6) derivative instruments for the transfer of credit risk;
(7) financial contracts for differences;
(8) options, futures, swaps, forward rate agreements and any other derivative
     contracts relating to climatic variables, freight rates, emission allowances or
     inflation rates or other official economic statistics that must be settled in cash
     or may be settled in cash at the option of one of the parties (otherwise than by
     reason of a default or other termination event); and
(9) any other derivative contracts relating to assets, rights, obligations, indices,
     and instruments not otherwise mentioned in Section C of MiFID, which
     have the characteristics of other derivative financial instruments, having
     regard to whether, *inter alia*, they are traded on a regulated market or an MTF,
     are cleared and settled through recognized clearing houses, or are subject to
     regular margin calls.

A coordinated management company may also provide investment advice with   **6.91**
regard to the instruments listed above[97] and can also provide services relating to the

---

[95] Art 77(3)(a), 2002 Act.
[96] Provided, in the case of physically settled commodities, that they are traded on a regulated
market and/or a multilateral trading facility (MTF).
[97] Art 77(3)(b), 2002 Act.

safekeeping and administration of UCI units[98] purchased by investors. The 2002 Act stipulates clearly that the advisory, safekeeping, and administration activities must remain incidental. A management company cannot be authorized to perform these functions if not authorized to provide discretionary portfolio management services.[99]

6.92 A management company may not carry on activities regulated by MiFID other than those referred to above. For example, it may not act as an agent for instruments mentioned in Section B of Annexe II to the 1993 Act except insofar as such services are part of the more general management of UCIs or authorized discretionary management services.[100]

6.93 As a rule, a management company may not provide domiciliation services[101] to third parties within the meaning of the amended Act of 31 May 1999 on company domiciliation. It may nevertheless provide domiciliation services to other management companies, investment companies and any other UCI having the legal form of a commercial company.[102] Within certain limits, it may also domicile advisory companies but in that instance the advisory company may, under its corporate object, provide advisory services to only one investment company and the investment company must be domiciliated with the same management company. By adopting this position, the CSSF seeks to ensure coordination of the various activities engaged in by the relevant advisory and investment companies to which a management company provides services.[103]

6.94 A management company may act as a head office agent for a SICAR or a pension fund, provided it has the necessary human and technical resources.[104]

6.95 In the performance of their additional functions, management companies are governed by rules that are very similar to those applicable to professionals of the financial sector offering the same services. They are, *inter alia*, subject to certain prudential rules and rules of conduct[105] as investment firms within the meaning of MiFID.[106] The organizational requirements laid down by MiFID differ little

---

[98] ibid.

[99] ibid.

[100] CSSF Annual Report for 2003, 80.

[101] When a company establishes a seat with a third party to conduct business there within the scope of its objects, domiciliary activities are those services associated with such business and provided by the said third party (Art 1, Act of 31 May 1999).

[102] CSSF Annual Report for 2004, 67; Art 1(4), Act of 31 May 1999.

[103] CSSF Annual Report for 2006, 81.

[104] CSSF Annual Report for 2004, 67.

[105] According to the principle of 'same activity—same treatment'.

[106] Art 77(4), 2002 Act insofar as it refers to Arts 10 and 11 of Directive (EEC) 93/22, which was repealed and replaced by MiFID (see in particular Art 66, MiFID, which makes applicable to the provision of those additional functions by management companies the initial capital endowment rules, the conduct of business rules, and the organizational requirements laid down in MiFID).

in essence from the prudential rules in the 2002 Act except insofar as they are more detailed. The general principles applicable to investment management, repeated in their entirety in the 2002 Act, are complemented by rules intended specifically to protect investors who have entrusted their funds or other assets to the management company.[107] The same applies to the rules of conduct specified in MiFID, to which the 2002 Act also refers. A few additional rules are applicable to a management company assuming the additional functions authorized by the 2002 Act, mainly prompted by the wish to protect individual investors.[108] To a large extent, recourse may be made to comitology[109] to adjust and specify these rules.

In this respect there is a difference in treatment between management companies **6.96** offering additional services and investment firms providing the same services. Directive 85/611, as amended by MiFID, refers only partly to the rules of conduct applicable to investment firms.

The 2002 Act extends the own funds requirements laid down by Directive 93/6 **6.97** of 15 March 1993 to management companies that provide services other than the management of UCIs.[110] The CSSF goes one step further and requires such companies to comply with the own funds requirements imposed by the 1993 Act.[111] The initial capital and the amount of own funds of such management companies are therefore equal to those required of professionals of the financial sector engaging in the same activities.

When management companies manage the portfolios of investors other than **6.98** UCIs, the 2002 Act subjects them to the provisions in the 1993 Act on investor compensation schemes, whereby they must participate in a compensation scheme to fund compensation payments to investors in the event of the inability of members of the compensation scheme to repay funds owed to investors or to return instruments owned by investors.[112]

When management companies carry on cross-border business, their additional **6.99** functions remain subject to prudential supervision in their home State. However,

---

[107] See 6.165 *et seq* below.
[108] ibid.
[109] Within Eurostat, comitology is a framework upon which the Community legislature generally relies when it designs the administrative process to be used in implementing legislation on statistics. For a more detailed analysis of this concept, see 12.86 *et seq* below.
[110] Art 77(4) of the 2002 Act, insofar as it refers to Art 8(2), Directive (EEC) 93/22 (repealed by MiFID), applies Council Directive (EEC) 93/6 of 15 March 1993 on the capital adequacy of investment firms [1993] OJ L141/1. Directive (EEC) 93/6 has meanwhile been replaced by Directive (EC) 2006/49 of the European Parliament and the Council of 14 June 2006 on the capital adequacy of investment firms and credit institutions (amended) [2006] L117/201.
[111] CSSF Annual Report for 2003, 80.
[112] Art 84(2), 2002 Act.

these management companies must comply with the rules of conduct imposed by their host State with respect to the additional functions.[113]

Ownership of management companies

6.100   Before approving a management company, the CSSF reviews its direct and indirect ownership. To this end it requires disclosure of the identity of shareholders with 'qualifying holdings' in the management company's capital, and the amount of their holdings.[114]

6.101   A holding is a 'qualifying' holding when it represents, directly or indirectly, 10 per cent or more of the capital or voting rights of the issued capital or enables significant influence to be exercised over the company's management.[115] In addition to the voting rights taken into account to determine the existence of a qualifying holding, the CSSF may consider holdings of a connected third party when, under the circumstances listed in the law,[116] such third party's voting rights may be used by a shareholder of the management company.

6.102   The CSSF may refuse authorization if it does not consider the holders of a qualifying interest in the management company capable of ensuring sound and prudent management.[117]

6.103   If a qualifying holding in the management company is held by a holding company on behalf of individuals who, in turn, have qualifying holdings, the identity (and ownership) of the ultimate shareholders will be considered by the CSSF in applying the requirements set out above. The CSSF may refuse authorization if the structure prevents it from carrying out its prudential supervision function.[118]

6.104   When a management company maintains close links with another natural or legal person, whether through a qualifying holding or through a parent company's controlling interest in a subsidiary, the CSSF needs to be convinced that this situation does not hamper the exercise of its supervisory role.[119] It may, *inter alia*, refuse to grant authorization to, or withdraw authorization from, a management company when parties with which the management company maintains close links are

---

[113]   Art 5.4, 6a point 4 and 6b point 3, Directive (EEC) 85/611; Arts 77(4), 88(4), and 89(3), 2002 Act.

[114]   Art 79(1), 2002 Act.

[115]   ibid Art 1(23).

[116]   Art 7 of the Act of 4 December 1992 on information to be disclosed when buying or selling a significant interest in a company listed on the stock exchange (*Mémorial* A 1992, 2558) to which Art 1(23) of the 2002 Act refers. This may be a controlling link with a third party with voting rights or an agreement on voting rights (beneficial ownership, provisional transfer for a financial consideration, concerted exercise of rights, etc).

[117]   Art 79(1), 2002 Act.

[118]   CSSF Annual Report for 2007, 75.

[119]   Art 78(2), 2002 Act.

established in a non-EEA country whose laws, regulations, or administrative rules, or difficulties encountered in seeking compliance with these provisions, render difficult supervision of the relevant management company by the CSSF.[120]

A consultation process between competent authorities takes place in the case of an **6.105** authorization request from a management company which is the subsidiary of another entity subject to EEA prudential supervision, ie another management company, an investment firm, a credit institution, or an insurance undertaking approved in a member country of the EEA.[121] The same procedure is followed when the management company is a sister company or otherwise subject to common control with such an entity.[122]

Own funds of management companies

The minimum required capital for a management company is €125,000.[123] **6.106** When the value of the portfolios managed by a management company exceeds €250 million, the management company must have additional own funds. The portfolios managed by a management company consist of the assets of FCPs under management, the assets of investment companies for which it is the designated management company, and the assets of other UCIs managed by it other than by delegation. This last case refers to circumstances where a management company manages assets under a mandate from another management company or a self-managed investment company.

In referring to UCIs under management, the 2002 Act does not distinguish **6.107** between UCIs that are coordinated UCITS and those that are not.

In determining the assets under management of a management company, the **6.108** assets of a feeder fund which invests its entire assets in a master fund managed by the same management company will not be taken into account in addition to those of the master fund. In this case, the feeder fund is merely used as a vehicle to access the assets of the master fund. In other words, its assets do not form a separate portfolio.

The additional amount of own funds required from a management com- **6.109** pany with a portfolio exceeding €250 million is 0.02 per cent of the portfolio value in excess of €250 million, subject to a maximum capital requirement of €10 million.[124]

---

[120] ibid.
[121] ibid Art 79(2)(a).
[122] ibid Art 79(2)(b) and (c).
[123] ibid Art 78(1)(a).
[124] ibid.

6.110   The own funds of a management company are notably defined as the subscribed and paid-up capital,[125] share premiums,[126] reserves,[127] profits and losses brought forward, and interim profits, provided they have been verified by the auditors.[128] This definition is taken directly from Directive 2000/12.[129] Here it is unfortunate that the authors of Directive 85/611 decided merely to refer to a Directive designed specifically for credit institutions. Because its content reflects the characteristics of such institutions, that Directive is unsuitable for the situation of management companies engaged in management of UCIs. A teleological analysis of its provisions is essential.

6.111   The CSSF accepts that subordinated loan capital may be considered as own funds.[130] However, the CSSF is adamant that a management company's capital should not come from bank loans made by its shareholders to fund capital requirements.[131]

6.112   A management company's own funds may never be less than one-quarter of the preceding year's fixed overheads.[132] When the company starts business, the benchmark overheads are those referred to in its business plan, as modified at the request of the CSSF.[133]

---

[125]   The subscribed capital is defined by Art 22, Council Directive (EEC) 86/635 of 8 December 1986 on the annual accounts and consolidated accounts of banks and other financial institutions [1986] OJ L372, as 'all amounts, regardless of their actual designations, which, in accordance with the legal structure of the institution concerned, are regarded under national law as equity capital subscribed by the shareholders or other proprietors'.

[126]   Excluding cumulative preferential shares (Art 34, Directive (EC) 2000/12 of the European Parliament and of the Council of 20 March 2000 relating to the taking up and pursuit of the business of credit institutions [2000] OJ L126/27 and 28 (as repealed and replaced by Art 57a of Directive (EC) 2006/48), except for application of the exception provided for by Art 36.3 of Directive (EC) 2000/12 as replaced by Art 64.3 of Directive (EC) 2006/48, to which the definition of own funds found in Art 1a of Directive (EEC) 85/611 refers).

[127]   Legal reserve, reserve for treasury stock, reserves under the articles of incorporation, and other reserves, including revaluation reserves (Art 34, Directive (EC) 2000/12 of the European Parliament and of the Council of 20 March 2000 relating to the taking up and pursuit of the business of credit institutions [2000] OJ L126/27 and 28, as replaced by Art 57a of Directive (EC) 2006/48, to which the definition of own funds found in Art 1a of Directive (EEC) 85/611 refers).

[128]   Title V, Ch 2, Section 1, Directive (EC) 2000/12 of the European Parliament and of the Council of 20 March 2000 relating to the taking up and pursuit of the business of credit institutions [2000] L126/27 and 28 as replaced by Directive (EC) 2006/48, to which the definition of own funds found in Art 1 a of Directive (EEC) 85/611 refers.

[129]   As repealed and replaced by Directive (EC) 2006/48.

[130]   CSSF Annual Report for 2007, 75.

[131]   ibid.

[132]   Annexe IV, Council Directive (EEC) 93/6 of 15 March 1993 on capital adequacy of investment firms and credit institutions [1993] OJ L141/1, to which Art 78(1)(a) of the 2002 Act refers. The same Annexe specifies that its capital adequacy requirement may be adjusted by the competent authorities in the case of a significant change in the company's activity compared with the previous year. Directive (EEC) 93/6 has been repealed and replaced by Directive (EC) 2006/49 of the European Parliament and the Council of 14 June 2006 on capital adequacy of investment firms and credit institutions [2006] OJ L177/201.

[133]   ibid.

The 2002 Act allows the CSSF to grant a management company that no longer **6.113** complies with these requirements a limited period to remedy the situation or to cease business, if justified by the circumstances.[134]

As the European legislature explains in the preparations for Directive 2001/107,[135] **6.114** the new requirements with regard to the own funds of management companies are not intended to offer investors a guaranteed minimum compensation should the investments of the UCITS turn out to be less profitable than expected. The market and credit risks connected with the investments of a UCITS are assumed exclusively by its investors, whose units may therefore lose value. In contrast, the management company assumes the operational risk connected with its activities. As described in the preparations referred to above, this risk, *inter alia*, covers 'the cost of human and computer errors in processing transactions or calculating closing values, disputes with a counterparty, internal fraud, etc'.[136] A 'minimum cushion'[137] of own funds is required to cover this risk. The amount of this minimum cushion factors in assets whose management has been delegated by the management company. As the European legislature specifies, this reflects the rule, also laid down by it in Directive 2001/107, that a management company cannot transfer legal liability for delegated activities to its agent.[138]

The Member States may authorize management companies to put up no more **6.115** than 50 per cent of the additional own funds required if the management company's obligations are guaranteed in the same amount by a credit institution or an insurance undertaking. This derogation not only applies to own funds as a percentage of assets under management but also to the obligation to hold an amount of own funds which is at least equal to one-quarter of the preceding year's fixed overheads.

To give a management company the benefit of a lower own funds requirement under **6.116** the 2002 Act, the credit institution or insurance undertaking must itself comply with certain provisions. The 2002 Act requires it to be established in a Member State of the European Union and thus to be subject to Community rules for its activities and prudential supervision. If this condition is not met because the credit institution or insurance undertaking is established in a non-EU country, the 2002 Act requires the

---

[134] Art 82(1), 2002 Act.
[135] Communication of the Commission to the European Parliament, point 3.2.2.4, SEC (2001) 1004 final (document available on the website of the European Parliament, under the heading 'Legislative Observatory').
[136] ibid.
[137] ibid.
[138] Art 5g(2), Directive (EEC) 85/611, mentioned in the Communication of the Commission to the European Parliament, point 3.2.2.5, SEC/2001/1004 final (document available on the website of the European Parliament, under the heading 'Legislative Observatory').

institution or undertaking to be subject to prudential rules which the CSSF considers are equivalent to those laid down under Community law.[139]

6.117 The guarantee in return for which a management company may have a partial derogation from the own funds requirement may take several forms. For instance, there seems to be no reason why it cannot take the form of insurance covering the management company's liability in the amount of own funds not supplied.

6.118 A management company authorized to perform certain additional functions is also required to comply with the capital requirements laid down by Directive (EC) 2006/49 of the European Parliment and the Council of 14 June 2006 on the capital adequacy of investment firms and credit institutions.[140] This includes the Directive's initial capital requirements. Once a management company has been organized and carries on additional activities, the required amount of own funds is calculated in accordance with Circular 2000/12.[141] The total amount of capital required may therefore exceed the ceiling of €10 million for management companies whose activities are limited to managing UCIs. As the legislature's objective is clearly to lay the groundwork for a level playing field between management companies with additional activities and professionals of the financial sector,[142] there is no reason why management companies should benefit from limits on capital requirements which do not apply to professionals of the financial sector.

6.119 The authorization of a management company authorized to carry on additional functions which does not comply with the capital requirements applicable to its additional activities may be revoked by the CSSF.[143]

Head office of management companies

6.120 Under the 2002 Act, the head office of a management company must be located in Luxembourg. This requirement is rooted in company law and not limited to management companies.

6.121 In view of its supervision duties towards management companies, the concept of head office is open to interpretation by the CSSF—in the same way as it has already

---

[139] Art 78(1)(a), 2002 Act.

[140] ibid Art 77(4), insofar as it refers to Art 8, para 2, Directive (EEC) 93/22 repealed by MiFID, which itself makes applicable Directive (EEC) 93/6, repealed and replaced by Directive EC 2006/49 of the European Parliament and the Council of 14 June 2006 on the capital adequacy of investment firms and credit institutions [2006] OJ L177/201.

[141] CSSF Circular 2000/12 of 31 March 2000, defining the capital ratios in application of Art 56, Act of 5 April 1993, amended, on the financial sector.

[142] See notably the Communication of the Commission to the European Parliament, point 3.2.2.4, SEC/2001/1004 final (document available on the website of the European Parliament under the heading 'Legislative Observatory').

[143] Art 82(1), 2002 Act.

interpreted this concept in the case of professionals of the financial sector—who may add certain rules in addition to those laid down by company law.

Head office in company law

The fact that management companies are required to locate their head office in Luxembourg comes from Directive 85/611, which stipulates that the head office and registered office of a management company must be located in the same Member State. **6.122**

The term 'head office' is used to mean 'principal place of business' or 'actual establishment'. This rule is mainly intended to avoid the fraudulent establishment of a registered office in a country other than the one in which the head office is established in order to avoid supervision by the latter's authorities. In fact, the registered office is merely a designated location in the articles of incorporation. There is no reason why a company should not establish its head office in another country. **6.123**

Any company wishing to claim residence in Luxembourg must establish and maintain its head office in Luxembourg[144]. A company's head office is defined as the 'place where it keeps its central accounting and archives and where its general meetings are held—in a nutshell, where the company's management activity is concentrated'.[145] **6.124**

The head office is the place where the company is managed. This place does not have to be in the same location as the place where the company carries on its commercial or industrial activities. Company law does not stop a management company from setting up an operational head office in a country other than that of its registered office and head office. **6.125**

Head office services and prudential supervision

Because management companies are subject to oversight by the CSSF, the CSSF is also authorized to impose specific requirements connected with head office services in Luxembourg. This is one of the objects of Circular 03/108. According to the CSSF, the concept of 'head office' embraces the human and technical infrastructure of a management company.[146] **6.126**

Every coordinated management company based in Luxembourg must always have the necessary human resources in Luxembourg. Although in principle required to hire its own personnel, it may, with authorization from the CSSF, use personnel seconded or assigned temporarily to it. Such secondments of personnel may be agreed between the management company and another entity of the same **6.127**

---

[144] Art 159(1), 1915 Act; Court of Appeal, 8 October 1947, Pas lux, 14, 346; District court of Luxembourg, 21 April 1971, Pas lux, 22, 63.
[145] C Resteau (n 75 above) para 21*quater*.
[146] Section I, 3, Circular 03/108.

group or a third company. The secondment agreement, which is subject to CSSF approval, lays down rules for managing conflicts of interest between an entity to which employees are seconded or assigned and the entity by which they are employed, if part of the same group as the management company.

6.128 The CSSF requires that it be kept informed of any personnel changes at management companies. It must also be informed of the names of the personnel responsible for supervising certain management aspects (such as risk control, verification of compliance with the applicable laws and regulations, supervision of delegated activities, and internal audit). The personnel responsible do not necessarily have to be the conducting persons of the company, nor do they have to reside in Luxembourg. They may act on behalf of the management company as part of a secondment of personnel,[147] provided their employer is not one of the delegates they are supposed to monitor.

6.129 A management company may delegate some of the tasks vested in it by a UCI to another entity. When it manages a coordinated UCITS,[148] delegation is subject to strict rules intended primarily to ensure that the management company preserves the ability to supervise and coordinate the delegated activities.

6.130 The CSSF subjects the technical infrastructure to few requirements. It must be given a description of the IT hardware, information sources, and software used, which enables it to check compliance with prudential rules calling for a reliable administrative, accounting, and IT organization.[149]

Status of conducting persons of coordinated management companies

6.131 Every management company must be headed by at least two people[150] who need not be directors of the management company. They are considered conducting persons from the moment they assume *de jure* or *de facto* responsibility for running the company's business.[151]

---

[147] Of course within the relevant limits set by labour law.

[148] Although its wording makes it impossible to state a definite opinion on this issue, Art 85(1), 2002 Act, when mentioning the UCIs to which it applies, appears to refer exclusively to UCITS. Circular 03/108 follows its lead even more clearly by expressly targeting only services supplied to UCITS (Section I, 3(a), Circular 03/108). A broader interpretation of Art 85(1), encompassing the delegation of any function involving UCITS or other UCIs, whether national or foreign, would nevertheless be possible. For this interpretation, see Elvinger and Schmit (n 83 above) 1530 and 1531. This would nevertheless go beyond Directive (EC) 2001/107 which governs only coordinated UCITS. The Luxembourg legislature could definitely have extended it to non-coordinated UCIs but the fact that it did not specify this in the law and in the Parliamentary work suggests that it did not intend to do so. Circular 03/108 confirms this conclusion.

[149] Section I, 3(b), Circular 03/108.

[150] Art 78(1)(b), 2002 Act.

[151] The conducting persons of the UCI and the depositary must also be of sufficiently good repute and experience for the type of UCI concerned. The CSSF must therefore be informed immediately of the names of the conducting persons and their replacements. 'Conducting persons' here

In requiring the appointment of two conducting persons, the Directive and the 2002 Act extend to management companies the 'four-eyes principle', already applied for many years to many other professionals of the financial sector.[152] This principle is an offshoot of the peer review principle used in many other areas (for example the presence of two pilots in aircraft) in order to reduce risk which may arise where decisions are made by only one manager.

6.132

Application of this principle to financial law is rooted in German law, where KWG (*KreditWesenGesetz*) introduced the '*Vier Augen Prinzip*' in 1976, following the bankruptcy of the Herstatt bank in 1974.[153] It was adopted by the Banking Directive of 1977 and has since been exported to all Member States.

6.133

There are two reasons for this principle:

6.134

- the mandatory presence of at least two conducting persons ensures a certain management control as either conducting person can monitor the management actions of his colleague;

- it is easier to maintain management supervision as the absence of one of the conducting persons can be cushioned by the presence of the other.

This two-fold objective explains why the two conducting persons are generally required to be at the same level of the occupational hierarchy. Neither must be able to impose his decisions on the other. They must be able to discuss issues as equals. This would be more difficult if, for example, one of the two is an employee while the other is a director.

6.135

Another restriction deriving from the 'four-eyes principle' is that the two conducting persons are not permitted to allocate tasks in such a way that either has reserved areas of competence from which the other is excluded.[154] In this case, there would be neither double oversight nor follow-up of management actions. However, a feasible division of tasks is one whereby one manager would have certain key functions, subject to supervision and, as applicable, replacement by

6.136

---

means anyone who, by virtue of the law or the constitutive documents, represents the UCI or the depositary or who effectively determines the conduct of the UCI's activity (Art 93(3), 2002 Act. See also Art 78(1)(b), 2002 Act).

[152] This requirement is rooted in Art 3(2), 3rd indent of the first banking directive, Directive (EEC) 77/780 of 12 December 1977 on the coordination of the laws, regulations and administrative provisions relating to the taking up and pursuit of the business of credit institutions, according to which the 'competent authorities only grant authorization to a credit institution if there are at least two persons who effectively direct the business of the credit institution'.

[153] *Bankrechts-Handbuch*, Hrsg H Schimansky, H-J Bunte, H-J Lwowski, CH Beck (Munich, 2001) Band III, §125, No 24, 4407; *KreditWesenGesetz-Kommentar zu KWG und Ausführungsvorschriften*, Hrsg K-H Boos, R Fischer, H Schulte-Mattler, CH Beck (Munich, 2000) §33, No 59, 801.

[154] J-W Van der Vossen, 'Authorization Requirements' in *Amsterdam Financial Series*, Banking and EC Law, 18–23.

the other. Indeed, this approach makes it possible to appoint highly-qualified experts in particular areas, enabling both conducting persons to offer the company the benefit of their particular expertise.

6.137 Do the functions assumed by the management company's conducting persons mean that daily management duties must be delegated to them? Not necessarily, although delegation of duties would certainly complement their work.

6.138 Daily management is defined in case law as 'the accomplishment of actions that are merely the daily execution of the line of conduct set out by the board and which must be accomplished on a daily basis to continue business and which, owing to their lack of importance and the need for immediate solutions, do not call for intervention by the board of directors itself'.[155] This definition obviously aligns with the concept of 'conduct of the company's activity' used in the 2002 Act[156] to define the conducting persons of a management company.

6.139 The delegation of daily management entails granting the power to represent the company with third parties in all actions included in this management concept. A special mandate is not required for each of these actions. Internally, restrictions on the powers of the daily management delegate may be imposed or agreed, but these will have no impact on third parties. A legal act entered into by the delegate with responsibility for daily management in violation of a restriction contained in the articles of incorporation or a contract is binding on the company. Ignorance of the articles or another agreement will only have internal consequences. The delegate will in principle incur liability for such violations.[157]

6.140 The foregoing shows both the advantages and the drawbacks of appointing a delegate with responsibility for daily management. The delegate does not constantly have to prove his authority towards third parties but could abuse his powers. However, this risk is very low as conducting persons have to be approved by the CSSF on the basis of their reputation and professional experience.

6.141 An alternative to the appointment of a delegate could be to appoint the two conducting persons as directors in charge of the company's ordinary business. However, this alternative does not offer any particular advantage over the appointment of a delegate with responsibility for daily management. When a director is given authority to represent the company vis-à-vis third parties, his actions commit the company without the need for a general or special power of attorney. General authority to represent the company avoids the need for both the company and third parties to establish or verify the director's powers in respect of

---

[155] Cour de Cassation b, 17 September 1968, Pas, 1969, I, 61; Cour, 18 March 1993, No 13501; see A Steichen, *Précis de droit des sociétés* (Luxembourg, Éditions Saint-Paul, 2006) 727 *et seq.*

[156] Art 78(1)(b), 2002 Act.

[157] For the liability of the daily management delegate, see 6.269 *et seq* below.

each commitment accepted on behalf of the company. In extreme cases this may nevertheless turn out to be a source of abuse.

Appointing conducting persons as directors in charge of ordinary business has a par-   **6.142**
ticular drawback owing to the specific rules on liability of board members. A director
can be held jointly liable with the other directors for acts or omissions of one or more
of their number.[158] This drawback—ie joint liability of directors for certain management errors—does not exist when the two conducting persons merely have the status
of a delegate of the company with responsibility for daily management.[159]

Moreover a combination of the role of conducting person with the functions of   **6.143**
director may lead to conflicts of interest. It may also give rise to doubts as to the
effectiveness of controlling functions assumed by a conducting person who is at
the same time a member of the board of directors in charge of supervising the
fulfilment of tasks delegated to individual persons. The use of a two-tier management structure helps to avoid such difficulties. In this case, the management board
vests daily management powers in an officer who also sits on the management
board. This combination of functions does not give rise to conflicts of interest,
since the officer is controlled by the supervisory board on which he may not sit.

Lastly, it is possible to make the two conducting persons agents of the company or its   **6.144**
board of directors only, without vesting them with general authority to represent the
company. Each conducting person would need a general or special power of attorney
in order to commit the company. Whenever engaging in an act with one of the conducting persons, a counterparty or contracting party would have to verify that the
conducting person in question had the necessary authority. The drawbacks of this
method are obvious. It not only generates significant practical constraints for both the
company and its contractors, it may also raise concrete problems due to the scope of
the daily management powers vested in the conducting persons pursuant to the law.
Moreover, the protection against misuse sought by the management company is very
limited. The theory of ostensible authority[160] could be applied successfully in many
circumstances to commit the company vis-à-vis third parties, even against its will.

Management of a management company may be entrusted only to persons who   **6.145**
can show the good repute and experience required for the type of UCI managed
by the company in question.[161] This is essential to preserve market and investor

---

[158] See 6.238 below.
[159] For the liability of the daily management delegate, see 6.269 *et seq* below
[160] As explained, *inter alia*, by P Wéry, *Droit des Contrats—Le Mandat* (Larcier, 2000) No 209, 246–248.
[161] The German law underlying this principle can be used as a guide. For example, it requires bank conducting persons to have the qualifications needed to manage credit institutions correctly. The skill required to manage an institution can, *inter alia*, be concluded from past experience, academic qualifications, and previous responsibilities. Thus, in contrast with the obligation of good repute, which is automatically assumed when no negative information is available (convictions,

confidence in UCITS. The CSSF must be advised of the names of the conducting persons and their replacements immediately to enable it to ensure compliance with these criteria.[162] Notification must in principle take place prior to a conducting person's appointment or replacement. If not, an appointment may not take effect before the CSSF has granted authorization, as the CSSF wishes to authorize conducting persons prior to their appointment[163].

6.146 Corporations are not barred from managing management companies. The parliamentary documents for the 1988 Act specify that 'when the conducting person is a corporation, it must appoint one or more natural persons as permanent representatives. Compliance with the criteria of professional qualifications and good repute may not be verified at the level of a legal person, since these concepts apply to natural persons'[164]. The concept of permanent representative of a corporation acting as a director is also to be found in the 1915 Act with respect to SAs.[165] The legal person appointed as a director must designate a permanent member acting in the name and on the account of such corporation. The appointment and revocation of the permanent representative must be registered with the trade and companies register. The revocation of such representative is conditional upon the appointment of a successor.

6.147 A permanent representative of a legal entity is subject to the same requirements as those applicable if he had been directly appointed director in place of the entity which he represents. Lastly, the representative incurs direct and personal liability while carrying out his management functions. Under the 1915 Act he incurs the same responsibility as if he had acted in his own name, without prejudice to the joint and several liability of the legal entity which he represents.

6.148 The CSSF requires direct access to the people who are running management companies to enable it to obtain all information it considers essential for prudential supervision. This does not apply solely to managers who are residing or carrying on their activities mainly in Luxembourg. That said, the CSSF specifies that at least one of the management company's conducting persons must, in principle, be locally available.[166] This obligation also applies to the second conducting person when a management company provides additional discretionary management services.

---

police record, etc), the required skill calls for positive proof. Moreover, according to German legal opinion, the conducting persons must have the necessary experience in theory and in practice. They must have acquired it in businesses with similar activities and of comparable size. In other words, German legal opinion holds that the requirements for heading a universal bank differ from those required (or considered adequate) to head an agricultural mutual society.

[162] ibid.
[163] Section I, 5, Circular 03/108.
[164] *Parliamentary doc* No 3172, Comments on the Articles, 52.
[165] Art 51*bis*, 1915 Act.
[166] Section I, 3(a), Circular 03/108; Circular 05/185.

This requirement is inspired by the rules laid down by the CSSF for professionals of **6.149** the financial sector, by virtue of which at least two conducting persons of such entities must reside in or near the borders of Luxembourg.[167] The CSSF takes a more relaxed line towards conducting persons of management companies, probably on the grounds that they manage coordinated UCITS, which are already subject to tight CSSF control.

How should the obligation to have a conducting person who is 'locally available' **6.150** be interpreted? 'Locally available' does not necessarily mean that they 'reside locally'. Granted, the CSSF wants to be able to contact and meet promptly with at least one locally available conducting person but residence in the Grand Duchy of Luxembourg is not the only way to comply with this obligation. For example, both conducting persons could reside in a foreign country and be in Luxembourg only part of the time. This could be the case with a conducting person acting on behalf of several entities, including at least one Luxembourg-based management company. Since he devotes only a limited number of working hours to the management of this company, he could restrict his presence in Luxembourg to the same portion of time, provided he can be reached and, in principle, easily attend meetings with the CSSF. In this case, residence in a neighbouring country should be acceptable if the conducting person is sufficiently present, accessible, and available for the CSSF.

The presence of a 'locally available' conducting person also creates substance in **6.151** Luxembourg and helps a management company to avoid classification as a letter-box entity. Is this the only criterion? Certainly not, according to Circular 05/185, which complements Circular 03/108 with regard to management companies whose activity is limited to collective portfolio management. A management company can also satisfy the 'locally available' requirement in other ways, such as when it actually occupies premises in Luxembourg, regularly holds board meetings in Luxembourg, shows that such meetings are mostly prepared for in Luxembourg, has directors residing in Luxembourg, has local employees, or exercises certain activities in Luxembourg, such as risk management control. These activities are not cumulative and are given only as examples. They reflect the wish to demonstrate corporate governance and risk control. Other activities may meet the criteria and can be discussed individually with the CSSF.

The conducting person of a management company is not necessarily employed by **6.152** his company. He may be self-employed, provided he has entered with the management company into a contract specifying his rights and, obligations and, as applicable, mentioning the person to whom he reports.[168]

---

[167] Art 7(2), 1993 Act; Circular CSSF 95/120 of 28 July 1995 on the head office function.
[168] ibid.

6.153 The CSSF also agrees to let a single person run several management companies if he can show that the exercise of several mandates does not affect his professional performance.[169]

6.154 The CSSF ensures that the appointment of conducting persons for a management company does not affect the legal principle that the company must remain independent of the depositaries of the coordinated UCITS managed by it. It will not approve the appointment of conducting persons employed by such depositaries.[170]

Organizational requirements

6.155 In principle, a management company is exclusively subject to the prudential supervision of the authorities in its home State.[171] This rule is not altered by the fact that a management company provides services in another Member State, whether directly or through a branch office. The Directive imposes certain prudential standards for the management of UCITS by the Member States.

6.156 The CSSF makes sure the management company has a reliable administrative and accounting organization and effective IT control and security systems. It further demands adequate internal control mechanisms in areas such as the personal transactions of employees, tracking transactions on behalf of UCITS under management, and compliance with investment policies.[172] Lastly, it makes sure the risk of conflicts of interest between UCITS under management and other clients of the management company is kept to a minimum.[173] These principles are rooted directly in Directive 85/611.[174] The 2002 Act did not extend them to the management of UCIs other than UCITS.

6.157 When a management company provides the additional services allowed under the 2002 Act, such as discretionary management and investment advice for investors other than UCIs, the organizational requirements of MiFID supersede those provided for by the 2002 Act.[175]

6.158 Where certain functions are delegated, the management company must remain capable of verifying compliance with these organizational rules by its agent and be able to withdraw its mandate with immediate effect whenever necessary.[176]

---

[169] ibid.
[170] ibid.
[171] Art 5d, point 2, Directive(EEC) 85/611; Art 82(2), 2002 Act.
[172] Art 84(1)(a), 2002 Act.
[173] ibid Art 84(1)(b).
[174] Art 5f, point 1, Directive (EEC) 85/611.
[175] Art 77(4), 2002 Act, which refers to Art 10, Directive (EEC) 93/22, which has now been replaced by MiFID (Art 66, which refers to Art 13, MiFID).
[176] Art 85(1)(f) and (g), 2002 Act.

Management companies must implement internal procedures and policies in order to ensure compliance with their legal and regulatory obligations and to oversee the personal transactions of employees, managers, and subcontractors in an appropriate manner. **6.159**

Human, administrative, and accounting resources must be organized in such a way as to guarantee the continuous and regular supply of investment services on offer. Management companies must adopt effective risk evaluation, control, and IT security mechanisms. Reasonable and useful organizational and administrative measures must also be adopted to prevent conflicts of interest. **6.160**

Measures intended to protect the funds and securities belonging to clients must be put in place. In particular, funds and securities belonging to clients have to be fully segregated from those belonging to the management company. That said, the management company may use financial instruments owned by clients for its own account with the clients' permission. **6.161**

Lastly, the delegation or subcontracting of certain essential functions to third parties is governed by special rules. Outsourcing of important operational functions may not significantly increase the operational risk or seriously affect the quality of internal control at the management company. In particular, it may not weaken the company's supervision by its supervisory authority.[177] **6.162**

Management companies which are subject to the organizational requirements laid down in MiFID must also communicate to the CSSF the names of the persons responsible for the compliance, risk management, and internal audit functions. A management company is also subject to CSSF Circular 04/155 on the compliance function.[178] **6.163**

Management companies must be able to adjust these organizational requirements rapidly to changes in service requirements or securities markets. The European legislature has also considered it desirable to encourage a dialogue between supervisory authorities about the interpretation of these rules. This explains why the Commission of the European Communities has been granted the right to adopt, by way of comitology, execution measures specifying the way in which these rules must be applied.[179] **6.164**

---

[177] Art 66, which refers to Art 13 of MiFID; also see Arts 5–23, Directive (EC) 2006/73, and Ch II of the Grand-Ducal Regulation of 13 July 2007.

[178] CSSF Annual Report for 2007, 75.

[179] The European legislature mentions 'the futility of trying to regulate the financial markets by hard-coding provisions in immutable legislation. In the light of the favourable responses of the European Council and European Parliament to the recommendations of the Lamfalussy committee, it is proposed to amend key provisions of the Directive to allow for adoption of legally binding implementing measures through the comitology procedure. This procedure will be used in strict conformity with the inter-institutional understanding between the European Parliament, Council and Commission' (Explanatory Memorandum to the proposal for MiFID [2003] OJ C71E/65).

Rules of conduct

6.165 Management companies must also comply at all times with the rules of conduct listed in the 2002 Act and further specified by the CSSF. These rules of conduct are applicable not only to the management of UCITS but also to any other activity the company is authorized to carry on,[180] and are intended to ensure compliance with at least the following five principles: (1) acting honestly and fairly in conducting its business activities in the best interests of its clients and the integrity of the market; (2) acting with due skill, care, and diligence; (3) having and efficiently employing the resources and procedures that are necessary for the proper performance of its business activities; (4) trying to avoid conflicts of interests and, when they cannot be avoided, ensuring that its clients are fairly treated; and (5) complying with all regulatory requirements applicable to the conduct of its business activities.[181]

6.166 These principles can be found *mutatis mutandis* in MiFID,[182] albeit complemented by additional rules introduced by MiFID and made applicable by the 2002 Act to coordinated management companies that provide additional services in the areas of discretionary management, investment advice, or the safekeeping and administration of UCI units.[183]

6.167 Under these additional rules of conduct, a coordinated management company offering such services must also inform itself about its clients. A management company must gather information about the client's knowledge of and experience with its products or services, the client's financial situation, and the client's investment objectives, to be able to recommend appropriate investment services and financial instruments.

6.168 The obligation to obtain information about the client's expertise and purposes is tied to the duty of transparency. When negotiating with a client, a management company must disclose all information the client may need. Such information must be provided in an appropriate manner, meaning that the management company must consider the client's experience in order to ensure the client fully understands the services offered.

6.169 All information sent by the management company to existing or potential clients must be correct and clear and may not be misleading. Advertising materials must be identifiable as such. Clients must be sent relevant and understandable data about the management company and its services and, as applicable, the proposed investment policy. This information must include a description of the financial

---

[180] Elvinger and Schmit (n 83 above)1525.

[181] Art 86, 2002 Act.

[182] Art 66, which refers to Art 19, MiFID. Also see (1) Arts 26–45 and 47–49 of Directive 2006/73; (2) Sections 1–4 and 6 and 8 of Ch III and Art 53 of the Grand-Ducal Regulation of 13 July 2007; and (3) CSSF Circular 07/307 laying down conduct of business rules in the financial sector.

[183] Art 77(4), of the 2002 Act, which refers to Art 11 of Directive 93/22 which has now been replaced by MiFID.

instruments that the company may buy and suitable warnings about the contemplated investment risks. Clients must also be given a description of the proposed execution systems and the cost of investment services offered or supplied. Management companies must send clients adequate reports about their services. Such reports must mention the cost, if any, of transactions and services.

Lastly, when a coordinated management company supplies additional cross-border **6.170** services in the areas of discretionary management, investment advice, or the safekeeping and administration of UCI units, it is subject to the rules of conduct laid down, implemented, and checked by the host State. The management company is informed of those rules by the competent supervisory authority in the host State during the notification procedure preceding establishment or authorization to provide services.[184]

Management companies are therefore subject to a hybrid system by virtue of **6.171** which they are subject to the rules of conduct adopted in their home State for the exercise of their core UCI management functions and to the rules of conduct established by the Member State into which they provide additional services on a cross-border basis.

Here, too, the Commission of the European Communities authorizes recourse to **6.172** comitology for the purpose of determining the strict application of these rules.[185] The objective of the European legislature is to limit MiFID to the major principles underlying the rules of conduct and to leave the actual implementation of these principles to the Commission of the European Communities. In doing so, the Commission is invited to take account of the type of service offered or supplied by the management company, the nature of the financial instruments in question, and the type of client.[186] Management companies must apply different standards of conduct according to the degree of sophistication and risk of their products and services, and the experience of their clients.

Delegation of functions by coordinated management companies

Management companies are not themselves required to carry out all activities **6.173** entrusted to them. They may delegate one or more duties to third party entities, provided this does not affect service quality or supervision of the management

---

[184] Art 88(4) and 89(3), 2002 Act; Art 6a, point 4 and 6b, point 3, Directive (EEC) 85/611.

[185] Within the framework of this procedure the 'CESR will prepare detailed technical advice, in the light of reactions to open consultation, to mandates issued by the Commission. This two-tier structure for securities law was proposed as a means of reconciling continuity in democratically established core regulatory principles, with detailed harmonisation required to support cross-border organisation of securities trading and services, and the flexibility needed to adapt to rapidly evolving market practice in fast-moving financial markets' (Explanatory Memorandum to the proposal for MiFID [2003] OJ C71E/66).

[186] See the description of 'professional clients' in Annexe II of MiFID.

company. In order to limit the risk of such negative consequences, the legislature subjects the right for management companies to subcontract their activities to compliance with a series of relatively strict conditions.

Scope of delegation

6.174 Neither Directive 85/611, nor the 2002 Act, nor CSSF circulars limit the activities management companies are authorized to delegate. For example, could a management company call on other service providers for its entire investment, UCI administration and marketing activities? A positive answer cannot be ruled out.

6.175 Directive 85/611 and subsequently the 2002 Act use the graphic expression 'letter-box entity' to emphasize that a management company is not authorized to delegate functions to the extent of becoming such an entity. The use of this expression in a legal text is highly unusual and raises questions about its legal scope. A review of the preparatory work for Directive 2001/107 offers further explanation. For instance, the supervisory authorities of the home State must be able to supervise the management company itself and must not have to deal with a 'shell company'. Directive 85/611 and the 2002 Act, which also uses the image of a 'letter-box entity', specify that delegation 'must not affect supervision of the management company'.[187] The preparatory work for the Directive indicates that references to the expression 'letter-box entity' actually summarize the conditions to which delegation of a management company's functions is subject.[188] This is confirmed by the content of the conditions themselves since they require, *inter alia*, that a management company must at all times be able to supervise delegated activities, give additional instructions, and withdraw its mandate with immediate effect. A management company that meets these conditions, which supervises and coordinates its delegated activities, is by definition not a shell company. In this case, the CSSF is, moreover, in a position to provide effective oversight. Because such a management company coordinates and checks the delegated activities, it can provide the CSSF with the required information and evidence. Provided these conditions are met, delegation of intellectual management, administration, and marketing activities is possible.

Delegation conditions

6.176 There are four types of delegation conditions, which are analysed below.[189]

6.177 **Information**   A management company wishing to delegate one or more of its activities must first inform the CSSF.[190] It must send the CSSF a description of the

---

[187] Art 5g, point 1(b), Directive (EEC) 85/611 and Art 85(1)(b), 2002 Act.

[188] Communication of the Commission to the European Parliament, point 3.2.2.5, SEC/2001/1004 final (document available on the web site of the European Parliament, under the heading 'Legislative Observatory').

[189] For the reasons for these rules, see Art 85, 2002 Act and Section I, 3, (c), Circular 03/108.

[190] Art 85(1)(a), 2002 Act.

functions proposed to be delegated and the proposed delegates. This description enables the CSSF to check that the contemplated delegation meets the applicable conditions. In particular, it provides the CSSF with information about the procedures used by the management company to supervise the subcontracted activities.[191]

The idea originally advocated at European level was to require prior approval of all delegation mandates. This requirement has been abandoned. The European legislature felt that it would make administration much too cumbersome.[192] **6.178**

The functions a management company is authorized to delegate must be disclosed in the complete prospectus and the simplified prospectus. The delegated entities must also be mentioned in the complete prospectus when the CSSF requires them to be published in the interest of the investors. This is, in principle, always the case when investment management is delegated.[193] **6.179**

Control Every delegation must be structured in such a way as not to hamper the CSSF's supervision of the management company. It must also be organized in such a way that the management company can act and the UCITS can be managed in the best interests of the investors. Lastly, a delegation does not affect compliance with the rules of conduct imposed on management companies, which must be verifiable at all times. **6.180**

Delegation does not mean that a management company can wash its hands of the delegated functions. Delegation does not release a management company's conducting persons from the obligation to supervise the delegated activities. Measures should be adopted to ensure permanent and effective supervision of subcontracted activities, including the right for conducting persons to access documents reflecting the way in which delegated activities are exercised. **6.181**

When a management company delegates intellectual management of investments, its conducting persons are given detailed reports enabling them to verify compliance with the investment policies and restrictions applicable to the UCITS in question.[194] The investment policies and restrictions are covered by specific clauses in agency agreements between management companies and delegated managers. Such clauses either list the policies and restrictions or merely refer to the prospectus of the relevant UCITS. They also set out the right of the management company's conducting persons to lay down particular rules for the delegated managers within the framework of the general investment policy. **6.182**

---

[191] Section I, 3(c), Circular 03/108.
[192] Explanatory Memorandum to the modified proposal for Directive (EC) 2001/107 (document available on the website of the European Parliament, under the heading 'Legislative Observatory')
[193] Ibid.
[194] From which it can be concluded that the control to be exercised by the management company is a form of *a posteriori* control (Elvinger and Schmit (n 83 above) 1515).

6.183 Other detailed reports to be submitted to the management company cover the risk management method, to enable the management company to check and measure at all times the risk connected with investment positions and their contribution to the general risk profile of the portfolio of each UCITS under management. They enable the management company's conducting persons to verify the existence and actual application of such a method.

6.184 Lastly, when the marketing of a fund's units is subcontracted, the management company must also request detailed reports enabling it to determine whether the marketing policy for the UCITS is being followed.

6.185 In line with its pragmatic approach, the CSSF does not specify the intervals at which such information must be sent to the conducting persons, on the grounds that this is primarily determined by the profile of the UCITS and its risks. For the same reason, it does not give a detailed description of the information to be provided in these reports.

6.186 The CSSF also makes sure the existing infrastructure enables the management company's conducting persons to access the accounting information about the UCITS in real time or on request.

6.187 Another aspect of the supervision exercised by the management company's conducting persons is that it must at all times be possible to issue additional instructions with respect to the subcontracted activities and even to withdraw the delegation with immediate effect. Contracts delegating management company activities are worded to reflect this and specify the conditions on which such rights may be exercised; in particular, the cases in which such contracts may be terminated immediately.

6.188 Does this framework allow for subcontracting arrangements with a limited term? A positive answer cannot be ruled out, provided the contract can be terminated at any time. A provision allowing a limited term of contract would have the benefit of requiring the management company and the delegate actively to consider, prior to expiry of the relevant term, whether the contract should be continued.

6.189 **Qualification** Delegation is allowed only when the beneficiary can show the necessary authorizations, qualifications, skills, and human and technical resources to conduct the activities entrusted to it.

6.190 This obligation is accompanied by one or even two other conditions when investment management is delegated. For the purpose of investor protection, firms to which investment management is delegated must be subject to permanent supervision in their home State by the supervisory authority provided for by law. When such firms are established in a non-EEA country, the 2002 Act also requires the existence of adequate cooperation between the CSSF and the supervisory authorities in question.[195] The CSSF determines whether or not each of these authorities meets this requirement.

Independence   As a general principle of the applicable rules of conduct, a man-   **6.191**
agement company must act in the best interests of its clients. This principle is most obvious in the obligation for management companies to avoid conflicts of interest. The duty of good conduct remains relevant and binding in the case of delegation. It governs not only the agent selected by the management company but also the way in which the agent carries on its activities.

To remove any doubt about the scope of the obligation to prevent conflicts of interest   **6.192**
when delegating investment management, the 2002 Act specifies that no mandate for this function may be granted to firms whose interests could conflict with those of the management company or the unitholders of the UCITS in question.[196] Such firms automatically include the depositary of a UCITS,[197] since the depositary is charged with checking certain management aspects of the UCITS and must remain entirely independent from the management company of an FCP.[198]

The 2002 Act limits the scope of the prohibition on delegation to the depositary   **6.193**
of mandates 'connected with the core function of investment management'. The qualifier 'core function' makes it possible to distinguish between investment management of a UCITS and of other investment portfolios on a discretionary and individual basis, one of the 'additional functions' now permitted for management companies. Reference to 'core function' in this context enables the legislature to distinguish between two types of activities covered by the general expression 'investment management'.

In Circular 03/108, the CSSF specifies the scope of the prohibition on delegating   **6.194**
investment management to the depositary.[199] This rule applies only to the depositary. It does not extend to other entities in the group of companies of which the depositary is a member. Delegation of investment management to another company in the same group as the depositary is allowed subject to measures intended to protect the interests of the management company and the unitholders. This type of delegation requires prior authorization from the CSSF, which verifies the existence of the measures required by the Circular to protect the interests of the management company and the investors.

---

[195] See the list of non-member countries proposed by Elvinger and Schmit (n 83 above) 1516. This list must not be considered exhaustive; the CSSF has already added other territories.
[196] Art 85(1)(e), 2002 Act.
[197] Ibid.
[198] Arts 20 and 66, 2002 Act.
[199] Section I, 3(c), Circular 03/108.

European passport

6.195 The authorization granted to a management company is valid for all Member States. [200] A management company authorized in a Member State, known as the 'home State', is allowed to carry on the activity for which it has been authorized in the territory of another Member State, known as the 'host State', whether directly, using its freedom to provide services, or indirectly through a branch set up for this purpose in the Member State in question[201]. In doing so, it may not be subject to an obligation to obtain authorization, to have a certain capital, or any other measure with equivalent effect, as such matters are regulated by its home State.[202] A management company's authorization to establish a branch or to provide services includes the right to market the UCI units managed by it in the host State.

6.196 The legal rules establishing the principle of a passport for the services supplied by management companies parallel the provisions set out in Article 46 of Directive 85/611. For many years, Directive 85/611 only introduced the principle of a 'product' passport. This passport was maintained when the 'management' passport was introduced in 2002. With the 'product' passport, units in coordinated UCITS may be marketed in any other Member State subject to notification to the authorities of the host State and compliance with certain rules in the host State in areas not covered by the Directive.[203] This 'product' passport remains useful whenever a UCITS wants to distribute its units in foreign countries without obtaining a 'management' passport.

6.197 The 'management' passport covers most of the services management companies are authorized to offer under Directive 85/611. In its Preamble, Directive 2001/107 lists the activities the passport introduced by it allows management companies to carry on in host States:

> '... to distribute the units of harmonised unit trusts/common funds managed by the company in its home Member State; to distribute the shares of harmonised investment companies managed by such a company; to perform all the other functions and tasks included in the activity of collective portfolio management; to manage the assets of investment companies incorporated in Member States other than its home Member State; to perform, on the basis of mandates, on behalf of management companies incorporated in Member States other than its home Member State, the functions included in the activity of collective portfolio management.'[204]

---

[200] Art 5.1, Directive (EEC) 85/611.

[201] ibid Art 6.1. 'A branch is defined as a place of business which is a part of the management company, which has no legal personality and which provides the services for which the management company has been authorised; all the places of business set up in the same Member State by a management company with its registered office in another Member State shall be regarded as a single branch'; Art 1(25), 2002 Act.

[202] Art 6.2, Directive (EEC) 85/611.

[203] ibid Arts 44 and 46.

[204] Preamble to Directive (EC) 2001/107, 7th Recital.

The general scope of the wording could be confusing. The breadth of the passport **6.198** is limited by certain principles, which are also found in the Directive. The first is particular to FCPs and reflects the provision in Directive 85/611 that the nationality of an FCP is that of the Member State in which the registered office of its management company is located.[205] An FCP may act only through a management company of the same nationality.

The second of these principles primarily concerns investment companies. Directive **6.199** 85/611 requires the head office of such companies to be located in the same Member State as their registered office. As interpreted by the CSSF, head office functions[206] may not be delegated to a management company established in a foreign country, even when that management company sub-delegates the head office services to an entity located in Luxembourg. In other words, a Luxembourg-based investment company may not appoint a foreign company for all management functions.[207] It will be considered self-managed unless these functions are delegated to a Luxembourg-based entity.

Because management companies with ancillary functions are subject to different **6.200** rules, the procedure to be followed when establishing a branch or providing services in a foreign country varies according to the activities a management company intends to carry on in such country.

Establishing a branch

Directive 85/611 establishes the procedure to be followed by a management com- **6.201** pany planning to open a branch in another Member State.[208] This procedure includes notification of the authorities in the home State and their cooperation with the authorities of the host State. The 2002 Act outlines this procedure for Luxembourg-based management companies wishing to use their freedom of establishment.[209]

According to this procedure, a management company must, in principle, wait for **6.202** a maximum of five months from the filing of an application to open a branch and carry on its activities in the host State.

Notification in the home State Companies based in Luxembourg must notify **6.203** the CSSF when planning to open a branch in an EEA member country, *inter alia*, informing the CSSF of the member country in which the branch would be set up,

---

[205] Art 3, Directive (EEC) 85/611.
[206] See 6.122 above.
[207] Position disputed by Elvinger and Schmit (n 83 above) 1508.
[208] Art 6a, Directive (EEC) 85/611; for further details about the right of establishment, see 12.33 *et seq* below.
[209] Art 88, 2002 Act.

the address at which documents may be obtained in the host State, and the names of the branch managers. This information must be accompanied by a programme specifying the services the company plans to offer and the proposed organizational structure of the branch.[210]

6.204 The CSSF has three months to examine such applications. Within this timeframe it must send this information to the competent authorities of the host State. When the management company in question offers services for which it must be a member of an investor compensation scheme if those services were provided in Luxembourg, the CSSF encloses the particulars of such a compensation scheme with its mailing.[211] The management company is informed when its application is forwarded.

6.205 The CSSF may decide not to send an application to the competent foreign authorities for any of the reasons listed in the 2002 Act. To reach such a decision the CSSF must have good reason to doubt the adequacy of the relevant management company's administrative organization or its financial health in view of the activities contemplated by the management company. The 2002 Act allows the CSSF only two months from receipt of the information from the management company in which to reject the application and to inform the management company in question.[212]

6.206 **Notification in the host State**   Following review of the relevant information by the CSSF and transmission to the host State, the authorities of the host State must review the relevant application. Directive 85/611 grants the host State a period of two months from receipt of the relevant documents from the authorities of the home State in which to organize supervision of the management company in question.[213]

6.207 The authorities of the host State may not refuse the establishment of a management company in their State. In principle, their only right is to enforce the company's compliance with certain principles set out in the Directive. The first of these principles is nevertheless very general and leaves the authorities practically free to decide which standards should apply to management companies established in their territory. The Directive refers to the conditions governing the exercise of activities 'in the interest of the general good'.[214] This basically covers all standards laid down by the supervisory authority, which is specifically charged with protecting investor interests. The Directive adds that these provisions in the interest of the general good encompass the rules applicable to foreign UCITS marketing their units in the State in question when such rules fall outside the areas covered by the Directive. They further include the State's advertising rules and the

---

[210]   ibid Art 88(2).
[211]   ibid Art 88(3).
[212]   ibid.
[213]   Art 6a, point 4, Directive (EEC) 85/611.
[214]   ibid.

measures required to ensure payments to participants, redemption of units, and dissemination of information.

In a number of circumstances, however, the authorities of the host State have the   **6.208**
right to refuse establishment, ie they may not allow a management company to
distribute in their territory the coordinated UCITS managed by it when the
method used to market these UCITS does not comply with the host State's rules
in areas not covered by Directive 85/611. They may also refuse authorization
when payments to participants, unit redemptions, and dissemination of information, as described by the management company, do not reflect their national standards. Their decision is communicated to the authorities of the home State[215] and
to the Commission of the European Communities.[216]

Within two months from receipt of the application file, the competent authorities   **6.209**
of the host State must notify the management company of the rules applicable to
it in conducting its activities in the host State and/or, when applicable, inform it
and the authorities of the home State of their refusal to allow marketing of the
coordinated UCITS.[217]

When a management company wants to offer discretionary portfolio manage-   **6.210**
ment services for investors other than UCITS, investment advice, or custodial
services via a branch in another host State, it is subject to the rules of conduct laid
down by the host State for these activities. The competent authorities in the host
State must send it the applicable rules of conduct within two months from the
date on which they receive the file from the CSSF.[218]

The management company may commence its activities in the host State as soon   **6.211**
as the competent authorities in that State have sent it the necessary information
about the applicable legal framework. If they fail to do so, the company must wait
until the expiry of a period of two months from the date on which such authorities
receive the file from the CSSF prior to commencing activities.[219]

Modification of the organizational structure   Delivery of a passport does not   **6.212**
end the notification procedure permanently. Further notifications are required
to be made whenever a management company changes the organizational structure of its branch, the scope of its activities in the host State, or the address at
which documents may be obtained from it in the host State. Notification to the
local regulator is also required whenever there is any change in branch management. Notification must be given in writing to the CSSF and the competent

---

[215] ibid Art 6a, point 5.
[216] ibid Art 6c, point 10.
[217] ibid Art 6a, points 4 and 5.
[218] ibid Art 6a, point 4; Art 88(4), 2002 Act.
[219] Art 6a, point 5, Directive (EEC) 85/611; Art 88(5), 2002 Act.

authorities in the host State no later than one month before they take effect.[220] During this period, the CSSF examines the information received and has the right to reject the proposed change for the reasons listed in the Directive.[221] During this same period, the authorities of the host State may inform the management company of the rules applicable to it after implementation of the contemplated changes.[222]

6.213   More generally, the CSSF informs the authorities of the host State of any change in the information sent to them during the first notification procedure.[223]

6.214   **Periodic information requirements**   In addition to the notification requirements outlined above, Directive 85/611 provides for the notification to the relevant authorities of periodic information.[224] Host States are authorized to request two types of information from foreign management companies established in their territory. First, if provided for by the national laws of the host State,[225] the host States may require management companies to provide periodic reports on the activities carried on in their territory. These reports are required for the establishment of statistics. The host States may also subject foreign management companies established in their territory to the same information constraints as their national management companies. Directive 85/611 puts a—rather vague—limit on this right to information. It may only be used to enable host States to exercise their responsibilities under the Directive.

6.215   **Right to penalize**   Although supervision of management companies is, in principle, conducted in the companies' home State, the authorities of the host State have certain powers to penalize companies operating in their territory. Directive 85/611 lays down three different procedures, based on the nature of the offences and the interests to be protected.

6.216   For example, it may be that a management company does not comply with the criteria set in the interest of the general good applicable in the host State and made known to it as part of the above-mentioned notification procedure. In this case, the relevant management company may be subjected to any appropriate measure intended to prevent or sanction such violations.[226] Directive 85/611 does not set limits on such measures. It expressly authorizes host States to prevent a management company from carrying out new transactions in its territory, ie to withdraw the company's right to use its passport in the territory of the host State.

---

[220]   Art 6a, point 6, Directive (EEC) 85/611; Art 88(6), 2002 Act.
[221]   See 6.204 above.
[222]   See 6.207 above.
[223]   Art 6a, point 7, Directive (EEC) 85/611; Art 88(7), 2002 Act.
[224]   Art 6c, points 1 and 2, Directive (EEC) 85/611.
[225]   This is the case with the Grand Duchy of Luxembourg by virtue of Art 90(1), 2002 Act.
[226]   Art 6c, point 6, Directive (EEC) 85/611.

It may also be that a management company does not comply with requests sent to **6.217** it by the authorities of the host State by virtue of their powers under Directive 85/611, such as legitimate requests for information. In such a case, the relevant management company violates the standards set by the supervisory authorities. Directive 85/611 provides for cooperation between supervisory authorities in view of the nature of the standards in question and to ensure compliance with the principle that a management company's supervision is, in principle, the responsibility of its home State.[227]

The right to penalize a management company that does not comply with the **6.218** measures adopted by a host State by virtue of the powers vested in it by Directive 85/611 rests in principle with its home State. The host State first orders the management company in question to terminate the irregular situation of which it is accused.[228]

If the management company concerned fails to take the necessary steps, the host **6.219** State informs the competent authorities of the home State, which are required to take prompt and appropriate measures to end such violations.[229] The home State authorities must also notify the competent authorities in the host State.

Nevertheless, cooperation between the host State and the home State may **6.220** ultimately fail to produce the desired results. For instance, a management company may persist in breaching the provisions in force in the host State despite injunctions to the contrary from the authorities in its home State or due to a lack of adequate measures on the part of those authorities. In these circumstances, the host State may substitute itself for the home State. Directive 85/611 authorizes it to take appropriate measures to prevent and penalize further irregularities or even to prevent the management company in question from operating in the future in its territory.[230] In this case, it must inform the home State[231] and the Commission of the European Communities[232] of its decisions.

Directive 85/611 also considers the possibility that the delays involved in coop- **6.221** eration between supervisory authorities could make it impossible to protect the interests of the management company's investors and clients in time. When such interests must be urgently protected, the authorities of the host State are authorized to adopt any precautionary measures necessary to achieve this.[233] They must report such measures promptly to the competent authorities of the other Member

---

[227] ibid Art 6c, points 3, 4, and 5.
[228] ibid Art 6c, point 3.
[229] ibid Art 6c, point 4.
[230] ibid Art 6c, point 5.
[231] ibid.
[232] ibid Art 6c, point 10.
[233] ibid Art 6c, point 8.

States concerned and to the Commission of the European Communities. The Commission is the only competent authority with power to order the host State to modify or repeal such precautionary measures, after consulting the authorities of the other Member States involved.[234]

6.222 As a general rule, any penalty or restriction on the activities of a management company, by or at the initiative of a host State, must be properly justified and communicated to the company concerned.[235] Every such measure is subject to a right of appeal to the courts in the Member State which adopted it.[236]

Freedom to provide services

6.223 The procedure to be followed by a Luxembourg-based management company wishing to use its freedom to provide services in the EEA is less cumbersome and faster than the one described above for the creation of branches. It allows a management company to offer all the services it is authorized to provide in any member country of the EEA.[237] This procedure also applies when a management company appoints a third party to market and distribute units in the host State.[238]

6.224 The first step of the procedure depends upon the management company. Before offering services in another EEA member country, the management company must send the CSSF a file, which must mention the host State and include a programme of the activities planned in that State.[239]

6.225 In contrast with the rules specified for establishment of a branch, the 2002 Act does not leave the CSSF any discretion regarding files received by it. The CSSF must send such files to the competent authorities of the host State within one month from receipt, together with particulars about the relevant investor compensation scheme applicable to such activites in Luxembourg, if any.[240]

6.226 On receipt of this information, the competent authorities in the host State inform the management company of the rules adopted in the interest of the general good applicable in the host State.[241] A management company is also informed of the rules of conduct applicable to it when it wishes to provide discretionary portfolio management, investment advice or safekeeping services in the host State.[242]

---

[234] ibid.
[235] ibid Art 6c, point 7.
[236] ibid.
[237] For further details about the freedom to provide services, see 12.26 *et seq* below.
[238] Art 6b, point 5, Directive (EEC) 85/611; Art 89(5), 2002 Act.
[239] Art 6b, point 1, Directive (EEC) 85/611; Art 89(1), 2002 Act.
[240] Art 89(2), 2002 Act; see also Art 6b, point 2, Directive (EEC) 85/611.
[241] Art 6b, point 3, Directive (EEC) 85/611; Art 89(3), 2002 Act.
[242] ibid.

Any change in the data forwarded to the CSSF must be reported to the CSSF and to the authorities of the host State prior to implementation.[243] No deadline is stipulated for this prior notification. Directive 85/611 specifies that the purpose of this requirement is to enable the authorities of the host State[244] to inform the management company of any new rule applicable to it. Management companies must be allowed the necessary time for notification. They must take this requirement into account when determining how much time to allow between notifying the supervisory authorities and implementing the contemplated modifications.   **6.227**

This is not necessarily the full extent of the dialogue between the authorities of the host State and management companies operating in their territory. The authorities may ask management companies to provide any other information they require in order to carry out their supervision duties with regard to such companies.[245] That said, their information requirements may not be more stringent than those imposed upon companies already established in their territory.   **6.228**

The procedures for penalizing irregularities committed by a management company in its host State do not differ according to whether the company is established in, or only provides cross-border services into, the host State. In this respect, please refer to the sanctions described in the section on the establishment of branches.[246]   **6.229**

Liability of management bodies and their delegates

There are several aspects to the liability of management bodies and their delegates. Liability differs according to the relevant party involved, namely the directors in the case of an investment company, the management company of an FCP and its directors, or the delegates of a UCI's management bodies. Each of these three cases will be examined separately. The liability in each case will be reviewed from three angles: contractual, quasi-tortious, and, as the case may be, criminal.   **6.230**

Liability of the directors, members of the management board, or members of the supervisory board of an investment company incorporated in the form of an SA

The liability of directors of an investment company incorporated in the form of an SA does not differ a lot from that of directors of traditional companies. The same is true with respect to the members of the management board and the supervisory board.   **6.231**

---

[243] Art 6b, point 4, Directive (EEC) 85/611; Art 89(4), 2002 Act.
[244] And not the home State, as suggested by an error in the French version of Directive (EEC) 85/611.
[245] Art 6c, point 2, Directive (EEC) 85/611.
[246] See 6.201 *et seq* above.

6.232   Similarly, whether an investment company is self-managed or not has little impact on the liability of directors. The board of directors (in a one-tier structure) or the management board and the supervisory board (in a two-tier structure) of an investment company remain in any event responsible for the supervision and coordination of delegated activities. Pursuant to company law, all delegated tasks are carried out under their oversight, within the framework and limits laid down by them. This principle is not affected by the designation of a management company. Directive 2001/107 does not make one party liable for another. In addition to the responsibilities of the board of directors, the management board, and the supervisory board, the Directive introduces a series of additional obligations for management companies and investment companies that have not designated a management company. The distinction between self-managed investment companies and investment companies with a designated management company applies only to the obligations introduced by Directive 2001/107 and does not affect company law, which the Directive does not intend to disapply. When an investment company with a designated management company is released from the additional obligations introduced by Directive 2001/107, its management bodies do not benefit from reduced liability rules and remain fully subject to company law.

6.233   The civil and criminal liability aspects of those management bodies are examined below.

Civil liability of the directors, members of the management board, and members of the supervisory board

6.234   There are three types of civil liability, each of which reflects a different regime:

    (1) contractual liability vis-à-vis the company for management faults;[247]

    (2) aggravated liability vis-à-vis the company and third parties for breaches of the 1915 Act or the company's articles of incorporation;[248] and

    (3) quasi-tortious liability under general law provisions.[249]

6.235   **Contractual liability for management faults**   The board of directors or the management board and the supervisory board of an investment company are obliged to manage their company with diligence. They are at fault when they do not act in the way a diligent and prudent board would in the same circumstances.[250]

---

[247] Arts 59, para 1, 60*bis*-10, para 1 and 60*bis*-16, para 1, 1915 Act.

[248] ibid Arts 59, para 2, 60*bis*-10, para 2 and 60*bis*-16, para 2.

[249] Arts 1382 and 1383, Civil Code.

[250] Faults are subject to marginal evaluation. Not every error amounts to a fault. Only errors that would not have been committed by a director acting with ordinary competence, diligence, honesty, and attention to the corporate interests of the entity managed by him can give rise to liability. For examples of such faults, see, *inter alia*, O Caprasse, 'La responsabilité civile professionnelle des administrateurs' (1997) *Act dr*, 486; or O Ralet, *Responsabilités des dirigeants de sociétés* (Larcier, 1996), para 62.

For example, the board of directors may commit a management fault for providing **6.236** inaccurate or inadequate information in the prospectus. The 2002 Act and the Act of 13 February 2007 require that the complete and the simplified prospectuses relating to the issue of units by a UCI should contain the data needed by investors to make an informed decision on the proposed investment.[251] However, they do not provide for specific liability in this respect, which means that the basic principles of general law apply. The directors may, *inter alia*, be held liable for incorrect notices or omissions, whether intentional or due to negligence, if these cause damage to the investors.

Similarly, the board of directors can be held liable for damage to a fund due to **6.237** market timing practices when it does not see to the implementation of procedures designed to prevent this type of transaction.[252]

The liability of the board of directors, the management board, and the supervisory **6.238** board for management faults may be individual or collective.[253] There is no joint liability.

The power to manage the company lies with the board of directors or with the **6.239** management board and the supervisory board as a collective body, not with each separate member.[254] A management fault is therefore generally committed by all directors making up the board or by all members of the management board and the supervisory board. That said, a person may incur individual liability, for example when the relevant person is individually at fault, for instance he fails to attend board meetings. Where a board is alleged to be liable, the directors or the members of the management board and the supervisory board may also be able to establish that they themselves are not guilty of any fault, for example because they opposed the decision concerned or were unaware of essential information and notified the general meeting as soon as possible as they became aware of the relevant information. In such circumstances, the courts may hold only some members of the management body liable. The authorization granted by the supervisory board to the management board does not relieve the members of the management board of liability.[255]

Only the company is authorized to claim contractual liability for manage- **6.240** ment faults.[256]. The decision to take legal action lies with the general meeting

---

[251] Art 110(1), 2002 Act; Art 53, Act of 13 February 2007.

[252] Circular 04/146.

[253] Ralet (n 250 above) para 42.

[254] Except in SAs with a single shareholder. In this case, the board of directors or the management board and the supervisory board can theoretically have only one member until the ordinary general meeting following the establishment of the existence of more than one shareholder (Arts 51, 60*bis*-2 and 60*bis*-14, 1915 Act). The CSSF, however, request that the board of an investment company be composed of at least three members.

[255] ibid Art 60*bis*-10, para 3.

[256] ibid Arts 59, para 1, 60*bis*-10, para 1 and 60*bis*-16, para 1.

of shareholders. If that meeting refuses or neglects to act, the individual or minority groups of shareholders have, in principle, no authority to do so.

6.241   A company's creditors are in a better position. They may act in the name of the debtor company by means of an *action oblique*[257] and plead liability on the part of one, some, or all members of the board of directors, the management board, or the supervisory board for management faults.[258]

6.242   Actions for contractual liability on account of management faults can succeed only if the plaintiff establishes the following:

(1) a damage suffered by him;
(2) a management fault; and
(3) a causal link between the fault and the damage.

6.243   Moreover, the general meeting of shareholders must not have officially discharged the directors or the members of the management board and the supervisory board from their management liability (as is the common practice in approving the company's annual financial statements), as this would make it impossible to successfully sue the various management personnel[259] unless it can be proved that the financial statements on which the discharge is based contained one or more omissions or incorrect information concealing the company's real situation.[260]

6.244   Lastly, the directors and the members of the management board and the supervisory board are liable only for damage that they could reasonably have foreseen, save in the event of fraud.[261]

6.245   **Aggravated liability for infringement of the 1915 Act or of the articles of incorporation**   The directors, the members of the management board, and the members of the supervisory board incur aggravated liability when they are liable for breaches of the 1915 Act or the company's articles of incorporation.[262] Such violations call for a heavier penalty, since they infringe 'provisions adopted in order to protect the public and the shareholders themselves'.[263] In that event, the directors,

---

[257] Art 1166 of the Civil Code defines an *action oblique*: 'Nevertheless, creditors may exercise all rights and causes of action of their debtor, save for those which are purely personal.'

[258] Fredericq, (n 71 above) Vol V, paras 438 and 439; Resteau, (n 75 above), Vol II, paras 944–947; Wauwermans (n 55 above) para 381.

[259] JR Nlend, *La responsabilité des dirigeants de sociétés en droit luxembourgeois*, Ecoconsult (SCP, 1997) 59.

[260] Art 74, 1915 Act.

[261] Art 1150, Civil Code limits contractual liability to damage that is or can be foreseen at the time when the contract is signed.

[262] Arts 59, para 2, 60*bis*-10, para 2 and 60*bis*-16, para 2, 1915 Act; District Court of Luxembourg, 30 May 1980 (1987) II *Bull François Laurent* 80–81; 23 December 1987 (1988) 13, *Bull Droit & Banque*, 40, overturned on appeal (for other reasons) by the Court of Appeal, 10 December 1993, not published; District Court of Luxembourg, 15 July 1993 (1994) 21 *Bull Droit & Banque* 51.

[263] Resteau (n 75 above) Vol II, para 962.

members of the management board, and members of the supervisory board are jointly liable and can escape liability for infringements only if they can prove that they did not take part in the acts and denounced them at the general meeting of shareholders.[264]

Moreover, the company is not the only party entitled to sue. Interested third par- **6.246** ties, such as creditors, may seek redress against the directors without resorting to an *action oblique*. Shareholders may also bring proceedings if they have suffered individual damage separate from the damage suffered by the company.

The authorization granted by the supervisory board to the management board **6.247** does not relieve the members of the management board of their liability.[265]

Quasi-tortious liability under general law provisions   The directors or the **6.248** members of the management board and of the supervisory board may incur quasi-tortious liability for any actions or omissions other than those committed in the performance of their management duties.[266] The conduct involved in such cases is not simply that attributable to the relevant person's management functions.[267]

Actions for quasi-tortious liability can be brought by the company or by any third **6.249** party, such as an individual shareholder or creditor who can prove damage as a result of an unlawful act or negligence by the management body or one of its members.[268] The fault in question must have caused personal damage to the plaintiff, distinct from the damage done to the company, and the causal link between the fault and the damage must be shown.

Criminal liability of the directors, members of the management board, and members of the supervisory board

In many cases, the facts giving rise to civil liability may also constitute criminal **6.250** offences, such as the use of forged documents, fraud, or breach of trust—all of which are covered and punished by the Criminal Code.

The 1915 Act also provides for specifically corporate criminal offences, such as **6.251** failure to publish financial and management reports by the statutory deadlines;[269]

---

[264] Arts 59, para 2, 60*bis*-10, para 2 and 60*bis*-16, para 2, 1915 Act; see also Resteau (n 75 above) Vol II, paras 964 and 965.

[265] Art 60*bis*-10, para 3, 1915 Act.

[266] Arts 1382 and 1383, Civil Code. Moreover, the company may incur liability for faults on the part of the management bodies. For example, a director is regarded as a body of the company vis-à-vis third parties, which means that the company directly incurs liability on the basis of Art 1382 of the Civil Code when the accusation concerns the faulty performance of an act which the body, by virtue of its functions, has the power or duty to accomplish (Fredericq (n 71 above), Vol V, para 432).

[267] Ralet (n 250 above) para 67.

[268] CA Luxembourg, 13 June 1990, *Pas Lux*, Vol XXVIII, 45.

[269] Arts 163 and 173*bis*, 1915 Act.

payment of fictitious dividends not taken from actual profits;[270] presentation of falsified balance sheets or profit and loss accounts;[271] and, more generally, the improper use of corporate assets.[272]

6.252 The 2002 Act[273] and the Act of 13 February 2007[274] lay down criminal penalties for UCIs, applicable to:

(1) The directors, members of the management board, or managers of an investment company other than a SIF who have not caused the issue and redemption price of the units or shares of the UCI to be determined at the specified intervals or who have not made such prices public in accordance with the law.

(2) The directors, members of the management board, or managers of an investment company who have violated the obligation to:

(a) issue and redeem an investment company's units or shares at the net asset value or, as regards SIFs, in breach of the principles set out in the constitutive documents;

(b) comply with the valuation principles and methods stipulated in the articles of incorporation and comply with the time limits fixed for payment in respect of issued and redeemed units or shares;

(c) redeem and sell assets at the price derived in accordance with the valuation criteria set out in the articles of incorporation;

(d) call an extraordinary general meeting of the shareholders in accordance with the law if the company's net asset value drops below the legal minimum;

(e) comply with the investment company's investment policy if governed by Part 1 of the 2002 Act;

(f) refrain from carrying out, or causing to be carried out, operations involving the receipt of savings from the public when the UCI for which they acted is not entered on the official list of UCIs or, in the case of SIFs, refrain from collecting or having agents collect funds from investors without applying for registration to the CSSF on behalf of the SIF for which they have acted within one month following the creation or constitution of the SIF; or

(g) refrain from issuing founder shares or similar securities for UCIs that are legally barred from issuing such securities.

---

[270] ibid Arts 167 and 173*bis*.

[271] ibid Arts 169 and 173*bis*.

[272] ibid Arts 171-1 and 173*bis*.

[273] Arts 120–126, 2002 Act; see also Art VIII, Act of 25 August 2006 under which: 'Any legal or regulatory provision concerning commercial companies and referring to the "board of directors" of an SA shall be understood as referring to the management board where such SA has a management board and a supervisory board, unless reference is made to the supervisory board due to the nature of the relevant mission'.

[274] Arts 60–65, Act of 13 February 2007.

Liability of the directors in the event of bankruptcy

In the event of a company's bankruptcy, any *de jure* or *de facto* conducting person, **6.253** whether visible or not and remunerated or not, and whether a natural or a legal person, who:

- under the cover of the company has engaged in commercial acts in his personal interest; or
- has disposed of corporate assets as though they were his own; or
- in his own interest, has wrongfully continued trading in circumstances in which the company would be unable to make payments due,

may be declared personally bankrupt,[275] on the understanding that, in that event, the company's liabilities are added to his own.

Moreover, when a company's bankruptcy reveals insufficient assets, the courts **6.254** may order its debts to be borne fully or partly, with or without joint liability, by the company's *de jure* or *de facto* conducting persons, whether visible or not and remunerated or not, in respect of whom serious and clear faults have been established that have contributed to the bankruptcy.[276]

The same conducting persons may be banned from carrying on, whether directly **6.255** or indirectly, a business activity as a director, manager, auditor, or any other function with the power to bind companies.[277] That penalty automatically accompanies judgments for ordinary or fraudulent bankruptcy.[278]

Liability of the management company of a common fund and its directors

Civil liability of the management company

The management company of an FCP 'must fulfil its obligations with the **6.256** diligence of a salaried agent; and is answerable to the unitholders for any loss resulting from the non-fulfilment or improper fulfilment of its obligations'.[279]

Neither the 2002 Act nor the Act of 13 February 2007 specifies the nature of the **6.257** contract between a management company and the investment company by which it is appointed. As a management company's designation requires it to enter into legal acts in the name of and on behalf of the investment company (acceptance of subscriptions of and applications for the redemption, purchase, and sale of financial instruments, etc), their contract should be considered a mandate and be governed by the applicable rules in the Civil Code.

---

[275] Art 495, Commercial Code.
[276] ibid Art 495-1.
[277] ibid Art 444-1.
[278] ibid.
[279] Arts 15 and 66, 2002 Act; Art 14, Act of 13 February 2007.

6.258   The management company of an FCP or an investment company is obliged to exercise all due skill and care, similar to that assumed by agents under the provisions of general law.[280] Any fault on its part must be properly established.

6.259   The 2002 Act derogates in one respect from the rules governing mandates in the case of coordinated management companies and their liability when they sub-delegate one of the functions entrusted to them.

6.260   Under the Civil Code,[281] a management company will not incur liability for the acts or omissions of a subcontractor provided it is entitled to use a subcontractor's services and has not designated an entity known to be insolvent or to have no legal capacity. Pursuant to the 2002 Act, a management company can incur liability even when it has authority to use delegates and does not designate an inappropriate entity.[282] This law stipulates that 'in no case shall the management company's and the depositary's liability be affected by the fact that the management company has delegated any functions to third parties . . . '.

6.261   This text is easy to understand insofar as it applies to the management company of an FCP. In this case, the management company is the legal representative of the FCP it has created and whose management rules it has developed. Unitholders have not had any role in the decision to delegate or the selection of delegates by the management company. It is therefore logical to hold the management company liable for the acts and omissions of its subcontractor. Such faults are ascribed to the management company itself, whether or not it has been negligent in connection with the sub-delegation.

6.262   This approach is less valid when a management company is designated by an investment company. In this case, the investment company —an independent entity with legal capacity— is positioned between the management company and the investors. It is therefore appropriate for the investment company, not its shareholders, to sue the management company for loss suffered as a result of the management company's acts or omissions.

6.263   It is difficult to imagine why an investment company might not permit the management company to delegate some of its functions. In certain cases, the

---

[280] 'Management of a portfolio is intrinsically a hazardous operation, the results of which cannot be guaranteed . . . It therefore seems necessary to hold the management company liable only for proven faults' (T Bonneau, 'Les fonds communs de placement, les fonds communs de créances, et le droit civil' (1991) *Rev trim dr civ* 44 and 45). Because of the legal instead of contractual nature of the powers vested in the management company, the nature of such liability is not clear (contractual or quasi-tortious). It could be contractual, since the unitholders, by acquiring units, are deemed to accept the management regulations and therefore the contractual document in which the management company is appointed.
[281]   Art 1994, Civil Code.
[282]   Art 85(2), 2002 Act.

investment company might even require the management company to delegate certain functions to particular entities. If so, the parties should be permitted to contract so as to limit the management company's role to coordinating and supervising the delegated activities. The management company's liability could reflect this feature and, by agreement between the parties, be limited to the management company's own faults or negligence. In other words, the management company would not be liable for the faults of its subcontractors as the parties would have derogated contractually from the 2002 Act, which does not stipulate that this is a matter of public policy.

The 2002 Act does not clearly define the scope of application of this onerous liability. Does it only apply to UCITS or does it also apply to all other UCIs, whether based in Luxembourg or other countries? As the Act does not mention any limit, these rules on liability for acts caused by others may possibly include the functions exercised by management companies on behalf of UCIs other than UCITS.[283] **6.264**

The management company acts in its own name vis-à-vis third parties but must indicate that it is acting on behalf of the FCP.[284] It may incur quasi-tortious liability. **6.265**

Civil liability of a management company's directors

A management company's directors cannot directly manage an FCP but may only do so through the management company. All the same, they are liable vis-à-vis the company and third parties on the terms set out in the 1915 Act and the Civil Code. **6.266**

Consequently, the management company's liability does not automatically entail liability on the part of its directors. In order to be liable, they must have been at fault within the meaning of the 1915 Act or the Civil Code. A case in point is the management company that has guaranteed repayment of the principal invested by an FCP's unitholders and which is no longer able to honour its commitment because it has lost the necessary financial resources. It could be held liable for such a breach, but its directors cannot if no fault can be attributed to them. **6.267**

Criminal liability of a management company's directors

As a legal entity, the management company does not incur criminal liability. However its directors may be punished under criminal law in the same way as an investment company's directors.[285] **6.268**

---

[283] For this interpretation see Elvinger and Schmit (n 83 above) 1531, which suggests selecting a non-coordinated management company to manage non-coordinated UCIs in order to remove any doubt in this respect.

[284] Arts 14(2) and 66, 2002 Act; Art 13(2), Act of 13 February 2007.

[285] See 6.250 above.

Liability of the delegates of management bodies

General delegates

6.269 The liability of the persons to whom a UCI's daily management has been delegated is governed by the ordinary rules applicable to agents.[286] This means that:

(1) delegates are liable vis-à-vis the UCI's management body (ie the principal) by virtue of the rules on agency relationships;[287]

(2) delegates cannot be released from liability in the same way as members of the board of directors;[288]

(3) unitholders cannot sue individually for redress for damage suffered by the UCI;[289] and

(4) delegates are liable vis-à-vis third parties by virtue of the general law provisions on quasi-tortious liability.[290]

6.270 Whether liability is several or joint when several persons assume the daily management of a UCI, for example in the case of a management committee, is debatable. According to the Civil Code:[291] 'Where the same instrument appoints several representatives or agents, they may incur joint liability only insofar as such liability is expressly provided for.'

6.271 The daily management delegates would therefore have individual contractual liability unless otherwise stipulated. Yet commercial law provides for joint liability subject to express derogation. However, this provision is unlikely to apply to the mandates held by management committee members. Nevertheless, to avoid any uncertainty in this respect, it is best to expressly exclude the joint liability of those delegates in the instrument by which they are appointed. It is advisable to mention this, particularly in the decision appointing the two conducting persons of the management company as daily management delegates.

6.272 Delegation may have two consequences for the liability of the management body itself:

• The members of the management body could be held liable vis-à-vis the UCI for the delegate's acts or omissions if the person chosen by them was clearly incompetent.

---

[286] Art 60, 1915 Act; Arts 1991 *et seq*, Civil Code; Fredericq (n 71 above) Vol V, No 459.

[287] Arts 1991 *et seq*, Civil Code.

[288] A Steichen, *Précis de droit des sociétés* (n 155 above) 824.

[289] However, were a shareholder to suffer individual damage separate from the company's damage, he could sue the delegate responsible for the fault on the grounds of the tortious liability provided for by Art 1382 of the Civil Code.

[290] ibid Arts 1382 *et seq*.

[291] ibid Art 1995.

• The management body may not grant the delegates absolute freedom. It still has the obligation to monitor them and to fix the limits of their autonomy.[292] Failure to perform that duty could be regarded as a management fault.

If the management body incurs liability for the acts of its delegate, it may take action against that delegate whilst remaining liable vis-à-vis the UCI and third parties.

It may be that daily management is delegated to an employee of the UCI. In that event, the delegate has a dual contractual relationship with the UCI: a daily management mandate and an employment contract in respect of his other functions.[293] In such cases, the applicable liability rules will depend on the nature of the act in question. If the fault has been committed in the person's capacity as an employee, employment law will apply. However, if the fault could only have been committed by a daily management delegate, its existence or consequences are determined according to the foregoing rules on the contractual liability of agents.   **6.273**

An employee's liability within the framework of his employment contract is defined by the law.[294] There is no liability vis-à-vis the employer (ie the UCI) except in the event of willful default or gross negligence.   **6.274**

Special delegates

Special delegates, such as the manager, the investment adviser, and the head office agent, provide services to the UCI or its management company pursuant to service agreements. The extent of their liability vis-à-vis the UCI depends on the content of those agreements and the general principles of contractual liability. As a general rule, they are under an obligation to use their reasonable endeavours rather than to achieve a specific result, which means that they are only liable for faults or negligence established by the plaintiff. Special delegates have quasi-tortious liability vis-à-vis third parties.   **6.275**

---

[292] Fredericq (n 71 above) Vol V, para 437; Resteau (n 75 above) Vol II, para 961.

[293] As regards such an accumulation of functions, see in particular Steichen's discussion (n 155 above) 733.

[294] Art 121-9, Labour Code (Act of 31 July 2006 on the introduction of a Labour Code (*Mémorial* A 2006, 2456 *et seq*), as amended by the Grand-Duchy Regulation of 22 December 2006 (*Mémorial* A 2006, 4119 *et seq*)) provides: 'The employer shall bear the risks generated by the company's business. The employee shall bear the consequences of any damage caused by his intentional acts or his serious negligence.'

Authorization of the conducting persons of UCIs

History

6.276   For the first time, the 1983 Act required a UCI's conducting persons to be authorized by the CSSF. It provided that the persons forming a UCI's management and supervisory bodies had to provide adequate assurances of probity and professional qualifications for the performance of their duties.

6.277   The same requirement was prescribed in identical terms for the conducting persons of an FCP's management company[295] and the managers of SICAVs.[296] However, it did not expressly refer to the conducting persons of other UCIs, from whom the supervisory authority was nevertheless entitled to receive 'comparable assurances',[297] including guarantees of probity and professional qualifications.

6.278   In the context of FCPs, the 1983 Act also required the main shareholders of the management company to provide adequate assurances of professional probity.[298] In the Parliamentary documents accompanying the 1983 Act, it even required such shareholders to prove their solvency and professional qualifications. Those requirements were ultimately withdrawn since they derogated from the provisions of general law,[299] and only the requirement of professional probity was retained.[300]

6.279   In the same Parliamentary documents, it was planned that the solvency of the conducting persons should be made a prerequisite. That proposal was ultimately rejected on the grounds that the conducting persons and management bodies are not personally liable for corporate liabilities.[301]

6.280   Lastly, it was proposed that the shareholders of the management company should jointly and severally ensure compliance with all terms and conditions contained in the management regulations, with the provisions of the 1983 Act and with the implementing regulations. The idea was to hold the shareholders of the management company responsible vis-à-vis the investors. Yet, the authors of the draft legislation recognized that joint liability would negate the very essence of the limited

---

[295]   Art 2(2)(d), 1983 Act.
[296]   ibid Art 26.
[297]   ibid Art 39.
[298]   ibid Art 2(2)(d).
[299]   *Parliamentary doc* No 2366, Opinion of the *Conseil d'État*, 54; *Parliamentary doc* No 2366[1], Position adopted by the government towards the opinion of the *Conseil d'État*, 1; *Parliamentary doc* No 2366[2], Opinion of the Chamber of Commerce, 3, and *Parliamentary doc* No 2366[3], Additional Opinion of the *Conseil d'État*, 3.
[300]   For the reasons behind this, see *Parliamentary doc* No 2366[8], Third additional opinion of the *Conseil d'État*, 6.
[301]   *Parliamentary doc* No 2366[4], Comments of the *Commissariat au Contrôle des Banques* on the additional opinion of the *Conseil d'État*, 2; and *Parliamentary doc* No 2366[6], Amendments proposed by the Special Commission, 3.

liability of an SA,[302] which is primarily why the proposal was rejected.[303] Moreover, the *Conseil d'État* pointed out that there was no reason why a shareholder who was not on the board of directors, and therefore held no influence over the company's business, should be held liable for failure to observe the management regulations and to comply with the law. It further stressed the difficulties created by such a requirement in the event of the disposal of shares in the management company.[304]

Authorization procedure

Conditions

The 2002 Act and the Act of 13 February 2007 reiterated that a UCI's conducting **6.281** persons must be authorized by the CSSF. As regards UCITS, this requirement supplements the rules governing the authorization of conducting persons of management companies or self-managed investment companies (which is justified, as designation as a management company does not release the board of the management company from its duty to control and supervise delegated activities). The conducting persons of a UCITS also play a role that requires prior authorization by the CSSF of their appointment.

The members of the board of directors, or management board, or a body equiva- **6.282** lent to the board of directors in companies other than SAs, must be authorized by the CSSF. They are authorized when they have the good repute and experience required to manage the UCI in question.

Under the 2002 Act, the identity of reference shareholders[305] of a management com- **6.283** pany, other than the management company of a UCITS, must be communicated to the CSSF.[306] Moreover, the CSSF takes the view that, insofar as those members actually determine the company's policy, they have the status of conducting persons and therefore require authorization with respect to UCIs other than SIFs.[307]

Procedure

To permit verification of the probity and experience of a UCI's conducting persons, **6.284** their names and those of any replacements must be communicated forthwith to the

---

[302] *Parliamentary doc* No 2366, Comments on the Articles, 25; and *Parliamentary doc* No 2366[1], Position adopted by the government towards the opinion of the *Conseil d'État*, 2.

[303] *Parliamentary doc* No 2366[2], Opinion of the Chamber of Commerce, 3; and *Parliamentary doc* No 2366[4], Comments of the *Commissariat au Contrôle des Banques* on the additional opinion of the *Conseil d'État*, 3.

[304] *Parliamentary doc* No 2366, Opinion of the *Conseil d'État*, 52 and 55 and *Parliamentary doc* No 2366[3], additional opinion of the *Conseil d'État*, 6.

[305] ie shareholders holding a majority stake in the management company's capital.

[306] Art 91(2)(c), 2002 Act.

[307] Ch N, II, Circular 91/75 and Circular 07/283 which confirms that only managers of the management company in the case of FCP-SIFs are to be considered as conducting persons.

supervisory authority.[308] In principle, such communication must be made prior to the conducting person's appointment or replacement. If that is not the case, authorization is required before his appointment or replacement can take effect.

The Depositary of a UCI

Rules governing the depositary's services

Historical background

Grand-ducal decree of 22 December 1972

6.285 The Luxembourg regulations have not always provided for the concept of a depositary for UCIs as we know it today. On the contrary, the Grand-Ducal Decree of 22 December 1972 concerning the supervision of investment funds, the first piece of legislation on the issue, did not in any way require Luxembourg-based UCIs to resort to a depositary's services.

6.286 Yet the Council of Europe's recommendation with respect to investment funds[309] had previously suggested the appointment of depositaries for FCPs. It was proposed that the task of such depositaries would be to protect the fund's assets, provide the management company with administrative assistance, and—to some extent an existing duty—to monitor transactions in the interest of the unitholders.[310]

6.287 Although their intervention was not required by any legislation, depositaries began to play an increased role in the 1970s, especially those involved with FCPs targeted at countries where the concept of depositary was already known. Under German law, for example, the authorization of Luxembourg-based FCPs in Germany was conditional on the appointment of a depositary charged with safeguarding their assets and monitoring their activities.

6.288 This development prompted the Banking Commissioner, from the start of the 1970s, to require, in respect of all FCPs, the appointment of a depositary having a very wide range of responsibilities.[311]

6.289 The depositary's role was to safeguard the FCP's portfolio and to keep the certificates of unissued units in custody. In that capacity, it was also responsible for carrying out

---

[308] Art 93(3) and (4), 2002 Act.

[309] Art 13 of Resolution (72)28 relating to investment funds, adopted by the Committee of Ministers on 19 September 1972 at the 213th meeting of the Ministers' Deputies.

[310] ibid Arts 13 and 14.

[311] For details of the history of depositaries and the development of administrative practices in the Grand Duchy of Luxembourg, see A Coussement, 'Le rôle de la banque de dépôt dans le fonctionnement des organes collectifs de placement', in *Les organes collectifs de placement dans la perspective de la place financière de Luxembourg,* Study Days of 11 and 12 December 1970, Université Internationale de Sciences comparées, Luxembourg, 69.

'all actions necessary for the proper administration of the portfolio',[312] ie collecting interest and dividends, exercising subscription rights, presenting securities for redemption or exchange, and closing out stock exchange transactions concerning portfolio items. It was also responsible for issuing and redeeming the FCP's units and collecting and paying the amounts relating thereto.

In contrast, for UCIs incorporated in the form of an investment company, the supervisory authority did not require the appointment of a depositary. In fact, most such companies nevertheless appointed a depositary, generally a foreign bank, the duties of which were limited to keeping their assets in safe custody and carrying out the instructions of the board of directors.[313] **6.290**

The difference in treatment between contractual and incorporated UCIs was justified by their different operating methods. An FCP's unitholders play a passive role since they cannot intervene in the management of the fund. Management authority is reserved by law to a company controlled by the promoter, and in the appointment of which the unitholders do not intervene. That situation very quickly revealed the need to vest a third party, the depositary, with clearly defined responsibilities in order to protect the investors. In contrast, an investment company is managed by a board of directors that is appointed and, where necessary, dismissed by the general meeting of shareholders. Under the circumstances, there did not seem to be any necessity to entrust the supervision of such UCIs to a depositary. **6.291**

The 1983 Act

Under the 1983 Act, 'all securities and liquid assets held by a common fund shall be kept in safe custody by a financial institution referred to as a "depositary bank", appointed by the management company and authorized by the supervisory authority'.[314] **6.292**

The 1983 Act imposed a minimum capital requirement on the depositary. It also required the bank's directors to meet probity and professional qualification criteria. Lastly, it required the bank's main shareholders to offer assurances of probity.[315] **6.293**

---

[312] ibid 77.
[313] ibid 81.
[314] Art 13(1), 1983 Act.
[315] ibid. At the time the draft Act was laid before the Luxembourg Parliament, that Article also required the main shareholders to provide guarantees of professional qualification in addition to guarantees of probity. The provision in question thus reproduced the provision concerning the authorization of an FCP's management company (Art 2(2)(d), 1983 Act), the shareholders of which also had to offer guarantees of probity and professional qualification. The initial text went so far as to require the shareholders of a management company to supply guarantees of solvency. During the preparation of the 1983 Act, those requirements were eliminated. As a result, only professional probity remained a prerequisite for approval of the main shareholders of both the depositary and the management company.

6.294   As a general rule, the 1983 Act applied the Council of Europe's recommendation concerning investment funds. Luxembourg's legislation concerning depositaries drew heavily on that recommendation, save in respect of a few details and some of its wording.

6.295   As previously, the 1983 Act required the appointment of depositaries only in the case of FCPs. Assignment to a financial institution of the duties of safekeeping and monitoring an FCP's portfolio was prompted by the wish to protect investors.[316] The scope of those duties was much broader than under the Grand-Ducal Regulation of 22 December 1972. The regime provided for in the 1983 Act anticipated much of that which was to be laid down in the 1988 Act.

The 1988 and 2002 Acts

6.296   The 1988 Act reiterated the contents of Directive 85/611, which makes it mandatory to appoint a depositary for FCPs and investment companies[317] and which sets out a depositary's minimum duties.[318] As Directive 85/611 has not been amended in this respect, the 2002 Act has not introduced any change in the depositary's missions and responsibilities.

6.297   Under the 2002 Act, safekeeping of the assets of any Luxembourg-based UCI must be entrusted to a depositary. That requirement applies to all UCIs regardless of their legal form—contractual or incorporated—or their status—coordinated UCITS governed by Part I of the 2002 Act, UCIs governed by Part II of the 2002 Act, or UCIs governed by the 1991 Act.[319] The depositary is subject to the specific supervisory obligations listed in the 2002 Act,[320] which are discussed in detail below.[321]

The Act of 13 February 2007

6.298   In order to make SIFs more attractive for promoters of alternative UCIs, the authors of the Act of 13 February 2007 relieved the depositary of the task of undertaking certain checks. Other than in this respect, the status, duties, and responsibility of a SIF's depositary are identical to those of any other UCI's depositary.[322]

---

[316]   *Parliamentary doc* No 2366, Comments on the Articles, 27.
[317]   Arts 7.1 and 14.1, Directive (EEC) 85/611.
[318]   ibid Arts 7.3 and 14.3.
[319]   Arts 17(1), 34(1), 40, 66, 71, and 75(6), 2002 Act; Arts 3, 5, and 6, 1991 Act, which has been repealed and replaced by the Act of 13 February 2007.
[320]   Arts 18(2), 34(3), 40, 66, 71, and 75(6), 2002 Act.
[321]   See 6.326 *et seq* below.
[322]   For further details about the role of a SIF's depositary, see Y Lacroix and L Tristan, 'Parties and service providers involved in specialised investment funds' in *Specialised Investments Funds* (Arendt & Medernach, 2007) 71; as regards a SIF's depositary using a prime broker, see H Schwabe and F Brülin, '*SIF hedge funds—opportunities to establish "unrestricted" hedge funds in a regulated environment*' in *Specialised Investment Funds* (Arendt & Madernach, 2007) 200 *et seq*.

Conditions of eligibility to act as a depositary

The legal status of depositaries

According to Directive 85/611, a depositary must either have its registered office   **6.299**
in the Member State in which the UCITS is situated or be established in that State
through a branch if its registered office is in another Member State.[323] The depositary must be subject to public control. It must 'furnish sufficient financial and
professional guarantees' to be able 'effectively to pursue its business as depositary'
and 'meet the commitments inherent in that function'[324]. Determination of the
types of institutions eligible, in principle, to act as depositaries is entrusted to the
Member States.

In the Grand Duchy of Luxembourg, the depositary must be a credit institution   **6.300**
incorporated in the form of a company under Luxembourg law or a branch of a
foreign institution.[325] In the case of a branch, the depositary is only authorized to
act as a depositary for a coordinated UCITS if the registered office of its parent
company is situated in a Member State of the EEA.[326] If not, it can only become a
depositary for UCIs other than coordinated UCITS.[327]

The depositary's infrastructure

Credit institutions are not automatically authorized to act as depositaries for   **6.301**
Luxembourg-based UCIs. Their selection by a UCI must be approved by the
CSSF.[328]

When an approval request is received, the CSSF examines the probity and profes   **6.302**
sional experience of the depositary's directors. It also asks the depositary to show
that 'it has the necessary infrastructure, ie adequate human and technical resources,
to accomplish all tasks connected with its function'.[329] The depositary must prove
that it has sufficient numbers of appropriately qualified employees and that it has
adequate IT facilities.

When seeking authorization for a UCI, the depositary asks the CSSF to approve   **6.303**
its skills in this area. A UCI's authorization is in fact subject to the CSSF's approval
of its choice of depositary, which differs from the general authorization of financial institutions. That may seem strange, inasmuch as the general authorization
basically covers all banking services. In fact, however, the functions of a UCI's

---

[323]   Arts 8.1 and 15.1, Directive (EEC) 85/611.
[324]   ibid Arts 8.2 and 15.2.
[325]   Arts 17(3), 35(2), 40, 66, 71, and 75(6), 2002 Act.
[326]   ibid Arts 17(2), 35(1), and 40.
[327]   ibid Arts 66, 71, and 75(6); those Articles do not, however, refer to Arts 17(2) and 35(1) of
the 2002 Act.
[328]   Art 93(2), 2002 Act; Art 42(2), Act of 13 February 2007.
[329]   Ch E, I, Circular 91/75.

depositary are so specialized that they require the setting-up of an infrastructure and the provision of specific professional and financial guarantees.[330]

6.304   In practice, approval for a bank to act as a depositary for UCIs remains valid indefinitely once it has assumed its duties for one UCI, except in the event of a change in circumstances.

The depositary's independence

6.305   Directive 85/611 does not permit the functions of an FCP's management company and depositary to be entrusted to one and the same entity.[331] The rule is the same for investment companies.[332] The reason for this is clear. The management and supervision functions must be exercised separately in any given UCI. The management company or the board of directors manages the assets, whereas the depositary retains custody of them and verifies the legality of management acts.[333]

6.306   The management company or, as the case may be, the investment company and the depositary are obliged to carry out their respective functions independently. This is expressly required by Directive 85/611, at least for FCPs.[334] The Directive does not repeat the constraint as such for investment companies. This omission seems to be due to an oversight.[335]

6.307   How should the depositary's independence vis-à-vis the management company be construed? In addition to the legal independence created by the existence of two separate entities, economic or financial independence might conceivably be required. That ingredient would, for example, be missing if the depositary held a direct or indirect interest in the capital of the management company. However, Directive 85/611 does not require economic or financial independence of the depositary and the management company or, as the case may be, the investment company. It merely requires legal independence, while specifying that the two entities must act independently.[336]

6.308   A depositary is not permitted to manage the assets of a coordinated UCITS whose assets it has in safekeeping whether the delegation is effected by the relevant management company[337] or by the investment company itself.[338]

---

[330]   Arts 8.2 and 15.2, Directive (EEC) 85/611.
[331]   ibid Art 10.1.
[332]   ibid Art 17.1.
[333]   'Towards a European market for UCITS' (n 40 above) No 57, 27.
[334]   Art 10.2, Directive (EEC) 85/611.
[335]   'Towards a European market for UCITS' (n 40 above) No 69, 32.
[336]   ibid. para 57, 27.
[337]   Art 85(1)(e), 2002 Act.
[338]   ibid Arts 27(2) and 40.

Directive 85/611 further requires the depositary to act solely in the interest of the **6.309** unitholders. That requirement is expressly stipulated for both FCPs and invest-ment companies.[339]

The Luxembourg legislature has accurately transposed the above-mentioned **6.310** Community requirements. The 2002 Act contains identical provisions to those found in Directive 85/611 for coordinated UCITS and they have been extended[340] to cover UCIs governed by Part II[341] and SIFs.[342]

The CSSF nevertheless does not allow the management companies of coordinated **6.311** UCITS to choose their conducting persons from among the depositary's employees.[343] The same principle was not extended to other management companies, governed by Chapter 14 of the 2002 Act. For such other management companies, Luxembourg has a flexible practice in this area. UCIs governed by Part II and SIFs are frequently promoted, managed, and controlled by a single financial institution established in the Grand Duchy of Luxembourg. The members of their management bodies are chosen from among the bank's officers and the bank acts as depositary. Such a situation does not create a conflict of interest provided that the depositary can act independently and the interests of the investors are safeguarded.

Replacement of a depositary

According to Directive 85/611, it is up to national law or a UCITS' constitutive **6.312** documents to establish the conditions for the replacement of the depositary and rules to ensure the protection of investors in the event of such replacement.[344] The 2002 Act and the Act of 13 February 2007 list several cases in which a depositary must cease to hold office.

The duties of an FCP's depositary naturally cease in the case of its withdrawal,[345] **6.313** whether at the initiative of the depositary or of the management company,[346] on the understanding that the withdrawal conditions and procedures are, in principle, laid

---

[339] Arts 10.2 and 17.2, Directive (EEC) 85/611.
[340] Except the asset management prohibition, which applies only to coordinated UCITS (Arts 85(1)(e), 27(2), and 40, 2002 Act).
[341] ibid Arts 20, 38, 40, 66, 71, and 75(6).
[342] Arts 18, 37, and 40(2), Act of 13 February 2007.
[343] Section I, 3(a), Circular 03/108.
[344] Arts 11 and 18, Directive (EEC) 85/611.
[345] Arts 21(b), and 66, 2002 Act; Art 19(b), Act of 13 February 2007.
[346] Art 21(b), 2002 Act; Art 19(b), Act of 13 February 2007. Arts 21(b), and 19(b), reproduce Art 16 of the 1983 Act and amend it slightly to make it clear that the contract may be cancelled at the initiative of either party, which the 1983 Act did not specify. Art 16 of the 1983 Act provided that cancellation was to be effected on the terms laid down in the management regulations (eg as regards the period of notice, etc). That detail was omitted in the 1988 and 2002 Acts and thereafter in the Act of 13 February 2007, as the legislature assumed it was implied. See *Parliamentary doc* No 3172, Comments on the Articles, 39.

down in the management regulations and in the depositary agreement between the parties. Those documents generally specify that a management company may not terminate its contract with the depositary without ensuring the depositary's replacement with a successor approved by the CSSF. Conversely, the management company may not, in principle, require a depositary to bind itself indefinitely to a fund. On the contrary, a depositary must be able to end its commitments, for example when a conflict arises with the management company. The 2002 Act and the Act of 13 February 2007 specify that a replacement depositary must in any event be appointed within two months,[347] in order to ensure investor protection. If a new depositary is not found within two months from expiry of the period of notice stipulated in the depositary agreement, the FCP is liquidated *ipso jure*.[348] To prevent the fund from drifting during those two months, the 2002 Act requires the depositary to 'take all necessary steps to ensure the proper preservation of the interests of the unitholders'.[349]

6.314   The duties of an FCP's depositary also cease in the event of the depositary being declared bankrupt or going into liquidation,[350] or if its authorization is withdrawn.[351] The same applies if the management company finds itself in one of those situations.[352]

6.315   Lastly, the depositary may be released from its duties in all other cases provided for by the management regulations,[353] which allows a certain degree of flexibility in the regulations in this respect.

6.316   The foregoing regime also applies to incorporated UCIs,[354] with one major difference: failure to replace the depositary within the two-month period does not automatically entail the UCI's liquidation. Insofar as an investment company's shareholders have a more active role than an FCP's unitholders, they may call a general meeting to adopt the necessary measures. For example, they may replace a board of directors that is slow to make the arrangements necessary to find a new depositary. In any event, the CSSF may at any time withdraw authorization and so bring about the judicial liquidation of a UCI that no longer has a depositary.[355]

---

[347]   Arts 21(b) and 66, 2002 Act; Art 19(b), Act of 13 February 2007.

[348]   Arts 22(1)(b) and 66, 2002 Act; Art 21(1)(b), Act of 13 February 2007.

[349]   Art 21(b), 2002 Act; Art 19(b), Act of 13 February 2007. The period of 2 months was already fixed in Art 16 of the 1983 Act. In the initial version of the text resulting in the 1983 Act, the period was set at 8 days. In response to an opinion issued by the Chamber of Commerce, it was extended to 2 months to facilitate replacement of the depositary by the management company (see *Parliamentary doc* No 2366², Opinion of the Chamber of Commerce, 7).

[350]   Arts 21(c) and 66, 2002 Act; Art 19(c), Act of 13 February 2007.

[351]   Arts 21(d) and 66, 2002 Act; Art 19(d), Act of 13 February 2007.

[352]   Arts 21(c) and (d) and 66, 2002 Act; Art 19(c) and (d), Act of 13 February 2007.

[353]   Arts 21(e) and 66, 2002 Act; Art 19(e), Act of 13 February 2007.

[354]   Arts 37, 40, 71, and 75(6), 2002 Act; Arts 36 and 40, Act of 13 February 2007.

[355]   Arts 94(2) and 104(1), 2002 Act; Arts 43(2) and 47(1), Act of 13 February 2007.

Dispensation from the obligation to have a depositary

In exceptional circumstances, Directive 85/611[356] allows investment companies to dispense with a depositary's services. However, detailed conditions must be met. **6.317**

The 2002 Act and the Act of 13 February 2007 do not afford this possibility. Although provided for by the 1988 Act[357] and made applicable to institutional UCIs by the 1991 Act,[358] the option was not used by any investment company and was therefore considered superfluous. **6.318**

Tasks of the depositary

The tasks of the depositary are threefold. [359] The first is to keep the assets in safe custody. The second is to monitor certain transactions by the UCI. Lastly, an FCP's depositary is also expressly charged with the day-to-day administration of the fund's assets. A SIF's depositary is only responsible for keeping the assets in safe custody. **6.319**

Custody of a UCI's assets

Pursuant to the 2002 Act and to the Act of 13 February 2007, the assets of any Luxembourg-based UCIs must be entrusted to a depositary for safekeeping. This is a general requirement, which applies to all UCIs, regardless of their legal form (contractual or incorporated) or status (coordinated UCITS governed by Part I of the 2002 Act, UCIs submitted to Part II of the 2002 Act, or SIFs).[360] **6.320**

Custody has two separate but complementary aspects, namely the safekeeping and the monitoring of a UCI's assets.

The safekeeping of a UCI's assets

The first aspect of custody is to physically keep the assets safe. In that capacity, the depositary takes delivery of and holds a UCI's assets (cash, transferable securities, or other instruments and assets). **6.321**

Pursuant to the Civil Code,[361] the depositary assumes two key obligations. It must first of all protect the deposited assets with the same care as it would its **6.322**

---

[356] Arts 14.4 and 14.5, Directive (EEC) 85/611.

[357] Arts 33(4) and (5), 39, 65, and 69(5), 1988 Act.

[358] Arts 5 and 6, 1991 Act respectively make Arts 65 and 69, of the 1988 Act applicable.

[359] For a description of the depositary's tasks in real estate and useful practical recommendations in this respect, see F Brausch, EF Henrion, and R Delcourt, 'Les devoirs de la banque dépositaire d'un fonds immobilier' (2008) *ACE* 18 *et seq.*

[360] Arts 17(1), 34(1), 40, 66, 71, and 75(6), 2002 Act; Arts 16(1), 33, and 40. Act of 13 February 2007.

[361] To which Art 11, Act of 1 August 2001 on the circulation of securities and other fungible instruments refers very broadly (*Mémorial* A 2001, 2180).

own assets.[362] Secondly, and above all, it must return those assets to the persons entitled.[363]

6.323   The safekeeping of a UCI's assets may also be entrusted to another professional appointed by the depositary or by the UCI in agreement with the depositary. Such a third party may hold the assets to the order of the depositary, in which case it is its correspondent or sub-custodian. It may also hold the assets directly to the order of the UCI, in which case it establishes an account relationship with the UCI. If an account is opened in the name of the UCI, the depositary must at all times know where the relevant assets are maintained, as discussed futher below.

6.324   The depositary and the UCI may also resort to the mechanism of a fiduciary agreement,[364] whereby the UCI (the *fiduciant*—settlor) transfers all or part of its assets (the fiduciary assets) to the depositary (the *fiduciaire*—trustee or fiduciary) under a fiduciary agreement between the two parties. The depositary holds those assets subject to certain obligations (the fiduciary liabilities), including the obligation to retransfer ownership, subject to compliance with certain conditions, to the UCI or to a third party appointed by the UCI. Insofar as the fiduciary is a credit institution, an investment undertaking, an investment company with variable or fixed capital, a securitization company, a management company of FCPs or securitization vehicles, a pension fund, an insurance or reinsurance undertaking, or a national or international public body operating in the financial sector, the fiduciary assets deposited with it must be accounted for off balance sheet and cannot be seized by its creditors in the event of bankruptcy.[365]

6.325   In practice, fiduciary agreements are a frequently used solution when a UCI deposits its cash with a depositary, because such a mechanism ensures that the UCI will recover its cash even if the depositary goes bankrupt. In that event, its cash would be immediately segregated from the bankrupt's assets and returned to the UCI. The main advantage for the depositary is that the fiduciary assets are not recorded on its balance sheet and do not affect the regulatory ratios to which it is subject by virtue of the 1993 Act.

Monitoring of a UCI's assets

6.326   The second element of custody is the monitoring of a UCI's assets. This has two aspects.

---

[362]   Art 1927, Civil Code.

[363]   ibid Art 1932.

[364]   Ch E, II, Circular 91/75.

[365]   Art 6, Act of 27 July 2003 regarding approval of The Hague Convention of 1 July 1985 on the Law Applicable to Trusts and on Their Recognition, with new regulations for fiduciary contracts and amending the Act of 25 September 1905 on the transcription of real property rights (*Mémorial* A 2003, 2620).

The first is the monitoring of the location of the assets. A depositary 'must know at all **6.327** times how the assets . . . are invested and where and how they are available'.[366] It must know at all times with which institution the UCI's assets are deposited. In that context, it is immaterial whether those assets are held in an account opened in the name of the UCI or of the depositary itself. Clearly, if the assets are deposited with the correspondent in the depositary's name, monitoring is easier than when the account is opened in the UCI's name. In the latter case, the correspondent does not have an account relationship with the depositary, which must therefore make sure that the third party keeps it at all times directly informed of the situation of the UCI's assets.

The second aspect is the monitoring of the qualifications and solvency of the cor- **6.328** respondents with which the UCI's assets are deposited. According to Circular 91/75,[367] the depositary fulfils its monitoring obligation when it is convinced, from the outset and during the entire term of the agreement, that the third parties with which the UCI's assets are deposited are of good repute and competent, and have adequate credit.

The depositary must choose its correspondents with care. When a UCI itself **6.329** determines the institutions with which it deposits its assets, the depositary must ensure that they meet the above-mentioned requirements.

A UCI's assets must be monitored by the depositary itself. That duty may not be **6.330** delegated to a third party. This is why the CSSF, in principle, opposes the appointment of a global sub-depositary to hold a UCI's assets. The reason for this rejection is that, when a global sub-depositary is appointed, the depositary is generally unable to communicate directly with the institutions charged with the safekeeping of the assets, nor can it intervene directly with those institutions in order to protect the UCI's interests. According to the CSSF, this makes it impossible for the depositary to supervise a UCI's assets and transactions effectively. Such a structure would violate the applicable laws and regulations 'since its object would be to render them meaningless' save where 'a single correspondent has been chosen for technical reasons', for example when the investments 'are made on a single market'.[368] That exception applies, *inter alia*, to UCIs that acquire securities only from issuers of a single country and money market funds that invest only in time deposits in several currencies.

Oversight of a UCI's transactions

The scope of the control duties entrusted to the depositary is determined by **6.331** Directive 85/611,[369] which assigns to the depositaries of UCITS distinct oversight

[366] *Parliamentary doc* No 3172, Comments on the Articles, 38; Ch E, II, Circular 91/75.
[367] Ch E, IV, Circular 91/75.
[368] ibid Ch E, III, 1.
[369] Arts 7.3 and 14.3, Directive (EEC) 85/611.

obligations the extent of which varies according to the legal status of the UCITS. Those oversight obligations are more extensive in the case of FCPs. In contrast with the shareholders of investment companies, investors in contractual UCIs need added protection because of their passive role in management.

6.332 The 2002 Act has faithfully transposed the applicable Community provisions into Luxembourg law.[370] It has also extended most of those provisions to the depositaries of UCIs governed by Part II of the Act.[371] However, those rules have not been incorporated into the Act of 13 February 2007. The legislature did not want to give depositaries of SIFs the same obligations to verify and monitor transactions, on the ground that investors in such UCIs are sufficiently capable of verifying the quality of services supplied to their UCI without a depositary's assistance. Such funds may, of course, choose to add these tasks contractually.

6.333 The depositary itself must directly fulfil its legal obligation to control transactions. That obligation may not be delegated save in the exceptional cases considered below.

Obligations incumbent on all depositaries of UCIs

6.334 According to the 2002 Act, the depositary of any UCI must ensure that certain transactions comply with the law or, as applicable, a UCI's constitutive documents. The term 'ensure' is taken from Directive 85/611. It means that the depositary must exercise due care in the fulfilment of certain duties but is not required to guarantee the outcome. The term 'ensure' also means that the depositary does not have to carry out such tasks itself. It has to verify only that they are correctly performed.[372]

6.335 **Obligations connected with the issue and redemption of units in UCIs**   The depositary must ensure that the sale, issue, redemption, and cancellation of units effected by or on behalf of a UCI are carried out in accordance with the law and with the UCI's constitutive documents.[373] That function primarily obliges the depositary to verify that the deadlines for paying the issue or redemption price stipulated in the constitutive documents are met. It further obliges the depositary to verify that bearer certificates are not delivered to subscribers before payment of the subscription price and, conversely, that redemption proceeds are not paid to the investor until after delivery of the corresponding certificate(s).

6.336 In a UCI organized as an umbrella fund or issuing classes of securities, such verification should also apply to the conversion of units from one sub-fund or category to another, even though this is not expressly stipulated in the 2002 Act. Technically, in fact, conversion amounts to redemption followed by a fresh subscription.

---

[370] Arts 18(2), 34(3), and 40, 2002 Act.
[371] ibid Arts 66, 71, and 75(6).
[372] Ch E, III, 1, Circular 91/75.
[373] Arts 18(2)(a), 34(3)(a), 40, 66, 71, and 75(6), 2002 Act.

Obligations connected with the transactions of UCIs The depositary must **6.337** ensure that, in transactions involving the assets of the UCI, any consideration is remitted to it within the usual time limits.[374] In practical terms, this means that a UCI, 'within the usual time limits', must receive the transferable securities or other portfolio items it has bought or, in the case of a sale, the monetary consideration.

That still makes it necessary to determine the meaning of 'the usual time limits'. If **6.338** the market in which a transaction takes place uses the practice of 'delivery versus payment', it is up to the depositary to ensure that securities are only delivered in return for payment of the sale price. Where such a practice does not exist,[375] additional time may be allowed between delivery and collection of the sale price.

Obligations connected with the allocation of a UCI's earnings The depositary **6.339** is under a duty to ensure that the income of a UCI is applied in accordance with its constitutive documents.[376]

To fulfil this obligation, the depositary must verify that the UCI complies with the **6.340** distribution policy described in its constitutive documents. A given UCI may propose to capitalize its income, whereas another may promise the unitholders regular dividends at fixed intervals or other dates. The depositary is responsible for ensuring that the stated policy is properly carried out.

The distribution policy of FCPs is described in the management regulations.[377] in **6.341** contrast with incorporated UCIs, where the general meeting has the ultimate decision-making power in relation to the distribution policy. The depositary must ensure that the investment company pays its shareholders only sums that are distributable.[378] It must also check that any relevant provisions in the articles of incorporation are observed. For example, the articles of incorporation may stipulate that dividends not collected by a given deadline will lapse and revert to the investment company. In such cases, the depositary must verify that this is done.

Additional obligations incumbent on the depositary of an FCP

Obligations connected with calculation of the FCP's net asset value The **6.342** depositary must ensure that the value of an FCP's units is calculated in accordance with the law and the management regulations.[379] That obligation involves verification of the calculation frequency, the correct application of the valuation rules, and the correct valuation of portfolio securities. This can be a difficult task when unlisted securities have to be valued.

---

[374] ibid Arts 18(2)(d), 34(3)(b), 40, 66, 71, and 75(6), 2002 Act.
[375] As is the case in certain emerging markets.
[376] Arts 18(2)(e), 34(3)(c), 40, 66, 71, and 75(6), 2002 Act.
[377] ibid Arts 13(2)(c), and 66, 2002 Act.
[378] In the specific meaning of such concept for investment companies. See 5.102–5.108 above.
[379] Art 18(2)(b), 2002 Act.

6.343   The depositary is obliged to check the calculation of net asset value only in respect of FCPs governed by Part I of the 2002 Act. That is not required for FCPs governed by Part II of the 2002 Act.[380] The Luxembourg legislature has not explained this omission. It seems likely that it did not wish to impose that specific duty, directly flowing from Directive 85/611, on the depositaries of FCPs other than coordinated UCITS.

6.344   **Obligations connected with the execution of instructions given by the management company of a common fund**   The depositary must carry out the management company's instructions unless they conflict with the law or the management regulations.[381] In principle this appears to require the depositary to verify, prior to execution, that instructions to pay or deliver securities when assets are purchased or sold do not infringe the investment restrictions applicable to the FCP under the 2002 Act or its management regulations. The depositary's duty is to check the lawfulness rather than the appropriateness of the management company's instructions.[382]

6.345   In practice, the depositary is frequently unable to conduct an *a priori* verification of its instructions, obliging it to carry out an *a posteriori* check. The CSSF considers this to be an acceptable approach while adding that such a situation does not affect the depositary's responsibility.[383]

6.346   Moreover, prior verification would be difficult for depositaries when asset managers are situated abroad in an entirely different time zone from that of the Grand Duchy of Luxembourg. The CSSF seems to recognize this difficulty and allows depositaries to delegate that verification function partly to agents located abroad. Circular 91/75 specifies that depositaries may use agency agreements in cases where a management company entrusts asset management to portfolio managers established in foreign countries.[384] In such cases, the relations between the depositary and its foreign agents must be organized in such a way that foreign agents have all the resources and data necessary to check beforehand that investment decisions are compatible with the law or management regulations.[385] If the depositary is not

---

[380]   Art 66 of the 2002 Act does not refer to subparagraph (b) of Art 18(2) of the 2002 Act.

[381]   ibid Arts 18(2)(c), and 66, 2002 Act.

[382]   See F Brausch, 'Les responsabilités du dépositaire d'OPCVM' (1994) *ALFI Yearbook* 229.

[383]   This solution does not seem entirely satisfactory. Even prior verification does not permit the depositary to guarantee a UCI's compliance with its investment restrictions. In fact, at the time of exercising such control, the securities transaction has already been entered into between the management company and the third party, which may in principle force the UCI to carry out the transaction, even if it falls outside the investment limits. Verification by the depositary will in any case be late if it is conducted only when the payment or delivery instruction is given. The only way to ensure perfect control would be to involve the depositary in the investment decision itself. However, that is not required by Directive (EEC) 85/611 and would be unrealistic in practice.

[384]   Ch E, III, 1, Circular 91/75. See also J-C Wolter, 'The Investment Funds Regulations in Luxembourg', in *Les fonds d'investissement, réglementation—fiscalité—évolution*, seminar of 24 and 25 November 1988, Association Luxembourgeoise des Juristes de Banque (ALJB), Institut Universitaire International Luxembourg (IUIL) 86.

[385]   Ch E, III, 1, Circular 91/75.

in a position to ensure that its agents conduct such prior verifications, it must, together with the head office agent based in the Grand Duchy of Luxembourg, organize inspection procedures designed to monitor on a post-trade basis that foreign transactions are regular and lawful.[386]

Day-to-day administration of an FCP's assets

Under the 2002 Act, a depositary is required to carry out all operations concerning the day-to-day administration of the FCP's assets.[387] This includes the collection of dividends, interest, and matured securities; the exercise of option and subscription rights; and, in general, all other transactions covered by the term 'global custody' in respect of a portfolio. Those tasks form part of the safekeeping obligation incumbent on all depositaries of UCIs by virtue of their depositary agreement.[388] **6.347**

According to Circular 91/75, a depositary may delegate such tasks when they concern assets that are not in its own safekeeping. In that case, it may entrust them to the third parties with whom the assets are actually deposited. Its only obligation in that case is to organize its relationships with the third parties in such a way that it is immediately informed of all transactions carried out as part of the day-to-day administration of the assets held by them on behalf of the FCP.[389] **6.348**

Civil liability of the depositary

Rules

The liability of the depositary as safekeeper

The depositary's liability as safekeeper is governed by the provisions of the Civil Code applicable to deposits.[390] **6.349**

Under the Civil Code,[391] the depositary is required to keep safe the assets entrusted to it. Where such assets are securities, the depositary must keep them in safe custody and **6.350**

---

[386] ibid.

[387] Arts 18(1) and 66, 2002 Act.

[388] See P Bourin, 'Droits et obligations du banquier dépositaire de titres', in *Droit bancaire et financier au Luxembourg* (Larcier, 2004) Vol 3, 1263 *et seq.*

[389] Ch E, III, 1, Circular 91/75.

[390] Arts 1915 *et seq*, Civil Code. These Articles have been made applicable to the custody of securities and other fungible financial instruments by Art 11 of the Act of 1 August 2001 on the circulation of securities and other fungible instruments (*Mémorial* A 2003, 2180). See Bourin, (n 388 above) 1248 and 1249; P Mousel and J Fayot, 'La circulation des titres', in *Droit bancaire et financier au Luxembourg* (Larcier, 2004) Vol 3, 1366 and 1367; and, for a more limited application of the custody rules in favour of the rules on hiring services and the administration mandate when the securities in question are paperless, Y Prussen, 'Le régime des titres et instruments fongibles', in *Droit bancaire et financier au Luxembourg* (Larcier, 2004) Vol 3, 1299.

[391] Art 1927, Civil Code.

collect the associated income. As interpreted by the courts,[392] safekeeping of deposited assets entails a reasonable endeavours obligation or even, when safekeeping of the deposit of an asset is remunerated, a 'supra' reasonable endeavours obligation where the burden of proving that it met the required standard rests with the depositary.[393]

6.351   At the UCI's request, the depositary must return the assets deposited with it.[394] They are returned in kind, except when the deposited asset has disappeared as a result of *force majeure*[395] or is fungible.[396] This is an absolute obligation.[397] When a depositary does not return the deposited asset, it can in principle avoid liability only by proving that its failure to do so is due to the fault of a third party or its client[398] or attributable to *force majeure*.[399]

6.352   There are two exceptions to the above principles:

- The depositary may use clauses in the agreement with the depositor in order to limit or even avoid liability. That said, such clauses are void in the event of gross negligence or intentional fault on the part of the depositary.

- The loss of fungible assets (such as cash) in the event of *force majeure* does not release the depositary from its restitution obligation. In that case, it must deliver equivalent assets to the depositor.[400] That principle does not, however, apply to securities deemed to be fungible because they are deposited without mention of numbers or other individual means of identification.[401] The loss of such securities through *force majeure* is borne by the depositor.[402]

6.353   When the depositary in turn deposits the assets entrusted to it with third parties, the foregoing principles continue to apply. However, in such cases the depositary

---

[392]   District Court, Luxembourg, 23 October 1985, No 513/85, *Pas lux*, Vol XXVIII, 51.

[393]   Court of Appeal, 8 November 2000, *Pas lux*, Vol XXXI, 399–403, for the opposite. In such a case, the burden of proof lies with the depositary, which must establish that it has not committed a fault (Bourin (n 388 above) 1259).

[394]   Art 1932, Civil Code.

[395]   In that case, a depositary that has received compensation for the loss is required to return such compensation instead of the destroyed assets (Art 1934, Civil Code).

[396]   In which case the deposit is qualified in principle as an 'irregular deposit'. In the case of the fungible deposit of securities and other financial instruments, however, Art 6 of the Act of 1 August 2001 on the circulation of securities and other fungible instruments (*Mémorial* A 2001, 2180) applies, by virtue of which the depositor of fungible securities preserves an intangible real right to all securities and other financial instruments of the same kind received on deposit or kept on account by his depositary.

[397]   CA, 14 July 1993, *Pas lux*, Vol XXIX, 257.

[398]   ibid CA, 26 March 1997 (1998) 27 *Bull Droit & Banque* 85; Cass Lux, 10 March 1983 (1984) 4 *Bull Droit & Banque* 33–8, note by MP Gillen.

[399]   CA, 14 July 1993 (n 397 above).

[400]   P Malaurie and L Aynès, *Cours de droit civil, Les contrats spéciaux* (Cujas, 1992) para 886.

[401]   Art 5, Act of 1 August 2001 on the circulation of securities and other fungible instruments (*Mémorial* A 2001, 2180).

[402]   Art 13, Act of 1 August 2001, cited above.

can avoid contractual liability only if its client has agreed to the sub-deposit arrangement. Moreover, the depositary may rely on a plea of *force majeure* only if it can show that the circumstances justifying reliance on that plea would have prevented restitution even if it had not delegated its obligations.[403] This last principle nevertheless does not apply to fungible securities. The depositary is only liable towards the UCI for the loss or destruction of fungible securities entrusted to it when the loss or destruction results from facts for which it can be held liable.[404]

The liability of depositary as to its obligation to monitor the assets and check the transactions of a UCI

The depositary's obligation to monitor the assets and check the legality of a UCI's transactions is rooted in the 2002 Act and, as regards the monitoring of the assets, in the Act of 13 February 2007. **6.354**

Pursuant to Directive 85/611, the depositary of a UCITS, because of the particular nature of its tasks, assumes liability in addition to that which it has incurred in respect of the simple safekeeping of assets. Directive 85/611 provides that a depositary, in accordance with the national law of the State in which the UCI's registered office is situated, is to be liable for any loss suffered by the UCI or the unitholders 'as a result of its unjustifiable failure to perform its obligations, or its improper performance of them'.[405] **6.355**

The 2002 Act transposed that Community requirement into Luxembourg law and extended it to the depositaries of UCIs governed by Part II. The Act of 13 February 2007 included it for SIFs.[406] **6.356**

The depositary is under a duty to exercise due skill and care in monitoring a UCI's assets and checking its transactions. The depositary must perform those obligations according to the 'prudent man' rule, with the diligence expected from a reasonably competent and circumspect professional placed in the same circumstances. It only incurs liability for faults proven by the plaintiff.[407] **6.357**

As a matter of public policy, the depositary cannot exculpate itself from responsibility for the performance of its monitoring and control functions. Thus any contractual provision limiting the depositary's liability in this respect it would be null and void.[408] Nor is the depositary's liability lessened by the fact that it has entrusted **6.358**

---

[403] *Encycl Dalloz, Droit civil*, see under 'Dépôt', para 121.
[404] Art 13, Act of 1 August 2001 on the circulation of securities and other fungible instruments (*Mémorial* A 2001, 2182).
[405] Arts 9 and 16, Directive (EEC) 85/611.
[406] Arts 17(1), 35 and 40, Act of 13 February 2007.
[407] See *Parliamentary doc* No 3172, Comments on the Articles, 38 (for FCPs) and 42 (for SICAVs); as regards SIFs, see Lacroix and Tristan, (n 322 above) 73.
[408] Ch E, IV, Circular 91/75.

safekeeping of the assets to a third party.[409] In the case of non-compliance with this monitoring obligation, the depositary cannot avoid liability by showing that the damage caused resulted from the acts or omissions of a sub-depositary.

Enforcement of a depositary's liability

Common funds

6.359 According to the 2002 Act and the Act of 13 February 2007, the liability of an FCP's depositary is invoked through the medium of the management company[410] or, if it fails to act, by the unitholders. Unitholders may exercise their rights to bring proceedings if the management company fails to act against the depositary within three months from service by them of formal notice calling upon it to do so.[411]

Investment companies

6.360 The 2002 Act provides, in respect of investment companies, that the depositary is liable 'to the shareholders',[412] whereas the Act of 13 February 2007 refers to investors.[413] These formulations are interesting when it comes to determining who may invoke liability. It is for the investment company, as the party that has contracted with the depositary, to take action against it. The investment company's management body is the appropriate body to issue proceedings against the depositary for damages. If the management body fails to act, it itself incurs liability and the general meeting of shareholders may appoint more diligent successors. Shareholders or investors do not have a right to act individually, despite the wording of the 2002 Act and of the Act of 13 February 2007, save that they may claim individually against the depositary for specific individual loss.[414] Such loss may not be due to the depositary's improper performance of its obligations vis-à-vis the investment company in respect of which the claimant would properly be the collective body of shareholders. In that respect, investment companies, because of their legal personality, have different rules from FCPs.

---

[409] Arts 17(4), 34(2), 40, 66, 71, and 75(6), 2002 Act; Arts 16(4), 34(3), and 40, Act of 13 February 2007, and *Parliamentary doc* No 5616³, Report of the Finance and Budget Commission, which draws attention to this point in respect of SIFs.

[410] Arts 19(2) and 66, 2002 Act; Art 17(2), Act of 13 February 2007. This is the so-called 'indirect' action provided for by Art 9 of Directive (EEC) 85/611, which leaves Member States the choice between actions for damages brought by the unitholders and actions brought through the intermediary of the management company. The Grand Duchy of Luxembourg has opted for the cumulative use of these two methods.

[411] Arts 19(2) and 66, 2002 Act; Art 17(2), Act of 13 February 2007.

[412] Arts 36, 40, 71, and 75(6), 2002 Act.

[413] Arts 35 and 40, Act of 13 February 2007.

[414] The *Parliamentary documents* accompanying the 1988 Act refer to the general company law provisions by way of explanation for the wording of Art 35 (*Parliamentary doc* No 3172, Comments on the Articles, 42). According to the 1915 Act, shareholders in an SA or SCA do not, in principle, have an individual right to sue a party that has contracted with the company.

The Head Office Agent of a UCI

Principles

The head office functions for a UCI comprise accounting and administrative **6.361** services,[415] which generally covers the following activities:

- keeping the accounts,
- calculating the net asset value,
- issuing and redeeming units or shares,
- keeping the register of unitholders or shareholders,
- collaborating on the preparation of documents to be sent to investors,
- sending the relevant documents to investors, and
- storage of the UCI's essential documents.

The 2002 Act and the Act of 13 February 2007 require the head office of Luxembourg- **6.362** based UCIs to be situated in the Grand Duchy of Luxembourg.[416] Accordingly, they require the human and technical resources necessary for the accounting and administration of such UCIs to be located in the Grand Duchy of Luxembourg.[417]

That requirement transposes a provision of Directive 85/611[418] into Luxembourg **6.363** law. The 2002 Act and the Act of 13 February 2007 go even further, as they apply the same principle to UCIs governed by Part II of the 2002 Act and to SIFs.

UCIs generally do not handle their head office functions themselves. They generally **6.364** assign those tasks to one or more third parties. There are several possible ways[419] in which this may be done. First, the entire head office may be entrusted to a single entity. In the case of an investment company, if entrusted to an approved management company together with intellectual management and distribution, it releases the investment company from the obligations of self-managed companies.[420]

That designated head office entity may itself perform all those functions or it may **6.365** delegate some of them, in which case it must assume responsibility for their coordination and general supervision and be answerable in that regard

A UCI may also entrust the head office functions to several third parties. In that **6.366** case, the UCI must itself coordinate and supervise the performance of all those

---

[415] As regards the head office functions for UCIs, see also C Kremer and M Eisenhuth, 'Banque dépositaire et administration centrale: aspects juridiques et pratiques' (1993) *ALFI Yearbook* 167 *et seq.*
[416] Arts 4 and 64, 2002 Act; Art 3, Act of 13 February 2007. See also Ch D, Circular 91/75.
[417] Chapter D, II, Circular 91/75.
[418] Art 3 provides that, in the case of UCITS, 'Member States must require that the head office be situated in the same Member State as the registered office', ie the Member State in which the registered office of the FCP's management company or of the investment company is situated.
[419] Ch D, II, Circular 91/75.
[420] Art 27, 2002 Act.

tasks, save where it entrusts that general supervision task to a third party. If it does so, the third party becomes the CSSF's counterparty for everything connected with the UCI's head office.

6.367 There is a limit to the extent to which the head office functions may be delegated to separate entities. In any event the delegation must not be prejudicial to the UCI. Excessive separation, which complicates the coordination and general supervision of tasks, is prohibited, as is any unjustified overlap of responsibilities that increases the UCI's management costs.[421] For that reason, the functions of keeping the register of unitholders or shareholders and of issuing and redeeming units or shares must, generally, be entrusted to the same service provider. Similarly, the accounting task may not, in principle, be divided up between two separate entities.

6.368 The head office agent is supervised by the CSSF, either as an approved management company or as a professional of the financial sector governed by the 1993 Act.[422] According to the 1993 Act, a head office agent can provide three types of services.

6.369 The first and main regulated activity is that of financial sector administrative agent. This activity, as defined by the 1993 Act, consists of providing a UCI under Luxembourg or foreign law with the administration services inherent to the activity of the UCI in question.[423] Because the 1993 Act defines this activity as 'connected with or complementary to a financial sector activity', it is not entitled to the European passport provided for by MiFID for professionals of the financial sector. It is nevertheless governed by the prudential rules and rules of conduct, and by the obligation of professional secrecy, laid down by the 1993 Act.[424] Since the Act of 13 July 2007, the share capital that a financial sector administrative agent must have has been reduced from €1,500,000 to €125,000.

---

[421] Ch D, II, Circular 91/78

[422] Art 29–2, 1993 Act.

[423] The activity of administrative agent is sometimes hard to distinguish from that of an IT systems and communications network operator in the financial sector ('OSIRC') as previously defined in Art 29-3, 1993 Act. Pursuant to the Act of 13 July 2007, Art 29-3, was replaced by two distinct provisions, ie Art 29-3 laying down rules for operators of primary computer systems in the financial sector and a new Art 29-4 applicable to operators of secondary computer systems and communication networks in the financial sector. The rationale for such amendment is to differentiate primary IT systems from those which are less essential, ie for which the operational risk is less important. For further detail and examples concerning the distinction between primary IT systems operators (OSIP) and secondary IT systems operators (OSIS), see CSSF Circular 08/350.

[424] Arts 36, and 36-1, and 39 to 41, 1993 Act. CSSF Circular 08/350 provides some guidance as to the application of prudential rules and rules of conduct by administrative agents in the financial sector and other professionals of the financial sector, also called 'support professionals of the financial sector', whose activity is closely related or ancillary to a financial sector activity. In addition to administrative agents in the financial sector, those professionals include company domiciliation agents, client communication agents, primary IT systems operators in the financial sector, secondary IT systems, and communications network operators in the financial sector, and professionals providing company formation and management services.

The second regulated activity carried on by head office agents is communication **6.370**
with the investors in the UCI. The 1993 Act imposes special authorization for
'client communication agents', defined as professionals who are responsible under
Luxembourg or foreign law for providing UCIs with certain investor communication services.[425] Since the Act of 13 July 2007, the share capital required for this
authorization is at least €50,000. Because by definition they carry on an activity
'connected with or complementary to a financial sector activity', client communication agents are not eligible for the European passport either but are governed by
the general standards for professionals of the financial sector contained in the
1993 Act, including the obligation of professional secrecy.[426]

The 1993 Act allows a notable exception to the obligation of professional secrecy for **6.371**
entities approved to act as administrative agents in the financial sector and for client
communication agents. Although such agents are themselves bound by this obligation of secrecy, other professionals communicating with them are released from the
professional secrecy provided for in the 1993 Act, provided the information to be
disclosed is supplied in the framework of a contract for the provision of services.[427]

Lastly, the third type of head office activity requiring specific authorization under **6.372**
the 1993 Act is the function of registrar, defined as 'a professional whose activity
consists in keeping the register of one or several financial instruments. Keeping the
register includes receiving and executing orders relating to those instruments; the
reception and execution of orders are a necessary adjunct to keeping the register'.
Since the Act of 13 July 2007, the legislature considers receiving and executing
orders incidental to the main activity of keeping the register. This clearly affects the
status of such professionals, since they may not be considered investment companies in the meaning of MiFID and be granted the benefit of a European passport.
Their minimum share capital is €125,000. Like administrative agents and client
communication agents, they are subject to the general prudential standards and
rules of conduct laid down by the 1993 Act.

---

[425] Art 29-1, 1993 Act. As defined in the Act of 13 July 2007, the activity of client communication
agents consists in providing one or more of the following services: (1) the production, in tangible form
or in the form of electronic data, of confidential documents intended for the personal attention of
clients of credit institutions, insurance companies, reinsurance companies, investors in UCIs or con-
tributors, members, or beneficiaries of pension funds; (2) the maintenance in archives or the destruction of the documents referred to under point (1) above; (3) the communication to the persons referred
to in the first point of documents or information relating to their assets and to the services offered by
the professional in question; (4) the handling of mails giving access to confidential data concerning the
persons referred to under point (1) above; (5) the consolidation, pursuant to an express mandate, of
positions held with diverse financial professionals by the persons referred to in the first point.
[426] See in particular Arts 36, 36-1, and 39 to 41, 1993 Act; CSSF Circular 08/350.
[427] Art 41(5), 1993 Act; see also Circular CSSF 06/240 of 22 March 2006 on the administrative and
accounting organisation; subcontracting of IT services and particulars about services requiring authorization as a support professional of the financial sector, Arts 29-1, 29-2, and 29-3 of the amended Act of 5
April 1993 on the financial sector; modification of IT subcontracting conditions of foreign branches.

6.373   It is possible to obtain a general authorization covering all three of the above activities. This is the authorization to act as a transfer agent. Under the 1993 Act, this authorization automatically entails the authorization to provide services as a financial sector administrative agent and as a client communication agent. Even if the head office agent prefers not to keep the register, it can opt for the status of financial sector administrative agent, which entails authorization to act as a client communication agent. In contrast, authorization to act as a client communication agent does not allow such an agent to carry on any other activity and does not entail authorization to engage in the other two activities.

6.374   The requirement that the head office be located in the Grand Duchy of Luxembourg does not rule out the use of an electronic data interchange network. In such cases, the data processing unit may be situated outside the Grand Duchy of Luxembourg. However, the head office agent must obtain the assurances listed in Circular 91/75[428] and, if the agent is a professional of the financial sector, in Circular 96/126 of 11 April 1996 on administrative and accounting organization, as amended by Circular 05/178. When a head office subcontractor has the associated status of professional of the financial sector, many of these assurances are automatically considered to have been satisfied.[429]

6.375   As a general rule, subcontracting must be covered by a detailed service agreement and detailed specifications, *inter alia*, setting out the responsibilities of both parties, aspects of subcontracting in tiers, internal and external control, continuity, and termination events.

6.376   These points must have been discussed and validated by the professional's board of directors. Subcontracting operations must be monitored on a daily basis by an employee appointed specifically for this purpose.

6.377   The operation of the head office must remain relatively independent from any foreign processing unit. It must be able to continue operating normally in the case of a breakdown at the processing unit, a breakdown in the means of communication, or other exceptional event. Similarly, the head office must at all times be able to transfer the subcontracted services to another provider or even to resume their management in-house.

6.378   When data management is delegated to a processing centre in a foreign country, it must belong to the same group as the head office entity. More precisely, it must be its parent company, one of its fellow subsidiaries, or another entity of the group (in the latter case it must also be specialized in data processing). The foreign delegate must also be subject to prudential control. This does not necessarily mean

---

[428] Ch D, III, 1, Circular 91/75.
[429] Section 4.5.2.4, Circular 05/178.

that the subcontractor must itself run or own the processing centre. The counter-party delegate is contractually responsible to the head office for the data processing activities carried on by the processing centre.

Circular 05/178 subjects delegation of data processing to many requirements, which reflect four main criteria. **6.379**

First, the head office agent must at all times be able to enter and retrieve data from the network. It must have immediate and unlimited access to information about the UCI administered by it. Similarly, it must be able to intervene directly in the processing of that information. At the end of each day, it must receive the daily balance of all accounts and all accounting movements.[430] **6.380**

Data is, in principle, entered in the network from the Grand Duchy of Luxembourg. However, a UCI's foreign representatives may enter data about transactions into the network. In that case, the head office agent must ensure that such representatives can access only information that is not protected by professional secrecy and which is necessary for the performance of their respective functions. Various mechanisms must also permit the UCI concerned to check management transactions in the light of the 2002 Act, its constitutive documents, and its prospectus. The IT liaison itself must be audited by the independent auditor and by the financial sector professional's internal audit department.[431] **6.381**

Secondly, access to the network by the various parties involved must not weaken the confidentiality of data relating to a UCI. A UCI's head office agent must ensure that there are adequate protection mechanisms in that respect.[432] No client name may be entered or recorded in a network to which third parties other than related professionals of the financial sector can have access. **6.382**

Thirdly, a UCI's head office agent must also be conversant with and check the software used by the network. It must be acquainted with the operations of the processing unit.[433] **6.383**

Lastly, the agent is responsible for storing the data recorded at the processing unit. When a processing unit is situated abroad, the data must be transferred at least once a week[434] to data storage media located in the Grand Duchy of Luxembourg.[435] **6.384**

---

[430] ibid Section 4.5.2.2.
[431] ibid.
[432] As regards confidentiality, see also Ch D, III, 3, Circular 91/75.
[433] Section 4.5.2.2 which refers to section 4.5.2.1, Circular 05/178.
[434] Or each time a UCI's assets are valued, if that happens more frequently (Ch D, III, 1, Circular 91/75).
[435] Such media must also be usable in the Grand Duchy of Luxembourg (Ch D, III, 1, Circular 91/75).

6.385 When the head office subcontracts certain tasks to a foreign entity, such subcontracting may be subject to less numerous constraints in the case of a SIF. Those constraints are based on the relevant rules established for SICARs. Each case is judged separately by the CSSF. However, the following conditions must be met as a minimum requirement:

(1) the head office must retain responsibility for, and coordinate, such delegation;

(2) the delegate must have adequate human and technical resources to carry out the tasks entrusted to it;

(3) the head office must have immediate and direct access to data processed abroad by the subcontracting entity and must control such data;

(4) the CSSF and the shareholders must be informed on the structure set up; and

(5) a seamless information flow between the relevant parties must be ensured.

Exercise of the main head office functions

Accounting

6.386 The accounts of Luxembourg-based UCIs must be kept in the Grand Duchy of Luxembourg. That constraint does not rule out the use of an electronic data interchange network for processing accounting data. However, the head office of a UCI other than a SIF must have the necessary resources in the Grand Duchy of Luxembourg to provide the processing unit of that network with information. In that case, the information in question may be processed by a unit located in a foreign country.[436]

Calculation of the net asset value

6.387 A foreign electronic data interchange network may be used to calculate the net asset value on the above-mentioned conditions. However, there are three types of operations that must be carried out in the Grand Duchy of Luxembourg, namely the charging, pro-rating, and provisioning operations necessary to finalize calculation of the net asset value. According to Circular 91/75,[437] this requirement stems from the head office agent's responsibility for the accuracy of the financial information relating to the UCI concerned.

6.388 In that respect, Circular 02/77 draws attention to the minimum guidelines to be followed in the event of errors in the calculation of net asset value.[438]

---

[436] Ch D, III, 1, Circular 91/75 and Section 4.5.2.2, Circular 05/178.
[437] Ch D, III, 1, Circular 91/75.
[438] Section I, Circular 02/77; see 8.92 *et seq* below.

Issue and redemption of units or shares

The head office agent's tasks in connection with the issue and redemption of units   **6.389**
or shares are as follows:[439]

(1) determining the issue and redemption prices of the UCI's units or shares;
(2) preparing the subscription and redemption forms;
(3) drawing up unit or share certificates if such certificates are issued; and
(4) sending those documents to the investors.

A UCI may appoint intermediaries to perform the foregoing functions but may   **6.390**
not provide that the intermediaries are the sole entities responsible for the receipt
and processing of subscription and redemption orders. Investors can contact the
UCI directly, which will then forward their subscription and redemption requests
to its head office. A UCI's prospectus must systematically inform investors of this
option.[440]

In accepting and processing subscription and redemption orders, a UCI's head   **6.391**
office is governed by the rules on the prevention of money laundering,[441] which
require the identity of any investor in a UCI to be verified.[442]

Keeping the register of unitholders or shareholders

In FCPs[443] and investment companies incorporated in the form of an SA[444] or   **6.392**
SCA,[445] the ownership of registered shares is evidenced by an entry in the share register. SARLs[446] must also keep a share register. In this case, ownership of registered
shares is not evidenced by an entry in such a register but by a personal investment
certificate.[447]

Under the 1915 Act, the share register is to be kept at the company's registered   **6.393**
office if the company is incorporated in the form of an SA[448] or SCA.[449] There is
no similar requirement for SARLs or FCPs. However, Circular 91/75 requires
shares or units to be registered, redeemed, and converted in the Grand Duchy

---

[439] Ch D, III, 2.1, Circular 91/75.
[440] ibid.
[441] See 10.02 *et seq* below.
[442] For more details of the standards and the procedures imposed by them, see 10.21 *et seq*
below.
[443] Arts 8(2) and 66, 2002 Act; Art 7(2), Act of 13 February 2007.
[444] Art 40, 1915 Act.
[445] Art 103, which refers to Art 40, 1915 Act.
[446] Article 185, 1915 Act.
[447] ibid Art 188.
[448] ibid Art 39.
[449] Art 103, which refers to Art 39, 1915 Act.

of Luxembourg.[450] Moreover, the register must at all times be available in the Grand Duchy of Luxembourg.

6.394 While all this does not rule out the use of an electronic data interchange network in which foreign distributors can enter information about subscription and redemption orders received, it is the head office agent that retrieves such information from the network in order to update the register.

Collaborating on the preparation of documents to be sent to investors

6.395 The head office agent must provide intellectual assistance with the preparation of the prospectus, financial reports, and other documents intended for investors. The services of foreign experts may be used only on a temporary basis.[451]

6.396 The head office agent may also provide physical assistance with the preparation of the above-mentioned documents, or may delegate that function to foreign entities. This task does not have to be carried out in the Grand Duchy of Luxembourg. For example, the printing of documents may be entrusted to foreign firms.[452]

Sending the documents to investors

6.397 In principle, the prospectus, financial reports and other investor documents must be sent from the Grand Duchy of Luxembourg. That rule reflects the head office agent's obligation of confidentiality. The head office agent may not send data concerning investors who have placed their orders directly in the Grand Duchy of Luxembourg or whose name is entered in the share register to any third party where this would constitute a breach of its professional secrecy.[453]

6.398 Exceptionally, documents may be sent from a foreign country, subject to supervision by the head office agent[454] and compliance with the agent's obligation of banking secrecy. For example, data concerning the registered shareholders of a SICAV could be sent to one of the head office's foreign correspondents. Under company law, such a transmission of information appears to be authorized when the foreign correspondent is itself a shareholder. That status gives it access to the register and to the information that it contains.[455] The same applies when the correspondent also distributes the UCI's units, insofar as its functions entitle it to know the identity of the investor whose name is recorded in the register.

---

[450] Ch D, III, 3, Circular 91/75.
[451] ibid Ch D, III, 4.
[452] ibid.
[453] ibid Ch D, III, 5.
[454] ibid.
[455] Art 39, 1915 Act.

Storage of a UCI's essential documents

A UCI's essential documents must be stored in the Grand Duchy of Luxembourg. **6.399**
That means that documents connected with foreign transactions must be sent
immediately to the Grand Duchy of Luxembourg.[456]

The documents to which this obligation applies are those necessary for the prepa- **6.400**
ration of the accounts and inventories and a UCI's deeds of title and claims. They
also include the documents used as the basis for allocating outstanding units or
shares. Lastly, they include the documents necessary to protect a UCI's general
interests, such as contracts between the UCI and its service providers.[457]

Prevention and elimination of late trading

Late trading, or late acceptance of an order, consists of the processing of a subscription, **6.401**
redemption, or conversion order issued after the cut-off time for accepting orders.[458]
This practice would allow investors to subscribe or redeem the units or shares of
UCIs with the benefit of information known only after expiry of the time limit for
acceptance of subscriptions and redemptions. In other words, such investors are
permitted to trade on a historic basis but with knowledge which only became
available after the dealing deadline by reference to which the dealing net asset
value was calculated.

Late acceptance of orders is in breach of the prospectus and, to a certain extent, the **6.402**
articles of incorporation or management regulations of the UCI in question. It
results in inequality between investors in that some have been able to take advantage of information not available when other investors were required to place their
orders. This has therefore never been tolerated in Luxembourg. Actions brought
by the US authorities[459] have nevertheless shown the extent to which it had become
commonplace and could be damaging. In order to remove any doubt about its
position and to strengthen prevention of this practice, CSSF Circular 04/146
imposes certain requirements on UCIs and their service providers in this regard.

---

[456] Ch D, III, 1, Circular 91/75.
[457] ibid.
[458] Circular 04/146.
[459] In 2002 and 2003, the US investment fund industry was seriously affected by many rumours
that late trading and market timing activities were widespread. The seriousness of these allegations
and their impact on investors prompted the Securities Exchange Commission and certain States to
sue the administrators of investment funds and their promoters. Investigations into US investment
funds have revealed that arbitragers had been exploiting the pricing weaknesses and inefficiencies
of investment funds for many years. The losses caused by these forms of arbitrage and late trading
amounted to US$4 billion a year according to an American study. For further information about
these phenomena, see the ALFI report entitled 'Fair Value Pricing and Arbitrage Protection', available at <http://www.alfi.lu> under the heading 'Publications'.

6.403   First of all, the time limit for accepting orders must be very clear in the prospectuses of UCIs. For example, it may not be described as 'after business hours'. It must be set in such a way that the net assest value is not and cannot be determined before or during its occurrence. The CSSF requires prospectuses to state that subscriptions, redemptions and conversions take place at unknown net asset value.[460]

6.404   As repeated many times in Circular 04/146, the criterion for determining late trading is the moment of issue of a subscription or redemption order. The order itself may be received after the deadline for accepting orders. It can, for instance, happen that orders issued before the time limit for acceptance reach a UCI's transfer agent after this time due to the time needed to route them through the UCI's distribution network. In this case, they may be processed at the net asset value applicable at the time of issue, provided they reach the transfer agent reasonably quickly. In such cases, the CSSF also requires the UCI to make sure that each distributor and sub-distributor provides a contractual undertaking that they will only send the transfer agent, orders for processing which were issued by the relevant investor prior to the time limit applicable for calculation of the relevant net asset value.[461] Sometimes an order is processed or even corrected after the time limit for acceptance. This is not a case of late trading if the order was issued before the time limit.[462]

6.405   The CSSF makes the transfer agent a major player in the prevention of late trading. The transfer agent has primary responsibility for preventing this practice from occurring, and must implement adequate prevention and control procedures. The independent auditor of the transfer agent or the UCI once again acts as a conduit for the supervisory authorities. Under Circular 04/146 he is expressly obliged to notify the CSSF if the transfer agent does not comply with the relevant time limits for accepting orders.[463] More generally, UCIs and all professionals supervised by the CSSF may not allow or practise late trading. The CSSF also imposes an obligation to report instances of late trading.[464]

6.406   Employees of a UCI's agents are given particular attention insofar as they may have access to inside information and be able to use such information to their personal advantage. Stakeholders must implement measures to prevent such conduct. The specific measures are not described in great detail in the circular and are therefore difficult to determine. Surveillance—even with permission—of transactions concluded by employees could run contrary to the rules on protection of privacy provided for in the European Human Rights Convention[465] and the Act of 11 August 1982 on

---

[460]   Section I(a), Circular 04/146.
[461]   ibid.
[462]   ibid.
[463]   ibid Section III.
[464]   ibid Section I(b).
[465]   Art 8, European Human Rights Convention, signed in Rome on 4 November 1950 under the auspices of the Council of Europe.

the protection of privacy.[466] The Act of 2 August 2002 on the protection of individuals in respect of the processing of personal data[467] must also be taken into account.

Late trading is considered a default by the errant party and entitles investors adversely affected by it to compensation. In his annual report, the UCI's auditor will evaluate whether the proposed compensation is adequate.[468]   **6.407**

Prevention and elimination of market timing

Market timing, or net asset value-based arbitrage, enables an investor to speculate in the very short term by exploiting time differences or inefficiencies in calculating net asset value. Market timing is similar to late trading. It enables the investor to speculate on the impact, on the net asset value of a UCI's securities, of events and information known to him at the time he placed his order, in the knowledge that such events and information have not yet been factored into the calculation of the net asset value applicable to his order.   **6.408**

Even if this practice does not breach any provision in a UCI's prospectus or documents, it has to be prohibited because it distorts market conditions and generates high transaction costs for the UCI. Like late trading, it is governed by particular prevention rules imposed by the CSSF in Circular 04/146.   **6.409**

There are many ways to avoid this practice. First, net asset value should be calculated according to the most recent prices. Moreover, subscription and redemption orders should not be accepted after calculation of net asset value has started, and ideally even after valuation of the fund's assets. Circular 04/146 specifies that the time limit for accepting orders, the valuation point at which the prices used for calculating net asset value are taken, and the time when net asset value is calculated must be set in such a way as to minimize the risk of arbitrage   **6.410**

Certain UCIs are more exposed to net asset value-based arbitrage than others, owing to the nature of their distribution network and the countries in which they invest.[469] Other UCIs may suffer from liquidity arbitrage due to the very low number of transactions in their portfolio securities (for example small caps and high yield bonds whose latest market price may not reflect fair value). Such UCIs are subject to more stringent obligations in order to discourage and prevent this practice. Their boards of directors will typically be vested with responsibility for adopting adequate measures, such as the introduction of subscription,   **6.411**

---

[466] Act of 11 August 1982 on the protection of privacy (*Mémorial* A 1982, 1840 *et seq*).

[467] Act of 2 August 2002 on the protection of persons in connection with personal data processing (*Mémorial* A 2002, 1836 *et seq*), as amended.

[468] Section III, Circular 04/146.

[469] This is especially the case with UCIs investing in countries with large time differences with Europe, such as America and East Asia.

redemption, and conversion fees when calculating the net assest value in order to discourage arbitrage or adjustment. It is advisable to monitor transactions in the securities of such UCIs more closely and as necessary to value their portfolio securities at fair value. The conducting persons of UCIs must also ensure that agents involved in the distribution of UCIs provide an undertaking that they will block transactions known or suspected to indicate market timing.[470]

6.412 Lastly, the effectiveness of the implemented procedures and controls is verified by the UCI's auditor, who states his opinion in his audit report.[471] The same report discusses the matter of compensation for investors harmed by this practice and states whether the proposed compensation is sufficient.

6.413 A UCI's prospectus must clearly show the conducting persons' intentions in this respect. It must point out that market timing is not authorized, that the orders of investors suspected of this practice may be rejected, and that any other measure may be adopted to protect investor interests.[472]

6.414 UCIs and their agents may neither encourage nor aid such practices, and the CSSF invites these stakeholders to report such practices to them promptly, with full supporting details.[473]

6.415 The obligation to prevent arbitrage is not expressed as an absolute obligation. It is not a performance obligation since UCIs cannot exercise total and infallible control over the reasons for and processes involved in subscription and redemption of their units or shares. Circular 04/146 stipulates a reasonable endeavours obligation. A UCI may be required to show that it has taken all reasonable measures in its power to prevent net asset value-based arbitrage. UCIs must not allow transactions suspected of involving market timing and must act within the limits of their resources to eliminate such practices.

Distributors of Units of UCIs

Principles

6.416 The distributor of a UCI's units is the intermediary charged by the UCI with collecting and, as the case may be, executing subscription and redemption orders for its units.[474] Such a contractual tie with one or more UCIs distinguishes it from a broker, which also handles buy and sell orders for financial instruments but which does not act on behalf of a UCI. The broker acts only at the request of a UCI's investors.

---

[470] Section I(a) Circular 04/146.
[471] ibid Section III.
[472] ibid Section I(a).
[473] ibid Section I(b).
[474] Ch D, III, 2.2.1, Circular 91/75.

In the Grand Duchy of Luxembourg, distribution of the shares and units of UCIs is **6.417** specifically regulated by the 1993 Act.[475] Distributors of shares and units of UCIs are, moreover, governed by MiFID. In that respect, they are subject to certain constraints, in exchange for which they are entitled to a European passport authorizing them to provide cross-border services and to establish branches within the EEA.

There is no restriction as to the countries in which the distributors of the units of **6.418** Luxembourg-based UCIs may be situated. However, the application of certain international anti-money laundering standards is an important factor for certain countries.[476]

For distributors situated outside the EEA, the CSSF ensures that they have **6.419** adequate financial resources and are sufficiently specialized in that profession to act with competence.

Distributors of shares and units of UCIs may provide UCIs with three types of **6.420** services. First of all, they may limit their service to acting as intermediaries between the UCI and investors. In that case, they are only involved in collecting subscription and redemption orders from investors. They may also manage the entire relationship between a UCI and the investors who buy the securities. In that case, they act as nominees and are involved as shareholders or unitholders vis-à-vis the UCI; the UCI deals only with them. They are responsible for forwarding information and, as the case may be, requesting voting instructions from their clients. Lastly, they may decide to buy the UCI's securities themselves in order to sell them directly to their clients. Conversely, they may buy such securities directly from interested investors and, as the case may be, request the UCI to redeem them. In that case, they are considered to be market makers. Each of those three types of service is governed by specific rules, which are examined below.

Conditions common to all distributors

Even where a distributor does not act as either a nominee or a market maker, it **6.421** may be appointed by a UCI to provide the following services:

(1) assistance with marketing the UCI's units or shares;
(2) receiving subscription and redemption orders from investors in its capacity as the UCI's agent;
(3) receiving and making payments connected with orders received;
(4) delivering or sending to investors bearer units or shares from its stock.

Such services are generally cumulative.

---

[475] Art 24-7, 1993 Act.
[476] For details concerning this point, see 10.10 below.

6.422 Circular 91/75 deals with a key concern as regards the handling of subscription and redemption orders by distributors, namely the forwarding of the relevant information to the head office agent appointed to execute such orders. It distinguishes between subscription and redemption documentation generally and documents relating to the identity of investors.[477]

6.423 Subscription and redemption documents do not necessarily have to be routed to the head office agent in the Grand Duchy of Luxembourg. That said, the agent must systematically be able to obtain such documents if it so wishes.[478]

6.424 In spite of the foregoing, there is one item of information that the head office agent of a UCI must know: the identity of registered shareholders and unitholders. Their names are recorded in the register of shareholders or unitholders. In contrast, the identity of the holders of bearer units or shares may remain unknown,[479] which facilitates the distributor's work. The distributor may offset subscription and redemption orders for the units or shares of the same UCI and send a global instruction to the UCI concerned. In that case, it acts as a subscriber from the viewpoint of the UCI's head office agent. The drawback of this approach is that it does not enable the head office to identify investors entitled to compensation in the case of errors in calculating net asset value or violation of investment restrictions, or to value the amount owed to each of these investors. In this case, the head office must make sure it has easy access to the information needed to perform its obligations under Circular 02/77.

6.425 Certain distributors may be called upon to receive and make payments in connection with subscription and redemption orders received by them. Circular 91/75 authorizes them in that case to pool and offset individual payments vis-à-vis the head office agent.[480]

Conditions applicable to distributors in their capacity as nominees

6.426 Nominees offer investors a more extensive range of services than the distributors discussed above. They agree to become shareholders or unitholders in the UCI in which their client investors have invested. As a result, the UCI does not know the identity of such clients and does not send them any documentation. The nominee informs its clients of the events with which it is acquainted in its

---

[477] Ch D, III, 2.2.1, Circular 91/75.

[478] Such access enables it, in particular, to identify the investors who are entitled to compensation as a result of an error in the calculation of the NAV, pursuant to Circular 02/77.

[479] Unless the head office agent requests the documents relating to the subscription and redemption of bearer units, in which case it is given the name and address of subscribers who have opted for bearer units.

[480] Ch D, III, 2.2.1, Circular 91/75.

capacity as a shareholder or unitholder and, where necessary, asks them for voting instructions.

As defined in Circular 02/77, the nominee is an 'intermediary between investors **6.427** and the UCI of their choice who offers nominee services that investors may use on the conditions set out in the UCI's prospectus'.[481]

Circular 91/75 authorizes Luxembourg-based UCIs to use nominees for distribu- **6.428** tion purposes. In that case, the promoters of the UCI concerned must ensure that the nominee has sufficient expertise and experience. Moreover, the promoters must set out contractually the respective obligations of the UCI, the nominee, the head office agent, and the investors. In that respect, their duty is to ensure that the contracts between investors and nominees contain a termination clause allowing the investors at any time to demand the return of the units or shares held on their behalf by the nominee.[482] They must further make sure that the nominee agrees to send the investors any compensation due for errors in calculating the net asset value or for infringement of the investment restrictions.[483] In practice, this kind of undertaking may be difficult to obtain.

Investors must be appropriately informed when a UCI decides to use the services **6.429** of a nominee. The nominee's role is described in the prospectus, which must also notify investors of their right to invest directly in the UCI without using the services of the nominee.[484]

The right of investors to address themselves directly to a UCI and, as necessary, to **6.430** terminate their agreement with a nominee does not apply where the services of that intermediary are indispensable or even mandatory by law, regulations, or binding practices.[485]

Conditions applicable to distributors in their capacity as market makers

Market makers do not act as intermediaries between the UCI and the investors. **6.431** They buy the UCI's units or shares in their own name and at their own risk for subsequent sale to investors. Conversely, they buy units or shares from investors and subsequently request redemption from the UCI.

---

[481] Sections I, 3(c) and II, Circular 02/77. The reference to the prospectus in this definition seems to rule out situations in which the interposition of a nominee has not been organized by the UCI itself but has been arranged at the investor's request without any participation by the UCI. In this case, the requirements imposed by Circular 02/77 on UCIs and their agents should normally not apply.
[482] Ch D, III, 2.2.2, Circular 91/75.
[483] Sections I, 3(c), and II, Circular 02/77.
[484] Ch D, III, 2.2.2, Circular 91/75.
[485] ibid.

6.432 The CSSF is adamant that this type of service should not harm investors in any way and therefore requires compliance with the following principles:[486]

(1) the prospectus must clearly describe the role of the market makers;

(2) the terms on which units or shares are sold to and bought from the market makers may not be less favourable than those applicable to the direct subscription and redemption of units or shares from the UCI;

(3) the market makers may not act as the counterparty for subscriptions or redemptions without the express permission of the investor originating the transaction. That effectively precludes purely speculative transactions without prior orders from clients.

6.433 There must be an efficient communication system between the market maker and the UCI's head office agent. The UCI's head office agent must be fully informed of transactions involving registered units or shares so that it can update the register and send investment certificates or confirmations to new investors.[487]

---

[486] ibid Ch D, III, 2.2.3.
[487] ibid.

7

MARKETING THE UNITS OF UNDERTAKINGS FOR COLLECTIVE INVESTMENT IN THE GRAND DUCHY OF LUXEMBOURG

The legal rules governing the marketing of a UCI's units differ according to **7.01** whether the UCI in question is a Luxembourg-based UCI or a foreign UCI. In the latter case, an additional distinction is made between UCIs governed by Directive 85/611 and other UCIs.

7.02 The marketing of units or shares by a Luxembourg-based UCI may be subject to certain provisions of, and regulations made under, the Act of 10 July 2005. These requirements are examined separately below. However, UCIs may alternatively be governed with respect to public offerings and admission to trading on a regulated market by the specific laws on UCIs. This topic requires a general introduction to the Act of 10 July 2005 and a description of its interaction with the 2002 Act and the Act of 13 February 2007.

Marketing the Units of Luxembourg-based UCIs

General presentation of the Act of 10 July 2005

7.03 The Act of 10 July 2005 is rooted in Directive 2003/71 and the Community objective of facilitating access by businesses to investment capital. To achieve this objective, Directive 2003/71 introduced the principle of a single passport for a prospectus issued in connection with an application for admission of securities to trading on a regulated market or of a public offering.

7.04 The Act of 10 July 2005 nevertheless does not just transpose the European standards. Article 1 of the Act specifies that the Act provides the legal framework for the 'drawing up, approval and distribution of the prospectus to be published when securities are offered to the public or admitted to trading on a securities market' whether or not these activities are referred to in Directive 2003/71.

7.05 The first parts of the Act of 10 July 2005 deal with the transposition of the Directive. Part I defines the legal terminology used and Part II focuses on transposition of Directive 2003/71. It contains a detailed description of the requirements applicable to the prospectus to be published when securities are offered to the public or admitted to trading on a regulated market (Part II, Chapter 1) and provides information about the conditions applicable to the prospectus passport (Part II, Chapter 2).

7.06 The Act of 10 July 2005 also provides for a particular legal framework for public offerings and admissions to trading on a regulated market not covered by Directive 2003/71 (Part III). This framework applies, *inter alia*, to issues of securities guaranteed by a Member State or one of its regional or local authorities, and securities issued by associations or non-profit organizations in order to raise the funds needed to achieve their not-for-profit purposes. Part III also governs offerings whose total amount is too low to be covered by Directive 2003/71, ie offerings which do not exceed €2,500,000 over twelve months.

7.07 Lastly, the Act of 10 July 2005 applies to securities admitted to a Luxembourg exchange which is not included in the list of regulated markets published by the Commission of the European Communities. In Luxembourg there is currently only one such market, the EuroMTF, which is operated by the Luxembourg Stock Exchange. As regards the admission of securities to trading on such market, the Act of 10 July 2005 refers primarily to the operating rules relating to the market operator in Luxembourg, ie to the internal rules of the Luxembourg Stock Exchange with respect to the EuroMTF.

The Act of 10 July 2005 is a framework law in that it provides a general legal frame-   **7.08**
work but depends upon other texts for its interpretation and implementation. Thus, at a European level, the following should be taken into consideration: Commission Regulation (EC) 809/2004 of 29 April 2004, Commission Regulation (EC) 1787/2006 of 4 December 2006, and Commission Regulation (EC) 211/2007 of 27 February 2007 which implement Directive 2003/71.

Several texts allow for a better understanding of the Act of 10 July 2005 and the   **7.09**
relevant EU regulations. In Luxembourg, the CSSF has issued several circulars, including Circular 05/225 on the concept of 'public securities offering' as defined in the Act of 10 July 2005. This Circular was followed by Circulars 05/226 and 06/267, which provide general guidance on the Act's requirements with respect to prospectuses and the CSSF's requirements with respect to the filing of documents and notices for public securities offerings and for admission of securities to trading on a regulated market.

To provide participants with more and better information on public offerings and   **7.10**
admission to trading on regulated markets, the CSSF has published on its website a document on the interpretation of the Act of 10 July 2005, entitled 'The New "Prospectus Regime" in 40 Questions and Answers'.[1]

At EU level, the Committee of European Securities Regulators provides opinions   **7.11**
and recommendations for a consistent interpretation of Directive 2003/71 by the different Member States.[2] Those opinions and recommendations are quite often very useful in interpreting the Act of 10 July 2005.

Lastly, as the title indicates, the Act of 10 July 2005 applies to securities prospec-   **7.12**
tuses. It does not govern the admission of securities as such to official listing or their admission to trading on a regulated market. The specific provisions applying to listing and admission to trading are laid down in the rules applicable to the market on which the securities are admitted to listing and trading.

---

[1] The number of questions and answers in this document has gradually increased, making this title a little too modest compared with the actual contents, which have been further enhanced with an additional section.

[2] The CESR's recommendations for the consistent implementation of the European Commission's regulation on prospectuses No 809/2004, CESR/05-054b, document available at <http://www.cesr-eu.org>. See also the 'Frequently asked questions' regarding Prospectuses: common positions agreed by CESR Members, CESR/06-296b, available at the same address.

7.13 In addition to the concept of a single passport, Directive 2003/71 introduces the concept of home Member State, namely the state in which the provisions of the local legislation transposing Directive 2003/71 will apply and the financial regulatory authorities of which will be responsible for the approval of prospectuses issued by funds entitled to the single passport.

7.14 The Act of 10 July 2005 also applies to prospectuses drafted in connection with a public offering of securities or an admission to trading on a regulated market for Luxembourg issuers.

7.15 An issuer's home Member State is determined by reference to its registered office and the type of securities offered or for which admission to trading on a regulated market is sought.

7.16 The passport contemplated by Directive 2003/71 is also limited to the prospectus. It is not associated with the product, ie the securities described in the prospectus. This reduces its scope considerably compared to the scope for UCITS. The possession of a passport for a prospectus does not in itself permit the making of a public offering in the European Union, nor does it guarantee admission to trading on a regulated market in a Member State. Each national authority and each market operator remains free to subject the authorization to offer securities publicly or admission of securities to trading on a regulated market to additional conditions, provided they are compatible with the Community principle of proportionality. The Community legislature is clear on this point: 'The mutual recognition of a public-offer prospectus and admission to official listings does not in itself confer a right to admissions'.[3] The competent authorities are expressly authorized to refuse admission of a security to an official market if its admission would be contrary to the interests of investors having regard to the issuer's situation.[4] The passport introduced by Directive 2003/71 grants the issuer or the seller of a security only the right to use a single prospectus for marketing operations in several Member States.

7.17 That said, such a passport can be used easily and rapidly under Directive 2003/71. At the request of the issuer or the author of the prospectus, the authority in the

---

[3] Directive (EC) 2001/34 of the European Parliament and of the Council of 28 May 2001 on the admission of securities to official stock exchange listing and on information to be published on those securities ([2001] OJ L184/8), as amended by Directive (EC) 2003/71, 17th recital. Also see Directive 2003/71, 15th recital: 'The disclosure requirements of the present Directive do not prevent a Member State or a competent authority or an exchange through its rule book to impose other particular requirements in the context of admission to trading of securities on a regulated market (notably regarding corporate governance). Such requirements may not directly or indirectly restrict the drawing up, the content and the dissemination of a prospectus approved by a competent authority'.
[4] Art 11.2, Directive (EC) 2001/34 of the European Parliament and of the Council of 28 May 2001 on the admission of securities to official stock exchange listing and on information to be published on those securities ([2001] OJ L184/8), as amended by Directive (EC) 2003/71.

home State provides the authority in the host State with an approval certificate attesting that the prospectus was drawn up in accordance with Directive 2003/71, together with a copy of the prospectus and, as applicable, a summary translation.[5] When this information has been provided to the host authority the prospectus may be used in the host State without any requirement for additional approval in that State. The competent local authorities in the host State may not require additions or adjustments to this document.[6]

Interaction of the Act of 10 July 2005 with the 2002 Act and the Act of 13 February 2007

The Act of 10 July 2005 applies in certain circumstances to public offerings **7.18** and admissions to trading on a regulated market of securities issued by UCIs. Such transactions are generally only governed by the 2002 Act or the Act of 13 February 2007.

Criteria for the application of the two Acts

Efforts to determine which situations are covered by which Act may be confusing **7.19** for professionals working with UCIs, since they do not use any of the ordinary classifications for UCIs, regardless of whether a UCI is organized in the form of an FCP or an investment company, is governed by Part I or Part II of the 2002 Act, or has a SIF status or not. Application of the Act of 10 July 2005 or of the law on UCIs is subject to different criteria, as indicated by three preliminary questions dealt with below.

Status of the UCI in question: closed-end or other than the closed-end type

The first question deals with a UCI's status and whether the UCI wishing to make **7.20** a public securities offering or seeking admission to trade on a regulated market is a closed-end UCI or a UCI other than the closed-end type. This question requires consideration of the concepts of closed-end UCIs and UCIs other than the closed-end type within the meaning of the Act of 10 July 2005.

A UCI other than the closed-end type or an 'open-end UCI' is defined in the Act of **7.21** 10 July 2005 and Directive 2003/71 as a UCI meeting the following cumulative criteria: (1) its object is to proceed with collective investment of capital provided by the public; (2) its operation is subject to the principle of risk spreading; and (3) its units are directly or indirectly redeemed or repaid out of its assets at the holder's request. UCIs governed by Part I of the 2002 Act are therefore always

---

[5] Art 18, Directive (EC) 2003/71; Art 19, Act of 10 July 2005.
[6] Art 17, Directive (EC) 2003/71; Art 18, Act of 10 July 2005.

UCIs other than the closed-end type. A great number of UCIs governed by Part II of the 2002 Act and the Act of 13 February 2007 must also be considered UCIs other than the closed-end type in that they market their units to the public[7] and allow their investors to redeem their units on request.

7.22 The definition of a closed-end UCI is based on the definition of a UCI other than the closed-end type given in the Act of 10 July 2005. The CSSF specifies therefore that it is relevant only within the framework of the Act of 10 July 2005. It does not affect the interpretation of provisions in the 2002 Act and the Act of 13 February 2007 other than those determining the scope of application of the relevant Act compared with the Act of 10 July 2005.

7.23 Under Circular 05/225, the CSSF specifies that a closed-end UCI is a UCI in which investors do not have any right to redeem their units. A UCI authorizing redemption at an investor's unilateral request even only once in its existence should be considered a UCI other than the closed-end type.

7.24 Although the CSSF does not specify this in its Circular, reference to the right to redeem units must be interpreted as referring only to the investors' right of redemption by unilateral request. As explained earlier in this text,[8] three types of redemption are possible at the level of a UCI: redemption at the investor's request, redemption with the consent of both the investor and the UCI, and redemption imposed by the UCI on the investor. A UCI that authorizes redemption which is not made at the holder's request must be considered to be of the closed-end type if investors are not permitted to request redemption during the scheme's life.

7.25 In light of those considerations, UCIs governed by Part I of the 2002 Act cannot be considered closed-end UCIs precisely because the 2002 Act obliges them to redeem units at the holder's request.

7.26 In contrast, it may be that certain UCIs governed by Part II of the 2002 Act or the Act of 13 February 2007 are considered closed-end. Once again, this does not mean that they can never redeem their units. They merely may not grant investors the right to request redemption. For example, this would be the case with UCIs whose underlying assets are illiquid and which therefore do not want to be forced to sell part of their portfolio to finance the redemption of units at an investor's request.

---

[7] Here used in the context of an unlimited group of investors; also see Art 48(1), Directive (EC) 2001/34 of the European Parliament and of the Council of 28 May 2001 on the admission of securities to official stock exchange listings and on information to be published on those securities ([2001] OJ L184/1 *et seq*) and Art 16 of 'Chapter II-Conditions for admission of financial assets to official stock exchange listing and rules for admission to trading on a market operated by the company', Rules and Regulations of the Luxembourg Stock Exchange (Mémorial A 2007, 1194). In practice, this provision is to be interpreted as requiring at least 5 investors in the UCI.

[8] See 5.171 above.

A UCI is also considered closed-end when marketing its shares or units exclusively **7.27** to a small number of investors, even though it authorizes their redemption. This would be the case with SIFs dedicated to a sole investor. This calls for a closer look at the terminology used in this area. 'Closed-end UCI' is an unfortunate classification because it may embrace funds that permit redemption but do not obtain funds from a large group of investors.[9]

Type of securities concerned: equity securities or other securities

The second question to be answered when determining the scope of application **7.28** of the Act of 10 July 2005 compared with the scope of the 2002 Act and the Act of 13 February 2007 concerns the securities involved in public offerings and requests for admission to trading on a regulated market. The 2002 Act and the Act of 13 February 2007 may be ruled out or applied depending on whether such securities are equity securities (shares or units) or other types of securities (such as debt securities and founder shares).

Type of transactions contemplated: public offering or admission to trading on a regulated market

The third and last question is the type of activity contemplated by the UCI. The Act **7.29** of 10 July 2005 will either apply or not, depending on whether the UCI is considering a public offering, admission to trading on a regulated market as published by the Commission of the European Communities, or admission to the EuroMTF (a regulated market but not mentioned in the list of regulated markets).

Consequences

The Act of 10 July 2005 applies in general to closed-end UCIs. It lays down rules **7.30** applicable to prospectuses issued with a view to the public offering by such UCIs of shares, units, and all other types of transferable securities within the meaning of its Article 2(1)(w). It also governs prospectuses issued with a view to the admission of units or other securities issued by a closed-end UCI to trading on a regulated market or on a Luxembourg market not included in the list of regulated markets, ie on the EuroMTF market.

The situation regarding an open-end UCI is less definite. The Act of 10 July 2005 **7.31** applies only to prospectuses issued with a view to a public offering of UCI securities other than equity securities (ie other than shares or units). Thus prospectuses issued

---

[9] An exchange traded fund, for example, may seek capital only from a very small pool of institutional investors, who in turn are responsible for organizing a secondary market for the fund's units. It may nevertheless be queried whether the secondary market for this type of fund should not be considered a primary market since the operation of such funds depends largely on the fact that the target public is not the entity or entities subscribing units on the primary market but investors buying units on the secondary market.

with a view to public offerings of bonds are governed by the provisions of the Act of 10 July 2005.

7.32 The admission of the shares or units issued by an open-end UCI to trading on the regulated market is also not covered by the Act of 10 July 2005. In this case, the prospectus to be drawn up by the UCI with a view to admission to trading is entirely governed by the 2002 Act or, as applicable, the Act of 13 February 2007.

7.33 In contrast, the Act of 10 July 2005 applies to prospectuses drafted with a view to the admission of transferable securities issued by an open-end UCI to trading on the EuroMTF, whether shares, units, or other types of securities.

Public offering

Public offering of shares or units in open-end UCIs

7.34 Luxembourg-based open-end UCIs other than SIFs may market their shares or units in the Grand Duchy of Luxembourg immediately after the CSSF has added them to its list of UCIs.[10] No additional steps are required. The Act of 10 July 2005 does not apply to the marketing of units of open-end UCIs or to the marketing of units of open-end SIFs.

Public offering of transferable securities issued by a UCI of the closed-end type or securities other than shares or units issued by a UCI of the open-end type

7.35 Under the Act of 10 July 2005, a UCI of the closed-end type which intends to offer transferable securities to the public in Luxembourg is required to issue a prospectus.[11]

7.36 Although this situation occurs only very rarely in practice, the public offering in Luxembourg by an open-end UCI of securities other than shares or units is also governed by the Act of 10 July 2005. For example, a fund issuing bonds to the public may have to draw up a prospectus governed by the Act of 10 July 2005.

Concept of public offering

7.37 The concept of a public offering, as used within the framework of the Act of 10 July 2005, is defined by the Act itself. Circular 05/225 provides additional details.

7.38 A public offering of transferable securities is a 'communication sent in any form and by any means to persons and which provides sufficient information about the

---

[10] Arts 93(1) and 94(1), 2002 Act.
[11] More particularly, by Part II of the Act of 10 July 2005 or, in the case of an offer of less than €2,500,000 over a period of 12 months, Part III, Ch I of the Act of 10 July 2005.

offering conditions and the securities to be offered to allow an investor to decide whether to buy or subscribe for these transferable securities'.[12]

In other words, the form of the offering and methods of the offering are unimportant. According to Circular 05/225,[13] the definition does not rule out any communication method or any medium. A public offering may be announced by notices in newspapers or in any other medium, by mailings to an unspecified number of persons, or by brochures made available at a location that is accessible to the public. A firm's correspondence to clients and the dissemination of documentation to a small group of potential investors may also be considered a public offering. **7.39**

The 'public' as used in the definition must also be considered in the broad meaning of the word. The definition refers to 'persons' without distinguishing whether these persons could consist of institutional investors or whether the term is intended to refer to non-professional clients. **7.40**

The definition of a public securities offering specifies that the communication constituting such an offer must provide 'sufficient information about the offering conditions and the securities to be offered to allow an investor to decide whether to buy or subscribe for these transferable securities'. According to Circular 05/225,[14] this means that the following three key elements need to be present: (1) the author of the offering must have the intention to make an offer; (2) he must provide a description of the transferable securities to be offered; (3) the document constituting the offering must determine or make it possible to determine the offering conditions (*inter alia*, including the price of the offered transferable securities). **7.41**

More precisely, the offer must provide at least succinct information on the securities offered (Circular 05/225 stipulates that it must mention the nature of the security and its main characteristics). The method that may be used to accept the offer and the offering period must also be indicated explicitly or implicitly. **7.42**

Consequently, the definition rules out certain operations, such as the disclosure of information on transferable securities and advice to buy such securities. These steps are, in principle, not a public offering. Similarly, a draft prospectus or a preliminary prospectus sent to potential investors without the purchase price of the securities concerned should, in principle, not be considered an offer if the price cannot be determined. The situation would be different if the preliminary document already gave a narrow price range allowing investors to determine the purchase price. In this case, the document could be considered a public offering and should as such comply with the requirements imposed by the Act of 10 July 2005. **7.43**

---

[12] Article 2.1(l), Act of 10 July 2005.
[13] Part I, 2(a), Circular 05/225.
[14] ibid Part I, 3.

Obligation to draw up a prospectus and exceptions

7.44   When a public offering of transferable securities issued by a UCI comes within its sphere of application, the Act of 10 July 2005 requires it, in principle, to draw up a prospectus meeting certain requirements. It nevertheless provides for important exceptions to the obligation to publish a prospectus when offers in certain categories are concerned.

7.45   First, the obligation to draw up a prospectus within the meaning of the Act of 10 July 2005 does not apply to securities offers addressed only to qualified investors. Qualified investors are defined in the Act of 10 July 2005.[15] This definition, directly inspired by the definition supplied by MiFID, covers institutional investors and all other categories of investors considered to be experienced.[16] Thus, SIFs only have to draw up a prospectus for their securities offerings in very limited cases. Equally, there is no obligation to draw up a prospectus within the meaning of the Act of 10 July 2005 when offering units or other securities reserved for institutional investors, even by a UCI governed by the 2002 Act.

7.46   A securities offering does not require a prospectus when a minimum subscription of at least €50,000 per investor applies to the offer of securities concerned. Similarly, a prospectus does not have to be drawn up by virtue of the Act of 10 July 2005 for securities offerings where the unit nominal value of the securities offered amounts to €50,000 or more.

7.47   Lastly, certain offers involve such small amounts that their originators are also exempt from the obligation to prepare a prospectus. These are offers whose total amount is less than €100,000 a limit calculated over a period of twelve months.

7.48   These exceptions to the obligation to publish a prospectus can be valuable to a UCI governed by the Act of 10 July 2005. The content of the prospectus specified by this Act is highly detailed and can impose serious constraints.

---

[15]   Art 2.1(j), Act of 10 July 2005.

[16]   Article 2.1(j), Act of 10 July 2005 lists the following: (1) legal persons authorized or regulated as operators in the financial markets, including: credit institutions, investment firms, other authorized or regulated financial institutions, insurance companies, undertakings for collective investment and their management companies, pension and retirement funds and their management companies, commodity dealers, and entities not so authorized or regulated whose corporate purpose is solely to invest in securities; (2) national and regional governments, central banks, international and supranational institutions such as the International Monetary Fund, the European Central Bank, the European Investment Bank, and other similar international organisations; (3) other legal persons which do not meet two of the following three criteria: fewer than 250 employees on average during the entire fiscal year, total assets of less than €43,000,000 and annual net sales of no more than €50,000,000; (4) natural persons recorded in a register of persons considered qualified investors within the meaning of Directive (EC) 2003/71 as implemented in a Member State; (5) small and medium-size enterprises recorded in a register of persons considered qualified investors within the meaning of Directive (EC) 2003/71 as implemented in a Member State.

Content of prospectus

Pursuant to the Act of 10 July 2005, a prospectus must contain 'all information **7.49** which, having regard to the particular nature of the issuer and the transferable securities offered to the public or admitted to trading on a regulated market, is required to allow investors to evaluate, with full knowledge of the facts, the assets and liabilities, financial situation, results and outlook of the issuer and its guarantors, if any, and the rights attached to such transferable securities'. This information must be presented in such a way that the investors for whom it is intended will find it easy to analyse and understand.[17]

Every prospectus is divided into three sections, each of which contains specific **7.50** information. At the issuer's discretion, these three sections may be part of a single document or several documents. If in the format of separate documents, the documents together form the prospectus.[18] The first section of the prospectus provides information about the issuer. When contained in a single specific document, this document is known as the registration document. The second section describes the securities offered. The particular document devoted to this, if any, is known as the securities note. The third part of the prospectus summarizes the main characteristics of the issuer, any guarantors, the securities offered, and the main risks connected with the proposed investment. This summary may also be contained in a separate document. The summary is not required for admissions to trading on a regulated market of securities other than in respect of capital securities with an accounting par value of at least €50,000.

Content of registration document   Commission Regulation (EC) 809/2004 of **7.51** 29 April 2004[19] lists the information to be included in the registration document of a closed-end UCI.[20] This document must, *inter alia*, contain a clear and detailed table of contents and a description of the risk factors connected with the issuer and the offered securities, and the following information:[21]

• the names of the persons responsible for the information contained in the document;[22]

---

[17]   Art 8.1, Act of 10 July 2005.
[18]   ibid Arts 8.2 and 8.3.
[19]   Regulation (EC) 809/2004 of the Commission of 29 April 2004 implementing Directive (EC) 2003/71 of the European Parliament and of the Council as regards information contained in prospectuses and the format, incorporation by reference and publication of such prospectuses and dissemination of advertisements [2004] L215/1.
[20]   Art 18, Regulation (EC) 809/2004, referred to above, which refers to certain provisions in Annexe I and Annexe XV of the same Regulation.
[21]   For the CSSF's position with regard to the presentation sequence of this information, see, 'The New "Prospectus Regime" in 40 Questions and Answers', Question 30, available at <http://www.cssf.lu> under the heading 'Securities markets'.
[22]   Annexe I, 1, Regulation (EC) 809/2004 (n 19 above).

- information about the statutory auditors;[23]
- financial information about the issuer;[24]
- information about the history and development of the issuer;[25]
- the organizational structure of the issuer's group;[26]
- a review of the issuer's financial condition and results;[27]
- as applicable, profit forecasts or estimates presented in the way indicated in Annexe I to the Regulation;[28]
- information about the conducting persons (name, criminal record, potential conflicts of interest, remuneration, and benefits);[29]
- a description of the operation of the administrative, management, and supervisory bodies;[30]
- information about major shareholders insofar as such information is available;[31]
- information about transactions with related parties;[32]
- a description of material contracts;[33]
- a list of documents available to the public;[34]
- information on significant interests held by the UCI;[35]
- a detailed description of the investment objective and policy;[36]
- a description of the standard profile of the investor targeted by the UCI;[37]
- measures taken when the investment restrictions are exceeded;[38]
- a detailed description of the investment restrictions;[39]
- as applicable, information about the underlying issuer[40]—this information must be very detailed, as if the underlying issuer were an issuer for the purposes of the minimum disclosure requirements for the UCI itself;[41]

---

[23] ibid Annexe I, 2.
[24] ibid Annexe I, 3, 20, and 21.
[25] ibid Annexe I, 5.
[26] ibid Annexe I, 7.
[27] ibid Annexe I, 9.
[28] ibid Annexe I, 13.
[29] ibid Annexe I, 14, and 15.
[30] ibid Annexe I, 16.
[31] ibid Annexe I, 18.
[32] ibid Annexe I, 19.
[33] ibid Annexe I, 22.
[34] ibid Annexe I, 24.
[35] ibid Annexe I, 25.
[36] ibid Annexe XV, 1.1.
[37] ibid Annexe XV, 1.4.
[38] ibid Annexe XV, 2.1.
[39] ibid.
[40] ibid Annexe XV, 2.2.
[41] In this case the UCI becomes transparent, ie the information about the fund must be complemented by the same information about the underlying issuer as though the securities issued by the underlying issuers were the direct object of the offer. Issuers subject to this requirement are those in which a UCI may invest more than 20% of its gross assets (Annexe XV, 2.2, Regulation (EC) 809/2004 (n 19 above) (an exception is made for UCIs with the status of 'index-linked' fund although this concept is not defined in Regulation (EC) 809/2004 (ibid Annexe XV, 2.10).

- information about risk spreading if the UCI may invest in excess of 20 per cent of its gross assets in other UCIs;[42]
- a description of the property held in the portfolio of property UCIs;[43]
- a description of derivatives techniques and instruments used for purposes other than hedging;[44]
- information about the UCI's service providers (direct or indirect remuneration, paid by the UCI or not, and potential conflicts of interest);[45]
- more particularly, as regards the manager, information about its regulatory status, history, performance, and experience;[46]
- a brief description of the investment advisers;[47]
- information about the custody of the UCI's assets and the depositary/ies;[48]
- a description of the principles and methods used to calculate the net asset value and of the circumstances in which valuations may be suspended;[49]
- information about cross-liabilities that could be incurred by umbrella UCIs within the meaning of Commission Regulation (EC) 809/2004,[50] ie UCIs issuing distinct classes of transferable securities; and
- a complete analysis of the UCI's portfolio.[51]

Content of securities note   This information on the issuer is complemented **7.52** by information on the issued securities. The information to be included in the securities note, whether by way of a separate document or a special section of the prospectus, is listed in specific annexes to Commission Regulation (EC) 809/2004 of 29 April 2004. The information required for shares and other equity securities[52] differs from the information required for debt securities.[53]

When the underlying issuer is itself a UCI, Regulation (EC) 809/2004 adds a few further qualifications. The underlying UCI must only disclose the information required by Regulation (EC) 809/2004 when its investments may include more than 40% of the gross assets of the UCI issuing the security (ibid Annexe XV, 2.5) or when the underlying UCI is itself authorized to invest more than 20% of its gross assets in other UCIs and is thus what is generally referred to as a 'fund of funds of funds' (ibid Annexe XV, 2.2). The principle of transparency of the UCI and the ensuing requirement of information about the underlying issuer also applies when the UCI is authorized to expose more than 20% of its gross assets to the credit risk of a single counterparty (ibid Annexe XV, 2.2). In this case, the same information must be disclosed with respect to the counterparty as the counterparty would be required to disclose if it were directly issuing the credit instruments included in the offer.

[42]   Annexe XV, 2.3, Regulation (EC) 809/2004 (n 19 above).
[43]   ibid Annexe XV, 2.7.
[44]   ibid Annexe XV, 2.8.
[45]   ibid Annexe XV, 3.
[46]   ibid Annexe XV, 4.1.
[47]   ibid Annexe XV, 4.2.
[48]   ibid Annexe XV, 5.
[49]   ibid Annexe XV, 6.
[50]   ibid Annexe XV, 7.
[51]   ibid Annexe XV, 8.2.
[52]   ibid Art 6 and Annexe III.
[53]   ibid Art 8 and Annexe V, for debt securities with an accounting par value of less than €50,000 and Art 16 and Annexe XIII, for debt securities with an accounting par value in excess of €50,000.

7.53 For example, the securities note for shares or the corresponding section in the prospectus must, *inter alia*, include the following:

- information about the persons responsible for the information given in the prospectus;[54]
- a declaration by those persons attesting that the information contained in the prospectus is in accordance with the facts and there are no omissions likely to affect its import;[55]
- a description of the risk factors associated with the securities being offered;[56]
- financial information about the issuer;[57]
- a description of potential conflicts of interest likely to have an impact on the offer;[58]
- a description of the reason for the offer and use of the proceeds;[59]
- a description of the rights attached to the shares being offered and the procedure for their exercise;[60]
- mention of any restrictions on the free transferability of the shares;[61]
- a description of the offer conditions, including the period during which the offer will be open and the price or the method used to determine the price;[62]
- information about any application for admission of the securities to trading on one or more regulated markets;[63]
- information about the offeror;[64] and
- information about the advisers, experts, and auditors involved in the preparation of the note or the corresponding section in the prospectus.[65]

7.54 **Content of summary** In addition to a summary of key information found in the other sections of the prospectus, the summary must include certain mandatory disclosures. The Act of 10 July 2005 lists the following:[66] (1) a notice that the summary must be considered as only an introduction to the prospectus; (2) a recommendation to read the prospectus carefully before deciding to invest in the securities in question; (3) a notice that the cost of translating the prospectus may be borne by the investor if the investor brings a legal action; and, lastly, (4) a notice that the

---

[54] Annexe III, 1.1, Regulation (EC) 809/2004 (n 19 above).
[55] ibid Annexe III, 1.2.
[56] ibid Annexe III, 2.
[57] ibid Annexe III, 3.
[58] ibid Annexe III, 3.3.
[59] ibid Annexe III, 3.4.
[60] ibid Annexe III, 4.5.
[61] ibid Annexe III, 4.8; see also ibid Annexe III, 7.3.
[62] ibid Annexe III, 5.
[63] ibid Annexe III, 6.
[64] ibid Annexe III, 7.
[65] ibid Annexe III, 10.
[66] Art 8.2, Act of 10 July 2005.

persons who have presented the summary are responsible for any error or contradiction in that text compared with the other parts of the prospectus.[67]

Special provisions The Act of 10 July 2005 does not rule out the possibility **7.55** that some of the information to be included in principle in a prospectus may turn out to be unsuitable or even harmful in the light of the characteristics of the contemplated offer.

It offers two alternatives in this respect. In practice, in the case of UCIs, if certain of the **7.56** information required to be presented in a prospectus by virtue of the law, the Directive, and its interpretative provisions is irrelevant because of the circumstances of the offer, the prospectus may replace this information with equivalent but more appropriate data.[68] In addition, the CSSF can grant exemptions in three cases prescribed by law. The first two cases concern the situations—relatively extreme and probably very rare for a UCI—in which certain disclosures would be contrary to the public interest[69] or could do material damage to the issuer.[70] The third case is less serious and concerns information of minor importance, not likely to affect the recipient's assessment of the financial situation and outlook of the issuer, the offeror, or the guarantor.[71]

Contrary to the registration document for UCIs of the closed-end type, the **7.57** registration document of a UCI of the open-end type or the corresponding part of the prospectus, when not made up of three separate documents, is not governed by particular provisions in Commission Regulation (EC) 809/2004 of 29 April 2004. The information to be included in this document needs to be looked for in the annexes to the Regulation dealing with the issue of securities. The following could, for example, be relevant: the provisions of the registration document on debt securities and derivatives with a unit nominal value of less than €50,000[72] and the provisions of the securities note dealing with debt securities with a unit nominal value of less than €50,000.[73] Other combinations are possible, based on the characteristics of the securities being offered.

---

[67] The content of the information listed above for the registration document and securities note is outlined in detail in Regulation (EC) 809/2004 (n 19 above), as complemented by the recommendations issued by the CESR in a document entitled 'CESR's recommendations for the consistent implementation of the European Commission's Regulation on Prospectuses No. 809/2004' (CESR/05-045b), available at <http://www.cesr-eu.org>. The list of information to be included in the prospectus, discussed in the foregoing paragraphs, is given for information only in order to provide the UCI professional with an idea of the requirements applicable to prospectuses governed by Directive (EC) 2003/71 and the Act of 10 July 2005. Anyone required to draw up such a prospectus needs to make a careful perusal of the provisions of the Directive, the Act of 10 July 2005, Regulation (EC) 809/2004, and the CESR recommendations.

[68] Art 10.3, Act of 10 July 2005.

[69] ibid Art 10.2(a).

[70] ibid Art 10.2(b).

[71] ibid Art 10.2(c).

[72] Art 7 and Annexe IV, Regulation (EC) 809/2004 (n 19 above).

[73] ibid Art 8 and Annexe V.

Admission to listing and/or trading

Admission to listing and/or trading on the regulated market of the Luxembourg Stock Exchange

General principles

7.58 As in the case of public offerings, the admission of securities issued by closed-end UCIs to trading on the regulated market of the Luxembourg Stock Exchange is generally governed by the Act of 10 July 2005. Thus this Act applies to prospectuses drafted with a view to admission to trading of units, shares, or any other securities issued by closed-end UCIs on the regulated market of the Luxembourg Stock Exchange. When it applies for a passport, a Luxembourg closed-end UCI could also use its prospectus drawn up in accordance with the Act of 10 July 2005 to apply for admission of its units to trading on a foreign regulated market. However, consideration of the issues relevant to such an application exceeds the scope of this work.

7.59 For open-end UCIs, the Act of 10 July 2005 governs only admission to trading of securities other than units or shares on the regulated market of the Luxembourg Stock Exchange. This does not mean that the shares or units issued by such UCIs cannot be admitted to trading on the regulated market of the Luxembourg Stock Exchange. Such transactions remain possible. In that case, the prospectus to be drawn up remains entirely governed by the 2002 Act or the Act of 13 February 2007. The Rules and Regulations of the Luxembourg Stock Exchange[74] are also applicable, *inter alia*, determining conditions for admission to trading on the regulated market other than the prerequisites for prospectuses. These are examined later in this section.

7.60 Contrary to its requirements with respect to public offerings, the Act of 10 July 2005 does not exempt any UCI seeking admission of its securities to trading on the regulated market of the Luxembourg Stock Exchange from the obligation to draw up a prospectus. A UCI of the closed-end type governed by the Act of 13 February 2007, for example, must draw up a prospectus in accordance with the Act of 10 July 2005 if it wishes to be admitted to trading on the regulated market of the Luxembourg Stock Exchange.

7.61 The Act of 10 July 2005 only relates to the obligation to publish a prospectus with a view to seeking admission to listing and to trading on the regulated market of the Luxembourg Stock Exchange. The Act of 10 July 2005 does not govern applications for admission which are covered by the provisions laid down by the relevant market authorities and by the rules applicable to that market.

---

[74] Rules and Regulations of the Luxembourg Stock Exchange (*Mémorial* A 2005, 1756 *et seq*).

Similarly, an open-end UCI seeking admission of its shares or units to listing and **7.62** trading must, in addition to the publication of a prospectus drafted according to the provisions of the 2002 Act or the Act of 13 February 2007, meet the requirements imposed by the relevant market and the rules applicable to such market.

Exceptions

The Board of Directors of the Luxembourg Stock Exchange may grant exemptions **7.63** from most of the conditions concerning admission to official stock exchange listing for units issued by open-end UCIs, ie other than the closed-end type within the meaning of the Act of 10 July 2005.[75]

As regards shares and units, the Rules and Regulations of the Luxembourg Stock **7.64** Exchange require, for example, a foreseeable market capitalization of at least €1,000,000.[76] A derogation can, however, be granted if the Luxembourg Stock Exchange receives an assurance that there will be an adequate market for the securities in question.[77]

The Rules and Regulations also require a UCI issuing shares or units to have been **7.65** in existence for at least three years. Here, too, derogations are possible on certain conditions. It is, *inter alia*, necessary for a derogation to be desirable in the interest of the UCI or its investors, that the investors have the necessary information to form an informed opinion about the UCI and the securities in question, and that they are provided regularly with financial information.[78]

Shares and units offered on the stock exchange must be negotiable.[79] This does **7.66** not rule out admission of partly paid-up securities, provided their negotiability is not hampered and the public is given adequate information. Securities whose transfer requires approval may also be admitted if the authorization clause does not disrupt trade. This should in principle be the case with a clause whose violation would not void a transfer but merely give rise to payment of compensation by the seller and, as applicable, the buyer.

Such shares and units must also benefit from adequate public distribution.[80] **7.67** The idea underlying this requirement is the need to ensure regular operation of

---

[75] ibid Art 12, Ch XII.

[76] ibid Art 3.A.2 and 12, Ch XII.

[77] ibid Art 3.A.2, Ch XII.

[78] ibid Art 3.A.3, Ch XII, to which Art 12 of the same chapter refers, allows the Board of Directors of the Luxembourg Stock Exchange to grant derogations. For admission to trading on the regulated market of the Luxembourg Stock Exchange, see also ibid Art 16.A.2, Ch XII.

[79] ibid Art 3.B.2, Ch XII, to which Art 12 of the same chapter refers, allows the Board of Directors of the Luxembourg Stock Exchange to grant derogations. For admission to trading on the regulated market of the Luxembourg Stock Exchange, see also ibid Art 16, Ch XII.

[80] ibid Art 3.B.4, Ch XII, to which Art 12 of the same chapter refers, allows the Board of Directors of the Luxembourg Stock Exchange to grant derogations. For admission to trading on the

the market. Distribution is considered adequate when at least 25 per cent of the capital is held as part of the public float. That said, a lower percentage is tolerated when it is established that the operation of the market is sufficiently regular owing to the high number of shares and units in this category and their public distribution.

7.68 Lastly, a request for admission to official stock exchange listing must cover all shares and units of the same category.[81] Exceptions to this principle are tolerated in the case of blocks of securities kept off the market to maintain control over the relevant company. Under the Rules and Regulations of the Luxembourg Stock Exchange, it is also possible to seek admission for securities that may not be transferred for a limited time. In this case, the Rules and Regulations require the public to be adequately informed of the fact that certain securities are not available on the market of the Luxembourg Stock Exchange. In such cases, partial admission must not damage the holders of the shares and units for which admission to the market of the Luxembourg Stock Exchange is requested.

7.69 Admission to listing and trading is also subject to the requirement for the issuer to publish information on a periodic basis or in specific circumstances. These requirements are set out in the Rules and Regulations of the Luxembourg Stock Exchange.[82] They are not applicable to investment companies other than the closed-end type. Although not expressly mentioned under this exception, FCPs should also be considered exempt from these requirements.[83]

Act of 11 January 2008

7.70 Since the enactment of the Act of 11 January 2008,[84] issuers whose securities are admitted to trading on a regulated market and whose home Member State is Luxembourg must comply with certain transparency obligations. These obligations notably include the disclosure of financial and other information which is periodic and ongoing, and the notification of certain thresholds which have been exceeded during the purchase or sale of investments in an issuer whose units are admitted to trading on a regulated market.

---

regulated market of the Luxembourg Stock Exchange, see also ibid Art 16.A.1, Ch XII.

[81] ibid Art 3.B.5, Ch XII, to which Art 12 of the same chapter refers, allows the Board of Directors of the Luxembourg Stock Exchange to grant derogations.

[82] ibid Ch XIII.

[83] The reference to the definition of an investment company other than the closed-end type in Art 1, Ch XIII is clearly an error since it refers to a non-existent provision. In all likelihood, this reference should be replaced by reference to Art 12, Ch XII of the Rules and Regulations, which defines UCIs other than the closed-end type.

[84] Act of 11 January 2008 on the transparency obligations of issuers whose securities are admitted to trading on a regulated market (*Mémorial* A 2008, 46).

However, the Act of 11 January 2008 only covers closed-end UCIs whose securities **7.71** are admitted on the regulated market of the Luxembourg Stock Exchange and whose home Member State is Luxembourg within the meaning of the said Act.

Admission to the EuroMTF

As regards the prospectus to be published with a view to seeking listing and trad- **7.72** ing on the EuroMTF, the Act of 10 July 2005 refers to the internal Rules and Regulations of the Luxembourg Stock Exchange. The analysis set out below is entirely based on the rules governing the drafting of prospectuses and admission to listing and trading on the EuroMTF, in other words on the Rules and Regulations of the Luxembourg Stock Exchange. Should other non-regulated markets be established, the rules governing those markets would apply to the drafting of prospectuses and admission to listing and trading of securities.

The contents of a prospectus issued in connection with the admission of securities **7.73** to trading on the EuroMTF is not regulated quite as strictly as the prospectus for admission to trading on a regulated market of instruments governed by Part II of the Act of 10 July 2005. As required by the Rules and Regulations of the Luxembourg Stock Exchange, it must include information that, 'having regard to the characteristics of the issuer and the financial assets concerned, is required to allow investors and their investment advisers to form an informed opinion about the assets, financial situation, results and outlook of the issuer and the rights attached to these financial assets'.[85] More precisely, it contains the information found in the tables attached to the Regulations, complemented, as applicable, by information on the particular features of the transaction, the issuer, or the financial securities being offered. The issuer may also opt for the tables described in Regulation (EC) 809/2004 of the Commission of the European Communities of 29 April 2004.[86]

The Rules and Regulations of the Luxembourg Stock Exchange are equally flexi- **7.74** ble as regards the remaining conditions for admission to trading on the EuroMTF. While imposing conditions for admission to trading on the regulated market of the Luxembourg Stock Exchange,[87] they authorize the Luxembourg Stock Exchange to exempt the issuer from the obligation to comply with all or part of these conditions.[88] Thus, the requirements of the Regulations can be adapted to the characteristics of the transaction in question.

The Rules and Regulations of the Luxembourg Stock Exchange subject admission **7.75** to official stock exchange listing on the EuroMTF market to the same specific

---

[85] Art 6, Ch XI, Rules and Regulations of the Luxembourg Stock Exchange.
[86] ibid.
[87] ibid Art 21, Ch XII.
[88] ibid Art 22, Ch XII.

requirements as admission to trading on the market of the Luxembourg Stock Exchange.[89]

Marketing the Units and Other Securities of Foreign UCIs

7.76 The most significant contribution made by Directive 85/611 concerns the cross-border marketing of units of coordinated UCITS organized pursuant to that Directive. Such UCITS may be marketed freely anywhere in the EEA without any requirement for additional authorization, save as regards aspects not connected with a UCITS' authorization, supervision, structure, or activities, or the information that such UCITS must publish.[90] Such UCIs are entitled to a European passport, in contrast with other UCIs, as we shall see below.[91]

Coordinated UCITS

Freedom of marketing: principles and limits

7.77 The freedom to market the units of a coordinated UCITS in the EEA is rooted in three principles set out in Directive 85/611.

7.78 First of all, a UCITS that markets its units in another Member State must comply with the laws, regulations, and administrative provisions in force in that Member State which do not fall within the scope of Directive 85/611.[92]

7.79 A Member State may not require coordinated UCITS marketed in its territory to comply with its national standards concerning the legal form, the depositary, the management company, the investment, or borrowing policy or the accounting of UCIs; nor may it subject them to special rules on the redemption of units or, to a certain extent, the circulation of information. In contrast, it may subject coordinated UCITS marketed in its territory to consumer protection rules and local tax regulations, since those issues are not dealt with by Directive 85/611. For example, the Grand Duchy of Luxembourg permits the creation of UCITS as umbrella funds. Since Directive 85/611 reserves determination of a UCITS' structure to the Member State from which the UCITS originates, the host Member State may not bar it from marketing its units on the grounds that its structure is not authorized under its national law.

---

[89]   ibid Art 24, Ch XII.
[90]   Fourth recital in the preamble to Directive (EEC) 85/611.
[91]   This topic is discussed in an article written by C Kremer and C Niedner, 'La commercialisation au Luxembourg de parts d'organismes de placement collectif étrangers' in *Luxemburger Wort*, 12 March 1999, ahead of the ALFI Conference held on 15 and 16 March 1999.
[92]   Art 44(1), Directive (EEC) 85/611.

In the Grand Duchy of Luxembourg, the standards expressly applicable to foreign **7.80**
coordinated UCITS include, *inter alia*, those dealing with consumer protection,
those connected with certain business practices, those designed to penalize unfair
competition, and those concerning door-to-door sales.[93]

The second principle underlying the freedom to market the units of coordinated **7.81**
UCITS is the freedom to advertise.[94] That freedom is nevertheless subject to the
above-mentioned principles. As Directive 85/611 does not govern this aspect of
unit offerings, the regulations of the host Member State are fully applicable.

Lastly, and above all, Directive 85/611 prohibits all discrimination between **7.82**
domestic and foreign coordinated UCITS.[95] Any standard imposed by a Member
State on foreign coordinated UCITS automatically applies to domestic UCITS,
thus reducing the temptation to discourage foreign coordinated UCITS from
entering its territory by means of unattractive legislation, since domestic UCITS
are subject to the same rules as foreign UCITS. Better still, the Member States
are prompted to create regimes that are favourable to the promoters of UCIs
and reassuring for the public, since those are the only elements of objective
competition between Member States authorized by the Directive.

Definition of the concept of marketing

Objective: investment by the public

Directive 85/611 refers to but does not define the concept of marketing. **7.83**
Nevertheless, it provides some guidance on the concept with two broad indicators.
In the preamble, the Directive provides first of all that it applies to UCIs 'which
promote the sale of their units to the public in the Community'.[96] In addition,
Article 2 provides that it does not apply to UCITS 'which raise capital without pro-
moting the sale of their units to the public within the Community or any part of it'.

To benefit from the status of coordinated UCITS, a UCITS must therefore either **7.84**
offer its units for sale to the public or promote the sale of its units to the public. The final
recipient of the offer must be the public. In that respect, it is immaterial whether the
offer is successful or not. The intention to place the units with the public is enough.

The *Petit Larousse*[97] defines the term 'marketing' as the act of 'putting on the mar- **7.85**
ket, launching, building up commercial distribution'. In other words, marketing
covers the entire process of promotion, regardless of its form or scope.

---

[93]   Ch O, Circular 91/75; see also Circular 07/277 and the website of the CSSF <http://www.
cssf.lu>, under the heading 'Marketing of UCITS > Marketing of units/shares of European UCITS
in Luxembourg', for more details of the rules applicable in Luxembourg.
[94]   Art 44(2), Directive (EEC) 85/611.
[95]   ibid Art 44(3).
[96]   Sixth recital in the preamble to Directive (EEC) 85/611.
[97]   *Le Petit Larousse* (Larousse, large format edition, 1999).

Methods: public offering or private placement

7.86 Luxembourg law on UCIs distinguishes between placements with the public and public offerings. The former encompasses a broader sphere than the latter. A placement is made with the public when targeted at potential investors in numbers greater than a 'restricted circle of persons'. As the CSSF wishes to reserve the right to judge each case individually, it has never fixed precise criteria as to the number of investors to be approached.[98] A placement with the public may take place by means of a private offering.[99]

Consequences of defining the concept of marketing

7.87 The absence of a definition of what constitutes marketing has a direct impact on the scope of Directive 85/611. Member States can interpret the concept to either expand or restrict the group of UCIs that are granted the status of coordinated UCITS. The absence of a definition of marketing has a second consequence. It restricts the scope of activities which may be conducted in Member States other than that in which the UCI is incorporated without triggering the obligation to notify the Member State's competent authorities. Those two consequences of the definition of marketing are sufficiently significant to give some cause for regret for the absence of a Community definition with uniform application from one Member State to the next.

7.88 The Grand Duchy of Luxembourg has adopted a broad interpretation of the concept of marketing. This has proved to be advantageous for Luxembourg-based UCIs, which are entitled to the status of coordinated UCITS even when their units are placed only with a specifically targeted and privately approached public.

7.89 Conversely, such an interpretation may restrict access to the Luxembourg market by UCITS registered in a foreign country which would be regarded as marketing their units in the Grand Duchy of Luxembourg, even if only in the form of private placements.

7.90 The effect of Luxembourg's definition of the concept of marketing could only be avoided if the Grand Duchy of Luxembourg were to practise reverse discrimination in favour of foreign coordinated UCITS. If so, private placement by such UCITS in the Grand Duchy of Luxembourg would not be considered as constituting the marketing of their units. Directive 85/611 does not appear to permit such discrimination.[100]

---

[98] For further details concerning the concept of placement with the public, see 1.06 *et seq* above.
[99] The Luxembourg legislature differs in this respect from those of other Member States of the EEA, which hold that a private placement may never be made in the form of a public offering.
[100] Art 44(3), Directive (EEC) 85/611 states that the provisions referred to in paras 1 and 2 of that Article 'must be applied without discrimination'. The Article does not distinguish between

Moreover, that is not the approach taken by the CSSF, which bases its assessment **7.91** on the criterion of those at whom an offer is targeted. When the CSSF notes that an offering targets the public—rather than a restricted circle of persons—it does not distinguish between public offering or private placement and requires the foreign UCITS to be registered with it.

According to Directive 85/611,[101] foreign coordinated UCITS only have to **7.92** register in the Member State in which their units are marketed when their units are offered *in* that State.

Marketing *from* a Member State does not require notification to the authorities **7.93** of that Member State. When the units of a foreign coordinated UCITS are exclusively promoted to the residents of one or more other Member States, there is no notification obligation in the Member State from which they are promoted. For example, a bank established in the Grand Duchy of Luxembourg could promote the sale of a German coordinated UCITS to its clients residing in Germany without triggering any obligation on the part of the German UCITS to notify the CSSF in accordance with the 2002 Act.

By the same token, notification is not required where a coordinated UCITS is **7.94** involved in activities other than marketing in one of the Member States. A bank or another professional of the financial sector established in the Grand Duchy of Luxembourg may provide its clients with securities accounts to hold the units issued by foreign coordinated UCITS. As long as those units are not offered for sale in the Grand Duchy of Luxembourg, the coordinated UCITS issuing the units does not have to register with the CSSF.

Notification procedure

According to the 2002 Act,[102] a foreign coordinated UCITS may not begin to **7.95** market its units in the Grand Duchy of Luxembourg prior to the expiry of two months after informing the CSSF of its intention to do so, on condition that the CSSF does not oppose its plan. If there is no reply from the authorities within two months, it is deemed to be accepted. In the Grand Duchy of Luxembourg, applications are generally examined long before expiry of that period, enabling UCITS to start marketing their units without expiry of the statutory period.[103]

---

discrimination that is unfavourable to foreign UCIs and reverse discrimination, which is unfavourable to domestic UCIs. It prohibits both types in the same way.

[101] ibid Art 44(1), as transposed in Art 58, 2002 Act.

[102] Art 60, 2002 Act.

[103] See also the guidelines of the CESR regarding the simplification of the notification procedure, available at <http://www.cesr-eu.org>, as well as Circular 07/277; within one week of receiving the complete documentation, the CSSF informs the relevant UCITS that the marketing of units/shares may commence in Luxembourg without any further delay.

7.96 In support of its application, a foreign coordinated UCITS must send the CSSF the following documents:[104]

(1) an attestation by the competent supervisory authorities of its home State to the effect that it fulfils the conditions laid down by Directive 85/611;

(2) the latest version of its constitutive documents;

(3) the latest version of its complete and simplified prospectuses;

(4) where appropriate, its latest annual report and any subsequent half-yearly report;

(5) information on the arrangements made for the marketing of its units in the Grand Duchy of Luxembourg.

7.97 It must also appoint a credit institution as 'paying agent' and instruct it to make the necessary payments to the shareholders or unitholders in the Grand Duchy of Luxembourg, generally dividend distributions or the proceeds of redemption of the UCI's units.

7.98 Moreover, the information required to be published in its home State must also be distributed in Luxembourgish, French, German, or English in the Grand Duchy of Luxembourg.[105]

7.99 Lastly, the UCITS must comply with Luxembourg's consumer protection legislation, including the rules on certain business practices, unfair competition, door-to-door sales, display of wares, and canvassing for orders.[106]

7.100 The CSSF may refuse an application for the marketing of units in the Grand Duchy of Luxembourg only when the planned arrangements do not comply with the foregoing requirements.[107]

Other UCIs

Principles

7.101 Public offers of the units of foreign UCIs without the status of coordinated UCITS in or from the Grand Duchy of Luxembourg are strictly regulated. These regulations are based on the 2002 Act for the units of open-end UCIs and on the Act of 10 July 2005 for closed-end UCIs. Private placements are not regulated and therefore are not subject to those constraints.

---

[104] ibid.

[105] Arts 59 and 61, 2002 Act.

[106] ibid Art 58, 2002 Act; Ch O, Circular 91/75; see also Circular 07/277 and the website of the CSSF <http://www.cssf.lu>, under the heading 'Marketing of UCITS > Marketing of units/shares of European UCITS in Luxembourg', for more details of the rules applicable in Luxembourg.

[107] Art 60, 2002 Act.

The 2002 Act[108] makes the public offering of securities of foreign UCIs of the **7.102** open-end type other than coordinated UCITS in or from the Grand Duchy of Luxembourg conditional on permanent supervision by a supervisory authority set up by law in their home State to ensure the protection of investors.[109]

Foreign UCIs of the open-end type that do not fulfil that requirement may **7.103** not display, offer, or sell their units publicly in or from the Grand Duchy of Luxembourg, nor target such actions from the Grand Duchy of Luxembourg at other countries. In contrast, private placements are always possible.

When a foreign UCI is closed-ended, it is not subject to the supervision **7.104** requirement imposed by the 2002 Act. Only the Act of 10 July 2005 applies to its securities offering in Luxembourg. If its offering prospectus has a European passport within the meaning of Directive 2003/71, the CSSF may not subject this prospectus to its approval procedure, provided the competent authority in the home State has notified the CSSF that it has approved this document in accordance with Directive 2003/71, as transposed into national law.[110]

If the foreign closed-end UCI has not drawn up a prospectus governed by **7.105** Directive 2003/71 because it has not yet made a public offering—in Luxembourg or elsewhere in the European Union—it falls within the sphere of application of the Act of 10 July 2005 when making a public offering within the meaning of this law in Luxembourg.

Concept of public offering under the 2002 Act

The concepts of displaying, offering, or selling units in open-end UCIs, ie other **7.106** than those of the closed-end type within the meaning of the Act of 10 July 2005, publicly in or from the Grand Duchy of Luxembourg, have never been defined in Luxembourg law.

That omission may be due to the difficulty of comprehensively and definitively **7.107** specifying the components of a public offering in a text. Units can be offered in many ways. Marketing techniques are changing continually. The distinction between information and promotion can be subtle. The Parliamentary documents accompanying the 1988 Act were already worded as follows: 'The concept of a public call for savings is not defined in any legislative text. Having regard to the complexity of the subject matter, formal determination of the concepts of public display, offer and sale of securities may not cover all cases.'[111]

---

[108] ibid Art 76.
[109] There are few countries whose UCIs fulfil this condition. They notably include the Member States of the EEA, Canada, the US, Hong Kong, Japan, and Switzerland.
[110] Art 18, Act of 10 July 2005.
[111] *Parliamentary doc* No 3172, Comments on the Articles, 52.

For that reason, reference to specific criteria, such as the number of target investors, is carefully avoided.

7.108 Directive 2003/71 gives a definition of public offering at European level. That definition, transposed in its entirety in the Act of 10 July 2005, is extremely general, making it possible to adapt its interpretation in CSSF circulars. The definition applies only to the concept of public offering used within the framework of the Act of 10 July 2005 and is irrelevant for units offered by open-end UCIs.

7.109 The Parliamentary documents accompanying the 1988 Act[112] are precise in one respect. They state that the 1988 Act does not apply to UCIs 'units of which are listed only on the Luxembourg Stock Exchange without active and direct canvassing of the public'.[113] According to that passage, UCIs listed on the Luxembourg Stock Exchange may be marketed only in foreign territories. In that case, they are not regarded as directly and actively canvassing the Luxembourg public. That may seem surprising. In principle, the listing of securities on a stock exchange should entail a public offering of such securities in the location where the stock exchange is established and where the transactions are conducted.[114]

7.110 The absence of a legal or regulatory definition does not mean that we cannot trace a rough outline of the concepts of public display, offering and sale.[115] For example, a report published in 1975 by the *Commissariat au Contrôle des Banques*, the banking commission, to commemorate the thirtieth anniversary of its creation, contains some interesting pointers.[116]

7.111 The report specifies, first, that the public or private nature of an issue is to be determined on a pragmatic basis. It then gives the following details: 'a securities offering, for subscription or sale, is public when announced for that purpose in the press (posters, notices, radio, television). The size of the print run or the circulation of a periodical is of little importance. News published in a financial newsletter for information purposes cannot necessarily be construed as a public offering'.

---

[112] Whose content remains relevant in this respect within the framework of the 2002 Act.

[113] ibid.

[114] This approach is confirmed in the Rules and Regulations of the Luxembourg Stock Exchange (*Mémorial* A 2005, 1756), which state that securities issued by foreign UCIs may be admitted to trading on the regulated market of the Luxembourg Stock Exchange without being the 'object of a display, public offering or public sale in or from Luxembourg' (Art 18, Ch XII, Rules and Regulations of the Luxembourg Stock Exchange).

[115] Such concepts appeared for the first time in Luxembourg law in Art 14 of the Grand-Ducal Decree of 19 June 1965 concerning banking and credit transactions and the issue of transferable securities (*Mémorial* A 1965, 612). That text provided: 'Any person intending to display for sale, to offer for sale or to sell publicly transferable securities must inform the *Commissaire au Contrôle des Banques* no later than two weeks in advance.' That was made applicable to UCIs by the Grand-Ducal Decree of 22 December 1972, which deals specifically with the supervision of investment funds (*Mémorial* A 1972, 2112), repealed by the 1983 Act.

[116] 'Le Commissaire au Contrôle des Banques 1945–1975', report published by the *Commissariat au Contrôle des Banques* (1975) 45 *et seq*.

It further explains that intention is decisive in this matter and that 'indication of the persons from whom subscriptions are received makes an offering public'.

According to the same report, notice that a message is published solely for information purposes and does not constitute a securities offering does not in itself rule out the possibility of a public offering. **7.112**

The report specifies the following with respect to the distribution of information: **7.113**

> A public offering is deemed to be made when private investors can obtain a prospectus dealing with the offer of the transferable securities concerned at one or more banks. The same applies to information given in circulars and brochures. In contrast, no public offering is deemed to be made, in principle, when a bank provides its customers personally with information under an express or implied mandate. The form of the bank's communication must be personal and made by: telephone, telex or a letter with a hand-written or stamped signature, duly addressed in a sealed envelope.'

Determination of the public or private nature of an offering therefore depends more on the form of the offering than on the number of potential investors contacted. A bank could promote the units of a foreign UCI in the Grand Duchy of Luxembourg by means of a letter sent to selected customers, based on mandates to receive information given by such customers. Such an operation would not be regarded as a public offering. In contrast, availability of the prospectus of that UCI at the bank's counters would always constitute a public offering, even when few prospectuses are distributed in that way. **7.114**

In conclusion, an offer is generally regarded as private when addressed to an existing customer base, regardless of the number of persons canvassed, and public when targeted at persons who are not customers at that time. **7.115**

Authorization procedure

A foreign UCI of the open-end type, subject in its country of origin to control by a supervisory authority that meets the conditions of the 2002 Act, may offer its units publicly in or from the Grand Duchy of Luxembourg only if it has received prior authorization from the CSSF.[117] **7.116**

A foreign UCI is required to follow the same procedure as that applying to Luxembourg-based UCIs. The CSSF examines the constitutive documents and verifies the expertise of the depositary.[118] It also ensures that the conducting persons of the management company or investment company and of the depositary have the probity and experience required for the performance of their duties[119] having regard to the type of UCI concerned. **7.117**

---

[117] Art 93(1), 2002 Act.
[118] ibid Art 93(2).
[119] ibid Art 93(3).

7.118 In practice, however, foreign UCIs other than those of the closed-end type are frequently authorized after a limited examination. A foreign UCI allowed to market its units in the Grand Duchy of Luxembourg is, by definition,[120] subject in its country of origin to supervision by a supervisory authority set up by law to ensure the protection of investors.[121] The CSSF is therefore entitled to rely, in reaching its decision, on a limited inspection of the local supervisory framework. The scope of its examination varies with the degree of supervision applied to the UCI in its country of origin. In many cases, the CSSF merely checks that the contemplated marketing conforms to Luxembourg's principles on the protection of public savings. It also ensures that the foreign UCI has appointed a credit institution to make payments to investors in the Grand Duchy of Luxembourg[122] and that it distributes its prospectus and its semi-annual and annual reports in the Grand Duchy of Luxembourg.[123]

7.119 A foreign UCI of the closed-end type is not subject to the above approval procedure.[124] Nevertheless, when making a public offering in Luxembourg within the meaning of the Act of 10 July 2005,[125] its prospectus must as applicable[126] be drawn up in accordance with this Act or follow the notification procedure set out in Directive 2003/71.

---

[120] ibid Art 76.
[121] ibid.
[122] ibid Arts 59 and 76.
[123] ibid Arts 61 and 109 *et seq*.
[124] ibid Art 93(1).
[125] See 7.37 above.
[126] ie it does not benefit from one of the exemptions from drawing up a prospectus provided for by the Act of 10 July 2005.

8

SUPERVISION OF UNDERTAKINGS FOR COLLECTIVE INVESTMENT

Powers of the CSSF

8.01   An offshoot of the former *Institut Monétaire Luxembourgeois*, the *Commission de Surveillance du Secteur Financier* (the CSSF) is the public body charged with the prudential supervision of UCIs in the Grand Duchy of Luxembourg.[1] The supervision exercised by the CSSF is an ongoing duty, which is carried out exclusively in the public interest.[2] The role of the CSSF starts when a UCI is created and ends after termination of the liquidation proceedings. It takes varied forms, depending on the undertaking involved. Most of the forms of supervision have already been discussed and will be mentioned only in passing. Others have not yet been described and will be reviewed in greater detail.

Powers of the CSSF during the creation of a UCI

8.02   In order to offer its units for sale to the public in the Grand Duchy of Luxembourg, a UCI other than a SIF[3] must be approved and entered in the list of UCIs by the CSSF.[4] A SIF may sell its units even though it has yet to be authorized, provided it files with the CSSF a dossier for registration on the official SIF list within one month of the creation or constitution of the SIF.[5]

---

[1]   For other comments on the prudential supervision exercised by the CSSF, see A Elvinger, 'Le rôle des autorités de surveillance' (1994) *ALFI yearbook* 33; C Kremer and J Baden, 'The role of the Luxembourg Monetary Institute in the supervision of undertakings for collective investment'(February 1995) 3 World Fund Industry/Gestion collective internationale 63; G Ludovissy, *La surveillance du secteur financier* (Éditions Promoculture, 2000).

[2]   Art 97, 2002 Act. The rule also applies to SIFs governed by the Act of 13 February 2007 (Art 41(2)).

[3]   And other than foreign coordinated UCITS.

[4]   Arts 93(1) and 94(1), 2002 Act.

[5]   Arts 41(1), 43(1), and 64, Act of 13 February 2007.

The CSSF's authority is therefore a mandatory and vital element during the start-up phase of a UCI. The CSSF has a wide range of powers.

The CSSF's first task in respect of an undertaking for which authorization is requested is to check that it satisfies the prerequisites for new UCIs.[6] Thus, it ensures that the exclusive object of applicant UCIs is to: **8.03**

- deal in collective investment,
- according to the principle of risk spreading,
- of capital obtained by the issue of units,
- from the public, provided that it is not a SIF.

Next, the CSSF determines the UCI's legal status. A UCI may be governed by Part I or Part II of the 2002 Act, in accordance with the criteria examined above.[7] A UCI that reserves its units for one or more well-informed investors is, in principle, governed by the Act of 13 February 2007. Categories are assigned by the CSSF, which determine the status of UCIs being formed. **8.04**

Once a UCI's legal framework has been fixed, derogations from certain investment or operating rules may be obtained. Once again, the CSSF has decision-making power in that respect. The scope of its power varies according to the legal framework concerned. **8.05**

A UCITS governed by Part I of the 2002 Act may obtain the following two derogations: **8.06**

- authorization to invest up to 100 per cent of its net assets in securities issued or guaranteed by a single State or its local authorities or by a public international body, subject to compliance with certain conditions;[8]
- authorization to publish its net asset value only once a month.[9]

The CSSF has much wider powers as regards UCIs governed by Part II of the 2002 Act or by the Act of 13 February 2007. In Circular 91/75, and with respect to SIFs in Circular 07/309, the CSSF lays down most of the rules applicable to such UCIs. As Circulars 91/75 and 07/309 are only recommendations, the CSSF is free to derogate from their provisions, within the confines of the law. **8.07**

The CSSF also examines a UCI's constitutive documents and promotional literature and the contents of the agreements the UCI intends to sign with its service providers, such as the depositary, the head office agent, and the **8.08**

---

[6] For details, see 1.01 *et seq* above.
[7] See 2.01 *et seq* above.
[8] Art 45(1), 2002 Act.
[9] ibid Article 116(1).

investment manager.[10] The 2002 Act and the Act of 13 February 2007 authorize the CSSF to request UCIs to provide any additional information it considers necessary.[11]

8.09   On completion of its examination, the CSSF decides whether or not to enter a UCI on its list. When a UCI is accepted for registration, the CSSF stamps the prospectus, the contents of which it has approved.[12]

Powers of the CSSF during the life of a UCI

Supervision of Luxembourg-based UCIs

8.10   Once a UCI has been approved and added to the list of UCIs, the CSSF verifies the UCI's compliance with its legal obligations. It uses several means to achieve that end.

8.11   First of all, any change in any of the documents submitted to the CSSF in order to obtain the UCI's authorization must first be approved by the CSSF.[13] That enables the CSSF to ensure that the law is observed and that the general interest of the unitholders is protected.

8.12   More generally, UCIs must send the CSSF their annual and semi-annual reports no later than the date on which they are published.[14] There are two reasons for this. First, it means that the CSSF is kept informed about the UCI's development and activities; secondly, it enables the CSSF to check the information sent to investors. Any error or omission in those reports may result in the publication of an amended report.[15]

8.13   Because annual and semi-annual reports are submitted only once every six months, they do not provide the CSSF with full information about a UCI's operations—hence the obligation to disclose information to the CSSF more frequently, ie monthly, pursuant to a legal provision authorizing the CSSF to ask UCIs for all information that it may consider necessary.[16] The type of information to be provided to the CSSF is identical for all UCIs, ie a list of financial items.

---

[10]   Arts 93(2) and 114, 2002 Act; Ch K, Circular 91/75.

[11]   Art 118, 2002 Act; Art 58, Act of 13 February 2007.

[12]   Ch L, I, 3, Circular 91/75.

[13]   Arts 93(4) and 114, 2002 Act; Arts 42(4) and 56, Act of 13 February 2007; Ch K, Circular 91/75.

[14]   Art 114, 2002 Act; Ch L, III, 3, Circular 91/75; Art 56, Act of 13 February 2007, which does not make reference to semi-annual reports, since the requirement to draft such reports is not imposed on SIFs.

[15]   Ch L, III, 3, Circular 91/75.

[16]   Art 118, 2002 Act; Art 58, Act of 13 February 2007.

UCIs have no obligation to publish such information.[17] In addition, it should be noted that the information provided monthly must also be supplied on an annual basis.[18] With respect to those communication obligations SIFs benefit from extensive disclosure derogations.

More generally, the CSSF may, directly or through appointees, examine a UCI's **8.14** accounting records, registers, or any other document.[19] Similarly, it may ask a UCI's independent auditor for all information or certificates on any matters of which the independent auditor has or should have knowledge in connection with the exercise of his office.[20] Lastly, it may order the independent auditor to check certain aspects of a UCI's activities and operations, at the UCI's expense.[21]

Non-compliance by a UCI with its obligation to follow the instructions of the **8.15** CSSF and to supply it with the requested information is an offence punishable under criminal law. In addition, the conducting persons of a UCI, other than a SIF, who refuse to produce the requested information or who provide incomplete, inaccurate, or false data may be fined.[22]

Supervision of foreign UCIs

The CSSF exercises less stringent supervision over foreign UCIs, which are subject **8.16** to supervision in their home State. The scope of the duties performed by the CSSF varies according to whether or not the UCI in question is a coordinated UCITS.

Coordinated UCITS are free to market their units anywhere in the EEA provided **8.17** that they inform the host Member State of their marketing plans and comply with certain local legal provisions.[23] The CSSF oversees compliance with such requirements. It verifies, *inter alia,* that the coordinated UCITS in question has appointed a Luxembourg-based banking or credit institution as paying agent responsible for making payments to the unitholders and redeeming units.[24] It also checks that the UCITS distributes in the Grand Duchy of Luxembourg the information that

---

[17] Circular IML 97/136 concerning financial information to be provided to the CSSF and to STATEC (*Service Central de la Statistique et des Études Économiques*). Circular IML 97/136 replaces and revokes Chapter M in Circular 91/75. As regards SIFs, see also Circular 07/310 on the financial information to be provided by SIFs.

[18] ibid.

[19] Art 118, 2002 Act; Art 58; Act of 13 February 2007.

[20] Art 113(3), 2002 Act; Art 55(3), Act of 13 February 2007.

[21] ibid.

[22] Art 108(1), 2002 Act.

[23] Arts 44–48, Directive 85/611; see also the guidelines of the CESR regarding the simplification of the notification procedure, available at <http://www.cesr-eu.org>.

[24] Art 59, 2002 Act.

must be published in its home State.[25] Lastly, it checks compliance by the UCITS with the applicable laws, regulations, and administrative provisions in force in Luxembourg that do not fall within the scope of the 2002 Act.[26]

8.18 If the CSSF finds that a foreign coordinated UCITS infringes the obligations incumbent on it in the Grand Duchy of Luxembourg, it may prohibit the marketing of the UCITS' units in Luxembourg.[27]

8.19 All other foreign UCIs, except closed-end funds within the meaning of the Act of 10 July 2005, may only offer their units publicly in or from the Grand Duchy of Luxembourg if previously authorized to do so.[28] Their constitutive documents and choice of depositary must be approved by the CSSF,[29] which also verifies that they fulfil the relevant conditions imposed by the 2002 Act, especially as regards the degree of supervision in their country of origin.[30]

8.20 Once a foreign non-coordinated UCI has been approved, the CSSF exercises the same level of supervision over it as is applied to Luxembourg-based UCIs,[31] on the understanding that it may rely on the forms of supervision exercised in the UCI's home State.

8.21 A foreign UCI qualifying as a closed-end fund within the meaning of the Act of 10 July 2005 may market its units or shares in the Grand Duchy of Luxembourg provided it complies with the European and national regulations on prospectuses for public offerings and admission to trading on a regulated market.

8.22 The right of the CSSF to obtain all such information it considers necessary for the performance of its duties also applies with regard to foreign UCIs. In that respect, provision is made for collaboration between the CSSF and the competent supervisory authorities as regards coordinated UCITS.[32]

8.23 The above-mentioned criminal penalties for Luxembourg-based UCIs are equally designed to ensure compliance by foreign UCIs (other than closed-end UCIs within the meaning of the Act of 10 July 2005) with their obligation to disclose information to the CSSF.[33]

---

[25] ibid Art 61, 2002 Act.
[26] ibid Art 58, 2002 Act; see also Circular 07/277 and the website of the CSSF <http://www.cssf.lu>, under the heading 'Marketing of UCITS > Marketing of units/shares of European UCITS in Luxembourg', for more details of the rules applicable in Luxembourg.
[27] Art 100(1), 2002 Act.
[28] ibid Art 93(1).
[29] ibid Article 93(2).
[30] ibid Article 76.
[31] ibid Art 93.
[32] Arts 50 and 52b, Directive 85/611. See 8.78 *et seq* below.
[33] Art 108(1), 2002 Act.

Powers of the CSSF during the liquidation of a UCI

The CSSF is also involved in the dissolution of Luxembourg-based UCIs. Where **8.24** a UCI is dissolved voluntarily, the CSSF approves the choice of liquidators[34] and continues to subject the UCI to general supervision.[35] The situation is different in the case of judicial liquidations, in which supervision is exercised by the District Court instead of the CSSF.[36]

Intermediaries Acting in Support of the CSSF's Supervisory Role

Intermediaries in Luxembourg-based UCIs

The two essential intermediaries supporting the CSSF's supervisory role: the depositary and the independent auditor

The CSSF does not carry out its task of supervisioning UCIs on its own. It **8.25** is broadly supported by two intermediaries, which are likewise responsible for keeping a close eye on UCIs.

The first of those intermediaries is the depositary. Appointed by the UCI and **8.26** approved by the CSSF, it is responsible for the performance of specific supervision duties, sometimes on a daily basis. The content of those assignments has already been analysed.[37]

The second of the intermediaries is the independent auditor. Like the depositary, **8.27** the independent auditor of a Luxembourg-based UCI is appointed by the UCI itself.[38] He must demonstrate adequate professional experience.[39] His involvement is less regular than that of the depositary. In principle, he becomes involved once a year during the four months following the end of the financial year[40] or six months following the year end in the case of SIFs.[41]

The task of the independent auditor of a Luxembourg-based UCI is more **8.28** extensive than that of the auditor of a traditional company, precisely because of his collaboration with the CSSF. It covers three aspects: auditing the accounts,

---

[34] ibid Art 106(1); Article 49(1), Act of 13 February 2007.
[35] Art 105(1), 2002 Act; Art 48(1), Act of 13 February 2007.
[36] Art 104, 2002 Act; Art 47, Act of 13 February 2007. See 9.32 below.
[37] See 6.319 *et seq* above.
[38] Art 113(2), 2002 Act; Art 55(2), Act of 13 February 2007. In an investment company, the auditor is appointed by the general meeting of shareholders (Section I, Circular 02/81).
[39] Art 113(1), 2002 Act; Art 55(1), Act of 13 February 2007.
[40] Art 109(2), 2002 Act.
[41] Art 52(2), Act of 13 February 2007.

verifying compliance with the specific laws and regulations concerning UCIs, and reporting to the CSSF. As explained below, the independent auditor may be required to provide the CSSF with detailed information about a UCI as part of that assignment. His status is therefore subject to special standards, which are also examined below.

Duties of independent auditors of UCIs

8.29 The independent auditor of a UCI has a broader mandate than an auditor at an ordinary company. His mandate is specified in detail in Circular 02/81. Under this Circular, the independent auditor's assignment is not limited to auditing accounting documents but includes analysis of a UCI's operations. The results of this analysis are recorded in a report reviewing the UCI's operations, which must deal with a number of matters listed in the Circular. Having regard to the number of matters to be reported on, the Circular is frequently referred to as the 'long-form report circular'. It does not apply to SIFs.

8.30 The long-form report, the report on the annual accounts, and the letter with recommendations for management (the 'management letter') form an important source of information for the CSSF in the performance of its supervisory duties.

8.31 The work of a UCI's auditor includes the following three basic assignments:

(1) auditing the annual accounts and drawing up a report on the annual accounts based on that audit;
(2) verifying the UCI's operations and the organization and procedures applicable to the UCI (the results of this verification are recorded in the long-form report); and
(3) reporting to the CSSF.

8.32 These assignments are set out in detail in a contract signed between the auditor and the UCI. The audits conducted by the auditor must be described in a report on the annual accounts and in a long-form report.

Report on the annual accounts

8.33 The independent auditor checks the accounting data in the following documents, which form the basis of a UCI's annual report.[42]

(1) the balance sheet;
(2) the profit and loss account;
(3) the report on the UCI's activities in the financial year in question;
(4) the information listed in Schedule B to the 2002 Act for UCIs governed by that Act, and in the Annexe to the Act of 13 February 2007 for SIFs;

---

[42] Art 110(5), 2002 Act; Art 52(4), Act of 13 February 2007.

(5) any significant information included in the annual financial statements that will enable investors to make an informed judgment on the development of the activities of the UCI and its results.

The independent auditor therefore makes sure that the annual report faithfully **8.34** reflects the assets, the financial situation, and the results of the UCI.[43] That assignment differs little from the audit assignments given to him by ordinary companies.[44] Applying a series of tests and checks, he verifies the quality of the financial information contained in the report. If he has any doubts about the quality of the financial information, he must immediately inform the CSSF.[45]

The annual accounts are audited according to the working recommendations **8.35** issued by the *Institut des Réviseurs d'Entreprises luxembourgeois* (IRE) based on the International Auditing Standards (IAS) published by the IFAC (International Federation of Accountants), adapted or complemented as necessary by national legislation or practice.

The results of the auditor's review of the annual report are recorded in an attesta- **8.36** tion attached to this report.[46] It is sent, together with the report, in duplicate,[47] to the CSSF.[48] Any irregularity noted by the auditor is reported in a 'management letter', in which the UCI's conducting persons are invited to explain the issue raised. This document is sent to the CSSF, which determines what steps to take.

Long-form report

The purpose of the long-form report is to set out the auditor's observations in **8.37** connection with the UCI's financial and organizational aspects, particularly its relations with the head office, the depositary, and the other intermediaries. The long-form report is not required for SIFs.

The audit focuses on all types of transactions, whether recorded on or off the bal- **8.38** ance sheet. The auditor's mandate may not exclude any transaction. He also reviews the organization and procedures applicable to the UCI, especially anti-money laundering procedures, procedures to verify compliance with investment restrictions, procedures for checking net asset value calculations, reconciliation procedures, and valuation methods and procedures.

---

[43] Art 113(1) and (3), 2002 Act; Art 55(1) and (3), Act of 13 February 2007.

[44] On the understanding, however, that the CSSF may impose special standards as regards the scope of his mandate and the contents of his report (Art 113(3), 2002 Act; Art 55(3), Act of 13 February 2007).

[45] Art 113(3), 2002 Act; Art 55(3), Act of 13 February 2007.

[46] Art 113(1), 2002 Act; Ch L, III, 1, Circular 91/75; Art 55(1), Act of 13 February 2007.

[47] Ch L, III, 3, Circular 91/75.

[48] Art 114, 2002 Act; Art 56, Act of 13 February 2007.

8.39 The auditor must give a detailed description of all oversights, errors, material problems, and breaches. He must provide precise information about weaknesses, gaps, and necessary improvements so as to allow the CSSF to assess the situation. These comments must be recorded in the report or in a management letter sent to the board of directors of the UCI or the management company, which in their turn may comment upon the auditor's remarks. All other documents issued by the auditor must be attached to the report.[49]

8.40 The long-form report must be submitted to the CSSF within four months from the end of the period under review. It must be concise, clear, and critical. It is not a public document, but is exclusively intended for the board of directors of the UCI or the management company and for the CSSF, and must enable them to make a precise and informed judgment on any issue raised. It is made up of six parts, analysed below.[50]

8.41 **Organization of the UCI**   The proper operation of a UCI requires specialized services in Luxembourg and other countries. The auditor of the UCI may refer to the audit reports drafted by the auditor of the depositary and the professional of the financial sector responsible for the head office tasks related to services provided to the UCI, provided his report stipulates on which audit report he has relied and provided he supplies the following data:

(1) the name of the auditor of the head office or the depositary;
(2) the date of the audit report; and
(3) if applicable, the audit report and the name of the auditor who has drawn up the report.[51]

8.42 If the auditor of the UCI does not use this right, he must conduct his own checks and verifications. In this case, he must inform the board of directors of the UCI or the management company of the matters on which he requires information. The board of directors forwards these requests for information to the audited entity.[52]

8.43 If the head office or the depositary has delegated some of its functions, the auditor must obtain access to the relevant information and refer to such information in his report. Moreover, he must specify the exact allocation of tasks between the different parties[53] and express an opinion on the adequacy of the coordination and general supervision procedures put in place.[54] His report must give a precise

---

[49] Section III, A, Circular 02/81.
[50] ibid.
[51] ibid Section III, C, 1.1.1 and 1.2.1.
[52] ibid Section III, C, 1.
[53] ibid Section III, C, 1.1.2.1.
[54] ibid Section III, C, 1 and 1.1.2.1.

description of the network of correspondent banks and the policy used by the entity to select counterparties.[55]

If the depositary also manages all or part of the head office functions, the report **8.44** must provide explanations on the separation of duties, specifically between depositary and head office duties.[56] He must further specify whether the head office and its delegates have a manual of procedures covering the aspects provided for in Chapter D of Circular 91/75[57] and whether they comply with the provisions of this Circular on accounting operations, calculation of net asset value, and the availability of basic documentation on the UCI and its transactions.[58]

The UCI's auditor must further express an opinion on the adequacy of the proce- **8.45** dures adopted by the depositary for reconciling the positions recorded by it and by the UCI.[59] He must comment upon the results of these reconciliations and give a detailed description of any serious problem encountered in this respect. He must also review the UCI's off balance sheet transactions.[60]

As regards the computer system, the auditor must give a brief description of the **8.46** software used. He must indicate any significant changes in the system and any problems encountered during migration from one system to another. He must further express an opinion on the adequacy of the computer system and human resources having regard to the volume of activities of the UCI in question,[61] and, as applicable, the pooling or co-management technique, if utilized by the UCI. He must also evaluate the adequacy of the net asset value calculation system having regard to the type of investments made by the UCI.

He must further verify that appropriate measures have been taken to safeguard the **8.47** confidentiality of information. He must outline the general principles of the contingency plan in the event of a breakdown of the system or problems with Internet connections.

Lastly, the auditor must verify the existence and adequacy of the internal **8.48** supervision procedures used to check the origin of funds, the investment policy and restrictions, and the accuracy of the net asset value calculation. His verifications must also cover the procedures used to value the securities portfolio, to register and settle subscription and redemption orders, and to validate and register securities purchases and sales.[62]

---

[55] ibid Section III, C, 1.2.2.1.
[56] ibid.
[57] ibid Section III, C, 1.1.2.1 and 1.2.2.1.
[58] ibid Section III, C, 1.1.2.2.
[59] ibid Section III, C, 1.2.2.3.
[60] ibid Section III, C, 1.2.1.
[61] ibid Section III, C, 1.1.2.1 and 1.2.2.2.
[62] ibid Section III, C, 1.1.2.1.

8.49   In the case of FCPs, the auditor must extend his checks and tests to the management company. In doing so, he may refer to the report of the management company's auditor. If he does not use this option, the board of directors of the management company must provide him with the necessary information about the services supplied by the management company to the FCP. The auditor must also check whether the management company performs its functions in accordance with the applicable laws and regulations.[63]

8.50   Within the framework of the UCI's relationships with other intermediaries, such as managers, transfer agents, distributors, etc, the auditor must indicate whether activities have been hampered by major operational problems. If so, he must describe them in detail to enable the CSSF to assess the situation.[64]

8.51   Supervision of the UCI's transactions   In this part of his long-form report, the auditor must check and verify the following points:

(1)   the adequacy of the special procedures developed and implemented to check the origin of funds;

(2)   the valuation of the securities portfolio by the accounting agent, with particular attention to unlisted and illiquid securities;

(3)   risk management;

(4)   the investment policy and restrictions; and

(5)   the accuracy of the net asset value calculation.

8.52   Since the head office of a UCI handles subscription, redemption, and transfer requests for the UCI's units or shares, the auditor must ensure compliance with the rules in the Circulars concerning the avoidance of money laundering and terrorist financing. If the UCI's auditor relies on the checks conducted in this area by the auditor of the head office in question, he must indicate the name of that auditor and the date of the report.[65] If not, the auditor must personally analyse the distribution channel for the UCI's units or shares in order to determine whether the head office performs its obligations in connection with the avoidance of money laundering and terrorist financing. More precisely, he must check whether the UCI is exempt from the identification obligation and verify whether the conditions laid down by Circular 05/211 have been met. The auditor must also check whether the head office monitors unusual transactions. In this context, he must indicate the selection method used, the sample files checked, and the percentage of total transactions covered.[66]

---

[63]   Section III, C, 1.3, Circular 02/81.
[64]   ibid Section III, C, 1.4.
[65]   ibid Section III, C, 2.1.
[66]   ibid.

The auditor must also check whether the valuation methods are applied in accor- **8.53** dance with the 2002 Act and the management regulations or the articles of incorporation and whether these methods are used consistently. He must, *inter alia*, check the application and fairness of the portfolio valuation rules (particularly focusing on unlisted and illiquid securities), securities lending/borrowing, repurchase and reverse repurchase agreements, sale with right of repurchase agreements, forward transactions, futures, swaps, and options.[67] He must further do sample tests to check whether these transactions were undertaken at arm's length.[68]

In his report, the auditor of the UCI must provide an analysis and assessment of **8.54** the risk management systems and must specify whether the existing risk supervision system is adequate at least as regards the risks inherent in the investment policy and risks of the UCI in question, such as credit/counterparty risk, market risk, settlement risk, foreign exchange risk, and, where appropriate, interest rate risk, liquidity risk, and risks relating to the use of derivative instruments.[69] The auditor must indicate the manager(s) or entity/ies entrusted with the supervision of these risks and the frequency with which such checks are made.[70]

As part of his assignment, the UCI's auditor must also check compliance with the **8.55** investment policy and investment restrictions.[71] The auditor must also check the net asset value calculation, and analyse all calculation errors and non-compliance with the investment rules. He must further report material errors and cases of non-compliance which should have been notified in accordance with Circular 02/77. If no material net asset value calculation error or non-compliance with the investment policy is detected, this is expressly mentioned in the report.[72] The auditor must indicate whether the net asset value has been published pursuant to Article 116 of the 2002 Act.[73]

The auditor must comment clearly and precisely on the items in the consolidated **8.56** balance sheet and the combined profit and loss account. He must certify their existence, their amounts, and the adequacy of their accounting treatment, and the consistent application of the accounting principles.[74] He must further review securities bought and sold during the two weeks preceding and following the end of the financial year[75] in order to identify the presence of transactions, if any,

---

[67] ibid Section III, C, 2.2.
[68] ibid.
[69] ibid Section III, C, 2.3.
[70] ibid.
[71] ibid Section III, C, 2.4.
[72] ibid.
[73] ibid Section III, C, 2.6.
[74] Section III, C, 2.5.
[75] This period may be extended when suspicious transactions are detected.

entered into for 'window-dressing' purposes.[76] He must further collect statistics on portfolio turnover in order to determine whether transactions have been entered into for the purpose of 'churning' .[77]

8.57 The auditor must request a list of all costs charged to the UCI, including transaction costs, where possible referring to the gross amount. He must verify whether the most significant costs have been calculated in accordance with the applicable contracts.[78] He must pay special attention to the performance fee paid to the manager.

8.58 Finally, the auditor must obtain the following attestations from the board of directors:

(1) an attestation that neither the managers nor their related parties have received rebates from brokers;

(2) an attestation as to whether any fees have been shared with other parties; and

(3) an attestation as to whether any arrangements have been made regarding the payment of soft commissions.[79]

The particulars of any soft commissions and shared commissions connected with a UCI's activity must be included in the report.[80]

8.59 **Internet** The long-form report must mention whether the UCI makes direct use of the Internet for communication or distribution purposes.[81]

8.60 **Investor complaints** The auditor must ask the board of directors of the UCI or the management company for the number of complaints received during the financial year under review by the head office in Luxembourg to which the UCI has had to respond. If no complaints have been received, this is specifically mentioned in the report.[82]

8.61 **Follow-up of problems identified in previous long-form reports** The auditor must indicate in his report what measures have been carried out to follow up on serious irregularities and weaknesses, gaps, and major problems identified in previous audits.[83]

8.62 **Opinion of the auditor** In the last part of the long-form report, the auditor must express an opinion on his overall assignment. To this end, he summarizes the

---

[76] Section III, C, 2.5, Circular 02/81.
[77] ibid.
[78] ibid.
[79] ibid.
[80] ibid.
[81] ibid Section III, C, 3.
[82] ibid Section III, C, 4.
[83] ibid Section III, C, 5.

material comments and conclusions in the report in order to provide an overview of the UCI's situation. He must also indicate the main recommendations and observations made to the board of directors of the UCI or the management company, and their response. If he has written a separate management letter, he must mention this and attach it to the report.[84]

Information for the CSSF

While checking the annual report or carrying out another assignment on behalf of a UCI, the independent auditor may have reason to doubt the quality of the financial information supplied on other occasions by the UCI to investors or to the CSSF. In that event, he must immediately notify the CSSF.[85] **8.63**

Moreover, pursuant to Directive 85/611, as subsequently amended and transposed into the 2002 Act,[86] the independent auditor is obliged[87] to inform the CSSF 'forthwith'[88] of any fact or decision that comes to his notice in the performance of his duties,[89] whether at the UCI itself or at a company that has a link of supervision with the UCI, which is such as to: **8.64**

(1) constitute a serious violation[90] of the 2002 Act or the regulations adopted for its execution;

---

[84] ibid Section III, C, 6.

[85] Art 113(3), 2002 Act; Art 55(3), Act of 13 February 2007.

[86] Act of 29 April 1999 (1) transposing Directive (EC) 95/26 concerning the reinforcement of prudential supervision into the Act of 5 April 1993 concerning the financial sector, as amended, and into the Act of 30 March 1988 concerning undertakings for collective investment, as amended; (2) partially transposing Art 7 of Directive (EEC) 93/6 on the capital adequacy of investment firms and credit institutions into the Act of 5 April 1993 concerning the financial sector, as amended; (3) making various further amendments to the Act of 5 April 1993 concerning the financial sector, as amended; (4) amending the Grand-Ducal Regulation of 19 July 1983 concerning the fiduciary contracts of credit institutions (*Mémorial* A 1999, 1301).

[87] An obligation was preferred to an option, in order to release independent auditors from all liability in that respect (*Parliamentary doc* No 4370, Comments on the Articles, 7).

[88] Art 113(3), 2002 Act. While the obligation to inform the CSSF forthwith does not bar the independent auditor from first discussing the matter with the managers of the UCI in question, it may not unduly delay notification of the CSSF (*Parliamentary doc* No 4370, Comments on the Articles, 7).

[89] Those terms must be understood broadly to include every assignment the independent auditor may be called upon to carry out for the undertaking, including the examination of any merger and demerger plans and the preparation of valuation reports on contributions in kind (*Parliamentary doc* No 4370, Comments on the Articles, 7).

[90] At first sight, the term 'serious' seems to be an addition by the Luxembourg legislature compared with the French version of Directive (EEC) 85/611, as amended by European Parliament and Council Directive (EC) 95/26 of 29 June 1995 amending Directives (EEC) 77/780 and (EEC) 89/646 in the field of credit institutions; Directives (EEC) 73/239 and (EEC) 92/49 in the field of non-life insurance; Directives (EEC) 79/267 and (EEC) 92/96 in the field of life insurance; Directive (EEC) 93/22 in the area of investment firms; and Directive (EEC) 85/611 in the field of undertakings for collective investment in transferable securities (UCITS) with a view to reinforcing prudential supervision [1995] OJ L168/7–13. The latter imposes on the independent auditor the

(2) put the UCI's future survival in jeopardy; or

(3) entail a refusal to certify the accounts, or the issue of a qualified audit opinion.[91]

This information obligation also applies to the independent auditors of a SIF.[92]

8.65 Lastly, the independent auditor has the even more general duty to send 'all information or certificates' required by the CSSF 'on any matters of which . . . [the auditor] has or should have knowledge in connection with the discharge of his duty'.[93] The CSSF may also instruct him to check one or more particular aspects of a UCI's activities and operations.[94]

Status of the independent auditor of UCIs

8.66 The importance of the independent auditor's role in the supervision of UCIs is clear from the above description. For that reason, the CSSF must have complete and unreserved confidence in him.[95] The 2002 Act and the Act of 13 February 2007 factor in that mandatory requirement and authorize the CSSF to withdraw from the list of authorized UCIs any UCI whose independent auditor does not satisfy the specified conditions[96] or does not discharge the obligations mentioned above.[97]

8.67 Although an intermediary of the CSSF, the independent auditor is appointed and remunerated by the UCI.[98] That state of affairs must not affect his independence.[99] His obligations vis-à-vis the CSSF take precedence over his duty of loyalty to the UCI by which he is appointed.

---

obligation to inform the CSSF of 'any fact or decision . . . which is liable to constitute a material breach of the laws or regulations that lay down the conditions governing authorisation or which specifically govern pursuit of the activities of financial undertakings' (Art 50a(1) of Directive (EEC) 85/611). It nevertheless seems that the above-mentioned Article 50a covers only those facts that could seriously affect a UCI's situation, as indicated in Recital (15) in the preamble to European Parliament and Council Directive (EEC) 95/26 of 29 June 1995, and the words *material breach of the laws* used in the English version of that Directive (*Parliamentary doc* No 4370, Comments on the Articles, 7).

[91] Art 113(3), 2002 Act.
[92] Art 55(3), Act of 13 February 2007.
[93] Art 113(3), 2002 Act.
[94] ibid. Such an inspection is carried out at the expense of the UCI in question.
[95] *Parliamentary doc* No 4612, Explanatory Statement, 3.
[96] Including adequate professional experience (Art 113(1), 2002 Act; Art 55(1), Act of 13 February 2007).
[97] Art 113(4), 2002 Act; Art 55(4), Act of 13 February 2007.
[98] Art 113(2), 2002 Act; Art 55(2), Act of 13 February 2007.
[99] Art 7 Act of 28 June 1984 concerning the organization of the profession of independent auditor (*Mémorial* A 1984, 1346; also see Y Lacroix and L Tristan 'Parties and service providers involved in specialised investment funds' in *Specialised Investment Funds* (Arendt & Medernach, 2007) 75.

The information obtained by the independent auditor in the performance of his **8.68** duties is covered by professional secrecy.[100] As described more fully in the Act of 23 December 1998 establishing a supervisory commission of the financial sector as well as in the 2002 Act,[101] that means that such information may be disclosed only in the following cases:

(1) within the limits imposed by Directive 85/611 and the 2002 Act, for the purposes of cooperation with the CSSF;
(2) in situations falling within the ambit of criminal law;[102]
(3) when presented in abridged form, in such a way that a UCI, management company, or depositary cannot be identified individually;[103]

Point (3) above does not apply:

(a) to information exchanges between the CSSF and the Central Bank;[104]
(b) to cases where persons referred to are called upon to testify in court, or, in the event of an appeal against a decision made by the CSSF, in fulfilment of its remit;[105]
(c) to disclosure permitted or required under law or regulation.[106]

There is one other case in which information obtained by an independent **8.69** auditor in the course of his audit duties may be disclosed. That case is not covered in the 2002 Act even though it is mentioned in Directive 85/611,[107] namely the disclosure, within the framework of civil or commercial proceedings, of information about a coordinated UCITS or the management company or depositary of a coordinated UCITS that has been declared bankrupt or has gone into judicial liquidation, provided that such information does not concern third parties involved in any rescue attempts.

The 2002 Act and the Act of 13 February 2007 release from all civil or criminal **8.70** liability an independent auditor who has sent to the CSSF, in good faith, the information he is required to disclose under the 2002 Act or the Act of 13 February 2007.[108]

---

[100] Art 9, of the Act of 28 June 1984 (n 99 above). See also Art 98(1), 2002 Act, which has no equivalent in the Act of 13 February 2007 and Art 16, Act of 23 December 1998 establishing a supervisory commission of the financial sector, as amended.
[101] Art 98(1), 2002 Act and Art 16, Act of 23 December 1998 establishing a supervisory commission of the financial sector, as amended.
[102] ibid.
[103] ibid.
[104] Article 16, Act of 23 December 1998 (n 101 above).
[105] ibid.
[106] ibid.
[107] Article 50.2, Directive (EEC) 85/611.
[108] Article 113(3), 2002 Act; Art 55, Act of 13 February 2007.

Intermediaries in foreign UCIs

Intermediaries in foreign coordinated UCITS

8.71 The services provided by depositaries and independent auditors vis-à-vis the supervisory authority in the home State of foreign coordinated UCITS are governed by precise provisions in Directive 85/611. Cooperation between those entities is subject to the rules laid down by the home State of the UCITS. In principle, the host State has no right to impose any additional requirements.

Intermediaries in UCIs other than coordinated UCITS

8.72 Like Luxembourg-based UCIs, non-coordinated foreign UCIs other than a closed-end UCI within the meaning of the Act of 10 July 2005 operating in the Grand Duchy of Luxembourg must have their annual report audited.[109] There is no express requirement that the auditor be an independent auditor ('*réviseur indépendant*' within the meaning of Luxembourg law). The 2002 Act refers more generally to an 'independent expert providing all required guarantees of probity and professional skill',[110] thus allowing the application of a UCI's national law. The role of the expert in question is the same as that of the independent auditors of Luxembourg-based UCIs.

Supervision of Luxembourg-based UCIs by Foreign Supervisory Authorities

8.73 Luxembourg-based UCIs that market their units in foreign countries are subject to supervision by the local competent authorities with respect to their marketing activities in the relevant host State, whose supervision is based on uniform rules when applicable to coordinated UCITS and carried out in a Member State of the EEA. In all other cases, the scope of supervision varies according to the type of UCI and the State in which the units are marketed.

8.74 Pursuant to Directive 85/611, a coordinated UCITS based in Luxembourg is free to market its units in other Member States of the EEA without obtaining local authorization. That said, it is required to observe certain formalities and constraints. For example, it must inform the CSSF in advance of its intention to market its units outside its national territory.[111] It must also notify the authorities of the States in which it intends to market its units and send them certain documents listed in Directive 85/611.[112]

---

[109] Art 113(6), 2002 Act.
[110] ibid.
[111] ibid Art 55.
[112] For such UCIs, the documents are as follows: an attestation by the CSSF that it qualifies as a coordinated UCITS; a notification letter; the latest version of its constitutive documents;

The supervisory authorities of the Member States concerned have two months to **8.75** examine all the documents presented for inspection and to decide on that basis whether to authorize the proposed marketing. If a reply is not received within two months, marketing may commence.[113]

In the event of refusal, the authorities must always give their reasons.[114] **8.76** Their decision may be based only on the reasons listed expressly in Directive 85/611, ie: failure to comply with the provisions of the host State in the areas not governed by Directive 85/611; failure to make the necessary arrangements for payments, redemption of units, or distribution of information to the unitholders in the host State; or unlawful arrangements.[115]

Once the units of a coordinated UCITS are allowed to be marketed, the **8.77** supervisory authority of the host State merely ensures that the UCITS complies with the provisions it must observe in that State pursuant to Directive 85/611, ie:

(1) the laws, regulations and administrative provisions in force in that State that do not fall within the field governed by Directive 85/611;[116]
(2) the provisions governing advertising in that State;[117] and
(3) the obligation to provide the necessary facilities in that State, in accordance with the prevailing requirements, for making payments to unitholders, redeeming units, and making available the information that UCITS are obliged to provide in the Grand Duchy of Luxembourg, in at least one language accepted by the host State.[118]

Collaboration between the CSSF and Foreign Supervisory Authorities

Many UCIs do not wish to limit their operations to the territory of their home **8.78** State, hence the need for cooperation between national authorities. The various agreements signed within the framework of the European Union and the EEA

---

the most recent version of its full prospectus and simplified prospectus; the latest annual report and any subsequent half-yearly report; and a description of the methods used to market its units in the other Member State (Art 46, Directive 85/611, as supplemented with the guidelines of the CESR regarding the simplification of the notification procedure, available at <http://www.cesr.eu>; see also Art 55, 2002 Act and Circular 07/277).

[113] Art 46, Directive 85/611.
[114] ibid.
[115] ibid.
[116] ibid Art 44.1.
[117] ibid Art 44.2.
[118] ibid Arts 45 and 47.

have enabled the organization of such cooperation within the framework of Directive 85/611, as amended in 1995.[119] The Directive applies only to cooperation as regards the supervision of coordinated UCITS and does not govern the supervision of other types of UCI.

8.79 Moreover, that legal framework is not binding on third party States, with whose competent supervisory authorities only specific bilateral agreements may be entered into. Directive 85/611 lays down only one requirement in that respect: the guarantee that their professional secrecy is at least equivalent to the secrecy imposed on the authorities of EEA Member States.[120]

8.80 The scope of collaboration between the authorities therefore varies according to two factors: their location and the type of UCI concerned.

Cooperation between the CSSF and the supervisory authorities of other Member States of the EEA

Cooperation with regard to the supervision of UCITS within the meaning of Directive 85/611

8.81 Cooperation between the supervisory authorities of EEA Member States as regards the prudential supervision of UCITS is governed by Directive 85/611.[121] The Directive provides, first of all, that cooperation between supervisory authorities must observe the obligation of professional secrecy binding each such

---

[119] European Parliament and Council Directive (EC) 95/26 of 29 June 1995 amending Directives (EEC) 77/780 and (EEC) 89/646 in the field of credit institutions; Directives (EEC) 73/239 and (EEC) 92/49 in the field of non-life insurance; Directives (EEC) 79/267 and (EEC) 92/96 in the field of life insurance; Directive (EEC) 93/22 in the area of investment firms; and Directive (EEC) 85/611 in the field of undertakings for collective investment in transferable securities (UCITS), with a view to reinforcing prudential supervision [1995] OJ L168/7–13. This amendment to Directive (EEC) 85/611 was transposed into the 1988 Act by the Act of 29 April 1999: (1) transposing Directive (EC) 95/26 concerning the reinforcement of prudential supervision into the Act of 5 April 1993 concerning the financial sector, as amended, and into the Act of 30 March 1988 concerning undertakings for collective investment, as amended; (2) partially transposing Art 7 of Directive (EEC) 93/6 on the capital adequacy of investment firms and credit institutions into the Act of 5 April 1993 concerning the financial sector, as amended; (3) making various further amendments to the Act of 5 April 1993 concerning the financial sector, as amended; (4) amending the Grand-Ducal Regulation of 19 July 1983 concerning fiduciary contracts of credit institutions (*Mémorial* A 1999, 1301).

[120] Art 50.4, Directive (EEC) 85/611.

[121] ibid Art 50. That Article governs general cooperation—internal and throughout the EEA—between the supervisory authorities of a UCI, the authorities charged with supervising other entities in the financial sector, and certain monetary authorities. The objective is to promote the exchange of information and to preserve the confidentiality of the data exchanged. This type of cooperation applies less directly to UCIs and is not discussed in this work.

authority.[122] It also circumscribes the use of information received, which is limited to the exercise of prudential supervision over UCITS,[123] ie

(1) to check that the conditions governing the status of coordinated UCITS, management company, and depositary and the exercise of the related activities (including efficient administrative organization and internal supervision) have been fulfilled;
(2) to impose penalties; and
(3) in administrative appeals or court proceedings against decisions of the supervisory authorities.

The 2002 Act designates the CSSF as the body in Luxembourg to whom the provisions of the Directive concerning cooperation apply.[124] It requires the CSSF, *inter alia*, to collaborate closely with the supervisory authorities of other Member States in order to supervise UCITS, 'within the meaning of' Directive 85/611.[125] The term 'within the meaning of' Directive 85/611 goes beyond the provisions of Directive 85/611, in that it embraces UCIs that are excluded from Part I of the 2002 Act on account of their investment or borrowing policy. It also includes UCIs from outside the EEA whose object and operations correspond to the definition of UCITS contained in Directive 85/611.[126] Directive 85/611 governs only cooperation between the supervisory authorities of UCITS that are 'subject to' it,[127] which rules out the above two types of UCITS. **8.82**

Collaboration in matters of supervision means that the CSSF must inform the supervisory authorities of the Member States in which the units of a Luxembourg-based UCITS are marketed of any serious measure it has decided to take against the UCITS concerned.[128] Such serious measures include, in particular, the withdrawal of authorization, although the suspension of redemption of a UCITS' units must also be reported. **8.83**

The CSSF must also inform the supervisory authority of the home State of a coordinated UCITS whose units are marketed in the Grand Duchy of Luxembourg of any decision to prohibit its marketing activities.[129] **8.84**

The CSSF may use confidential information received by it only for certain purposes listed in the 2002 Act, which repeats Directive 85/611 almost word **8.85**

---

[122] Art 50.3, Directive 85/611.
[123] ibid Art 50.5, as transposed into Art 98(4), 2002 Act.
[124] Art 98, 2002 Act.
[125] ibid Art 98(2).
[126] Art 1.2, Directive 85/611.
[127] ibid Art 2.
[128] Art 103, 2002 Act.
[129] ibid Art 100(2).

for word.[130] The authorization to use such information in legal proceedings is even more restrictive than under Directive 85/611, which refers to any court action concerning a decision taken 'in respect of a UCITS pursuant to the laws, regulations and administrative provisions adopted in accordance with this Directive' and to the remedies available if no decision is taken within six months of the submission of an application by a UCITS.[131] The 2002 Act adopts a more restrictive position as in the context of legal proceedings, confidential information may be used only in an action challenging a decision refusing authorization or a decision withdrawing authorization.[132]

8.86 Conversely, information received from the CSSF may be used only within the strict limits set out in Directive 85/611.[133]

Cooperation with respect to the supervision of UCIs other than UCITS within the meaning of Directive 85/611

8.87 Prior to its amendment in 1999, the 1988 Act[134] required the CSSF to collaborate with foreign supervisory authorities as part of its duty to supervise UCIs in general. That obligation is now limited to the supervision of UCITS within the meaning of Directive 85/611. Strict interpretation of the 2002 Act means that information sent[135] and received[136] by the CSSF may be used only for the purposes of supervision of UCITS within the meaning of Directive 85/611. Far too strict in both principle and consequences, such a solution must be interpreted in the light of the overriding Community principle of fair cooperation between national administrations, which requires mutual assistance

---

130 See 8.81 above.
131 Art 51.2, Directive 85/611.
132 Art 98(4), 2002 Act.
133 Art 50.5, Directive 85/611.
134 Art 76(2), 1988 Act, as amended by the Act of 29 April 1999: (1) transposing Directive (EC) 95/26 concerning reinforcement of prudential supervision into the Act of 5 April 1993 concerning the financial sector, as amended, and into the Act of 30 March 1988 concerning undertakings for collective investment, as amended; (2) partially transposing Art 7 of Directive (EEC) 93/6 on the capital adequacy of investment undertakings and credit institutions into the Act of 5 April 1993 concerning the financial sector, as amended; (3) making various further amendments to the Act of 5 April 1993 concerning the financial sector, as amended; (4) amending the Grand-Ducal Decree of 19 July 1983 concerning the fiduciary contracts of credit institutions (*Mémorial* A 1999, 1301).
135 Art 98(2), 2002 Act: 'for that purpose alone'.
136 ibid Art 98(4). The *Parliamentary documents* accompanying the above-mentioned Act of 29 April 1999, which amends the 1988 Act, explain that: 'Communication of information is implicitly subject to the condition that the receiving authorities use it exclusively within the limits and for the purposes specified in paragraph (4) . . . That condition was not included in the text of the draft law because the EU Member States are deemed to have defined, in their internal law, the use their authorities may make of information received from other supervisory authorities within the Community, in accordance with Article 12.4, Directive 89/646/EEC' (*Parliamentary doc* No 4370, Comments on the Articles, 4).

between supervisory authorities so that there is efficient collaboration between those authorities, whether the object of their attention is a UCITS or not. In other words, cooperation is necessary even in the absence of an express legal provision.[137] This also applies to SIFs, even though the Act of 13 February 2007 is silent on this question.

Cooperation between the CSSF and the supervisory authorities of countries outside the EEA

Cooperation with regard to the supervision of UCITS within the meaning of Directive 85/611

Cooperation between the supervisory authorities of EEA Member States and of countries outside the EEA is governed by Directive 85/611, which states[138] that the communication of information to foreign authorities is permitted provided that the receiving authority observes the same degree of professional secrecy as provided for in Directive 85/611. **8.88**

The 2002 Act[139] repeats that obligation, which it further clarifies and supplements. According to the 2002 Act, the requirement of at least the same degree of professional secrecy on the part of the foreign authority obliges that authority, in particular, to limit the utilization of information received to the same sphere as that covered by the restrictions imposed on the CSSF. The foreign authority may therefore use information received only in order to supervise UCITS within the meaning of Directive 85/611. The 2002 Act ties professional secrecy to the obligation of reciprocity. In other words, foreign authorities must generally grant the CSSF the same right to information. **8.89**

Similarly, information received by the CSSF from foreign authorities may, in principle, be used only for the supervision of UCITS within the meaning of Directive 85/611.[140] Directive 85/611 itself does not impose this restriction. That is due to an error in the transcription of the Directive, which limits the use of information gathered by the CSSF in the Grand Duchy of Luxembourg to the supervision of UCITS. In the 2002 Act, reference to information of Luxembourg origin[141] was replaced by a reference to information from non-EEA countries.[142] The Community principle that national laws must be construed according to **8.90**

---

[137] The Community principle of fair cooperation between national administrations applies in this case and requires mutual assistance between supervisory authorities.

[138] Art 50.4, Directive 85/611.

[139] Art 98(3), 2002 Act.

[140] ibid Art 98(4), 2002 Act.

[141] ie ibid Art 98(1).

[142] ie ibid Art 98(3).

European law[143] could nevertheless be used here. The 2002 Act should be interpreted as not limiting the use of information received from non-EEA countries to the supervision of coordinated UCITS.

Cooperation with regard to the supervision of UCIs other than UCITS within the meaning of Directive 85/611

8.91 Until the amendment of 1999, the 1988 Act required the CSSF to collaborate with foreign supervisory authorities. That collaboration obligation is now reserved for the supervision of UCITS governed by Directive 85/611. The absence of legal constraints allows the CSSF to organize cooperation with supervisory authorities outside the EEA in its best interests.

Treatment of Errors in the Calculation of Net Asset Value and Non-Compliance with Investment Rules

8.92 The supervisory authorities of Luxembourg have long held that any error in the calculation of the net asset value of a UCI, regardless of its impact, must be reported and—save in exceptional cases—must give rise to compensation of the injured parties.

8.93 At the proposal of the Luxembourg investment fund industry, based on the example of other countries such as the United States, the United Kingdom, Ireland, and France, the CSSF, aware of the counter-productive impact of an excessively rigid approach, agreed some years ago to apply the principle of materiality to the treatment of net asset value calculation errors. This is the background to Circular 2000/8, issued on 15 March 2000, which established minimum rules of conduct for collective management professionals in the Grand Duchy of Luxembourg in the case of errors in the calculation of net asset value[144] or non-compliance with the investment rules applicable to UCIs.[145] The purpose of Circular 2000/8 was to correct such errors and failures and to ensure rapid and fair compensation for the injured UCI and investors. It was designed to be a pragmatic instrument, easy to implement and geared to economic realities. Its authors endeavoured to combine protection of investor interests with solutions to avoid unnecessarily cumbersome procedures with disproportionate costs. In its successive annual reports, the CSSF specified and developed certain rules laid down in the Circular in order to simplify its practical application.

---

[143] See 12.42 below.
[144] Section I, Circular 2000/8.
[145] ibid Section II.

On 27 November 2002, Circular 2000/8 was replaced by Circular 02/77. **8.94**
Circular 02/77 repeated most of the content of Circular 2000/8 subject to a few
changes of form. It further introduced a simplified procedure applicable when
the damage caused by a calculation error or non-compliance with investment
rules does not exceed a certain amount.[146] The following discussions are primarily
based on the above sources.

Circular 07/77 does not apply to SIFs. Insofar as an error in the calculation of the **8.95**
net asset value or the non-compliance with an investment rule is at the origin of a
damage suffered by an investor or creditor of a SIF, the latter must be indemnified
in accordance with the principles of civil liability. Otherwise, SIFs are not covered
by the provisions therein regarding the treatment of errors in the calculation of net
asset value and the non-compliance with investment rules.

Definitions and scope of application

Errors in the calculation of the net asset value

Errors in the calculation of the net asset value may be due to one or more factors **8.96**
related to inadequate internal control procedures, management shortcomings,
faults or deficiencies in the operation of the IT, accounting, or communication
systems, or non-compliance with the valuation rules contained in the constitutive
and sales documents of UCIs.[147]

The CSSF classifies calculation errors in four categories according to their origin, **8.97**
ie valuation errors, accounting errors, errors in the calculation of costs, and provisions and other errors, such as errors in the valuation of swaps or futures.[148]

It is presumed that the net asset value is correctly calculated where the rules **8.98**
provided for its determination in the constitutive and sales documents of the UCI
are strictly applied, consistently and in good faith, on the basis of the most current
and most reliable information available at the time of the calculation.[149]

Based on the observation that the net asset value calculation process is not an exact **8.99**
science and that the result of the calculation merely constitutes the closest possible
approximation of the true market value of the assets of a UCI, Circular 02/77
adopts the principle of materiality. Only errors with a material impact on the net

---

[146] Without contrary guidelines on the part of the CSSF, the particulars and analyses of the rules
of Circular 2000/8 in the CSSF's annual reports for 2000, 2001, and 2002 apply as-is to Circular
02/77. This principle has been expressly confirmed for excess bond positions (CSSF Annual Report
for 2002, 80).
[147] Section I, 1, Circular 02/77.
[148] CSSF Annual Report for 2000, 71.
[149] Section I, 1, Circular 02/77.

asset value, ie whose percentage compared with the net asset value reaches or exceeds a certain threshold, known as the materiality or tolerance threshold, must be dealt with according to the procedure laid out in the Circular.[150]

8.100 The materiality threshold is not always determined individually. The impact of several net asset value calculation errors may be considered collectively in order to determine to what extent the materiality threshold has been crossed. Thus, the concept of material errors covers not only isolated calculation errors with a significant impact on the net asset value but also unprocessed simultaneous or successive calculation errors, which remain separately below the materiality threshold but which, taken together, reach or exceed this threshold.[151] Although this is not specified in the Circular, only errors with an impact on the same net asset value calculation day should reasonably be aggregated.

Non-compliance with investment rules

8.101 Circular 02/77 also covers non-compliance with investment rules which is classified as 'active' or 'intentional' or 'advertent'. Such non-compliance with investment rules embraces investments in violation of the investment policy set out in the UCI's constitutive and sales documents and investments in excess of the investment or borrowing limits provided for by law and by the UCI's constitutive and sales documents.

8.102 Passive or 'inadvertent' non-compliance, ie non-compliance for reasons beyond the UCI's control, is not penalized.[152] Passive non-compliance may be due to market fluctuations, requests for the subscription or redemption of large volumes of the UCI's units, or any other event not under the control of the UCI's manager. Conversely, active non-compliance with investment rules is due to transactions carried out by the manager in violation of the rules applicable to the UCI.

Materiality thresholds

Net asset value calculation error

8.103 Imprecision is an inherent factor in the net asset value calculation process. The degree of precision with which the net asset value is calculated depends on a series of external factors such as the volatility of the markets on which a significant fraction of the UCI's assets is invested, the timely availability of up-to-date information on market prices and other elements used to calculate the net asset value, and the reliability of the available information sources. Thus, the CSSF requires to be notified only of calculation errors whose percentage compared with

---

[150] See 8.103 *et seq* below.
[151] Section I, 3, Circular 02/77.
[152] Art 49(2), 2002 Act.

the net asset value reaches or exceeds a certain threshold. The CSSF also holds that only these errors may give rise to compensation of the UCI and investors according to the procedure set out in the Circular.

In order to reflect the fact that the external factors determining the precision of the net asset value calculation are more or less linked to the complexity of each UCI, the Circular defines the tolerance threshold according to a differentiated approach. It sets materiality thresholds in the form of a net asset value percentage whose rate varies according to the investment policy of the UCI in question. **8.104**

The CSSF defines four categories of UCIs, to which the following materiality thresholds are applicable: 0.25 per cent of the net asset value for UCIs investing in money market instruments and cash; 0.50 per cent for UCIs investing in bonds or similar debt instruments; 1 per cent for UCIs investing in shares or other financial assets; and 0.50 per cent for UCIs with a mixed investment policy.[153] **8.105**

These are, in principle, general and abstract categories.[154] For example, the materiality threshold applicable to bond UCIs is, as a general rule, set at 0.50 per cent regardless of the degree of risk inherent in the bonds making up the UCI's bond portfolio. It applies equally to UCIs that mainly hold government securities and to UCIs that invest in bonds with higher solvency and volatility risks, such as securities issued in emerging countries. **8.106**

In the same way, UCIs with a mixed investment policy are subject to a materiality threshold of 0.50 per cent regardless of the proportions in which the different types of securities—shares, bonds, derivatives instruments, etc—are represented in the portfolio. **8.107**

Lastly, as a money market or bond fund of funds remains a fund of funds, it is subject to the threshold of 1 per cent even if the net asset value calculation of such a UCI does not present any of the difficulties sometimes encountered in determining the value of the units of an underlying fund. **8.108**

However, the CSSF tempers its position towards UCIs using derivatives. It agrees to consider the underlying assets of those derivatives in order to determine the materiality threshold, provided that their return is prominent for the performance of the UCI. This is the case when such return accounts for at least 80 per cent of the performance of the UCI.[155] **8.109**

As the purpose of Circular 02/77 is to provide investors with minimum protection, the promoter of a UCI may apply stricter materiality thresholds than those **8.110**

---

[153] Section I, 2, Circular 02/77.
[154] CSSF Annual Report for 2000, 73.
[155] CSSF Annual Report for 2007, 84.

defined in the Circular or even not apply any. In that case, the promoter does not have to comply with the correction procedures set out in the Circular.

8.111 Foreign countries in which the UCI's units are marketed may also have compensation procedures. The materiality thresholds applied to net asset value calculation errors could conflict with their requirements. In that case, the competent foreign authority could refuse to recognize and apply the Luxembourg concept of materiality and, even in the case of an insignificant net asset value calculation error, require the UCI to indemnify the injured investors under its supervision.[156] Insofar as these investors are indemnified by the UCI, the other investors must benefit from the same advantages by virtue of the principle of equal treatment incumbent upon the UCI. The fact that certain investors are not protected by the foreign authority that requires indemnification does not mean that the other investors are not entitled to the same indemnification.

8.112 In contrast, entities such as the manager, the depositary, and the head office of the UCI are not subject to these rules. Insofar as compensation is paid by these entities, acting in their own name and for their own account, it should not necessarily be extended to all other investors in the UCI.

Non-compliance with investment rules

8.113 In the past, the CSSF consistently rejected application of the principle of materiality in the case of active non-compliance with investment rules applicable to UCIs.

8.114 More recently, the CSSF has reviewed its position, reflecting changes in the legislative framework for UCIs and the growing sophistication of the financial markets. Compliance with investment rules has become much more complex than in the past. Today, it would be difficult to consider investment policies as an exact science. This is why—as with net asset value calculation errors—an error in the investment policy should also benefit from a predetermined tolerance threshold.

8.115 At the proposal of the Luxembourg investment fund industry, the CSSF therefore adopted an interpretation of the Circular that to some extent accepts application of the principle of materiality in the case of non-compliance with investment rules.

8.116 Advertent breaches of investment rules entail application of the following principles, which differ according to whether they apply to the indemnification of the UCI or to losses suffered by investors in connection with subscriptions and redemptions.

---

[156] This difficulty should only arise in connection with non-EEA countries. See 8.181 *et seq* below.

In the case of losses caused by investment breaches and excess positions and charges **8.117** due to, for example, unauthorized borrowings, the UCI must always be indemnified regardless of the impact of the non-compliance. Application of the principle of materiality is not allowed in this context.[157]

In the case of losses arising in the case of subscriptions and redemptions processed **8.118** during the period of non-compliance, the investors having subscribed or redeemed and suffered those losses must be indemnified according to the procedure applicable to net asset value calculation errors, including the principle of materiality.[158] Thus, recalculation of the net asset value determined during the period of non-compliance and compensation of the injured parties are only required when the impact on the net asset value exceeds the materiality thresholds stipulated in the Circular.

Correction measures

When a material calculation error or advertent breach of investment rules has **8.119** been determined, the necessary correction measures must be effected as soon as possible in order to return the UCI to the situation it would have been in if the error or non-compliance had not occurred. First, the error or non-compliance matter must be corrected and its impact must be determined. Secondly, the UCI and the injured investors must be compensated.

Correction of errors

Material calculation error

When a material calculation error occurs, the head office of the UCI recalculates **8.120** net asset values determined during the period of the error, ie the period between the date on which the error became material and the date on which the error was corrected.[159] That said, incorrect net asset values should only be recalculated when subscription or redemption requests have been processed during this period.

Based upon the corrected net asset values, the head office calculates the damage **8.121** suffered by the UCI and its investors. Circular 02/77 recommends distinguishing between investors who invested in the UCI before the period during which the error occurred and who redeemed their units during this same period, and investors who subscribed units in the UCI during the period of error and who held

---

[157] Section II, Circular 02/77, which rules out application of this principle to remedy the damage suffered by a UCI.
[158] Circular 02/77 refers to the rules applicable to NAV calculation errors, including materiality thresholds.
[159] Section I, 3(b), Circular 02/77.

their units until after this period.[160] These are, of course, merely basic categories since other investors may be concerned. There are two possibilities in this situation.

8.122 First, the net asset value may have been understated. In this case, investors who subscribed for units of the UCI before the error period and who redeemed their units during this same period must be compensated for the difference between the corrected net asset value and the understated net asset value applied to the redemption. The UCI must be compensated for the difference between the corrected net asset value and the understated net asset value applied to units subscribed during the error period and that are still outstanding.

8.123 The net asset value may also have been overstated. In this case, investors who subscribed for units in the UCI during the error period and who retained their units after this period must be compensated for the difference between the overstated net asset value applied to the subscription price for the units and the correct net asset value. The UCI must be compensated for the difference between the correct net asset value and the overstated net asset value applied to units issued before and redeemed during the error period.

8.124 Two methods can be used to determine the financial impact of a calculation error. The first is a simplified method, which does not consider the fact that the UCI and its investors should have been compensated when the error occurred and not when the error was discovered. The impact of such a 'carry-back' on subsequent subscriptions and redemptions is therefore not taken into account. Thus, the simplified method should only be applied when the impact of indemnifying the UCI and the investors is not significant. A more complex method must be used where there were significant dealings in UCI units.

8.125 When the impact of the indemnification of the UCI and its investors on subsequent subscriptions and redemptions is not significant, the head office may use either method at its discretion. Nevertheless, it is up to the administration to show consistent use of the method and to justify the method used.

Advertent breaches of investment rules

8.126 Correction of advertent breaches of investment rules consists of two steps. First, the conducting persons of the relevant UCI must regularize the situation having regard to the investment rules applicable to the UCI. Secondly, the financial impact of this non-compliance must be determined in order to calculate the resulting damage for the UCI and its investors.

---

[160] ibid.

Regularization of a UCI's situation   In the case of advertent breaches, the   **8.127**
situation of the UCI must be regularized immediately. Investments in violation
of the investment policy or in excess of investment limits must be sold. Excess
borrowings must be reduced to the authorized limit.

The obligation to sell positions exceeding the investment restrictions applicable   **8.128**
to the UCI is governed in particular by the following principles:

(1) First, the excess position to be sold is determined by reference to the excess
securities held on the day the limit was crossed. In other words, on the day the
situation is regularized, the sales obligation is limited to the portion of the
excess position attributable to the position which initially exceeded the relevant
limit. Any portion of the excess position which may be ascribed to a decrease
in the value of the UCI's other assets or an increase in the value of the investment fraction that did not exceed the limit need not be rectified immediately
as it is considered to result from passive non-compliance and is an 'inadvertent' breach. It does not have to be sold immediately but must be corrected at
an appropriate time in the interests of the investors.[161]

(2) The obligation to sell the excess position exists only during the period of
the excess position. It ends on the day the situation has been regularized,
regardless of the reasons for correction. For instance, it is not important
whether its regularization is due to a change in the value or the volume of
assets held by the UCI.

(3) If the initial excess holding is again in excess due to market fluctuations or a
large volume of subscription or redemption requests after the UCI's situation
has been regularized, the new excess position is considered as an inadvertent
breach.

(4) The obligation to sell the initial excess position is limited to the excess
fraction on the day the situation is regularized. In other words, if the initial
excess position was larger than the excess position on the day the situation is
regularized, the sales obligation is limited to the latter.

(5) Finally, when an excess position relates to several combined investment
limits, the situation can be regularized by focusing on an asset different from
that which was at the origin of the excess position. For instance this may be
the case when a UCITS does not comply with the restriction providing that
the value of certain instruments in which it invests more than 5 per cent of its

---

[161] Under Art 49 of the 2002 Act, in the case of passive non-compliance with investment limits
the primary aim of a UCITS' sales transactions must be to regularize the situation with the interests
of the participants in mind. In other words, the manager of a UCITS must consider investor interests when selling excess positions. In practice, this means that he does not have to sell the excess position immediately if, for example, market conditions are unfavourable. This relatively flexible rule
reflects the fact that indemnification is not required in the case of passive non-compliance, making
it even more important to limit the damage, if any, suffered by the UCI and its investors.

assets may not exceed 40 per cent of the value of its assets. When an UCI decides to sell another asset than that which caused the excess position, it must be able to establish that such action is in the shareholders' interests.[162]

Determining the financial impact

8.129 *Damage suffered by the UCI* The damage suffered by the UCI due to advertent breaches of investment rules has two aspects. The UCI must be compensated for losses suffered during the regularization of its situation. It must further receive compensation for damage caused by subscriptions processed during the period of non-compliance based on an understated net asset value and redemptions processed during the same period based on an overstated net asset value.

8.130 When there are several simultaneous cases of non-compliance, the indemnification of the UCI will depend upon the net regularization proceeds for all non-compliance events. If the net proceeds are positive, the profit goes to the UCI.

8.131 The damage suffered by the UCI due to regularization of its situation is in principle determined according to the so-called 'accounting' method.[163] In the case of excess investments and investments in violation of the investment policy, the UCI must be indemnified for the loss resulting from the disposal of the unauthorized position on the day on which the correction is effected. In the case of 'passive' regularization of the UCI's situation after a change in the asset value or volume, the damage corresponds to the unrealized loss on the day the situation of the UCI was regularized, ie the loss that would have been caused by divestment of the unauthorized position on the day the UCI's situation was regularized. In the case of excess borrowing positions, indemnification corresponds in principle to debit interest and other charges on the unauthorized loan fraction.

8.132 While UCIs generally use the 'average cost' method to determine the result of sales transactions, in the event of non-compliance with investment rules head offices apparently prefer the LIFO (last in-first out) method. They often feel that, in this case, the proceeds must be determined by reference to the security that caused the non-compliance.[164]

8.133 The CSSF holds that while UCIs can select the method they want to apply, they must continue to apply the same method during their entire existence. If the method used in the case of non-compliance with investment rules differs from that normally used to calculate the result of sales transactions, a UCI's conducting persons must make sure the IT system can handle such a method.

---

[162] CSSF Annual Report for 2007, 84.
[163] Section II, Circular 02/77.
[164] CSSF Annual Report for 2000, 74.

If the limit applicable to a bond position is exceeded, the regularization result can **8.134** be determined by adding the interest received or to be received by the UCI to the sale price for the bond. When a capital loss is realized on an excess position, the income accrued and collected on this position during the excess period could be taken into consideration. It would further be necessary to verify whether, during the period in question, any unrealized capital losses on the bonds were at any time offset by accrued interest—due or not yet due—on those securities.[165]

Provided valid reasons are given, methods other than the accounting method may **8.135** be used to calculate the damage suffered by a UCI during regularization. Circular 02/77 refers in particular to the method according to which the damage suffered by a UCI is determined in light of the performance that would have been achieved if the unauthorized investments had undergone the same changes as a portfolio invested in accordance with the investment policy and the investment limitations laid down by law and by the sales documents of the UCI.

In order to ensure fairness among investors, the CSSF believes that there must be **8.136** continuity in the application of the chosen method.[166] This should not prevent a UCI that has applied one method to a particular violation of investment rules from using another method in the future if there are valid reasons, particularly when fairness requires application of the new method under new circumstances.

Damage suffered by investors   Investors must be compensated for the loss suffered **8.137** on subscriptions processed during the excess period based on an overstated net asset value and redemptions processed during the same period based on understated net asset value. The directives given by the Circular for errors in net asset value calculations apply *mutatis mutandis.*

When investment restrictions are exceeded, the principles described below in **8.138** particular govern compensation of investors. In principle, investors who have subscribed for units in the UCI before or during the excess period without requesting redemption during the same period need not be indemnified. Their loss is compensated by the increase in the UCI's net asset value after payment of compensation to the UCI.

There are three cases in which investors suffer damage distinct from that covered **8.139** by indemnification of the UCI.

- The first case is where the value of the securities making up the excess position on the relevant subscription date was higher than the value of those securities on the day the breach occurred[167] and the date on which the UCI

---

[165]   CSSF Annual Report for 2001, 76 and 77; CSSF Annual Report for 2002, 80.
[166]   CSSF Annual Report for 2000, 74.
[167]   Which preceded the subscription date.

was indemnified. In this case, the investor must be compensated for the difference between the compensation received by the UCI and the relative loss of value of his holding arising from the excess position between the subscription date and the date on which the UCI was indemnified.

- The second case is where the investor who has redeemed his securities during the breach period must be compensated if the value of the securities making up the excess position has dropped between the day on which the breach occurred and the date of redemption.

- The third case concerns the investor who has subscribed and redeemed securities during the breach period. Assuming that the value of the securities making up the excess interest has dropped between the subscription date and the redemption date, the investor must be indemnified for the proportionate unrealized loss suffered on the redemption day, arising from the notional sale of the excess holding.

Indemnification

Applicable principles

8.140 The general law provisions on civil liability apply to errors in the net asset value calculation or non-compliance with investment rules. The question of liability is generally settled contractually. If liability for errors is not agreed contractually, the additional rules in Luxembourg's Civil Code apply. The party at fault indemnifies the UCI and its investors for their damage. If the party at fault is unable to indemnify the injured parties, the CSSF requests the promoter to substitute itself for the defaulting party.[168]

8.141 Injured investors may be indemnified by the UCI when the amounts owed to them correspond to those the UCI has unduly received or kept, provided such indemnification does not affect the interests of other investors.

8.142 When a UCI is negatively affected by subscriptions processed on the basis of an understated net asset value or redemptions based on an overstated net asset value, can it require investors to repay the amount not paid by them in respect of units/ shares subscribed by them or to repay the excess sums received by them in respect of units/shares redeemed?

8.143 The CSSF raises this problem in Circular 02/77. It stresses that this is a controversial issue to which no clear response can be given in the absence of a court precedent. It concludes that the injured UCI should not request investors who have benefited unduly from an error or non-compliance to

---

[168] See 4.09 above.

repay excess sums received on redemption or to pay an additional amount in respect of subscriptions processed at an undervalue. However, this remains a possibility when the investors concerned are institutional investors or other well-informed investors who may agree in full knowledge of the circumstances to cover the losses suffered by the UCI.[169]

It would be up to the head office of the UCI or to the promoter to substitute itself **8.144** for investors who have benefited from the error and to make the payments due to the UCI in their place.

Insofar as this is not formally prohibited by the Circular, the provisions of **8.145** Luxembourg's Civil Code with regard to undue payments[170] and the general legal principle with regard to unjust enrichment[171] should, on certain conditions, allow the UCI or, as applicable, the head office or the promoter of the UCI to require the investors concerned pay the amounts not paid by them or to repay any excess amounts received by them.

De minimis rule

The Circular authorizes UCIs to apply a *de minimis* rule to indemnification of **8.146** investors.[172] According to this rule, investors need not be indemnified when indemnification involves amounts not exceeding a certain threshold, known as the *de minimis* amount. This avoids paying investors an indemnification whose amount is so small that the payment costs (cost of cheque collection or bank transfer) are higher and in effect negate the value of the financial compensation.

However, a UCI may not impose application of the *de minimis* rule on an **8.147** investor who, although the indemnification to which he is entitled is less than the *de minimis* amount, expressly states that he wishes to obtain this amount.

The Circular does not stipulate a fixed amount. As most Luxembourg-based UCIs **8.148** are marketed abroad, transfer costs vary significantly from one UCI to the next, depending upon the country of residence of the investors. Each UCI determines a fixed amount by reference to its characteristics, which it submits to the CSSF. This fixed amount factors in bank costs and other costs assumed by investors when receiving payments.

A UCI may decide to grant investors new units or fractions of units rather than **8.149** compensation paid by cheque or bank transfer. This solution is recommended

---

[169]   Section I, 3(b), Circular 02/77.
[170]   Arts 1235 and 1376, Civil Code.
[171]   See in particular G Bonet, 'Quasi-contrats — Enrichissement sans cause Arts 1370–1381, *Jurisclasseur, Code civil*, 1st Vol, 1988 and F Terré, P Simler, and Y Lequette, *Droit Civil—Les obligations* (Précis Dalloz, 7th edn, 1999) 895.
[172]   Section I, 3(c) Circular 02/77.

insofar as it avoids bank charges for investors. In this case, the *de minimis* rule is unnecessary and does not apply. UCIs that indemnify investors by granting new units or fractions of units may not charge fees or other front-end costs on such units.

Indemnification of nominees

8.150 A policy of indemnification of investors who have subscribed or redeemed units through nominees[173] is liable to raise problems. A UCI does not know the identity of the underlying investors and is unable to pay them the amounts owed. In this respect it is dependent upon the nominee, which it generally does not control. Nominees are ordinarily not supervised by the CSSF and do not necessarily see the interest of indemnification and therefore identification and payment of injured investors, which may turn out to be a costly and cumbersome procedure. In this case, it is up to the UCI, working in principle through its head office, to use its resources to inform such investors that they are owed indemnification. If applicable, it may contemplate publication of the relevant issue in the countries in question.

8.151 A nominee may send a UCI an omnibus subscription and redemption order, in which the nominee has offset individual subscription and redemption requests and converted them into a single instruction. In order to calculate the indemnification owed to the UCI and the investors, the head office must in this case be given at least the aggregate amount of both subscriptions and redemptions received on each valuation day affected by the error or the non-compliance.

8.152 The head office should have the information needed to determine the indemnification owed to each investor. This would be the case when the impact of an error or an excess position on the net asset value exceeds the materiality thresholds stipulated in Circular 02/77. The head office would in this case have to know the securities transactions carried out by the investors in the UCI in order to calculate the exact amount to be paid to each.

8.153 If the nominee refuses to provide the requested information and does not confirm that indemnification would be lower than the *de minimis* amount, the head office could, for instance, publish a notice in the countries in which the UCI is distributed to invite investors to present themselves. In the mean time, it could put the funds in escrow or deposit them with the *Caisse de Consignation*.

8.154 The Circular requires nominees to forward any sums they receive to the beneficial owners.[174] If, despite all efforts, the UCI or its head office is unable to obtain

---

[173] For this concept, see 6.420 above.
[174] ibid.

reasonable assurance that the amounts to be paid to the nominee will actually be transferred to the beneficiaries, it should have the right to settle this obligation by paying the sums in question to the *Caisse de Consignation*.

Umbrella UCIs

When a UCI has several sub-funds, indemnification is due to the UCI as a whole, **8.155** since sub-funds are not considered to be legal entities, after which the UCI allots it to the sub-fund that has been affected by the error or non-compliance.

Correction procedures

The Circular lays down the main steps in the correction process and the conduct **8.156** to be adhered to when rectifying material errors in the net asset value calculation. The Circular distinguishes two regimes, depending upon the amount of the indemnification. The Circular outlines a general procedure but permits application of a simplified procedure instead when the indemnification amount does not exceed €25,000 and when the amount to be repaid to each investor does not exceed €2,500.

These procedures are outlined below and apply *mutatis mutandis* to the treatment **8.157** of active non-compliance with the investment rules applicable to the UCI.

The CSSF further authorizes a fast-track procedure in the case of material **8.158** calculation errors if there have been no subscription and redemption requests during the error period.

General procedure

Information to be supplied to the promoter and the depositary of the UCI and to the CSSF

When a material calculation error is identified, the head office of the UCI in **8.159** question must immediately notify the promoter, the depositary, and the auditor of the UCI and the CSSF.[175]

The head office presents the promoter and the CSSF with a plan to correct the **8.160** causes of the error and the measures proposed or adopted to correct the error and to prevent such problems from arising in the future. The corrective action plan focuses primarily on the following points:

(1) improvements in the existing administrative and supervision structures;
(2) identification of the different categories of investors affected by the error;

---

[175] Section I, 3(a) Circular 02/77.

(3) recalculation of the net asset values applied to subscription and redemption requests processed during the error period;

(4) determination of the amount of compensation to be paid to the UCI and to the affected investors;

(5) notification of the supervisory authorities in countries in which the units of the UCI are authorized for distribution, when required by those authorities; and

(6) notification of the injured investors.

8.161 When the calculation error is discovered by the auditor, he must at once notify the head office of the UCI and request it immediately to inform the promoter, the depositary, and the CSSF. If the head office does not do so, the auditor must inform the CSSF.[176]

8.162 These rules apply *mutatis mutandis* to non-compliance with investment rules applicable to the UCI.[177] The head office is responsible for organizing the administrative aspects of the correction process but it is not responsible for verifying compliance with the investment rules applicable to the UCI. This supervisory duty is incumbent upon the UCI's board of directors or management company.[178] In other words, the UCI's management body ensures notification of the parties involved when it detects a violation of the investment rules. Similarly, it is this body that draws up a corrective action plan with the measures required to remedy the weaknesses that caused the non-compliance.

Correction of the error or non-compliance

8.163 As soon as a material calculation error or active non-compliance with investment rules is detected, the necessary measures must be adopted to correct the error or breach and compensate the injured parties.

8.164 The head office of the UCI may implement the correction process without prior permission from the CSSF.[179] The CSSF nevertheless demands to be informed of the measures adopted and reserves the right to intervene on an ex-post basis if it considers this necessary to safeguard the interests of the UCI or the affected investors. Circular 02/77 stresses that the costs generated by the correction process may in no circumstances be charged to the UCI's assets.[180]

---

[176] ibid Section I, 3(d).

[177] ibid Section II.

[178] Thus, Circular 02/81 specifies that the board of directors of the UCI or its management company must arrange the control environment necessary to ensure compliance with the UCI's investment restrictions and policies. The board of directors may delegate the application of these controls to one or more third parties, such as the manager of the UCI.

[179] Section I, 3(c), Circular 02/77.

[180] ibid Section I, 4.

Once the amount of the damage resulting from the calculation error or the **8.165** non-compliance has been established, the head office records the data necessary to cover the payments to be received and made by the UCI.[181]

When the independent auditor has finalized his special report on the relevance **8.166** and reasonableness of the correction process, the head office pays out the due indemnifications.[182]

Review of the correction process by the independent auditor

The auditor's involvement results in principle in three separate reports. **8.167**

First, the auditor draws up a report in which he gives an opinion on the adequacy of **8.168** the methods that the head office or, as applicable, the conducting persons of the UCI intend to use during the correction process, especially as regards the following points:

(1) identification of the categories of investors concerned;
(2) recalculation of the net asset values applied to subscription and redemption requests processed during the error period; and
(3) determination of the indemnification to be paid to the injured parties.[183]

This document is attached to the corrective action plan.

Next, when the head office has recorded the data necessary to correct the error or **8.169** non-compliance, the auditor draws up a special report in which he expresses an opinion on the relevance and reasonableness of the correction process. He states his opinion on the methods used during the correction process, the recalculated net asset values and the damage suffered by the UCI and its investors.

The head office sends copies of this report to the CSSF and, if so required, to the **8.170** supervisory authorities in the countries in which the UCI's units are authorized for distribution.

The procedure culminates in an attestation by the auditor certifying that the **8.171** due amounts of indemnification have been paid to the UCI and to the injured investors. A copy of this attestation must be forwarded to the CSSF and, if so required, to the supervisory authorities in the countries in which the UCI's units are authorized for distribution.

In his annual report, the auditor must moreover mention net asset value calcula- **8.172** tion errors and non-compliances with investment restrictions identified during his audit and not reported to the CSSF in accordance with the Circular.[184]

---

[181] ibid Section I, 3(b).
[182] ibid Section I, 3(d).
[183] ibid.
[184] Section III, A, Circular 02/81.

Communications to investors entitled to indemnification

8.173 The investors concerned must be informed of the occurrence of a material calculation error or active non-compliance with the investment rules applicable to the UCI. They must be given particulars of the error or non-compliance and the correction and indemnification measures adopted.[185]

8.174 Such communications may be supplied through individual notices or by publication in the press. They must first be submitted to the CSSF, which has the right to change them if necessary. If so required, they must also be sent to the supervisory authorities in the host countries.

Simplified procedure

8.175 When the aggregate amount of the indemnification does not exceed €25,000 [186] and the amount owed to each investor does not exceed €2,500, the Circular provides for a simplified procedure that derogates in some respects from the general procedure.

8.176 In these circumstances it is not necessary to submit a corrective action plan to the CSSF. The head office or, as applicable, the conducting persons of the UCI must nevertheless notify the CSSF of the calculation error or the advertent breach of investment rules. They must rapidly take the necessary steps to correct the error or breach and pay compensation for the damage according to the procedure stipulated in the Circular.[187]

8.177 In the case of the simplified procedure, a special auditor's report is not required. In his annual report, the auditor examines the correction process and states whether it is relevant and reasonable,[188] in particular, giving an opinion on:

- the methods used during the correction process,
- the accuracy of the recalculated net asset values,
- the damage suffered by the UCI and/or its unitholders, and
- payment of compensation.

The head office must pay the indemnification as soon as the amounts to be paid have been determined.

---

[185] Section I, 3(e), Circular 02/77.
[186] Circular 02/77 merely specifies what must be covered by the compensation in question. It may reasonably be assumed that this is the total amount of compensation owed to the UCI and its investors.
[187] Section I, 3(a) and (c), Circular 02/77.
[188] ibid Section I, 3(d).

Fast-track procedure

The CSSF allows for a fast-track procedure when there have been no subscription **8.178**
or redemption requests at the start or during the period of a material calculation
error.[189]

The head office of the UCI must report the occurrence of such an error to the **8.179**
promoter, the depositary, the CSSF, and the independent auditor of the UCI, and
correct it.

In this case, the auditor merely draws up an attestation confirming that the **8.180**
calculation error has been corrected and that there were no subscriptions or
redemptions during the error period in question.

Cross-border consequences of Circular 02/77 within the EEA

Certain foreign countries in which the units of a Luxembourg-based UCI are dis- **8.181**
tributed do not recognize the Luxembourg concept of materiality. Thus, a foreign
supervisory authority could hold the service providers of a Luxembourg-based
UCI responsible for indemnifying investors for an error not considered material
in Luxembourg. This is not always the case. A distinction needs to be made between
UCIs governed by Directive 85/611 and other UCIs.

Coordinated UCITS

Coordinated UCITS are, in principle, entitled to mutual recognition of the legis- **8.182**
lation applicable to them in their home country. Pursuant to Directive 85/611,
the supervisory authorities of the EEA Member States are obliged to recognize
Circular 02/77 when applicable to a Luxembourg-based coordinated UCITS.

Directive 85/611 lays down common basic rules for the authorization, supervi- **8.183**
sion, structure, and activities of UCITS based in a Member State and for the
information they are obliged to disclose. These rules deal, *inter alia,* with their
approval, their structure, their management, their investment and borrowing
policies, their asset valuation rules, the information they are required to disclose,
and their supervision. Directive 85/611 further lays down the rule that a UCITS
must be supervised by the authorities of the Member State in which the UCITS is
situated. Moreover, a Member State in which a foreign UCITS distributes its
units may, in principle, not subject that UCITS to its own rules in areas already
covered by Directive 85/611. Any violation of the law, the articles of incorporation, or the prospectus of the UCITS in one of these areas can be penalized only
by the supervisory authorities in its country of origin.

---

[189] CSSF Annual Report for 2000, 73.

8.184 Circular 02/77 applies to two aspects covered by Directive 85/611, ie the investment and borrowing policies of UCITS (since it governs the indemnification due to investors when either is violated) and asset valuation rules (since it lays down the procedure to be followed in the case of an error in the net asset value calculation). That is why it falls within the sphere of application of Directive 85/611. The supervisory authorities of the EEA Member States are therefore obliged to recognize its effects and may not substitute their own rules.

UCIs other than coordinated UCITS

8.185 For UCIs not governed by Directive 85/611, Circular 02/77 must be recognized by the supervisory authorities of the EEA Member States in accordance with the EC Treaty, and more particularly in the freedom of establishment, the free movement of capital, and the freedom to provide services provisions found in this Treaty. These freedoms mean that no Member State can subject an entity established in another EEA Member State to rules whose objectives and consequences are similar to those found in the home Member State. Thus, no rule other than the one imposed by Circular 02/77 can govern the indemnification due and the procedures to be followed by a Luxembourg-based UCI or its agents in the case of a net asset value calculation error or violation of investment restrictions. In addition to these freedoms—of establishment, movement of capital, and provision of services— the principle of fairness recognized in the EC Treaty calls for close cooperation between national authorities. According to this principle, supervisory authorities within the EEA must recognize each other's duties and facilitate their accomplishment. The refusal of a supervisory authority in the EEA to apply Circular 02/77 would violate this principle.

Cross-border consequences of Circular 02/77 outside the EEA

8.186 The supervisory authorities of countries outside the EEA do not have to comply with these Community freedoms and principles and could therefore impose other indemnification rules than those laid down in Circular 02/77 on UCIs based in Luxembourg.

9

DISSOLUTION AND RESTRUCTURING OF UNDERTAKINGS FOR COLLECTIVE INVESTMENT

Dissolution and Liquidation of a UCI or of a Sub-fund of a UCI

Dissolution and liquidation of a UCI

The liquidation of UCIs is governed by the relatively distinct rules explained below because of the two different types of structures for collective investment schemes which may be established either as an incorporated vehicle in the case of SICAVs and SICAFs or a contractual vehicle in the case of FCPs. Only the principal features of the regime will be examined. For further information, the reader is referred to the more detailed explanations contained in books and articles **9.01** devoted more specifically to company liquidations.[1] The liquidation of FCPs does not appear to have been the main subject of any publications.[2]

Types and causes of dissolution

9.02 There are three types of dissolution for both investment companies and FCPs, dissolution by operation of law, voluntary dissolution, or judicial dissolution (or regulatory dissolution in the case of FCPs). The type of dissolution differs according to the structure of the relevant UCI.

Reasons for the dissolution of investment companies

9.03 **Dissolution arising by operation of law**   There are two reasons why investment companies may be dissolved by operation of law, both based on the articles of the Civil Code applicable to companies. The first is the expiry of the company's term.[3] This applies only to companies with a limited term that has not been extended. The second is extinction of the reason for incorporation,[4] which is a textbook case for both investment companies and other types of companies.[5]

9.04 When one of the two above-mentioned eventualities occurs, a company is dissolved and wound up without the need for a decision by its management bodies or any authority. Such a company cannot be extended[6] or change its object retroactively.

9.05 **Voluntary dissolution**   A company can be dissolved by virtue of a decision of its general meeting of shareholders. It may, for example, start to question its long-term future if the value of its assets drops below certain thresholds. The general meeting called to vote on the liquidation must always be held in the presence of a notary. In principle, dissolution may be decided only by a general meeting voting with the quorum and majority required to amend the articles of incorporation.[7]

---

[1] See, in particular, E de Bie and G de Leenheer, *Liquidation des sociétés après la loi du 13 avril 1995* (Ced Samsom, 1995); H Du Faux, 'La liquidation des sociétés commerciales', *Rép not*, Vol XII, Book VI (Larcier, 1994); B Roland, 'La liquidation' in *Traité pratique de droit commercial*, Vol 4 (Kluwer Éditions juridiques Belgique, 1998) 1091.

[2] However; as regards the liquidation of SIFs in general, see M Hoffmann and C Jacobs, 'Liquidation and merger of investment funds under the new law on SIFs' in *Specialised Investment Funds* (Arendt & Medernach, 2007) 162.

[3] Art 1865(1), Civil Code.

[4] Art 1865(2), Civil Code.

[5] B Roland, 'Les causes de dissolution' in *Traité pratique de droit commercial*, Vol 4, (Kluwer Éditions juridiques Belgique, 1998) 1070.

[6] Cass, 24 May 1985 (1986) *JDF* 228, note by M Buydens; P Van Ommeslaghe and X Dieux, 'Examen de jurisprudence (1979 à 1990), Les sociétés commerciales' (1994) 178 *RCJB* 772 and 773.

[7] Arts 99, 103, and 180-1, 1915 Act. Note that this differs in SARLs (see Arts 142 and 199, 1915 Act).

The situation is different if an investment company generates such losses that its **9.06** net asset value drops below certain thresholds. It should be noted here that the 2002 Act and the Act of 13 February 2007 deviate from the 1915 Act, which also contains provisions concerning that type of situation.

The first threshold at which an investment company's conducting persons are **9.07** obliged to call an extraordinary general meeting of shareholders is when the company's share capital corresponds to an amount less than two-thirds of the minimum capital.[8] In this case a general meeting of shareholders must be held within forty days from the date on which that loss is ascertained.[9] There is no quorum requirement for such a meeting.[10] A simple majority vote by the shareholders present or represented is sufficient to dissolve the company.[11]

The second threshold at which an extraordinary general meeting of shareholders **9.08** must be held is when the capital corresponds to an amount less than one-quarter of the minimum capital. In that case a general meeting of shareholders must also be held within forty days from the date on which the loss is ascertained.[12] There is no quorum requirement for this meeting and the company will be dissolved if one-quarter of the shareholders present or represented votes in favour of dissolution.[13]

Pursuant to the 1915 Act,[14] the directors or the members of the management **9.09** board of an SA or the managers of an SCA who fail to call a general meeting which they are obliged to convene may be held personally and jointly liable vis-à-vis the company for all or part of any increase in the losses suffered as a result of the failure to convene the relevant meeting. That principle also applies to investment companies, as neither the 2002 Act nor the law on SIFs provides for any derogation.

Judicial dissolution In certain cases laid down by law, a competent court is **9.10** authorized to order the dissolution of an investment company. Three of those cases are specifically framed for investment companies and based on the 2002 Act and the Act of 13 February 2007. The others are governed by the general law relating to commercial companies.

The three cases of judicial dissolution listed in the 2002 Act and the Act of **9.11** 13 February 2007 relate to the obligation for UCIs to be registered on the list of UCIs kept by the CSSF. The first is the situation in which a UCI does not apply

---

8   The minimum capital of an investment company is €1,250,000.
9   Arts 30(3), 40, 71, and 74(4), 2002 Act; Arts 30(3) and 39(4), Act of 13 February 2007.
10   Arts 30(1), 40, 71, and 74(2), 2002 Act; Arts 30(3) and 39(4), Act of 13 February 2007.
11   ibid.
12   Arts 30(3), 40, 71, and 74(4), 2002 Act; Arts 30(1) and 39(2), Act of 13 February 2007.
13   Arts 30(2), 40, 71, and 74(3), 2002 Act; Arts 30(2) and 39(3), Act of 13 February 2007.
14   Arts 100 and 103, 1915 Act.

for registration within one month from the date of incorporation.[15] The second is the situation in which registration is unconditionally refused.[16] The third is the situation in which a UCI's registration is unconditionally withdrawn.[17]

9.12 In each of those three situations, dissolution is applied for by the State Prosecutor, who may act *ex officio* or at the request of the CSSF.[18] Investors are not entitled to ask the court directly to dissolve a UCI for failure to register. They can apply only to the State Prosecutor, who has unfettered discretion to decide whether to proceed or not.[19] Judicial dissolution takes place only once the decision refusing or withdrawing registration has become final.

9.13 The process by which the decision of the CSSF becomes final may take some time, pending which measures must be taken to protect the UCI's assets.[20] Such measures are only necessary in respect of UCIs withdrawn from the list. By assumption, a UCI that has been refused admission has not yet begun its activities, unless it is a SIF which does not require approval of the CSSF prior to its creation.

9.14 For that reason, the 2002 Act[21] and the Act of 13 February 2007[22] subject UCIs withdrawn from the list to close supervision by a 'supervisory commissioner'. That function is in principle fulfilled as of right by the CSSF. However, the CSSF is free to refuse the appointment, in which case the court appoints another person, whose powers it limits as necessary.

9.15 Withdrawal from the CSSF's list automatically results in the suspension of payments by the UCI in question and a prohibition on taking any measures other than protective measures except with the written authorization of the supervisory commissioner. Actions in violation of that prohibition are null and void. The supervisory commissioner is authorized to submit any proposals he considers necessary or expedient for deliberation by the corporate decision-making bodies or, in the case of FCPs, the management company. Lastly, he is entitled to attend the meetings at which those proposals are discussed.

9.16 Such supervision ceases if the withdrawal decision is overturned or when that decision has become final and is followed by judicial liquidation. In that case, the liquidator takes over from the supervisory commissioner.

---

[15] Art 104(11), 2002 Act; Art 47(11), Act of 13 February 2007.
[16] Art 104(1), 2002 Act; Art 47(1), Act of 13 February 2007.
[17] ibid.
[18] ibid.
[19] *Parliamentary doc* No 2366, Comments on the Articles, 42.
[20] *Parliamentary doc* No 2366[7], Second supplementary opinion of the *Conseil d'État*, 10.
[21] Art 99(3), 2002 Act.
[22] Art 46, Act of 13 February 2007, which, however, does not apply to SIFs whose application for registration on the list kept by the CSSF has not been made within the relevant time frame or has been rejected by the CSSF, although they had already started their activities.

An investment company may also be judicially dissolved if a shareholder[23] is able to show valid reasons for the dissolution.[24] That may be the case, in particular, when a disagreement between shareholders blocks the company's entire decision-making process. Dissolution is an extreme solution and may only be ordered when there is no alternative.[25] **9.17**

Judicial dissolution may also be ordered to penalize a commercial company whose activities are in violation of the criminal law or in serious breach of the 1915 Act.[26] Imposition of that penalty on a UCI nevertheless seems unlikely, since the CSSF intervenes both to prevent unlawful activities and to impose specific penalties in respect of them. **9.18**

Since the Act of 25 August 2006, the right to request dissolution of an SA or SCA which has had only one shareholder for more than six months may no longer be applied.[27] **9.19**

SARLs may also be judicially dissolved for a specific reason, namely where the shareholders refuse to approve certain share transfers.[28] **9.20**

Reasons for dissolution of common funds

Dissolution by operation of law FCPs do not possess legal personality as such and act through their management company. However, in certain cases, the management regulations provide for specific things to happen without the need for a decision on the part of the management company. That is the case with liquidation. An FCP automatically goes into liquidation on expiry of the term stipulated in the management regulations[29] and in all other cases provided for by those regulations.[30] **9.21**

The management company is entirely free to specify in the management regulations the situations which will result in the FCP's liquidation, provided, as always, that it acts in the exclusive interest of the unitholders.[31] **9.22**

FCPs are also liquidated if the management company or the depositary has ceased to exercise its functions and has not been replaced within two months.[32] In addition, **9.23**

---

[23] A Benoit-Moury, 'Des justes motifs de dissolution des sociétés commerciales—De l'article 1871 du Code Civil à l'article 102 des lois coordonnées' Liber Amicorum Jan Ronse (E Story-Scienta, 1986) 163; I Corbisier, *Droit des sociétés* Vol 6 (UCL, Bruylant, 1996) 219.

[24] Art 1871, Civil Code; Arts 99, 103, and 180-1, 1915 Act.

[25] Corbisier (n 23 above) 204 *et seq.*

[26] Art 203, 1915 Act.

[27] Arts 101(3) and 103, 1915 Act, before the relevant amendment made by the Act of 25 August 2006.

[28] Art 189, paras 4 and 5, 1915 Act.

[29] Arts 22(1)(a) and 66, 2002 Act; Art 20(1)(a), Act of 13 February 2007.

[30] Arts 22(1)(e) and 66, 2002 Act; Art 20(1)(e), Act of 13 February 2007.

[31] Arts 14(1), 20, and 66, 2002 Act; Arts 13(1) and 19, Act of 13 February 2007.

[32] Arts 22(1)(b) and 66, 2002 Act; Art 20(1)(b), Act of 13 February 2007.

an FCP is dissolved if its management company is declared bankrupt, even if another management company is ready to take over the functions of the bankrupt company.[33]

9.24 Lastly, FCPs are automatically liquidated if their net assets fall below one-quarter of the legal minimum for more than six months.[34]

9.25 **Voluntary dissolution** In contrast with the shareholders of companies, unitholders of FCPs have, in principle, no management powers whatsoever. The only way in which they may show their disagreement is to sell or have their units redeemed. The management regulations may nevertheless increase their rights in that respect and authorize them to vote on certain decisions, such as dissolution of the FCP. The management regulations specify the cases in which they may exercise that right and the conditions on which they may take that decision.

9.26 The management company may also decide to liquidate an FCP on the conditions set out in the management regulations.

9.27 **Judicial dissolution** The courts will dissolve FCPs in the three specific cases mentioned above with regard to investment companies.[35] Each of those situations concerns the non-registration of a UCI on the list kept by the CSSF, ie:

(1) if application for registration is not made within one month of an FCP's creation;[36]

(2) if there is a definitive refusal to register an FCP;[37]

(3) if registration is definitively withdrawn.[38]

As with investment companies, FCPs that have been withdrawn from the list are managed under the supervision of a supervisory commissioner.[39]

9.28 **Regulatory dissolution** As unitholders in principle have no powers in an FCP, it is important for the CSSF to protect them in certain serious situations. That is the position where an FCP's losses are so large that its net assets are reduced to less than two-thirds of the legal minimum. The management company must immediately notify the CSSF of such a situation. The CSSF may demand the dissolution of the FCP if that is justified by the circumstances.[40]

---

[33] Arts 22(1)(c) and 66, 2002 Act; Art 20(1)(c), Act of 13 February 2007.

[34] Arts 22(1)(d) and 66, 2002 Act; Art 20(1)(d), Act of 13 February 2007. The legal minimum value of an FCP's net assets is €1,250,000.

[35] See 9.11 above.

[36] Art 104(11), 2002 Act; Art 17(11), Act of 13 February 2007.

[37] Art 104(1), 2002 Act; Art 47(1), Act of 13 February 2007.

[38] ibid.

[39] Art 99(3), 2002 Act; Art 46, Act of 13 February 2007.

[40] Arts 24 and 66, 2002 Act; Art 22, Act of 13 February 2007.

Liquidation regime

General principles

Both the 2002 Act and the Act of 13 February 2007, in addition to the 1915 Act, apply to the liquidation of UCIs. The 2002 Act and the Act of 13 February 2007 apply, in particular, to the judicial liquidation of UCIs, a regime relatively similar to that prescribed by the 1915 Act for the liquidation of companies. The non-judicial liquidation of FCPs is not covered by any law, whereas the non-judicial liquidation of investment companies is governed by the 1915 Act. **9.29**

There are two basic liquidation regimes for UCIs. The first governs liquidation other than judicial, referred to below as 'contractual'. It differs depending on whether it applies to investment companies or FCPs. The second governs the judicial liquidation of UCIs. Its application is very similar, whether it involves FCPs or investment companies. **9.30**

As a general rule, dissolved UCIs do not disappear entirely and immediately. They are deemed to exist for liquidation purposes.[41] In practice, that means they are only authorized to carry on the activities necessary for the purposes of the liquidation. They no longer have any legal existence for the purpose of conducting other activities. It is not always easy to determine what activities are authorized, especially if the liquidator temporarily continues the UCI's business.[42] **9.31**

During liquidation, a UCI remains under supervision. In the case of a judicial dissolution, that supervision is exercised by the court that has ordered the liquidation of the fund. In all other cases, it is exercised by the CSSF.[43] All documents issued by such a UCI must indicate that it is in liquidation.[44] **9.32**

Lastly, amounts and assets not claimed by unitholders on termination of the liquidation are paid into a special account. Such amounts and assets are deposited at the *Caisse de Consignation*.[45] **9.33**

Contractual liquidation of UCIs

Contractual liquidation of investment companies   The liquidation of investment companies is almost entirely governed by the 1915 Act. The 2002 Act and the Act of 13 February 2007 cover only two specific aspects of the procedure, namely the appointment of a liquidator and closure of the liquidation process. **9.34**

---

[41] Art 105(1), 2002 Act; Art 48(1), Act of 13 February 2007.
[42] Roland, 'La liquidation' (n 1 above) paras 1509 and 1520. According to the Parliamentary documents accompanying the 1983 Act (*Parliamentary doc* No 2366, Comments on the Articles, 44), 'the undertaking for collective investment . . . no longer has the capacity to accept new commitments'.
[43] Arts 104 and 105(1), 2002 Act; Arts 47 and 48(1), Act of 13 February 2007.
[44] Art 105(2), 2002 Act; Art 48(2), Act of 13 February 2007.
[45] Art 107, 2002 Act; Art 50, Act of 13 February 2007.

9.35   All other aspects of the contractual liquidation of investment companies are governed by the general law provisions concerning the liquidation of commercial companies laid down in the 1915 Act. Only the key phases are summarized below. There is an important exception to the general law provisions on companies. Under traditional rules, three consecutive general meetings must be held. In the case of UCIs, the second general meeting also closes the liquidation.[46]

9.36   The liquidator is, in principle, appointed by the general meeting of shareholders voting to dissolve the company. That general meeting may also appoint a panel of several liquidators. Each liquidator must be authorized by the CSSF and provide guarantees of probity and professional skill.[47] If a liquidator is not authorized or does not accept the appointment, the district court dealing with commercial matters must appoint another liquidator at the request of the CSSF or any other interested party. The court's judgment is provisionally enforceable on production of a copy of the judgment and before registration, notwithstanding any appeal or objection.[48]

9.37   The liquidator collects receivables, settles liabilities and, as the case may be, disposes of the UCI's assets in order to generate liquidity.

9.38   The liquidator requires prior authorization from the general meeting of shareholders to perform certain actions,[49] especially to contribute the company's assets to other companies.[50] That constraint may slow down the liquidation process or make it difficult to take advantage of promising opportunities. For that reason, the articles of incorporation or the general meeting appointing the liquidator frequently authorize him in advance to carry out such actions.

9.39   The general meeting of shareholders is convened at least once a year during the course of the liquidation.[51] In fact, the shareholders in general meeting must be informed once a year of the results of the liquidation and the reasons that have prevented its conclusion. That general meeting differs from an ordinary general meeting, which may no longer be held. Consequently, it may be held on a date other than the date fixed under the articles of incorporation for ordinary general meetings.

---

[46]   Art 113(5), 2002 Act; Art 55(5), Act of 13 February 2007.

[47]   Art 106(1), 2002 Act; Art 49(1), Act of 13 February 2007. The purpose of this requirement is to provide the contractual liquidation of UCIs with guarantees in respect of liquidators that are similar to those prescribed in the case of judicial liquidations (*Parliamentary doc* No 2366, Comments on the Articles, 44).

[48]   Art 106(2), 2002 Act; Art 49(2), Act of 13 February 2007.

[49]   Art 145, 1915 Act.

[50]   Where appropriate, through the more flexible procedure described in Art 148*bis*, 1915 Act and Art 104(5), 2002 Act, and Art 47(5), Act of 13 February 2007. As to the application of this provision to contractual liquidations, see 9.55 below.

[51]   Art 150, 1915 Act.

On completion of the liquidation, the liquidator calls a general meeting of share- **9.40** holders.[52] Its agenda is as follows:

- liquidator's report on application of the assets;
- report on the liquidation by the UCI's auditor;
- approval of the liquidation accounts;
- discharge of the liquidator;
- closure of the liquidation;
- decision on the location at which the company's books and documents are to be stored;
- the deposit procedure for undistributed funds, including those it has not been possible to remit to the creditors and shareholders.

Such a general meeting does not have to be held in the presence of a notary[53] and decisions are taken by ordinary majority of the shareholders present or represented at the meeting.

Closure of the liquidation ends the company's existence. It may nevertheless be the **9.41** subject of judicial actions during the five years following closure of its liquidation.[54] The company may be sued through its liquidators, who are considered to be its representatives.

The liquidators are liable vis-à-vis the company and third parties for the perfor- **9.42** mance of their office and for any faults committed under their management.[55] That liability lapses five years after the occurrence of the facts or, if those facts were fraudulently concealed, after their discovery.[56]

For a long time the acquisition of all the shares by a single party has been a **9.43** frequently used method of putting investment companies into contractual liquida- tion. It is now seldom used. In this method one person[57] acquires or holds all the shares issued by the company. In his capacity as a shareholder, he decides in the pres- ence of a notary to dissolve the company and to appoint himself as a liquidator.[58] Assuming that all the liabilities have been fully settled, he may immediately decide

---

[52] ibid Art 151; Art 113(5), 2002 Act; and Art 55(5), Act of 13 February 2007, pursuant to which the institution of liquidation assessors was abolished for all investment companies based in Luxembourg. Once the liquidation process is finished, the auditor draws up a liquidation report, which is presented to the general meeting during which the liquidators report to the shareholders. The same general meeting votes on approval of the liquidation accounts, discharge, and closure of the liquidation process.

[53] Except when it entails the allocation of real property to the shareholders (J Van Ryn and J Heenen, *Principes de droit commercial* (Bruylant, 2nd edn, 1981) Vol II, 139).

[54] Art 157, 1915 Act.

[55] ibid Art 149.

[56] ibid Art 157.

[57] Who is often the investment company's promoter.

[58] This appointment must be published, pursuant to Art 11*bis*, 3(c), 1915 Act.

to close the liquidation process. The dissolution and liquidation closure meetings are recorded in the same notarial instrument. A commissioner's report is not required, as the liquidation did not involve any transactions.

9.44 A company which is the sole shareholder of another company should not itself assume the liabilities of its subsidiary, since that could be regarded as a merger by absorption. If the absorbing company is a Luxembourg-based company, the transaction could be governed by the 1915 Act[59] and therefore be subject to the specific requirements and formalities applicable to corporate mergers.[60]

9.45 Liquidation by the transfer of all shares to a single owner may be an attractive option for a UCI that has not yet been marketed and where the promoter of the UCI has decided not to proceed with the launch of the scheme, as it is a swift and inexpensive liquidation method.[61]

9.46 **Contractual liquidation of common funds**   The liquidation procedure for FCPs is not subject to specific legal criteria except in the event of judicial dissolution. Hence, the liquidation procedure is conducted by reference to the rules laid down in the management regulations. If the regulations are silent on the point, it is governed by the general principles applying to liquidations, ie the creditors are paid and the remaining assets are divided between the participants in proportion to the number of units respectively held by them.

9.47 The liquidation is handled by a liquidator, who is authorized by the CSSF and who must therefore provide guarantees of probity and professional skill.[62] That function is frequently assumed by the management company, which is the FCP's legal representative.

9.48 The liquidator may be appointed by the court at the request of any interested party or of the CSSF. The court's appointment of a liquidator is provisionally enforceable on production of a copy of the judgment and before registration, notwithstanding any appeal or objection.[63]

9.49 Once the event resulting in liquidation occurs, an FCP may no longer issue units. Transactions conducted in violation of that prohibition are void.[64] In contrast, redemption remains possible, provided that the equal treatment of unitholders is respected.[65]

---

[59] Art 278, 1915 Act. See also Art 24 of the Third Council Directive (EEC) 78/885 of 9 October 1978 based on Art 54(3)(g) of the Treaty concerning mergers of public limited liability companies [1978] OJ L295/36–43.

[60] Du Faux (n 1 above) 46.

[61] See Roland, 'La liquidation' (n 1 above) para 1568.

[62] Art 106(1), 2002 Act; Art 49(1), Act of 13 February 2007.

[63] Art 106(2), 2002 Act; Art 49(2), Act of 13 February 2007.

[64] Arts 22(3) and 66, 2002 Act; Art 20(3), Act of 13 February 2007.

[65] ibid.

The absence of any specific provisions covering contractual liquidation raises the **9.50** question of the nature of the powers of a liquidator other than the management company. In fact, neither the 2002 Act nor the Act of 13 February 2007 appear to grant liquidators any general power to represent unitholders. That power is referred to only in the provisions governing judicial liquidation.[66] Should liquidators appointed for non-judicial liquidation purposes therefore be considered to be the representatives of each unitholder? That construction could lead to considerable practical difficulties.

The problem could be solved by a wide interpretation of the provisions of the 2002 **9.51** Act and the Act of 13 February 2007 applicable to judicial liquidation, so as to extend the scope of those provisions to non-judicial liquidation. However, such an interpretation may be problematic, as the provisions in question refer expressly to judicial liquidation.[67] The Parliamentary documents accompanying the 1983 and 1988 Acts are contradictory in that respect[68] and do not assist in interpretation.

A possible solution would be to arrange for the judicial dissolution of an FCP the **9.52** management company of which does not wish to, or cannot, act as the liquidator. That case is not mentioned in the grounds for judicial dissolution of FCPs. However, the list of grounds is not necessarily exhaustive and, for that reason, a court hearing an application to that effect may order the liquidation of an FCP if its management company does not assume the role of liquidator

The 2002 Act and the Act of 13 February 2007 do not define the responsibilities **9.53** of an FCP's liquidator in contractual liquidations, nor do they specify the period

---

[66] Art 104(2) and (3), 2002 Act; Art 47(2) and (3), Act of 13 February 2007.

[67] Art 104(2), 2002 Act and Art 47(2), Act of 13 February 2007 require authorization from the court, whereas Art 104(3), 2002 Act and Art 47(3), Act of 13 February 2007 refer to the judgment putting the fund into liquidation.

[68] Certain comments state, in fact, that Art 80 of the 1988 Act, or rather the equivalent of Art 80 in the 1983 Act, applies to the judicial liquidation of UCIs (see in particular *Parliamentary doc* No 2366, Opinion of the *Conseil d'État*, 60 and Opinion of the *Commissariat au Contrôle des Banques*, 98, and *Parliamentary doc* No 3172, Comments on the Articles, 54), while not limiting to that type of liquidation the principle that an FCP in liquidation is represented by its liquidators (see eg *Parliamentary doc* No 2366, Opinion of the *Conseil d'État*, 56, Opinion of the *Tribunal d'Arrondissement de Luxembourg*, 101 and Opinion of the *Parquet du Tribunal d'Arrondissement de Luxembourg*, 103; and *Parliamentary doc* No 2366[1], Position taken by the Government concerning the Opinion of the *Conseil d'État*, 5). An excerpt from the Parliamentary documents accompanying the 1983 Act is revealing in this respect, stating, *inter alia*, that 'it is important that the fund can be represented by the liquidators independently of the fate of the management company, whether or not the latter continues to exist, is placed into liquidation or declared bankrupt'. The next sentence contains the significantly more restrictive statement that 'From the moment the fund is ordered into liquidation by a judicial decision, it is important that the judicial authority can appoint liquidators authorised to represent the fund, both actively and passively and both judicially and extra-judicially' (*Parliamentary doc* No 2366, Opinion of the *Conseil d'État*, 52). A few pages further on, the text states that 'moreover, an undertaking for collective investment that is placed in liquidation by a court order is represented by its liquidator(s) for liquidation purposes, both judicially and extra-judicially.' (*Parliamentary doc* No 2366, Opinion of the *Conseil d'État*, 61).

during which he may be sued, either as the FCP's representative or personally. The legal provisions governing those matters[69] are included in the general provisions covering the judicial liquidation of UCIs. On first analysis, they do not seem to apply to contractual liquidations. Yet they may be construed as also applying to that type of liquidation, for two reasons:

- First, the wording of the provisions has been kept general, so that they govern both judicial and contractual liquidations.
- Secondly, the Parliamentary documents accompanying the 1983 and 1988 Acts state that those provisions apply to all types of liquidation.[70]

9.54 These texts can therefore be used as the basis for a broad interpretation. That would limit the period during which liability suits can be brought against liquidators to five years and would also put a five-year limit on actions brought against liquidators as the representatives of an FCP.

9.55 The 2002 Act and the Act of 13 February 2007 also contain general provisions on the contribution of assets to other UCIs,[71] worded in such a way as to seemingly apply to both judicial liquidations and liquidations of contractual UCIs. The Parliamentary documents accompanying the 1983 Act do not expressly limit those provisions to judicial liquidation.[72] Hence, it may be convincingly argued that it also applies to the liquidation of contractual UCIs.

Judicial liquidation of UCIs

9.56 The liquidation of a UCI following its judicial dissolution is, in principle, governed by uniform rules, regardless of the form of the UCI. The 2002 Act and the Act of 13 February 2007 do not distinguish between UCIs in describing the regime applicable to a judicial liquidation.[73]

9.57 The judicial liquidation regime for UCIs is largely based on the provisions of the 1915 Act concerning the liquidation of companies and the judicial dissolution of companies that have committed serious violations of company law or criminal law.[74] The court appoints one or more liquidators and a '*juge-commissaire*' or bankruptcy judge.

---

[69] Art 104(8) and (10), 2002 Act; Art 47(8) and (10), Act of 13 February 2007.

[70] *Parliamentary doc* No 2366, Comments on the Articles, 43: 'The legal form used for the organisation of an undertaking for collective investment should have no impact on the duration of the liquidator's liability. That regime should be uniform. That is why the regime created by Art 157 of the Companies Act has been extended to cover the liquidators of FCPs.'

[71] Art 104(5), 2002 Act; Art 47(5), Act of 13 February 2007.

[72] *Parliamentary doc* No 2366, Opinion of the *Conseil d'État*, 61; *Parliamentary doc* No 2366², Opinion of the Chamber of Commerce, 9; *Parliamentary doc* No 2366⁶, Amendments proposed by the Special Commission, 12; *Parliamentary doc* No 2366⁸, Special Commission's report, 15.

[73] As regards judicial dissolution of UCIs, see G Baden and Y Baden, 'Diagonales en matière de liquidation des établissements de crédit et fonds d'investissement' in *Droit bancaire et financier au Luxembourg* (Larcier, 2004) Vol 1, 177.

[74] *Parliamentary doc* No 2366, Opinion of the *Conseil d'État*, 61.

It also determines the liquidation method.[75] Its judgment is provisionally enforceable[76] and is published in several newspapers, including the *Mémorial*.[77]

Judicial dissolution terminates all attachments effected at the behest of unsecured creditors. As from the date of the judgment, any pending legal action or enforcement procedure may be pursued only against the liquidators.[78]   **9.58**

The liquidators carry out the transactions necessary to complete the liquidation.[79] Significant acts, such as the mortgaging or pledging of a UCI's assets, or the disposal of those assets, require authorization from the court.[80] In line with the procedure for ordinary companies, the court should be able to grant such authorizations in advance, when it appoints the liquidators.   **9.59**

The contribution of a UCI's assets to another UCI requires prior authorization from a general meeting of shareholders or unitholders, voted with a special quorum and majority.[81] At least half of all outstanding units or share capital must be represented and the decision must be taken by a two-thirds majority vote of the shareholders or unitholders present or represented. As the 2002 Act and the Act of 13 February 2007 do not refer to the 1915 Act with respect to requirements as to quorum and majority,[82] it must be presumed that a second general meeting cannot validly arrive at any decision unless a similar quorum is present.   **9.60**

The general meeting convened to vote on the contribution is called by the liquidator, whether on his own initiative or at the request of shareholders or unitholders representing at least one-quarter of the undertaking's assets.[83]   **9.61**

The above rules on asset contributions are similar to those laid down in the 1915 Act.[84] The 1915 Act is even more flexible, as it also allows liquidators to contribute liabilities. However, the 2002 Act and the Act of 13 February 2007 specifically rule out the contribution of liabilities to another UCI.[85]   **9.62**

---

[75] Art 104(1), 2002 Act; Art 47(1), Act of 13 February 2007. This freedom allows the court to 'organise an original, particular and appropriate liquidation where an undertaking's characteristics so require' (*Parliamentary doc* No 2366, Opinion of the *Tribunal d'Arrondissement de Luxembourg*, 101).

[76] Art 104(1), 2002 Act; Art 47(1), Act of 13 February 2007.

[77] Art 104(6), 2002 Act; Art 47(6), Act of 13 February 2007.

[78] Art 104(3), 2002 Act; Art 47(3), Act of 13 February 2007.

[79] Art 104(2), 2002 Act; Art 47(2), Act of 13 February 2007.

[80] ibid.

[81] See 9.38 above in relation to investment companies. In contrast to corresponding provisions in the 1915 Act (Art 145), neither Art 104(2), 2002 Act nor Art 47(2), Act of 13 February 2007 mention the contribution of corporate assets among the transactions that liquidators are authorized to carry out.

[82] Art 67-1, 1915 Act.

[83] Art 104(5), 2002 Act; Art 47(5), Act of 13 February 2007.

[84] Art 148*bis*, 1915 Act.

[85] The Parliamentary documents accompanying the 1983 Act include the following passage: 'Since, pursuant to Article 148*bis* of the Act of 10 August 1915, a merger is also a method of liquidation, that case will be governed by special provisions' (*Parliamentary doc* No 2366, Opinion of the *Conseil d'État*, 61).

9.63   Once a UCI's liabilities have been settled or the necessary sums have been paid into court, the unitholders receive their due share of the net assets.[86]

9.64   A liquidation is closed in two phases.[87] The liquidators report to the court on the allocation of the UCI's assets, such allocation being supported by the accounts and other relevant documents. The court appoints auditors[88] to examine those documents[89] and to produce a report on their mission.

9.65   Following receipt of the auditors' report, the court sits again in order to give a ruling on the liquidators' management and the closure of the liquidation.[90] The judgment pronouncing closure of the liquidation is published in various newspapers, including the *Mémorial*.[91] Such publication informs third parties of the place at which the UCI's books and records will be kept for at least five years, and the measures taken to pay into court the amounts due to the creditors and to the shareholders or unitholders.[92]

9.66   As with ordinary companies, the liquidators are answerable to the UCI and third parties for the discharge of their duties and are liable for defaults in the course of their management.[93] They may be sued in that respect within a period of five years, from either the date of the defaults giving rise to the claim or, if the facts in that respect were fraudulently concealed, from the date of their discovery.[94]

9.67   As with ordinary companies, the UCI survives passively for five years following publication of closure of the liquidation.[95] During that period, the UCI may be sued through its liquidators, in their capacity as liquidators, ie as the representatives of the liquidated UCI.

Liquidation of sub-funds of a UCI

Straightforward liquidation of sub-funds

9.68   Liquidation of a sub-fund of a UCI is the procedure by which the assets of a sub-fund are distributed in kind or in cash among the relevant sub-fund's shareholders

---

[86]   Art 104(4), 2002 Act; Art 47(4), Act of 13 February 2007.
[87]   The legislature appears to have omitted reference to judicial liquidation when it simplified the voluntary liquidation procedure for UCIs in the Act of 17 July 2000.
[88]   It is nevertheless generally accepted that the general meeting appoints a single auditor (P Wauwermans, Manuel pratique des sociétés anonymes (Bruylant, 7th edn, 1933) para 999).
[89]   Art 104(9), 2002 Act; Art 47(9), Act of 13 February 2007.
[90]   ibid.
[91]   ibid.
[92]   ibid.
[93]   Art 104(8), 2002 Act; Art 47(8), Act of 13 February 2007.
[94]   Art 104(10), 2002 Act; Art 47(10), Act of 13 February 2007.
[95]   ibid.

or unitholders. It does not terminate the UCI's existence but merely that of one of its economic subdivisions.[96]

In the course of its duty to supervise UCIs, the CSSF has issued a memorandum[97] **9.69** setting out the terms and conditions governing the liquidation or termination of sub-funds of an umbrella collective investment scheme. Thus, it has placed limits on the autonomous right of a UCI's competent bodies to decide on such a measure. In particular, it imposes the requirement to publish the exact redemption terms prior to implementation of the liquidation decision, requires liquidation proceeds that cannot be distributed to be deposited, requires examination by an auditor of the process, and requires the inclusion of specific notices in the UCI's annual report.

According to the memorandum issued by the CSSF, the articles of incorporation **9.70** must stipulate which body of an investment company is competent to decide on liquidation of a sub-fund.[98] That may be the general meeting of shareholders of the company, the general meeting of shareholders of the sub-fund concerned, or the company's board of directors.

If the articles of incorporation confer that power on the general meeting, they **9.71** must stipulate the quorum and majority required for such decisions. They may grant the right to adopt resolutions without the need for a quorum and with a simple majority vote.

In FCPs, the competent entity is, in principle, the management company. The **9.72** management regulations may nevertheless subject the liquidation decision to approval by a general meeting of unitholders. Such a meeting may be attended by the unitholders of a sub-fund or of all sub-funds combined, depending on what is stipulated in the management regulations, which will also set out the quorum and majority to be met, although they may grant the right to adopt resolutions without the need for a quorum and with a simple majority vote.

If authority is vested in the board of directors, the articles of incorporation must **9.73** specify the situations in which a sub-fund may be liquidated. The situations do not have to be listed in detail. The articles of incorporation may simply refer to a change in the economic or political situation affecting the sub-fund's assets, or even to a minimum size below which the sub-fund can no longer operate efficiently. The same requirement applies to an FCP's management regulations. In other words, intervention by the management company is subject to analogous rules.

---

[96] See Hoffmann and Jacobs (n 2 above)170 *et seq.*

[97] Memorandum issued on 29 March 1993 by the CSSF concerning the procedure for closing a sub-fund of a UCI with several sub-funds.

[98] The validity vis-à-vis third parties of such a provision in the articles of incorporation reflects the general rules set out in the 1915 Act (see above 6.44).

9.74 Next, the liquidation decision is published. Its text, which must, *inter alia*, set out the reasons for liquidation and the liquidation procedure, is first submitted to the CSSF. Once it has been approved, the text is published in accordance with the rules stipulated in the prospectus for the notification of shareholders or unitholders.

9.75 Pending implementation of the liquidation decision, a UCI may continue to redeem its securities unless otherwise decided by its management company or, as the case may be, its board of directors or the general meeting. In that case, the redemption price must be equal to the net asset value of each unit, from which no redemption fee or any other type of cost may be deducted. The net asset value must take account of the liquidation costs and, as applicable, the writing-off of any start-up costs that are still not fully amortized.

9.76 Assets that the fund has been unable to distribute are initially deposited with the depositary for a period of no more than six months, after which they must be deposited with the *Caisse de Consignation*.

9.77 The liquidation procedures, particularly the liquidation costs, are verified by the UCI's auditor as part of his audit of the annual report. The annual report must refer to the liquidation decision and describe the progress of the liquidation.

Merger of a sub-fund with another sub-fund of the same UCI

9.78 In the case of a merger of two sub-funds in the same UCI, legally, the assets and liabilities of the contributed sub-fund do not change owner. That distinguishes 'mergers' of sub-funds from mergers between companies. The 1915 Act does not apply to mergers of sub-funds.

9.79 The merger really constitutes an internal asset transfer in exchange for units in the sub-fund into which the assets are transferred. Thus, in return for the transfer of his proportionate share of assets in one sub-fund to another sub-fund, the investor receives shares or units from the sub-fund to which the assets are transferred.

9.80 The terms and conditions imposed by the CSSF on merger procedures are very similar to those described above for the liquidation of sub-funds. In other words, the authority to merge sub-funds by virtue of the articles of incorporation or the management regulations must comply with the same requirements as those laid down by the CSSF for the liquidation of sub-funds.[99] The conditions governing publication of the merger decision are also the same.

9.81 The merger notice, which is verified by the CSSF, must inform the unitholders about two additional points. First of all, it must inform them of their right to withdraw cost-free from the sub-fund to be liquidated during a period of at least

---

[99] See 9.70–9.73 above.

one month from the date of publication of the merger notice. Secondly, it must describe the differences between the two sub-funds involved in the transaction. That description focuses primarily on the investment policy and objectives, the allocation of income, subscription and redemption fees, management fees, and the frequency of redemption of shares or units in each sub-fund.

Once the decision is published, the investors in the sub-fund to be liquidated have **9.82** at least one month in which to redeem their units at net asset value, without any charge. That right must be set out in the UCI's constitutive documents within the foregoing limits. The right for unitholders to redeem free of charge from a sub-fund that is to be merged with another protects them from a forced transfer to a sub-fund that they do not wish to join.

Mergers of sub-funds and compliance with the required procedures must be veri- **9.83** fied during the course of the UCI's annual audit. In particular, the auditor must verify the calculation of the equality of exchange on the basis of the respective net asset values of the two sub-funds at the merger date. The annual report records the merger decision. It also contains a description of the conditions of the transaction and the composition of the transferred assets.

Merger of sub-funds with other UCIs governed by Luxembourg law

The merger of a sub-fund of one UCI with another UCI resembles an ordinary **9.84** liquidation, inasmuch as it likewise involves a reduction of the assets of the con-tributing UCI and the number of shares or units issued by that UCI. It is also similar to a merger of sub-funds. In both cases, the shareholders or unitholders are involved in an exchange of UCI shares or units rather than a liquidation.

The UCI that decides to close one of its sub-funds contributes the assets and, if **9.85** permitted under the relevant governing law, the sub-fund's liabilities to another UCI. The other UCI issues shares or units in consideration of the contribution, which the contributing UCI allocates in turn to the shareholders or unitholders of the sub-fund to be closed.

There are many similarities between the liquidation and merger of sub-funds within a **9.86** single UCI and the liquidation and merger of sub-funds with other UCIs. Nevertheless, certain special features exist, mainly driven by the need to protect the holders of the shares or units transferred from one UCI to another as a result of the contribution.

The primary concern of the CSSF[100] is to prohibit the contribution of a sub-fund **9.87** of a coordinated UCITS to another type of UCI. The CSSF treats the contribution of a sub-fund to another UCI as the conversion of a UCI and therefore subjects it

---

[100] Memorandum issued on 29 March 1993 by the CSSF on the procedure for closing a sub-fund of an umbrella UCI.

to the prohibition precluding a coordinated UCITS governed by Part I of the 2002 Act from converting into a UCI governed by Part II of the same Act.[101]

9.88 The criteria laid down for the liquidation and merger of sub-funds also apply to the decision-making powers vested in the board of directors or the management company, or alternatively the general meeting of all shareholders or unitholders or the general meeting of investors in the sub-fund concerned. The CSSF nevertheless makes one important reservation, namely that an investment company's decision to contribute a sub-fund to an FCP 'is binding only on those shareholders who have voted in favour of the merger'.[102] Accordingly, each shareholder has three choices. He can become a participant in the FCP to which the contribution is made; he can keep his shares in the sub-fund to be closed; or he can request redemption.[103] The merger of an entire sub-fund is impossible without the consent of, or a redemption request from, each individual shareholder.

9.89 The CSSF defines the contents and publication conditions of the merger decision, in the same way as for the merger of sub-funds within the same UCI.

9.90 As with the merger of sub-funds within the same UCI, the constitutive documents must grant a cost-free redemption right to investors in the sub-fund that is contributed to another UCI. That allows investors who are opposed to the merger to withdraw before the decision takes effect. As explained above, they may also decide to remain in the sub-fund to be closed when the merger is of a sub-fund of an investment company with an FCP. In that case, the investment company has no choice but to maintain or liquidate the sub-fund or merge it with another of its sub-funds. The last two decisions do not require the shareholder's individual consent.

9.91 Contributions by a UCI to a company incorporated in the form of an SA or SCA always require an auditor's report, which examines and describes the planned merger and the valuation techniques used. It indicates whether the value arrived at by means of those techniques corresponds at least to the number and nominal value or, in the absence of a nominal value, the accounting par value and, as the case may be, the issue premium applying to the shares to be issued in consideration of the merger.[104]

9.92 The CSSF has extended the obligation of verification by an auditor to all UCIs to which a sub-fund is contributed, regardless of their form. The checks to be carried out by the auditor in the case of investment companies are in addition to those described in the foregoing paragraph.[105]

---

[101] Art 2(5), 2002 Act.
[102] Memorandum issued on 29 March 1993 by the CSSF on the procedure for closing a sub-fund of an umbrella UCI.
[103] See 9.90 below.
[104] Arts 26-1(3) and 103, 1915 Act.
[105] Memorandum issued on 29 March 1993 by the CSSF on the procedure for closing a sub-fund of an umbrella UCI.

The audit report must include an opinion on the accuracy of the equality of exchange **9.93** as between the shares or units of the two UCIs concerned based on the net asset value of the shares or units at the time the merger is effected. The auditor also expresses an opinion on the adequacy of the methods used to determine the equality exchange.

The merger will be described in the UCI's annual report. In view of the auditor's **9.94** prior verification, the description of mergers with other UCIs in the annual report remains relatively general and limited to the conditions of the transaction, without giving details of the composition of the assets contributed to effect the merger.

Can a merger of a sub-fund of one Luxembourg UCI to another Luxembourg **9.95** UCI be compared to a contribution of a branch of activity within the meaning of Article 308*bis*-3 of the 1915 Act? As defined in the 1915 Act, a branch of activity is 'a division which from a technical and organisational point of view exercises an independent activity and is capable of functioning by its own means'.[106]

A contribution of a branch of activity consists in the transfer of the assets and **9.96** liabilities attaching to the branch of activities in exchange for the issue of shares or corporate units of the recipient company. Any Luxembourg company with a legal personality may determine to submit such a contribution to the provisions governing the demerger of companies, in which case the assets and liabilities attached to the branch of activities are transferred ipso jure.[107]

It would be difficult to consider a UCI sub-fund as a branch of activity. A sub-fund **9.97** is an asset subdivision rather than a whole which can be operated independently. The concept of branch of activities rather applies to industrial operators. As a fiscal and accounting concept, it focuses on the production capacity of a given unit.[108]

Could the provisions of the 1915 Act on the transfers of professional assets apply **9.98** to mergers of sub-funds of two Luxembourg UCIs? Professional assets may be transferred wholly or in part. Such a process consists in the transfer of assets and liabilities of a professional estate to another person within the framework of a professional assignment.[109] It is subject to the provisions governing the demerger of companies when effected between companies with legal personality and where the members of the transferring company receive shares or units of the receiving company.[110] It may also be effected with a foreign entity, provided the latter's national law does not prohibit such a transaction.[111]

---

[106] Art 308*bis*-3, 1915 Act.
[107] ibid.
[108] See in this respect H Michel and C Delginiesse, 'Titre X: Les restructurations de société' in *Traité pratique de droit commercial*, Vol 4, (Kluwer Éditions Juridiques Belgique 1996) para 1279, 919.
[109] Art 308*bis*-6, 1915 Act.
[110] ibid.
[111] ibid.

9.99 The transfer of a professional estate automatically implies the transfer of assets and liabilities attached to such estate. Such transfer, its enforceability by operation of law against creditors, and the circumstances in which such transfer will be null and void, are subject to specific provisions in the 1915 Act.[112] Assets and liabilities included in a UCI's sub-fund could be considered to be a professional estate. Their transfer by an investment company to another vehicle subject to Luxembourg law (investment company or FCP) would then be automatically subject to the rules governing the transfer of a professional estate as described in para 9.98 above. Such rules would supplement the CSSF's conditions laid down in the memorandum issued on 29 March 1993 by the CSSF.

Merger of sub-funds with other UCIs governed by foreign law

9.100 The CSSF has reservations regarding the merger of sub-funds of Luxembourg UCIs with UCIs governed by foreign law. It does not regulate such transactions but limits its involvement to requiring the consent of each individual shareholder or unitholder to the transfer of his shares or units.

9.101 The rules governing the transfer of professional assets, as discussed above, could apply to the contribution by an investment company of one of its sub-funds to a foreign company, provided the national law of that foreign entity does not prohibit such transaction.

Merger and Demerger of UCIs

9.102 The 2002 Act and the Act of 13 February 2007 do not contain any specific provisions concerning the merger or demerger of UCIs.[113] Consequently, such operations are governed by the 1915 Act[114] when they are effected by investment companies. In other cases, the general civil law determines the terms and conditions on which a UCI's assets and liabilities may be transferred to one or more other entities.

Conversion of UCIs

9.103 The traditional distinction between FCPs and investment companies is somewhat overturned in the area of conversion. In contemplating conversion into another investment company, a distinction must be drawn between FCPs and

---

[112] Arts 308*bis*-7 and 308*bis*-14, 1915 Act.

[113] Save in so far as Art 104(5), 2002 Act and Art 47(5), Act of 13 February 2007 can be regarded as governing mergers between UCIs (see 9.60 above). However, that seems doubtful, as these Articles are limited to asset transfers whereas a merger also entails contribution of the liabilities of the merged entity.

[114] Arts 257–308, 1915 Act. For further details concerning the relevant provisions and their application to SIFs, see Hoffmann and Jacobs, (n 2 above) 173 *et seq*.

SICAFs, on the one hand, and SICAVs, on the other. SICAVs and SICAFs nevertheless share the same fate when converted into FCPs.

A second distinction to be borne in mind is that between UCITS governed by Part I **9.104** of the 2002 Act and UCIs governed by Part II of the same Act. Transformation may in no event result in a coordinated UCITS regulated under Part I of the 2002 Act becoming subject to Part II of the 2002 Act.[115] Moreover, UCITS governed by Part I of the 2002 Act may not be converted into SIFs. The reverse is possible, however.

Conversion into a SICAV

When the legislature created the SICAV in 1983, it considered the new legal **9.105** structure to be both more appropriate and safer for investors.[116] It therefore logically sought to facilitate the conversion of existing UCIs into that new legal form, for which it used two mechanisms. The 2002 Act and the Act of 13 February 2007 subsequently adopted that system without change. SICAFs and FCPs may therefore be converted into SICAVs. In the case of a SICAF, the voting requirements for the general meeting of shareholders are reduced[117] and there is no quorum for such meetings. The conversion resolution must be passed by two-thirds of the votes of the shareholders present or represented at the meeting. Conversion of an FCP into a SICAV can be effected on the same terms.[118] The conversion from a SICAF or an FCP to a SICAV is therefore relatively easy.

Conversion into a SICAF

The authors of the 1983 Act, the 2002 Act, and the Act of 13 February 2007 did **9.106** not expressly address the conversion of SICAFs. The 1915 Act applies if the entity to be converted is a SICAV. If the initial UCI is an FCP, it is in principle only possible to use general contract law, although the process can be considerably simplified by setting up an intermediate SICAV. The procedure to be followed for those two types of conversion is explained below.

A SICAF may take one of various different forms of a commercial company. The **9.107** most frequently used forms are the SA and the SCA. An SARL is also conceivable.

In contrast, a SICAV must always be incorporated as an SA or an SE, except **9.108** when it adopts the status of a SIF, allowing it to opt for other legal forms such as the SCA and the SARL. A SICAV may be converted into a SICAF in two ways.

---

[115] Art 2(5), 2002 Act.
[116] See *Parliamentary doc* No 2366³, Supplementary opinion of the *Conseil d'État*, 19.
[117] Art 132(1), 2002 Act; Art 70(1), Act of 13 February 2007.
[118] Art 132(2), 2002 Act; Art 70(2), Act of 13 February 2007.

If the contemplated host structure has been incorporated in the same legal form, it will only have to adapt the articles of incorporation, applying the traditional rules for amending the articles of incorporation as laid down in the 1915 Act. If the target structure has not adopted the same legal form, the company must follow the procedure for conversion into another company. As regards the necessary amendments to the articles of incorporation of an SA or an SCA, the 1915 Act requires not only the quorum and majority needed for amendment of the articles of incorporation[119] but also the individual consent of the shareholders, whose liability becomes unlimited, and of any bondholders.[120] Where the host structure is an SA or an SCA, conversion is tantamount to incorporating an SA or an SCA, as the case may be, and is therefore subject to the rules applicable to incorporation,[121] such as those covering the valuation of the SICAV's assets other than cash[122] and the liability of the founders.[123]

9.109   Conversion of a SICAV into a SICAF does not entail the creation of a new legal person. The original entity continues to exist. Only its form is modified.

9.110   Conversion of an FCP into a SICAF is, in principle, more complex, involving the FCP's liquidation, the incorporation of a company, and the contribution to the new company of the FCP's assets. That process will require the consent of each unitholder, who will become a shareholder in the SICAF by virtue of the contribution to the SICAF of his share of the assets and subsequent issue to him of shares in the SICAF.

9.111   The 2002 Act and the Act of 13 February 2007 nevertheless afford a way of circumventing the need for unanimous approval. The FCP may be converted into a SICAV. As explained above, that decision requires the approval of two-thirds of the unitholders attending or represented at a general meeting. The SICAV may subsequently be converted into a SICAF by amending the articles of incorporation.

Conversion into an FCP

9.112   As with the conversion of a SICAV or an FCP into a SICAF, conversion of a SICAV or SICAF into an FCP was not dealt with by the legislature in 1983, 1988, or 2002, and is therefore governed by general law provisions.

---

[119]   As necessary through application of Art 68 of the 1915 Act, concerning modification of the respective rights of share classes.

[120]   Arts 67-1(3) and 103, 1915 Act.

[121]   ibid Arts 103 and 31-1.

[122]   ibid Arts 103 and 26-1.

[123]   ibid Arts 103 and 31(1).

The change from an investment company to an FCP invariably involves three steps:

(1) liquidation of the company;
(2) distribution of the company's assets among the shareholders; and
(3) contribution of the assets of the company (or a proportionate part) to a newly created FCP by those shareholders who wish to do so.

The liquidator of an investment company is not authorized to exchange the assets **9.113** of the investment company for an FCP's units or to impose such transfer on the shareholders. Neither the 1915 Act nor the 2002 Act nor the Act of 13 February 2007 authorizes him to effect this. Moreover, the CSSF takes the view that the voting rights of shareholders in incorporated UCIs may not be withdrawn without their consent. For that reason, the consent of each shareholder is required when a sub-fund of an investment company is converted into a sub-fund of an FCP.[124] That also applies when the decision to contribute the assets applies to the entire investment company.

---

[124] Memorandum issued on 29 March 1993 by the CSSF on the procedure for closing a sub-fund of an umbrella UCI.

10

UNDERTAKINGS FOR COLLECTIVE INVESTMENT AND CRIMINAL LAW

UCIs may be confronted with criminal law in various situations, notably when **10.01** their conducting persons violate certain strict rules set out in the 1915 and 2002 Acts and in the Act of 13 February 2007. That aspect has already been discussed[1] and will not be examined further in this chapter. UCIs are also concerned by criminal law insofar as they must make sure they are not used for money laundering or

---

[1] See 6.250 and 6.266 above.

terrorist financing purposes and that their conducting persons or certain service providers may come into possession of information protected by professional or banking secrecy.

UCIs and the Combating of Money Laundering and Terrorist Financing

10.02 The offence of money laundering is not specific to UCIs. In particular, banks and other service providers in the financial sector are also faced with that crime in their business dealings. The fact that the product used for money laundering is a unit in a UCI does not change either the nature or the scope of the issue.

10.03 Over the last fifteen years, and partly at the initiative of the EU authorities, the Luxembourg legislature has introduced various measures designed to prevent the use of the financial system for money laundering purposes.

10.04 What made Luxembourg's initiative remarkable was that it preceded most international initiatives. The Financial Action Task Force on money laundering (FATF) had barely started work[2] and Council Directive 91/308 of 10 June 1991 on prevention of the use of the financial system for the purpose of money laundering did not yet exist. Promulgated in 1991,[3] this European Directive required credit institutions and similar financial institutions, and life insurance companies to identify their clients in order to help to combat efforts to launder the proceeds of organized crime.

10.05 Luxembourg's regulations consist of two parts. The first focuses on prevention, the second on punishment. The prevention of money laundering and terrorist financing is the primary objective. This aim underlies most existing laws and regulations in the area. The competent authorities have organized a general money laundering and terrorist financing prevention and detection system based on compliance by certain professionals with obligations relating to identification, follow-up of transactions, retention of documents, and the making of reports to the competent authorities. The professionals concerned must be able to reach an informed judgment on their clients, particularly as regards the origin of the money that their clients entrust to them and the reasons for their business relationships with such professionals. Failure to comply with money laundering and terrorist financing prevention and detection obligations and actual money laundering and terrorist financing transactions are punishable under criminal law.

---

[2] The FATF was instituted in 1989 by the Fifteenth Economic Summit of the G7 in Paris and is domiciled at the OECD. The FATF's mission is to develop and promote strategies to fight money laundering and terrorist financing.

[3] Council Directive (EEC) 91/308 of 10 June 1991 on prevention of the use of the financial system for the purpose of money laundering [1991] L166/77–83.

The professional obligations apply, *inter alia,* to transactions such as the subscrip- **10.06**
tion and redemption of units in UCIs.

The scope of the professional obligations is defined in the applicable laws and **10.07**
regulations. In the financial sector, in addition to the Act of 12 November 2004,
Circular 05/211 applies insofar as it specifies and complements certain laws and
regulations. It applies to professionals of the financial sector and to entities supervised by the CSSF, and in some respects goes beyond the Act of 12 November
2004 in that it extends certain obligations to entities not expressly targeted by the
applicable laws and regulations. It supersedes and repeals earlier Circulars.

This chapter deals first of all with the professional obligations relating to the combat- **10.08**
ing of money laundering and terrorist financing, first in the financial sector in general
and secondly in connection with UCIs. It then looks at the applicable criminal sanctions, and, lastly, it briefly discusses the difficulties in implementing the various rules.

Outline of the Luxembourg regulations in the combating of money laundering and terrorist financing

Prevention: professional obligations

The Luxembourg regulations subject a series of professionals to obligations **10.09**
intended to prevent or, if applicable, to report offences connected with money
laundering and terrorist financing. The activities targeted by these obligations are
listed exhaustively in the Act of 12 November 2004. Below we will examine only
the implementation of these obligations by financial sector service providers.

Professionals concerned

The Act of 12 November 2004 provides an exhaustive list of professionals with pre- **10.10**
ventative obligations in the combating of money laundering and terrorist financing.
In addition to financial sector service providers, the legislation applies to such professions as lawyers,[4] notaries,[5] auditors,[6] organizers of games of chance,[7] casino operators,
real estate agents, tax and financial advisers, and dealers in high value goods.[8]

---

[4] Art 2(1), para 12, Act of 12 November 2004.
[5] Also see Arts 12-1 and 12-2, Act of 9 December 1976 on the organization of the notarial
profession, as amended by the Act of 11 August 1998 introducing organized crime and the offence
of money laundering into the Criminal Code (*Mémorial* A 1998, 1456).
[6] Also see Arts 9-1 and 9-2, Act of 28 June 1984 on the organization of the independent audit
profession, as amended by the Act of 11 August 1998 which introduced organized crime and the
offence of money laundering into the Criminal Code (*Mémorial* A 1998, 1456).
[7] Also see Art 13-1, Act of 20 April 1977 on the operation of games of chance and betting games
at sports events, as amended by the Act of 11 August 1998 which introduced organized crime and
the offence of money laundering into the Criminal Code (*Mémorial* A 1998, 1456).
[8] Art 2(1), para 15, Act of 12 November 2004.

10.11   Financial sector service providers subject to obligations relating to the prevention of money laundering are primarily professionals covered by the Act of 12 November 2004 and subject to CSSF supervision, ie credit institutions and other professionals of the financial sector allowed to carry on their business in the Grand Duchy of Luxembourg,[9] pension funds subject to supervision by the CSSF,[10] management companies that market the units or shares of UCIs or which carry on additional or ancillary activities in the meaning of the 2002 Act,[11] and UCIs that market their units or shares.

10.12   UCIs that market their units or shares are defined in the preparatory work for the Act as those UCIs that distribute their own units or shares.[12] Circular 05/211 reflects the same approach when it describes them as UCIs 'in direct contact with investors insofar as they market their units without using the services of other professionals'.[13]

10.13   Even if a UCI does not market its own units or shares it is still subject to obligations with regard to the prevention and punishment of money laundering and terrorist financing.

10.14   Circular 05/211 goes beyond the Act of 12 November 2004 and also applies to UCIs which distribute their units through third-party intermediaries. This reflects the position already adopted by the CSSF in Circular 94/112 in the light of the general scope of the legislation related to drug addiction, which is applicable to UCIs. The Circular extended professional obligations to prevent money laundering to UCIs.

10.15   Extension of these obligations to UCIs that do not market their own units or shares reflects the CSSF's general prudential control powers.[14]

10.16   Professionals governed by the Act of 12 November 2004 are obliged to ensure compliance by their branches and subsidiaries in Luxembourg and foreign countries with the professional obligations imposed by the Act. Nevertheless, the scope of application of this obligation has been limited in two respects.[15] First, it extends

---

⁹ ibid Art 2(1).

¹⁰ ibid Art 2(1), para 6.

¹¹ ibid Art 2(1), para 5.

¹² *Parliamentary doc* No 5165¹¹, Report of the Legal Commission, Comments on the Articles, 7.

¹³ Para 15, Circular 05/211.

¹⁴ Art 2, Act of 23 December 1998 on the creation of a *Commission de Surveillance du Secteur Financier* (*Mémorial* A 1998, 2985). Ch D, III, 2.3, Circular 91/75 describes the professional rules to follow concerning money laundering in connection with the distribution of UCI units. It refers secondarily to the content of former IML Circular 89/57 and states that this Circular is also applicable to UCIs. In the meantime, Circular 89/57 was replaced by Circular 94/112, which made the money laundering provisions in Circular 91/75 superfluous. Circular 94/112 has now been replaced by Circular 05/211.

¹⁵ Art 2(2), Act of 12 November 2004.

only to the branches and subsidiaries of those professionals which are under their control.[16] Next, this extension applies only 'insofar as these branches and subsidiaries are not subject to equivalent professional obligations under the laws applicable in the place where they are established'. In other words, the existence of equivalent anti-money laundering and terrorist financing legislation in the country in which the subsidiary or branch is established limits the obligations of the Luxembourg professional with respect to its foreign subsidiaries and branches. Thus the obligation will not apply in the case of subsidiaries and branches in EEA Member States and FATF member countries where equivalent legislation applies. For other countries, a case-by-case verification is required.[17]

As the CSSF specifies in Circular 05/211, the obligations imposed by the Act of **10.17** 12 November 2004 are part of public policy. Thus they are also binding upon any entity operating in Luxembourg under the rules governing the freedom to provide services from an establishment based in a foreign country.[18]

Professional obligations

The Act of 12 November 2004 basically introduces four types of professional **10.18** obligation: the obligation to know and monitor clients; the obligation to examine certain transactions with particular care;[19] the obligation to have an appropriate internal organization; and the obligation to cooperate with the authorities.[20]

For the actual implementation of these obligations, professionals are advised to **10.19** assess the real risk of activities conducted for money laundering or terrorist financing purposes.[21] This assessment determines the scope of their investigations.

The 1993 Act obliges credit institutions and other professionals of the financial **10.20** sector to include the originator's name or account number in remittances and transfers of funds and any messages relating thereto.[22]

Obligation to identify clients

General rules

Principle The obligation to 'know your client' obliges professionals within the **10.21** meaning of the Act of 12 November 2004 to identify their clients and, as applicable, the persons (beneficiaries) on whose behalf they are acting. When establishing

---

[16] See in this respect para 17, Circular 05/211.
[17] ibid para 18.
[18] ibid para 16.
[19] Art 3(9), Act of 12 November 2004.
[20] In addition to these obligations there is the obligation to keep certain documents (Art 3(8), Act of 12 November 2004 and paras 107–110, Circular 05/211).
[21] Para 4, Circular 05/211.
[22] Art 39, 1993 Act; para 145, Circular 05/211.

business relations, especially when opening an account or savings book or offering asset custody services, clients must be identified by means of an official document and other information sources.[23] When the client acts on behalf of another party, known as the 'beneficial owner', the latter must also be identified.[24]

10.22 The identification requirement also applies to occasional or 'one-off' clients with whom no long-term business relationship is established whenever counter transactions have a value of €15,000 or more.[25]

10.23 The concept of beneficial owner is not defined in either the Act of 12 November 2004 or Circular 05/211. In contrast, Directive 2005/60[26] supplies a definition. According to the Directive, the beneficial owner is 'the natural person(s) who ultimately own(s) or control(s) the customer and/or the natural person on whose behalf a transaction or activity is being conducted'.[27] In other words, a beneficial owner within the meaning of the anti-money laundering legislation is never a legal person.

10.24 *Procedure* Every financial professional must know his clients.[28] Except for the 'material execution' thereof, he may not delegate the identification of clients. That would go against the spirit of the law, as he would 'thereby avoid his obligation to know his clients and the responsibility resulting from such knowledge'.[29] According to the CSSF, professionals are required by law to form their own judgment of their client before entering into business relations. As a general rule, professionals may not, for example, base their judgment on a certificate drawn up by a third party, attesting that he knows the client in question.[30] The alertness of professionals

---

[23] Art 3(1), Act of 12 November 2004; paras 23 and 27, Circular 05/211.

[24] Art 3(2), Act of 12 November 2004.

[25] ibid Art 3(3).

[26] Directive (EC) 2005/60 of the European Parliament and of the Council of 26 October 2005 on the prevention of the use of the financial system for the purpose of money laundering and terrorist financing [2005] OJ L309/15.

[27] ibid Art 3(6). More particularly, according to the same Article, the concept of beneficial owner includes at least '(a) in the case of corporate entities: (i) the natural person(s) who ultimately own(s) or control(s) a legal entity through direct or indirect ownership or control over a sufficient percentage of the shares or voting rights in that legal entity, including through bearer share holdings, other than a company listed on a regulated market that is subject to disclosure requirements consistent with Community legislation or subject to equivalent international standards; a percentage of 25% plus one share shall be deemed sufficient to meet this criterion; (ii) the natural person(s) who otherwise exercise(s) control over the management of a legal entity: (b) in the case of legal entities, such as foundations, and legal arrangements, such as trusts, which administer and distribute funds: (i) where the future beneficiaries have already been determined, the natural person(s) who is(are) the beneficiary of 25% or more of the property of a legal arrangement or entity; (ii) where the individuals that benefit from the legal arrangement or entity have yet to be determined, the class of persons in whose main interest the legal arrangement or entity is set up or operates; (iii) the natural person(s) who exercise(s) control over 25% or more of the property of a legal arrangement or entity'.

[28] See a description of the implementation of this obligation in paras 23–94, Circular 05/211.

[29] Para 82, Circular 05/211.

[30] ibid para 85.

needs to be adjusted to the risk of abuse of assets for money laundering purposes. A politically exposed client[31] or a client residing in a non-cooperative territory (under the FATF rules on money laundering and terrorist financing) must be subjected to more stringent identification and follow-up procedures.[32]

The client identification procedure differs according to whether the professional is dealing with a natural person[33] or a legal person.[34] **10.25**

A client who is a natural person must be identified through production of an official document certifying his identity. Circular 05/211 mentions a passport, an identity card, a driving permit, a residence permit, or any other official document with a photo permitting definite identification of the client in question. On receipt of the necessary documents, the professional must verify that the document produced in fact identifies the client and make a copy. He must further ensure that the client fills out the documents needed to start a business relationship.[35] **10.26**

If his client is a legal person, the professional must identify it on the basis of documents establishing, *inter alia,* its existence and legal status (articles of incorporation or other constitutive documents). He must also require the presentation of documents such as a recent certificate from the trade register (or a similar document) with the name of the company, the names of the directors and other conducting persons, representation powers, and the address of the company's registered office. The company's representatives must also be identified. These are the people representing the company vis-à-vis the Luxembourg-based professional. **10.27**

The obligation to know your client sometimes requires a professional to look beyond the immediate entity to whom services are to be provided and identify the person on whose behalf the client is acting. Circular 05/211 provides some information on the manner in which this obligation should be exercised. Here, it distinguishes between prospective clients who are natural persons[36] and legal persons.[37] **10.28**

When dealing with a natural person, the professional of the financial sector must obtain a written declaration that the client is acting in his or her own name. The production or not of such a declaration can enable the professional of the financial sector to conclude that the prospective client and the beneficial owner of the transaction are **10.29**

---

[31] The concept of 'politically exposed persons' is defined in Directive (EC) 2005/60 of the European Parliament and of the Council as 'natural persons who are or have been entrusted with prominent public functions and the immediate family members, or persons known to be close associates, of such persons' (ibid Art 3(8)).
[32] Paras 34 and 61–76, Circular 05/211.
[33] ibid paras 36–38.
[34] ibid paras 39–42.
[35] For the details of this procedure, see ibid para 37.
[36] ibid paras 53 and 54.
[37] ibid paras 57–59.

one and the same, or it may convince him that an as yet unidentified beneficial owner will benefit from the transaction. He may also suspect the existence of an undeclared beneficial owner. If this suspicion cannot be satisfied through a negative declaration on the part of the apparent client or a declaration by a third party that he or she is the beneficial owner, the professional may decide to stop acting for this client or even to report his suspicion to the State Prosecutor.

10.30 If the professional is certain of the existence of a beneficial owner, he is advised to ask his apparent client for documents allowing him to identify the beneficial owner and, preferably, a written declaration on the part of the beneficiary himself confirming the information supplied by the apparent client.

10.31 When dealing with a legal person, such as a company, the professional must first endeavour to understand the company's general structure and obtain information about the company's owners and, as applicable, the group of which it is part. If a natural person owns more than 25 per cent of the capital of the legal person, whether directly or through other structures, the natural person and, as applicable, the beneficial owner, if any, acting through that natural person must also be identified according to the procedure described in the foregoing paragraph. Circular 05/211 advises the professional to be particularly alert to the existence of shell corporations, suggested by such indicators as a small number of shareholders, no commercial activity, and no stock exchange listing.

10.32 Accounts may be opened at a distance without any physical encounter between the professional and his client. In that case, the professional must receive complete and satisfactory answers to all his questions, such that he may make an informed judgment in relation to the client. The Act of 12 November 2004 specifies that, in such cases, professionals must take specific and adequate measures to protect themselves against the increased risk of money laundering or terrorist financing. These measures must be such as to ensure identification of the client. The professional is requested to take one of the following two additional measures to ensure this. He may request certification of the documents establishing the identity of his client.[38] Alternatively, he may require the first transfer to be made from an account opened in the client's name at a credit institution subject to an equivalent identification obligation. The CSSF considers it acceptable when a bank established in Luxembourg directly sends the client's bank a transfer order signed by the client together with a reference number. This allows the Luxembourg-based bank to verify on receipt of the funds that they were sent from an account kept by the client at the bank of origin. It carries out this verification with the help of the reference number and the account number.[39] Other procedures are possible, subject to prior

---

[38] ibid para 63.
[39] ibid.

permission from the CSSF. The professional may also have to request other documentary evidence, such as proof of the client's activity, the origin of the funds, or the client's address.[40]

The obligation to know your client is not limited to identification by reference to documents produced. In addition to obtaining documents, the Luxembourg-based professional is requested to inquire into the client's identity and activities and the purpose of the business relationship. This is the type of information that could alert the professional and enable detection of suspicious transactions. **10.33**

The law confirms the principle that clients must be monitored: professionals must monitor their clients continually throughout the period of their business relationship.[41] This obligation must be adjusted to take account of the risk of money laundering and terrorist financing by the particular client. **10.34**

In identifying a client, the professional is authorized to delegate, on certain conditions, the 'material execution' of the identification obligation to qualified professional partners.[42] The Act does not specify the duties in question, which are presumably to gather and authenticate papers or other documents from clients based in foreign countries and to gather information on the client, with whom the professional partner has often maintained a close connection for many years, and to ensure that they are sent to the Grand Duchy of Luxembourg. Such delegation of tasks does not relieve the professional of his responsibilities. He remains responsible for the final decision to enter into a business relationship. It is merely a practical approach in the chain of procedures leading to identification of a client, as justified by constraints of space or time. **10.35**

This type of delegation is covered in an agency agreement whose content must comply with the requirements laid down by the Act of 12 November 2004 and Circular 05/211. This agreement must precisely define the delegated duties, taking account of the standards in Luxembourg or their equivalent in foreign countries and giving a detailed description of the documents and information to be requested and verified by the delegated agents.[43] It must also allow the professional to access the identification documents during the legal retention period and the right to obtain these documents on request.[44] **10.36**

The law requires that a copy of all identification documents be delivered to the professional before entering into any business relationship.[45] When entering into **10.37**

---

[40] ibid para 65.
[41] Art 3(9), Act of 12 November 2004; paras 104–106, Circular 05/211.
[42] For details see, paras 82–89, Circular 05/211.
[43] ibid para 83.
[44] ibid para 86.
[45] Art 3(7), Act of 12 November 2004.

a business relationship at a distance, copies of identification documents must be duly certified.[46]

10.38   Under the law, national or foreign professionals in the same sector and subject to an equivalent identification obligation are authorized to act as delegated agents. The Circular provides a few particulars in this respect.[47]

10.39   Among professionals in Luxembourg, eligibility is therefore limited to credit institutions and other professionals of the financial sector authorized to carry on business in Luxembourg, insurance undertakings authorized to conduct business in Luxembourg, UCIs marketing their own units or shares, management companies marketing units or shares of UCIs or carrying on additional or ancillary activities in the meaning of the 2002 Act, and pension funds subject to the CSSF's prudential supervision.

10.40   Eligible foreign professionals must be comparable to those listed above and be subject to an identification obligation equivalent to that provided for by the laws of Luxembourg. According to the CSSF, this last condition is automatically satisfied when the professionals are based in an EEA Member State or an FATF member country. As regards the support from professionals situated in other countries, the Luxembourg-based professional is responsible for verifying whether they are subject to equivalent identification obligations. If verification shows that the foreign professional is not subject to equivalent obligations in his own country, the Luxembourg-based professional must contractually impose such obligations on him and ensure compliance with them.[48]

10.41   *Exemption from the identification obligation*   There is one exception to the obligation to identify clients. Where the client is itself a national or foreign financial institution subject to an equivalent identification obligation, it may reasonably be assumed that there is no risk of money laundering or terrorist financing. In that case, it can be presumed that the origin of the funds used has already been verified pursuant to similar laws. The Act of 12 November 2004 therefore waives the requirement of a second verification.[49]

10.42   This exception applies only when the financial institution maintains in its own name the business relationship with the professional governed by the Act of 12 November 2004. That, for example, is not the case when the financial institution in question introduces some of its clients to the professional in the role of intermediary.

---

[46] Para 85, Circular 05/211.
[47] ibid paras 87 and 88.
[48] ibid para 88, Circular 05/211.
[49] Art 3(5), Act of 12 November 2004; see also paras 90–94, Circular 05/211.

The financial institutions that may be exempted from identification requirements **10.43** are described in Circular 05/211. This is a smaller category than the 'eligible delegated agents' category mentioned above.

Among national financial institutions, the Circular selects credit institutions, other **10.44** professionals of the financial sector and insurance undertakings authorized to carry on their activity in Luxembourg, and UCIs marketing their own units or shares.[50]

Foreign professionals must be professionals similar to those mentioned above, who **10.45** are subject to an identification obligation equivalent to that laid down by the laws of Luxembourg. According to the CSSF, this last condition is automatically satisfied when they are based in an EEA Member State or an FATF member country. As regards professionals situated in other countries, the Luxembourg-based professional is responsible for verifying whether they are subject to equivalent identification obligations. According to Circular 05/211,[51] this condition may be satisfied when the parent company of the foreign professional subjects the foreign professional to obligations equivalent to those imposed on the parent company itself and which are imposed on the branch or subsidiary by virtue of a legal provision or the group's own internal rules.

Special rules for UCIs that do not market their own units or shares Although **10.46** not covered by the Act of 12 November 2004, UCIs that do not market their own units or shares must also comply with the provisions of Circular 05/211. However, the Circular lays down special rules for such UCIs in view of their marketing methods.[52]

Such UCIs are exempt from the identification obligation when the intermediary **10.47** used by them to market their units is a national or foreign financial institution as defined above in respect of whose clients the UCI does not have an identification obligation (on the basis that the financial institution itself is obliged to verify its clients' identity). If the intermediary is not such an institution, the UCI has an identification obligation.

Several features of the way in which a UCI's units are distributed justify particular **10.48** rules. Units in UCIs are generally offered for sale in a large number of countries. That requires the establishment of a complex system of distributors and sub-distributors, including different types of professionals in many countries. The normal identification procedure described above would have considerably slowed the marketing of Luxembourg UCIs.

---

[50] Circular 05/211 specifies in this respect that if the client of the professional is a UCI that does not market its own units, a management company or a Luxembourg-based pension fund, the client must be identified on the basis of its constitutive documents (ibid para 91(c)).

[51] ibid para 92.

[52] ibid para 15.

10.49 Circular 05/211 therefore creates a fundamental difference between the duties of banks and other professionals of the financial sector in traditional business relationships, on the one hand, and in connection with the distribution of UCI units, on the other.

10.50 The general rules do not exempt banks and other professionals of the financial sector from the obligation to identify a client, save where the client is itself a financial institution subject to a specific identification obligation. Moreover, professionals of the financial sector may delegate only certain tasks connected with the identification of clients, albeit such delegation does not in any case release them from liability.

10.51 In contrast, under Circular 05/211, a UCI that does not market its own units or shares is subject to more relaxed rules, which should extend to professionals responsible for distributing this UCI and to any professional who, as a UCI's head office agent, manages its subscription and redemption orders. These professionals should be exempt from the obligation to identify investors and should not incur criminal liability, provided the orders were received via a financial institution that has its own legal identification obligation and is included in the list given for this purpose in Circular 05/211.

10.52 It may be asked what the situation is for management companies which are not included among the 'eligible delegated agents' listed in Circular 05/211. According to Circular 05/211, a UCI that entrusts them with the distribution of its units is not exempt from the investor identification obligation. It can only delegate to certain entities—including the management company—the physical performance of the identification obligations, without transferring final liability for investor identification to the intermediary.

10.53 That is why a coordinated UCITS wishing to appoint a management company is advised not to entrust it directly with the distribution of its units or shares but to call on the services of an 'eligible delegated agent' in the meaning of Circular 05/211, who would operate under the supervision of the management company. The three parties could sign an agreement for this purpose, which would remove any uncertainty as to the UCI's status under Circular 05/211.

Obligation to pay special attention to certain transactions

10.54 The obligation to monitor transactions is specified: professionals must pay close attention to any transaction they consider particularly likely to be connected with money laundering or terrorist financing because of its intrinsic characteristics, its circumstances, or the capacity of the persons involved.[53]

---

[53] See also ibid paras 95–103.

Among suspicious transactions, the CSSF particularly mentions: complex **10.55** transactions; transactions involving unusually high amounts, or repeated at unusually short intervals; transactions that deviate from those generally carried out by the client; and transactions with certain risk factors, especially the countries concerned or the activities being financed.[54]

The context of a transaction must also be examined. The Luxembourg-based **10.56** professional needs to obtain information about the status of the parties and the circumstances of the transaction.[55] He must also implement procedures and systems to detect suspicious clients and transactions.[56]

In the case of doubt or suspicion, the professional should not carry out the trans- **10.57** action and may even terminate the business relationship. As necessary, he must send a suspicious transaction report to the competent authorities.[57]

Obligation to have an appropriate internal organization

Professionals must adopt adequate internal control and communication procedures.[58] **10.58** They must also take appropriate measures to raise staff awareness and to train employees on the applicable laws and regulations.[59]

Obligation to report money laundering

Professionals must cooperate with the Luxembourg authorities responsible for **10.59** combating money laundering and terrorist financing. They are required on their own initiative to inform the State Prosecutor at the Luxembourg District Court of any events indicating money laundering or terrorist financing and to provide him on request with all necessary information.[60] They are not authorized to carry out transactions known or suspected to be connected with money laundering or terrorist financing without first notifying the State Prosecutor,[61] and may not warn the client concerned or any third party that the authorities have been informed.[62]

In Circular 05/211, the CSSF requires entities under its supervision to send it the **10.60** same information as was submitted to the State Prosecutor.[63]

---

[54] ibid para 97; see also the non-exhaustive list of this type of transaction in Appendix II to the Circular.
[55] ibid para 98.
[56] ibid paras 101 and 102.
[57] ibid para 100.
[58] Art 4(a), Act of 12 November 2004; para 113, Circular 05/211.
[59] Art 4(b), Act of 12 November 2004; paras 114 and 115, Circular 05/211.
[60] Art 5(1), Act of 12 November 2004; paras 117–144, Circular 05/211.
[61] Art 5(3), Act of 12 November 2004.
[62] ibid Art 5(5). However, Circular 05/211 specifies that the professional may refer to any counter-instruction received from the State Prosecutor to explain his refusal to carry out the client's order if the client requests the reasons for his refusal (para 141).
[63] Para 137, Circular 05/211.

Penalties: money laundering and terrorist financing offences

Offence of money laundering

10.61 The criminal offence of laundering the proceeds of an unlawful activity was introduced in Luxembourg by the Act of 7 July 1989.[64] At the time, the law only targeted efforts to launder the proceeds of drug trafficking. The new law mainly added to the Act of 19 February 1973 on the sale of drugs and the combating of drug addiction,[65] a new Article 8-1 that, *inter alia,* punished those who 'contributed in any way to the placement, layering or conversion of the proceeds from such an offence'.

10.62 Luxembourg's drug trafficking legislation was enhanced by the Act of 17 March 1992[66] approving the UN Convention against Illicit Traffic in Narcotic Drugs and Psychotropic Substances.[67]

10.63 Other basic modifications were introduced by the Act of 11 August 1998,[68] which enhanced the Criminal Code with a new Article 506-1 that defined the offence of money laundering. According to the Article, those who 'contribute to the placement, layering or conversion of the direct or indirect proceeds' of one or more of the following offences are engaged in money laundering:[69]

(1) crimes or misdemeanours committed as part of or in conjunction with a gang or criminal organization;[70]

(2) kidnapping of minors;[71]

---

[64] Act of 7 July 1989 amending the Act of 19 February 1973, as amended, on the sale of pharmaceutical substances and the combating of drug addiction (*Mémorial* A 1989, 923).

[65] Act of 19 February 1973 on the sale of pharmaceutical substances and the combating of drug addiction (*Mémorial* A 1973, 319).

[66] Act of 17 March 1992 (1) approving the UN Convention against Illicit Traffic in Narcotic Drugs and Psychotropic Substances, adopted in Vienna on 20 December 1998; (2) amending and completing the Act of 19 February 1973 on the sale of pharmaceutical substances and the combating of drug addiction; (3) amending and completing certain provisions in the Criminal Investigation Code (*Mémorial* A 1992, 698).

[67] Adopted in Vienna by the Sixth Plenary Session of the United Nations Conference, held on 19 December 1988.

[68] Act of 11 August 1998 introducing organized crime and the offence of money laundering into the Criminal Code and amending: (1) the Act of 19 February 1973, as amended, on the sale of pharmaceutical substances and the combating of drug addiction; (2) the Act of 5 April 1993, as amended, on the financial sector; (3) the Act of 6 December 1991, as amended, on the insurance sector; (4) the Act of 9 December 1976, as amended on the organization of the notarial profession; (5) the Act of 20 April 1977 on the operation of games of chance and betting games at sports events; (6) the Act of 28 June 1984 on the organization of the independent audit profession; (7) the Criminal Investigation Code (*Mémorial* A 1998, 1456).

[69] See Appendix I, Circular 05/211 for a brief description of this information.

[70] Arts 322–324*ter*, Criminal Code.

[71] ibid Arts 368–370.

(3) sexual offences against minors;[72]

(4) procuring;[73]

(5) corruption;[74]

(6) offences under the legislation on arms and munitions.[75]

The Acts of 12 November 2004 and 23 May 2005[76] extended this list to include fraud against the financial interests of the State and international institutions.[77]

Offence of terrorist financing

The Criminal Code defines terrorist financing as 'the supply or collection, directly **10.64** or indirectly, unlawfully and willingly, of funds or goods of any type with the intention that they be used or in the knowledge that they are to be used, in full or in part, to carry out one or more of the offences of terrorism[78] and hostage taking[79] even if not actually used to commit one of these offences'.[80]

Breach of professional obligations

Professionals of the financial sector, insurance companies, notaries, independent **10.65** auditors, casinos, organizers of games of chance, and other professionals with legal obligations to help prevent money laundering and terrorist financing may be sanc-

---

[72] ibid Art 379.

[73] ibid Arts 379 and 379*bis*.

[74] ibid Arts 246–253, 310 and 310-1.

[75] See also the Act of 15 March 1983 on arms and munitions (*Mémorial* A 1983, 694).

[76] Act of 23 May 2005 approving: (a) the Convention based on Art K.3 of the Treaty of the European Union on the combating of corruption involving public officials of the European Communities or public officials of Member States of the European Union, signed in Brussels on 26 May 1997; (b) the second Protocol based on Art K.3 of the Treaty of the European Union, on the Convention on the protection of the financial interests of the European Communities, signed in Brussels on 19 June 1997; (c) the Criminal Law Convention on Corruption, signed in Strasbourg on 27 January 1999; (d) the Protocol signed in Strasbourg on 15 May 2003; amending and completing certain provisions in the Criminal Code (*Mémorial* A 2005, 1176).

[77] Arts 496-1–496-4, Criminal Code.

[78] An act of terrorism is punishable with maximum imprisonment of at least three years or a more serious penalty if, owing to its nature or context, such act may seriously harm a country, an organization or an international body and has been committed deliberately in order to: (1) seriously intimidate a population; (2) force the public authorities, an organization, or an international body unduly to accomplish or to refrain from accomplishing any act; or (3) seriously destabilize or destroy the fundamental political, constitutional, economic, or social structures of a country, an organization, or an international body (Art 135-1, Criminal Code).

[79] A hostage taker is someone who 'has kidnapped, arrested, held or sequestered or has had another party or other parties kidnap, arrest, hold or sequester a person, regardless of his or her age, in order to prepare or facilitate the commitment of a crime or misdemeanour or in order to assist the escape or ensure the impunity of the perpetrators of or accomplices in a crime or a misdemeanour or in order to have the kidnapped, arrested, held or sequestered person execute an order or meet a condition' (Art 442-1, Criminal Code).

[80] Art 135-5, Criminal Code.

tioned for failure to carry out their professional obligations even when they had no intention of participating in a money laundering transaction and even when no money laundering or terrorist financing offence was actually committed.

Penalties

10.66 The situation with regard to criminal penalties has changed. The original version of Article 8-1 of the Act of 19 February 1973 relating to drug addiction required imprisonment for one to five years and/or a fine of Lux Fr 5,000 to Lux Fr 50 million, for those convicted of participating in a money laundering operation 'whether deliberately or by neglecting their professional obligations'.[81]

10.67 The revised version of the same Article[82] subsequently required participation to be 'deliberate' and omitted the involuntary offence due to mere negligence by the professional.[83] Thus, deprivation of liberty may only be imposed on a natural person who has knowingly participated in a money laundering or terrorist financing transaction.[84]

10.68 Professionals who have deliberately failed to perform their anti-money laundering or terrorist financing obligations may, however, be fined a minimum of €1,250 up to a maximum of €125,000.

Difficulties concerning the application of the special rules applicable to UCIs

10.69 Since the adoption of Circular 94/112, financial sector service providers in the Grand Duchy of Luxembourg have encountered certain difficulties in applying

---

[81] Art 8-1 as introduced by the Act of 7 July 1989 amending the Act of 19 February 1973, as amended, on the sale of pharmaceutical substances and the combating of drug addiction (*Mémorial* A 1989, 923).

[82] As introduced by the Act of 11 August 1998 introducing organized crime and the offence of money laundering into the Criminal Code and amending: (1) the Act of 19 February 1973, as amended, on the sale of pharmaceutical substances and the combating of drug addiction; (2) the Act of 5 April 1993, as amended, on the financial sector; (3) the Act of 6 December 1991, as amended, on the insurance sector; (4) the Act of 9 December 1976, as amended on the organization of the notarial profession; (5) the Act of 20 April 1977 on the operation of games of chance and betting games at sports events; (6) the Act of 28 June 1984 on the organization of the independent audit profession; (7) the Criminal Investigation Code (*Mémorial* A 1998, 1456).

[83] Art 8-1(2) of the Act of 19 February 1973, as amended, on the sale of pharmaceutical substances and the combating of drug addiction as introduced by the Act of 11 August 1998 (n 82 above).

[84] In the Grand Duchy of Luxembourg, legal persons such as companies and partnerships do not have liability under criminal law and cannot be punished under criminal law. Only the natural person working for them who has committed the offence can be convicted under criminal law (Luxembourg Court of Cassation, 22 March 1962, *Pas lux*, Vol XVIII, 450). See also A Jonckheere, M Capus-Leclerc, V Willems, and D Spielmann, *Le blanchiment du produit des infractions en Belgique et au Grand-Duché de Luxembourg*, Larcier, collection 'Les dossiers du Journal des Tribunaux' (No 9) (1995) 115.

the legislative and regulatory obligations in connection with money laundering. It is not proposed here to give a detailed description of those practical difficulties; that would exceed the scope of this work.[85] Nevertheless, it is worth taking a closer look at two of the problems.

The first difficulty is how to determine those countries whose national laws impose equivalent identification standards on domestic financial service providers. Initially, the CSSF limited its list to those countries that had transposed Council Directive 91/308 of 10 June 1991 on money laundering,[86] and to FATF member countries.[87] The CSSF subsequently added other countries[88] without wishing to produce or approve an official overall list, on the grounds that it would be up to Luxembourg professionals of the financial sector to examine the regulations applicable to foreign professionals in cases not expressly regulated by the CSSF.

10.70

The second problem concerns the meaning to be applied to the concepts of 'financial institution' and 'equivalent identification obligation'. Whilst the term 'financial institution' has a precise legal meaning for Luxembourg professionals pursuant to Circular 05/211, that is not necessarily the case with foreign professionals. Professionals in the Grand Duchy of Luxembourg must determine on a country-by-country and case-by-case basis, whether their delegated agent qualifies as a financial institution that is comparable to its Luxembourg peers, without any support from Luxembourg's laws and regulations.

10.71

Moreover, even if foreign financial institutions can be considered eligible as such, it remains to be determined whether their national legislation subjects them to equivalent identification obligations. There are few reliable references capable of

10.72

---

[85] In 1993, the Luxembourg Association of Banks and Bankers (ABBL) issued a set of practice directions and recommendations designed to prevent the use of UCIs for money laundering purposes. Whilst that document was intended to cover aspects not provided for in IML Circular 94/112, it does not have regulatory force. It was subsequently amended and enlarged, and issued in March 2000 as a joint recommendation of the ABBL and the ALFI.

[86] Council Directive (EEC) 91/308 of 10 June 1991 on the prevention of the use of the financial system for the purpose of money laundering [1991] OJ L166/77–83.

[87] Currently, the following countries are FATF members: Argentina, Australia, Austria, Belgium, Brazil, Canada, China, Denmark, Federation of Russia, Finland, France, Germany, Grand Duchy of Luxembourg, Greece, Hong Kong, Iceland, Ireland, Italy, Japan, Mexico, Netherlands, New Zealand, Norway, Portugal, Singapore, South Africa, Spain, Sweden, Switzerland, Turkey, United Kingdom and United States, and the following international organisations: EC Commission, Gulf Cooperation Council. In a circular issued on 26 June 2006 (CSSF Circular 06/250), the CSSF drew attention to the decision adopted at the FATF Plenary Meeting held from 20 to 23 June 2006 with regard to the list of non-cooperative countries and territories. Currently the list mentions no country. The CSSF stressed that transactions with business counterparts in such countries or territories should be examined particularly closely in accordance with paras 73 *et seq*, Circular 05/211.

[88] Including Monaco, the Czech Republic, and Hungary.

giving the financial service providers concerned adequate legal certainty. International harmonization in this area would be desirable.

UCIs and Professional and Banking Secrecy

Scope of the application of professional and banking secrecy

10.73 Professional secrecy[89] and its specific application to the banking and financial community,[90] ie banking secrecy, do not apply to UCIs as such, except in tax matters. UCIs merely have an obligation to maintain confidentiality, which gives rise, where applicable, to civil liability.

10.74 In fact, according to the Criminal Code,[91] professional secrecy applies to the medical profession and to anyone who, by virtue of his status or profession, becomes the custodian of the secrets entrusted to him. As a general rule, a UCI's status or function does not make it the custodian of confidential information. Hence, it is not subject to the rules on professional secrecy.

10.75 Banking secrecy applies only to the directors, members of the management and supervisory bodies, conducting persons, employees, and other persons at the service of credit institutions and professionals of the financial sector governed by the laws of Luxembourg. It also applies to the personnel of foreign credit

---

[89] On this subject, see in particular R Hoffmann, 'Réflexions sur le fondement du secret professionnel' (1983) 2 *Bull Droit & Banque* 3; P Lambert, *Le secret professionnel* (Éditions Nemesis, 1985).

[90] As described, *inter alia*, by M Elvinger, 'Les conflits entre l'obligation au secret bancaire instituée par la loi luxembourgeoise et l'obligation de déclaration imposée par une loi étrangère' (1997) 26 *Bull Droit & Banque* 5; G Harles, 'Luxembourg' in *International Bank Secrecy* (Sweet & Maxwell, 1992) 471; D Spielmann, *Le secret bancaire et l'entraide judiciaire internationale pénale au Grand-Duché de Luxembourg*, Larcier, collection 'Les dossiers du Journal des tribunaux' (No 20) (Lancier, 1999) and (No 62) (2007); A Steichen, 'Le secret bancaire face aux autorités publiques nationales et étrangères' (1995) 24 *Bull Droit & Banque* 24; N Wagner, 'Le secret professionnel en droit luxembourgeois' in *Diagonales à travers le droit luxembourgeois, Livre jubilaire de la conférence Saint-Yves 1946–1986* (Luxembourg, 1986) 901; A Serebriakoff, 'Le caractère d'ordre public du secret bancaire: conviction ou réalité?' in *Droit bancaire et financier au Luxembourg* (Larcier, 2004) Vol 1, 283; J-L Schiltz and F Schiltz, 'Le secret bancaire face aux tiers devant le juge civil' in *Droit bancaire et financier au Luxembourg* (Larcier, 2004) Vol 1, 307; L Thiel 'La protection du client de banque—un secret à revoir' (2004) *Codex* 170; P Kinsch, 'L'affaire des fichiers volés de la Kredietbank luxembourgeoise devant la Cour d'appel et la Cour de cassation—Observations sous l'arrêt de la Cour d'appel du 2 avril 2003 et l'arrêt de la Cour de cassation du 18 mars 2004' (2003) 35 *Bull Droit & Banque*, 52; A Schmitt and E Omes, *La responsabilité du banquier en droit bancaire privé luxembourgeois* (Larcier, 2006), 61 *et seq*; C Liebertz and C Schmidt, 'Le secret bancaire face au mandat dans la perspective du banquier' (Hors Série, 2005) *Bull Droit & Banque* 37; O Poelmans, 'Le secret bancaire luxembourgeois et l'attestation négative' (2007) 40 *Bull Droit & Banque* 60.

[91] Art 458, Criminal Code, which punishes violation of professional secrecy with a prison sentence ranging from 8 days to 6 months and a fine of €500 to €5,000.

institutions and other professionals of the financial sector within or outside the EEA and operating in the Grand Duchy of Luxembourg. Hence it applies to most professionals who supply UCIs with services. In contrast, the advisers and managers of Luxembourg-based UCIs covered by the 2002 Act or by the Act of 13 February 2007 are not subject to banking secrecy;[92] nor are persons whose business may only be started and carried on by virtue of special laws.[93]

Like professional secrecy, banking secrecy covers information received by credit institutions and professionals of the financial sector in the context of their professional activities.[94] **10.76**

In the area of taxation,[95] professional and banking secrecy applies broadly to credit institutions and other professionals of the financial sector established under Luxembourg law, to holding companies governed by the 1929 Act,[96] and to UCIs within the meaning of the 2002 Act.[97] Consequently, the tax authorities may not request information from any of the above-mentioned entities for taxation purposes. However, tax secrecy does not apply to the collection by the Luxembourg authorities[98] of registration and succession duties. **10.77**

History of professional and banking secrecy

Professional secrecy is an essential corollary of many professions and was included in the first Criminal Code promulgated in the Grand Duchy of Luxembourg. The applicable Article expressly refers to doctors, surgeons, health inspectors, pharmacists, and midwives. In addition to those medical professions, it refers to 'all other persons who, by virtue of their status or profession, are the custodians of the **10.78**

---

[92] Arts 41 and 13(2), 1993 Act.

[93] ibid.

[94] ibid Art 41, which punishes violation of banking secrecy in accordance with Art 458 of the Criminal Code.

[95] Para 178*bis* of the General Tax Act, as introduced by the Grand-Ducal Regulation of 24 March 1989 specifying banking secrecy in tax matters and outlining the investigation rights of the tax authorities (*Mémorial* A 1989, 182). As regards the international tax aspects of banking secrecy, see Spielmann, 2007 (n 90 above) 82 *et seq*; and Steichen (n 90 above) 24 *et seq*.

[96] And also to so-called 'milliardaire' holding companies within the meaning of the Grand-Ducal Decree of 17 December 1938 (*Mémorial* 1938, 1325), as amended by the Grand-Ducal Decree of 15 November 1947 (*Mémorial* 1947, 931).

[97] To which should be added the SIFs (Art 75, Act of 13 February 2007).

[98] Art 1 of the Grand-Ducal Regulation of 24 March 1989 specifying banking secrecy in tax matters and outlining the investigation rights of the tax authorities (*Mémorial* A 1989, 182). The applicable legislation here is the Act of 28 January 1948 concerning the fair and exact collection of registration and succession duties (*Mémorial* A 1948, 180). As regards the banker's obligations in this area, see C Kremer, 'Le banquier luxembourgeois face aux droits de succession' in *Droit bancaire et financier au Grand-Duché de Luxembourg* (Larcier, 1994) Vol 2, 730.

secrets entrusted to them'.[99] That notably includes priests and lawyers. The banker's situation was less obvious.[100]

10.79 For that reason, the legislature adopted a clear position in 1981. It extended the application of professional secrecy to bankers by referring in the Banking Act of 23 April 1981[101] to the provision of the Criminal Code dealing with professional secrecy.

10.80 A further step was taken in 1993. Banking secrecy was officially provided for in the 1993 Act, which also covered information received by professionals of the financial sector, other than banks, in the performance of their duties.

Lifting of banking secrecy

10.81 The possibility of credit institutions or other professionals of the financial sector breaching the obligation of banking secrecy raises delicate problems when not expressly authorized by the 1993 Act. Although necessary and justified in certain cases, it runs counter to the idea promoted during the preparations for the 1993 Act, according to which banking secrecy is a matter of public policy.

10.82 One therefore has to begin by examining those cases in which disclosure of information is authorized by the 1993 Act and subsequently analyse the right to lift banking secrecy in situations not expressly covered by the 1993 Act.

Lifting of banking secrecy in cases covered by the 1993 Act

10.83 The 1993 Act lists several situations in which banking secrecy ceases to exist. In all those cases, the information concerned may only be used for the purposes for which disclosure is authorized by law.[102]

Disclosure authorized or imposed by or further to a legislative provision

10.84 Pursuant to the 1993 Act,[103] 'the obligation to maintain secrecy ceases when the disclosure of information is authorised or required by a legislative provision, even if that provision predates the present law'.

10.85 This applies, *inter alia,* to money laundering. The Act of 12 November 2004 obliges credit institutions and other professionals of the financial sector, and their

---

[99] Art 458, Criminal Code.

[100] See Spielmann, 2007 (n 90 above) 19 and the references cited on this page.

[101] Art 16(1), Act of 23 April 1981 implementing the first Directive of the Council of the European Communities of 12 December 1977 on the coordination of laws, regulations and administrative provisions relating to the taking up and pursuit of the business of credit institutions (*Mémorial* A 1981, 615).

[102] Provided the applicable rules in criminal matters are complied with (Art 41(6), 1993 Act).

[103] Art 41(2), 1993 Act.

directors and employees, to inform the authorities of any circumstances that they suspect of being connected with money laundering.[104]

Under the Criminal Code, evidence given before the courts constitutes another **10.86** legal exception to the obligation requiring credit institutions and other professionals of the financial sector to keep information about clients secret.[105]

According to certain scholars and case law, banking secrecy may only be lifted **10.87** pursuant to a provision enshrined in Luxembourg law.[106]

Disclosure within the framework of prudential supervision

The 1993 Act permits the disclosure of confidential information to the 'national **10.88** or foreign authorities charged with the prudential supervision of the financial sector when performing their supervisory duties within the framework of their legal powers, provided that the information disclosed is protected by the professional secrecy imposed on the supervisory authority receiving the same'.[107] The use of such information and cooperation between supervisory authorities is covered by a specific provision in the 1993 Act.[108]

When a foreign authority requests information directly from an entity subject to **10.89** banking secrecy without going through the CSSF, the information is communicated via the parent company or a shareholder or partner subject to supervision by the foreign authority.[109]

Banking secrecy might also impede the exercise of supplementary supervision of **10.90** credit institutions and investment companies in a financial conglomerate.[110] Such supplementary supervision encompasses the financial position of the financial conglomerate and its capital adequacy in particular. It also covers risk concentration, intra-group transactions, internal control mechanisms, and risk management processes set up at the level of the group. Supplementary supervision is conducted by a supervisory authority, the coordinator, which must be provided with any relevant information in the context of its duty. Under the 1993 Act this information must be provided by any entity in a financial conglomerate, whether or not

---

[104] Art 5(1), Act of 12 November 2004.
[105] Art 458, Criminal Code.
[106] See Elvinger (n 90 above) 11 and 12; Luxembourg, 2 April 2003 (2003) 34 *Eull Droit & Banque* 52 *et seq*; Opinion of the Advocate-General P Léger delivered on 23 April 2002, Case C-153/00, Criminal proceedings against Paul der Weduwe, Rec I-2002, 11319, para 48 Luxembourg, 18 March 2004 (2004) 35 *Bull Droit & Banque* 57: 'Banking secrecy, protected by the penalties in Article 458 of the Criminal Code, which, according to Article 41, paragraph 2 of the Act of 5 April 1993, can only be lifted by the law, is part of public policy'.
[107] Art 41(3), 1993 Act.
[108] ibid Art 44.
[109] ibid Art 41(3).
[110] As regards such supervision, see ibid Arts 51-9–51-26.

regulated, in respect of which the CSSF is the coordinator.[111] More generally, the 1993 Act disapplies banking secrecy to the sharing of information among entities in a financial conglomerate, provided that such information is necessary for the supplementary supervision of the group. In this context the coordinator may be the CSSF or a foreign supervisory authority.[112]

Intra-group disclosure

10.91 Banking secrecy does not apply to the reference shareholder of a credit institution or another professional of the financial sector, subject to certain conditions. The reference shareholder is the shareholder 'whose status is one of the conditions for authorisation of the institution in question'.[113] The only information not covered by secrecy is 'information needed for the sound and prudent management of the institution, provided that such information does not directly reveal the institution's commitments vis-à-vis clients other than professionals of the financial sector'.[114]

10.92 A typical example of that exception is the situation in which a bank informs its reference shareholder of the amount of loans granted to another professional of the financial sector.

10.93 Without access to specific information, there can be no efficient internal supervision within a financial group, which can prevent legal risks and reputational risks in connection with money laundering or the financing of terrorism. For that reason, banking secrecy may not operate to counteract the activities of internal supervision bodies of financial groups. This, however, only applies to the extent necessary to prevent money laundering or the financing of terrorism.[115]

Disclosure to certain professionals of the financial sector

10.94 Article 41 of the 1993 Act may not be used to prohibit delegation of activities between professionals of the financial sector. It provides for disclosure of information to certain professionals of the financial sector, ie client communication agents, administrative agents in the financial sector, primary IT systems operators in the financial sector, and secondary IT systems and communications networks operators in the financial sector. Banking secrecy may be lifted subject to one condition: it must be within the context of a service agreement with one of the above-mentioned authorized business lines.[116]

---

[111] ibid Art 51-21.
[112] ibid Art 41(5*bis*).
[113] ibid Art 41(4).
[114] ibid.
[115] ibid.
[116] ibid Art 41(5). See also Title 1 of Circular 96/240 of 22 March 2006 as regards the lifting of banking secrecy during assignments entrusted to an IT systems and communication networks operator.

Thus, this provision authorizes a registration and transfer agent to send a client **10.95**
communication agent the names and addresses of shareholders recorded in the
register kept by him on behalf of the investment company. This allows him to
sub-delegate, on his own initiative or on the instructions of the investment company, the mailing and receipt of correspondence with these shareholders. This
option also makes it easier for an investment company to entrust these activities
directly to a client communication agent, since the law allows it to ignore the
banking secrecy imposed on the registration and transfer agent in this case.

Lifting of banking secrecy in cases not covered by the 1993 Act

According to the Parliamentary documents accompanying the 1993 Act concern- **10.96**
ing banking secrecy, 'the legislature has given that obligation a legal rather than a
contractual basis and has linked compliance to the criminal penalties laid down in
Article 458 of the Criminal Code, thereby rendering it a matter of public policy
to which only the law may make exceptions'.[117]

Although that statement by the legislature has at times been criticized,[118] it cannot **10.97**
be ignored.[119] Whilst its rationale is justified and most of its consequences are beneficial, it sometimes causes practical difficulties that have to be overcome in the interests
of the financial market. Its absolute liability provisions must sometimes make way
for other values and interests that are just as legitimate as those it is seeking to protect.
The best way to moderate the consequences of the public policy character of banking secrecy could be to insist on judicious application of the principle of proportionality, as explained below. That means that the interests protected by the public policy
nature of banking secrecy must be considered and identified. The principle of
proportionality can be used to weigh and reconcile those interests with those of the
financial markets in the event of a conflict between them.

Interests protected by banking secrecy

In order to be a matter of public policy, a law must be 'in the essential interests of **10.98**
the State or the community' or lay down 'in private law, the basic legal foundations underpinning the economic or moral order of a given society'.[120]

---

[117] *Parliamentary doc* No 3600, Comments on the Articles, 8; *Parliamentary doc* No 3600[4],
Report of the Finance and Budget Committee, 13. Luxembourg, 2 April 2003 (2003) 34 *Bull
Droit & Banque* 52 *et seq*; Luxembourg, 18 March 2004 (2004) 35 *Bull Droit & Banque* 57 *et seq*:
'Banking secrecy, protected by the penalties in Article 458 of the Criminal Code, which, according to Article 41, paragraph 2 of the Act of 5 April 1993, can only be lifted by the law, is part of
public policy'.
[118] Spielmann 1999 (n 90 above), 36–41; in contrast, in favour of the force of public policy, see
Harles (n 90 above) 477; Hoffmann (n 90 above) 3; Steichen (n 90 above) 29; Liebertz and Schmidt
(n 90 above) 40 and 41.
[119] Parliamentary documents are recognized sources for the interpretation of laws: H de Page,
Traité élémentaire de droit civil belge (Bruylant, Vol I, para 214, B).
[120] de Page (n 119 above) para 91.

10.99   That applies, notably, to the provisions on banking secrecy. The absolute force of banking secrecy has been an integral part of the growth of Luxembourg's financial market. The confidence of the saving public and investors in the discretion of their financial intermediaries in Luxembourg is an important feature in entrusting the financial intermediaries with their funds.[21]

10.100   A key feature of the public policy nature of banking secrecy is that banking secrecy in Luxembourg protects a series of private interests.[122] Its general 'public' benefit flows from the protection it offers to private interests. Those two types of interest may conflict, in which case they may be settled according to the principle of proportionality.

Principle of proportionality

10.101   The principle of proportionality is a general legal principle[123] and must be respected when preparing and implementing legal standards.[124] Application of the principle to the implementation of legal standards can have two consequences. It may either moderate the exercise of a right (prohibitive effect) or authorize actions or decisions that are at first sight prohibited (authorizing effect).[125] It is the latter use of the principle of proportionality that could limit the application of banking secrecy. It would make it possible to moderate certain extreme consequences of the absolute nature of the secrecy rules by authorizing bankers to disclose information when this is justified by legitimate interests.

10.102   The practical application of the principle of proportionality to banking secrecy calls for a series of verifications.[126]

10.103   It is first of all necessary to check whether the lifting of banking secrecy is justified by a legitimate interest. In most cases, that legitimate interest is the client's interest. In some cases, it may even be the banker's interest.

10.104   Next, it is necessary to examine whether the lifting of banking secrecy is justified. Three cumulative tests are conducted to verify whether a waiver of banking secrecy is justifiable: (1) Does the waiver permit continued protection of the legitimate interest in question? (2) Is it necessary to protect that interest insofar as there is no

---

[121]   See the CSSF Annual Report for 2003, 198 *et seq*.

[122]   See the decision of the Luxembourg District Court of 24 April 1991 (*Pas lux*, Vol XXVIII, 176), according to which the 'obligation of secrecy results from considerations of both public and private interest'; also see the CSSF Annual Report for 2003, 198 *et seq*.

[123]   F Schockweiler, 'Les principes généraux du droit en droit communautaire et en droit administratif luxembourgeois' in *Mélanges dédiés à Michel Delvaux* (Luxembourg: Cercle Michel Delvaux, 1990) 230.

[124]   P-E Partsch and I Lebbe, 'Principe de proportionnalité et droit des sociétés' (1996) *JT* 609.

[125]   Partsch and Lebbe (n 124 above) 610.

[126]   As regards the test of proportionality in general, see W Van Gerven, 'Principe de proportionnalité, abus de droit et droits fondamentaux' (1992) *JT* 305–9.

other effective means with a less adverse impact on the public policy considerations underlying banking secrecy? (3) Do the benefits of a waiver favourably balance any damage caused to the public policy considerations underlying the principle of banking secrecy?

The authorizing effect of the principle of proportionality has already been applied **10.105** in various situations, particularly those involving matters of public policy,[127] because the absolute force of such general prohibitive standards would result in an outcome contrary to the interests protected by those standards, or even other interests the protection of which is just as important. Flexibility should be possible, notably by means of the conclusion of private agreements.

Lifting of banking secrecy in the client's interest

Designed to protect the client's interest and thereby the public interest in the **10.106** Grand Duchy of Luxembourg, the absolute enforcement of banking secrecy may sometimes work against the intended beneficiary of secrecy laws. Investors may require information about them to be sent directly to a third party by a credit institution subject to banking secrecy in Luxembourg.

For example, someone may instruct an agent to perform certain tasks requiring **10.107** access to information protected by banking secrecy. In that case, an agent is generally allowed access to confidential information about his client, provided that such access is justified by the performance of his agency agreement.[128]

An agent may also have to disclose information about a client to a third party, for **10.108** example when a financial intermediary trades on the stock exchange and has to disclose the identity of his client. Such disclosure should be permitted since it is required in order to place orders on those markets and is therefore of necessity accepted by the client.

---

[127] This is, for example, the case with the public law principle of the free disposal of goods, as enshrined in the Civil Code (Arts 544, 1048 *et seq*). Violation of that principle by inalienability clauses has been held to be lawful, provided that such clauses protect a legitimate interest and are limited in time (French Supreme Court, Civil Section, 20 April 1858, *D*, 1858, 1, 154, Summary, 1858, 1, 589). Similarly, voting agreements have been accepted in company law, provided that they are in the company's interest, are not fraudulent, and do not negate the shareholder's right to take part in company decisions (Belgian Supreme Court, 13 April 1989 (1990) *JT* 751 *et seq*, note by D Michiels (1991) *RCJB* 205 *et seq*, note by J-M Nelissen Grade). This derogation, which reflects the principle of proportionality, has been accepted despite the public policy considerations underlying the shareholder's freedom to vote (Partsch and Lebbe (n 124 above) 610).

[128] According to Spielmann (n 90 above) 41, the information obtained by the agent may not go beyond the specific object of his mandate; as regards banking secrecy and the agency agreement, see also the article by Liebertz and Schmidt (n 90 above) 38 *et seq*, and the CSSF Annual Report for 2004, 118.

10.109   In all these examples, derogation from banking secrecy is justified since its positive effects outweigh its negative consequences, ie that it weakens the absolute force of banking secrecy.

10.110   Banking secrecy is therefore currently waived in the interest of the client of the professional of the financial sector where it satisfies the test of proportionality. The interest protected by that mechanism is not only legitimate but in such situations disclosure of information may also be necessary and more advantageous to the client than non-disclosure so as to preserve banking secrecy. For those reasons, it should justify derogation from the public policy considerations underlying banking secrecy.[129]

10.111   A memorandum issued on 1 March 2004 by the CSSF's committee of lawyers and published in the CSSF's annual report for 2003 also accepts a relatively flexible interpretation of banking secrecy in Luxembourg.[130] According to this memorandum, banking secrecy falls within the sphere of public policy. Banking secrecy not only protects the interests of the person affected by the information entrusted to the financial professional but also society's general interests. First, banking secrecy enables confidence to be maintained between the custodians of the relevant confidential information and the protected parties and so helps to preserve the authority of the financial profession. Secondly, it helps to protect privacy when bulk processing personal information.

10.112   The authors of this memorandum have identified an element constituting a breach of banking secrecy from which they draw fundamental conclusions as to the extent of the secrecy obligations. This element is lack of consent on the part of the person whose information is maintained under banking secrecy rules. There can be no accusation of a breach of banking secrecy in the case of 'permissive consent', ie where the 'relevant person' has given advance agreement to a disclosure which may affect his rights or interests.[131] This 'permissive consent' would differ from a contractual waiver of secrecy because of its specific nature and the capacity of the protected person to withdraw it freely at any time.[132]

10.113   This consent must be free and informed and satisfy at least the following conditions, which are not necessarily cumulative:

---

[129] In its judgment of 24 April 1991, cited above (*Pas lux*, Vol XXVIII, 173), the Luxembourg District Court even goes so far as to authorize any lifting of banking secrecy at the client's request. However, that judicial decision predates the Parliamentary documents accompanying the 1993 Act, according to which banking secrecy is a matter of public policy and hence mandatory.

[130] CSSF Annual Report for 2003, 196 *et seq.*

[131] ibid 200.

[132] Except in the case of abuse of law.

(1) it must concern specific information as opposed to 'general information of any kind';
(2) the recipient of the information must be precisely identified;
(3) the client's objective in granting consent must be mentioned;
(4) it may not be granted without time limit.

The committee of lawyers clearly advises the professional to inquire into the client's objective when the client requests him to send certain pieces of information, in order to ensure that disclosure does not break the law. It further advises the professional should assume that consent no longer exists when the purpose for which consent was given no longer exists or has been fulfilled.[133] It also stresses the client's interests and contends that 'it is logical and in accordance with the principles of professional secrecy to grant priority to the interests of the protected person in all considerations regarding the limits of secrecy. Any other attitude exposes the professional to the risk of crossing the line and committing an offence whenever the client's mood or interest changes'.[134]   **10.114**

The criteria allowing the professional to assume that he has not violated banking secrecy are those of the proportionality test discussed earlier in this text. Disclosure of information at the client's request serves a legitimate interest. Moreover, it seems to be necessary and appropriate to disclose information to achieve the client's purpose but disclosure should be strictly limited to the stated purpose (the information to be sent must be clearly defined (interest received) and the recipients must be identified). Under particular circumstances, this is a better solution than strict application of banking secrecy.   **10.115**

Lifting banking secrecy in the interests of the custodian of the secret

Banking secrecy can sometimes impose an excessively heavy burden on credit institutions or other professionals of the financial sector. Although that may seem a theoretical situation in connection with UCIs, it is discussed briefly below. It occurs essentially when a credit institution or another professional of the financial sector has to set aside banking secrecy in order to protect its own rights. In that case, its interest conflicts with the interest of its client and the general interest protected by the absolute force of banking secrecy. The principle of proportionality likewise offers an appropriate solution for that type of conflict.   **10.116**

---

[133] These principles are illustrated by a few examples, including disclosure of information under a 'Qualified Intermediary Agreement' and the Directive on Savings Taxation (CSSF Annual Report for 2003, 203. See also L Thiel, 'La protection du client de banquier—un secret à revoir' (n 90 above) 174, which advocates a review of the banking secrecy rules. It may be in the client's interest to ask his bank to disclose certain data to his tax administration in order to reduce the taxes he would otherwise have to pay).

[134] CSSF Annual Report for 2003, 201.

10.117   A judgment delivered by the Luxembourg District Court[135] is particularly revealing in this respect. As part of its defence in the legal proceedings, a bank produced
a number of documents and statements of account protected by banking secrecy.
The plaintiffs argued that those documents were inadmissible as evidence.
The court dismissed their argument on grounds rooted directly in the principle
of proportionality.[136] The court accepted at the outset the legitimacy of the bank's
interest in revealing certain data: 'Refusing the bank the right to disclose secrets in
the case of a conflict with its client would amount to depriving it of the means to
defend itself and would expose it to serious damage'. However, it immediately
confined that exception to secrecy to a strictly limited sphere. Disclosure of secrets
is only possible in the case of 'clear involvement of a banker's ownership interests;
the possibility of non-pecuniary damage is therefore not enough'. Moreover,
disclosure may only take place 'within the framework of contested legal proceedings and must be limited to information needed to support the claim in question'.
As all steps of the test of proportionality had been taken successfully, the court
ruled that the documents in question could be lawfully produced.

10.118   As a general rule, the lifting of banking secrecy must be used 'prudently and within
the very narrow limits of what is necessary to protect the interests of the bank (or
the banker), whether as plaintiff or defendant'.[137] Such conditions correspond to
those applicable to the principle of proportionality.

---

[135]   Luxembourg District Court of 26 June 1981 (1983) 2 *Bull Droit & Banque* 36.
[136]   See, to the same effect, Spielmann 1999 (n 90 above) 44.
[137]   Spielmann 1999 (n 90 above) 43.

11

UNDERTAKINGS FOR COLLECTIVE
INVESTMENT AND TAX LAW

Tax Treatment of UCIs

History of the tax treatment of UCIs

Origins

11.01 Historically, Luxembourg-based UCIs have enjoyed tax breaks not enjoyed by corporations governed by the provisions of general tax law. Prior to the 1983 Act, the tax regime for investment funds[1] was closely tied to the rules governing holding companies as defined in the 1929 Act.[2] Like such companies, investment funds were only subject to capital duty and subscription tax, to the exclusion of all other taxes.

---

[1] Prior to the 1983 Act, UCIs were generally known as *fonds d'investissement* in the Grand Duchy of Luxembourg, a literal translation of the English term 'investment fund'.

[2] For a detailed description of the tax regime applicable to investment funds under the rules prior to the 1983 Act, see B Delvaux, 'Questions actuelles concernant la loi de 1929 sur le régime fiscal des sociétés de participations financières' (1956) XVI *Pas lux*, 146; B Delvaux, 'Les sociétés d'investissement du type ouvert au Grand-Duché de Luxembourg' (1961) XVIII *Pas lux* 35; B Delvaux, 'Régime fiscal luxembourgeois assurant une juste perception des impôts', in *Les organes collectifs de placement dans la perspective de la place financière de Luxembourg,* Study Days of 11 and 12 December 1970, Université Internationale de Sciences Comparées, Luxembourg, 33; A Elvinger, 'Statut fiscal des fonds communs de placement et des sociétés d'investissement au Grand-Duché de Luxembourg' in *Les organes collectifs de placement dans la perspective de la place financière de Luxembourg,* Study Days of 11 and 12 December 1970, Université Internationale de Sciences Comparées, Luxembourg, 25; A Elvinger, 'Historique du droit bancaire et financier luxembourgeois' in *Droit bancaire et financier au Grand-Duché de Luxembourg* (Larcier, 1994) Vol 1, 3.

General discussion of capital duty and subscription tax

Capital duty and subscription tax are types of registration duty, levied, *inter alia*, **11.02**
on the conveyance (or transfer) of movable and real property.

Capital duty is charged on capital paid into *sociétés civiles* (non-commercial **11.03**
companies) and *sociétés commerciales* (commercial companies). The consideration
for the contribution of funds to a company is the issue of new shares in the capital
of the company. The issue of capital in exchange for such contributions is subject to
a duty payable by the company that is proportional to the value of the contribution/
capital issued.

Capital duty was harmonized at Community level by a European Directive **11.04**
adopted in 1969.[3] In the Grand Duchy of Luxembourg, it has been governed by
a special law since 1971.[4] Based on Community law, it replaces the earlier rules
dating from the First World War.[5]

Subscription tax is registration duty in another form. Registration duty is charged **11.05**
on the transfer of company securities.[6] Subscription tax was also introduced at the
time of the First World War.[7] It was initially levied on the transfer of every type of
security. As the authorities found it difficult to keep abreast of assignments of
bearer securities, the tax was subsequently converted[8] into a duty paid by companies on the transfer of their securities. Like a subscription tax, this lump-sum tax
is intended to cover all types of transfers of securities. It is an *ad valorem* tax based
on the total average stock market value of a company's outstanding securities

---

[3] Directive (EEC) 69/335 of 17 July 1969 concerning indirect taxes on the raising of capital
[1969] OJ L249/25.

[4] Act of 29 December 1971 concerning the taxation of capital contributions to non-commercial
and commercial companies (*Mémorial* A 1971, 2733). That law was amended by the Act of 3
December 1986 amending the Act of 29 December 1971 concerning the taxation of capital contributions to non-commercial and commercial companies and revising certain legislative provisions
governing the collection of registration duty (*Mémorial* A 1986, 2274), in application of Directive
(EEC) 85/303 of 10 June 1985 [1985] OJ L156/23. Moreover, under the Act of 25 January 1872,
newly issued securities in Luxembourg-based companies were subject to stamp duty corresponding
to 0.10% of their accounting par value. Stamp duty was abolished by the above-mentioned Act of
29 December 1971.

[5] Act of 23 December 1913 amending the laws governing taxes collected by the Luxembourg
registration authority (*Mémorial* of 29 December 1913, 1341). The rate of capital duty has changed
since the creation of this tax. The initial rate of 0.32% was raised several times with a preferential
rate for holding companies, and was raised to a uniform 1% on 1 January 1973. UCIs benefit from
a special regime, as we shall see later in this section.

[6] The statement of reasons is contained in an administrative decision of 8 September 1939,
mentioned in the Tax Code, Vol 5, Ch XII, 40.

[7] Act of 23 December 1913 amending the laws governing taxes collected by the Luxembourg
registration authority (*Mémorial* of 29 December 1913, 1341).

[8] Act of 7 August 1920 increasing registration duty (*Mémorial* A 1920, 923).

during a given year or, if that value cannot be determined, their nominal value or estimated value.[9]

Treatment of UCIs

11.06 The fact that, prior to 1983, investment funds were treated as holding companies within the meaning of the 1929 Act primarily reflected the practice of the Luxembourg registration authority, the supervisory authority for that type of company. They were treated in the same way for both capital duty and subscription tax.

11.07 **Capital duty** Capital contributions to investment companies were subject to capital duty. Capital duty also applied to capital contributions to the management companies of FCPs. Both types of contributions were taxed at the rate for holding companies. In contrast, the issue of units by an FCP was not subject to capital duty. That rule was logical, as FCPs are merely undivided pools of securities and contributions did not involve any transfer to a company, which ruled out the application of capital duty.[10]

11.08 **Subscription tax** Based on case-by-case decisions, the Luxembourg registration authority accorded FCPs and their management companies the same treatment as that applicable to holding companies within the meaning of the 1929 Act.

11.09 In an initial decision dated 17 October 1955,[11] the Service agreed to subject FCPs, like holding companies, only to subscription tax and not to any other taxes imposed on ordinary corporations. The tax rate was fixed at 0.06 per cent per annum, which was lower than the rate set for holding companies. The basis of assessment was a fund's net asset value. The subscription tax thus collected included the tax owed by the management company, which was exempt on the understanding that it formed an inseparable economic whole with its fund.

---

[9] In 1986, the subscription tax was abolished for bonds (Act of 19 December 1986 reforming certain direct and indirect tax provisions (*Mémorial* A 1986, 2330)). In 1990 (Act of 6 December 1990 (*Mémorial* A 1990, 1014)) it was abolished for all company securities, except holding companies governed by the 1929 Act and UCIs. For holding companies, the subscription tax rate is currently 0.20% of the value of its shares, save for so-called 'milliardaire' holding companies. They are exempt from subscription tax but subject to a substitute tax referred to as 'income tax', a sliding-scale levy on revenues distributed.

[10] See B Delvaux, 'Questions actuelles concernant la loi de 1929 sur le régime fiscal des sociétés de participations financières' 169; A Elvinger, 'Statut fiscal des fonds communs de placement et des sociétés d'investissement au Grand-Duché de Luxembourg', Vol 1, 27.

[11] Quoted by Delvaux (n 10 above) 166 and 172.

In a subsequent decision dated 13 February 1959,[12] the Service made the **11.10** preferential treatment of FCPs subject to the condition that their management company did not manage more than one FCP.

Investment companies were treated in exactly the same way as holding companies. **11.11** They paid subscription tax at the same rate as holding companies, ie 0.20 per cent per annum,[13] based on the value of their issued shares during the past year.

The 1983 Act

The 1983 Act introduced a special tax regime for UCIs, which were finally **11.12** removed from the scope of the tax rules for holding companies within the meaning of the 1929 Act.

In the initial form of the Bill, the regime for holding companies continued to **11.13** apply to investment companies and other types of UCIs that were neither FCPs nor SICAVs.[14] That idea was subsequently abandoned and superseded by a special regime introduced for all types of UCIs. There were three reasons for that decision:[15]

(1) safeguarding UCIs against criticism of the tax treatment of Luxembourg-based holding companies and likely changes following pressure from within the Community;

(2) enabling UCIs to distinguish themselves from holding companies for the purposes of double taxation treaties, from which holding companies were traditionally excluded; and

(3) removing obstacles to the introduction of a transparent taxation regime for residents of the Grand Duchy of Luxembourg who held investments in Luxembourg-based UCIs.[16]

While the tax regime introduced by the 1983 Act continued to limit the taxation **11.14** of UCIs to capital duty and subscription tax, the basis of assessment to tax of UCIs was radically modified.

---

[12] Quoted by B Delvaux, 'Les sociétés d'investissement du type ouvert au Grand-Duché de Luxembourg', 49.

[13] This rate, fixed initially at 0.16%, was raised to 0.20% by the Act of 30 November 1978 amending certain provisions governing income tax, business tax for financial holding companies, and stamp duty (*Mémorial* A 1978, 973).

[14] *Parliamentary doc* No 2366, Comments on the Articles, 48.

[15] *Parliamentary doc* No 2366[3], Supplementary opinion of the *Conseil d'État*, 18; *Parliamentary doc* No 2366[8], Report of the Special Parliamentary Committee, 2 *et seq*. See also A Elvinger, 'Historique du droit bancaire et financier luxembourgeois' (n 2 above) Vol 1, 92.

[16] Bill No 2379 of 30 January 1980 was intended to provide for the taxation of co-owners of property or investments in UCIs. That Bill was not taken further at the time and the issue remains dormant to this day (see 11.132 below).

The 1988 Act

11.15 The regime introduced by the 1983 Act was not amended by the 1988 Act but was initially faithfully reproduced[17] and then amended when new tax breaks were added.[18]

The 2002 Act

11.16 The 2002 Act did not change the tax rules in force under the 1988 Act, so that the tax regime for UCIs governed by the 2002 Act and those that remain governed by the 1988 Act (until its repeal in 2007) is the same.

The Act of 13 February 2007

11.17 Under the Act of 13 February 2007 the tax treatment of UCIs governed by the 2002 Act was transposed to SIFs without amendment.[19]

Features of the tax regime for UCIs

Principle

11.18 The 2002 Act and the Act of 13 February 2007 apply to all UCIs situated in the Grand Duchy of Luxembourg. An FCP is situated in the Grand Duchy of Luxembourg if the registered office of its management company is located in the Grand Duchy of Luxembourg.[20] An investment company is situated in the Grand Duchy of Luxembourg if its registered office is located in the Grand Duchy.[21]

11.19 The tax regime applicable to such UCIs is set out in the 2002 Act and in the Act of 13 February 2007, which provide that, apart from capital duty and subscription tax, 'no other tax shall be payable by the undertakings for collective investment referred to in this Act'.[22]

Scope

11.20 The tax regime for Luxembourg-based UCIs constitutes a *sui generis* regime. It derogates from the general tax provisions introduced by the LIR (income tax law) in that it limits the taxation of Luxembourg-based UCIs to capital duty and

---

[17] The 1988 Act reproduces Arts 62–66 of the 1983 Act, renumbered Arts 105–109.
[18] For the chronological sequence of successive modifications, see 1.38 *et seq*.
[19] For further details on the tax treatment applicable to SIFs, see A Goebel and B Gasparotto, 'Tax aspects of SIFs' in *Specialised Investment Funds* (Arendt & Medernach, 2007) 148 *et seq*.
[20] Arts 4 and 64, 2002 Act.
[21] ibid.
[22] ibid Art 127(1); Art 66(1), Act of 13 February 2007.

subscription tax. It also differs from the provisions applicable to holding companies within the meaning of the 1929 Act, since its taxation procedures and tax rates are not the same.

Hence, Luxembourg-based UCIs, regardless of their status or legal form, do not pay direct taxes as imposed on normal trading corporations, such as, in particular, corporation tax, local business tax, and wealth tax. **11.21**

Limits

The foregoing preferential regime does not mean that Luxembourg-based UCIs do not pay any tax whatsoever except capital duty and subscription tax. The Parliamentary documents accompanying the 1983 Act specified that UCIs would be subject to all 'taxes normally referred to as indirect taxes, including property tax'.[23] **11.22**

A similar guideline can be found in the following passage contained in the Parliamentary documents accompanying the 1988 Act:[24] **11.23**

> The *Conseil d'État* fears that certain promoters may conclude from this legislation that all transactions, regardless of their nature, carried out by undertakings for collective investment are exempt from all levies and taxes. That is not the case. In fact, to the extent that transactions carried out by a UCI are directly subject to tax, such as VAT and property transfer duty, such levies and taxes fall outside the sphere of the tax exemption accorded to UCIs by Article 105(1).

These sources show that the seemingly general wording of the 1988 Act must be considered having regard to the particular tax in question. **11.24**

Value added tax

General Services are liable to VAT in Luxembourg if they fall within the scope of VAT due to their territorial and physical characteristics.[25] **11.25**

From the physical angle, a service may only be subject to VAT in Luxembourg when it is supplied by a taxpayer, ie 'any person who independently and routinely carries out transactions falling within the scope of a general economic activity, regardless of the object, results or place of that activity'.[26] The taxpayer plays an essential role, as it is responsible for collecting the tax due. **11.26**

---

[23] *Parliamentary doc* No 2366, Comments on the Articles, 47.

[24] *Parliamentary doc* No 3172[1], Opinion of the *Conseil d'État*, 14.

[25] Art 2(a), Act of 12 February 1979 on VAT (Tax Code, Vol VI). For a more detailed analysis of the impact of VAT in the context of UCIs, see C Kremer and B Gasparotto, 'La TVA dans les structures d'organismes de placement collectif et de véhicules apprentés' in *Droit fiscal luxembourgeois, Livre Jubilaire de l'IFA Luxembourg*, ouvrage collectif (Bruylant, 2008) 691 *et seq*.

[26] Art 4(1), Act of 12 February 1979 on VAT (Tax Code, Vol VI).

11.27 The mechanism of VAT deductions paid 'upstream' allows the taxpayer to avoid the financial burden of VAT billed 'downstream'. To be authorized to deduct VAT paid upstream, the taxpayer must carry out an economic activity subject to VAT deduction and, in principle, report sales subject to VAT. If all or part of the taxpayer's sales are not subject to VAT, the taxpayer is respectively known as a 'taxpayer without the right to deduction' or a 'taxpayer with a partial right to deduction'. Thus, the following distinction must be made with regard to sales posted by the taxpayer:

(1) VAT may be deducted from:[27]
   (a) operations (provision of goods and services) which are actually subject to VAT in Luxembourg;
   (b) operations carried out abroad and which would have been subject to VAT in Luxembourg if they had fallen within the sphere of Luxembourg's territory;
   (c) operations subject to exemption for intra-Community and international supplies;[28]
   (d) banking, financial, and insurance operations carried out with a client established outside the European Community, or directly related to goods which are intended to be exported to a country outside the European Community.[29]

(2) VAT may not be deducted from:[30]
   (a) operations that are exempt from VAT (such as banking, financial, and insurance operations within the European Community);[31]
   (b) operations which do not fall within the scope of VAT.

11.28 For territorial purposes, a service is subject to VAT in Luxembourg when the service is deemed to be provided in Luxembourg. The location of a service is determined by several factors, such as the type of service and the client's status.[32] According to the general rule, a service is supposed to take place at the location where the service provider establishes the head office of the commercial business delivering the service.[33]

Example 1. A taxpayer in Luxembourg (a lawyer) provides an advisory service to a private client who does not pay tax in Luxembourg and resides in Germany. In this

---

[27] Art 49(2), Act of 12 February 1979 on VAT (Tax Code, Vol VI).
[28] Those operations benefit from exemption under the provisions of Art 43 of the Act of 12 February 1979 on VAT (Tax Code, Vol VI).
[29] Those operations benefit from exemption under the provisions of Art 44(1)(c) and (i), Act of 12 February 1979 on VAT (Tax Code, Vol VI).
[30] Art 49(1), Act of 12 February 1979 on VAT (Tax Code, Vol VI).
[31] ibid Art 44.
[32] See the rules on the location of service providers listed in ibid Art 17.
[33] ibid Art 17(1).

case, the service is deemed to be provided in Luxembourg and Luxembourg VAT is charged.

For certain categories of services—of which the law provides an exhaustive list[34]— the place where the service is provided is deemed to be the place where the client is established, provided that the client is a taxpayer established in a EU Member State other than that of the service provider or when the client is established outside the European Union. According to this principle (known as 'reverse charge'), the VAT on the service is declared by the taxable client, who shows a VAT receivable. Provided the taxable client's right to deduction is not limited, the VAT declared as a 'reverse charge' may be deducted upstream by the client.[35] The reverse-charge VAT may be carried over as a VAT which is due and deductible, as the case may be, through the client's VAT return. **11.29**

The service categories covered by the reverse-charge principle notably include the following: **11.30**

(1) the services provided by lawyers, consultants, external accountants, engineers, and design firms, and similar activities;
(2) data processing and the supply of information;
(3) banking, financial, insurance, and reinsurance operations except for the rental of safe deposit boxes.

Example 2. A taxpayer in Luxembourg (a lawyer) provides an advisory service to a German taxpayer. This service is not subject to VAT in Luxembourg The German client declares the German VAT on the service, which, depending on the scope of his right to deduction in Germany, may be recoverable.

Example 3. A German taxpayer (a lawyer) provides an advisory service to a Luxembourg taxpayer. This service is subject to VAT in Luxembourg. The Luxembourg client declares the Luxembourg VAT on the service, which, depending on the scope of his right to deduction in Luxembourg, may be recoverable.

However, when a client for one of these service categories is not subject to VAT, Example 1 applies (para 11.28 above), which stipulates that VAT is paid where the service provider is established.

When a client for one of these service categories is not a taxpayer and is domiciled and residing habitually outside the European Union, service is deemed to be provided at the location of this domicile or this habitual residence,[36] so that no European VAT is due on the service provided. **11.31**

---

[34] ibid Art 17(2)(e).
[35] For a more detailed description of location rules, see B Vanderstichelen and B Gasparotto, *TVA Luxembourg— guide pratique 2006* (Kluwer, 2005).
[36] Art 17(2)(e), Act of 12 February 1979 on VAT.

Example 4. A taxpayer in Luxembourg (a lawyer) provides an advisory service to a private client established in the United States. This service is not subject to VAT in Luxembourg.

11.32 **Status of participants in UCIs with regard to VAT**   For many years, the Luxembourg registration authority[37] did not consider UCIs to be taxpayers, on the grounds that they did not have an economic activity but limited themselves to managing their own assets. This position was wiped away following a decision handed down by the European Court of Justice (ECJ) in the Banque Bruxelles Lambert (BBL) case.[38] The ECJ held that collective investment in transferable securities of capital raised from the public constitutes an activity exceeding the mere acquisition and sale of securities and is intended to generate income on a continuing basis. The ECJ therefore concluded that SICAVs are taxpayers, whether they have an integrated management function or refer management to an authorized outside service provider. SICAVs carry on an economic activity for VAT purposes since they use the capital deposited by subscribers when buying units to constitute and manage securities portfolios on their behalf and in exchange for remuneration. Thus, the ECJ put an end to certain divergent interpretations between the Member States. Although the BBL decision concerned a coordinated SICAV, it also covers, in principle, non-coordinated UCIs of the incorporated type. It should be noted that Circular 723 of 29 December 2006, issued by the registration authority, confirms that the following entities are eligible as VAT taxpayers:

(1) UCIs which are subject to supervision by the CSSF (eg Luxembourg UCIs or foreign UCIs distributed in Luxembourg);
(2) Luxembourg pension funds;
(3) SICARs;
(4) SIFs;
(5) securitisation vehicles.

The status of FCPs is clarified insofar as the management company and not the FCP itself qualifies as a VAT taxpayer.

11.33 Circular 723 specifies that where taxpayers are not authorized to deduct VAT paid on the purchase of goods as well as on services provided, they are exempt from the obligation to be VAT registered. However, if they benefit from 'intellectual' or 'intangible' services (such as legal or tax advisory services) delivered by providers established outside Luxembourg, or if they acquire goods transported from a Member State to Luxembourg for an amount in excess of €10,000 on an

---

[37] *Administration de l'Enregistrement.*
[38] C-8/03, *Banque Bruxelles Lambert SA (BBL) v État belge*, 21 October 2004, ECJ.

annual basis,[39] those investment vehicles are required to register in Luxembourg for VAT purposes. Provided that they are liable for Luxembourg VAT on the purchase of goods or services provided from abroad, UCIs must register for VAT purposes, submit a (simplified) annual VAT return, and pay the corresponding tax to the Treasury.

Most other service providers in the UCI sector, such as depositaries and head office agents, are subject to VAT.   **11.34**

Exemption from VAT of services related to the management of UCIs   Pursuant   **11.35**
to a special VAT provision, many UCI-related services rendered by service providers established in the Grand Duchy of Luxembourg are not subject to VAT in Luxembourg.[40] According to the provision in question, VAT is not charged on 'the management of UCIs, including SICARs and SIFs, and pension funds subject to supervision by the CSSF or the Commissariat aux Assurances, and securitisation vehicles situated in Luxembourg'.[41] Management services for UCIs are therefore exempt from VAT in Luxembourg. That exemption applies to the management of all UCIs, whether incorporated or contractually based.

The laws of Luxembourg do not define the concept of 'management'. Another   **11.36**
case at Community level has made some important clarifications. In the *Abbey National* decision,[42] the ECJ ruled that the concept of 'management' has its own independent meaning in Community law which Member States may not amend or deviate from.[43] According to this approach, a Member State cannot use its own definition and so give its own fund sector a competitive edge over those of other Member States.

The ECJ has ruled that the concept of 'management of undertakings for collective   **11.37**
investment' covers the services performed by a third party manager in respect of the administrative and accounting management of a fund if, viewed broadly, they form a distinct whole, and are specific to, and essential for, the management of that fund.

In contrast, this concept does not cover the custody and control services incumbent   **11.38**
upon depositaries by virtue of Directive (EEC) 85/611. The ECJ therefore holds that the regulatory texts, particularly Directive 85/611 can be usefully applied to determine which activities are specific to and essential for the management of a

---

[39] Art 18(2), first indent, Act of 12 February 1979 on VAT.
[40] ibid Art 44(1)(d).
[41] Art 52(3), Act of 22 March 2004 on securitization and amending the Act of 12 February 1979, as amended, on value added tax and Art 38 of the Act of 15 June 2004 on the risk capital investment company (SICAR) have extended the scope of application of exemption to management of securitization vehicles established in Luxembourg and to SICARs supervised by the CSSF.
[42] C-169/04, *Abbey National plc, Inscape Investment Fund v Commissioners of Customs & Excise*, 4 May 2006 ECJ (hereinafter the *'Abbey National'* decision).
[43] *Abbey National* (n 42 above) point 43.

UCI. Therefore, apart from portfolio management tasks, the scope of the exemption from VAT also covers the administration of UCIs themselves, such as the tasks set out in Annexe II to Directive 85/611, under the heading 'Administration',[44] which are functions specific to UCIs.[45]

11.39 The ECJ has further specified that application of a VAT exemption does not in principle preclude the management of UCIs from being broken down into a number of separate services that may come within the meaning of 'management of undertakings for collective investment' in that provision, and benefiting from exemption, even when they are provided by a third party manager.[46]

11.40 However, to be regarded as exempt transactions, services performed by a third party manager in respect of the administrative and accounting management of UCIs must, viewed broadly, form a distinct whole, fulfilling in effect the specific, essential functions of a management service for UCIs. The services supplied must therefore concern specific essential elements of the management of UCIs. The mere provision of equipment or technical services, such as making available an IT system, are not exempt.

11.41 The position of the Luxembourg registration authority with regard to the subcontracting of management services for UCIs[47] has not been fundamentally challenged by the judgment handed down by the ECJ in the *Abbey National* case, since its application conditions are the same.

11.42 In 1996, the Luxembourg Minister of Finance decided to extend the benefit of VAT exemption to subcontracts, subject to compliance with certain conditions. These exemption conditions were worded as follows:

> The following are exempt from VAT: management services provided under a direct contract between the service provider (bank, trustee, etc.) and the undertaking for collective investment. Subcontracts are not exempt except for contracts for finished services, i.e. a situation in which the subcontractor delivers management services to the main service provider and the latter's role is strictly limited to re-invoicing said services as such to the undertakings for collective investment.[48]

---

[44] The following services are listed under the heading 'Administration': (a) legal and accounting management services to the fund; (b) requests for information from clients; (c) portfolio valuation and calculation of the unit value (including tax aspects); (d) verification of compliance with regulations; (e) maintaining the register of unitholders; (f) allocation of revenues; (g) issue and redemption of units; (h) settlement of contracts (including mailing of certificates); (i) registration and storage of transactions.

[45] *Abbey National* (n 42 above) point 64.

[46] *Abbey National* (n 42 above) points 67 *et seq.*

[47] Ministerial Decision of 11 October 1996.

[48] ibid.

In this case, management services do not have to be covered by a direct contract between the UCI and the service provider in order to benefit from exemption. That said, such services are not automatically exempt from VAT.

In fact, such services must be 'finished', ie management services delivered by the **11.43** subcontractor to the main service provider, whose role is limited to re-invoicing them to the UCI. The principal manager may re-invoice such services to a UCI only when they are segregated and provided on behalf of a particular UCI.

Other services   All services other than management services supplied to UCIs **11.44** by service providers established in the Grand Duchy of Luxembourg (such as lawyers' and auditors' services or the printing of prospectuses) are subject to VAT at the applicable rate.

Aspects of territoriality   Only services considered to be provided in the Grand **11.45** Duchy of Luxembourg for VAT purposes are subject to Luxembourg's VAT rules.

As explained above,[49] the place where the service is provided is generally the loca- **11.46** tion of the principal place of business from which the service provider supplies the service (or any other permanent establishment from which the service is provided).[50] There are exceptions to that principle (for example in the banking and financial sectors) for cross-border services to recipients subject to tax in the Grand Duchy of Luxembourg. In such cases, the recipient's location is deemed to be the country in which the recipient is established.[51] If an EU recipient is not subject to VAT, the place in which the service is provided is the principal place where the foreign service provider is established.[52]

There are several possibilities in connection with UCIs. In the vast majority, VAT **11.47** is not due in Luxembourg. For instance, if a foreign service provider supplies a service to a taxpayer in the Grand Duchy of Luxembourg, that is the place at which the service is rendered. As all management services provided to UCIs are exempt from VAT under Luxembourg law, the foregoing service is also exempt from VAT in Luxembourg. That is, *inter alia,* the case if foreign investment advisers supply investment management services to Luxembourg-based management companies or SICAVs.

Examples   In a purely internal situation in the Grand Duchy of Luxembourg, **11.48** there are two possible cases whose only difference is whether or not the main service provider is subject to VAT.

---

[49]   See 11.28 above.
[50]   Art 17(1), Act of 12 February 1979 on VAT.
[51]   ibid Art 17(2)(e).
[52]   ibid Art 17(1).

Example 5. An administrator based in Luxembourg provides services to a Luxembourg UCI and subcontracts, among other tasks, the registrar's function to another entity in Luxembourg. Such services are VAT exempt to the extent that they must, viewed broadly, form a distinct whole, fulfilling, in effect, the specific and essential functions of a management service provided to the UCI. The subcontractor delivers a finished service to the main service provider, which does not pay upstream non-deductible VAT.

	Management service		Management service	
Subcontractor	->	Main service provider	->	UCI
	Exemption		Exemption	

Example 6. In the same situation as described above, the administrator also subcontracts certain accounting functions (not specific to or essential for the management of UCIs) to another entity based in Luxembourg. These accounting services cannot be considered management services provided to UCIs. The VAT billed by the subcontractor on such services is considered upstream non-deductible VAT and therefore may not be deducted by the main service provider (unless the administrator in turn invoices those accounting fees or allocates them to an activity in respect of which VAT is deductible).

Subcontractor	->	Main service provider	->	UCI
	VAT		Exemption	

There are several possibilities in a situation with extraneous factors:

Example 7. In the same situation as described in Example 5 above, the administrator subcontracts a portion of the registrar's function to an entity based in a foreign country, whether an EU Member State or not. As the main service provider and the beneficiary of the subcontracted service is subject to VAT in Luxembourg, the subcontracted services are deemed to be provided in Luxembourg. However, the service is exempt as the subcontractor delivers a service which, viewed broadly, forms a distinct whole, fulfilling, in effect, the specific and essential functions of a management service provided to the UCI.

	Management service		Management service	
Foreign subcontractor	->	Main service provider	->	UCI
(EU – non EU)		subject to tax in Luxembourg		
	Exemption		Exemption	

Example 8. When an activity subcontracted to a foreign entity concerns a taxable service, such as certain accounting functions (not specific to or essential for the management of UCIs), or legal functions, and since the main service provider and the beneficiary of the subcontracted service is subject to VAT, the subcontracted services are deemed to be provided in Luxembourg. As this service cannot be exempt, the main service provider must declare the upstream VAT on this service as a reverse charge. The upstream VAT cannot be deducted (unless the main service provider in turn invoices those accounting fees or allocates them to an activity in respect of which VAT is deductible).

Foreign subcontractor	->	Main service provider	->	UCI
(EU – non EU)		subject to tax in Luxembourg		
		and VAT registered		
	Reverse charge VAT		Exemption	

Registration duty

Real estate property funds have to pay registration duty when they directly acquire **11.49** buildings in the Grand Duchy of Luxembourg. Such property conveyances are subject to proportional or *ad valorem* registration duty calculated on the value of the building in question, with such duty being paid by the buyer, even if it is a UCI.[53] In contrast, if the building concerned is contributed to a UCI in consideration for the issue of shares, registration duty is not chargeable. That type of transaction is covered by the fixed capital duty paid when the UCI is formed.

Property tax

Are UCIs entitled to claim exemption from property tax? The 1983 Act and **11.50** subsequent laws on UCIs are silent in that respect. A study of the Parliamentary documents leads to inconclusive results.

The Parliamentary documents accompanying the 1983 Act did not exempt UCIs **11.51** from property tax, on the grounds that it is an indirect tax. That is debatable. Legal opinion holds that property tax is a direct tax, as opposed to taxes on the legal circulation of assets, which are categorized as indirect taxes.[54] Property tax is a real tax. It is not levied according to the taxpayer's status but according to the nature and location of the property. It is charged on buildings located in the Grand Duchy of Luxembourg.[55]

Indeed, the Parliamentary documents accompanying the 1983 Act are some- **11.52** what contradictory in this respect. They acknowledge that UCIs should be exempt from local business tax. However, business tax is also a real tax, levied on

---

[53] The rate of registration duty charged on the conveyance of real property in the Grand Duchy of Luxembourg is 6%, plus 1% transcription duty, and, if the property is located in the territory of the City of Luxembourg, a municipal surtax of 3% (para IX of the Act of 7 August 1920 increasing registration duty, Tax Code, Vol 5, Title 2, Ch V; para II of the proportional scale of rates annexed to the Act of 7 August 1920 on registration duty, Tax Code, Vol 5(a), Title 5, Ch XIII; tax regulation of 14 March 1988 on registration duty paid on all real property conveyances (*Mémorial* A 1988, 567)).

[54] J Olinger, *Introduction à l'étude du droit fiscal luxembourgeois* (Études fiscales, Éditions de l'Imprimerie Saint-Paul, 1974) 18.

[55] Para 3, Act of 1 December 1936 on property tax, (Tax Code, Vol 4, Title II). Property tax is levied at a rate that varies from one municipality to another. For example, in the City of Luxembourg, the rate is currently about 10% of the unit value of buildings.

businesses located in the Grand Duchy of Luxembourg.[56] That makes it difficult to understand why property tax should be treated differently.

11.53 The *Conseil d'État* uses another distinction in the Parliamentary documents accompanying the 1988 Act. According to the criteria used by the *Conseil d'État*, certain transactions effected by UCIs are taxable *per se*. However, property tax should be excluded even according to those criteria, since its application is not linked to specific transactions.

11.54 Real estate property funds investing directly in buildings located in the Grand Duchy of Luxembourg appear to be paying property tax at this time. That does not conform to the law.

Tax treatment of UCIs on their formation

Incorporated UCIs

11.55 The 2002 Act and the Act of 13 February 2007 subject UCIs to 'capital duty levied on the contribution of capital to *sociétés civiles* [non-commercial companies] and *sociétés commerciales* [commercial companies]'.[57] The legislation authorizes the applicable rate to be determined by Grand-Ducal Regulation, while specifying that it must be a fixed charge the amount of which may not exceed €1,250.[58]

11.56 The Grand-Ducal Regulation of 14 April 2003 fixed capital duty at €1,250. That duty is collected on incorporation and covers all future capital contributions, particularly capital increases.[59]

Contractual UCIs

11.57 FCPs are undivided pools of assets. Hence they are not subject to capital duty, which is only charged on capital contributed to companies.[60] The rules relating to the capital duty paid by an FCP's management company are discussed below.[61]

---

[56] The real character of commercial tax and property tax is recognized by the Luxembourg direct tax authority: see the General Tax Act of 22 May 1931 (Tax Code, Vol 1, note §4).

[57] Art 127(1), 2002 Act; Art 66(1), Act of 13 February 2007.

[58] Art 128(1) and (3), 2002 Act; Art 67(1) and (3), Act of 13 February 2007.

[59] Art 1 of the Grand-Ducal Regulation of 14 April 2003 prescribing the fixed duty applicable to capital contributions to undertakings for collective investment governed by Art 128 the Act of 20 December 2002 concerning such undertakings (*Mémorial* A 2003, 1004).

[60] This conclusion can be drawn from the Parliamentary documents accompanying the 1983 Act, expressed as follows: 'The capital duty to be collected is that provided for by the Act of 29 December 1971. For the FCPs defined in Article 1 of this Act, the levying of capital duty is limited strictly to capital contributions and increases concerning the management company. Payments made to a common fund are not liable to the duty on capital contributions'. *Parliamentary doc* No 2366, Comments on the Articles, 47.

[61] See 11.87 *et seq* below.

Ongoing tax treatment of UCIs

Application of subscription tax

What makes the tax regime of Luxembourg-based UCIs special is that it exempts **11.58** them from every tax on income and wealth imposed on ordinary corporations. The ordinary revenues obtained by a UCI from domestic or foreign sources and both realized and unrealized capital gains are exempt from taxes paid by corporations in general.

The only tax paid annually by UCIs is subscription tax. This is a type of capital **11.59** tax, in that it is based on a UCI's net asset value. It is imposed on both incorporated and contractual UCIs, whether they make distributions to investors or capitalize all or part of their revenues.

Subscription tax rate

Normal rules

The normal subscription tax rate payable by UCIs governed by the 2002 Act is **11.60** 0.05 per cent.[62] It is 0.01 per cent for SIFs.[63] Neither rate varies depending on a UCI's status and legal form.

Preferential regimes

Funds of funds UCIs are exempt from subscription tax on the value of assets **11.61** represented by units in other UCIs, provided the underlying UCIs are themselves subject to the subscription tax provided for in the 2002 Act or in the Act of 13 February 2007.[64]

This tax break not only applies to UCIs which are funds of funds. On the contrary, **11.62** every UCI holding units in other Luxembourg-based UCIs is exempt from subscription tax in respect of that holding.

Money market funds

Principle The subscription tax rate is reduced from 0.05 per cent to 0.01 per cent **11.63** for UCIs the exclusive object of which is collective investment in money market instruments and in deposits held with credit institutions. Such preferential

---

[62] Art 129(1), 2002 Act.

[63] Art 68(1), Act of 13 February 2007; Art 129(2), 2002 Act.

[64] Art 129(3), 2002 Act; Art 68(2)(a), Act of 13 February 2007. This exemption was introduced by the Act of 23 December 1994 concerning the State revenue and expenditure budget for the 1995 fiscal year (*Mémorial* A 1994, 2481). In 1995 and 1996, a reduced rate of 0.03% applied to the proportion represented by such assets. But since double taxation subsisted, even at that low rate, the government decided simply to abolish subscription tax on the value of any investment in other Luxembourg-based UCIs with effect from 1 January 1997 (Act of 24 December 1996 amending certain direct and indirect tax provisions (*Mémorial* A 1996, 2303)). This system was adopted without change by the 2002 Act.

treatment also applies if a UCI exclusively invests in deposits held with credit institutions.[65] Although not specified in the 2002 Act, the preferential regime will also apply when a UCI invests only in money market instruments.

11.64 The meaning of 'money market instruments' is provided for in a Grand-Ducal regulation.[66] The scope is very broad and covers 'any debt securities and instruments, irrespective of whether they are transferable securities or not, including bonds, certificates of deposit, deposit receipts and all other similar instruments'.[67] That wording makes application of the tax break compatible with the investment restrictions applicable to coordinated UCITS investing in transferable securities other than money market instruments stipulated in Article 1 of the 2002 Act, ie instruments normally traded on the money market.

11.65 Because it aims to promote UCIs investing in financial instruments (transferable securities or other securities), the yield on which is close to the money market rate, the Grand-Ducal regulation provides that the initial or residual maturity of such securities must not exceed twelve months at the time of acquisition by a UCI. If such securities carry a floating interest rate, the terms of issue governing those securities must provide that the applicable interest rate is to be adjusted at least annually in accordance with market conditions.[68]

11.66 A security's maturity may be varied 'synthetically' by means of derivatives. Pursuant to the Grand-Ducal regulation in question, the relevant financial instruments are to be taken into account when calculating its maturity.[69] UCIs may use that mechanism to buy money market instruments the residual period to maturity of which exceeds twelve months, provided that they also hold derivatives—such as put options—enabling them to sell the instruments concerned within twelve months.

11.67 According to the interpretation of the law by the CSSF, money market funds the average portfolio maturity of which does not exceed twelve months also qualify for the reduced subscription tax rate. The reduced subscription tax rate applies

---

[65] Art 129(2)(a) and (b), 2002 Act. This reduction was introduced by the Act of 23 December 1994 concerning the State revenue and expenditure budget for the 1995 fiscal year (*Mémorial* A 1994, 2481). At the time, the reduced rate was 0.03%. The Act of 24 December 1996 amending certain direct and indirect tax provisions (*Mémorial* A 1996, 2303) lowered the rate to 0.02% for 1997 and 0.01% from 1 January 1998. This system was adopted without change by the 2002 Act.

[66] Grand-Ducal Regulation of 14 April 2003 determining the conditions and criteria for the application of the subscription tax referred to in Art 129 of the Act of 20 December 2002 on undertakings for collective investment (*Mémorial* A 2003, 1003).

[67] Art 1 of the Grand-Ducal Regulation of 14 April 2003 determining the conditions and criteria for the application of the subscription tax referred to in Art 129 of the Act of 20 December 2002 on undertakings for collective investment (*Mémorial* A 2003, 1003).

[68] ibid.

[69] ibid.

mutatis mutandis to the money market sub-funds of umbrella funds.[70] The reduced subscription tax rate takes effect once a UCI is entered on a list prepared by the CSSF. That list includes all UCIs and the sub-funds that meet the legislative and regulatory prerequisites.[71]

Exception   Certain types of money market funds are entirely exempt from subscription tax provided they comply with certain criteria.[72]   **11.68**

First, the securities of such a UCI must be reserved solely for institutional investors. **11.69** It is not necessary that the UCIs concerned be governed by the Act of 13 February 2007 but, if governed by the 2002 Act, they must simply make sure their units are not held by non-institutional investors. As regards SIFs the concept of institutional investor is replaced by that of well-informed investor within the meaning of the Act of 13 February 2007.[73] In addition, the UCI's objective should be restricted exclusively to investment in money market instruments or very short-term bank deposits, fixed by the law at a maximum of 90 days in terms of the portfolio's weighted residual maturity. Moreover, the money market fund must have the highest possible rating from a recognized rating agency.[74] The exemption also applies to eligible sub-funds of an umbrella UCI. When a UCI issues units in several categories, exemption applies only to those categories—of the sub-fund or the UCI—reserved for institutional investors and, with respect to SIFs, for other well-informed investors.

Sub-funds and classes of units in UCIs reserved for instituational investors **11.70** Where an umbrella fund subject to the 2002 Act reserves one or more of its sub-funds for institutional investors, the relevant sub-fund is entitled to pay subscription tax at the reduced rate of 0.01 per cent, regardless of the applicable investment policy.

The reduced rate of 0.01 per cent, also applies when a UCI subject to the 2002 Act **11.71** issues classes of units reserved for institutional investors, whether within a sub-fund or otherwise.[75] The concept of institutional investor must be interpreted in the same way as in the context of an institutional UCI within the meaning of the 1991 Act.[76]

---

[70]   Second paragraph of Art 2 of the Grand-Ducal Regulation of 14 April 2003 determining the conditions and criteria for the application of the subscription tax referred to in Art 129 of the Act of 20 December 2002 on undertakings for collective investment (*Mémorial* A 2003, 1003).

[71]   ibid first paragraph of Art 2.

[72]   Art 129(3) of the 2002 Act, introduced by the Act of 19 December 2003 on the revenue and expenditure budget for the 2004 fiscal year (*Mémorial* A 2003, 3687); Art 68(2)(b), Act of 13 February 2007.

[73]   Art 68(2)(b), Act of 13 February 2007.

[74]   Such as Aaa (Moody's) or AAA (Standard & Poor's).

[75]   This extension of the reduced subscription tax is based on the Act of 17 July 2000 amending certain provisions of the 1988 Act (*Mémorial* A 2000, 1226). It continues to apply within the framework of the 2002 Act (Art 129(2), 2002 Act).

[76]   See 2.63 *et seq* above.

The concept is more restrictive than that of well-informed investor within the meaning of the Act of 13 February 2007, which repealed and replaced the 1991 Act.

11.72 **Pension fund pooling vehicles** UCIs whose securities are reserved for institutions for occupational retirement provision or similar investment vehicles are entirely exempt from subscription tax.[77] The purpose of this provision is to encourage multinationals to accumulate the assets held by them to meet retirement liabilities vis-à-vis their employees in Luxembourg-based UCIs established as pension fund pooling vehicles. The technique is to pool, in a single investment vehicle, the similar pension assets held by various entities within a multinational group.

11.73 This structure is of interest for several reasons. One is that it can be used to set up complementary pension schemes or pension funds according to local legal requirements while pooling asset investments in a single vehicle, making it possible to generate economies of scale. In other words, the assets held under different pension schemes organized locally by a particular group can be grouped and managed within a single investment vehicle, permitting better asset allocation, broader risk spreading, and access to certain investments that may not have been accessible in the absence of critical mass. This technique further strengthens control at group level, giving it an overview of its full commitments.

11.74 In Luxembourg, the FCP structure has been the vehicle traditionally used for pooling assets. As an FCP is not itself taxable, it would therefore appear to be the ideal vehicle to hold the pension assets held by various entities across a multinational group. Businesses and pension funds investing in tax-transparent funds are in the same position as regards the tax authorities as if they had invested directly in the assets held through the fund.

11.75 That said, the subscription tax paid by such funds is an additional cost in the area of complementary pension schemes (as in other areas). The subscription tax charged on the assets of Luxembourg-based UCIs used to be a significant competitive disadvantage.[78]

11.76 Nowadays, Luxembourg-based UCIs (regardless of their legal form—common fund or investment company) are exempt from subscription tax, provided the relevant scheme is dedicated to pooling assets held to finance pension payments. The exemption also applies to SIFs to which the exemption has been extended,

---

[77] Art 129(3)(c), 2002 Act, introduced by the Act of 15 June 2004; Art 68(2) and (5), Act of 13 February 2007.
[78] Great Britain and Ireland have adopted specific laws for pension pooling vehicles. In 1996, Great Britain created a dedicated 'pension fund pooling vehicle', which was a new type of fiscally-transparent unit trust. In 2003, Ireland created the 'common contractual fund', similar to Luxembourg's FCP, which was transparent for tax purposes and which can be used for pension pooling activities.

and individual sub-funds and share classes of such UCIs.[79] The exemption expressly refers to assets obtained directly from businesses operating an internal pension scheme and assets obtained from pension funds financing external pension schemes.

Within the framework of the 2002 Act, the only UCIs eligible for exemption are those that reserve the issue of their securities to entities within the same group. According to the preparatory works for the law introducing this regime,[80] the concept of 'group' has the meaning already provided for by the 2002 Act. A group consists of all companies that are consolidated within the meaning of Directive 83/349 on consolidated accounts[81] or according to recognized international accounting rules. The situation of SIFs is somewhat different in this respect. A SIF may reserve its securities for issue to the trustees of group pension schemes established by one or several employers.[82]   **11.77**

Another difference between UCIs governed by the 2002 Act and SIFs lies in the potential for mixing the funding of pension schemes with other investment policies for the benefit of distinct investors.   **11.78**

In order to benefit from the exemption, a UCI governed by the 2002 Act must be solely used to pool assets. A SIF, however, may dedicate one of its sub-funds to this technique while offering the rest of its sub-funds to other private or institutional investors. That type of UCI, if governed by the Act of 13 February 2007, is entitled to exemption at the level of the dedicated sub-fund.   **11.79**

Exemption from subscription tax is available to an umbrella UCI governed by the 2002 Act which is exclusively dedicated to pension pooling but offers its subfunds to several groups of companies.   **11.80**

Neither the wording of the law nor that of the Parliamentary documents appears to rule out this flexible interpretation. The concern of Parliament to exclude mixed vehicles from the scope of the exemption is still respected in the case of a UCI dedicated to pooling the assets of several groups. The logical corollary of this would be a shift in Luxembourg's administrative practice towards the development of 'multi-employer' pension funds.[83]   **11.81**

---

[79] Art 68(2) and (5), Act of 13 February 2007.
[80] *Parliamentary doc* No 5201[2], Government amendments, 3.
[81] Seventh Directive (EEC) 83/349 of the Council of 13 June 1983, based on Art 54, paragraph 3(g) of the Treaty, with regard to consolidated accounts [1983] OJ L193/1.
[82] Art 68(2) and (5), Act of 13 February 2007.
[83] For multi-employer pension funds, see C Kremer and A Contreras, 'Les fonds de pension soumis au contrôle prudentiel de la Commission de surveillance du secteur financier' in *Droit bancaire et financier au Luxembourg* (Larcier, 2004) Vol 4, 1768 *et seq.*

Basis of assessment for subscription tax

11.82   The basis of assessment for calculation of subscription tax is the value of the total net assets of the UCI or sub-fund in question, as valued on the last day of each quarter.[84] On the formation or dissolution of a UCI, the subscription tax is pro-rated according to the number of days between the date on which the UCI is entered on the list and the end of the first quarter, or the number of days between the start of the last quarter and dissolution of the UCI. However, that exception does not apply to the creation and dissolution of sub-funds, since an umbrella UCI forms a single legal entity.

Tax treatment of UCIs on dissolution or restructuring

11.83   The dissolution of a UCI does not have particular fiscal consequences. The distributed liquidation surplus is not subject to a deduction at source.[85]

11.84   Mergers and demergers of Luxembourg-based UCIs or sub-funds are also not taxed in Luxembourg. Likewise no taxation is levied when an incorporated UCI changes its legal form and when a contractual UCI is converted into an incorporated UCI. When a UCI governed by the 1988 Act or by the Act of 13 February 2007 is converted into a UCI governed by the 2002 Act, its conversion does not give rise to a new contribution tax.[86]

11.85   If a UCI is converted into a company outside the scope of the 2002 Act, such as a family estate management company (*'société de gestion de patrimoine familial'*—'SPF') within the meaning of the Act of 11 May 2007,[87] a proportional capital duty equal to 0.5 per cent (1 per cent before 31 December 2007) of the real value of the contributions is charged at the time of 'migration', notwithstanding the fixed duty of €1,250 already paid when the UCI was created.[88]

Tax rules for management companies of UCIs

11.86   The legal and regulatory status of management companies of UCIs has already been discussed earlier in this work.[89] The applicable tax rules are discussed below.

---

[84]   Art 129(5), 2002 Act; Art 68(4), Act of 13 February 2007.

[85]   Art 127(2), 2002 Act; Art 66(2), Act of 13 February 2007.

[86]   Art 3 of the of the Grand-Ducal Regulation of 14 April 2003 prescribing the terms and amount of the fixed duty applicable to liquidated capital governed by Art 128 the Act of 20 December 2002 concerning undertakings for collective investment (*Mémorial* A 2003, 1004).

[87]   Act of 11 May 2007 introducing a *société de gestion de patrimoine familial*—'SPF' (*Mémorial* A 2007, 1608 *et seq*).

[88]   Art 5 of the Grand-Ducal Regulation of 14 April 2003 (n 86 above).

[89]   See 6.31–6.40, 6.48–6.55, and 6.83–6.229 above.

General

The tax status of the management company of a UCI depends upon its activity. The **11.87** 1983 Act limited a management company's activity to a single FCP.[90] Under the 1988 Act, the activities of a management company must be limited to the management of UCIs, 'the administration of its own assets being only an ancillary activity'.[91]

The 1988 Act extended the permitted sphere of activity for several reasons. First **11.88** of all, the Grand Duchy of Luxembourg could not be more restrictive in this area than Directive 85/611. Secondly, a wider sphere would permit economies of scale, since it would not be necessary to set up a new management company for every new FCP. The 1988 Act nevertheless did not permit management companies to carry on activities other than the management of UCIs.[92]

The 2002 Act significantly extended the scope of permitted activities for **11.89** management companies under the new rules introduced by Directive 2001/107. Nowadays, Luxembourg-based management companies fall into two categories:

(1) those that manage coordinated UCITS and, as applicable, other UCIs;[93] and
(2) those that manage only UCIs other than coordinated UCITS.[94]

Management companies in the second category have, by and large, the same **11.90** permitted activities as those existing under the 1988 Act. Management companies in the first category are essentially set up to manage coordinated UCITS. Such companies may, moreover, carry on so-called 'additional' activities, such as the management of individual investment portfolios, and 'ancillary activities', such as individual investment advice and custody and administration services for UCI units.[95, 96]

Neither the 2002 Act nor the 1988 and 1983 Acts defined the tax treatment of **11.91** these management companies, which is determined by the changing practices of the tax administration.

---

[90] Art 2(2)(a), 1983 Act.
[91] Arts 6(2)(a), and 61, 1988 Act. This limitation reflects Art 6, of Directive (EEC) 85/611, which provides: 'No management company may engage in activities other than the management of common funds and of investment companies.'
[92] The Parliamentary documents accompanying the 1988 Act justify the solution chosen by the legislature as follows: 'Based on Art 6 of the Directive, paragraph (2) allows a management company to manage several separate UCIs. It was considered expedient to adopt that provision, which differs from Luxembourg's existing regime, which is justified primarily by fiscal reasons. That said, its activities must be limited to the management of UCIs. The object of this is to protect investors, since it tends to guarantee an optimum degree of specialisation by the management company and to avoid any risk of a conflict of interest with other activities' (*Parliamentary doc* No 3172, Comments on the Articles, 35).
[93] Under Ch 13, 2002 Act (Arts 77 and 90, 2002 Act).
[94] Under Ch 14, 2002 Act (Arts 91 and 92, 2002 Act).
[95] ibid Art 77(3).
[96] For a detailed description of these rules, see 6.39 above.

Tax status proper

Management company with reduced activity

11.92 Management companies with reduced activity are those whose articles of incorporation limit their corporate object to the management of a single FCP, ie those that limit their activity to the sphere imposed by the 1983 Act.

11.93 For the purpose of calculating capital duty and subscription tax, the tax authorities treat the management company and the FCP, including the latter's sub-funds, if any, as a single taxpayer. When the FCP is created, the tax authorities therefore levy a fixed capital duty of €1,250, regardless of the share capital of the management company.[97] The subscription tax is calculated on the basis of the fund's net asset value.

Management company with extended activity

11.94 According to the tax authorities,[98] a management company whose corporate object extends beyond the management of a single FCP is a commercial company subject to the provisions of general law. The same goes for a management company 'designated' by an investment company with the status of a UCITS. Hence, the management company must pay a capital duty of 0.5 per cent (1per cent before 31 December 2007) on all capital contributions received. It is, moreover, subject to all income and wealth taxes imposed on ordinary corporations.

11.95 The authorities base their position on the Parliamentary documents accompanying the 1988 Act.[99] They argue that the legislature implicitly intended not to amend the pre-existing tax regime for management companies. However, that regime was based on the principle that a management company can manage only one fund. The position of the authorities has been the subject of criticism and legal proceedings, the final results of which are not yet known.[100]

Legal and tax rules for advisory companies

11.96 As with management companies, the tax regime of so-called 'advisory' companies is closely tied to their sphere of activity, which means that those two aspects cannot be dissociated and will be discussed together below.

---

[97] The capital duty is payable by the management company. However, since it was created to manage only one FCP, the FCP's management regulations may provide for payment of the capital duty from the fund's assets. That does not mean that the creation of the FCP itself should be construed as a capital contribution subject to capital duty.

[98] Position (1995) adopted in writing by the Luxembourg registration authority (Corr TVA/F/18251).

[99] *Parliamentary doc* No 3172, Comments on the Articles, 56.

[100] For discussion of this controversy, see A Steichen, *Précis de droit fiscal de l'entreprise* (Editions Emile Borschette, 3rd edn, 2004) 326.

Concept

Luxembourg-based UCIs are directed by their management bodies. In the case **11.97**
of investment companies, that task devolves mainly upon the board of directors
or the manager, whilst FCPs are run by a management company. Those undertakings may in turn delegate the management of investments to any managers
of their choice, who are also regarded as conducting persons and as such must
be authorized by the CSSF.[101] In practice, such conducting persons frequently
seek assistance from one or more investment advisers. Such specialists have
specific knowledge of, and experience in, the particular geographical, economic,
or industrial sectors targeted by their client UCI. They are remunerated in the
form of an advisory fee charged to the UCI's assets or paid by the manager.

Investment advisers are not regarded as conducting persons within the meaning **11.98**
of the 2002 Act or the Act of 13 February 2007, since their service is limited to
giving opinions and making recommendations. They are not directly involved
in the decision-making process, which is reserved for the conducting persons.
For that reason, the CSSF does not subject them to the same authorization
criteria as conducting persons. Unless their remuneration is paid directly by a
UCI, it does not have to mention them in its promotional literature. At their
own expense, such advisers are frequently assisted by other specialists known as
'sub-advisers', who generally have even more specialized experience in the UCI's
target areas.

Practical experience has resulted in the emergence of so-called advisory firms, **11.99**
which act as investment advisers for Luxembourg-based UCIs whilst enjoying the
preferential tax status provided for in the 1929 Act.

Permitted sphere of activities

The tax regime for the advisory company of an incorporated UCI was created in **11.100**
1968, when the tax authorities decided that holding companies governed by the
1929 Act could also supply investment companies with advice. The following
conditions must be met:[102]

(1) the object of the advisory company must be limited to the acquisition of
    actual holdings and to advising a single investment company;
(2) the share capital of the advisory company may not be less than €75,000;[103]

---

[101] Art 93(3), 2002 Act.
[102] Letter of 17 October 1968 from the Treasury Minister, quoted by B Delvaux and E Reiffers,
Les sociétés holding au grand-duché de Luxembourg (Imprimerie de la Cour Victor Buck, 5th edn,
revised and expanded with the assistance of R Elter and J Delvaux, 1969) 39.
[103] The equivalent, at the time, of three million Luxembourg francs required by the Ministerial
Decision of 17 October 1968, referred to in n 102 above.

(3) 5 per cent of the share capital (with a minimum of €50,000) must be invested in the shares of the client investment company.[104] Thus the advisory company's advice increases the value of its interest in the investment company.

11.101 More recently, the authorities have confirmed that the advisory company of an FCP may also assume the status of holding company within the meaning of the 1929 Act, subject to compliance with the foregoing conditions.[105]

Tax status

11.102 An advisory company that meets the above conditions may opt for the tax status of a holding company within the meaning of the 1929 Act. Like UCIs, holding companies governed by the 1929 Act pay only capital duty and subscription tax. That said, the assessment base for holding companies differs from that of UCIs: capital duty at the full rate of 1 per cent was levied on the value of all contributions and subscription tax is imposed at a rate of 0.20 per cent on the share value.[106] [107]

Changes to the tax rules

11.103 The tax rules for holding companies within the meaning of the 1929 Act have for some time been severely criticized by the European Commission. In a decision dated 19 July 2006,[108] it held that the tax treatment of these companies amounted to a State aid regime that was incompatible with the common market.[109]

---

[104] Originally, there were two additional conditions, which were subsequently abolished. The first was to prohibit an advisory company from acquiring interests other than in the company advised (this is no longer required in administrative practice). The second was the obligation for advisory companies to invest 2.5% of their share capital (with a minimum of Lux Fr 1m) in Luxembourg public funds (abolished in a position (1989) adopted in writing by the Luxembourg registration authority (Corr No 297/89)).

[105] Position (2000) adopted in writing by the Luxembourg registration authority (Corr ENR/1704/00).

[106] For a detailed description of the holding company rules, see G Bernard, *Les sociétés holding au Grand-Duché de Luxembourg* (Institut universitaire international, 1979); Delvaux and Reiffers (n 102 above).

[107] An Act of 21 June 2005 modifying Art 1 of the Act of 31 July 1929, as amended, on the tax regime for companies with financial holdings (*Mémorial* A 2005, 1635) amended the rules for holding companies governed by the 1929 Act. According to this law, the benefit of the tax regime provided for by the 1929 Act will not be available to any holding company for which, during a given financial year, the dividends received from interests in companies established in jurisdictions with low tax rates account for 5% or more of the total amount of dividends collected (Art 1, Act of 21 June 2005 referred to above). This law will have its full impact on consulting firms. The new rules will not apply to holding companies existing on its effective date (1 July 2005) before 1 January 2011 (Art 2, Act of 21 June 2005 referred to above).

[108] Decision of the European Commission of 19 July 2006 on the aid scheme C3/2006 implemented by Luxembourg in favour of '1929' holding companies and 'milliardaire' holding companies (*Mémorial* B 2006, 836).

[109] For a critical analysis of the procedure launched by the European Commission, see T Lesage and P-E Partsch, 'Le droit communautaire est-il une menace pour l'avenir des holdings 1929' (May 2006) 1 *ACE Magazine* 7.

In response to the criticism by the European Commission, the Luxembourg **11.104** government expressed its willingness to repeal the tax regime in question, 'because, in return, it was granted a long transition period'.[110] According to the government, this transition period, which lasts until 31 December 2010, 'should give businesses in the sector the legal certainty needed to restructure themselves'.[111] As a result, the Grand Duchy of Luxembourg was obliged to bring an end to the tax treatment of holding companies within the meaning of the 1929 Act. This has been effected under the Act of 22 December 2006.[112]

Repeal of the tax regime for 'holding companies under the 1929 Act' entails aban- **11.105** donment of the equivalent regime for firms specializing in advisory services to Luxembourg UCIs. Those still in existence will have to be dissolved and liqui- dated before the end of the transition period, while new consulting firms will no longer be allowed for future UCIs.

Eligibility of UCIs to Benefit from Double Taxation Treaties

The application to UCIs of double taxation treaties is a complex issue, which has **11.106** been extensively discussed.[113] While the question is clear, the answers given so far are still not entirely satisfactory. An exhaustive survey of all aspects of this issue would exceed the scope of this work. What follows is therefore only a summary of the topic and an overview of existing solutions.

Luxembourg-based UCIs are directly concerned by this issue, since they invest in **11.107** countries with which the Grand Duchy of Luxembourg has signed tax treaties. It is also relevant for foreign UCIs insofar as they invest in the Grand Duchy of Luxembourg. These two aspects are discussed below.

Conditions under which Luxembourg-based UCIs are eligible to benefit from tax treaties

The double taxation treaties signed by the Grand Duchy of Luxembourg are **11.108** mostly based on the OECD model tax treaty, the provisions of which apply to

---

[110]   Declaration of the Treasury Minister of 24 July 2006, available at <http://www. gouvernement.lu>.

[111]   ibid.

[112]   Act of 22 December 2006 regarding the '*sociétés de participations financières*' (*Mémorial* A 2006, 4834 *et seq*).

[113]   This issue has been analysed in detail by J-P Winandy, C Kremer and E Fort, 'L'imposition des fonds de placement', National report by Luxembourg for the IFA congress in New Delhi in 1997, *Cahiers de droit fiscal international* (Kluwer, 1997) Vol LXXXII b, 589 *et seq*; P Hoss and P Kinsch, 'Conventions fiscales internationales et organismes de placement collectif en valeurs mobilières', Proceedings of the Belgo-Luxembourg and French working groups at the IFA convention held in Luxembourg on 15 and 16 May 1992; J Schaffner, *Droit fiscal international* (Éditions Promoculture, 2nd edn, 2005) 565 *et seq*.

'persons who are residents in one of the contracting States or both contracting States'.[114]

11.109 Eligibility for the benefit of a tax treaty requires the fulfilment of two preconditions. First, the benefit must be claimed by a person[115] within the meaning of the tax treaty. Next, that person must be a resident[116] of one or both of the contracting States. These two conditions are supplemented by a third—negative—condition: the convention must not exclude the person concerned from its protection.

Concepts of person and residence as applied in the tax treaties

Contractual UCIs

11.110 Can an FCP be regarded as a resident of the Grand Duchy of Luxembourg for the purpose of tax treaties signed by Luxembourg? Legal opinion is divided on this point.[117] In practice, it is necessary to determine whether an FCP is itself not taxable (fiscally transparent) or whether it may claim the status of taxpayer, despite the lack of legal status, and so benefit from the tax treaties.

11.111 According to some, an FCP is a form of allocated assets[118] or so-called 'vacant' assets.[119] That interpretation holds that FCPs are tax-opaque and non-transparent. Such funds would be a sort of business centre, regarded as a legal person for tax purposes. According to the comment on the articles of the OECD model treaty,[120] the benefit of tax treaties must accrue to all taxpayers who may be qualified as a legal person for taxation purposes, even if such taxpayers do not have legal personality. In other words, FCPs, like foundations, would be eligible. They would meet the condition of residence insofar as they are situated in the Grand Duchy of Luxembourg.

---

[114] Art 1 of the OECD model treaty on income and wealth, OECD Tax Affairs Committee, July 2005.

[115] Art 3.1 of the OECD model treaty (n 114 above): 'For the purposes of this Convention, unless the context otherwise requires: a) the term "person" includes an individual, a company and any other body of persons; b) the term "company" means any body corporate or any entity that is treated as a body corporate for tax purposes.'

[116] ibid Art 4.1: 'For the purposes of this Convention, the term "resident of a Contracting State" means any person who, under the laws of that State, is liable to tax therein by reason of his domicile, residence, place of management or any other criterion of a similar nature, and also includes that State and any political subdivision or local authority thereof. This term, however, does not include any person who is liable to tax in that State in respect only of income from sources in that State or capital situated therein.'

[117] In favour of a tax status for FCPs: P Hoss and P Kinsch (n 113 above) 2 *et seq*; Steichen (n 100 above) 451; A Steichen, *Manuel de droit fiscal* (Éditions Saint-Paul, 2002) Vol 2, 382; against, Winandy, C Kremer and Fort (n 113 above) 603.

[118] Known in German as *Zweckvermögen*.

[119] Known in German as *nichtrechtsfähiger Verein*.

[120] OECD model treaty (n 114 above) commentary on Art 3, point 2.

According to others, the major obstacle arises from the fact that FCPs are subject **11.112** only to capital duty and subscription tax, which are not expressly referred to in Luxembourg's tax treaties. According to those authors, since an FCP does not have a legal personality, it cannot be regarded as a 'person' within the meaning of the OECD model treaty. That treaty implies that tax residents claiming the status of 'person' must be subject to the taxes referred to in it, ie income tax and wealth tax. That is not the case with FCPs. The obligation to pay capital duty and subscription tax would not be enough to regard FCPs as legal persons for taxation purposes. Because they are not persons within the meaning of the tax treaties, the question of their residence does not arise.

The Luxembourg tax authorities take the view that an FCP, being an undivided **11.113** pool of assets, does not constitute a resident within the meaning of the tax treaties.[121] Consequently, FCPs are not currently eligible for the benefits of those treaties. In contrast, the authorities acknowledge that there is no bar to an FCP's participants claiming the benefit of such treaties personally, if they are residents of the Grand Duchy of Luxembourg.[122]

Incorporated UCIs

Legal opinion and the tax authorities in Luxembourg agree that incorporated **11.114** UCIs are persons within the meaning of the tax treaties, in that they are legal entities which are taxable corporations. Most are incorporated as an SA with fixed or variable capital, or as an SARL or an SCA. Does this mean that they are residents under such tax treaties and therefore subject to tax? Most authors believe so,[123] for the following reason: double taxation treaties are not only designed to eliminate actual double taxation but also potential double taxation. Thus a person merely has to have subjective ties that could result in actual taxation. Whether that person is ultimately taxed or not is irrelevant.[124]

Luxembourg's tax authorities appear to support this analysis, mainly because the **11.115** OECD model treaty does not make actual taxation a prerequisite. Indeed, if that were to be made a prerequisite, it would result in legal uncertainty and oblige tax offices to verify in each individual case whether the condition of actual taxation had been met. The authorities have therefore announced that they are willing to certify the tax residence of UCIs incorporated in the form of corporations, in cases permitted by interpretation of the text of the treaty or when the other contracting

---

[121] Circular issued by the director for direct taxes, 15 February 2000 (No II/1425-S16 HE/CG).

[122] ibid.

[123] Hoss and Kinsch (n 113 above) 6; Winandy, Kremer and Fort (n 113 above) 604.

[124] K Vogel, *Doppelbesteuerungsabkommen*, (CH Beck, 4th edn, 2003) 420 para 26. Also see J-P Winandy, *Les impôts sur le revenu et sur la fortune* (Promoculture, 4th edn, 2002) 201.

State expressly permits application of the tax treaty to investment companies based in Luxembourg.[125]

Clauses excluding Luxembourg-based UCIs from the benefit of double taxation treaties

11.116 Most bilateral treaties against double taxation signed by the Grand Duchy of Luxembourg with other States contain direct or indirect clauses providing for certain exclusions from their benefit.[126]

'Subject to tax' clause

11.117 The 'subject to tax' clause permits the contracting State to limit the benefit of a treaty to cases in which a person is actually taxed in the country of residence.[127] The tax treaty between the Grand Duchy of Luxembourg and France contains such a clause,[128] as does the treaty with Austria, save that the tax authorities of the Grand Duchy of Luxembourg and Austria, in subsequent correspondence, have agreed to grant incorporated UCIs the benefit of the treaty.[129]

Clause excluding holding companies

11.118 All treaties signed by the Grand Duchy of Luxembourg contain a clause excluding holding companies, which can be found either in the text of the treaty itself or in correspondence between the competent authorities. The scope of the exclusion clause varies from one treaty to another.

11.119 Certain treaties limit the exclusion to holding companies within the meaning of the 1929 Act and the 'milliardaire' holding companies referred to in the Grand-Ducal Decree of 17 December 1938.[130] They are not prejudicial to UCIs, which have been governed since 1983 by a special tax regime, entirely separate from the tax regime for holding companies.

11.120 Other treaties use broader wording. They exclude all companies enjoying the benefit of a regime similar to that for holding companies within the meaning of the

---

[125] Circular issued by the director for direct taxes, 15 February 2000 (No II/1425-S16 HE/CG).

[126] For a more detailed analysis of this topic, see Schaffner (n 113 above) 451 *et seq*.

[127] OECD model treaty (n 114 above), commentary on Arts 23A and 23B, point 35.

[128] Art 10*bis* of the Franco-Luxembourg tax treaty of 1 April 1958 (*Mémorial* 1959, 1063 *et seq*), as amended by Art 6 of the amendment of 8 September 1970 (*Mémorial* A 1971, 1756).

[129] Protocol of 21 May 1992 (*Mémorial* A 1993, 1033) to the treaty of 18 October 1962 between the Grand Duchy of Luxembourg and the Republic of Austria to avoid the double taxation of income and wealth (*Mémorial* 1963, 734 *et seq*).

[130] Grand-Ducal Decree of 17 December 1938, as amended, on the tax regime of holding companies that receive contributions comprising assets of foreign companies with a value of at least Lux Fr 1bn (*Mémorial* A 1938, 1311).

1929 Act and introduced by a law after the effective date of the treaty.[131] Such treaties may affect UCIs, since their tax regime resembles that of holding companies. Certain authors[132] feel that such an interpretation should be rejected. In their opinion, the treaties in question are designed merely to ensure the exclusion of companies covered by laws substituted for and offering similar advantages to the 1929 Act.

Clause excluding incorporated UCIs

Certain recent treaties signed by the Grand Duchy of Luxembourg avoid all interpretation problems, since they exclude UCIs from their scope. That is, *inter alia*, the case with the treaties signed with Sweden and the United States.[133]   **11.121**

Practice of Luxembourg's tax administration

According to Luxembourg's tax authorities, the scope of application of bilateral tax treaties cannot be determined unilaterally by only one of the two contracting States. The position adopted by the other contracting State must also be taken into account. The tax authorities accordingly opt for dialogue with the foreign States concerned. According to the tax authorities, tax treaties should apply to UCIs incorporated in the form of corporations. However, they generally refuse to provide such UCIs with certificates of residence before obtaining the agreement of the competent foreign authorities except where the text of the treaty itself is clear.   **11.122**

Investment companies under Luxembourg law may currently claim the benefit of the tax treaties signed with the following countries: Austria, China, Finland, Germany, Indonesia, Ireland, Israel, Malaysia, Malta, Morocco, Mongolia, Poland, Portugal, Republic of Korea, Romania, Singapore, Slovak Republic, Slovenia, Thailand, Trinidad and Tobago, Tunisia, Turkey, Uzbekistan, and Vietnam.[134] The same applies to the treaties signed with Spain[135] and Denmark.[136]   **11.123**

---

[131] Such clauses are, for example, included in the treaties signed between the Grand Duchy of Luxembourg and Belgium, Brazil, Ireland, South Korea, and the United Kingdom.

[132] Hoss and Kinsch (n 113 above) 12.

[133] Protocol of 14 October 1996 (*Mémorial* A 1998, 52) to the treaty between the Grand Duchy of Luxembourg and the Kingdom of Sweden to avoid double taxation and to prevent the evasion of income and wealth taxes; Art 24.10 of the new treaty between the Grand Duchy of Luxembourg and the United States of America concerning income and wealth taxes, 5 April 1996 (in force from 2001) (*Mémorial* A 1999, 634 *et seq*), *Parliamentary doc* No 4335, Interpretation Memorandum, 37.

[134] Circular issued by the director for direct taxes, 15 February 2000 (No II/1425-S16 HE/CG). Also see the official list published by the Luxembourg direct tax authority at <http://www.impotsdirects.public.lu/dossiers/conventions/opc/sicav/index.html>.

[135] Circular issued by the director for direct taxes, 10 May 2000 (LG Conv DI No 52). Also see the official list published by the Luxembourg direct tax authority at <http://www.impotsdirects.public.lu/dossiers/conventions/opc/sicav/index.html>. The agreement with Spain is limited to coordinated UCITS duly authorized by the competent authority of each State and marketed in the other State.

[136] Exchange of letters of 30 December 2005 and 15 February 2006 between the Danish and Luxembourg tax authorities.

11.124 In contrast, they are excluded from the tax treaties signed with South Africa, Belgium, Brazil, Canada, Estonia, the United States, France, Hungary, Iceland, Japan, Latvia, Lithuania, Mauritius, Mexico, Norway, the Netherlands (except for collective requests by unitholders who are Luxembourg residents), the Czech Republic, the United Kingdom, and Sweden.[137]

11.125 Lastly, the situation vis-à-vis the following countries has not yet been settled: Bulgaria, Greece, Italy, the Russian Federation, and Switzerland.[138]

Conditions determining the eligibility of foreign UCIs to benefit
from tax treaties

11.126 In practice, the benefit of tax treaties between the Grand Duchy of Luxembourg and foreign countries applies only rarely to investments made by foreign UCIs in the Grand Duchy of Luxembourg. However, a foreign UCI may benefit if it receives dividends from a Luxembourg-based company taxed at the full rate.

11.127 In that instance, the foregoing principles should apply to such foreign UCIs. Thus:

- If a foreign UCI can be regarded as the equivalent of a Luxembourg-based FCP, the tax treaty with its country of residence applies only if that country treats the UCI as a resident person within the meaning of the treaty, on the understanding that, in the event of failure to apply the treaty, the investor should be able to claim the benefit of the treaty, if any, between his State of residence and Luxembourg.

- If a foreign UCI can be regarded as the equivalent of a Luxembourg-based corporation, the treaty between Luxembourg and the UCI's country of residence should apply regardless of whether or not that UCI is actually taxable.

Taxation of Participants in Luxembourg-based UCIs

11.128 The tax treatment of investors in Luxembourg-based UCIs depends primarily on the applicable national laws. The situation is simple for UCIs: distributions to investors are not subject to deduction at source,[139] regardless of whether they are Luxembourg residents or not. For other aspects, it is generally necessary to refer to the laws in force

---

[137] Circular issued by the director for direct taxes, 15 February 2000 (No II/1425-S16HE/CG). Also see the official list published by the Luxembourg direct tax authority at <http://www.impotsdirects.public.lu/dossiers/conventions/opc/sicav/index.html>.

[138] ibid.

[139] Art 127(2), 2002 Act.

in the investor's country of residence and, as necessary, to the double taxation treaty in force between the Grand Duchy of Luxembourg and that country.

Situation of non-resident investors in Luxembourg

Pursuant to the 2002 Act, amounts distributed by UCIs are never taxable in the Grand Duchy of Luxembourg if received by non-residents.[140] The same applies to capital gains on disposals, save in the exceptional event that a non-resident investor holds more than 10 per cent of the share capital of a UCI incorporated in the form of a corporation and disposes of the investment within six months from its acquisition date.[141] This exceptional rule should not apply to contractual UCIs, which are not corporations.   **11.129**

Non-residents do not pay wealth tax in Luxembourg on investments in a Luxembourg-based UCI; nor do they pay estate duty[142] or gift tax[143] on units in UCIs. In principle, therefore, non-resident investors are not subject in the Grand Duchy of Luxembourg to direct or indirect taxes on investments in the units of Luxembourg-based UCIs.   **11.130**

We should nevertheless not lose sight of the significant impact—described below—that the European Directive on the taxation of savings income can have on the distribution and redemption of units.[144]   **11.131**

Taxation of Luxembourg residents

Principles

The tax treatment of residents investing in UCIs—whether Luxembourg-based or foreign—has never been covered by specific legislation. Two successive attempts failed.   **11.132**

---

[140] ibid.

[141] Art 156(8), LIR

[142] For a more detailed analysis of this issue, see C Kremer, 'Le banquier luxembourgeois face aux droits de succession' in *Droit bancaire et financier au Grand-Duché de Luxembourg* (Larcier, 1994) Vol 2, 711.

[143] As regards gift duties, the situation would only be different in the exceptional event that the gift of units in a UCI was recorded in a deed executed before a notary in the Grand Duchy of Luxembourg. See C Kremer and J Elvinger, 'La double imposition internationale des successions et des donations', National report by Luxembourg for the IFA Congress held in London in 1985, *Cahiers de droit fiscal international*, Vol LXX b: International Double Taxation of Inheritances and Gifts (Kluwer, 1985) 441.

[144] See 11.165 *et seq* below.

11.133   The first was the draft law of 30 January 1980,[145] which was designed to make such UCIs fiscally transparent vis-à-vis their participants. The second attempt was made in 1990 as part of the fundamental tax reform carried out in that year.[146] The initial draft of that reform provided for the general fiscal transparency of UCIs, including incorporated funds. The draft legislation provided that participants would be taxed directly on income from a UCI's investments (mainly interest and dividends), including income not paid out to the participants, under the tax regulations applicable to dividends. In contrast, private taxpayers (ie natural persons) would be exempt from tax on capital gains realized on portfolio sales, regardless of the time period during which the UCI realized the gain. Private taxpayers normally pay tax on capital gains on movable assets, including transferable securities, realized during a period of six months, known as the 'speculation period' between the purchase date and the sale date. No capital gains tax is paid after six months, except where such transferable securities are shares in a corporation in which the private investor holds more than 10 per cent of the capital.[147] The solution proposed by the draft legislation, modelled on the regime in force at the time in Germany, would have given private investors an incentive to buy units in UCIs, since capital gains realized on directly held portfolio securities would have become exempt after only six months.[148]

11.134   The purpose of the proposed reform was to give residents investing in Luxembourg-based UCIs the benefit of the tax treaty signed between the Grand Duchy of Luxembourg and the country of investment and to enable them to obtain a credit for foreign withholding taxes. That part of the tax reform of 1990 was nevertheless abandoned.

11.135   The commentary on the articles of the draft reform legislation of 1990 stressed that FCPs should be regarded as fiscally transparent even without a reform of the tax system.[149] Investors in FCPs should normally pay income tax in the year in which the income is generated by the fund, not in the year in which it is made available in the form of dividends. The capitalization of income in UCIs should therefore have no impact on the timing of their tax liabilities.

11.136   Historically, Luxembourg's tax authorities nevertheless seem to have opted consistently for another practice,[150] according to which unitholders are taxed on

---

[145]   Draft Act of 30 January 1980 concerning the taxation of persons with co-ownership titles or investments in UCIs (*Parliamentary doc* No 2379).

[146]   Act of 6 December 1990 reforming certain direct and indirect tax provisions (*Mémorial* A 1990, 1014) (*Parliamentary doc* No 3431).

[147]   Arts 99, 99*bis,* and 100, LIR.

[148]   *Parliamentary doc* No 3431, Comments on the Articles 94.

[149]   ibid 95.

[150]   See A Elvinger, 'Statut fiscal des fonds communs de placement et des sociétés d'investissement au Grand-Duché de Luxembourg' (n 2 above), 31; Winandy, Kremer and Fort (n 113 above) 601.

distributions by FCPs at the time they are made, unless the taxpayer wishes to claim that the FCP is fiscally transparent. Administrative practice is not opposed to treating FCPs in the same way as investment companies, where dividends distributed become subject to tax on payment to the beneficiary.

UCIs governed by the Rau Act

History

In 1984, the 'Rau' Act[151] established certain tax breaks in favour of individual Luxembourg residents with shares or units in Luxembourg-based corporations taxed at the full rate. Those preferential measures incidentally extended to the acquisition of units in Luxembourg-based UCIs investing mostly in the capital of such corporations. **11.137**

The initial regime under the Act of 27 April 1984 was modified by the Act of 22 December 1993.[152] Finally, the Act of 21 December 2001[153] abolished the Rau Act regime and laid down a gradual repeal process described below, for information, as it is likely to have consequences until 2009.[154] **11.138**

Provisions of the Rau Act

Pursuant to the Rau Act, a tax break may be granted to private residents who buy units in Luxembourg-based UCIs. The tax break is granted on two conditions. First, the units in question must form a portion of the taxpayer's private assets[155] and secondly, in accordance with the undertaking's internal regulations, more than 75 per cent of the portfolio must be invested in the securities and rights of resident corporations taxed at the full rate.[156] The target companies must be SAs or SARLs. SCAs in particular are excluded.[157] **11.139**

Analysis of the legislative texts leaves some doubts about the meaning of certain rules. To begin with, the Rau Act does not specify the legal form of a UCI. The text **11.140**

A Steichen, *Manuel de droit fiscal* (Imprimerie Saint-Paul, 2002) Vol 2, 286. Also see S Trausch-Schoder's comments on this issue in *Le traitement fiscal de l'épargne mobilière* (Études fiscales, Éditions de l'Imprimerie Saint-Paul, 1994), 18.

[151] Act of 27 April 1984 adopted to promote capital expenditure and the creation of jobs by promoting savings in transferable securities (*Mémorial* A 1984, 611 *et seq*), known as the 'Rau Act' as it was adopted at the initiative of the Member of Parliament, Fernand Rau. The Rau Act was extended until 31 December 1992 and amended by the Act of 7 June 1989 extending and amending the Act of 27 April 1984 (*Mémorial* A 1989, 743) and by Art 8 of the Act of 6 December 1990 reforming certain direct and indirect tax provisions (*Mémorial* A 1990, 1014).

[152] Act of 22 December 1993 adopted to revive investment in the interests of economic development and introducing Art 129(c), LIR (*Mémorial* A 1993, 2020 *et seq*).

[153] Act of 21 December 2001 reforming certain direct and indirect tax provisions (*Mémorial* A 2001, 3312).

[154] See 11.146 below.

[155] Art 129(c)(1), LIR

[156] ibid 129(c)(2)(2)(c).

[157] ibid 129(c)(2)(1).

simply refers to the 'undertaking's internal regulations'. As the Act is not restrictive, it could apply to both contractual and incorporated UCIs with the text insofar as it relates to contractual UCIs being deemed to refer to the management regulations and, with respect to incorporated UCIs, to the UCI's articles of incorporation.

11.141 Next, the Rau Act requires 75 per cent of the portfolio to be invested in Luxembourg securities. In a circular,[158] the tax administration defined the term 'portfolio' as comprising all securities (including deposits, bank accounts, etc) held by a UCI. This means that the figure of 75 per cent must be calculated by reference to all of a UCI's assets.

11.142 Furthermore, the Rau Act refers to the 'securities and rights' to be bought by the UCI in the target companies. Those terms are not defined. According to existing administrative practice, that can apparently only mean shares or units, and excludes bonds issued by such companies. The restriction seems to reflect the legislature's intention to promote investment in the share capital of Luxembourg-based companies.

11.143 Lastly, despite the reference to 'buying' units in UCIs, the tax breaks apply only when such shares or units are subscribed directly into the UCI in question.[159]

11.144 The tax breaks may only be claimed if the units are held until the end of the fourth tax year after the year of purchase.[160] Disposal or early redemption of the units during the mandatory ownership period will result in an adjustment assessment, except when occasioned by the taxpayer's death, disability, or permanent inability to work.[161]

11.145 The tax break consists of a rebate at the time of investment: taxpayers may apply for an income tax rebate on a first tranche of €1,500 or all securities covered by the Rau Act bought during the fiscal year in question. That first tranche of €1,500 is doubled (ie an additional €1,500) in the case of joint taxation for spouses.[162]

Gradual repeal of the Rau Act

11.146 According to the legislature, the Rau Act failed to achieve its primary objective, which was to encourage retail investors to invest their savings in the capital needed

---

[158] Instruction 2.4 contained in Circular No 94 issued by the director for direct taxes on 4 July 1984, reproduced in the Tax Code, 2b *sub* A1, further to the Act of 27 April 1984. Instruction 2.4 in that Circular should still be valid today despite the repeal of the Act of 27 April 1984 and its replacement by the Act of 22 December 1993, since Art 129(2)(2) (c) reproduces, word for word, Art 2.2 of the Act of 27 April 1984.

[159] Art 129(c)(2)(2)(c), and Art 129(c)(5)(a), LIR.

[160] Art 129(c)(5)(c), LIR.

[161] ibid.

[162] Art 129(c)(4), LIR.

by businesses. The Parliamentary documents for the Act of 21 December 2001 state: 'the vast majority of investment tax allowances was made available on purchases of units in SICAVs, which invested these funds in eligible shares by buying existing securities others were ready to sell without generating new capital'.[163] The legislature held, moreover, that exclusively promoting investments in the national economy could be incompatible with European legislation since the tax breaks would be granted only to taxpayers investing in fully taxable resident corporations or in certain authorized investment vehicles.[164]

The gradual repeal regime was divided into two phases. First, the allowance for investors was reduced to €1,000 for 2003, and to €500 for 2004, and ceased entirely in 2005. Secondly, the obligation for eligible UCIs to invest 75 per cent of their portfolio in fully taxable resident corporations was lowered to 50 per cent for 2003 and 25 per cent for 2004. During the gradual repeal phase, the obligation to hold securities for four years remains in force. **11.147**

Sale and redemption of units in Luxembourg-based UCIs

When a private investor residing in the Grand Duchy of Luxembourg sells all or part of his shares in a Luxembourg-based investment company to a third party or when he switches his investment from one sub-fund to another sub-fund,[165] any resulting capital gain is only taxed if the sale or the switch takes place within six months from the date of purchase.[166] Capital gains are no longer taxable after that 'speculation period'. **11.148**

Based on the known practices of the tax authorities in this area, that rule should also apply to FCPs, even though strict application of the principle of tax transparency should lead to different conclusions. **11.149**

Capital gains realized by private investors on the sale of shares in Luxembourg-based investment companies remain taxable after six-months' ownership but at a preferential rate, in the exceptional event that the vendor owns more than 10 per cent of the investment company's share capital.[167] That rule should not apply to FCPs, since they are not corporations. Nor should it prevent investors from holding more than 10 per cent of the shares in a sub-fund of an incorporated UCI, provided that such investments do not total more than 10 per cent of the **11.150**

---

[163] *Parliamentary doc* No 4855, Comments on the Articles, 22.
[164] ibid.
[165] Under Circular LIR 100/1 issued on 13 July 2007 by the director for direct taxes, moving out from one sub-fund to another is to be considered as selling shares or units held in one sub-fund and then acquiring shares or units in another sub-fund.
[166] Art 99*bis*, LIR.
[167] ibid Arts 100 and 132.

share capital of the overall entity, all sub-funds combined.[168] If units in UCIs are held as assets of a business, the transferor is in principle liable to tax on capital gains, regardless of the period of ownership.

11.151 When units are sold by means of direct redemption by the UCI, the above rules remain unchanged in principle. The only difference between redemption by a UCI and sale to a third party is the status of the counterparty.

11.152 Those rules must be qualified where a redemption has the effect of reducing the capital. While this is not possible in common funds which have no capital, in the case of investment companies, redemption may reduce the capital, especially if the redeemed shares are cancelled.

11.153 The LIR does not automatically exempt resident shareholders from liability to pay tax on the proceeds of a capital reduction. If the capital reduction is not motivated by 'serious economic reasons',[169] the shareholder is taxed on the resulting reimbursement as income from investment capital. That is, *inter alia*, the case when ordinary commercial companies with substantial reserves reduce their capital. This principle enables the tax authorities to counter abuse.

11.154 Such a penalty should not apply to SICAVs.[170] Redemption followed by cancellation is part of their normal operation. It is reflected in the corresponding reduction of the share capital, which is equal to the fund's net asset value.[171] In that case, the 'serious economic reasons' should be construed as the SICAV's operating procedure, without the need for shareholders to give detailed individual reasons.

11.155 There is no good reason to treat the shareholders of SICAFs differently, since redemption of a SICAF's shares does not in principle reduce the SICAF's share capital and the economic reasons are the same, ie to allow shareholders to realize their investment in the way traditionally provided for in respect of this type of product.

11.156 The foregoing rules should also apply to conversion from one UCI sub-fund to another. In fact, conversion, generally regarded as a single transaction, actually consists of redemption followed by subscription in a new sub-fund.

---

[168] The director for direct taxes has adopted a similar position in Circular LIR 100/1 of 13 July 2007 and considers that benefits from the sale of more than 10% of the shares or units relating to a specific sub-fund of a UCI could be tax exempt under Art 100 LIR, provided that such participation does not represent more than 10% of the shares or units of the entire share capital of the UCI.

[169] Art 97(3), LIR.

[170] For a contrary view see Steichen (n 100 above) 466.

[171] Arts 25 and 69, 2002 Act.

Application of tax treaties to investors in Luxembourg-based UCIs

The question of whether the network of tax treaties signed by the Grand Duchy of **11.157** Luxembourg applies to Luxembourg-based and foreign UCIs has already been discussed.[172] The same question may be asked in relation to investors in such UCIs.

Where a tax treaty signed between the Grand Duchy of Luxembourg and a foreign **11.158** country applies to UCIs, the residents of the foreign country may claim its benefit for their investments in Luxembourg-based investment companies. However, that remains a theoretical benefit. As far as dividends are concerned, treaties against double taxation are mainly intended to reduce withholding taxes, but no such taxes are imposed on distributions by Luxembourg-based UCIs.

Conversely, Luxembourg residents should also be able to apply such agreements **11.159** to their investments in incorporated UCIs domiciled in those countries.

Tax Supervision of UCIs

The Luxembourg registration authority is responsible for the fiscal supervision of **11.160** UCIs.[173] That rule was introduced by the 1983 Act.[174] The legislature of 1983 wished to entrust the fiscal supervision of UCIs to the Luxembourg registration authority for the reason that a UCI's activities are very similar to those of holding companies, which are likewise monitored by that authority.[175]

Where the Luxembourg registration authority finds that a UCI is carrying out a **11.161** transaction falling outside the sphere of activities authorized by the 2002 Act or by the Act of 13 February 2007, the favourable tax provisions specified in the 2002 Act or in the Act of 13 February 2007 cease to apply.[176] That raises two questions: from what point in time should the penalty be applied, and what are the main consequences of its application?

The 2002 Act does not specify when the special tax regime for UCIs ceases to **11.162** apply. According to the 1929 Act, which prescribes the same penalty for holding companies, the date on which the preferential rules cease to apply is the day on which the administration gives notice of, or serves, its withdrawal decision.[177] There is every reason to assume that the same solution applies to UCIs.

---

[172] See 11.106 *et seq* above.
[173] Art 131, 2002 Act; Art 69, Act of 13 February 2007.
[174] Art 66, 1983 Act; Art 69, Act of 13 February 2007.
[175] *Parliamentary doc* No 2366, Comments on the Articles, 47.
[176] Art 131, 2002 Act.
[177] Art 1 of the 1929 Act, as amended by Art 2 of the Act of 12 July 1977, amending and supplementing the 1929 Act (*Mémorial* A 1977, 1280).

11.163 Such a change in a UCI's status has two fiscal consequences when applied to a company. First, the company must pay additional capital duty at the rate applicable to ordinary companies. Secondly, it is regarded as a normal taxpayer subject to the provisions of general law.

11.164 While contractual UCIs are not affected as regards capital duty, they must often be liquidated judicially or otherwise, since the status of FCP is reserved for UCIs and securitization vehicles.[178] Moreover, UCIs engaged in tax evasion may be fined 0.02 per cent of the total value of their assets.[179]

Impact on UCIs of the European Directive on the Taxation of Savings Income

Presentation of Directive 2003/48

A necessary normative instrument

11.165 For many years, the EU Member States in principle treated savings income in the form of interest payments as taxable income. However, the free movement of capital established by the EC Treaty[180] allowed the residents of one EU Member State to avoid any taxation of interest received in other Member States. This situation generated *de facto* tax competition, which went against the desire to build a uniform Europe underlying the common market.

11.166 Thus the idea of a Directive providing for the common tax treatment of savings income was gradually shaped over several years of negotiations before a text was finally agreed. Indeed, the draft Directive went through a tough period of gestation, to say the least, from the first rough proposal which was rejected in 1998 to the first common position adopted by the European Council of Feira in 2000 and the ECOFIN Council meeting held on 3 June 2003 in Luxembourg, which adopted the final version of the Directive.[181]

---

[178] See 14.22 below.
[179] Art 131, 2002 Act.
[180] Arts 56–60, EC Treaty. The authors want to thank their colleague, Maître J Le Gall for his valuable contribution to this section.
[181] More precisely, the Directive is based on the consensus adopted during the European Council of Feira held on 19 and 20 June 2000 and the subsequent ECOFIN meetings of 26 and 27 November 2000, 13 December 2001 and 21 January 2003. Directive (EC) 2003/48 was adopted as part of the 'tax package' initiated in 1997 during Luxembourg's presidency of the EU and aimed at countering tax competition within the EU. There were 2 other aspects to this tax package: a code of conduct for the taxation of companies and a Directive on interest and royalty payments between associated companies in Member States.

The ultimate aim of Directive 2003/48 'on the taxation of savings income in the   **11.167**
form of interest payments' is to enable savings income in the form of interest
payments made in one Member State to beneficial owners who are individuals
resident in another Member State to be made subject to effective taxation in
accordance with the laws of the latter Member State.[182]

Although the aims of the Directive are clearly and explicitly stated, they would   **11.168**
have remained ineffective if the European legislature had not implemented an
enforceable system, mainly consisting of the automatic exchange of information
between Member States or, during a transitional period, of a 'withholding'
system.

Formal adoption of a method: harmonization by exchange of information

Directive 2003/48 makes the exchange of information between Member States   **11.169**
the tool for coordinating the taxation of savings income at a European level.[183]
According to this text, all Member States will finally have to automatically
exchange information about interest payments made in their territory to
individuals who are resident in another Member State.

More stringently, Directive 2003/48 stipulates that when the beneficial owner of   **11.170**
savings income in the form of interest is resident in an EU Member State other
than that in which the paying agent is established, the paying agent must report
a certain minimum amount of information to the competent authority in the
beneficial owner's Member State of establishment.

However, these general rules are subject to a temporary exception. During a   **11.171**
transitional period the Directive affords certain countries—Austria, Belgium,
and Luxembourg—an alternative to the information exchange procedure, ie to
apply a withholding tax to the income paid by a paying agent established in
one of those countries to a beneficial owner resident in another Member
State.

In other words, while the general and the alternative system follow different   **11.172**
methods, both hinge on the importance of the two roles of paying agent and
beneficiary, as explained below.

Key players in the new systems

In its introductory provisions, Directive 2003/48 provides extremely detailed   **11.173**
definitions for identifying the paying agent and the beneficial owner of interest
payments.

---

[182] Preamble to Directive (EC) 2003/48, 8th Recital.
[183] ibid 14th Recital.

11.174 **The paying agent** Directive 2003/48 defines the paying agent as any economic operator who pays interest to or secures the payment of interest for the immediate benefit of the beneficial owner, whether the paying agent is the debtor of the entitlement that produces the interest or the operator charged respectively by the debtor or the beneficial owner with paying interest or securing the payment of interest as the case may be.[184] Consequently, the economic operator cannot be a paying agent when allocating the payment of interest to an intermediary of the beneficial owner.

11.175 According to the Explanatory Memorandum to Directive 2003/48,[185] an economic operator is any legal or natural person who pays interest as part of his profession or his commercial business. Thus, occasional interest payments between natural persons may be considered to fall outside the scope of the Directive.

11.176 In the special situation where interest is received from a coordinated UCITS, the paying agent is the party appointed by the UCITS or the beneficial owner to secure the payment of the interest. Depending upon the structure of the UCITS in question, the paying agent might therefore be the depositary, the registrar, or the administrative agent. Moreover, any 'entity' established in a Member State and to which the interest is paid in favour of the beneficial owner is also a paying agent at the time the interest is paid.[186] Such an entity is more generally known as the 'residual entity'.

11.177 In contrast, such an entity is not considered a paying agent when:

(1) it is a legal person (other than specified legal persons);[187] or
(2) its profits are taxed under the general corporate tax rules; or
(3) it is an authorized UCITS under Directive 85/611.

11.178 A residual entity may opt to be treated as an authorised UCITS pursuant to Directive 85/611 to avoid being categorized as a paying agent on receipt of interest and having to report interest payments. Each Member State has been given the right to determine the internal applications of this option. The Luxembourg Act of 21 June 2005 transposing Directive 2003/48[188] lays down the principle that every residual entity established in Luxembourg must be considered an authorised UCITS pursuant to Directive 85/611.

---

[184] Art 4, Directive 2003/48.
[185] [2001] OJ C270E/259.
[186] The concept of 'entity' is not defined in Directive (EC) 2003/48. Certain commentators refer to the criterion of 'material unity' to characterize an entity (see *Handbook sur la fiscalité de l'épargne*, collective work (ABBL-KPMG, February 2005, 79).
[187] Under Art 4.5, Directive (EC) 2003/48, these legal persons are: Voin yhtiö (Ay) and kommandiittiyhtiö (Ky)/öppet bolag and kommanditbolag (Finland); handelsbolag (HB) and kommanditbolag (KB) (Sweden).
[188] See 11.187 *et seq* below.

The beneficial owner   Directive 2003/48 defines a beneficial owner as any   **11.179**
individual resident for tax purposes in a Member State who receives an interest
payment or any individual to whom an interest payment is attributed, unless he
provides evidence that it was not received or attributed for his own benefit, that is
to say that:

(1) he acts as a paying agent; or
(2) he acts on behalf of a legal person, an entity taxed on its profits under
    the general arrangements for business taxation, a UCITS authorized in
    accordance with Directive 85/611; or
(3) he acts on behalf of another individual who is the beneficial owner and
    discloses to the paying agent the identity of that beneficial owner.

In other words, it is not the objective of the European legislature to tax corporate
income. Thus, receipt of interest by legal persons falls outside the scope of the
Directive.

When a paying agent has information suggesting that the individual who receives   **11.180**
an interest payment or to whom an interest payment is attributed may not be
the beneficial owner, it must take reasonable steps to establish the identity of the
beneficial owner.[189]

Each Member State may determine the procedures necessary to allow the paying   **11.181**
agent to identify the beneficial owners and their place of residence, subject to
compliance with minimum standards pursuant to Directive 2003/48. Here, the
Directive distinguishes between contracts entered into between the paying agent
and the beneficial owner before and after 1 January 2004. If entered into before
1 January 2004,[190] it refers to Directive 91/308 on prevention of the use of the
financial system for the purpose of money laundering.[191]

Type of information exchanged

In accordance with Directive 2003/48[192] the paying agent must provide the com-   **11.182**
petent authority of the Member State in which it is established with its name and
address, the name and place of residence of the beneficial owner, the account number of the beneficial owner, or, where there is none, identification of the debt claim
giving rise to the interest, and information concerning the interest payment.

The exchange of information is then effected by the competent authority in   **11.183**
the Member State of the paying agent, which is responsible for reporting this

---

[189] Art 2(2), Directive (EC) 2003/48.
[190] ibid Art 3(a).
[191] Directive (EEC) 91/308 of 10 June 1991 on the prevention of the use of the financial system
for the purpose of money laundering [1991] OJ L166/77.
[192] Art 8, Directive (EEC) 2003/48.

information at least once a year to its counterpart in the Member State in which the beneficial owner is resident.[193]

A system limited to savings income in the form of interest payments

11.184 Directive 2003/48 lists the different types of income considered to be 'interest payments', including:

(a) interest paid or credited to an account, relating to debt claims of every kind, whether or not secured by a mortgage and whether or not carrying a right to participate in the debtor's profits, and, in particular, income from government securities and income from bonds, or debentures, including premiums and prizes attaching to such securities, bonds, or debentures (excluding penalty charges for late payments);

(b) interest accrued or capitalized on the sale, repayment, or redemption of the debt claims referred to in (a);

(c) income deriving from interest payments either directly or through a residual entity, distributed by a UCITS authorized in accordance with Directive 85/611 or entities that have opted to be treated as authorized UCITS or UCIs established in third countries;

(d) income realized upon the sale, repayment, or redemption of shares or units in the above-mentioned undertakings and entities, if they invest directly or indirectly, via other undertakings for collective investment or entities referred to above, more than 40 per cent of their assets in debt instruments as referred to in (a). This provision also applies to direct or indirect investments intended to avoid application of the Directive.

11.185 The threshold of 40 per cent (see point (d) above) will be reduced to 25 per cent on 1 January 2011. When the paying agent is unable to verify whether the condition for the threshold of 40 per cent has been met, the percentage of such assets is deemed to exceed 40 per cent.

11.186 By way of derogation, Member States have the option of excluding from the definition of interest payment any income from UCITS or other entities established in Luxembourg when the investment of such undertakings or entities in the debt assets referred to in point (a) above does not exceed 15 per cent of their assets. Luxembourg has opted for this solution in the Act of 21 June 2005 transposing Directive 2003/48.[194] This minimum threshold of 15 per cent allows UCITS or other entities to exclude marginal investments in fixed-income products.

---

[193] ibid Art 9(2).
[194] See 11.206 below.

Transposition of the Directive into Luxembourg law

Accurate transposition by the Act of 21 June 2005

The Act of 21 June 2005 transposing Directive 2003/48 into Luxembourg law **11.187** faithfully follows the wording of the Directive. The foregoing discussion of the text of the Directive also applies to the Act of 21 June 2005.

Moreover, Luxembourg has signed a number of agreements with associated and **11.188** dependent territories of EU Member States and third countries under which they apply withholding taxes in accordance with the rules in force in Luxembourg. Some of these agreements have been approved by the Act of 21 June 2005.[195]

Benefit of transitional provisions

Like Austria and Belgium, the Grand Duchy of Luxembourg is subject—for an **11.189** unspecified period—to the transitional provisions stipulated in Directive 2003/48[196] and reproduced in the body of the Act of 21 June 2005. As provided for in Directive 2003/48, the term of the transitional period depends on:

- the conclusion of agreements on the exchange of information 'on request' with respect to interest payments between the European Union and each of the following countries: the Swiss Confederation, the Principality of Liechtenstein, the Republic of San Marino, the Principality of Monaco, and the Principality of Andorra and the application, by those countries, of a withholding tax at the rates stipulated in Directive 2003/48 for the transitional period; and

- an undertaking by the United States to exchange information 'on request' with the European Union with respect to interest payments.

Luxembourg negotiated the benefit of these transitional provisions in order to **11.190** preserve its tradition of stringent banking secrecy, which would have been weakened by the information exchange procedure.[197] This transitional period offers Luxembourg the option of deferring implementation of an automatic information exchange procedure and adoption of a withholding system instead.

Introduction of withholding tax and revenue sharing

Withholding mechanism

Withholding tax is a traditional method of collecting income tax, especially in **11.191** Luxembourg where it is the norm for natural persons. Directive 2003/48 and,

---

[195] Act of 21 June 2005 approving agreements in the form of exchanges of letters with regard to the tax treatment of savings income in the form of interest payments between the Grand Duchy of Luxembourg and certain other countries and territories (*Mémorial* A 2005, 1547).

[196] Ch III, Directive (EC) 2003/48.

[197] In this respect, see *Parliamentary doc* No 5297, Explanatory Statement, 2.

correspondingly, the Act of 21 June 2005, stipulate a specific withholding feature as they require the paying agent to levy the withholding tax on behalf of the Luxembourg Treasury. In other words, any paying agent established in Luxembourg and paying interest to a beneficial owner must itself apply a withholding tax to the payment.

11.192 The withholding tax rate is predetermined and will gradually increase according to a set timetable. The rate is 15 per cent until 30 June 2008, after which it rises to 20 per cent until 30 June 2010 and 35 per cent from 1 July 2011. Withholding tax is paid once a year.

11.193 The Act of 21 June 2005 sets out the exact rules applicable to paying agents in respect of withholding tax.[198] Similarly, the Act provides the necessary particulars about the amounts to be subjected to withholding tax.[199]

11.194 In certain exceptional situations, withholding tax is not charged, ie when:

- the beneficial owner or the entity[200] grants the paying agent a special mandate to disclose information in accordance with the law, in which case this authorization covers all interest paid by the paying agent to the beneficial owner;
- the beneficial owner provides his paying agent with a certificate, as described in the Act, issued in his name by the competent authority in the State in which he is resident for tax purposes.[201]

11.195 Thus, a beneficial owner who wants to be exempt from withholding tax can use either of two types of procedures. The first is to authorize the paying agent expressly to exchange information with the competent authority in his State of residence, as provided for by the general procedure. The second is to provide the paying agent with a certificate issued by the same authority. The Act of 21 June 2005 sets out the minimum information to be disclosed by the paying agent.[202]

Revenue sharing procedure

11.196 According to this procedure, Luxembourg keeps 25 per cent of the withheld revenues and transfers 75 per cent to the Member State in which the beneficial owner of the interest is resident.[203] The total sum due must be transferred to the foreign

---

[198] Art 7, Act of 21 June 2005.
[199] ibid.
[200] See 11.179 above.
[201] This is Luxembourg form No 911.
[202] Art 9.2, Act of 21 June 2005.
[203] ibid Art 8.

treasury in question no later than 30 June of the year following the end of the calendar year in which the deduction is made.

Despite this redistribution, revenues from withholding taxes levied in Luxembourg remain income of Luxembourg itself.[204] **11.197**

Differing treatment of UCIs under the law

UCIs were belatedly included in the scope of application of Directive 2003/48, when it was still in draft form. At the time, the text distinguished between funds which distributed and those which capitalized income. The European legislature subsequently changed its approach, making the type of financial transaction rather than the nature of the fund the relevant criterion. **11.198**

In the final version, Directive 2003/48 endeavours to determine particular interest payment situations and does not make the nature of a fund the overriding criterion.[205] **11.199**

Criteria to determine UCIs whose revenues or distributions may be taxed

There are two cumulative criteria. **11.200**

(1) First criterion: the UCI. The Act of 21 June 2005 potentially targets:
  (a) UCITS authorized under Directive 85/611, ie SICAVs and FCPs governed by Part I of the 2002 Act;
  (b) so-called 'residual' entities, which must always be treated as UCITS governed by Directive 85/611; and
  (c) investment funds established outside the European Union.[206]
(2) Second criterion: the financial transaction. The Act of 21 June 2005, which strictly replicates the terms of the Directive, states that the UCIs and entities

---

[204] Luxembourg receives 75% of the withholding tax collected on interest received by its residents in the following Member States and territories: Austria, Belgium, Switzerland, Liechtenstein, Andorra, San Marino, Monaco, Jersey, Guernsey, Isle of Man, Dutch Antilles, British Virgin Islands, Turks and Caicos Islands.

[205] For more complete information about the practical aspects set out in this section, the reader is referred to two particularly valuable publications: '*Handbook sur la fiscalité de l'épargne*' (ABBL-KPMG, February 2005), complemented by an update in August 2005, and the recommendations and interpretations published by ALFI: '*The European Savings Directive, ALFI's interpretations and recommendations*' (June 2005).

[206] These funds must be UCIs. This is a major difficulty for the paying agent: how can he make sure that a foreign entity is in fact a fund and, if so, a UCI? A number of 'objective' criteria are used to determine this in the absence of a universal definition of funds and UCIs. For example, is the purpose of the fund the collective investment in securities of capital received from the public according to the risk-spreading principle (which is not an absolute principle)?

referred to above can only receive interest payments which give rise to a withholding tax in two cases:[207]

(a) when such UCIs and entities distribute, directly or through another entity, revenues received from due interest payments as defined by the law;[208]

(b) on the sale, repayment, or redemption proceeds for units or shares in UCIs and entities as referred to above which in turn invest either directly or through other UCIs and entities as referred to above in assets represented as to 40 per cent or more by debt instruments.[209] This 40 per cent rule applies automatically. In other words, indirect investments need to be added to direct investments in order to determine whether revenues from the sale, repayment, or redemption of units or shares in the UCI in question are liable to withholding tax.

The foregoing can be used to determine which UCIs and income distributions are included within the scope of the Act.

11.201 For the purpose of applying the withholding tax, the percentages (explained below) of 15 per cent (*de minimis* threshold) and 40 per cent (investments in claims in the form of interest payments) must primarily be judged having regard to the investment policy defined in the management rules or in the constitutive documents of the UCIs in question. When the investment policy cannot be used to determine whether the above-mentioned thresholds have been crossed or not, the Act requires their application to be based on the actual portfolio composition.

UCIs and revenues falling within the scope of the Act

11.202 The Act of 21 June 2005 covers two categories of UCIs and revenues.

11.203 The first category includes revenues distributed by UCITS authorized in accordance with Directive 85/611 or by 'residual' entities, which must always be treated as UCITS governed by Directive 85/611, or by investment funds established outside the European Union, and connected with claims in the form of interest payments.

11.204 Not all revenues are treated as claims in the form of interest payments. Revenues from real property and from derivative instruments should not be considered interest payments.[210] Until 31 December 2010, the following cannot be

---

[207] Arts 6.1(c) and (d), Act of 21 June 2005.

[208] Arts 6.1(a) and 6.1(b), Act of 21 June 2005. However, the revenues distributed in this way are only treated as interest payments when received by the UCITS itself.

[209] See 11.184 above.

[210] The '*Handbook sur la fiscalité de l'épargne*' published by ABBL-KPMG proposes four criteria to determine whether a product can be considered as a claim generating interest revenues within the

considered interest payments: domestic and international bonds and other negotiable debt instruments issued originally prior to 1 March 2001 or whose original
prospectus was issued before that date by the competent authorities within the
meaning of Council Directive 80/390[211] or by the competent officials of third
countries, provided no new securities have been issued since 1 March 2002.

The second category covers revenues received on the sale, repayment, or redemp- **11.205**
tion of units or shares in the undertakings and entities referred to above when such
undertakings and entities invest directly or indirectly, through other UCIs or
entities, more than 40 per cent of their assets in interest bearing accounts or claims
of any kind. It is irrelevant whether such claims are linked to mortgage guarantees
or clauses providing for a share in the debtor's profits. This category includes, in
particular, revenues from public bonds, including the premiums attached to them
(but excluding penalties for late payment).

UCIs and distributions outside the scope of the Act

Withholding tax is not levied on: **11.206**

(1) distributions by SICAVs governed by Part II of the 2002 Act or by the Act of
13 February 2007;[212]
(2) revenues from 'excluded products', ie not covered by the Act of 21 June 2005
as claims in the form of 'interest payments',[213] such as shares in listed and
privately held companies, life insurance products, structured products, and
derivative instruments;
(3) UCIs that invest less than 15 per cent of their assets in the claims listed
exhaustively in the Act (*de minimis* threshold).

Consequences for the operational environment of UCIs

The provisions of the Act of 21 June 2005 obviously have relatively significant **11.207**
consequences for the internal organization of service providers for UCIs. The
entire chain of service providers is affected, from development to distribution.
Upstream, promoters of UCIs need to determine whether they agree to the 'tax
waste' generated by the withholding tax or whether they want to be positioned

---

meaning of the Act of 21 June 2005: qualification of revenues received on money lent, the existence
of an underlying claim, a guarantee to repay the money, and the absence of recognition in hidden
reserves or goodwill.

[211] Council Directive (EEC) 80/390 of 17 March 1980 coordinating the requirements for the
drawing up, scrutiny, and distribution of the listing particulars to be published for the admission of
securities to official stock exchange listing [1980] OJ L100/1.

[212] An FCP governed by Part II of the 2002 Act, intrinsically without legal personality, is considered a residual entity. It is therefore assumed to have opted automatically for treatment as a UCITS
in compliance with Directive (EEC) 85/611.

[213] Art 6, Act of 21 June 2005.

outside the scope of the Directive. Similarly, cross-border distribution involves a tax risk not associated with distribution to local residents.

11.208 The withholding tax mechanism itself requires a certain internal organization at the service providers. The depositary pays interest by debiting the UCI's accounts in favour of the account of the beneficial owner, the custody account keeper makes sure it has the necessary information about the identity of the said beneficiary and the administrative agent in charge of calculating net asset value must be familiar with the nature of the payment in order to identify the fraction of 'interest' that may be subject to a withholding. Experience can be expected to refine the roles of the various service providers.

12

UNDERTAKINGS FOR COLLECTIVE INVESTMENT AND EUROPEAN LAW

The influence of Community law on UCIs is evident mainly from Directive **12.01**
85/611, amended by Directives 2001/107, 2001/108, and more recently
2007/16.[1,2,3]

---

[1] In preparing this part, the authors benefited from the valuable support of Maître P-E Partsch, partner in Arendt & Medernach in charge of European law, professor in European banking and financial law at the University of Liège, visiting professor at the University of Luxembourg, and former legal secretary at the ECJ, who kindly guided them in their examination of Community legal opinion and case law and whose comments provided the authors with a better understanding of certain aspects of this issue.

[2] If we except Directive (EC) 2005/1 of the European Parliament and of the Council of 9 March 2005, amending Directives (EEC) 73/239, (EEC) 85/611, (EEC) 91/375, (EEC) 92/49 of the Council and Directives (EC) 94/19, (EC) 98/78, (EC) 2001/34, (EC) 2002/83 and (EC) 2002/87 organizing the competent financial services committees according to a new structure, [2005] OJ L79/9, abrogating Art 53 and amending Art 53a of Directive (EEC) 85/611 on the implementation powers of the Commission of the European Communities (see 12.75 *et seq* below).

[3] Commission Directive (EC) 2007/116 of 19 March 2007 implementing Council Directive (EEC) 85/611 on the coordination of laws, regulations and administrative provisions relating to undertakings for collective investment in transferable securities (UCITS) as regards the clarification of certain definitions.

12.02 The successive versions of this Directive have been transposed into national law by the EU Member States. The Directive also gives guidance on the interpretation of the provisions in the national laws transposing the Directive.[4] If a State fails to transpose all or part of the Directive, an economic operator or a private citizen may claim its provisions against the public authorities when the provisions are clear, precise, and unconditional.[5]

12.03 The application of Community law to UCIs is, however, not limited to Directive 85/611. Here, three comments may be made.

12.04 First, Directive 85/611 must be evaluated having regard to Community law and its standards, ie the provisions of the EC Treaty and the general principles of Community law. These provisions and principles have precedence over legislation derived from the Treaty. This has two consequences.

12.05 On the one hand, the Directive—and therefore the national provisions transposing it—must be interpreted in the light of these overriding standards of Community law. In the event of a conflict with these standards, the Directive must give way. This possibility cannot be ruled out on an *a priori* basis. Directive 85/611 is more than twenty years old, which is a considerable age for any legal instrument in Community law concerning financial matters. Revisions of the EC Treaty and case law of the ECJ since 1985 may have made certain provisions of the Directive obsolete. For example, the provisions of the EC Treaty on the free movement of capital have been significantly liberalized since the adoption of Directive 85/611. On the other hand, the overriding standards of Community law are also available to fill gaps in Directive 85/611.

12.06 This Directive was the first framework Directive for European banking and financial law. It does not cover the entire legal regime applicable to UCITS. In certain areas, it is necessary to judge whether national law is compatible with the provisions of the EC Treaty organizing the relevant freedoms of movement. For example, direct taxation is not harmonized. Consequently, any restrictions on marketing UCITS units within the European Community under a national law in this regard must be considered in conjunction with the Community principle of freedoms of movement.

12.07 The following standards and principles may also apply to the UCITS governed by Directive 85/611:

(1) the provisions of the EC Treaty on the free movement of capital, freedom to provide services, and freedom of establishment;

---

[4] In the event that a Member State fails to transpose all or part of the Directive, an economic operator or a private citizen may claim its clear, precise, and unconditional provisions against the public authorities in the general meaning of the term.

[5] According to criteria based on ECJ case law.

(2) the principles of the EC Treaty,[6] such as the principle of close cooperation;

(3) the general principles of Community law, such as the principle of proportionality.

Secondly, Directive 85/611 governs only certain types of UCITS. Non-coordinated UCIs are governed only by the general framework of Community law outlined above. Thus, to market its units in other EU Member States, a non-coordinated UCI under Luxembourg law may not rely on the European passport created by the Directive but must instead use the provisions in the EC Treaty on free movement of capital. **12.08**

Lastly, UCIs, whether coordinated or not, may be affected, incidentally or not, by other Community Directives, such as the sixth VAT Directive,[7] which exempts management of 'investment funds as defined by the Member States'. Such instances are increased by the adoption of many other banking and financial directives, such as MiFID, Directive 2003/71, known as the Prospectus Directive, and Directive 2003/6, known as the Market Abuse Directive. Such directives can raise delicate problems of coordination with Directive 85/611. **12.09**

The aim of this chapter is not to comment in detail on Directive 85/611. Its material provisions are already analysed indirectly in the other chapters of this work. This chapter will focus on other standards of Community law liable to have an impact on the legal regime of UCIs and on the institutional provisions of the Directive insofar as these touch upon the implementing powers of the European Commission. **12.10**

This chapter will begin by looking at the scope of Community freedoms in connection with capital, services, and establishment. The principle of close cooperation will be discussed separately. **12.11**

Next it will analyse some practical consequences of those principles and freedoms, such as the potential conflict between certain provisions of Directive 85/611 and the rules laid down in the EC Treaty. It will also comment on the options open to a host State to block the offering of units in foreign UCIs, whether coordinated or not, in its territory. The implementing powers of the Commission of the European Communities will be discussed separately. **12.12**

---

[6] As set out in Arts 1–16 of the EC Treaty.

[7] Sixth Council Directive (EEC) 77/388 of 17 May 1977 on the harmonization of the laws of the Member States relating to turnover taxes—common system of value-added tax—uniform assessment basis [1997] OJ L145/1. This exception has been interpreted in the decision rendered on 4 May 2006, *Abbey National*, C-169/04, Rec I-4027.

Applicable Community Standards

Free movement of capital

12.13 Capital consists of invested wealth and wealth that can be invested. It is used for financial transactions targeted primarily at investment.[8] Such transactions are referred to as 'movements of capital' and concern the free circulation of capital when involving more than one Member State.

12.14 The concept of the free movement of capital[9] has a significant impact on UCIs, notably when collecting capital, subscribing, redeeming, or repurchasing a UCI's units in the European Union and when a UCI buys or sells financial instruments insofar as these involve intra-Community exchanges or exchanges between a Member State and a third country.

12.15 Transactions in the units of UCIs is, moreover, one of the headings in the nomenclature of capital movements annexed to Directive 88/361 of the Council.[10] That nomenclature provides the only firm indication of the concept of capital movements in Community law. Even though Directive 88/361 was implicitly repealed by the Maastricht Treaty, its nomenclature remains entirely topical. As the European Court of Justice (ECJ) has held,[11] it retains its interpretative value, on the understanding—as explained in its introduction—that it is not exhaustive.

12.16 According to that nomenclature, transactions in units of UCIs include both transactions in such units[12] and their admission to the capital markets. As used in the nomenclature, the concept of UCIs is broader than that of coordinated UCITS. It also covers UCIs not governed by Directive 85/611.

12.17 In contrast with other freedoms, the free movement of capital does not just benefit EU residents living within the Community. It applies whenever one element of

---

[8] ECJ, judgment of 31 January 1984 in Joined Cases 286/82 and 26/83 *Luisi and Carbone* [1984] ECR 377, paras 21 and 22.

[9] Arts 56–60, EC Treaty. The free movement of capital between the Member States of the European Free Trade Association (Iceland, Norway, and Liechtenstein) and between those Member States and third countries is governed by provisions with a slightly different content, ie Arts 40–45 of the Agreement on the European Economic Area, signed in Porto on 2 May 1992.

[10] Council Directive (EEC) 88/361 of 24 June 1988 for implementation of Art 67 of the Treaty [1988] OJ L178/5.

[11] Judgment of 16 March 1999 in Case C-222/97 *Trummer and Mayer* [1999] ECR I-1661, para 21.

[12] That is to say: (1) the acquisition by non-residents of units of national undertakings dealt in on a stock exchange; (2) the acquisition by residents of units of foreign undertakings dealt in on a stock exchange; (3) the acquisition by non-residents of units of national undertakings not dealt in on a stock exchange; (4) the acquisition by residents of units of foreign undertakings not dealt in on a stock exchange.

a transaction is located in the Community, regardless of the domicile of the operators or any conditions of nationality.

Any restrictions on movements of capital are in principle prohibited,[13] including **12.18** restrictions on international capital movements and measures which, while they may apply under the law without any distinction made between domestic and capital movements, in fact have a more prejudicial impact on international transactions than on purely internal transactions within the Member State concerned.[14]

The entities bound by the free movement of capital are not only the Member **12.19** States but also the European Union itself when it adopts secondary legislation, such as European Directives. For example, Directive 85/611 must comply with the principles laid down by the EC Treaty on the free movement of capital. However, it would be an error to place the Member States and the Community institutions on the same level. In line with what is happening with other Community freedoms, the ECJ can be expected to show more leniency vis-à-vis secondary legislation than vis-à-vis unilateral measures taken by the Member States. In fact, it takes account of the Community origin, and therefore of the unifying nature, of the provisions of secondary legislation and their contribution to the achievement of the single market.[15]

The question of whether the ban on the creation or maintenance of restrictions on **12.20** movements of capital is binding on all or some private operators is the subject of debate. Nevertheless, in the years ahead, the ECJ may well judge that the provisions on the free movement of capital apply to credit institutions and even to the relationships between UCIs and their clients.

Despite the prohibition on restrictions on the movement of capital, the EC **12.21** Treaty[16] nevertheless authorizes Member States to derogate from this principle on several grounds. In addition to measures justified on grounds of public policy or public security, Member States may lay down restrictions necessary to prevent infringements of their national laws and regulations. They may lay down procedures for the declaration of capital movements for administrative or statistical information purposes.[17] They may also distinguish for tax purposes between

---

[13] Art 56, EC Treaty. As regards the free movement of capital, see PE Partsch, 'Les capitaux et les paiements', in *Commentaire Article par Article des traités UE et CE* (Helbing & Lichtenhahn, Dalloz, Bruylant, 2000) 478–527.

[14] The ECJ has confirmed this point in the above-mentioned decision of 16 March 1999, *Trummer and Mayer*, regarding an Austrian provision that required registration of mortgages in the Austrian land survey register in the national currency.

[15] P Oliver, 'La législation communautaire et sa conformité avec la libre circulation des marchandises' (1979) *Cah dr eur* 245.

[16] Art 58, EC Treaty.

[17] ibid Art 58(1)(b).

taxpayers who are not in the same situation with regard to their place of residence or the place where their capital is invested.[18]

12.22 Moreover, a Member State may take any measures to restrict the movement of capital, provided that the measures apply without distinction, are justified by overriding factors in the public interest, are capable of achieving the objective pursued, and (pursuant to the principle of proportionality) do not go beyond what is necessary for those purposes. For example, the need for transparent mortgage rules and the protection of lower-ranking creditors[19] or concerns about town and country planning[20] may, in absolute terms, justify restrictions on movement of capital.

12.23 The ECJ is relatively strict in its assessment of the proportionality of national measures restricting the free movement of capital. For example, it opposes prior authorization systems,[21] partly because they delay movements of capital and partly because they subject the free movement of capital to the discretion of administrative authorities.[22]

12.24 However, prior authorization systems are not condemned in absolute terms. They would, for example, be allowed if they were necessary to protect public policy or public security.[23] Direct foreign investments could therefore be blocked initially for control purposes, as they could be too difficult to identify after the capital had entered a Member State.[24]

12.25 In evaluating the need for restrictions on the movement of capital, the ECJ could reasonably be expected to apply an equivalence test. It already uses such a test when assessing the need for a barrier to the freedom to provide services. According to that test, a host State may not impose constraints on a service provider if the interests protected by such constraints are secured via comparable guarantees in the home State of the service provider. The host State must take

---

[18] ibid Art 58(1)(a).

[19] See the judgment in *Trummer and Mayer* (n 11 above).

[20] ECJ, judgment of 1 June 1999 in case C-302/97 *Konle* [1999] ECR I-3099 *et seq.*

[21] Thus, the ECJ has held a national law making the export of cash conditional on the grant of prior authorization and a national regulation subjecting the purchase of real property in a mountainous tourist area to prior authorization to be contrary to the free movement of capital. In the latter case, the ECJ observed that there are alternatives less damaging to the free movement of capital. Infringement of national legislation on secondary residences may be penalized by a fine or by a decision requiring the acquirer to terminate the unlawful use of the land forthwith under penalty of its compulsory sale or by a declaration that the sale is void (judgment of 1 June 1999 in *Konle*, (n 20 above) para 47).

[22] See ECJ, judgment of 23 February 1995 in Joined Cases C-358/93 and C-416-93 *Bordessa* [1995] ECR I-361, paras 24 and 25.

[23] ECJ, judgment of 14 March 2000 in Case C-54/99 *Church of Scientology* [2000] ECR I-1335, para 19 concerning an investment plan of the British branch of the church in France.

[24] ibid para 20.

such guarantees into account.[25] To date, the ECJ has not yet been called on to determine that aspect of the free movement of capital.

Freedom to provide services

Freedom to provide services[26] may be defined as the right of every national of a EU Member State to offer and supply services as an independent business across EU borders. Construed as intangible activities, such services could be offered and supplied on the following conditions:

12.26

- the service provider moves temporarily to the recipient's Member State or another Member State in order to offer and/or supply a service;

- the service provider offers and/or supplies services from his home Member State to recipients in other Member States;

- the service provider and the recipient move to another Member State in order to provide the services there.

For example, a resident from one Member State who subscribes for a UCI's units in another Member State may be considered as benefiting from the UCI manager's financial expertise, equivalent to indirectly providing a service to the unitholder. Moreover, the marketing of UCI units in other Member States involves a number of services to investors to enable them to exercise their rights.

12.27

Initially, the provisions on freedom to provide services were construed as prohibiting only discrimination based on nationality or residence. In 1991, the ECJ ruled that they also prohibited 'any restriction, even if it applies without distinction to national providers of services and to those of other Member States, when it is liable to prohibit or otherwise impede the activities of a provider of services established in another Member State where it lawfully provides similar services'.[27] That development was confirmed by the Treaty of Amsterdam.[28]

12.28

As with the free movement of capital, the ECJ allows the Member States to subject freedom to provide services to restrictions justified by reasons of public interest other than those expressly provided for in the EC Treaty. These reasons range from consumer protection to fairness in commercial transactions and preservation of

12.29

---

[25] According to the ECJ, 'the freedom to provide services, as one of the fundamental principles of the Treaty, may be restricted only by provisions that are justified by the general good . . . in so far as that interest is not safeguarded by the provisions to which the provider of a service is subject in the Member State of his establishment' (judgment of 4 December 1986 in Case 205/84 *Commission v Germany* [1986] ECR 3802, para 27).

[26] Arts 49–55, EC Treaty; Arts 36–39 of the Agreement on the European Economic Area, signed in Porto on 2 May 1992.

[27] ECJ, judgment of 25 July 1991 in Case C-76/90 *Säger* [1991] ECR I-4222.

[28] See Art 49, EC Treaty.

the reputation of the financial sector,[29] on two conditions. First, they must be legally applicable without distinction to service providers established in the Member State concerned or in other Member States. Secondly, they must be proportionate and necessary in order to achieve the objective in question. That is not the case if the equivalence test shows that the objective is already achieved by measures applicable to the service provider in his home State.[30]

12.30 A typical example of a national measure affecting freedom to provide services is the obligation for economic operators to have a permanent establishment in the host State. This effectively makes it impossible to exercise that freedom, except by setting up a secondary establishment.[31] That type of requirement is permitted only when it is essential in order to achieve the objective pursued.

12.31 For example, in the area of direct insurance, Germany required all documents needed for the purposes of supervision by its authorities to be located physically in its territory. That requirement was overruled by the ECJ,[32] which held that it was not enough that the requirement made it easier for the supervisory authorities to perform their task. Germany also had to prove that those authorities could not carry out their supervisory tasks effectively without such a measure. It could not prove this.

12.32 Similarly, the ECJ found that Italy had infringed the EC Treaty by requiring operators wishing to build up a brokerage business in transferable securities in its territory to be established there.[33]

The right of establishment

12.33 The right of establishment[34] is the right of residents of one EEA Member State to settle permanently in a Member State other than that to which they are tied by nationality or professional qualifications, in order to carry on—in that Member State—an independent economic activity.[35] The right of establishment may be exercised in two ways: either the operator in question moves its centre of activity to another Member State (exercise of right of primary establishment) or it creates

---

[29] EJC, 10 May 1995, *Alpine Investments*, C-384/93, *Rec*, p I-144, point 45.

[30] See, ECG judgment of 4 December 1986 in *Commission v Germany* (n 25 above) para 27.

[31] See, *inter alia*, ECJ, judgment of 26 November 1975 in Case 39/75 *Coenen* [1975] ECR 1547; judgment of 29 October 1998 in Case C-114/97 *Commission v Spain* [1998] ECR I-6718.

[32] See ECJ judgment of 4 December 1986 in *Commission v Germany* (n 25 above) paras 54–56.

[33] ECJ judgment of 6 June 1996 in Case C-101/94 *Commission v Italy* [1996] ECR I-2691.

[34] Arts 43–48, EC Treaty; Arts 31–35 of the Agreement on the European Economic Area, signed in Porto on 2 May 1992.

[35] L Truchot, 'Le droit d'établissement', in *Commentaire Article par Article des traités UE et CE (Helbing & Lichtenhahn, Dalloz, Bruylant,* 2000) 379.

a second permanent centre of activity in another Member State, known as the right of secondary establishment. This involves the incorporation of subsidiaries or the opening of branches, agencies, or offices without legal personality in the host Member State.

In the area of UCIs, the right of establishment has a practical effect for depositaries **12.34** and management companies. It allows a financial institution to act as the depositary of a UCI established in a particular Member State without being a resident. It needs to have only a secondary establishment in the said State. Since Directive 2001/107, management companies are to some extent allowed to carry on activities in other Member States by creating a secondary establishment with a European passport.

As a general rule, however, the right of establishment is only of limited interest for **12.35** UCIs themselves. First, a UCI is allowed to market its units within the European Union without setting up a branch or opening an agency or an office. Secondly, a UCI will not find it easy to use the right of establishment, owing to the fact that its head office and registered office, or the registered office of its management company and at least the depositary's secondary establishment, must be located in the UCI's home State. The case law of the ECJ in this area is similar to that concerning freedom to provide services.

Restrictions on the right of establishment are national measures that, whilst appli- **12.36** cable without distinction, are liable to hamper or to render less attractive the exercise of freedom of establishment.[36] For example, the right to carry on certain self-employed activities may be subject to compliance with certain conditions in the public interest, such as rules on organization, qualifications, professional ethics, supervision, and liability.[37] However, such rules could hinder exercise of the right of establishment without good reason in that they do not take account of the knowledge and qualifications already acquired by someone in his home State.[38]

Recently, the ECJ has made a notable application of the idea that Article 43 of the **12.37** EC Treaty prohibits any unjustified restriction on the right of establishment, even where there is no discrimination. In the *Caixabank* decision of 5 October 2004,[39] it ruled that the French prohibition on paying interest on current accounts

---

[36] ECJ, judgment of 31 March 1993 in Case C-19/92 *Kraus Dieter v Land Baden Würtenberg* [1993] ECR I-1689.

[37] ECJ, judgment of 30 November 1995 in Case C-5/94 *Gebhard* [1995] ECR I-4165; judgment of 20 May 1992 in Case C-106/91 *Ramrath v Luxembourg Minister of Justice* [1992] ECR I-3351.

[38] ECJ, judgment of 7 May 1991 in Case C-340/89 *Vlassopoulou* [1991] ECR I-2357 and Directive (EC) 2005/36 on the recognition of professional qualifications [2005] OJ L255/22.

[39] ECJ, judgment of 5 October 2004, in Case C-442/02 CaixaBank France [2004] ECR I-8961.

restricted exercise of the right of establishment and obstructed the collection of capital from the public by the French subsidiaries of foreign companies by depriving them of one of the most effective methods of competition for a new operator wishing to enter the market of a Member State.

12.38 The ECJ further held that the prohibition in question was disproportionate to the reasons of public interest claimed by the French government, ie consumer protection and the wish to encourage long-term savings.[40]

The principle of close cooperation

12.39 As enshrined in the EC Treaty[41] and interpreted by the ECJ, the principle of close cooperation imposes two types of obligations on the Member States. First, the States must take all appropriate measures to ensure fulfilment of the obligations arising out of the EC Treaty or resulting from action taken by institutions of the Community. They are required to facilitate achievement of the European Union's tasks. Secondly, they have the duty to abstain from any measures that jeopardize attainment of the objectives of the EC Treaty.

12.40 The Member States must adopt the measures necessary for effective implementation of Community acts. It is their responsibility to take the consequences of their membership of the European Union into account in their internal legal infrastructure and, as the case may be, in certain national rules of law.

12.41 For example, the accurate transposition of Directives necessitates respect for the meaning of the terms and concepts used in such secondary legislation, in order to ensure its uniform interpretation and application throughout the European Union despite semantic and conceptual differences between national legal systems. Each Member State must guarantee the complete, clear, and precise transposition of Directives. Where a Directive is intended to create rights for individuals, the persons concerned must be in a position to ascertain the full extent of their rights and to rely on them before the national courts.[42]

12.42 In line with that reasoning, the ECJ has concluded that the EC treaty[43] imposes on the judicial authorities of Member States the obligation to construe national law having regard to the Directives by applying the 'conformed

---

[40] For a comment on this decision, see P-E Partsch, 'Droit bancaire et financier européen: Chronique de jurisprudence de l'année 2004' (2005) 36, *Bull Droit & Banque* 42–56.

[41] Art 10, EC Treaty. See J Verhoeven, *Droit de la Communauté européenne* (Larcier, 1996) 333 *et seq.*

[42] See, in particular, ECJ, judgment of 18 November 1995 in Case C-433/93 *Commission v Germany* [1995] ECR I-2317 para 18; judgment of 20 March 1997 in Case C-96/95 *Commission v Germany* [1997] ECR I-1679, para 35.

[43] Art 10, EC Treaty.

interpretation' precept.[44] The scope of that obligation is wide. First, it applies to all national legislation, including that existing prior to the Directives and not subsequently amended.[45] Secondly, it applies even to disputes between individuals.[46]

The principle of close cooperation must also govern relations between the respec- **12.43** tive administrative authorities of the Member States insofar as a situation falls within the sphere of application of the EC Treaty. Non-compliance with this principle by a Member State may lead to a procedure for a declaration of failure on the part of the Member State to fulfil an obligation.[47] Thus, every Member State is under a duty to assist every other Member State that is under an obligation under Community law.[48]

Consequences of Community Law for UCIs

Compatibility of Directive 85/611 with the Treaty of the European Communities

Directive 85/611[49] provides that where a UCITS proposes to market its units in a **12.44** Member State other than that in which it is situated, it must inform the competent authorities of that other Member State. It may begin to market its units in that other Member State two months after such communication unless the authorities of the Member State concerned establish, before the expiry of that period of two months, that the arrangements made for the marketing of units do not comply with the provisions of Directive 85/611.

---

[44] 'The national courts, in applying their national law, are required to interpret it in the light of the wording and the purpose of the Directive in order to achieve the result referred to in the third paragraph of Article 189 of the Treaty' (judgment of 7 November 1989 in Case 125/88 *Nijman* [1989] ECR 3546 para 6; see also the judgments of 10 April 1984 in Case 14/83 *von Colson and Kamann* [1984] ECR 1909, para 26, and of 20 September 1988 in Case 31/87 *Beentjes* [1988] ECR 4662, para 39).

[45] See ECJ, judgment of 16 December 1993 in Case C-34/92 *Miret* [1993] ECR I-6932, para 21.

[46] See, *inter alia*, ECJ, judgment of 10 April 1984 in *von Colson and Kamann*, (n 44 above) para 26; judgment of 13 November 1990 in Case C-109/89 *Marleasing* [1990] ECR I-4159, para 8. What makes that case law especially remarkable is that the Court has thus far refused to recognise the horizontal direct effect, ie the effect between individuals, of Directives that have not been transposed or have been transposed incorrectly (see, *inter alia*, the judgments of 26 February 1986 in Case 152/84 *Marshall* [1986] ECR 749, para 48; of 14 July 1994 in Case C-91/92 *Faccini Dori* [1994] ECR I, 3355-3356, paras 20 and 24; and of 7 March 1996 in Case C-192/94 *El Corte Inglés* [1996] ECR I-1303 *et seq*, paras 15–21).

[47] ECJ, 2 June 2005, *Commission/Luxembourg*, C-266/03, *Rec*, I-4805.

[48] ECJ, judgment of 27 September 1988 in Case 235/87 *Matteucci* [1988] ECR I-5611, paras 18 and 19.

[49] Art 46, Directive (EEC) 85/611.

12.45 A prior authorization system has, therefore, been implemented. While such systems are generally disapproved of by the ECJ, it is unlikely to disapprove in this case. There are three reasons for this.

12.46 First, the administrative authorities of the host State do not have discretionary powers, since the grounds for refusing marketing authorization are laid down in Directive 85/611.

12.47 Secondly, prior authorization is required under Directive 85/611 itself. The Community institutions have a degree of leeway in legislating. Hence, the ECJ generally applies less stringent control to their legislative measures than to national measures.

12.48 Thirdly, there are good reasons for such prior control by the authorities of the host State. If a foreign UCITS were to market its units in violation of rules adopted by the host State to protect investors, it could be difficult to return to the pre-existing situation. It might not, for example, be easy to trace those investors who had suffered as a result of the actions of the UCITS concerned.[50]

12.49 Pursuant to Directive 85/611,[51] the depositary must either have its registered office in the same Member State as that of the management company or the investment company, or be established in that Member State. This rule is justified by the scope of the depositary's task. The depositary also provides important assistance for the supervisory authority of the coordinated UCITS.[52] In the investors' interest, it checks certain transactions carried out by the UCITS.[53] If it notes an irregularity, it takes the measures necessary for correction. The assistance function of the depositary is essential, since the supervisory authority of the UCITS does not have the necessary resources to check the operations of a UCITS frequently and thoroughly.

12.50 The inspection duties entrusted to the depositary can only be exercised correctly when three conditions are met.

(1) The depositary must know the operating conditions of the UCITS concerned. It must know the legislative, regulatory, and prudential standards applicable to the UCITS. It must also master the language used for business purposes by that UCITS. Lastly, it must know and have rapid access to the

---

[50] For a similar argument, see the judgment of the ECJ of 14 March 2000, Case C-54/99 *Church of Scientology* [2000] ECR I-1335, para 20, according to which, 'in the case of foreign direct investments, the difficulty of identifying and blocking capital once it has entered a Member State may make it necessary to prevent at source any transactions that would violate public policy or affect public society'.

[51] Arts 8(1) and 15(1), Directive (EEC) 85/611.

[52] See 8.25 above.

[53] Arts 7(1), 7(3), 14(1), and 14(3), Directive (EEC) 85/611.

persons responsible for the administration of the UCITS. Those requirements are easiest to satisfy when the depositary is established in the same
Member State as the UCITS.

(2) The depositary's duties must be governed by the same laws as those applicable
to the UCITS. For that reason, it is preferable that depositaries should come
under the same legal system as the UCITS monitored by them.[54]

(3) The supervisory authority with which the depositary liaises must be able to
supervise it easily.[55] It must also be able to communicate with it without
difficulty or unnecessary cost. That is the case if a depositary is established in
the same State as its UCITS.

Despite all these considerations, the Legal Affairs and Citizens' Rights Committee
of the Council published an opinion on 26 July 1993 that challenged compatibility between the EC Treaty and the rule that the registered office of the UCITS and
that of the depositary must be established in the same State.[56] According to the
Council, that rule violates the principle of freedom to provide services enshrined
in the EC Treaty, especially since the activity of depositaries of transferable
securities was liberalized by Directive 93/22. **12.51**

The opinion emanating from the Council's Legal Service is debatable.[57] First of
all, the particular duties of a UCITS depositary justify application of the rule that
the registered office of a UCITS and that of its depositary must be in the same
State and the derogation in that respect from the principle of freedom to provide
services.[58] In fact, the task of the depositary of a UCITS is much wider in scope
than that of the securities depositary legislated for in the Directive on investment
services. The depositary of a UCITS is required, first and foremost, to monitor
certain operations of the UCITS, whereas a securities depositary is merely charged
with the physical custody of securities. That makes it impossible to invoke the
Directive on investment services in this case. **12.52**

Next, its role as an interface with the public authorities explains why the
depositary must be established in the home State of the UCITS. In a decision
dated 5 October 1994 (*van Schaick*), the ECJ held that the effectiveness of **12.53**

---

[54] See *Dictionnaire permanent—Droit européen des affaires*, Undertakings for collective
investment in transferable securities (UCITS), sheet 26 of 2 December 1995, No 19.

[55] ibid.

[56] Legal Affairs and Citizens' Rights Committee, session documents of the European Parliament,
1 October 1993, A3-0268/93.

[57] In this respect it is important to note that the rule that the registered office must be established in the same State is maintained in Directives (EC) 2001/107 and (EC) 2001/108 amending
Directive (EC) 85/611.

[58] In this respect, see J-M Gollier and M Van der Haegen, M Waelbroeck, 'Obligation pour le
dépositaire d'être établi dans le même État que l'OPCVM—Libre prestation de services' (1994),
ALFI Yearbook 105.

periodic control of investment vehicles calls for supervision, which can only be exercised in the national territory by the national authorities[59]. For the same reasons, the CSSF can only maintain effective supervision over depositaries established in its territory. This argument is strengthened by MiFID. Deviating from the traditional principle of home country control, it assigns the authorities of the Member State in which a branch is established the responsibility to monitor compliance with its rules of conduct, since those authorities are closer and therefore in a better position to exercise supervision. The same solution, based on the same reasons, was adopted for Directive 2001/97 on money laundering.

12.54 We should, moreover, not forget that a depositary's activity is only one of the elements of the complex economic phenomenon of UCITS.

12.55 In that the depositary's exclusion from the freedom to provide services is essential for the successful operation of this collective savings mechanism, it is not a restriction on the freedom to provide services prohibited by Article 49 of the EC Treaty.[60]

12.56 Lastly, the requirement that the depositary must be established in a UCITS' home State does not appear to be either unjustified or disproportionate in view of the overall contribution of Directive 85/611 to the freedom to market UCITS units in Europe and the leeway left to the Community institutions, particularly as regards the harmonization of such delicate issues.[61]

Marketing coordinated UCITS in the EEA

12.57 The primary object of Directive 85/611 is to facilitate 'the removal of the restrictions on the free circulation of the units of collective investment undertakings in the Community'[62] as 'such coordination will help to bring about a European capital market'.[63]

12.58 Directive 85/611 therefore created a European passport, by virtue of which authorization for a coordinated UCITS to carry on an activity in an EEA Member State is valid in all other Member States.[64] When a coordinated UCITS wishes to

---

[59] ECJ, 5 October 1994, Case C-55/93 *van Schaik* [1994] ECR I-4858, para 20.

[60] For the same view, see the ECJ judgment of 11 April 2000, Case C-191/97 *Deliège* [2000] ECR I-2620, para 69.

[61] For the existing situation and possible developments in the regulations on UCITS depositaries in Member States, see the communication of 30 March 2004 from the Commission to the Council and to the European Parliament, COM (2004) 207 final, available on the website of the European Commission).

[62] Preamble to Directive (EEC) 85/611, 3rd recital.

[63] ibid.

[64] ibid Art 4(1).

market its units in the territory of a Member State other than the State in which it is authorized, the host State may not check whether that UCITS satisfies the conditions to which Directive 85/611 subjects authorization of the status of coordinated UCITS. It must rely on the authorization received by that UCITS in its home State.[65]

Any other solution would deprive Directive 85/611 of most of its effect, since it would permit a return to segregated markets. In that case, each Member State could subject UCITS marketed in its territory to specific requirements based on its own interpretation of Directive 85/611. **12.59**

The constraint laid down by Directive 85/611 does not remove all the remedies available to a Member State wishing to dispute the authorization accorded to a foreign coordinated UCITS. The supervisory authorities concerned can discuss the matter. It is also possible to bring an action for infringement of Directive 85/611 before the ECJ.[66] Lastly, the ECJ, as a provisional measure, may also grant the right to bar a fund from marketing its units.[67] **12.60**

A coordinated UCITS wishing to market its units in the territory of a Member State other than the State in which it is authorized is required to send certain documents to the competent supervisory authority in the host Member State, which will be used by that authority to verify compliance with certain marketing standards.[68] It has two months in which to bar the coordinated UCITS from marketing its units in its territory.[69] **12.61**

Certain EEA Member States also subject the marketing of units in new sub-funds of coordinated UCITS to that procedure, even if they have already authorized the UCITS to sell its units in their territory. That practice is not supported by any provision in Directive 85/611 and seems debatable. As explained in the text of Directive 85/611, a marketing authorization applies to a UCITS in its entirety **12.62**

---

[65] The Belgian *Conseil d'État* confirmed this position in a judgment delivered on 4 June 1997 (judgment No 66556, *Fleming Flagship v État belge*, (1997) 8 *Rev Banque* 538 *et seq*, note by M Tison; see also the annual reports of the *Commission bancaire et financière*, 1995–1996, 132 and 133; 1996–1997, 140–142). In that case, the *Commission bancaire et financière*, the supervisory authority for UCIs in Belgium, refused to allow a Luxembourg-based UCI to market the units of one of its sub-funds in Belgium on the grounds that the sub-fund did not comply with an essential investment restriction established by Directive (EEC) 85/611. In contrast, the CSSF considered that the UCI had complied with Directive 85/611 and had therefore authorized it. The *Conseil d'État* held that the authorization of the CSSF was binding on the *Commission bancaire et financière*, pursuant to Directive (EEC) 85/611.

[66] Art 226, EC Treaty.

[67] ibid Art 242 and 243. See in that regard, Tison's note (n 65 above) accompanying the decision of 4 June 1997 (1997) 8 *Rev Banque* 593.

[68] See 7.78 above.

[69] See the report entitled '*CESR's guidelines to simplify the notification procedure of UCITS*', ref 06-120b (June 2006).

rather than to each of its sub-funds. There can be no reason to disallow a sub-fund. Only a UCITS' marketing methods require approval by the supervisory authority in the host State. As long as those methods remain the same, the marketing authorization should automatically cover any new sub-fund.

12.63   More generally, the host State may not impose constraints that are not strictly necessary to verify compliance with the marketing standards in force in its territory.

12.64   The prior notification and authorization procedures prescribed by Directive 85/611 come into play when units are 'marketed'[70] in a Member State other than the State in which the issuing UCITS is located.

12.65   The concept of marketing is not defined at European level.[71] As a result, every Member State has developed its own interpretation. A coordinated UCITS wishing to offer its units in any Member State must first acquaint itself with that Member State's interpretation in order to determine whether or not it is subject to the notification obligation provided for by Directive 85/611. This aspect would benefit from European harmonization, whether by the insertion of further particulars in Directive 85/611 or by the case law of the ECJ.

12.66   Pursuant to Directive 85/611, a UCITS that markets its units in another Member State must comply with any local laws, regulations, and administrative provisions not covered by Directive 85/611.

12.67   That obligation to comply with applicable local provisions must be qualified. According to case law of the ECJ concerning freedom to provide services, if the home State applies legislative, regulatory, and administrative requirements to coordinated UCITS, they must be taken into account by the host State. In that case, the host State may not require compliance with standards that are different but designed to achieve the same result.[72]

Marketing other UCIs in the EEA

12.68   UCIs other than coordinated UCITS are not eligible for the European passport under Directive 85/611. Their marketing in the EEA is subject only to the principles of the free movement of capital and the freedom to provide services.

---

[70]   Arts 44–47, Directive (EEC) 85/611.
[71]   Nevertheless, as regards the location of the offer and despite a different context, see the interpretative communication from the Commission of the European Communities entitled 'Freedom to provide services and the general interest in the Second Banking Directive' [1997] C 209/04/6.
[72]   See 7.82 above.

By virtue of these two freedoms, a non-coordinated UCI, such as a UCI **12.69**
investing in risk capital, may, in principle, market its units anywhere in the EEA,
subject only to any restrictions adopted in the public interest (such as those concerning the protection of public savings) in accordance with the principle of
proportionality.

In practice, application of the test of proportionality—including the equivalence **12.70**
test—frequently results in the elimination of national measures restricting the marketing of units in non-coordinated UCIs. As every Member State wants to protect
its nationals, the organization and marketing of non-coordinated UCIs are governed in many States by strict standards. The host State of a non-coordinated UCI
may not ignore the existence of a system of strict standards in the home State of
such UCI. If the object of the standards adopted by the host State is already achieved
by the standards established in the home State, the host State must take those into
account and may not apply its national standards to the UCI in question.

Communication between supervisory authorities

Cooperation between the authorities responsible for supervising UCIs is rooted **12.71**
in two legal principles.

The first, which applies without distinction to both coordinated UCITS and **12.72**
other UCIs, is the principle of close cooperation, as laid down by the EC Treaty
and interpreted by the ECJ. Under the principle of close cooperation, the Member
States are obliged, in particular, to facilitate achievement of the objectives of the
EC Treaty, including the free movement of capital. To that end, they must ensure
that their respective administrative authorities assist each other and send each
other the information necessary for the prudential supervision of UCIs marketing
their units in their territory.

The second legal basis for cooperation between the supervisory authorities of UCIs **12.73**
is Directive 85/611,[73] the scope of that cooperation is limited to the supervision of
coordinated UCITS. The authorities that may be sent information—in principle
confidential—concerning UCITS and their depositaries are covered in detailed
provisions. The use that may be made of those provisions is also limited.[74]

Whereas close cooperation is only required between the administrative **12.74**
authorities of the Member States, Directive 85/611 also governs the relations
between the authorities of the Member States and their counterparts in non-EEA
countries.

---

[73] Art 50, Directive (EEC) 85/611.
[74] See 8.85 *et seq* above.

Implementing powers of the Commission of the European Communities as regards UCIs

Principles

12.75 In its resolution on more effective securities market regulation in the European Union, the European Council of Stockholm of 23 and 24 March 2001 requested the implementation of the four-level approach proposed in the Committee of Wise Men's report, better known as the 'Lamfalussy Report'.

12.76 The 'Committee of Wise Men on the Regulation of European Securities Markets' had been commissioned to submit proposals to make the EU legislative process with regard to securities more flexible, more effective, and more transparent. The recommended procedure distinguished four levels:

- Level 1 would be the level of basic legal instruments, ie directives or regulations decided by co-decision of the Council and the European Parliament. These two institutions would also determine the nature and scope of execution measures (level 2) to be adopted in the light of Commission proposals.[75] The basic legal instruments would embrace the framework principles for regulation, which would be general but sufficiently precise standards reflecting basic political choices.

- Level 2 would embrace the adoption of technical implementation measures, primarily in application of comitology decisions.

- Level 3 would mainly be intended to guarantee consistent and timely implementation of level 1 and 2 measures thanks to enhanced cooperation and networking among EU securities regulators through the Committee of European Securities Regulators.[76]

- At level 4, the European Commission and the Member States would have to enforce stricter application of Community legislation.

12.77 Again according to the recommendations of the Lamfalussy report, this approach would have to be underpinned by two committees.

12.78 The first would be a new securities regulators committee made up of top-level representatives of the national supervisory authorities. It would be responsible for strengthening cooperation and exchanges between the national authorities in order to agree on common implementation standards in the area of securities (level 3).

12.79 The second committee would have two roles:

- The first role would be an advisory function, conferred upon it by decision of the European Commission, as part of which it would provide the Commission with advice on legislation (level 1).

---

[75] Which is not an innovation.
[76] For details of this Committee, see 12.80 below.

- The second would be a comitology role, vested in it by law, as part of which it would help the European Commission to exercise its implementing powers (level 2) in accordance with the regulation procedure laid down in Article 5 of the comitology decision.

On 6 June 2001, therefore, the European Commission adopted Decisions **12.80** 2001/527[77] and 2001/528,[78] respectively instituting the Committee of European Securities Regulators (CESR) and the European Securities Committee (ESC). The CESR was created to carry out level 3 tasks and to provide the European Commission with technical advice regarding basic instruments (level 1) and implementing measures (level 2). The ESC's mission is to advise the European Commission on the policy to be followed and on possible securities laws. It consists of high-level representatives of the Member States.

Directive 2005/1 of the European Parliament and the Council of 9 March 2005 **12.81** extended the Lamfalussy approach to other financial sectors,[79] *inter alia*, amending Directive 85/611 in order to reorganize the structure of the competent financial services committees.

Pursuant to Article 9 of Directive 2005/1, Section X of Directive 85/611 is now **12.82** entitled 'European Securities Committee' and no longer 'Contact Committe'. Moreover, Directive 2008/18 amended Article 53, as already amended by Directive 2005/1.[80]

Scope of implementing powers

In order to determine the exact scope of the implementing powers vested in the **12.83** Commission, it is necessary to take account of the principles of the EC Treaty in this area, the Comitology Decision as defined at para 12.86 below and the wording of Directive 85/611.

---

[77] Commission Decision (EC) 2001/527 of 6 June 2001, instituting the Committee of European Securities Regulators [2001] OJ L191/43.

[78] Decision (EC) 2001/528 of 6 June 2001 instituting the European Securities Committee [2001] OJ L191/45.

[79] Directive (EC) 2005/1 of the European Parliament and of the Council of 9 March 2005 amending Directives (EEC) 73/239, (EEC) 91/675, (EEC) 92/49, and (EEC) 93/6 of the Council and Directives (EEC) 94/19, (EC) 98/78, (EC) 2000/12, (EC) 2001/34, (EC) 2002/83 and (EC) 2002/87 reorganizing the structure of the competent financial services committees [2005] OJ L79/9.

[80] Art 53a was replaced by the following text: 'The Commission shall adopt technical amendments to this Directive in the following areas: (a) clarification of the definitions in order to ensure uniform application of this Directive throughout the Community; (b) alignment of terminology and the framing of definitions in accordance with subsequent acts on UCITS and related matters. Those measures, designed to amend non-essential elements of this Directive, shall be adopted in accordance with the regulatory procedure with scrutiny referred to in Article 53b(2). Article 53b 1. The Commission shall be assisted by the European Securities Committee instituted by Commission Decision 2001/528/EC 2. Where reference is made to this paragraph, Article 5a(1) to (4) and Article 7 of Decision 1999/468/EC shall apply, having regard to the provisions of Article 8 thereof.'

12.84 First, it is important to note that legislative power, within the Community legal order, is vested in the Council and the European Parliament, although the European Commission has, in principle, a monopoly of initiatives.

12.85 Moreover, implementing power is vested basically in the Council. However, as the Council is unable to exercise this power effectively, delegation of implementing powers to the European Commission has become the rule. Article 202, third indent, of the EC Treaty stipulates:

> To ensure that the objectives set out in this Treaty are attained the Council shall, in accordance with the provisions of this Treaty, . . . confer on the Commission, in the acts which the Council adopts, powers for the implementation of the rules which the Council lays down. The Council may impose certain requirements in respect of the exercise of these powers. The Council may also reserve the right, in specific cases, to exercise directly implementing powers itself. The procedures referred to above must be consistent with principles and rules to be laid down in advance by the Council, acting unanimously on a proposal from the Commission and after obtaining the opinion of the European Parliament.

12.86 The conditions by reference to which the implementing powers conferred upon the European Commission are exercised, were laid down in Council Decision 1999/498 of 28 June 1999,[81] hereafter referred to as the 'Comitology Decision'.

12.87 In addition, the provisions of the underlying legislation, ie Article 53a of Directive 85/611, confer the implementing powers upon the European Commission, subject to compliance with the third indent of Article 202 of the EC Treaty and the Comitology Decision.

12.88 The European Commission and its committees are not directly empowered by Article 202, third indent, of the EC Treaty and the Comitology Decision. These provisions merely determine the maximum scope of the implementing powers granted under the basic legal instruments. The Comitology Decision specifies that one of the implementing procedures, the regulatory procedure, may be used only to ensure application of the essential provisions of a basic instrument or to make it possible to adapt certain non-essential provisions of a basic instrument.

12.89 Lastly, according to ECJ case law, an implementing measure may not alter the scope of the obligations imposed upon the Member States by the basic Directive, nor may it affect the scope of the principles set out in the basic Directive. An implementing measure that modifies or contradicts the conception underlying the basic Directive is liable to be struck down.

---

[81] Council Decision (EC) 1999/468 of 28 June 1999 laying down the procedures for the exercise of the implementing powers conferred upon the Commission [1999] OJ L184/23.

The first indent of paragraph 1 of Article 53a of Directive 85/611 grants a first **12.90** implementing power consisting of the 'clarification of the definitions in order to ensure uniform application of this Directive throughout the Community'.

This power should be limited to definitions, ie only to concepts explained in the **12.91** Directive. This is shown by three elements of the Directive:

(1) The German version of Article 1a of the Directive, introduced by Directive 2001/107, begins with the following sentence: '*Für die Zwecke dieser Richtlinie gelten folgende Definitionen: . . .*'.
(2) An indicator of a definition is that the term defined in the Directive is placed in quotation marks. Such terms are moreover often presented in a sentence of the following kind: 'For the purposes of this Directive, . . . shall be . . .'.
(3) The second indent of paragraph 1 of Article 53a grants the implementing powers of 'harmonization of terminology' and 'reformulation of definitions'. The juxtaposition of these expressions implies both that the concept of 'definition' is more restrictive than that of 'terminology', and that definitions require adaptation efforts different to those concerning terminology, ie 'reformulation' rather than 'harmonization'.[82]

Clarification of certain simple concepts used by the Directive, such as derivatives, head office, prudential supervision, and marketing of units, is therefore not possible.

This view is not shared by the services of the European Commission, as discussed **12.92** in the CESR report of 28 October 2005. According to the Commission, the definitions should not be limited to Articles 1 and 1a of the Directive because such a formal approach would be inappropriate. This is an unconvincing argument.

According to Article 1 of Decision 1999/468,[83] organizing the comitology pro- **12.93** cess, the implementing powers are conferred upon the European Commission pursuant to the relevant provisions in the basic instrument, ie Directive 85/611. It is therefore irrelevant that the services of the European Commission feel it

---

[82] According to this approach, the clarification power therefore applies only to formulas explaining the following concepts in the Directive: (1) UCITS (Art 1.2); (2) common funds managed by investment companies (Art 1.3, para 2); (3) transferable securities (Art 1.8); (4) money market instruments (Art 1.9); (5) depositary (Art 1a, point 1); (6) management company (Art 1a, point 2); (7) management company's home Member State (Art 1a, point 3); (8) management company's host Member State (Art 1a, point 4); (9) UCITS home Member State (Art 1a, point 5); (10) UCITS host Member State (Art 1a, point 6); (11) branch (Art 1a, point 7); (12) competent authorities (Art 1a, point 8); (13) close links (Article 1a, point 9); (14) qualifying holdings (Art 1a, point 10); (15) ISD (Art 1a, point 11); (16) parent undertaking (Art 1a, point 12); (17) subsidiary (Art 1a, point 13); (18) initial capital (Art 1a, point 14); (19) own funds (Art 1a, point 15); (20) directors (Art 4, section 3, para 3); (21) activities of management of unit trusts/common funds and of investment companies (Art 5, section 5, para 2 and Annexe II).

[83] Council Decision (EC) 1999/468 (n 81 above).

would have been better if the implementing powers had been defined more broadly than they are in fact defined by the European legislature in this Directive.

12.94 Clarification is only allowed when a text is ambiguous, obscure, or inaccurate. According to case law of the ECJ, the clarification process may not add obligations to those stipulated in the basic instrument in question or modify the scope of that instrument. It must be limited to specifying and explaining the definitions concerned and should not create new obligations for the Member States.[84] For example, clarification may be necessary in the case of a vague definition requiring a clearer explanation.

12.95 Again according to the case law of the ECJ, an implementing measure involving essential elements of a Directive, such as its definitions, must contain simple procedures for implementing the basic Directive. It may not affect the scope of the principles defined in the Directive. An implementing measure that modifies or contradicts the premise underlying the basic Directive is liable to be struck down.[85]

12.96 The second implementation mission assigned to the ESC is to harmonize the terminology and reformulate definitions in the light of subsequent legal instruments on UCITS and related issues. This mission raises problems of validity under Article 2 of the Comitology Decision.

12.97 According to this provision, the European Commission and the ESC are only allowed to modify provisions of secondary importance ('non-essential provisions') in a basic legal instrument. Moreover, this modification right may only be used for adaptation and updating purposes, which suggests that factual or legal circumstances have changed since adoption of the provisions in question. Lastly, the right of adaptation may not be used for all non-essential provisions of a basic instrument but must be limited to certain of those non-essential provisions.

12.98 The implementation mission of harmonization of terminology and reformation of defintions entrusted to the ESC by Article 53a seems to overcome these restrictions. First, it is not expressly limited to non-essential provisions in Directive 85/611. Most of the definitions affected by the right of reformulation concern basic concepts of the Directive as described from its first provisions onwards. It may, moreover, be difficult to maintain that the entire technical vocabulary ('terminology') used in the Directive without definition does not concern essential

---

[84] See the ECJ decision of 20 March 1997, Case C-57/95 *France v Commission* [1997] ECR I-1650–1651, paras 19 and 23.

[85] See the ECJ decision of 18 June 1996, Case C-303/94 *European Parliament v Council* [1996] ECR I-2971 and 2972, paras 30 and 33, and the conclusions of Advocate General Tesauro in this case, paras 12 and 20.

provisions of the Directive. Secondly, the right of adaptation conferred upon the ESC does not appear to be limited to certain non-essential provisions in Directive 85/611.

In order to ensure that this right remains relatively useful, its application should **12.99** be limited to harmonization of terminology and reformulation of definitions of non-essential provisions in Directive 85/611.

Review and outlook

Looking beyond the legitimacy of the committees, discussed above, it seems **12.100** appropriate to begin taking stock of their activities despite their relatively recent creation. While the overall results are positive, they vary from one committee to the next.

The Contact Committee had *a priori* been granted sufficient authority to harmo- **12.101** nize the European regulations. In practice, these prerogatives did not give all of the expected results. Recognizing the relative failure of this committee, on 3 December 2002, the Council invited the European Commission to take the measures needed to transfer the missions and powers of this committee to existing bodies in the securities sector, particularly CESR.[86]

The acknowledged success of CESR is underpinned by the number and **12.102** quality of the reports produced by its expert groups, systematically chaired or supervised by a member of the committee and working on each issue according to precise terms of reference.

To convince the reader of CESR's efficiency, it may be useful to take an **12.103** example and to describe the operating method of the expert group on asset management.[87]

Initially conferred upon the Contact Committee, the responsibilities connected **12.104** with UCITS and management companies were assumed in practice by CESR during 2003. At the time, this committee took its mission fully in hand by orga- nizing a meeting attended by the main players in the investment fund industry. Based on information exchanged at this meeting, CESR subsequently distrib- uted a written consultation to review and determine the principles governing its

---

[86] The Commission has thus proposed a Directive that, *inter alia*, amends Directive (EEC) 85/611 and provides for repeal of the mission entrusted to the UCITS Contact Committee. As this amend- ment requires a corresponding and simultaneous amendment of the competences of the Committee of European Securities Regulators, as stipulated in Art 2 of Decision (EC) 2001/57, the Commission adopted the relevant decision on 5 November 2003 ((EC) 2004/7) [2004] OJ L3'32.

[87] Investment Management Group chaired by Lamberto Cardia (on the publication date of this work), who also chairs the Italian market authority.

services to the UCITS sector and to propose a list of priority projects.[88] The CESR consultation sparked a host of constructive replies that enabled the committee to see the real expectations of the investment funds market.[89]

12.105 This initial dialogue led to further consultations, allowing the experts in the area of asset management—and therefore UCITS—to propose, for example, ways to simplify the notification procedure referred to in Article 46 of the 1985 Directive.[90]

12.106 The proposals, recommendations, and calls for contributions issued by CESR have, on the whole, been responsible for the main advances towards a single market for investment funds since adoption of the 'UCITS III' Directives.[91] This is, at least, the opinion of the market players themselves, who see the organization of CESR as a major step towards harmonization,[92] and of the European Commission, which has acknowledged that the expert groups have made a decisive contribution.[93]

---

[88] 'CESR's Consultation on the role of CESR in the regulation and supervision of UCITS and Asset Management activities in EU', ref 03-441(5 November 2003).

[89] 'Results of CESR's public consultation on the role of CESR in the regulation and supervision of UCITS and Asset Management activities in EU', ref 03-499 (19 December 2003).

[90] 'CESR's guidelines to simplify the notification procedure of UCITS', ref 06-120b (June 2006).

[91] The following CESR publications are particularly important: *'Level 3 Guidelines on the classification of hedge fund indices as financial indices'* (17 July 2007); *'CESR's guidelines concerning eligible assets for instruments by UCITS'* (19 March 2007); *'CESR's guidelines to simplify the notification procedure of UCITS'* (29 June 2006); *'CESR Recommendation on Alternative Performance Measures'* (3 November 2005); *'CESR's recommendations for the consistent implementation of the European Commission's Regulation on Prospectuses No. 809/2004'* (10 February 2005); *'CESR's guidelines for supervisors regarding the transitional provisions of the amending UCITS Directives'* (3 February 2005); *'Recommendation for additional guidance regarding the implementation of International Financial Reporting Standards "IFRS"'* (30 December 2003); *'A European Regime of Investor Protection—The Professional and Counterparty Regimes'* (8 June 2002); *'A European Regime of Investor Protection— The Harmonisation of Conduct of Business Rules'* (9 April 2002). CESR has also launched many consultations, including: *'Second consultation regarding CESR's guidelines for supervisors regarding the notification procedure according to Section VIII of UCITS'* (1 June 2006); *'Consultation on CESR's recommendations for Alternative Performance Measures'* (11 July 2005); *'Second Consultation Paper on CESR's Draft Technical Advice on Possible Implementing Measures of the Directive 2004/39/EC on Markets in Financial Instruments'* (4 April 2005); *'Consultation on CESR's technical advice to the European Commission on possible measures concerning credit rating agencies'* (1 February 2005); *'Concept Paper on how CESR intends to measure equivalence between Third Country GAAP and IAS/IFRS'* (22 February 2004); *'CESR consults on Minimum Disclosure requirements for Sovereign Issuers and Financial Information on Prospectus'* (30 October 2003). All these documents are available at <http://www.cesr-eu.org>.

[92] See the interview with Xavier Musca, Director General of the Treasury and Economic Policy, 'Europe financière: recréer une dynamique' (2005) 217 *Revue L'Hémicycle* 8. See also Olivia Dufour, 'L'harmonisation européenne est en marche' (March 2007) 667 *Revue Banque*, where the author states that 'the largest obstacle to modernisation of the UCITS Directive was removed when management was added to the scope of competence of the CESR, allowing it to use the Lamfalussy procedure'.

[93] *The Green Paper of the European Commission on the enhancement of the EU framework for investment funds*, issued on 12 July 2005, SEC (2005) 947. In this paper, the Commission specifies that 'good cooperation and the commitment of the national supervisory authorities acting within the

This success obviously calls for a few unavoidable changes in the investment fund **12.107** industry. Some stakeholders have already urged that CESR should be granted the right to take direct EU-level decisions on highly integrated market activities.[94] However, this should not affect either the division of legislative power between the Council, the European Parliament, and the Commission or its organization, nor should it allow the Commission to exceed its powers under Directive 85/611, the EC Treaty, and the Comitology Decision.

Whether upstream from or incidental to the 'traditional' use of its powers, the **12.108** European Commission intervenes regularly in the environment of UCIs without going through either of the above-mentioned committees.

The Commission's Green Paper on the 'enhancement of the EU framework for **12.109** investment funds', published in July 2005, illustrates its aim (to boost the development of the fund sector) and the method currently favoured (broad consultation with stakeholders on a proposal for a Directive). This Green Paper advocates a prudent and concerted approach by the Commission.

The European Commission begins by describing the principal requirements to **12.110** improve the legislative framework governing UCITS. Briefly put, the European Commission urges better use of the potential offered by existing legislation[95] rather than a radical overhaul of existing legislation. The Green Paper further poses a series of questions to investment fund players in order to gather their complaints and suggestions. Finally, the Green Paper announces the creation of two expert groups, one for researching market inefficiencies, the other for studying alternative investment funds.[96]

Both expert groups have already presented their reports to the Commission. They **12.111** have subsequently been discussed at a public hearing attended by the authorities and industry representatives[97] and have been the subject of ample comment.

These reports exemplify the quality of the initiative taken by the European **12.112** Commission. In response to demands from the main players, the experts have

---

framework of the CESR thus appear to be a key ingredient of the search for pragmatic solutions to implementation problems'.

[94] CESR report 'Which supervisory tools for the EU securities markets?' (25 October 2004) (known as the 'Himalaya Report').

[95] See *The Green Paper of the European Commission on the enhancement of the EU Framework for investment funds* (issued on 12 July 2005, SEC (2005) 947) Introduction, 2.

[96] Commission Decisions of 5 December 2005, C(2005) 4653 and C(2005) 4654.

[97] See '*Report of the Expert Group on Investment Fund Market Efficiency*'; '*Report of the Alternative Investment Expert Group— Managing, Servicing and Marketing Hedge Funds in Europe*'; '*Report of the Alternative Investment Expert Group—Developing European Private Equity*' published in July 2006. The public hearing was held in Brussels on 19 July 2006. The purpose of this type of hearing is to allow the authorities and other stakeholders to respond to expert reports from a perspective other than that of the industry.

highlighted the difficulties of this market segment, making it possible to look beyond the necessary development of common definitions for particular concepts (such as 'private equity', 'alternative investments' and so on) and to align the structures of specific funds (such as hedge funds and private equity funds) and to facilitate their marketing across Europe.

12.113 Lastly, these reports and the responses to them have enhanced the keenly awaited White Paper on investment funds that the European Commission published in November 2006.[98]

---

[98] Commission White Paper of 15 November 2006 on enhancing the single market framework for investment funds (COM (2006) 686 final, available on the Commission's website). The report starts from the premise that Directive (EEC) 85/611 is no longer able to support the fund industry to meet new competitive challenges and the changing needs of investors. Therefore, the White Paper proposes several ways of improving the Directive: the Commission wants to remove administrative barriers to cross-border marketing, facilitate cross-border fund mergers and asset pooling, establish a European passport system dedicated to management companies, and strengthen supervisory cooperation. As regards the interests of the end-investor, the Commission wants to simplify further the rules applicable to prospectuses and improve the distribution of funds through MiFID. Lastly, with respect to non-harmonized retail funds, the Commission would also like to establish a European passport system, yet there are numerous obstacles hindering such establishment.

13

RISK CAPITAL INVESTMENT COMPANIES

Legal Framework

Origin

13.01   Luxembourg is no newcomer to investment in risk capital.[1] Since the beginning of the 1980s, successive laws on UCIs have invariably allowed this type of investment. Circular 91/75 provides a framework of particular rules[2] to UCIs 'the principal object of which is the investment in risk capital'.

13.02   Moreover, Luxembourg has traditionally been home to risk capital companies not governed by the legislation on UCIs. As we have seen,[3] an investment vehicle can avoid the status of UCI—even when it invests according to the principle of risk spreading—if it does not raise money from the public. In this case, it opts for the status of an unregulated company. Such a company may be organized to invest in risk capital without being subject to the CSSF's prudential supervision.

13.03   So why resort to the SICAR to invest in risk capital? There are several good reasons to do so, owing to certain shortcomings in the laws governing UCIs and in general company law.

13.04   When a risk capital company opts for the 2002 Act, it cannot avoid certain disadvantages of operating under the Act and the corresponding regulations which can hamper the organization and growth of such vehicles.

13.05   First, the Act requires recourse to a reputable promoter, as defined by the CSSF, without whose services no UCI can be created in Luxembourg under the 2002 Act. Next, the 2002 Act lays down a series of rules that are easily complied with by traditional UCIs but which should be more flexible to cater for the particular features of the life cycle and operation of companies investing in risk capital. Such companies are often organized for a limited period. They arrange to obtain funds from investors during the initial commitment or subscription phase and call funds as and when they make their investments. In view of the processes used to select and monitor target companies, the risks of such companies are more concentrated than those of traditional UCIs. Once they have invested their capital, they frequently keep their investments on a long-term basis. Occasionally, stakes may be sold and a portion of the sales proceeds distributed to investors by repaying capital or distributing income with the balance being reinvested in a new investment. These features often make the normal operating rules of traditional UCIs unsuitable.

---

[1]   The content of this chapter is based on an article by C Kremer and I Lebbe entitled 'Les sociétés d'investissement en capital à risque' *Luxembourger Wort*, 24, 25, 26, and 28 June 2004.

[2]   Ch I, I, Circular 91/75.

[3]   See 2.85 and 2.86 above.

In addition, the provisions for risk capital funds in Circular 91/75 no longer **13.06** reflect subsequent developments in private equity structures. The concept of risk capital has evolved in ways not foreseen by the regulations at the time of drafting.

Circular 91/75 defines risk capital as investment 'in securities of companies that **13.07** either have been recently formed or that are still in the course of development'.[4] This definition covers only a portion of a broader segment of unlisted companies that cannot access the stock market for a variety of reasons, not necessarily their degree of maturity, and includes companies whose capital is held by a small group of entrepreneurs who do not want to, or are unable to, open the capital to a larger group of investors, thus putting the stock exchange out of reach. These are often family firms whose owners do not want too many outside investors. The category of start-ups or venture capital companies is part of a broader class of private equity companies, which includes investment in more mature companies. The regulation introduced by Circular 91/75 does not provide the qualifications or nuances needed to provide a suitable framework for this type of product.

The legislature initially contemplated a refinement of Circular 91/75. This plan **13.08** was finally abandoned on the grounds that it would be more useful to adopt a special law.

As compared with the 2002 Act, the Act of 13 February 2007 on SIFs represents **13.09** a more attractive framework for private equity investment strategies.[5] Many of its provisions directly come from the Act of 15 June 2004 on the SICAR. However, since a SIF is a UCI, it remains subject to the risk-spreading principle. This principle, as interpreted by the CSSF,[6] usually requires investment to be made in at least three target entities. Moreover a SIF does not benefit from a specific 'private equity' label, as it makes it possible to implement very different investment policies. Lastly, SIFs are subject to the tax rules applicable to UCIs. In some circumstances, those rules may be less favourable than those governing SICARs.

The use of a normal company for risk capital investment is not without drawbacks **13.10** either. The general provisions of company law may turn out to lack flexibility in certain respects, such as with respect to changes in share capital, payment of dividends, and the repurchasing of shares from investors. Moreover, a company whose object is to invest in risk capital according to the principle of risk spreading cannot raise money from the public without being reclassified as a UCI.

---

[4] Ch C, II, 4.1, Circular 91/75.
[5] C De Boeck and E d'Anterroches 'SIF: a new investment vehicle suitable for private equity' in *Specialised Investment Funds* (Arendt & Medernach, 2007) 220.
[6] Circular 07/309.

13.11   Both these flaws in the 2002 Act and in general company law, as well as the observation that investment in risk capital is a growing business, prompted the preparation and adoption of the Act of 15 June 2004. From inception it was agreed that it would not supersede the existing regime for UCIs and non-regulated companies investing in risk capital but provide a streamlined new framework for private equity investment in the widest meaning of the term.

13.12   A working group was set up at the initiative of ALFI and the ABBL with the participation of other professional organizations with links to the financial sector. The work of this group culminated in a summary report, which was discussed with the CSSF and then followed by the preparation of the Bill[7] leading to the Act of 15 June 2004 on risk capital companies (SICARs).

Legal and regulatory status

13.13   The status of a SICAR is not easy to define. It is a hybrid version of the UCI and an unregulated company, and may resemble either.

13.14   At first sight, the SICAR could be considered a UCI governed by a special law, such as SIFs. Like traditional UCIs, SICARs require prior authorization from the CSSF. They are also subject to permanent prudential supervision throughout their existence. Their head office must be situated in Luxembourg. The custody of their assets must be entrusted to a depositary. Their capital may be variable. Many of the principles governing their operation are taken directly from the 2002 Act or influenced heavily by that Act. They have also been taken up in the Act of 13 February 2007 and apply to SIFs. The SICAR/SIF regime distinguishes companies established as SICARs and SIFs from normal unregulated companies whose creation and operation are not subject to the same rules and constraints.

13.15   That said, a SICAR cannot be considered a UCI within the meaning of the term in Luxembourg. It is not obliged to meet one of the criteria determining the status of UCI in that its investment policy is exempt from the principle of risk spreading. This reflects the object of a SICAR and the legislature intentionally refrains from specifying risk spreading as a requirement for SICARs in the Act of 15 June 2004.[8] This distinguishes the SICAR from UCIs, which are subject to the principle of risk spreading, and makes it similar to—but not identical with—ordinary unregulated companies.

13.16   To distinguish them clearly from the rules for UCIs and the general law provisions applicable to commercial companies, SICARs were subjected to a special law, ie the

---

[7] *Parliamentary doc* No 5201.
[8] Art 1(1), Act of 15 June 2004.

Act of 15 June 2004. The concept of risk capital within the meaning of this law was subsequently explained in Circular 06/241.

Organization

Basic features

Object

According to the Act of 15 June 2004, the object of a SICAR must be 'to invest its **13.17** assets in securities representing risk capital in order to provide its investors with the benefit of the result of the management of its assets in consideration for the risk they incur …'.[9]

Investment activity

As its name indicates, the SICAR is an investment company. Its object is to carry **13.18** on an investment activity[10] as opposed to a holding activity. The SICAR buys financial assets in the risk capital category with the aim of selling them at a profit. It is not a holding company, which can restrict itself to keeping assets acquired by it. According to the CSSF,[11] the 'holding period' is a key factor in determining whether the planned investment falls within the sphere of a SICAR's object. This factor is assessed differently depending on the type of target asset. For example, while a SICAR specialized in venture capital may buy into a start-up and keep its stake for several years in its portfolio—during the initial growth phase—a SICAR investing in a more mature company can reasonably be expected to sell its interest in the shorter term.

Holding companies and SICARs each have their own special status in Luxembourg **13.19** and carry on different activities. Does this mean that a holding company cannot be converted into a SICAR? Not necessarily. A holding company may be converted into a SICAR provided it changes its object or at least adopts activities falling within the scope of the Act of 15 June 2004.

Investment in risk capital

General Investment in risk capital is defined as 'the direct or indirect contribu- **13.20** tion of assets to entities with a view to their launch, their development or their listing on a stock exchange'.[12] According to the Parliamentary documents for the

---

[9] ibid.
[10] ibid.
[11] Section I, Circular 06/241, 3.
[12] Art 1(2), Act of 15 June 2004.

Act of 15 June 2004, this definition is merely given as an example. An investment in risk capital is a high-risk investment for its investors, in return for which they hope to earn higher profits than those that would have been generated by a more traditional investment. The risks connected with risk capital investment include the risk of limited liquidity and high volatility due to the lack of maturity of the target companies.[13]

13.21 The definition is extremely general and covers the area of both venture capital and private equity. According to the authors of the Act of 15 June 2004, these two concepts are not identical but require similar techniques in practice. Venture capital means 'capital made available to start-ups or high-growth sectors', whereas private equity is defined 'broadly as any investment in an unlisted privately held company'.[14]

13.22 In fact, both definitions are too narrow. Private equity is a generic term and covers a range of activities, primarily including venture capital.[15] The wide range of investments available to private equity investors explains the difficulty of defining once and for all this multi-faceted concept.[16] Without claiming to be exhaustive, the following paragraphs give a few criteria and examples to facilitate understanding of this term.

---

[13] *Parliamentary doc* No 5201, Comments on the Articles, 22.

[14] ibid Explanatory statement, 1.

[15] 'The venture capital fund is the archetypal private equity fund' (JM Schell, *Private Equity Funds: Business Structure and Operations* (Law Journal Press, 2004) §1.03); 'The venture capital refers to equity investments made for the launch, early development, or expansion of a business' (U Grabenwarter and T Weidig, *Exposed to the J-Curve, Understanding and Managing Private Equity Fund Investments* (Euromoney Books, 2005) 19).

[16] eg the European Private Equity & Venture Capital Association (EVCA) defines private equity as follows: 'The universe of all venture investing, buyout investing and mezzanine investing. Fund of fund investing and secondaries are also included in this broad term' (definition available on the EVCA website at <http://www.evca.com> under the heading: 'Glossary of terms'). G Sharp explains how difficult flexibility makes such a definition: 'Although the definition is straightforward, a closer examination will reveal the flexibility—not to mention the potential for immense complexity—which lies behind such a superficially simple concept. It will also begin to explain why the private equity markets have seen enormous growth since the early 1980s and are now such a significant element of corporate finance activity across Europe' (G Sharp, *European Private Equity: a practical guide for vendors, managers and entrepreneurs* (Euromoney Books, 2002)). As a result, certain authors prefer to base their definition of private equity on the list of activities embraced by this concept. Thus, JM Schell writes: 'it is worth emphasizing that there is no single "market" for private equity funds. . . . The literature on private equity funds is too limited for there to be any conventional listing of private equity fund categories. Nonetheless, it is likely that many participants in the private equity fund arena would accept the following list as representing distinct categories of private equity funds: Venture Capital Funds, Leveraged Buy-out, Hedge Funds, Funds of Funds, Real Estate Funds' (Schell (n 15 above) §1.02[2]. See also Grabenwarter and Weidig (n 15 above) 3; in a more original, yet too general way C Demania defines private equity as 'an equity or quasi-equity fund investment . . . for a fixed maximum period of time . . . involving specific risks . . . aiming at high profitability . . . made for qualified investors' (*Introduction to private equity* (Paris: Revue Banque Editions, 2006) 18).

Investment in private equity is driven by the need for an entity to finance a project **13.23** or a particular business plan that is too risky for a loan by a credit institution and too large to be financed internally.[17] Private equity financing is riskier than more traditional loans but promises significant returns linked to the results of the target entity.[18] Private equity investors frequently do not merely contribute fresh capital but involve themselves more or less directly in the management of the target entity. In this respect, they resemble entrepreneurs.[19]

The liquidity of a private equity investment is low due to the lack of a market in **13.24** the securities issued by the financed entity. This is why such investments are often made with a long-term view.

Venture capital is a sub-category of private equity and its historical forerunner.[20] **13.25** In 1946, it was formally defined by the investment firm American Research and Development. Its characteristics have, by and large, remained the same ever since. Eligible target entities had to develop new technologies, new sales principles, or new products. Their staff had to be particularly skilled and their products or manufacturing techniques had to be adequately protected by intellectual property rights such as patents, trademarks, and patterns.[21] They had to grant investors relatively significant power to intervene in their management so as to allow them to contribute not just fresh capital but also their experience, network of contacts, and know-how. Lastly, the securities acquired by venture capital investors had to be transferable after a few years, whether as part of a public offering, a listing, or a private sale.

---

[17] Grabenwarter and Weidig (n 15 above) Introduction, xv; G Mougenot, *Tout savoir sur le capital investissement* (Gualino, 3rd edn, 2005) 15.

[18] 'Private equity financing is fundamentally different from loan agreements, under which lenders receive interest, wait for repayment of the lent capital and are generally priority creditors. Private equity financing is a capital transaction whose profitability depends upon the growth and earnings capacity of the financed business' (M Eisenhuth and A Gosset, 'Les Private Equity Funds' in *Droit bancaire et financier au Luxembourg* (Larcier, 2004) Vol 4, 1707). As the CSSF writes in Circular 06/241, 'the primary purpose of the SICAR is to develop and/or to "create value" at the level of the entities in which it invests'; Mougenot (n 17 above) 17.

[19] See the research conducted by Global Insight, Inc, 'Venture Impact 2004: Venture Capital benefits to the US Economy', at the request of the National Venture Capital Association (NVCA): 'Venture capital addresses the funding needs of entrepreneurial companies that generally do not have the size, assets, and operating histories necessary to obtain capital from more traditional sources, such as public markets and banks. Far from being simply passive financiers, venture capitalists foster growth in companies through their hands-on involvement in the management, strategic marketing, and planning of their portfolio companies. Venture capitalists invest alongside management and employees through equity financing and the practice of using stock option plans to motivate all workers. They are entrepreneurs first and financiers second'.

[20] Eisenhuth and Gosset (n 18 above) 1701.

[21] JW Bartlett, *Fundamentals of Venture Capital* (Madison Books, 1999) 3; see also the example of risk capital with regard to Silicon Valley, as explained by E Dubocage and D Rivaud-Danset, *Le capital-risque* (Paris, Editions La Découverte, 2006) 61 *et seq.*

13.26 Capable of generating high returns, investment in venture capital entails major risks owing to the fact that it essentially targets new projects or young, developing activities.[22] This was followed by the development of other forms of private equity that were less risky for investors, such as investment in companies in a more advanced growth phase following the lack of certainty of survival surrounding the start-up of their activities.[23]

13.27 The geographical location of a target entity does not by itself determine whether an investment should be classified as risk capital. Each case needs to be analysed individually. Classification as risk capital may stem from political risk in addition to other particular risks. Investment in companies in regions with a high political risk seems possible provided there is evidence of sufficient growth to create value at the target company.[24]

13.28 **Variants of risk capital** Risk capital therefore groups an array of different activities, presented below in chronological sequence of the entity to be financed.[25]

13.29 In the very first stage, seed capital is injected to fine-tune a new concept or product.[26]

13.30 Once this first step has been completed, another form of finance may be needed to develop the concept or new product and to prepare its marketing. This type of financing is generally known as start-up funding.

---

[22] See in particular Grabenwarter and Weidig (n 15 above) 19: 'Venture capital investments are riskier than later-stage private equity investments from various perspectives. Companies financed through venture capital are typically not self-sustainable at the time of investment. Especially in the seed and early-stage phase they are often cash burning. Their aim is to develop a product with a market potential that later in the company's life hopefully outweighs the losses accumulated in the early years of existence. During this development phase, venture capital-financed companies are exposed to a series of risks that are ultimately borne by the venture capital investor such as: (i) technology risk—the company's product or service may prove to be unviable or obsolete by the time it is marketed; (ii) timing risk—competitors might come up with a similar or identical product in a shorter time; (iii) refinancing risk—the company may be unsuccessful in getting the funding required to bring its product to the market; and (iv) risk of lacking management quality—these companies' business concepts often depend on a deep, sometimes scientific, knowledge of the products underlying technology. The departure of key individuals may put an end to the company's development potential.'

[23] 'Private equity, put simply, is an investment option that provides equity capital to (mostly) unlisted enterprises and companies at various stages of the business cycle. Private equity is sourced away from public markets and is typically used for: early stage venture capital opportunities, to expand working capital, to make strategic acquisitions, or to assist in the restructure, change or ownership, or partial sale of a business' (P Hodgson, 'Private equity investing: your guide to this emerging asset class', in *Fundamental, Invesco's education supplement*, May 2002, Issue No 2, document available at <http://www.invesco.com.au>.

[24] Section II, Circular 06/241.

[25] See also 'Report of the Alternative Investment Expert Group' (July 2006) published by the European Commission and available at <http://ec.europa.eu> under the heading 'Internal market'.

[26] This is the type of financing that made it possible to test and develop, for example, the game *Trivial Pursuit* prior to marketing.

Lastly, a product or concept that is already marketed is not immediately profitable, **13.31** which may justify another call for funds known as early-stage financing.

These three activities are undeniably venture capital operations in that they focus **13.32** on the very first phases of a product or concept launch.[27] An investor specialized in this type of financing shows special characteristics and specific expertise. He not only provides a business with finance, he generally also contributes his management, marketing, and recruitment experience. Often referred to as business angels,[28] such investors are normally themselves entrepreneurs. In addition to their financial and intellectual contributions to the entity they finance, their participation frequently acts as a catalyst for other investors. Companies targeted for investment by investors specialized in venture capital will subsequently find it easier to attract other private equity investors.

Once a company's product has been marketed and has generated profits, that **13.33** company may need additional financing to boost its product development, increase its production capacity, or extend its geographical coverage. This kind of financing falls into the category of private equity rather than venture capital. Such investments are less risky than those needed to launch a product or to start an activity. They may in fact be made on the basis of financial data that was not previously available.

Private equity can also be used to finance the replacement of a shareholder **13.34** ('replacement capital'), such as when a group is restructured or when, as a result of a decision of anti-trust authorities, a business is ordered to dismantle a dominant position and sell part of its business to third parties.

A frequent example of private equity is the financing of management buy-outs **13.35** and management buy-ins.

Lastly, private equity may be used to bail out troubled companies, in which case it **13.36** is known as rescue or turnaround financing.

---

[27] '[Venture capital] comprises the sub-classes seed financing, start-up financing and expansion financing. Seed financing typically refers to the financing provided for research and the development of an initial business concept. The start-up segment targets companies in the development phase of their product up to the initial marketing. In this phase, companies may have some revenues from cooperation agreements but typically have no commercial revenues. The expansion phase segment finally provides finance for the marketing of the product. Companies in this phase have significant revenues although they may still be cash burning.' (Gravenswarter and Weidig (n 15 above) 19).

[28] 'High net worth investors who directly invest in new and/or growth businesses typically adopt a hands-on approach, providing the target company with a significant strategic contribution through their business experience, their skills and their relations', A Schmitt, 'La société d'investissement en capital risque en droit luxembourgeois' in *Droit bancaire et financier au Luxembourg* (Larcier, 2004) Vol 4, 1660 and 1661; 'Business angels . . . are usually entrepreneurs or former entrepreneurs and their experience is at least as valuable as their money' (Mougenot (n 17 above) 19).

13.37   Under certain circumstances, the financing of listed companies may amount to a risk capital investment. A typical example is the leveraged management buy-out or buy-in, in which a listed company repurchases its shares and withdraws its listing to become privately held (known as a public-to-private buy-out).

13.38   More generally, the purchase of shares in a listed company may indicate the characteristics of a private equity investment owing to higher-than-average risk and unusually high yield expectations. When such a company has lost value and could regain value after a restructuring or a management reshuffle, a private equity investor could acquire control, make the necessary improvements, and sell it a few years later. In this case, it may not be desirable to de-list it in order to preserve the liquidity of its securities and to allow the investor to divest at the appropriate time.

13.39   The CSSF pays careful attention to risks of abuse when a SICAR acquires securities from a listed company in order to de-list those securities. The SICAR must have exit strategies with respect to the investment, in the event of the takeover bid being unsuccessful.

13.40   The purchase of listed securities may also take the form of a private equity investment when the securities are traded on a stock exchange that does not meet the criteria applicable to regulated markets. The same situation exists when securities listed on a regulated market have been issued by a risk capital entity. For instance, investments in listed small companies could be eligible investments for a SICAR, as the initial public offering of such a company will not necessarily make the investment unattractive to a SICAR.[29]

13.41   Indeed, the Act of 15 June 2004 and its preparatory documents do not rule out investment in listed securities. Article 1(2) specifies that a risk capital investment is to be understood as 'the direct or indirect contribution of assets to entities with a view to their launch, their development or their listing on a stock exchange'. The references to companies in the start-up and initial public offering phases primarily concern the funding of unlisted companies. In contrast, the reference to companies in the development phase provides for investment in companies with a certain maturity—and possibly already listed—but entering a new development phase, for example connected with the marketing of new products, the acquisition of another company, or the conquest of a new market.

13.42   This interpretation is confirmed by the preparatory work for the Act of 15 June 2004. Thus, the *Conseil d'État* has specified that 'investment in an already listed company

---

[29]   Section II, Circular 06/241.

is eligible if it is made when the company is launched or when the company enters a new development phase'.[30]

It is impossible to make an exhaustive inventory of the many different forms of private equity. The important factor in all these examples is the SICAR's objective of contributing to the development of the entities in which it invests. The concept of development is used in the general meaning of the term as value creation at the level of the target company, which can take different forms.[31] **13.43**

In general, investments made by SICARs represent development capital for the target entity. However, an injection of fresh capital is not always required. Risk capital securities acquired on the secondary market are also eligible. **13.44**

In order to maximize returns, SICARs often help to manage target companies, by providing advice or being represented on management bodies. They will endeavour to create value by restructuring and modernization measures, and will promote any measures intended to improve the allocation of resources. **13.45**

The active involvement of SICARs in order to create value at the target companies is nevertheless not always required, as other factors—such as the financing method or the nature or remuneration of the stakeholders—may show that a risk capital investment is involved. However, when a SICAR invests in only one target company, active involvement in management is a key criterion. **13.46**

Private equity real estate   Does the concept of private equity cover real estate investments? The answer is yes, provided certain conditions are met. In this respect, Anglo-Saxon practice distinguishes between what it calls private equity real estate and traditional property investment. The former activity involves higher risks than traditional real estate, permitting its qualification as private equity. Although the relevant criteria need to be assessed in each individual case and are liable to change, they can be summarized as follows: **13.47**

- *Risk profile.* Private equity real estate investments generally target assets with a higher risk than traditional property investments. However, a particularly high investment risk or a location in a country with a certain political risk does not in itself qualify investment in real estate as a risk capital investment. Such a special risk may, for instance, lie in the fact that the building is hard to lease or situated in a disaster stricken or down-market area. While not always a decisive

---

[30] *Parliamentary doc* No 5201[4], Opinion of the *Conseil d'État*, 5. See also Comments on the Articles, according to which 'paragraph (2) of Article 1 of the Act of 15 June 2004 defines risk capital as an investment of funds, which may be more or less direct, in entities in order to drive their launch, development, initial public offering or expansion'. The reference to companies in the expansion phase definitely seems to include listed companies embarking upon a new growth phase.

[31] Section I, Circular 06/241; for a comment on the application of this circular to the real estate sector, see P Goebel, 'La SICAR en tant que véhicule d'investissement immobilier' (2008) *ACE* 3.

factor, the political risk may also be taken into consideration. In contrast, the price risk generated by soaring prices in certain property markets is not an adequate criterion, unlike the transfer risk and legal risk that may result from the geographical location of the underlying buildings.[32]

- *Value creation.* This is the intention of developing the purpose or use of the buildings and therefore going beyond the mere collection of income generated by the buildings. Value creation at the level of the underlying building can be defined broadly as a change in existing conditions. It can take several forms, such as efforts to increase the value of the building by means of renovations, renegotiation of contracts, changing tenants, and restructuring of the portfolio.

- *Management method.* Entities investing in private equity real estate generally hold their property assets for less than five years, in contrast with vehicles investing in traditional property, whose object is to hold property with stable revenues for the long term. Vehicles investing in private equity real estate are therefore normally managed more actively than vehicles investing in traditional real estate, which have more static portfolios. As a SICAR is an investment company, its object should be to buy in order to sell at a profit. For example, a SICAR's policy could not just be to hold or manage real estate portfolios or property owned by a family, business, or group.[33]

- *Projected returns.* The returns targeted for private equity real estate are higher than those projected for traditional real estate. Certain authors set the projected returns at 15 per cent per annum.[34]

- *Liquidity.* Investments in private equity real estate are generally less liquid than traditional property investments.

- *Use of leverage.* Vehicles looking for maximum returns and investing in private equity real estate often use larger leverage than vehicles investing in traditional real estate. Leverage for vehicles in private equity real estate frequently exceeds 70 per cent of their assets.[35]

- *Investment by the promoter/manager.* Another characteristic of entities specializing in private equity real estate is that their promoter/manager generally holds an interest, ensuring that the promoter/manager's interests are compatible with those of the investors.

- *Target investors.* As investment in private equity real estate is generally riskier than investment in traditional property, vehicles investing in private equity real estate are reserved for well-informed and seasoned investors.

---

[32] ibid.
[33] ibid.
[34] P Linneman and S Ross, 'Real estate private equity funds' (Spring 2002) *Wharton Real Estate Review* 7.
[35] ibid.

A SICAR can therefore engage in two types of real estate investments. Either by **13.48** investing in privately held companies specializing in real estate or buying its own private equity real estate. Such purchases are of necessity made by financing intermediate vehicles. A SICAR cannot invest directly in a building as the Act of 15 June 2004 only allows it to finance 'entities'.[36] A building does not constitute a legal 'entity'.

Exclusion of risk capital   Not every risky activity constitutes a risk capital **13.49** investment within the meaning of the Act of 15 June 2004. For instance, investment in high-risk distressed debt assets or in high-risk junior tranches issued by securitization vehicles do not themselves qualify as a risk capital activity under the Act of 15 June 2004.[37] The issuer or the assets underlying such securities must always be eligible by virtue of the above criteria. While junior debt securities do not represent risk capital in themselves, they could under certain conditions be accepted as a means of financing an eligible entity.

Investment in works of art normally does not qualify as risk capital either. While **13.50** this activity may have a 'risk' factor, it is not accompanied by the wish to develop the business and to create value. This is why SICARs are not allowed to carry on this activity.[38]

The boundary between hedge fund type activities and private equity type activities **13.51** is more obscure. Many hedge funds engage in private equity investments, closing the gap between these two business lines. Certain authors are already categorizing hedge funds as private equity,[39] although there is no consensus as yet. Like the above-mentioned investment in works of art, the purpose of investment in derivatives is not to develop or to create value at the level of the assets underlying such instruments. In view of this uncertainty, the CSSF does not allow SICARs to pursue a policy of investing in derivatives for speculative purposes. Derivatives may only be used for hedging purposes and in pursuance of risk capital investment policies.

Other aspects   In referring to the concept of direct or indirect investment, the **13.52** legislature has not limited the form that risk capital can take. It may take the form of investment in shares, bonds, or other securities issued by target companies. Moreover, the Act of 15 June 2004 does not rule out loan finance, including mezzanine loans, bridging finance, convertible bonds, and other non-securitized receivables.

A SICAR may pursue its investment policy indirectly, ie through intermediate **13.53** vehicles. Several cases are possible.

---

[36]   Art 1(2), Act of 15 June 2004.
[37]   Section II, Circular 06/241.
[38]   Circular 06/241.
[39]   See Schell (n 15 above) §1.02[2].

13.54   A SICAR may be used as a feeder in a master/feeder structure. In this case, the master must be eligible as a pure private equity fund. However the CSSF does not require complete compatibility between the SICAR's investment policy and the SICAR Act.[40] The SICAR's prospectus describes the contemplated investment in such a way that the 'risk' and 'development' components are mentioned to investors. The SICAR's annual report indicates the investments made by the master fund.[41]

13.55   A SICAR may also act as a fund of funds in investing in a number of private equity UCIs. In this case, the SICAR's annual report indicates the names and main features of the target funds. It does not necessarily include an exhaustive list of the investments made by those funds.[42]

13.56   Lastly, a SICAR often invests in a target company through an intermediary or 'special purpose vehicle' (SPV). In that case, the CSSF considers that the SPV is transparent. Having regard to the Act of 15 June 2004, the eligibility of the investment is established taking into account the target entity. It is the same target entity which is described in the SICAR's annual report.[43]

13.57   When a SICAR holds funds and is required to wait before investing them, it may nevertheless invest those funds. The investment must ensure the invested capital is maintained. The CSSF authorizes, for example, demand or term deposits or investments in money market instruments or in liquid bonds issued by high-quality issuers. However, it does not recommend that investments should be made in shares or other related securities.[44]

13.58   The methods by which SICARs may divest entities in which they have invested are not regulated either. Thus it is possible to sell holdings or assets, to transfer them to another entity, or even to divest them by means of an initial public offering.[45]

No obligation to spread risks

13.59   A SICAR is not obliged to comply with the principle of risk spreading when selecting investments. This is one of the most salient differences from the legislation on UCIs. One of the key features of a UCI is the obligation to invest according to the principle of risk spreading. This is the case regardless of a UCI's status (coordinated UCITS or other type of UCI) or the category of investor it targets (publicly distributed UCI within the meaning of the 2002 Act or SIFs). In contrast, a SICAR is authorized to hold, for example, only one or two companies in an

---

[40] CSSF Annual Report for 2007, 96.
[41] CSSF Annual Report for 2006, 105.
[42] ibid.
[43] ibid.
[44] CSSF Annual Report for 2007, 97.
[45] Section I, Circular 06/241, 3

extremely small niche market, for instance in biotechnology or geological prospecting. According to the Parliamentary documents for the Act of 15 June 2004, this is justified by the 'difficulties and length of time involved in the selection of and support for the development of target companies'.[46] Assistance to a start-up may, for example, require such a large investment of financial and human resources that a SICAR may very well decide not to make other risk capital investments. In such cases, the CSSF will allow a SICAR to hold a single target company if it can give good reasons for this limitation. The CSSF will, *inter alia,* check that the SICAR actually has the intention and resources to involve itself actively in the management of the target entity.[47]

Eligible investors

The legislature wants a SICAR's increased risk to be understood and accepted by the SICAR's investors. This is why SICARs must reserve their securities for well-informed investors.[48] The concept of informed investor is the subject of a detailed definition.   **13.60**

According to the Act of 15 June 2004,[49] a well-informed investor is: **13.61**

- an institutional investor;
- a professional investor; or
- any other investor who, while not an institutional or professional investor, gives certain assurances demonstrating his understanding of the increased risk connected with investment in the SICAR.

The assurances to be given by an investor who is not an institutional or professional investor can be given in either of two ways: **13.62**

(1) the investor confirms in writing that he is a well-informed investor and agrees to invest at least €125,000 in the SICAR; or
(2) the investor has obtained an assessment by a third party certifying his expertise, experience, and knowledge in adequately appraising a risk capital investment.

The third party in question can only be a credit institution, an investment company within the meaning of MiFID, or a management company within the meaning of Directive 2001/107. The written assessment by a professional of the financial sector may be conducted by agreement with the client, for example under a discretionary mandate in the case of the provision of wealth management   **13.63**

---

[46] *Parliamentary doc* No 5201, Comments on the Articles, 22.
[47] Section I, Circular 06/241.
[48] Art 1(1), 3rd indent, Act of 15 June 2004.
[49] ibid Art 2.

services by the professional of the financial sector.[50] The qualification of informed investor reflects the relevant recommendations from the Forum of European Securities Commissions,[51,52] now included in Annexe II to MiFID.

13.64 In its current version, the Act of 15 June 2004 provides that the eligibility conditions imposed on investors do not apply to the general partners of *sociétés en commandite* (limited partnerships and partnerships limited by shares). This exemption has turned out to be too restrictive in that other parties may contribute to the management of a SICAR. Moreover, the SICAR may have been incorporated in a legal form different from that of a *société en commandite*. Company managers and members of the board of directors should not be required to meet the definition of well-informed investor. Hence the proposal to exempt 'all conducting persons and other persons involved in the management of a SICAR'. That proposition is expected to lead to the amendment of Article 2 of the Act of 15 June 2004. The conducting persons are those persons who are governed by Article 12(3) of the Act of 15 June 2004. The persons involved in management are the persons 'who actually manage a SICAR's investments, including those who are employed by a management company'.[53]

13.65 Neither the Act of 15 June 2004 nor the relevant Parliamentary documents define the categories of institutional or professional investors.

13.66 For the first category, we refer to the interpretation given in connection with the Act of 13 February 2007 and, previously, with the 1991 Act.[54,55]

13.67 The category of professional investors is defined as follows in Annexe II to MiFID:

(1) entities that are required to be authorized or regulated in order to operate in the financial markets, ie credit institutions, investment firms, other authorized or regulated financial institutions, UCIs and their management companies, pension funds and their management companies, insurance companies, dealers in commodities and their derivatives, certain local businesses, and other institutional investors requiring the same type of authorization;

---

[50] *Parliamentary doc* No 5201, Comments on the Articles, 24.
[51] ibid 23 and 24.
[52] 'Implementation of article 11 of the ISD: categorisation of investors for the purpose of conduct of business rules', FESCO document (March 2000), available at <http://www.cesr-eu.org> under the heading 'Documents'. The Forum of European Securities Commissions (FESCO), made up of representatives from 17 prudential supervision authorities in the EEA, has prepared a paper on the categorization of investors for the purpose of the conduct of business rules adopted in application of Art 11 of Directive (EEC) 93/22 on investment services in the securities field.
[53] *Parliamentary doc* No 5842, Comments on the Articles, 6.
[54] See 2.63 *et seq* above.
[55] *Parliamentary doc* No 5616.

(2) large corporations that individually meet the following criteria:
   (a) balance sheet total: €20 million,
   (b) net turnover: €40 million,
   (c) shareholders' equity: €2 million;
(3) national governments, central banks, international and supranational institutions such as the World Bank, the International Monetary Fund, the European Central Bank, the European Investment Bank, and other similar international organizations;[56]
(4) other institutional investors whose core business is to invest in financial instruments, especially entities engaged in the securitization of assets or other financing transactions.

The concepts of institutional investor and professional investor sometimes tend to be synonymous with each other. Annexe II to MiFID does not refer to the institutional investor as such and uses the term 'professional' for certain entities that are classified as institutional pursuant to the Act of 13 February 2007.

13.68

It may be that an intermediary company is used between the SICAR and its investors. For example, the CSSF authorizes the investment in a SICAR by a Luxembourg or foreign UCI. Such a UCI is a professional investor as defined in Annexe II to MiFID. This also applies to large corporations as described in the Annexe. Similarly, an ordinary commercial company or an investment company may acquire securities of the SICAR, provided that such investment is made on an ancillary basis.[57] Yet, the CSSF wants to avoid abuses. An entity may on no account be used between the investors and a SICAR to avoid the restriction whereby only well-informed investors may acquire securities of a SICAR.[58] It is the SICAR's duty to check the absence of abuse and to confirm such absence to the CSSF, as the case may be.

13.69

Intentional adoption of SICAR status

For the authors of the Act of 15 June 2004, it was essential to make sure that adoption of the status of SICAR was intentional and not accidental. In other words, the regime in the Act of 15 June 2004 is not intended to replace the rules governing other vehicles investing in risk capital. It coexists with the 2002 Act and the Act of 13 February 2007, pursuant to which UCIs may still be formed. Nor does it bar companies governed by the general provisions of the 1915 Act from carrying on a risk capital activity even though they do not have the status of either a UCI or a SICAR.

13.70

---

[56] FESCO document referred to above, para 10.
[57] CSSF Annual Report for 2007, 98.
[58] ibid.

Structure and operation

Company law aspects

Legal forms

13.71 Owing to its legal form, a SICAR's founders can choose between the following structures:[59],[60]

- *société anonyme*—SA;
- *société à responsabilité limitée*—SARL;
- *société en commandite simple*—SCS;
- *société en commandite par actions*—SCA;
- cooperative society organized in the form of an SA.

This calls for several observations.

13.72 First, as its name indicates, a SICAR must be incorporated as a commercial company. It may not be constituted as an FCP. The exact reasons for this restriction are difficult to determine. The Parliamentary documents for the Act of 15 June 2004 do not discuss this issue. A possible explanation is that the FCP structure was reserved for UCIs. The legislature may have wanted to avoid extending a legal form reserved for UCIs to the 'hybrid' regime for SICARs. The legislature may also have based itself on foreign precedent in the area of risk capital and therefore have preferred the form of an SCS or an SCA, closer to the limited partnership of Anglo-Saxon law.

13.73 A SICAR may adopt the legal form of a cooperative society organized in the form of an SA, under the 1915 Act as amended in 1999, when Luxembourg law was enhanced with specific legislation for pension funds.[61] Although this form preserves the basic features of a cooperative (the fact that partners can withdraw, make variable investments in the company, and, in principle, cannot transfer their shares), it is governed by rules inspired directly by those governing the organization and operating method of SAs.[62] In practice, it has been used very infrequently, if at all.

---

[59] Art 1(1), 1st indent, Act of 15 June 2004.

[60] Since there is no official translation into English of the above-listed structures, the latter have been maintained in French. However, as mentioned in the section entitled 'Acronyms and Abbreviations', an SA may be referred to as a limited company; an SARL, as a private limited company; an SCS, as a limited partnership; and an SCA, as a partnership limited by shares.

[61] Act of 10 June 1999 amending the 1915 Act (*Mémorial* A 1999, 1469); Act of 8 June 1999 creating pension funds in the form of a *société d'épargne-pension à capital variable* (pension savings company with variable capital—SEPCAV) and an *association d'épargne-pension* (pension savings association—ASSEP) (*Mémorial* A 1999, 1476), as amended by the Act of 1 August 2001 (*Mémorial* A 2001, 2194).

[62] See C Kremer and A Contreras 'Les fonds de pension soumis a contrôle prudentiel de la commission de surveillance du secteur financier' in *Droit bancaire et financier au Luxembourg* (Larcier, 2004) Vol 4, 1747 *et seq*.

Lastly, a SICAR can adopt the traditional form of an SA or an SARL.   **13.74**

Any SICAR, regardless of its legal form, remains subject to the general rules   **13.75**
governing commercial companies under the 1915 Act, insofar as these are not
expressly disapplied by the Act of 15 June 2004.[63] This means that all features of
a particular type of company must be taken into account, even if the company in
question is a SICAR. This is, *inter alia*, the case with the restrictions on the right
to transfer shares in an SCS or an SARL.

SICARs are often created on behalf of a limited number of investors who wish to   **13.76**
retain maximum control over their structure. The *société en commandite* is an
excellent legal form to achieve this aim. The promoter, who, as the general partner,
has unlimited liability as well as far-reaching management powers, coexists with
the investors, who are limited partners and play a more passive role. Depending
upon whether the company is incorporated as an SCS or an SCA, it is either
considered a partnership or a corporation. Lastly, an SARL may be a suitable legal
form if the aim of the investors is to keep their group small. The legal restrictions
on the right to transfer shares ensure that the structure remains 'captive'. Finally,
the legal form of the SA has proven its value in the area of UCIs and was therefore
considered a useful option for SICARs.[64]

Share capital

Variability   With one exception, any SICAR, other than a SICAR established in   **13.77**
the form of an SCS, may stipulate in its articles that its capital is variable.[65] In this
respect, the Act of 15 June 2004 differs from the legislation on UCIs, under which
only SAs may vary their capital.

SICARs created in the form of an SCS are not entitled to vary their capital. The   **13.78**
reason for this lies in the specific features of the legal system applicable to SCS. As
a partnership, an SCS is not subject to the formal rules governing incorporation
and changes in the share capital of SAs. An SCS can be formed by means of a private
agreement, without the obligation to use a notary. The same method may be used
to amend the constitutive documents, including capital increases and decreases.
There is no mandatory pre-emptive right. Only excerpts of the constitutive
document and its amendments are published in the *Mémorial*. This fast-track
procedure reflects the unlimited and joint liability of the general partners, which
makes protection of the share capital less critical. Thus, the legislature did not
deem it useful to derogate from this procedure by providing for variable capital.

---

[63] Art 3, Act of 15 June 2004.
[64] The operating rules of these different types of company have already been discussed in other
sections of this work, to which the reader is referred. See in particular 2.129 *et seq* above.
[65] Art 4(2), Act of 15 June 2004.

13.79 However, constraints linked to capital increases in SCS should also have been taken into account. First, only a general meeting of partners may decide on a capital increase. Such decision necessitates amendment of the constitutive instrument and requires the unanimous approval of the partners, unless the latter provide for a specific (simple, absolute, two-thirds . . .) majority vote in the articles of incorporation. The validity of such statutory clauses is nevertheless subject to divergent positions.[66] Moreover, the information on partners' contributions as well as on the amounts to be paid up to the company on contributions must be made public. The 1915 Act requires the publication of an extract of the company instruments containing at least 'the amount of the corporate capital and details of the assets contributed or to be contributed to the SCS, with details of the corporate capacity in which they have been contributed or promised; . . . a precise designation of the limited members who must contribute assets, with details of the obligations of each of them'.[67] Any amendment to those provisions must also be published.[68]

13.80 When they are applied to the SICAR, those voting and information requirements create considerable complexity for the process of raising and making calls on capital. The funding of a SICAR is usually made through the subscription commitments of investors. The names of investors as well as the amounts committed must be made public pursuant to the law. Currently no derogation from this obligation seems possible.

13.81 Once it has collected commitments to subscribe from its investors, the SICAR calls the committed funds as and when necessary. The payment of those funds is made through a subscription of shares or units. Within an SCS each of those calls must be decided by a general meeting of partners, since it entails a increase of the capital of the company. When the funds have been paid, a new publication is necessary to inform third parties on the amounts contributed to the company as well as on the outstanding amounts to be paid by each of the partners. Publication is also necessary whenever the payment is made to the company of amounts initially subscribed.

13.82 Distributions to partners are subject to the same rules when they take the form of capital repayments and reduce the capital of the SCS.

13.83 All those requirements do not really meet the need for flexibility, promptness, and discretion of the relevant parties in private equity and most probably explain the reasons why very few SICARs are incorporated in the form of SCS.

---

[66] J Van Rijn and J Heenen Vol I, para 307 are against; see, however, C Matray and F Ringlheim, 'La société en commandite simple', in *Traité pratique de droit commercial* (1998) Vol 4, para 134, according to whom 'the articles of incorporations of SCS often include a clause organising general meetings on the basis of the operating rules of deliberative boards'.
[67] Art 6, 1915 Act.
[68] ibid Art 11*bis*, 1(2).

For all these reasons, a legislative amendment extending the benefit of variable **13.84** capital to SCS and derogating from the publication requirements regarding the amounts contributed or promised by the partners has been proposed by the Luxembourg Chamber of Commerce[69] and the Luxembourg *Conseil d'État*.[70] It would encourage the use of this corporate form and the tax transparency which it permits.

This said, a SICAR incorporated as an SCS is free to borrow funds from its partners. **13.85** Such borrowings are legally distinct from contributions.[71] They are not included in the corporate capital and therefore they are not subject to the rules described above.

Minimum capital A SICAR's subscribed share capital, together with issue **13.86** premiums,[72] may not be less than €1,000,000.[73] This is a slightly lower amount than is stipulated for UCIs,[74] whose capital may not be less than €1,250,000. This minimum threshold must be reached within twelve months from authorization of the SICAR.[75] This is twice the time available to UCIs governed by the 2002 Act[76] and adds flexibility to the financing of SICARs.

Legal reserve SICARs are not obliged to set up a legal reserve.[77] The rule is the **13.87** same as for SICAVs, who likewise are not obliged to establish a legal reserve.[78] The variable nature of the capital makes it unnecessary to impose an intangible legal reserve.

The Act of 15 June 2004 releases SICARs from the obligation to build a legal **13.88** reserve even when their articles do not provide for variable capital. This distinguishes them from UCIs, particularly SICAFs, which remain subject to the legal reserve requirement.

---

[69] *Parliamentary doc* No 5842, Opinion of the Chamber of Commerce, 10–11.

[70] ibid Opinion of the *Conseil d'État*, 4–5.

[71] G Ripert, R Roblot, under the direction of M Germain, Traité de droit commercial, (Paris: LGDJ, 18th edn, 2002) paras 1056–1057, 1222, and 1605. The author notably points out that 'in some cases, it is quite difficult to distinguish a *commandite* from a loan with participation in profit. The distinction lies in the obligation to participate in losses which may imply a contribution loss'; Matray and Ringelhim (n 66 above) para 124.

[72] Once Art 4(1), Act of 15 June 2004 has been amended as proposed in *Parliamentary doc* No 5842, so that issue premiums can be taken into account in the calculation of the minimum capital. In this respect, it is worth mentioning that, in contrast to corporate capital, the amount of issue premiums must be directly and fully paid up (Art 32-2, 1915 Act), which considerably limits the practical interest of this funding method.

[73] Art 4(1), Act of 15 June 2004.

[74] Arts 27(1) and 70, 2002 Act for SICAVs; Arts 23 and 74(1), 2002 Act for other types of UCI; Arts 21, 27, and 39(1), Act of 13 February 2007.

[75] Art 4(1), Act of 15 June 2004.

[76] Arts 23, 27, 70, and 74(1), 2002 Act. That period is also 12 months for SIFs (Arts 21, 27, and 39(1), Act of 13 February 2007).

[77] Art 6(1), Act of 15 June 2004.

[78] Art 32(2), 2002 Act.

13.89   The Act of 15 June 2004 draws few distinctions between SICARs with variable capital and SICARs with fixed capital. The main difference between these SICARs lies in the fact that, as regards SICARs with variable capital, 'variations in the capital shall be effected . . . *ipso jure* and without the necessity for compliance with measures regarding publication and entry in the trade and companies register'.[79] Increasing or reducing the share capital of a SICAR with fixed capital therefore requires a decision to that effect as well as compliance with several publication measures.

13.90   As for the rest, provisions regarding subscriptions,[80] distributions,[81] and repayments[82] to investors apply without distinction to both structures. Does this imply that SICARs with fixed capital and SICARs with variable capital may be subject to identical rules, save for the provisions governing the process and publication of a variation in the capital? SICARs with fixed capital benefit from a greater level of flexibility, as compared to SICAFs, with respect to subscriptions, distributions, and repayments to investors.

Distributions and repayments to investors

13.91   Distributions and other repayments to investors by SICARs are not subject to restrictions other than those stipulated in their articles,[83] which may, *inter alia*, provide for payment of interim dividends.

13.92   This is a much more flexible regime than that for SICAVs and SICAFs, whose payouts may never reduce the net assets below certain thresholds, which vary depending on their legal form.[84]

13.93   Moreover, in the case of SICAFs, distributions and other repayments to shareholders may be financed only by means of 'distributable' reserves and may not affect certain accounting ratios between assets and shareholders' equity.[85] SICAFs are further subject to particular conditions and formalities with regard to interim dividends.[86] These rules, taken partly from the 1915 Act, have been lifted for SICARs.

13.94   Lastly, the Act of 15 June 2004 does not specifically provide for the redemption of a SICAR's shares. Since such a transaction amounts to a repayment to investors, any restriction the shareholders would like to impose on redemptions would have to be stipulated in the articles of incorporation.

---

[79]   Art 4(2), Act of 15 June 2004.
[80]   ibid Art 5(1).
[81]   ibid Art 6(2).
[82]   ibid.
[83]   ibid Art 6(2) and (3).
[84]   See 5.102–5.108 above.
[85]   ibid.
[86]   ibid.

Securities

Securities that may be issued   No provision in the Act of 15 June 2004 lists or **13.95** restricts the securities a SICAR is authorized to issue, allowing full application of the 1915 Act in this respect. Based on its own needs and those of its investors, a SICAR organized in the form of an SA or SCA may issue participating shares, founder shares, bonds, and other securities pursuant to the 1915 Act. Here, too, the Act of 15 June 2004 is less restrictive than the 2002 Act, which prohibits any UCI other than a SICAF governed by Part II of this same Act from issuing founder shares or similar securities.[87]

A SICAR with the status of an SARL has the same scope as a SICAR established **13.96** as an SA or an SCA with respect to the type of share capital that may be issued, with a few minor differences. It is not barred from issuing founder shares, even if not expressly provided for in the 1915 Act. The 1915 Act nevertheless limits financing by means of bonds or equity securities.[88] Equity securities may not be issued to more than forty investors,[89] while bonds may not be issued to the public.[90] Although these restrictions are not necessarily an obstacle for a SICAR wishing to work with a limited group of investors, they must not be overlooked when plans are made to open up the SICAR to a larger public.

Issue of securities   A SICAR may issue new securities according to the procedures **13.97** and in the forms provided for in the articles of incorporation.[91] The authors of the Act of 15 June 2004 wanted SICARs to have considerable flexibility in their search for capital. In this respect, the rules for SICARs are quite different from those applicable to UCIs.

The issue price of shares in a SICAV governed by the 2002 Act must in principle **13.98** reflect net asset value, ie the SICAV's net assets divided by the number of shares in issue.[92] This rule becomes a genuine obstacle when investors make their payments according to a timetable geared to the company's investment needs.

In the case of UCIs investing in risk capital, capital adjusted to the company's **13.99** investment needs is often financed according to the so-called subscription commitment technique. At the time of the initial offering the investor agrees to

---

[87] Arts 31, 40, and 71, 2002 Act. This interdiction was not incorporated in the Act of 13 February 2007.

[88] Art 188, 2002 Act.

[89] This limit may only be exceeded when shares are transferred in the case of death or partition of a marital community (Art 181, 1915 Act).

[90] Art 188, 2002 Act.

[91] Art 5(1), Act of 15 June 2004.

[92] For a detailed description of the rules governing the issue of shares by investment companies governed by the 2002 Act, see 5.123 *et seq* above. This regime does not apply to SIFs, which are free to determine the issue price of their shares (Arts 8 and 28(2), Act of 13 February 2007).

subscribe a certain amount of shares. Whenever funds are called, payments are offset by new share issues based on net assets at the time of issue.

13.100 New securities can only be issued at the net asset value. However, when the holdings bought by the investment company are not listed, their successive valuations only rarely reflect their real value. Any error or inaccuracy in valuing assets is likely to dilute (or enhance) the earnings of existing investors compared with new investors.

13.101 To overcome this drawback, the investment company could consider issuing partly paid-up shares, which would be paid up as and when funds are called. However, according to the 2002 Act, shares issued by a SICAV must be fully paid up.[93] While this restriction does not apply to SAs with fixed share capital, the 1915 Act nevertheless requires at least one-quarter of each share to be paid up,[94] which is often more than the company needs to make its first investments.

13.102 These difficulties are avoided by the regime for SICARs. First, shares do not necessarily have to be issued at the company's net asset value. A SICAR's articles of incorporation are free to stipulate another calculation reference, such as a predetermined nominal value or the accounting par value, possibly combined with an issue premium. Secondly, the Act of 15 June 2004 sets the minimum share fraction that has to be paid up at 5 per cent.[95] This makes the regime far more flexible since it lowers the traditional minimum payment of 25 per cent to a percentage that is better geared to the requirements and constraints of risk capital investment vehicles.

13.103 SIFs benefit from the same rules as those governing SICARs on these points.[96]

Umbrella SICARs

13.104 The original version of the Act of 15 June 2004 did not provide for the creation of SICARs with multiple sub-funds. This has quickly turned out to be a major drawback. SICAR practitioners have proposed an amendment to the Act of 15 June 2004 to authorize SICARs to set up an 'umbrella' structure. The regime would be the same as for UCIs, to which it refers without comment.[97]

Regulatory aspects

Supervision by the CSSF

13.105 The CSSF is responsible for the prudential supervision of SICARs.[98] The Act of 15 June 2004 specifies the nature of this supervision, stipulating that the CSSF

---

[93] Arts 28(8) and 71, 2002 Act.
[94] Art 26(1), 4, 1915 Act.
[95] Art 5(2), Act of 15 June 2004.
[96] Art 28(2) and (3), Act of 13 February 2007.
[97] *Parliamentary doc* No 5842, Art II. For further details on umbrella structures, see 2.166 *et seq* above.
[98] Art 11(1), Act of 15 June 2004.

must ensure that SICARs and their conducting persons comply with the applicable legal and contractual rules.[99]

Initial authorization   A SICAR is not allowed to carry on its activities without initial authorization.[100] The Act of 15 June 2004 provides for the principle of authorization but does not require it to be granted before a SICAR is actually launched.[101] Nevertheless, the collection of savings from investors when a SICAR has not yet been entered in the CSSF's list of SICARs is a criminal offence.[102] This distinguishes SICARs from SIFs. SIFs may collect subscriptions or subscription commitments from investors, even if not yet authorized by the CSSF. **13.106**

As in the case of UCIs, the CSSF approves the constitutive documents and the choice of depositary.[103] Authorization further requires evidence that the SICAR's head office is based in Luxembourg.[104] However, the CSSF is nevertheless less demanding in this respect than vis-à-vis UCIs and notably allows delegation of net asset value calculation to a foreign entity.[105] Once approved, the SICAR is entered on a list maintained by the CSSF.[106] **13.107**

Permanent supervision   Like UCIs, SICARs are subject to permanent prudential supervision by the CSSF. The rules are lighter than for UCIs, as explained below. **13.108**

When they are being authorized, SICARs receive a circular letter from the CSSF asking them to send to the CSSF semi-annual financial information. This information must at least cover: **13.109**

(1) the SICAR's assets and liabilities, including the total amount of its assets;
(2) detailed information on the SICAR's portfolio;
(3) the amount of the subscribed capital, the paid-up capital, and the aggregate subscription commitments;
(4) the type of investors who have subscribed for shares of the SICAR;
(5) as the case may be, information on the level of indebtedness of the SICAR.[107]

Such information must be provided to the CSSF within forty-five days from the reference date. Moreover, the CSSF requires to be furnished with a copy of the financial reports as sent by the SICAR to its investors.[108] **13.110**

---

[99] ibid Art 11(3).
[100] ibid Art 12(1).
[101] ibid.
[102] ibid Art 42.
[103] ibid Art 12(2). As for the list of documents to be provided to the CSSF, see the CSSF Annual Report for 2006, 90 and 91, and the CSSF Annual Report for 2007, 98.
[104] Art 12(5), Act of 15 June 2004.
[105] CSSF Annual Report for 2005, 91.
[106] Art 13(1), Act of 15 June 2004.
[107] CSSF Annual Report for 2005, 91.
[108] ibid 92.

Status of conducting persons and promoter

13.111   A SICAR's conducting persons must be authorized by the CSSF.[109] Although inspired by the rules applicable to UCIs governed by the 2002 Act, the authorization procedure is fundamentally different in two respects.

13.112   The 2002 Act not only requires authorization of a UCI's formal conducting persons (directors of the investment company or the management company of an FCP) but also of all those 'who effectively determine the conduct of the activities' of the UCI.[110] Thus the CSSF has extended the authorization procedure to the promoters and managers of the UCI.[111]

13.113   For a SICAR, authorization is only required for those who formally represent the company, such as general partners at SCAs and SCS, company directors at SAs and managers at SARLs. These conducting persons are subject to the CSSF's prior verification of their probity and professional experience,[112] based on their track record and an excerpt from their police record or a similar document. The CSSF also asks to be provided with a statement sworn by the proposed conducting persons stating that they have not been convicted of criminal offences and that they are currently not being prosecuted for criminal offences.[113] The CSSF also requires an initiator's representative or an independent expert in private equity to be included among the conducting persons.

13.114   Under the rules on SICARs, the CSSF does not verify the 'status and financial situation of the manager to whom the conducting person may have delegated management', on the grounds that 'all investors in a SICAR are institutional, professional or informed investors and are therefore sufficiently experienced to judge for themselves the qualifications of the manager and the potential consequences from his possibly restricted financial experience'.[114]

13.115   Moreover, in contrast with the rules on UCIs governed by the 2002 Act, the CSSF does not require that a SICAR has a promoter and does not subject promoters of SICARs to prior authorization and special responsibility towards investors.[115]

13.116   According to the Parliamentary documents for the Act of 15 June 2004, the proposed regime 'also takes account of the fact that such promoters and managers do not necessarily have the financial experience of promoters and managers approved by

---

[109]   Art 12(3), Act of 15 June 2004.
[110]   Art 93(3), 2002 Act.
[111]   For a detailed discussion of this issue in the regime for UCIs, see 4.07 above.
[112]   *Parliamentary doc* No 5201, Comments on the Articles, 28 and 29.
[113]   CSSF Annual Report for 2007, 98.
[114]   *Parliamentary doc* No 5201, Comments on the Articles, 29.
[115]   ibid. For the concept of promoter in the context of UCIs, see 4.01 *et seq* above.

the CSSF'[116] for UCIs. For the same reasons the legislature applied identical rules to SIFs with respect to their conducting persons and promoters.

Correspondents of the CSSF

Depository   The custody of a SICAR's assets must be entrusted to a depositary.[117]   **13.117**
The requirements for this function are very similar to those applicable to UCIs.

As in the case of UCIs other than coordinated UCITS, the depositary must have   **13.118**
its registered office in Luxembourg or else must be established in Luxembourg
through a branch, with no obligation for the parent company to have its registered
office within the EEA. The depositary must be a credit institution within the
meaning of the 1993 Act.[118] The depositary's role is similar to that of a depositary
of a UCI. The concept of custody has the same meaning as under the rules for
UCIs, to which the law refers in full.[119]

The Act of 15 June 2004 entrusts the depositary with the following tasks, with   **13.119**
respect to the supervision of transactions undertaken by SICARs:

(1) ensuring that the subscription price of the SICAR's securities is received by
     the SICAR within the times stipulated in the constitutive documents;
(2) ensuring that, in transactions involving the SICAR's assets, consideration is
     paid or delivered within the customary times; and
(3) ensuring that the SICAR's income is allocated in accordance with its constitutive
     documents.

It is currently proposed that the depositary should be no longer obliged to   **13.120**
perform those tasks. The proposed new legislature wants to align the respective
sets of rules governing SICARS and SIFs on that issue. In particular, the legislature
considers that such tasks do not correspond to any specific need of private equity
structures.[120]

The rules governing the liability of SICAR depositaries have also been aligned   **13.121**
with those applicable to UCIs, with the difference that a SICAR's depositary
incurs liability vis-à-vis the investors through the SICAR. If the SICAR does not
take action, despite an investor's written request to this effect, the investor may
directly invoke the depositary's liability within three months of the date of the
request to the SICAR to take action.[121] These rules are the same as those applicable

---

[116] *Parliamentary doc* No 5201, Explanatory statement, 3.
[117] Art 8(1), Act of 15 June 2004.
[118] ibid.
[119] See 6.320 *et seq* above.
[120] *Parliamentary doc* No 5842, Art II.
[121] Art 9(3), Act of 15 June 2004.

to FCPs pursuant to the 2002 Act and the Act of 13 February 2007.[122] Despite similar wording, an equivalent right to take action directly has not been granted to the shareholders of investment companies governed by the 2002 Act or the Act of 13 February 2007. The right to sue the depositary belongs exclusively to the company itself and not to its individual shareholders.[123]

13.122 **External auditor** SICARs are obliged to use the services of an external auditor to check the accounting data in their annual report.[124] This is the same requirement as for UCIs and does not call for particular discussion.[125]

13.123 In his audit of the financial reports, the external auditor verifies the increase in value of the SICAR's assets. Where there is a divergence between such value and his valuation results while using the same calculation method, the external auditor alerts the shareholders by issuing a specific document, the so-called 'matter of emphasis'.

13.124 With respect to investments made by the SICAR, the CSSF also assigns a 'whistle blowing' duty to the external auditor. The CSSF asks the auditor to be informed 'forthwith and on the external auditor's initiative if he becomes aware that the SICAR's assets are not or have not been invested in accordance with the rules provided for by law or in the articles of incorporation'.[126]

13.125 Lastly, the CSSF calls for the management letters issued by the auditor in his auditing of the annual accounts to be transmitted to it as soon as the SICAR receives those letters. If no management letter has been sent to the SICAR, the CSSF asks to be provided with a written declaration by the auditor confirming that no management letter has been issued for the relevant SICAR.[127]

Head office

13.126 Like UCIs, SICARs must have their registered office and their head office in Luxembourg. The Act of 15 June 2004 does not discuss the relevant criteria, which it leaves to the CSSF to set out in detail. The criteria are less stringent than those governing the head office of UCIs. Here, once again, the CSSF does not feel the same need for strict intervention, owing to the profile of the target investors.

13.127 A SICAR's head office agent need not necessarily be a professional of the financial sector, in contrast with the requirements for UCIs set out in the 1993 Act.[128] The CSSF merely needs to be shown that the relevant entity has the human and technical resources needed to manage the head office services of the SICAR in question.

---

[122] Arts 19(2) and 66, 2002 Act; Art 17(2), Act of 13 February 2007.
[123] Arts 36, 40, 71, and 75(6), 2002 Act; Arts 35 and 40(2), Act of 13 February 2007.
[124] Art 27(1), Act of 15 June 2004.
[125] For further details, see 8.29 *et seq* above.
[126] CSSF Annual Report for 2007, 97.
[127] ibid 98.
[128] Art 29-2, 1993 Act.

Functions may be delegated to foreign entities as long as they do not lead to **13.128**
complete—or almost complete—relocation of the head office to a foreign country.
For example, the calculation of the net asset value may be made elsewhere than in
Luxembourg.[129]

Information for investors

Prospectus and annual report   The prospectus of a SICAR must contain the **13.129**
information necessary to enable investors make an informed assessment on the
proposed investment.[130] The provisions in the Act of 15 June 2004 are very similar
to those in the 2002 Act and the Act of 13 February 2007, to which it refers.

In its Annual Report for 2006,[131] the CSSF gives its interpretation of the legal **13.130**
requirements relating to the content of the prospectus. In this respect, it formulates
some requirements and also provides a series of recommendations. The prospectus
of a SICAR must provide investors with transparent and adequate information on
the following:

• the investment policy;
• the risks inherent in such policy;
• the decision-making processes;
• the rules regarding the distribution of dividends;
• the remuneration of managers;
• other costs and commissions to be borne by the investors.

Moreover, the CSSF recommends that the prospectus should inform investors on **13.131**
the relevant procedure and conditions for any major change to the operation of the
SICAR. Changes to the characteristics of the SICAR or the composition of its managing bodies, or the replacement of a service provider, are mentioned as examples.[132]
This would also apply to any change in the investment policy.

The essential data in the prospectus has to be updated only when additional secu- **13.132**
rities are issued.[133] Here, the legislature is more flexible than with respect to UCIs
governed by the 2002 Act, which have the ongoing obligation to keep the contents
of their prospectus continually up to date.[134] For their part, SIFs are subject to very
similar rules in this respect.[135]

---

[129] CSSF Annual Report for 2005, 91.
[130] Art 24(1), Act of 15 June 2004.
[131] CSSF Annual Report for 2006, 104.
[132] ibid.
[133] Art 26, Act of 15 June 2004. This provision would also have to be amended according to
SICAR practitioners. The requirement to update a prospectus should only apply in the case of
additional securities issued for 'new investors'. When additional securities are issued exclusively for
existing investors, such an update should not be necessary.
[134] Art 112, 2002 Act.
[135] Art 54, Act of 13 February 2007.

13.133 Moreover, in contrast with the 2002 Act, the Act of 15 June 2004 does not include an annex describing the minimum content of the prospectus or a precise outline of the contents of the annual report.[136]

13.134 The SICAR must prepare and publish an annual report for each financial year. The annual report must be published within six months from the end of the period under review.[137] This six-month period is identical to that for SIFs.[138] However, it is longer than the four months applicable to UCIs.[139] It reflects the fact that a SICAR may require more time to value its holdings in unlisted companies.[140] The SICAR is not obliged to detail the content of its portfolio in its annual report.

13.135 In contrast with UCIs governed by the 2002 Act, SICARs are not obliged to publish a semi-annual report. Lastly, again in contrast with UCIs governed by the 2002 Act,[141] SICARs are not obliged to keep the annual report available for investors at a place mentioned in the prospectus.[142]

13.136 **Other information** UCIs governed by the 2002 Act must publish the issue, sales, and redemption price of their shares whenever they issue, sell, or redeem shares. Coordinated UCITS must do so at least twice a month and other UCIs in principle once a month.[143] SIFs are not obliged to publish such information.

13.137 No such constraint exists for SICARs either. The Act of 15 June 2004, requires SICARs to inform investors of the net value of their shares if investors request this information, in which case the information must be provided at least once every six months and free of charge. This does not oblige SICARs to calculate the net asset value of these securities at the same frequency. The net asset value can be calculated once a year. This obligation to supply information should be withdrawn under the proposed amendment to the Act of 15 June 2004, on the grounds that the concept of net asset value is seldom significant in the context of private equity.[144]

Valuation of assets

13.138 Valuation of a SICAR's assets is always based upon fair value. This value is determined according to the procedure set out in the articles of incorporation.[145]

---

[136] Art 110(2) and (4) and Annex I, Sch A and B, 2002 Act.
[137] Art 23(2), Act of 15 June 2004.
[138] Art 52(2), Act of 13 February 2007.
[139] Art 109(2), 2002 Act.
[140] *Parliamentary doc* No 5201, Comments on the Articles, 31.
[141] Art 115(3), 2002 Act.
[142] Art 29(2), Act of 15 June 2004.
[143] Art 116(1) and (2), 2002 Act.
[144] *Parliamentary doc* No 5842, Art II.
[145] Art 5(3), Act of 15 June 2004. In its current version, the Act of 15 June 2004 requires the use of the probable sales value for the calculation of the SICAR's assets. According to SICAR

A SICAR invests mainly in unlisted entities about which there may be very little **13.139** information available for valuation purposes. The articles of incorporation refer mostly to valuation principles developed by such industry organizations as the European Venture Capital Association (EVCA), and in particular the international private equity and venture capital valuation guidelines. These principles are designed to determine 'fair value', defined as the amount for which an asset could be traded or a liability extinguished between well-informed, consenting parties dealing at arm's length. Generally, several criteria are proposed to determine this amount.

Thus, when a significant transaction has occurred in the shares of a company held **13.140** in a portfolio whose reference price has been set on arm's length conditions, this transaction can be used to value the SICAR's investment.

In the absence of a significant transaction in portfolio securities, the securities of **13.141** a company acquired during the twelve months preceding the valuation date are valued at the purchase price unless a material change has occurred in the company's financial situation.

In other cases, different methods may be used, such as valuation based on the **13.142** earnings multiples and cash flows of comparable listed companies, multiples reflecting known transactions of comparable companies, valuation based on the company's net assets or on the company's discounted future cash flow or the cash flow expected from the investment, or any other valuation method used for the initial investment in the company. The short-term prospect of a sale of the company's shares or any other significant transaction in these shares may also be taken into account.

Investments in underlying funds are traditionally valued at net asset value. **13.143** However, this should not prevent adjustment when a significant transaction in the fund's securities has occurred on arm's length conditions. Similarly, in the case of recently created funds, it should be possible to ignore unrealized capital losses due only to administrative and management costs.

Investment restrictions

The Act of 15 June 2004, which exempts SICARs from the obligation to apply the **13.144** principle of risk spreading to their investments, does not supply more information about applicable limits in terms of percentage and investment or borrowing ratios. In this respect, promoters of SICARs are free to organize the regime they want to offer investors.

---

practitioners, reference to the probable sales value should be replaced by reference to the fair value, which is more appropriate in the context of SICARs. See *Parliamentary doc* No 5842, Art II.

Provisions under criminal law

13.145   The applicable rules are directly based on those applicable to UCIs, to which the law refers.

Liquidation

13.146   The provisions in the Act of 15 June 2004 governing a SICAR's liquidation are directly copied from the regime for SICAVs and SICAFs in the 2002 Act.[146]

Taxation

General

13.147   When defining the taxation of SICARs,[147] the legislature wanted to achieve three objectives. Underlying these objectives was the establishment of a new risk capital regime with an attractive tax framework for the investing public. The tax regime for UCIs transpired to be inadequate for these kinds of investments, particularly due to the fact that UCIs are not always entitled to claim the benefits of tax treaties concluded by Luxembourg. The ordinary tax regime for companies under the general law provisions did not provide an appropriate framework either as the lack of tax relief penalizes investors who do not invest directly in risk capital.[148]

13.148   The first objective of the legislature was to offer the investing community two types of companies, one fiscally transparent, the other opaque.

13.149   The first category includes the SCS which, under Luxembourg law, is fiscally transparent for income and wealth taxes.[149] In these respects, the SCS is not a taxable person and therefore not subject to the taxes levied on the income and wealth of corporations. Its income is directly allocated to the partners, in whose hands it becomes taxable irrespective of any formal distribution thereof. Thus there is no double taxation between the company and its partners.

13.150   The second category includes all other legal forms available to SICARs, ie SAs, cooperative societies organized in the form of an SA, SARLs, and SCAs. These companies, referred to as corporations in tax law, are taxable persons and thus taxed in addition to and separately from their shareholders or partners.[150]

---

[146]   See 9.29 *et seq* above.

[147]   The content of this section has been taken from an article by C Kremer and T Lesage entitled 'Investment Company in Risk Capital ("SICAR"), Response to Venture Capital and Private Equity', in *Derivatives & Financial Instruments, International Bureau of Fiscal Documentation* (January/February 2005).

[148]   See also 'Report of the Alternative Investment Expert Group', European Commission (July 2006) available at <http://ec.europa.eu> under the heading 'Internal market'.

[149]   Art 11, *Steueranpassungsgesetz* of 16 October 1934.

[150]   Art 159, LIR.

The second objective of the legislature was to create a more lenient tax regime for SICARs adopting the form of a corporation, while avoiding subjecting non-resident investors in fiscally transparent vehicles that do not realize Luxembourg-source income to Luxembourg taxes. **13.151**

The third objective of the legislature was to ensure that SICARs organized in the form of corporations could claim the benefit of the network of treaties signed by the Grand Duchy of Luxembourg to avoid double taxation. **13.152**

Direct taxes

SICARs organized in the form of a corporation

Corporate income tax and municipal business tax

SICARs are subject to the ordinary taxes imposed on Luxembourg resident corporations governed by general law provisions, ie corporate income tax and municipal business tax.[151] This point establishes a clear difference between SICARs and UCIs. UCIs benefit from a personal or subjective tax exemption and therefore are not subject to either corporate income tax or municipal business tax.[152] **13.153**

However, SICARs are subject to corporate income and municipal business tax but enjoy an objective exemption in respect of income from transferable securities and income generated by the sale, contribution, and settlement of these assets. Equally, capital losses on the sale of transferable securities and unrealized capital losses recognized on such securities are not tax deductible business expenses.[153] **13.154**

The term 'transferable securities' must be interpreted broadly and covers shares, bonds, and other debt securities, as well as all other negotiable instruments giving their owner the right to buy the above-mentioned transferable securities.[154] **13.155**

Consequently, the taxable profits of SICARs incorporated in the form of a corporation include only the financial profits derived from assets other than transferable securities (particularly bank deposits) and the non-financial profits, primarily profits from the management of subsidiaries (attendance fees, management fees, etc). **13.156**

For tax purposes, the purchase price is the ceiling for valuing assets (unrealized profits are not taken into consideration). If the valuation rules applied by SICARs result in recognition of unrealized gains in their annual reports, the profits to be taken into account for tax purposes will be adjusted accordingly.[155] **13.157**

---

[151] The applicable maximum overall rate is currently 29.63%, ie a corporate income tax of 22.88% (22% plus 4% for the employment fund) and a municipal business tax of 6.75% in the city of Luxembourg.

[152] Art 127(1), 2002 Act; Art 66(1), Act of 13 February 2007.

[153] Art 34(2), Act of 15 June 2004.

[154] *Parliamentary doc* No 5201, Comments on the Articles, 33.

[155] Arts 23 and 40, LIR.

13.158 During the preparatory work for the Act of 15 June 2004, commentators stressed that, in the case of private equity vehicles, there is often a waiting period between the receipt of capital from investors and the investment made by the vehicle. In order to allow SICARs to invest their resources with sufficient flexibility, an amendment was introduced to maintain the tax exemption for profits from funds held pending their investment in risk capital. This exemption applies only for a maximum period of twelve months preceding the risk capital investment, provided it can be established that these funds were actually invested in risk capital.[156]

13.159 In contrast with what is demanded for the exemption of profits derived by parent companies from their subsidiaries under the participation exemption,[157] the objective exemption available to SICARs is not subject to a minimum holding period,[158] a minimum investment threshold,[159] or the tax status or legal form of the subsidiary. Consequently, even though the SICAR is entitled to the benefit of the participation exemption, like any other company under general tax provisions, it does not need to claim this right since its objective exemption regime is more advantageous.[160]

13.160 In order to counter the risk of abuse, a SICAR cannot be subjected to corporate income tax as part of a consolidated group with other Luxembourg-based companies or permanent establishments of foreign companies established in the territory of Luxembourg.[161]

13.161 A SICAR incorporated in the form of a corporation is subject to municipal business tax on the same tax assessment basis as for corporate income tax.[162] By way of exception, the remuneration or profit share of the general partners of SCAs is treated as a non-deductible expense for the purpose of municipal business tax.[163] This addition to the municipal business tax assessment basis only results in an actual levy of the municipal business tax insofar as the remuneration has offset a taxable profit.

---

[156] Art 34(3), Act of 15 June 2004. The government initially proposed a period of 3 months: see *Parliamentary doc* No 5201², Government amendments, 1.

[157] Transposed into Luxembourg law by Art 166 of the LIR and the Grand-Ducal Regulation of 21 December 2001 on the implementation of Article 166, paragraph 9, number 1 of the amended Act of 4 December 1967 on income tax.

[158] 12 months.

[159] A direct holding of at least 10% or €1,200,000 (€6,000,000 for exemption from capital gains) in the capital of an eligible subsidiary.

[160] But see the discussion at 13.198 below.

[161] Art 34(1)(d), Act of 15 June 2004 introducing a fifth paragraph in Art 164*bis*, LIR.

[162] Para 7 of the Act on the municipal business tax (*Gewerbesteuergesetz* of 1 December 1936).

[163] ibid para 8(4).

Moreover, as the general partner of an SCA can itself be a Luxembourg-resident **13.162** corporation subject to municipal business tax, any risk of double taxation is avoided. In fact, the Act of 15 June 2004 specifies that the general partner's remuneration and profit share may be deducted from the municipal business tax base if they are included in the operating profit as determined for municipal business tax purposes, provided such remuneration and profit share has been added to the municipal business tax assessment basis at the level of the SCA.[164] If its addition at the level of the SICAR does not create a municipal business tax assessment basis, the deductibility of this same remuneration at the level of the general partner enables the aggregate tax rate paid by the partner to be reduced, with a liability arising only in respect of corporate income tax.

Wealth tax

Luxembourg resident corporations are in principle subject to a wealth tax at a rate **13.163** of 0.5 per cent, charged annually on the assessed unitary value of the corporations in question. However, a subjective exemption from wealth tax was introduced in favour of SICARs incorporated in the form of a corporation.[165] Whereas certain investments held by a SICAR might not be eligible for the exemption under the participation exemption between parent companies and subsidiaries,[166] the authors of the Act of 15 June 2004 felt that application of a wealth tax would have excessively reduced the competitiveness of SICARs compared with companies taxed under foreign legislation.[167]

Fiscally transparent SICARs

Income tax and wealth tax

Under Luxembourg law, the SCS is considered a transparent entity for the **13.164** purpose of corporate income tax and wealth tax. If an SCS does not carry on its own commercial activity, the income of every investor in the SCS is qualified in principle according to his personal tax situation. Consequently, the income attributable to a resident private investor is generally not classified as business profit (but instead, for example, as rental income or income from capital transfers), whereas an entrepreneur's income is classified as business profit. By way of

---

[164] Art 36(b), Act of 15 June 2004, introducing number 2(b) in para 9 of the Act on the municipal business tax (n 162 above).

[165] Art 35, Act of 15 June 2004, introducing number 5 in the first part of para 3 of the Act on wealth tax (*Vermögensteuergesetz* of 16 October 1934).

[166] Para 60, Act on the valuation of goods and securities (*Bewertungsgesetz* of 16 October 1934) requiring a holding of at least 10% or €1,200,000 in the share capital of an eligible subsidiary (without a waiting period).

[167] *Parliamentary doc* No 5201, Comments on the Articles, 34.

exception, when at least one of the general partners of an SCS is a corporation resident in the Grand Duchy of Luxembourg, the income derived by all investors is considered as business profit.[168]

13.165 In order to avoid this requalification in connection with SICARs and, more generally, in order to avoid any risk that a SICAR's income may be requalified as business profit, the Act of 15 June 2004 specifies that SICARs with the legal form of an SCS are not considered as commercial companies.[169] This measure ensures that non-resident investors are not taxed in Luxembourg solely because of their investment in a SICAR. Such an investment alone may not lead to a permanent establishment in Luxembourg.[170]

13.166 The above-mentioned tax treatment combines complete tax neutrality with sufficient flexibility to apply the tax rules in force in the investor's state of residence. This alternative of a tax transparent vehicle may provide for an even more favourable treatment for non-resident investors than investment in a SICAR incorporated in the form of a corporation (for example a lower capital gains tax rate, tax credits, etc).

Municipal business tax

13.167 Municipal business tax is a real tax. It is levied on the business itself, regardless of its legal form. No fiscal transparency is therefore applicable at the municipal business tax level. However, a SICAR constituted in the form of an SCS is not subject to municipal business tax, regardless of the place of residence and the tax status of its investors.[171]

Withholding tax

Income received by the SICAR

13.168 In principle, dividends distributed by a Luxembourg resident corporation are subject to a withholding tax of 15 per cent. Withholding tax also applies to certain interest payments (certain types of participating bonds and silent partnership agreements).[172]

13.169 Dividends distributed by a Luxembourg resident corporation to a SICAR are as a rule subject to the 15 per cent withholding tax although certain exemptions are available under the ordinary rules. In particular, dividends paid by a Luxembourg resident corporation to a SICAR incorporated in the form of an SA, an SCA, or

---

[168] Art 14(4), LIR; this rule is based on the 'immersion theory' (*Geprägetheorie*).
[169] Art 34(1)(a), Act of 15 June 2004 introducing a new final sentence in Art 14(1), LIR.
[170] *Parliamentary doc* No 5201[1], Opinion of the Chamber of Commerce, 5.
[171] Article 36(a), Act of 15 June 2004, introducing number 4 in section 2 of para 2, Act on the municipal business tax (n 162 above).
[172] Art 146(1), LIR.

an SARL are exempt from withholding tax provided the SICAR holds or commits itself to hold a qualified shareholding in the capital of the subsidiary (at least 10 per cent or a minimum purchase price of €1,200,000) for an uninterrupted period of at least twelve months.[173]

Final withholding taxes levied in Luxembourg on dividents distributed to SICARs incorporated in the form of a corporation are creditable against the corporate income tax due, and any excess may be repaid to the SICAR.[174]   **13.170**

At the level of transparent SICARs, the investor needs to file an application to obtain a reduction of, or exemption from, withholding taxes on income levied in Luxembourg on local profits. Investors resident in a state that has concluded a treaty on double taxation with Luxembourg must directly claim the relevant provisions of the treaty.   **13.171**

Income distributed by the SICAR

Dividends and liquidation proceeds distributed by a SICAR are not subject to a withholding tax. Whereas the absence of a withholding tax on liquidation pay-outs is a shared characteristic of all corporations based in Luxembourg, the Act of 15 June 2004 has introduced a specific exemption for dividend payments in order to preserve tax neutrality vis-à-vis non-resident investors.[175] Like UCIs, dividends distributed by SICARs are therefore exempt from withholding tax.   **13.172**

Capital gains realized on the disposal of shareholdings in Luxembourg resident corporations are not subject to withholding tax either. The Act of 15 June 2004 further eliminated the possibility of a Luxembourg income tax liability for non-residents in cases where, according to Luxembourg's tax rules, the capital gain realized on the disposal of a substantial shareholding (more than 10 per cent) in a Luxembourg resident corporation would have been taxable in Luxembourg by way of assessment should the non-resident taxpayer not be covered by a treaty to prevent double taxation.[176]   **13.173**

The above exemption and non-taxation rules, introduced by the Act of 15 June 2004, do not distinguish between the dividends and profits generated by entities incorporated in the form of a corporation and those generated by fiscally transparent companies. This is perhaps self-explanatory, as the exemption or absence of liability to taxation arose from the transparency regime itself.   **13.174**

---

[173] ibid Art 147(2), but see the discussion at 13.198 *et seq* below.
[174] ibid Art 154.
[175] Art 34(1)(b), Act of 15 June 2004 amending Art 147, LIR.
[176] Art 34(1)(c), Act of 15 June 2004, introducing Art 156(8)(c), LIR. The non-resident investor in question is obviously supposed not to be carrying on a professional activity in Luxembourg through a permanent establishment or a permanent representative.

Indirect taxes

Capital duty

13.175 Contributions made to the share capital and the share premium of Luxembourg companies is, in principle, subject to an *ad valorem* capital duty of 0.5 per cent[177] under the law on capital duty.[178]

13.176 As for UCIs,[179] an exception to the above-mentioned provisions was introduced for SICARs. Instead of an *ad valorem* capital duty, contributions to a SICAR are subject to a one-off, fixed duty of €1,250. The capital duty must be paid when the SICAR is constituted. Its scope is determined by a Grand-Ducal regulation of 10 September 2004.[180]

Value added tax

13.177 Article 44(1)(d) of the amended VAT Act dated 12 February 1979[181] stipulated that the management of UCIs, pension funds supervised by the CSSF or by the Insurance Commission, and securitization vehicles situated in Luxembourg are exempt from VAT.

13.178 The scope of this VAT exemption was extended to the management of SICARs. While this issue was not debated in Parliament, the exemption appears to be based on Article 13B(d)(6) of the Sixth VAT Directive,[182] which grants Member States the right to define 'special investment funds' whose management is exempt from VAT. The term 'management' is here used to mean an activity with the same types of management services as provided to UCIs.[183]

13.179 In this respect, the European Court of Justice ruled in the *Abbey National* case[184] that the notion of 'management services' encompasses the tasks of portfolio management and also those of administering UCITS themselves, such as those set

---

[177] During his speech on the State of the Nation, held on 22 May 2008, the Luxembourg Prime Minister announced the abolition of capital duty by 2009 and a Bill to abolish capital duty as from 1 January 2009 is currently being prepared.

[178] Amended Act of 29 December 1971 concerning taxation of capital gathering in civil and commercial companies and amending certain legal provisions governing the collection of registration duty.

[179] Art 128(1), 2002 Act; Art 67(1), Act of 13 February 2007.

[180] Art 37 of the Act of 15 June 2004 and Grand-Ducal Regulation of 10 September 2004 determining the conditions and amount of the fixed duty on contributions paid by virtue of Art 37 of the Act of 15 June 2004 on risk capital investment companies (SICAR) (*Mémorial* A 2004, 2475).

[181] Tax Code, Vol 6.

[182] Sixth Directive (EEC) 77/388 of 17 May 1977 on the harmonization of the laws of the Member States relating to turnover taxes—Common system of value added tax: uniform basis of assessment [1977] OJ L145/1, replaced by Directive (EC) 2006/112 of November 2006 as from 1 January 2007.

[183] L Nevelsteen and R Van Den Plas, *Undertakings for Collective Investment and VAT in the EU*, VAT Monitor, International Bureau of Fiscal Documentation (November/December 2003) 461.

[184] C-169/04, *Abbey National plc, Inscape Investment Fund v Commissioners of Customs & Excise*, 4 May 2006.

out in Annex II to the UCITS Directive under the heading 'Administration'. The services set out under this heading are the following:

- legal and fund management accounting services;
- customer inquiries;
- valuation and pricing (including tax returns);
- regulatory compliance monitoring;
- maintenance of unit-holder register;
- distribution of income;
- unit issues and redemptions;
- contracts settlements (including certificate dispatch);
- record keeping.

In case of sub-contracting part of these management services, the European Court of Justice ruled in the same case that the services performed by a third party manager in respect of the administrative management of the funds come within the concept of 'management of special investment funds' if, viewed broadly, they form a distinct whole, and are specific to, and essential for, the management of special investment funds. **13.180**

The European Court of Justice also ruled that the VAT exemption does not cover the functions of depositary of undertakings for collective investment, such as those set out in Articles 7(1) and (3) and 14(1) and (3) of the UCITS Directive. **13.181**

The Luxembourg registration authority has released a Circular[185] in view of shedding light on the VAT treatment of collective investment structures (including the SICARs) and their management services.[186] In particular, the Circular takes the view that SICARs should be considered as a taxable person for VAT purposes with no right of input VAT deduction. In principle, SICARs are not required to register for VAT purposes in Luxembourg. However, any Luxembourg SICAR receiving legal or tax services by a service supplier established outside Luxembourg will be required to register for VAT in Luxembourg (under a simplified procedure) in order to pay the Luxembourg VAT due (15 per cent) on the receipt of such taxable services from abroad. **13.182**

The managing partners of SICARs constituted in the form of an SCS or an SCA are clearly considered to be taxable persons for VAT purposes. In this context, they should not be obliged to register for VAT when supplying VAT-exempt management services to the SICAR, except upon receipt of taxable services (such as legal or tax services) from abroad.[187] **13.183**

---

[185] Circular No 723 of 29 December 2006.
[186] The provisions of the Circular are applicable as from 1 April 2007.
[187] Art 1, Grand-Ducal Regulation of 21 December 1979 on the VAT declaration at the start, change or cessation of an economic activity (*Mémorial* A 1979, 2121).

Tax regime for resident investors in SICARs incorporated in the form of a corporation

Natural persons

13.184   Dividends distributed by a SICAR are taxed by way of assessment through income tax returns as income from movable assets[188] at the level of the individual shareholder.[189]

13.185   Capital gains realized on the disposal of SICAR shares are taxed as speculative income, but only if the period between the purchase and disposal of the shares does not exceed six months or if the disposal of the shares precedes their purchase[190].

13.186   Taxable speculative profits are pooled with profits from other categories and together subjected to normal progressive tax rates and to the 1.4 per cent dependence contribution. The deduction of realized capital losses is subject to restrictions.

13.187   If a SICAR's shares have been held for more than six months, the realised capital gain is not taxed provided the investor (alone or together with his/her spouse and/or minor children) has not held a substantial participation, ie more than 10 per cent of the SICAR's share capital.[191] When an investor disposes of a substantial participation more than six months after acquisition, any capital gains realized will be taxed as extraordinary income benefiting from the half-global rate.[192] Such investors have two further benefits. First, the purchase price of their securities is revalued according to certain inflation-adjusted coefficients and, secondly, they are entitled to a deduction of €50,000 (€100,000 for jointly taxed spouses).[193]

---

[188]   The theoretical situation in which a SICAR's shares are held professionally is not analysed.

[189]   Art 97, LIR. The first tranche of €1,500 of income from movable assets is exempt. This tranche is €3,000 in the case of collective taxation within the meaning of Art 3, LIR (spouses taxed collectively) (Art 115(15), LIR). As the SICAR is considered to be a fully taxable corporation (see the discussion at 13.189 below), 50% of the dividends paid to the shareholders is exempt (Article 115(15a), LIR).

[190]   Art 99*bis*, LIR. Speculative gains realized during a given year are only taxable if their total amount reaches €500.

[191]   An investor is also considered to have held a substantial participation if he has obtained, without providing financial consideration, in the 5 years preceding the divestment, a participation which was itself considered substantial for the transferor (or the transferors in the case of successive free transfers in the same period of 5 years). In order to determine the transferor's ownership fraction, shares held in both a private capacity and in a professional capacity must be aggregated. Both direct holdings and indirect holdings (such as those held in trustee capacity) must be taken into account. Ownership of a holding through a corporation in which the taxpayer holds the majority of voting rights is considered an indirect holding (Art 100, LIR).

[192]   Maximum marginal rate of 19.475% calculated in accordance with Art 131(1)(c), LIR.

[193]   Arts 102(6) and 130(4), LIR. This rebate is available once every 10 years for the income covered by Arts 99*ter*–101, LIR.

Corporations

Profits (dividends or liquidation income received), including capital gains, realized on shareholdings in SICARs are, in principle, subject to corporate income tax and municipal business tax according to the ordinary rules. SICARS constituted in the form of an SA, an SCA, or an SARL must obviously be classified as corporations. **13.188**

By way of exception, these profits are exempt under the participation exemption between parent companies and subsidiaries insofar as the relevant conditions have been met.[194] In this respect, it must be determined whether a SICAR should be considered a fully taxable corporation. This issue is not discussed in either the Act of 15 June 2004 or the accompanying Parliamentary documents. **13.189**

Income tax law does not give any definition of the term 'fully taxable'. Based on the Parliamentary documents relating to this law, the term should be interpreted as 'not entitled to total or partial subjective exemption'.[195] SICARs are entitled to a partial exemption which should be considered objective rather than subjective, ie they are entitled to an exemption—rather than being exempt from tax themselves—on certain profits. Consequently, SICARs should fall within the scope of the above definition. Moreover, the omission of specific exclusions suggests that the legislature did not intend to prevent SICARs from taking advantage of the participation exemption between parent companies and subsidiaries.[196] **13.190**

It can therefore be concluded that SICARs are fully taxable companies for the purpose of the participation exemption regime between parent companies and subsidiaries.[197] **13.191**

Change of company form

Conversion of an ordinary company into a SICAR

The status of SICAR is not reserved for newly incorporated companies. Any ordinary company can convert itself into a SICAR if it complies with the conditions set out in the Act of 15 June 2004. The adoption of the SICAR status triggers an obligation on the SICAR to pay a fixed capital duty.[198] **13.192**

Whether the adoption of the SICAR status has a neutral impact on corporate income tax and municipal business tax needs to be examined more closely. The adoption **13.193**

---

[194] Art 166, LIR and Grand-Ducal Regulation of 21 December 2001 (mentioned at n 157 above) and para 60 of the amended Act of 16 October 1934 on the valuation of goods and securities.

[195] *Parliamentary doc* No 571[16], Opinion of the *Conseil d'État*, 98.

[196] In contrast with securitization vehicles, for which a Grand-Ducal Regulation of 31 March 2004 introduced a special exclusion with regard to capital gains.

[197] However, this should not prevent the tax authorities from refusing to grant the benefit of these provisions in the case of abuse, in the meaning of para 6 of the Tax Adaptation Act.

[198] Art 2 of the Grand-Ducal Regulation of 10 September 2004.

of a subjective exemption regime (for example a UCI) by an ordinary company is treated as a liquidation for tax purposes.[199] Since a SICAR preserves its legal status and legal form[200] and remains subject to corporate income tax and municipal business tax, it can be concluded that the adoption of SICAR status does not trigger liquidation in terms of corporate income tax and municipal business tax, unless adoption of the SICAR status is exclusively motivated by the avoidance of taxation of unrealized capital gains. In this case, the authorities may refuse to accept the tax neutrality of the conversion pursuant to section 6 of the Tax Adaptation Act.

Conversion of a SICAR into an ordinary company

13.194 The conversion of a SICAR into an ordinary company triggers an obligation to pay the *ad valorem* capital duty that would have been due when the company was originally incorporated. The fixed duty paid previously will not be allocated against the duty owed.[201] A loss of the SICAR status does not affect the fund's corporate income tax and municipal business tax status.[202]

The SICAR and the international tax environment

SICARs and double taxation treaties

13.195 Owing to their subjective exemption rules, UCIs constituted in the form of companies (SICAVs and SICAFs) are not always considered to be Luxembourg residents for the purpose of double taxation treaties. Their right to benefit from such treaties is determined by bilateral negotiations between Luxembourg and each of the states in question. So far, about twenty-six of the more than fifty states that have signed such treaties with Luxembourg have agreed to extend their application to SICAVs and SICAFs.[203]

13.196 The situation is different for SICARs organized in the form of a corporation, which are subject to corporate income tax and municipal business tax. These SICARs belong clearly to categories of entities resident in Luxembourg covered by the double taxation treaties. They are therefore fully entitled to the benefits of these treaties unless their application is specifically excluded or restricted.[204]

---

[199] Art 169, LIR. Also see R Molitor, *Le régime fiscal des sociétés mères et filiales* (Etudes Fiscales, Imprimerie Saint-Paul, 1994) 61.

[200] Unless the legal form is modified at the same time.

[201] Art 3, Grand-Ducal Regulation of 10 September 2004.

[202] It may nevertheless be asked whether such a change would give rise to a revaluation of securities for exemption purposes (ie are the unrealized capital gains embedded in the securities on the day the status is changed definitively exempt?).

[203] See 11.114 above.

[204] Notably a restriction on benefits within the framework of the double taxation treaty between Luxembourg and the US (Art 24).

At the level of fiscally transparent SICARs, the benefits of double taxation treaties **13.197** should be requested by the investors themselves, assuming that the source state accepts the transparency. For income and profits whose source is in Luxembourg, Luxembourg grants treaty benefit to investors in fiscally transparent SICARs who are resident in states with which Luxembourg has concluded a double taxation treaty.

SICARs and the Directive on parent companies and subsidiaries

To benefit from the provisions of the Directive on parent companies and **13.198** subsidiaries,[205] the company in question must comply with the conditions set out in Article 2 of the Directive.

The eligibility of SICARs incorporated in the form of an SA, an SCA, or an SARL **13.199** depends upon whether they are subject to corporate income tax 'without right of option or exemption'. In this context, there can be no doubt that SICARs are subject to corporate income tax in the absence of exercise of the option and the absence of a subjective exemption. That said, the objective exemption regime allows SICARs to benefit from a preferential regime compared with other Luxembourg resident corporations.

Article 2(c) of the Directive does not appear to require effective payment of tax. **13.200** This Article requires companies to be 'subject to tax' rather than the effective taxation of income.[206] The objective exemption should therefore not exclude a SICAR from the benefits of this Directive.

Consequently it is necessary to analyse every case individually in order to determine **13.201** whether a company resident in an EU Member State can actually claim the benefit of national rules transposing the Directive to its shareholding in a SICAR. Certain Member States require a company resident in another Member State actually to pay tax in significant amounts. Such Member States may base this requirement on Article 1(2) of the Directive, which allows Member States to introduce anti-abuse provisions.[207]

---

[205] Council Directive (EEC) 90/435 of 23 July 1990 on the common system of taxation applicable in the case of parent companies and subsidiaries of different Member States [1990] OJ L225/6–9.

[206] G Maisto, *Shaping EU Company Tax Policy: Amending the Tax Directives*, European Taxation, International Bureau of Fiscal Documentation (August 2002) 268

[207] ibid. In early 2005, the European Commission received a complaint that the tax regime for SICARs and for securitization vehicles was incompatible with Community law. This complaint was underpinned by the assertion that these tax regimes amounted to unauthorized government aid. At the time of going to press, this complaint, whose validity is very far from having been established, has not yet been settled by the European Commission.

14

SECURITIZATION VEHICLES

Introduction

As its name indicates, securitization allows the conversion of various instruments **14.01** into negotiable securities by assigning them to a separate asset pool (the securitization vehicle) which issues securities to investors. The cash flow generated by these instruments is used to finance distributions on and redemptions of the securities issued by the vehicle, which are in turn secured by the instruments.[1]

Several types of securitization have been developed over the years. A distinction **14.02** should be drawn between synthetic securitization and true-sale securitization. True-sale securitization involves the assignment of the underlying assets to a financial vehicle. Synthetic securitization does not involve such an asset assignment but only transfer of the risks connected with the underlying assets.

In true-sale securitization, assets are assigned to a securitization vehicle that is dis- **14.03** tinct and legally independent from the assignor.[2] Acquisition of the assets is financed by issuing securities, which may be issued by the securitization vehicle itself or possibly another vehicle, established solely for the purpose of issuing securities while

---

[1] See B Rauis, *Produits dérivés de crédit, Applications et Perspectives* (Larcier, 2003) 32.
[2] However, the Act of 22 March 2004 does not make it unlawful for the assignor to hold the securitization vehicle.

the assets will be held in the asset acquisition vehicle.[3] Securities issued for securitization purposes are secured by the assets acquired by the vehicle. Such securities are generally given a rating, often enhanced through a variety of credit enhancement techniques, such as a third party guarantee, the use of escrow arrangements, overcollateralization of the vehicle, subordination, etc.

14.04   More specifically, subordination results from the issue of securities belonging to several categories or 'tranches'. These categories are distinguished by the degree of risk borne by each, ranked according to the three traditional levels: a junior tranche, most exposed to the risk of default of the underlying assets; an intermediate or mezzanine tranche; and a senior tranche; which assumes the least risk.

14.05   The transfer of risks under a synthetic securitization is often effected through the use of a credit default swap. The securitization vehicle agrees a credit default swap with the assignor, pursuant to which it assumes the credit risk connected with certain assets in return for payment of a premium. It also issues securities, for which it generally seeks a rating.

14.06   Further classification of true-sale securitizations reveals several sub-categories reflecting the type of underlying assets acquired.

14.07   When the underlying assets consist of mortgage credits, the securities issued by the securitization vehicle are categorized as mortgage backed securities (MBSs). Other underlying assets are conceivable, such as consumer loans, credit card outstandings, car loans, property loans, and intellectual property rights. Securitizations in transactions involving a bond portfolio or loans are known as collateralized debt obligations (CDOs) and, more specifically, collateralized bond obligations (CBOs) if they relate to a bond portfolio, while transactions involving a loan portfolio, are known as collateralized loan obligations (CLOs). Depending upon whether the underlying portfolio remains unchanged or may be adjusted, the CDO is either static or dynamic. Securitization can serve several objectives.

14.08   First, securitization allows the assignor to obtain funding on attractive conditions.[4] Because the securities issued by the securitization vehicle are, in principle, backed by the instruments being financed and assigned to the vehicle, this type of refinancing benefits from better financial terms than a simple loan in the same amount. Securitization also allows the assignor to diversify its financing sources. Because the assignor assigns risk, it may not have to recognize the asset

---

[3]   Art 1(2), Act of 22 March 2004.
[4]   J Deacon, *Global Securitization and CDOs* (Wiley Finance, 2004) para 1.2; WA Roever and F Fabozzi, 'A Primer on Securitization' (Summer 2003) *The Journal of Structured and Project Finance* 7 and 8.

assigned in its accounts, thereby improving its balance sheet and, in particular, its debt-to-equity ratio.[5]

Secondly, securitization allows the investor to access more diversified sectors and businesses than those accessed through markets in such securities as bonds, certificates of deposit, and other negotiable debt instruments.[6] The flexibility of the legal framework for such transactions makes it possible to use them for a wide variety of assets and to adapt them to the needs of investors by offering securities whose risks and income are tiered. Securitization can be used to grant 'tailor-made' finance, generally secured by the assets assigned by the assigning business. **14.09**

Although practised for many years in the Grand Duchy of Luxembourg, securitization did not benefit from an ad hoc legal framework until the Act of 22 March 2004, which provides a flexible, innovative, and attractive legal and tax framework, together with the legal certainty required for securitization structures, their promoters, and investors.[7] **14.10**

Scope of Application

One of the most obvious features and advantages of the Act of 22 March 2004 is the extensive scope of its application. Reflecting the economic and financial approach advocated by the legislature, its scope is extremely broad, primarily because it treats securitization as an asset pooling and refinancing technique and does not try to regulate the subject matter of the securitization, which may comprise any type of instrument.[8] **14.11**

Securitization, as defined by the Act of 22 March 2004, means a transaction pursuant to which a securitization vehicle acquires or assumes, directly or through another undertaking, the risks relating to claims, other assets or obligations owned by third parties or inherent in all or part of the activities of third parties, by issuing securities whose value or yield depends on such risks.[9] **14.12**

As worded by its authors, the Act of 22 March 2004 is 'available for the securitization of any type of risk, in the general meaning of the term, whether inherent in **14.13**

---

[5] Deacon (n 4 above) 4; H Hovasse, *La Titrisation* (Juris-classeurs, 1991) Vol 2260, 2.

[6] See also Hovasse (n 5 above) 3.

[7] For a more detailed description of the Act of 22 March 2004, see A Gudmannsson, 'Luxembourg: New law on securitization' (July 2004) *International Securitisation Report* 2; 'Cross-Border securitization in Luxembourg' (2004/2005) *Global Securitization Review* 152; N Kayser 'Fiducie ou SPV—Quelques aspects de la titrisation en droit luxembourgeois' in *Droit bancaire et financier au Luxembourg* (ALJB, Larcier, 2004) Vol 2, 857.

[8] CSSF Annual Report for 2007, 101.

[9] Art 1(1), Act of 22 March 2004.

receivables or in any other type of asset or obligation or any kind of activity'.[10] Securitization has evolved rapidly since the advent of traditional receivables securitization, and can, *inter alia,* be used to hold all types of existing and future receivables and any other tangible and intangible assets, including commodities and other assets with similar characteristics,[11] in a dedicated vehicle. It can also be used for the synthetic transfer of various risks (insurance risks, credit risks, risks linked to the commercial activity of a third party, etc).

14.14   This flexibility permitting any type of securitization is confirmed by the text of the Act of 22 March 2004 itself. According to the Act, 'risks relating to the holding of assets, whether movable or immovable, tangible or intangible, and risks resulting from the obligations assumed by third parties or relating to all or part of the activities of third parties are capable of being securitised'.[12] Furthermore, the Act of 22 March 2004 does not limit the techniques that may be used to transfer risks connected with assets, obligations, and activities to the securitization vehicle.

14.15   This flexibility, however, does not turn a securitization vehicle into an undertaking. The CSSF points out that:

> ... due to the specific nature of a securitisation vehicle's activity, the risks securitised by the securitisation vehicle shall exclusively result from assets or receivables or commitments assumed by third parties and wholly or partly inherent in the activities carried on by third parties; they shall however not be generated by the securitisation vehicle or result in whole or in part from the activity of the securitisation vehicle acting as an entrepreneur or a trader.[13]

14.16   Therefore, with the exception of securitization vehicles having as their object the management of a portfolio of financial assets, any management of third parties' activities, receivables, or assets by securitization vehicles which generates a risk additional to the risk linked to securitization activities, receivables, or assets, or which aims at creating additional wealth or achieving the commercial development of the securitization vehicles' activity, would be incompatible with the purpose of the Act, notwithstanding the fact that the actual management of such activities, receivables, or assets has been delegated to an external service provider.

14.17   The role of a securitization vehicle must be limited to the management of financial flows related to securitization transactions as well as to the prudent management of its risk portfolio, with the exception of any activity which would make the securitization vehicle eligible as an entrepreneur or a trader.[14]

---

[10] *Parliamentary doc* No 5199, Comments on the Articles, 20.
[11] See, however, the limits which the CSSF set out in this respect in its annual report for 2007, 102.
[12] Art 53, Act of 22 March 2004.
[13] CSSF Annual Report for 2007, 101.
[14] ibid.

The CSSF allows, under defined conditions, structures where the securitization **14.18** vehicle itself grants credits rather than acquires existing credits. A securitization vehicle may also securitize existing portfolios of partly drawn credits and revolving credits. Here, too, strict conditions must be met in order to prevent the securitization vehicle from being used as a credit institution.[15]

The use of derivative techniques and instruments by a securitization vehicle must **14.19** remain limited. Such use is possible only insofar as is necessary for a securitization transaction or as an integral part of the relevant transaction.[16]

A securitization vehicle issues securities in order to obtain finance.[17] Borrowing by **14.20** a securitization vehicle is also possible but under strict conditions,[18] especially when it is planned to borrow on a long-term basis.

Securitization Vehicles

When a securitization vehicle is organized as a company, it can take the form of **14.21** any of the three most common commercial companies, ie the SA, the SCA, or the SARL.[19] However, incorporation as an SARL means that the company may not issue bonds intended for the general investor public.[20] The Act of 22 March 2004 also allows the organization of a securitization vehicle in the form of a cooperative society organized as an SA.[21] This type of company, rarely used in practice, comes with certain particular constraints, such as the obligation to have at least seven shareholders.[22]

Securitization vehicles may also be organized in the form of co-ownerships or **14.22** fiduciary estates.[23] In either case, securitization will require the services of a management company charged with administering and managing the fund's assets.[24]

Whether the securitization vehicle is organized as a company or contractually, the **14.23** use of sub-funds is allowed.[25] This will enable the vehicle to carry out different types

---

[15] ibid, 102.
[16] ibid, 103.
[17] For a definition of the concept of security in the context of the Act of 22 March 2004, see the CSSF Annual Report for 2007, 103.
[18] ibid, 104.
[19] Art 4(1), Act of 22 March 2004.
[20] Art 188, 1915 Act.
[21] Art 4(1), Act of 22 March 2004.
[22] Art 114, para 2, 1915 Act.
[23] Art 6(1), Act of 22 March 2004.
[24] ibid Art 6(2).
[25] ibid Arts 5 and 8; in its annual report for 2007 (at 105), the CSSF notes that in such cases, financial statements must be drawn up for each sub-fund.

of transactions with different assignors. In this case, each sub-fund is considered to be a separate entity vis-à-vis shareholders of the other sub-funds and creditors. Several classes of securities may be issued by a single sub-fund (in particular, tracker shares).[26]

Authorization and Supervision

14.24 Only securitization vehicles that 'continually' issue transferable securities intended for the public have to be authorized by the CSSF.[27] 'Continually' means that the securitization vehicle issues securities at least three times a year. The entire securitization vehicle (including all of its sub-funds) is considered in order to appraise such frequency. Similarly, the CSSF does not necessarily consider that the implementation of an issuance programme represents a single issue. The CSSF can come to that conclusion by examining the nature of the programme as well as the features of the different series of issues.[28]

14.25 As for the public nature of an issue, the CSSF has adopted and made public several criteria to determine what constitutes a 'public' issue. These criteria principally assist in determining what does not constitute a public issue. The CSSF distinguishes two types of issues which are not public issues, ie issues intended for professional clients within the meaning of Annexe II of MiFID and issues distributed in the form of private placements.[29]

14.26 A securitization vehicule which ceases to satisfy one of the two criteria related to the continuous issue and 'public' issue may request that its name be removed from the list of authorized securitization vehicles. In the case of such a request, the CSSF will verify that all the issued securities placed with the public have matured and have been repaid.[30]

14.27 Authorized securitization vehicles are subject to supervision by the CSSF, which ensures that they comply with their legal and contractual obligations. The authorization procedure for securitization vehicles is very similar to that for SIFs and SICARs. The initiator of the vehicle submits to the CSSF an application package including the sales documents, the constitutive documents, and the main agreements

---

[26] Art 63, Act of 22 March 2004.
[27] ibid Art 19.
[28] CSSF Annual Report for 2007, 106.
[29] ibid 107. In this respect, the CSSF recalls that its practice is to appraise on a case-by-case basis the private nature of a placement, taking into account the means of communication and distribution used. It also notes that a subscription made by a financial intermediary in order to place the subscribed securities with the public cannot be considered to be a private placement.
[30] ibid 106.

to be entered into by the vehicle.[31] The CSSF also verifies the probity and professional experience of the proposed conducting persons.

The supervision effected by the CSSF is continuous. It involves reporting require- **14.28** ments which are similar to those for SIFs and SICARs. In this context, a bi-annual reporting on the financial situation of the vehicle and on the future, current, or matured issues is implemented. Any change in the information provided to the CSSF under the authorization procedure must be notified to the CSSF and requires its prior agreement in most cases.[32]

Securitization vehicles are also supervised to some extent by independent **14.29** auditors. The accounts of any securitization vehicle, whether authorized or not, must be audited by an independent auditor.[33]

Securitization vehicles are required to appoint a bank to hold their assets. **14.30** This function may be performed only by credit institutions established or having their registered office in Luxembourg.[34] A securitization vehicle may appoint a different depositary bank for each of its sub-funds.[35]

At the administrative level, the CSSF requires the securitization vehicle to **14.31** have the appropriate infrastructure in addition to any personnel and other significant resources needed for its activities.[36] This does not prevent the securitization vehicle from delegating the management of its assets and the structuring of the technical aspects of transactions to certain professionals. The delegates appointed by the securitization vehicle may be located abroad. In this case, the CSSF sees to it that there is a sufficient information flow between the professionals involved.[37]

Particular Provisions on the Assignment of Receivables

In order to facilitate the securitization of receivables, the Act of 22 March 2004 **14.32** gives legal effect to the assignment of existing receivables both as between the parties to the assignment and vis-à-vis third parties from the moment the assignment agreement is entered into, subject to the application of the laws of the State in which the assignor is situated with regard to the legal enforceability of the

---

[31] For further details, see ibid 107 *et seq.*
[32] ibid 109.
[33] Art 48, Act of 22 March 2004.
[34] ibid Art 22.
[35] CSSF Annual Report for 2007, 108.
[36] ibid, 107.
[37] ibid.

assignment against third parties.[38] It also regulates the assignment of future receivables, which it permits even in the event of bankruptcy proceedings.[39]

14.33   Also pursuant to the Act of 22 March, unless otherwise agreed, assignment to or by a securitization vehicle will result in the transfer of the guarantees and security interests relating to the assigned receivables and enforceability of the transfer of such guarantees and security interests by operation of law against third parties.[40]

14.34   Lastly, because it is important to allow the assigning creditor to maintain contact with its clients, the creditor may be given the responsibility of collecting the receivables. Alternatively this task may be entrusted to any other third party.[41]

Subordination and Protection against Bankruptcy

14.35   The Act of 22 March 2004 authorizes the issue of securities whose repayment is subordinated to the repayment of other securities, certain receivables or even certain share categories.[42] Moreover, creditors other than investors can subordinate the enforcement and payment of their claim to those of other claims or certain investors.[43] In other words, all possible combinations for structuring the capital and debts of a securitization vehicle are permitted, thereby enabling the securitization vehicle to use the structure best suited to the needs of the capital markets.

14.36   Securitization vehicles are further protected against bankruptcy by recognition of the validity of non-recourse covenants given by investors and creditors with respect to the vehicle and their agreement not to petition for its bankruptcy.[44]

Fiduciary Representative

14.37   The Act of 22 March 2004 creates a new function whereby the investors are represented as a body, based on the legal mechanisms governing mandates and trusts, in order to provide investors and creditors with the necessary protection and the securitization vehicle with the necessary stability and equilibrium. This function is performed by the fiduciary representative.[45]

---

[38] Arts 55(1) and 58, Act of 22 March 2004.
[39] ibid Art 55(2) and (3).
[40] ibid Art 56(2).
[41] ibid Art 60.
[42] ibid Arts 63 and 64.
[43] ibid Art 64.
[44] ibid Art 64(2).
[45] In view of the formalities required for authorization of the fiduciary representative, the *Conseil d'État* asked itself whether this was a new type of professional of the financial sector, which would

The appointment of such a representative by securitization vehicles is optional[46] **14.38** and is made in accordance with the terms of an agreement with the investors and creditors whose interests he has agreed to protect.[47] He is granted a general representation power for this purpose.[48] He may also be called upon to hold rights, guarantees, and security interests or to receive payments on behalf of the investors or the creditors who appointed him.[49] The securitization vehicle may also assign certain contracts, rights, and actions arising under agreements to the fiduciary representative, who is responsible for managing them in the best interests of the investors.[50]

The CSSF also allows the appointment of a foreign trustee to represent and **14.39** protect the interests of shareholders.[51]

Tax Treatment

The tax treatment of securitization vehicles differs according to whether the vehi- **14.40** cle is organized in the form of a company or contractually. However, in either case, the legislature wanted to keep the transaction neutral for taxation purposes.

The contributions paid into a securitization vehicle on incorporation are subject **14.41** to a fixed capital duty of €1,250.[52] This amount, collected on incorporation, covers all capital transactions, including any subsequent capital increase, any change in the corporate form of the securitization company, and any merger.

Securitization companies are fully taxable in Luxembourg and therefore subject to **14.42** corporate income tax and to municipal business tax at a maximum overall rate of 29.63 per cent[53] on their net profit for accounting purposes. However, distributions

---

have had a series of legal consequences that would not necessarily have been desirable within the framework of the Bill. Art 86 of the Act of 22 March 2004 confirmed the position of the Finance and Budget Commission and specified that fiduciary representatives were not professionals of the financial sector in the meaning of the 1993 Act. See in particular, *Parliamentary doc* No 5199[5], Report of the Finance and Budget Commission, Comments on the Articles (Arts 79 and 86) 11. For several details on the appointment of the fiduciary representative, see CSSF Annual Report for 2007, 105.

[46] Art 67, Act of 22 March 2004.
[47] ibid Art 68.
[48] ibid Art 69.
[49] ibid Art 71.
[50] ibid Art 72.
[51] CSSF Annual Report for 2007, 105.
[52] Art 51, Act of 22 March 2004; Grand-Ducal Regulation of 29 April 2005 establishing the terms and amount of the fixed capital duty payable pursuant to Art 51 of the Act of 22 March 2004 (*Mémorial* A 2005, 931).
[53] During his speech on the State of the Nation, on 22 May 2008, the Luxembourg Prime Minister announced a progressive reduction of the maximum overall rate to 25.5%.

and other income allocated to investors and other creditors are tax deductible business expenses.[54] The Act of 22 March 2004 does not distinguish between the different types of transferable securities issued to investors, which may be bonds, shares, founder shares, and other debt or equity securities. In the case of shares and founder shares, any distribution (regardless of the form of the distribution under company law, ie whether a dividend or redemption) is a tax deductible business expense. Securitization companies and exempt from wealth tax.[55]

14.43 Moreover, distributions (dividend or interest) paid by a securitization vehicle to non-resident investors and other creditors are not subject to withholding tax, subject to the provisions of Directive 2003/48 on taxation of savings income in the form of interest payments.[56]

14.44 Securitization funds are subject to the accounting and tax rules governing FCPs under the 2002 Act.[57] Like UCIs, securitization funds are therefore exempt from corporate income tax, municipal business tax and wealth tax. However, in contrast with UCIs, securitization funds are not liable to subscription tax.

14.45 Moreover, management services to securitization vehicles are exempt from VAT.[58]

14.46 Lastly, in order to avoid certain abuses, the legislature has ruled out tax consolidation for securitization vehicles.[59] It has also maintained the tax neutrality of exchanges of securities.[60]

Securitization and UCIs/SICARs

14.47 Together, the features of the legal rules governing securitization make it very similar to certain other structures, such as UCIs and SICARs. A securitization vehicle may issue securities, with a value and return linked to the performance of indices, baskets of securities, or derivatives. It may also be dedicated to the management of portfolios of assets such as actively managed collateral debt obligations.[61] In that case, the constitutive documents or the offering documents set out the selection criteria and the composition of the portfolio under management.

---

[54] Art 89(d), Act of 22 March 2004.
[55] Art 90, Act of 22 March 2004.
[56] See 11.165 *et seq* above.
[57] Art 50, Act of 22 March 2004.
[58] ibid Art 52(3).
[59] ibid Art 89(e).
[60] ibid Art 89(a).
[61] CSSF Annual Report for 2007, 102.

The description of the portfolio composition can be limited to mentioning the categories of assets held.[62] The conditions for selling assets must also be provided for.[63]

The CSSF limits the use of securitization vehicles for asset management purposes. **14.48**
Securitization vehicles are not allowed to intervene in the management of the entities held in their portfolios.[64] This prohibition is similar to that imposed upon coordinated UCITS. However, an equivalent prohibition does not apply to UCIs governed by Part II of the Act of 2002 or by the Act of 13 February 2007. It does not apply to SICARs either.

Apart from this prohibition on intervention in management, what are the **14.49**
elements allowing a distinction to be drawn between a securitization vehicle and a SICAR? A joint ALFI/ABBL working group has identified certain criteria in this respect.

The following criteria reflect the findings of this group. Each individual case needs **14.50**
to be analysed separately. In themselves, whether taken alone or together, they do not definitively determine application of the Act of 22 March 2004.

Objectives

The organization of a securitization vehicle generally caters to the needs of a bank **14.51**
or a (re)financing company seeking to refinance certain of its assets by issuing securities representing these assets. This kind of activity also offers two advantages. First, it improves the balance sheet structure of the assigning business and, secondly, it exploits the credit enhancement of the securitized assets. Economically, securitization constitutes the 'refinancing of a set of assets in order to reduce the risks assumed by the holder of the assets in respect of its debtors'.[65]

In contrast, the purpose of UCIs and SICARs is to collect savings from investors **14.52**
for the purpose of collective investment.

In the case of a securitization vehicle, the project gives effect to the wish to transfer **14.53**
certain assets for refinancing purposes. In the case of a UCI or SICAR, the project is the offering of a service to certain categories of investors. The securitization vehicle is therefore generally a financing and risk management tool, whereas UCIs and SICARs are primarily investment and investment management instruments.

---

[62] ibid.
[63] Art 61, Act of 22 March 2004; see the CSSF Annual Report 2007, 104, according to which the constitutive documents may refer to provisions of the offering documents.
[64] CSSF Annual Report for 2007, 103.
[65] *Parliamentary doc* No 5199[1], Opinion of the *Conseil d'État*, General considerations, 1.

14.54   Their objectives, therefore, are basically different. The organization of a securitization vehicle mostly reflects the wish of an institution to refinance itself or to assign the risks attached to certain assets by transferring these specific assets or risks.[66] UCIs and SICARs mostly reflect the wishes of their investors to invest their savings in a variety of assets.[67]

14.55   It must nevertheless be acknowledged that it is not always possible to determine the nature of a particular transaction based on its objective alone. In other words, a securitization transaction may therefore also serve certain investment management objectives.

Redemption

14.56   Whereas 'the essence of securitization is to secure the rights of investors to the assets financed by their investment',[68] because the value of or return on securities issued by the vehicle depends on the underlying assets, and because a securitization vehicle does not primarily provide investment services to investors, it should not be capable of offering extensive redemption facilities at the request of investors in respect of securities it has issued.[69]

14.57   This criterion needs to be assessed prudently, as the Act of 22 March 2004 implicitly allowed securitization vehicles to redeem their shares, and in this respect did not rule out the application of the laws governing commercial companies to securitization vehicles.[70]

14.58   In practice, however, the fact that the Act of 22 March 2004 refers to the 1915 Act significantly complicates redemption by a securitization vehicle at the request of its shareholders. Hence, few securitization vehicles want to use this option.

Management of underlying assets

14.59   In contrast with a UCI, the main objective of a securitization vehicle is normally not to engage in active asset portfolio management. In principle, it does not invest

---

[66]   Deacon (n 4 above) 4 *et seq.*
[67]   See T Bonneau, 'Les fonds communs de placement, les fonds communs de créances, et le droit civil' (1991) *Rev trim dr civ* 5: 'The *fonds commun de placement* (common fund) was created in order to attract a category of retail investors to businesses without the trouble of having to manage a securities portfolio. The purpose of *fonds commun de créance* (receivables securitization funds) is quite different and appears to be two-fold. First, the fund must enable credit institutions to refinance themselves. . . . Second, it must lastingly improve the balance sheet structure of banks. . . . Thus, the aims of receivables securitization funds are different from those of investment funds'.
[68]   *Parliamentary doc* No 5199, Comments on the Articles, 33.
[69]   For France, see also Hovasse (n 5 above) 4, point 13.
[70]   Art 4, Act of 22 March 2004.

permanently in diversified assets which are traded on an ongoing basis.[71] This feature was stressed in the preparatory documents for the Act of 22 March 2004, which state that the objective of securitization is to 'organise a framework for investment in homogeneous risk clusters'.[72]

There are, however, special securitization structures that to some extent manage their underlying assets. These structures are gradually gaining ground. The returns promised to the holders of their securities do not depend upon the income generated by the assets held by the securitization vehicle but upon separate criteria, such as a variable interest rate. **14.60**

Active management is restricted by the collateral provided in principle by the assets held by the securitization vehicle. The Act of 22 March 2004 stipulates that, although securitization vehicles may buy receivables and other assets, in one or more transactions or on a continuous basis, they are not authorized to assign them except in accordance with their articles of incorporation or their management rules.[73] Here, the preparatory documents for the Act of 22 March 2004 are clear: 'The purpose is to protect [the investors] from the potentially adverse consequences of an assignment of or granting of a pledge over these assets by the securitisation vehicle'; 'the security offered to investors is mainly underpinned by the transparency with which assignments must take place. Such assignments must be provided for, at least in principle, by the constitutive documents of the securitisation vehicle'.[74] **14.61**

The text of the law therefore does not prohibit securitization vehicles from adjusting their portfolio composition to suit market conditions.[75] This right is nevertheless subject to certain rules and it is clear that a UCI manager has more scope for discretion than a securitization vehicle manager, who is generally bound by strictly defined structures and formulas.[76] **14.62**

---

[71] Bonneau (n 67 above) 6. However, see CSSF Annual Report for 2007, 102, in which securitization vehicles dedicated to the management of a portfolio of assets are included among authorized structures.

[72] *Parliamentary doc* No 5199, Comments on the Articles, 19.

[73] Arts 54 and 61(1), Act of 22 March 2004. However, the CSSF allows that the constitutive documents make reference to provisions of the offering documents with respect to the decision-making process and the conditions for the sale of assets (CSSF Annual Report for 2007, 104).

[74] *Parliamentary doc* No 5199, Comments on the Articles, 33.

[75] See Dr J Benjamin, *Interests in Securities* (Oxford University Press 2000) para 12.20: 'First, at closing, the portfolio consists in large part (or even wholly) of the proceeds of the issue of notes, and this cash invested in (interests in) bonds over a "ramp up" period (of six months to one year). Secondly, during a reinvestment period (of a number of years), redemption monies will be reinvested in new (interests in) bonds. Further, when existing (interests in) bonds fail to perform against defined criteria, there is provision for them to be disposed of, and others substituted. Thus, the pool of assets underlying the CBO is not only mixed, but changing from time to time'.

[76] Benjamin (n 75 above) paras 12.22, 12.53 and associated notes, 12.54, 12.65, and 12.66. Also see CSSF Annual Report for 2007, 102.

14.63   In view of the growing sophistication of securitization operations, therefore, the essential functional difference between investment funds and a securitization structure does not so much lie in the right to manage underlying assets actively, as in the degree of freedom with which the manager can vary the composition of the vehicle's portfolio.

Permanent investment

14.64   The Act of 22 March 2004 allows securitization vehicles to buy assets continuously.[77] However, securitization typically involves a specific transaction in predetermined assets, held for a limited time. Moreover, as the assets held by the vehicle represent the investor's security, there are unlikely to be major changes in the portfolio composition that would weaken the effectiveness of this guarantee.[78]

14.65   Promoters may nevertheless use securitization vehicles such as repackaging structures to carry out several transactions within a single struture in order to reduce transaction costs and to shorten the time needed to implement refinancing transactions.[79]

14.66   The right to invest on a permanent basis, expressly provided for in the Act of 22 March 2004, should be interpreted having regard to the right offered by this law to create sub-funds within the same vehicle. Thus, the permanence of an investment would be judged at the level of the overall vehicle, whereas in practice each sub-fund would be created to hold a specific transaction.[80]

---

[77] Art 54, Act of 22 March 2004.

[78] See Deacon (n 4 above) paras 4.1 and 4.2: 'A consideration of the eligibility or substitution criteria for introducing new assets into a deal is essential'. Moreover, 'the eligibility criteria for a deal are designed to ensure that, on replenishment of new assets in a deal which permits the reinvestment of proceeds from receivables (or on substitution of new assets into a deal generally), the asset quality of the portfolio is not eroded'.

[79] ibid 5.9; CSSF Annual Report for 2007, 102.

[80] In early 2005, the European Commission received a complaint that the tax regime for SICARs and for securitization vehicles was incompatible with Community law. The complaint was underpinned by the assertion that such tax regimes amounted to unauthorized government aid. At the time of going to press, this complaint, whose validity is very far from having been established, has not yet been settled by the European Commission.

SELECT BIBLIOGRAPHY

Arendt, E, 'Statut juridique des fonds communs de placement et des sociétés d'
investissement au Grand-Duché de Luxembourg' in *Les organes collectifs de placement
dans la perspective de la place financière de Luxembourg*, Study Days of 11 and 12
December 1970, Université Internationale de Sciences Comparées, Luxembourg, 7

Baden, G and Baden, Y, 'Diagonales en matière de liquidation des établissements de crédit
et fonds d'investissement' in *Droit bancaire et financier au Luxembourg* (Larcier, 2004)
Vol 1, 177

Bartlett, JW, *Fundamentals of Venture Capital* (Madison Books, 1999)

Benjamin, Dr J, *Interests in Securities* (Oxford University Press, 2000)

Benoit-Moury, A, 'Des justes motifs de dissolution des sociétés commerciales. De l'article
1871 du Code civil à l'article 102 des LCSC' in *Liber Amicorum Jan Ronse* (E Story-
Scientia, 1986) 147

Bernard, G, *Les sociétés holding au Grand-Duché de Luxembourg* (Institut Universitaire
International, 1979)

Besseau, E, 'La réforme des Opcvm et ses limites' (February 2003) 644 *Banquemagazine* 70

Bonet, G, 'Quasi-contrats—Enrichissement sans cause', *Jurisclasseur, Civil Code*,
Vol 1, 1988.

Bonneau, T, 'Les fonds communs de placement, les fonds communs de créances,
et le droit civil' (1991) *Rev trim dr civ* 1

Bourin, P, 'Droits et obligations du banquier dépositaire de titres' in *Droit bancaire
et financier au Luxembourg* (Larcier, 2004) Vol 3, 1243

Boys, P and Emery, J-L, 'La nouvelle directive Opcvm' (February 2003) 644
Banquemagazine 44

Brausch, F, 'Les responsabilités du dépositaire d'OPCVM' (1994) *ALFI Yearbook* 223
_____ Henrion, E-F, and Delcourt, R, 'Les devoirs de la banque dépositaire d'un fonds
immoblier' (January 2008, No 1) *ACE* 18

Bucher, F, 'Du bon usage de la commandite par actions' (1994) *Rev Soc* 415

Bussière, F and Courant, E, 'La réforme de la directive Opcvm 85/611/CEE du
20 décembre 1985', Part One (November–December 2002) 86 *Banque & Droit* 6

Caprasse, O, 'La responsabilité civile professionnelle des administrateurs' (1997)
Act dr 484

Chabardes, P and Delclaux, F, *Les produits dérivés* (Gualino Editeur, 1999)

Chartier, Y, 'Les nouveaux fonds communs de placement (commentaire du titre
Ier de la loi No. 79-594 du 13 juillet 1979 et de ses textes d'application)' (1980)
JCP 3001.

Chèvremont, M-J, 'Évolution de l'industrie des fonds d'investissement en Europe et au
Luxembourg en particulier' in *Les fonds d'investissement, réglementation—fiscalité—évolution*,
Seminar of 24 and 25 November 1988, Association Luxembourgeoise des Juristes de
Banque (ALJB), Institut Universitaire International Luxembourg (IUIL), 5

Coipel, M, 'Réflexions sur le portage d'actions au regard de l'article 1855 du Code civil.
Le porteur et le lion' (1986) *RCJB* 542

_____ 'Encore l'article 1855, alinéa 2 du Code civil: réflexions additionnelles en faveur d'une interprétation renouvelée d'un texte controversé' (1995) *RDC* 132

Commentaire article par article des traités UE et CE (Helbing & Lichtenhahn, Bruylant, 2000)

Contreras, A and Fassin, J-N, 'Supervision' in *Specialised Investment Funds* (Arendt & Medernach, 2007) 77–9

Corbisier, I, *Droit des sociétés* (Université Catholique de Louvain, Bruylant, 1996) Vol 6

Cottier, P, *Hedge Funds and Managed Futures* (Haupt, 3rd edn, 2000)

Courant, E, 'Utilisation des produits dérivés de gré à gré par les Opcvm' (July–August 2000) 72 *Banque & Droit* 16

_____ and Bussière, F, 'La réforme de la directive Opcvm 85/611/CEE du 20 décembre 1985', Part Two (November–December 2002) 89 *Banque & Droit* 14

Coussement, A, 'Le rôle de la banque de dépôt dans le fonctionnement des organes collectifs de placement' in *Les organes collectifs de placement dans la perspective de la place financière de Luxembourg*, Study Days of 11 and 12 December 1970, Université Internationale de Sciences Comparées, Luxembourg, 69

Dandois, M and Meynial, A, 'Les fonds immobiliers au Grand-Duché de Luxembourg ou le réveil de la pierre: Aspects juridiques et fiscaux' in *Droit bancaire et financier au Luxembourg* (Larcier, 2004) Vol 4, 1539

Das, S, *Swaps/Financial Derivatives—Products, Pricing, Applications and Risk Management*, Vol 2 (Wiley Finance, 3rd edn, 2003)

Deacon, J, *Global Securitisation and CDOs* (Wiley Finance, 2004)

De Bie, E and de Leenheer, G, *Liquidation des sociétés après la loi du 13 avril 1995* (Ced Samsom, 1995)

De Boeck, C and d'Anterroches, E, 'SIF: a new investment vehicle suitable for private equity' in *Specialised Investment Funds* (Arendt & Medernach, 2007)

De La Mettrie, L and Lambion, M, 'UCITS III: Quel avenir pour les sociétés "sandwich"?' *AGEFI*, Luxembourg, April 2002

Delattre, E, *Les nouveaux instruments financiers*, series: 'Que sais-je?' (Presses universitaires de France, 1994)

Deliège, A, 'Inaliénabilité' in *Rép not*, Vol II, book 7 (Larcier, 1979)

Delvaux, B, 'Questions actuelles concernant la loi de 1929 sur le régime fiscal des sociétés de participations financières' (1956) XVI *Pas lux* 197

_____ 'Les sociétés d'investissement du type ouvert au Grand-Duché de Luxembourg' (1961) XVIII *Pas lux* 37

_____ 'Régime fiscal luxembourgeois assurant une juste perception des impôts' in *Les organes collectifs de placement dans la perspective de la place financière de Luxembourg*, Study Days of 11 and 12 December 1970, Université Internationale de Sciences Comparées, Luxembourg, 35

_____ and Reiffers, E, *Les sociétés holding au Grand-Duché de Luxembourg* (Imprimerie de la Cour Victor Buck, 5th edn, reviewed and expanded with the assistance of Elter, R and Delvaux, J, (Sirey, 1969)

Delvaux, J, *Le droit des sociétés au Grand-Duché de Luxembourg* (Université de Luxembourg, 1999)

De Page, H and Dekkers, R, *Traité élémentaire de droit civil belge* (Bruylant, 1975)

De Vauplane, H and Bornet, J-P, *Droit des marchés financiers* (Litec, 1998)

De Wolf, P and Feron, B, 'Les conventions d'actionnaires: une évolution inachevée' (1991) 21 *DAOR* 29

Dubocage, E and Rivaud-Danset, D, *Le capital-risque* (Editions La Découverte, 2006)

Dubourdieu, I, Moreau, F and Baratelli, A, 'Functioning of the SIF structure' in *Specialised Investment Funds* (Arendt & Medernach, 2007) 109

Du Faux, H, 'La liquidation des sociétés commerciales' *Rép not*, Vol XII, book VI (Larcier, 1994)

Eisenhuth, M and Gosset, A, 'Les Private Equity Funds' in *Droit bancaire et financier au Luxembourg*, Vol 4 (Larcier, 2004) 1707

Elvinger, A, 'Statut fiscal des fonds communs de placement et des sociétés d'investissement au Grand-Duché de Luxembourg' in *Les organes collectifs de placement dans la perspective de la place financière de Luxembourg*, Study Days of 11 and 12 December 1970, Université Internationale de Sciences Comparées, Luxembourg, 25

_____ 'Le rôle des autorités de surveillance' (1994) *ALFI Yearbook* 33

_____ 'Historique du droit bancaire et financier luxembourgeois' in *Droit bancaire et financier au Grand-Duché de Luxembourg* (Larcier, 1994) Vol 1, 3

Elvinger, J and Schmit, IM, 'Les sociétés de gestion d'organismes de placement collectif en droit luxembourgeois' in *Droit bancaire et financier au Luxembourg* (Larcier, 2004) Vol 4, 1495

Elvinger, M, 'Les conflits entre l'obligation au secret bancaire instituée par la loi luxembourgeoise et l'obligation de déclaration imposée par une loi étrangère (1997) 26 *Bull Droit & Banque* 5

Embrechts, P and Furrer, H, 'VaR, stress testing and related risk management techniques for hedging funds' in *The new generation of risk management for hedge funds and private equity investments* (Institutional Investor Books, 2003) 399

Feron, B and Wouters, H, 'La directive 93/22 concernant les services d'investissement dans le domaine des valeurs mobilières et son impact sur la loi du 4 décembre 1990' (1999) *Rev prat soc* 209

Fonctionnement et contrôle des établissements financiers internationaux, collective work, Working Document of the European Parliament, Economic Affairs series ECON 118 FR, Vol 1 (February 2001)

Foriers, P-A, 'Les situations de blocage dans les sociétés anonymes' (1992) *RDC* 477

_____ 'Portage et clause léonine (observations sur le champ d'application de l'article 1855 du Code civil)' in *Hommage à Jacques Heenen* (Bruylant, 1994)

Fredericq, L, *Traité de droit commercial belge* (Editions Fecheyr, 1950)

Geens, K, 'Quelques aspects de la clause d'agrément dans la société anonyme' (1989) *Rev prat soc* 325

Goebel, A and Gasparotto, B, 'Tax aspects of SIFs' in *Specialised Investment Funds* (Arendt & Medernach, 2007) 147

Gollier, J-M, Van der Haegen, M and Waelbroeck, M, 'Obligation pour le dépositaire d'être établi dans le même Etat que l'OPCVM. Libre prestation de services' (1994) *ALFI Yearbook* 105

Grabenwarter, U and Weidig, T, *Exposed to the J-Curve, Understanding and Managing Private Equity Fund Investments* (Euromoney Books, 2005)

Gudmannsson, A, 'Luxembourg: New law on securitization' (July 2004) *International Securitisation Report* 2

_____ 'Cross-Border securitization in Luxembourg' (2004/2005) *Global Securitization Review* 152

Handbook sur la fiscalité de l'épargne (ABBL/KPMG, collective work, February 2005)

Hansenne, J, *Les Biens*, Vol I (Collection Scientifique de la Faculté de Droit de Liège, 1996)

Harles, G, 'Luxembourg' in *International Bank Secrecy* (Sweet & Maxwell, 1992) 471

Hodgson, P, 'Private equity investing: your guide to this emerging asset class' in (May 2002) 2 *Fundamental* XX, Invesco's education supplement

Hoffmann, M and Jacobs, C, 'Liquidation and merger of investment funds under the new law on SIFs' in *Specialised Investment Funds* (Arendt & Medernach, 2007) 162

Hoffmann, R, 'Réflexions sur le fondement du secret professionnel' (1983) 2 *Bull Droit & Banque* 3

Hoss, P and Kinsch, P, 'Conventions fiscales internationales et organismes de placement collectif en valeurs mobilières', Proceedings of the symposium of the Belgo-Luxembourg and French groups of the IFA, Luxembourg, 15 and 16 May 1992

Hovasse, H, *La Titrisation*, Vol 2260 (Juris-classeurs, 1991)

Hull, JC, *Options, futures and other derivatives* (Prentice Hall, 5th edn, 2002)

Jonckheere, A, Capus-Leclerc, M, Willems, V and Spielmann, D, *Le blanchiment du produit des infractions en Belgique et au Grand-Duché de Luxembourg*, Larcier, series: 'Les dossiers du Journal des tribunaux', No 9 (Larcier, 1995)

Juncker, G and Wigny, J, 'Nouvelles politiques et restrictions d'investissement pour les OPCVM' in *Droit bancaire et financier au Luxembourg* (Larcier, 2004) Vol 4, 1627

Kayser, N, 'Fiducie ou SPV—Quelques aspects de la titrisation en droit luxembourgeois' in *Droit bancaire et financier au Luxembourg* (ALJB, Larcier, 2004) Vol 2, 857

Kemp, M and Martougin, C, 'Real estate SIFs—New opportunities for investments in real estate properties' in *Specialised Investment Funds* (Arendt & Medernach, 2007) 182

Kinsch, P, 'L'affaire des fichiers volés de la Kredietbank luxembourgeoise devant la Cour d'appel et la Cour de cassation—Observations sous l'arrêt de la Cour d'appel du 2 avril 2003 et l'arrêt de la Cour de cassation du 18 mars 2004' (2004) 35 *Bull Droit & Banque* 52

Kirkpatrick, J, 'Le régime de la cession d'actions futures d'une société anonyme en droit positif belge et *de lege ferenda*' in *Hommage à Jacques Heenen* (Bruylant, 1994) 221

Kremer, C, 'Le banquier luxembourgeois face aux droits de succession' in *Droit bancaire et financier au Grand-Duché de Luxembourg* (Larcier, 1994) Vol 2, 711

_____ and Baden, J, 'The role of the Luxembourg Monetary Institute in the supervision of undertakings for collective investment' (February 1995) 3 *World Fund Industry/ Gestion collective internationale* 63

_____ and Baden, J, 'L'investissement par les organismes de placement collectif luxembourgeois dans les marchés émergents' (March–April 1996) 56 *Notes financières de la Banque Générale du Luxembourg* 20

_____ and Contreras, A, 'Les fonds de pension soumis au contrôle prudentiel de la Commission de surveillance du secteur financier' in *Droit bancaire et financier au Luxembourg* (Larcier, 2004) Vol 4, 1743

_____ and Eisenhuth, M, 'Banque dépositaire et administration centrale: aspects juridiques et pratiques' (1993) *ALFI Yearbook* 167

_____ and Eisenhuth, M, 'Fonctions et responsabilités des organes d'administration et de gestion des OPC et de leurs délégués' (1994) *ALFI Yearbook* 201

_____ Eisenhuth, M and Ueberecken, J-M, 'Impact of the law of 25 August 2006 concerning the European company on Luxembourg undertakings for collective investment' *Tageblatt*, 26 September 2006

_____ and Elvinger, J, 'La double imposition internationale des successions et des donations', National Report by Luxembourg for the IFA Congress in London in 1985, *Cahiers de droit fiscal international*, Vol LXXb: *International Double Taxation of Inheritances and Gifts* (Kluwer, Rotterdam, 1985) 441

600

_____ and Gasparotto, B, 'La TVA dans les structures d'organismes de placement collectif et de véhicules apparentés' in *Droit fiscal luxembourgeois, Livre jubilaire de l'IFA Luxembourg, ouvrage collectif* (Bruylant, 2008)

_____ and Lebbe, I, *Les organismes de placement collectif en droit luxembourgeois* (Larcier, 1st edn, 2001)

_____ and Lebbe, I, 'Les sociétés d'investissement en capital à risque' *Luxemburger Wort*, 24, 25, 26, and 28 June 2004

_____ and Lesage, T, 'Investment Company in Risk Capital ("SICAR"), Response to Venture Capital and Private Equity' in *Derivatives & Financial Instruments*, International Bureau of Fiscal Documentation (January/February 2005)

_____ and Niedner, C, 'L'utilisation par les organismes de placement collectif de techniques et instruments dérivés', in *Portfolio*, special issue published for the annual ALFI-NICSA Congress (October 1997)

_____ and Niedner, C, 'La commercialisation au Luxembourg de parts d'organismes de placement collectif étrangers' *Luxemburger Wort*, 12 March 1999

Kremer, R, 'Les organismes de placement collectif sur la place financière luxembourgeoise' in *Livre Jubilaire* for the 75th anniversary of the Luxembourg Stock Exchange (Bourse de Luxembourg, 2004)

Lacroix, Y and Tristan, L, 'Parties and service providers involved in specialised investment funds' in *Specialised Investment Funds* (Arendt & Medernach, 2007) 71

Lambert, P, *Le secret professionnel* (Editions Nemesis, 1985)

Lebbe, I, 'La vente d'un fonds de commerce ou la cession de titres de sociétés—Aspects du droit commercial' (1994) 4 *Act dr* 833

_____ and Partsch, P-E, 'L'article 1855, alinéa 2, du Code civil et les opérations sur titres' (1997) *Rev prat soc* 81

Les fonds d'investissement, réglementation—fiscalité—évolution, Seminar of 24 and 25 November 1988, Association Luxembourgeoise des Juristes de Banque (ALJB), Institut Universitaire International Luxembourg (IUIL)

Les organes collectifs de placement dans la perspective de la place financière de Luxembourg, Study Days of 11 and 12 December 1970, Université Internationale de Sciences Comparées, Luxembourg

Lesage, T and Partsch, P-E, 'Le droit communautaire est-il une menace pour l'avenir des holdings 1929' (May 2006) 1 *ACE* 7

Linneman, P and Ross, S, 'Real estate private equity funds' (2002) *Wharton Real Estate Review* 7

Ludovissy, G, *La surveillance du secteur financier* (Editions Promoculture, 2000)

Maisto, G, 'Shaping EU Company Tax Policy: Amending the Tax Directives', *European Taxation*, IBFS, Amsterdam (August 2002) 9

Malaurie, P and Aynès, L, *Cours de droit civil, Les contrats spéciaux* (Cujas, 1992)

Merriman, CO, *Unit trusts and how they work* (Pitman & Sons, 2nd edn, 1959)

Metzler, L, *Le régime juridique et fiscal des sociétés à responsabilité limitée dans le Grand-Duché de Luxembourg* (Imprimerie de la Cour Victor Buck, 1933)

Moles, P and Therry, N, *The Handbook of International Financial Terms* (Oxford University Press, 1999)

Molitor, R, *Le régime fiscal des sociétés mères et filiales* (Etudes fiscales, Imprimerie Saint-Paul, Luxembourg, 1994)

Morel, A and Omes, E, 'L'obligation d'information et de conseil du banquier' in *Droit bancaire et financier au Luxembourg* (Larcier, 2004) Vol 2, 481

Moulla, M and Chantalangsy, M, 'Presentation of the law of 2007 compared to other existing legislation governing collective investment structures—historical overview of the law of 2007' in *Specialised Investment Funds* (Arendt & Medernach, 2007) 14

Mousel, P and Fayot, J, 'La circulation des titres' in *Droit bancaire et financier au Luxembourg*, Vol 3 (Larcier, 2004) 1319

Musca, X, Director General of the Treasury and Economic Policy (France), 'Europe financière: recréer une dynamique' (June 2005) 217 *Revue L'hémicycle* 8

Nejman, G, *Les contrats de produits dérivés—Aspects juridiques* (Larcier, 1999)

Nelissen Grade, J-M, 'De la validité et de l'exécution de la convention de vote dans les sociétés commerciales' (1991) *RCJB* 214

Nevelsteen, L and van den Plas, R, 'Undertakings for Collective Investment and VAT in the EU', *VAT Monitor*, International Bureau of Fiscal Documentation (November/December 2003) 456

Niedner, C and Kass, F, 'Les fonds alternatifs en droit luxembourgeois' in *Droit bancaire et financier au Luxembourg* (Larcier, 2004) Vol 4, 1581

Nlend, JR, *La responsabilité des dirigeants de sociétés en droit luxembourgeois* (Ecoconsult SCP, 1997)

Olinger, J, *Introduction à l'étude du droit fiscal luxembourgeois* (Etudes fiscales, Imprimerie Saint-Paul, 1974)

Oliver, P, 'La législation communautaire et sa conformité avec la libre circulation des marchandises' (1979) *Cah dr eur* 245

Partsch, P-E, 'Dans quelle mesure le conseil d'administration d'une société anonyme belge peut-il adopter des décisions sans réunion physique de ses membres?' (1995) *Rev prat soc* 201

_____ 'Les capitaux et les paiements' in *Commentaire article par article des traités UE et CE* (Helbing & Lichtenhahn, Dalloz, Bruylant, 2000) 478

_____ 'Droit bancaire et financier européen: Chronique de jurisprudence de l'année 2004' (2005) 36 *Bull Droit & Banque* 42

_____ and Lebbe, I, 'Principe de proportionnalité et droit des sociétés' (1996) *JT* 609

Pierlot, V and Benizri, Y, 'A specialised investors fund?' in *Specialised Investment Funds* (Arendt & Medernach, 2007) 24

Prussen, Y, 'Le régime des titres et instruments fongibles' in *Droit bancaire et financier au Luxembourg* (Larcier, 2004), Vol 3, 1287

Ralet, O, *Responsabilités des dirigeants de sociétés* (Larcier, 1996)

Rauïs, B, *Produits dérivés de crédit, Applications et Perspectives* (Larcier, 2003)

Resteau, C, *Traité des sociétés anonymes* (Éditions Swinnen, 3rd edn (by Benoit-Moury, A and Grégoire, A), 1982) Vol 2

Reuter, A-M and Berck, N, 'Available Structures' in *Specialised Investment Funds* (Arendt & Medernach, 2007) 37

Ripert, G and Roblot, R, *Traité de droit commercial* (LGDJ, 15th edn (by Germain, M), 1993) Vol 1

Roever, WA, and Fabozzi, F, 'A Primer on Securitization' (Summer 2003) *The Journal of Structured and Project Finance* 7

Roland, B, 'Les causes de dissolution' in *Traité pratique de droit commercial* (Kluwer Editions juridiques Belgique, 1998) Vol 4, 1061

_____ 'La liquidation' in *Traité pratique de droit commercial* (Kluwer Editions juridiques Belgique, 1998) Vol 4, 1091

Schaffner, J, *Droit fiscal international* (Editions Promoculture, 2nd edn, 2005)

Schell, J M, *Private Equity Funds: Business Structure and Operations*, (Law Journal Press, 2004)

Schiltz, J-L and Schiltz, F, 'Le secret bancaire face aux tiers devant le juge civil', in *Droit bancaire et financier au Luxembourg* (Larcier, 2004) Vol 1, 307

Schmitt, A, 'La société d'investissement en capital à risque en droit luxembourgeois' in *Droit bancaire et financier au Luxembourg* (Larcier, 2004) Vol 4, 1657

Schockweiler, F, 'Les principes généraux du droit en droit communautaire et en droit administratif luxembourgeois' in *Mélanges dédiés à Michel Delvaux* (Luxembourg, 1990) 230

Schwabe, H and Brülin, F, 'SIF hedge funds—opportunities to establish "unrestricted" hedge funds in a regulated environment' in *Specialised Investment Funds* (Arendt & Medernach, 2007)

Serebriakoff, A, 'Le caractère d'ordre public du secret bancaire: conviction ou réalité?' in *Droit bancaire et financier au Luxembourg* (Larcier, 2004) Vol 1, 283

Sharp, G, *European Private Equity: a practical guide for vendors, managers and entrepreneurs* (Euromoney Books, 2002)

Specialised Investment Funds (Arendt & Medernach, 2007)

Spielmann, D, *Le secret bancaire et l'entraide judiciaire internationale pénale au Grand-Duché de Luxembourg*, Larcier, series: 'Les dossiers du Journal des tribunaux', No 20 (Larcier, 1999)

Steichen, A, 'Le secret bancaire face aux autorités publiques nationales et étrangères' (1995) 24 *Bull Droit & Banque* 24

_____ *Manuel de droit fiscal* (Imprimerie Saint-Paul, Vol 1, 2nd edn, 2000; Vol 2, 1st edn, 2002).

_____ *Précis de droit fiscal de l'entreprise* (Editions Emile Borschette, 3rd edn, 2004)

_____ *Précis de droit des sociétés* (Imprimerie Saint-Paul, 2006)

Terré, F, Simler, P and Lequette, Y, *Droit civil—Les obligations* (Précis Dalloz, 7th edn, 1999)

The European Savings Directive, ALFI's interpretations and recommendations (June 2005)

Thiel, L, 'La protection du client de banque—un secret à revoir' (2004) *Codex* 170

Tilquin, T, 'Le renouveau de la société en commandite par actions' (1991) *Rev Banque* 89

_____ 'Quelques aspects de la transmission et de la continuité des sociétés familiales' in *Transmission et protection des entreprises familiales* (Fédération des Entreprises de Belgique, 1992) 69

_____ and Simonart, V, *Traité des sociétés*, Vol I (Kluwer Editions juridiques Belgique, 1996)

Towards a European market for undertakings for collective investment in transferable securities, Comments on the provisions of Directive 85/611, Office of Official Publications of the European Communities (1988)

Traité pratique de droit commercial (Kluwer Editions juridiques Belgique, 1998) Vol 4

Trausch-Schoder, S, *Le traitement fiscal de l'épargne mobilière* (Etudes fiscales, Imprimerie Saint-Paul, 1994)

Truchot, L, 'Le droit d'établissement' in *Commentaire article par article des traités UE et CE* (Helbing & Lichtenhahn, Dalloz, Bruylant, 2000) 45

Van der Vossen, J-W, 'Authorization Requirements', in *Amsterdam Financial Series*, Banking and EC Law (2002) 18

Van Gerven, W, 'Principe de proportionnalité, abus de droit et droits fondamentaux' (1992) *JT* 305

Van Hille, J-M, *La société anonyme, Aspects juridiques et pratiques*, supplement (Bruylant, 1992)

Van Ommeslaghe, P, 'Les conventions d'actionnaires en droit belge' (1989) *Rev prat soc* 309

_____ and Dieux, X, 'Examen de jurisprudence (1979 à 1990), Les sociétés commerciales (suite)' (1993) *RCJB* 716

Van Ryn, J, *Principes de droit commercial* (Bruylant, 1st edn, 1954) Vol I

_____ and Heenen, J, *Principes de droit commercial* (Bruylant, 2nd edn, 1981) Vol III

Vanderstichelen, B and Gasparotto, B, *TVA Luxembourg—guide pratique 2006* (Kluwer, 2005)

Verhoeven, J, *Droit de la Communauté européenne* (Larcier, 1996)

Viandier, A, 'Les nouveaux fonds communs de placement' (1980) *Rev soc* 249

Vogel, K, *Doppelbesteuerungsabkommen* (CH Beck, 4th edn, 2003)

Wagner, M, 'Le secret professionnel en droit luxembourgeois' in *Diagonales à travers le droit luxembourgeois, Livre jubilaire de la conférence Saint-Yves 1946–1986,* (Imprimerie Saint-Paul, 1986) 901

Wauwermans, P, *Manuel pratique des sociétés anonymes* (Bruylant, 7th edn, 1933)

Wéry, P, *Droit des contrats—Le mandat* (Larcier, 2000)

Winandy, J-P, *Les impôts sur le revenu mandat et sur la fortune* (Promoculture, 4th edn, 2002)

_____ *Manuel de la TVA au Luxembourg* (Portalis Editions, 2005)

_____ Kremer, C and Fort, E, 'L'imposition des fonds de placement', National Report by Luxembourg for the IFA Congress in New Dehli in 1997, *Cahiers de droit fiscal international* (Rotterdam: Kluwer, 1997) Vol LXXXIIb 589

Wolter, J-C, 'The Investment Funds Regulations in Luxembourg' in *Les fonds d'investissement, réglementation—fiscalité—évolution,* Seminar of 24 and 25 November 1988, Association Luxembourgeoise des Juristes de Banque (ALJB), Institut Universitaire International Luxembourg (IUIL) 84

INDEX